AF653880

FOUNDATIONS AND APPLICATIONS
OF
INDIAN PSYCHOLOGY

Foundations and Applications of Indian Psychology

Edited by
R. M. Matthijs Cornelissen
Girishwar Misra
Suneet Varma

Pearson

Associate Editor-Commissioning: Moutushi Mukherjee
Production Editor: Vamanan Namboodiri

Copyright © 2014 Dorling Kindersley (India) Pvt. Ltd

All right reserved. This book is sold subject to the condition that it shall not, by way of trade or otherwise, be lent, resold, hired out, or otherwise circulated without the publisher's prior written consent in any form of binding or cover other than that in which it is published and without a similar condition including this condition being imposed on the subsequent purchaser and without limiting the rights under copyright reserved above, no part of this publication may be reproduced, stored in or introduced into a retrieval system, or transmitted in any form or by any means (electronic, mechanical, photocopying, recording or otherwise), without the prior written permission of both the copyright owner and the above-mentioned publisher of this book.

Although the author and publisher have made every effort to ensure that the information in this book was correct at the time of editing and printing, the author and publisher do not assume and hereby disclaim any liability to any party for any loss or damage arising out of the use of this book caused by errors or omissions, whether such errors or omissions result from negligence, accident or any other cause. Further, names, pictures, images, characters, businesses, places, events and incidents are either the products of the author's imagination or used in a fictitious manner. Any resemblance to actual persons, living or dead or actual events is purely coincidental and do not intend to hurt sentiments of any individual, community, sect or religion.

In case of binding mistake, misprints or missing pages etc., the publisher's entire liability and your exclusive remedy is replacement of this book within reasonable time of purchase by similar edition/ reprint of the book.

ISBN: 978-93-325-2636-5

First impression

This edition is manufactured in India and is authorized for sale only in India, Bangladesh, Bhutan, Pakistan, Nepal, Sri Lanka and the Maldives. Circulation of this edition outside of these territories is UNAUTHORIZED.

Published by Pearson India Education Services Pvt. Ltd, CIN: U72200TN2005PTC057128.

Head Office: 1st Floor, Berger Tower, Plot No. C-001A/2, Sector 16B, Noida - 201 301, Uttar Pradesh, India.

Registered Office: 6th Floor, Tower A, Unit A and B, International Tech Park, CapitaLand Chennai, 200 Feet Radial Road,Zamin Pallavaram, Old Pallavaram Chennai – 600117, Tamil Nadu, India

Website: in.pearson.com; Email: companysecretary.india@pearson.com

Digitally printed in India by Trinity Academy for Corporate Training Ltd, New Delhi in the year of 2026.

Contents

Foreword

Karan Singh

Apart from its other achievements, the ancient Indian civilization undertook the most profound examination of the human mind that has ever been attempted anywhere. The entire process of *yoga*, particularly the system based on Patanjali's *Yogasutras*, developed a methodology for 'stilling the modifications of the mind'. The *Bhagavad Gita* also contains specific instructions for stilling the mind, and thereby accessing the deeper reaches of our psyche. Indian psychology therefore has a firm base and a profound underlying philosophy.

Due largely to centuries of Western domination, we have tended to be unduly influenced by the West, even in the area of psychology. This is not in any way to denigrate the great breakthroughs of Western psychology, particularly those of Sigmund Freud and C. G. Jung. Indeed, post-Jungian psychology, especially Transpersonal Psychology, which has developed in recent years in California and around the world, are welcome efforts to delve deeper into the mysteries of the mind. What is really needed is a creative fusion between the Indian psychological traditions and the newer Western methodologies.

As they do in so many other areas, Sri Aurobindo's writings throw a flood of light upon various elements connected with the quest for the inner light. He has used *Vedic* symbolism to postulate a highly original interpretation, which places Indian psychology at the heart of the entire study. It is important that Indian insights become part of mainstream psychology around the world, and not be treated merely as an esoteric phenomenon.

The editors of *Foundations of Indian Psychology* deserve warm commendations for having brought together a broad and rich spectrum of articles dealing with various aspects of psychology, including social, psychological, educational, health and emotional dimensions. This book represents a valuable contribution to world psychological studies and will be of great value to students of psychology around the world. Recent research on the brain and the mind-brain relationship has thrown fascinating light upon how the human mind functions. Indian psychology, of course, goes beyond the mind into what we would call the spiritual centre of our being. The co-relation of these various elements and dimensions represent a fascinating field for study.

Living as we are in an age of great stress and tension, the psychological aspects of human welfare and individual happiness can no longer be neglected. I take great pleasure in recommending this book not only to professional psychologists, but also to the general reader interested in delving deeper into the marvels and mysteries of the human mind.

Acknowledgements

The list of people to whom we owe an immense gratitude begins early. In fact, it begins with the ancient *ṛṣis* who composed the beautiful verses of the *Ṛg Veda,* and it continues right into our present times through a long, uninterrupted lineage of *yogis*, poets, sages, philosophers and common men and women, who together developed the theory and practice on which Indian psychology is based.

Amongst our contemporaries, there are again too many great individuals to name all, but we would like to mention at least a few. The first who come to mind are no doubt the authors of the chapters in this book. They have not only borne with us during the long period of gestation *Foundations and Applications of Indian Psychology* took to come out, but they have also contributed in many other ways to the development of Indian psychology as a science. Then there are the many others have not contributed directly to the text, but who have worked for Indian psychology in other ways, whether by writing, research or the organization of seminars, workshops and conferences. We would like to mention, for example, George Mathews, Janak Pandey, S. Narayanan, Usha Ram, Indrani Sanyal, P. Krishna Rao, Krishna Mohan, Sonali Bhatt Marwaha, Ramana Kumar Kanuri, H. R. Nagendra and his colleagues at SVYASA, and in Pondicherry A. S. Dalal, Panch Ramalingam, Soumitra Basu, Larry Seidlitz and Ananda Reddy, but there are so many others.

Special mention need be made of Kireet Joshi, who in the early years of this century gave his unstinting moral and financial support to the development of Indian psychology as the then Chairman of the Indian Council of Philosophical Research. Similarly, we are grateful to K. Ramakrishna Rao, who personally and in his many official capacities has made a unique contribution to the development of Indian psychology. During the last ten years, the ICPR and ICSSR have enabled almost every seminar related to Indian psychology in India. In this connection we also want to express our gratitude to Rajiv Malhotra and the Infinity Foundation.

Finally there are those at the Sri Aurobindo Ashram and the Indian Psychology Institute who have helped with the production of this book: Neeltje Huppes, without whose continuous support the book might not have come out at all, Vladimir Iatsenko who provided us with the Glossary, and Lynn Crawford, Divya Parasher and Jyoti Dalal who proofread and typeset the texts. We owe a similar gratitude to the staff of Pearson Education and to the many others who by their interest, silent support or hard work have helped with the development of Indian psychology and the production of *Foundations and Applications of Indian Psychology*.

We are grateful to the Sri Aurobindo Ashram Trust for giving us permission to use quotations from Sri Aurobindo's writings.

Introduction to the second edition

R. M. Matthijs Cornelissen
Girishwar Misra
Suneet Varma

What do we mean by Indian psychology?

By Indian psychology we mean an approach to psychology that is based on ideas and practices that developed over thousands of years within the Indian sub-continent. In other words, we use the word 'Indian' to indicate and honour the *origin* of this approach to psychology—the origin of the underlying philosophy, the conceptual framework, the methods of enquiry, and the technology of consciousness that it uses to bring about psychological change and transformation. It may be useful to make explicit that we do not use the word 'Indian' to localize or limit the *scope* of this approach to psychology; we do not mean, for example, 'the psychology of the Indian people', or 'psychology as taught at Indian universities'. We hold that Indian psychology as a meta-theory and as an extensive body of related theories and practices has something essential and unique to contribute to the global civilization as a whole.

It may also be useful to make explicit that this volume is not about the past, but about the present and the future. You will look in vain for chapters about the history of Indian philosophy or religion as they developed over the ages. Many such texts are already available, but this is not one of them. This volume has contributions that demonstrate how ideas and practices from the Indian tradition can be used to tackle issues in contemporary psychology and constructively inform its disciplinary practice by helping theory building and application.

Psychology as taught at present, all over the world, is still amazingly unicultural. This is rather remarkable if we consider the intensity and ease of international communications, and the fact that it is almost half a century since the political decolonization of Asia and Africa was completed. Though the large component of European and American thought in psychology is understandable historically, it is not any longer excusable. For it is not that the rest of the world has not thought about human nature, and it is definitely not that contemporary psychology has found the one and only correct way of doing so. In this context, one could argue that Indian psychology will be relevant particularly to Asian, African, or Latin-American countries which share alternative non-Western world views about mind, psyche and various psychological phenomena such as healing, health, self, or personality; but we strongly believe that in spite of all cultural differences, there is a large common core to human nature, and that, to the extent that Indian psychology deals with that common core, it should be of interest to all members of the human family.

In short, we do not look at Indian psychology as something that belongs only to India or the past, but as a rich source of psychological insight and know-how that can be utilised to create a better future for the whole of humanity.

What the Indian civilization can contribute to psychology

The unique contribution which the Indian civilization can make to modern psychology can be looked at as consisting of three distinct elements—a sophisticated and well-worked out, psychology-based meta-theoretical framework, a wide repertoire of psychological practices, and a rich treasury of psychological theories. These three are, obviously, closely interconnected, and it may be clear that none of them can be fully understood without a fairly complete understanding of the other two. Yet, as language is inevitably linear, we will give here a separate short introduction to each of them.

A psychology-friendly meta-theoretical framework

The first major contribution the Indian civilization can make to psychology is a psychology-friendly meta-theoretical framework. To delineate the underlying theory, the basic 'paradigm' of the Indian tradition is, of course, a pretentious undertaking fraught with possibilities of error. The Indian civilization is immensely complex, and, given the abundance of different—often contrary—voices it harbours within itself, it is hard to state anything about it that cannot be contradicted with a striking counter-example. And yet, it is useful to give it a try, for the simple reason that without this background it is impossible to fully understand its psychological practices and its theories.

When one looks at the Indian civilization as it developed over the ages, it becomes quickly clear that within it there exists such a huge variety of distinct cultural traditions, that one may doubt whether it actually makes sense to speak of a single Indian tradition and whether it would not be more accurate to speak of Indian traditions in the plural. The doubt is understandable, but we would contend that in case of the Indian tradition, singularity and multiformity are not necessarily mutually exclusive. A rich variety of expressions does not preclude the possibility of a common thread, a single foundation supporting the variety, and we are inclined to think that especially in India such a common core indeed does exist. In fact, the idea of a single truth supporting a variety of manifestations is itself one of the core-characteristics of the deep view of reality that underlies the whole wide gamut of Indian traditions. One of the most-often-quoted aphorisms expressing this acknowledgment of divergent views in spite of a single underlying reality is probably: *ekam sad viprā bahudhā vadanti*, which means, 'the truth is One, but the wise call it by different names'. An interesting aspect of this saying is that the differences are not described as errors: it is the wise that give different names to the one truth. Moreover, one would miss the point if one were to take this saying as no more than a polite exhortation for religious tolerance. It rests on a deep, psychological understanding of the human condition, which says that reality as it really is, will always remain beyond our limited mental capacity to grasp, and that each individual can perceive of that reality only as much as their individual capacity and inclination will allow.

There is another ancient saying which goes a step further. It deals with the different perceptions that arise from affirmative and agnostic approaches to reality. It says—and one can immediately see how close some ancient Indian thinkers came to postmodern constructivism—that not only the name we give to an experience, but even the experience itself is determined by our 'set'. The *Taittirīya Upaniṣad* (2.6.1), for instance, says, *asann eva sa bhavati, asad brahmeti veda cet, asti brahmeti ced veda, santam enaṁ tato viduḥ*, meaning, 'whoever envisages it as existence becomes (or realizes) it as existence, and whoever envisages it as non-being becomes (or realizes) that non-existence'. It may be noted that in the Indian tradition such differences are not attributed only to the different cultural priming; they are attributed primarily to the different type, level and quality of the internal state of the observer. And this brings us to what might well be described as the most important difference between the Indian and the Western paradigm.

The differences. Western psychology is largely confined to two dimensions which are both fully accessible to the ordinary waking consciousness—the physical and the social.

Genetics, neurophysiology and the cognitive sciences are typical for sub-disciplines with a focus on the physical dimension, and the various offshoots of psychoanalysis, social constructivism and cross-cultural psychology could be considered typical for those who focus on social factors. Between the two, there is still, in spite of many attempts at 'softening' psychology, a widespread tendency to take the physical dimension more seriously than the social. Even in the field of consciousness studies, the existence of physical reality tends to be taken for granted, while the ontological 'reality' of consciousness and subjective experience is open for discussion. Their apparent existence needs some kind of justification, and both are commonly considered epiphenomenal products of material processes. Related to this, in terms of epistemology, the ordinary waking consciousness is considered the only acceptable state for the researcher to be in, and a clear rational mind is taken as the ultimate arbiter of truth. In fact, non-ordinary states of awareness are primarily associated with drugs and somewhat frivolous new-age activities. Finally, in terms of practical methodology, objectivity is taken as the ultimate ideal, and first-person, subjective observations are taken seriously only if they are embedded in statistics and third-person objective measures to counteract their inherent weaknesses. Obviously all this is a simplification and there are exceptions to this pattern—one could, for example, think of phenomenology—but still, a strong physicalist bias, an absolute faith in the ordinary waking consciousness and a total reliance on objective methods are so much part of mainstream psychology that amongst psychologists, they are commonly considered indispensable elements of the scientific method.

The intellectual tradition of India starts from radically different assumptions. Ontologically, the most fundamental reality is not matter, but spirit; or more precisely, the indivisible unity of *saccidānanda*, of absolute existence, consciousness and delight. In other words, the Indian tradition includes psychological phenomena like consciousness and joy as core-elements of reality, and in fact it takes not physics, but 'knowledge of the self' (*adhyātma-vidyā*) as the fundamental science. Accordingly, the possibility and cosmic importance of an absolutely silent, transcendent consciousness are hardly ever doubted, while there are major schools of thought that do doubt the importance and even the reality of the material pole of existence. While Western science has come to terms with the fact that there are many different types of physical energies and substances, of which some are not directly perceptible by the human senses, the Indian tradition takes it for granted that there are also various types and levels of non-physical existence—entire inner 'worlds' which are not directly perceptible to the ordinary waking consciousness, but that are ontologically as real, or even more real than the ordinary physical world. These non-physical realities are considered to be intermediate planes of conscious existence between the absolute, silent consciousness of the transcendent and the apparent unconsciousness of matter. As a result, physical and social factors are accepted as part of causal networks, but not as the full story—events are thought to be influenced by a wide variety of forces that include factors belonging to non-physical realities. Similarly, epistemologically, a rational mind is appreciated and cultivated, but it is understood that there are higher sources of knowledge and the possibility of a direct, intuitive apprehension of truth. Finally, objective, sense-based knowledge is considered a minor form of knowledge (or even ignorance, *avidyā*) and an immense collective effort has gone into the development of processes that can make us more open to the subtle worlds, and especially to the pre-existing inner knowledge, *vidyā*.

It may be clear that these two basic views of reality lead to a very different sense of what psychology is about, how it is to be conducted, and what can be expected from it. For those under the influence of the physicalist worldview, psychology deals either with outer behaviour or with mental processes that happen within the neuro-physiological apparatus of individual human beings; even those who stress social influences, tacitly assume that such influences are transferred by physical means. It is taken for granted that consciousness, whether individually or socially determined, depends on working neural systems.

Non-physical realities are illusionary and parapsychological phenomena are 'anomalous'. For an eternal soul there is no place (except as a belief of others, not as an 'objective' reality that exists in itself). Methodologically, one has to rely on statistics and sophisticated third-person methods of research. In terms of application, one aims at (behaviourally verifiable) changes in others.

For those under the influence of the Indian system, consciousness is primary. It is taken to be all-pervasive, and as existing within space and time, as well as beyond both. The borders of the individual are porous, and the individual consciousness is found to extend through space and time, to others, to all kinds of inner worlds, and even to what is beyond all manifestation. As a result, non-physical realities and parapsychological phenomena fit perfectly within this explanatory framework, and there is no difficulty accepting an eternal soul as our real self. For research in Indian psychology, sophisticated first person methods are the natural first choice. In terms of application, Indian psychology aims primarily at the mastery and transformation of oneself.

When one lists these differences in this manner, the two systems seem to belong to different worlds, and not only serious misunderstandings, but even a certain mutual distrust appears almost inevitable. Historically this has indeed been the case. In the Indian tradition, right from the *Upaniṣads* and the stories of the *Purāṇas*, the basic ontological and epistemological assumptions of modern psychology are looked at as beginners' errors, remnants of an ordinary, naive way of looking at the world that stand in the way of a deeper understanding of how the human mind, consciousness in general, and even the physical reality actually work. Seen from the other side, from the perspective of mainstream psychology, giving up its positivist, constructivist, or agnostic assumptions looks like a return to a superstitious past, a giving up of the most valuable accomplishments of the European Enlightenment, a recipe for disaster.

Roads to reconciliation. There are several factors that may, however, help to overcome these difficulties. The first is that the inability of modern science to deal effectively with non-physical realities and 'the divine', may not be intrinsic to science as such. Future generations, who are likely to have a more globally informed cultural background, may ascribe this inability largely to the vagaries of European history. It might well be found that in the early years of modern science, Europe left these inner realms aside, not because it is intrinsically too difficult to research them in an intelligent and open-minded manner, but simply because they were too encrusted in the religious environment of the time. It is true that neither alchemy, nor the later efforts of parapsychology have led to sufficiently concrete results to convince the sceptics; but that might well be because their studies were hampered on the one side by the lack of a sufficiently supportive philosophical framework, and on the other by their failure to develop effective powers within the inner realms they purported to study.

As we will try to present in this volume, the Indian tradition might be able to provide both. Though the Indian civilization has had its own difficulties—800 years of foreign interference not the least of them—such a dramatic split between the physical and the inner domains is not part of the Indian story. In fact, the social structures and mental attitudes supporting spiritual pursuits in India are much closer to those of European science than to those of European religion. Even Śaṅkara—who arguably comes closest to what in the Christian tradition would have been called a church-father, given his role in founding centres of religious authority and power—in the end puts personal experience (*anubhava*) above tradition. In his *Bhagavad Gītā Bhāṣya* he says, for example (18, 66), 'Even a hundred scriptural passages will not become authoritative when they, for instance, announce that fire is cool or dark' (Rao, 1979, p. 65). The methods of *yoga* and meditation are nowadays primarily looked at soteriologically, that is, as a means for salvation, as a means to arrive at *samādhi* or *nirvāṇa*—at least if they are not seen as a means to arrive at physical health and the survival of a corporate lifestyle. In the culture of origin, however, they are part of a coherent knowledge system and they are clearly looked at as a way to arrive at reliable knowledge. This is most clear in the case of *jñānayoga* (the *yoga* of knowledge); but one can easily discern elements of the pursuit of truth even in *karma-* and *bhaktiyoga* (the paths of works and devotion), which also, in their own way, have methods to reduce the distortions of perception and affect that are part of the ordinary human consciousness.

The good news then is that modern scientific and ancient Indian approaches to psychology may not be so much contradictory as complementary. It is true that they are based on different ontological and epistemological assumptions, that they use different methods, and to some extent, that they look at different sides of the human enterprise, but in the end, they are based on the same human urge for true knowledge, pure love, effective power and happiness. It may not be easy to come to mutual respect and understanding, but the effort will be worth it, for our preoccupation with knowledge and power in the physical domain has not solved humanity's problems. On a global scale, suffering due to poverty, violence and disease is still rampant, and we have added a considerable risk of sudden environmental self-destruction. One could well argue that the one thing we need most at present is a more comprehensive understanding of our own nature. As editors of this volume, we would like to argue that Indian psychology can make a valuable contribution to that endeavour.

Psychological practices

According to a survey commissioned by the *Yoga Journal*, there were in February 2008, some 15.8 million practitioners of (*haṭha*) *yoga* in the USA alone, and amongst the rest of the adult population, another 8 per cent, or eighteen million people, were 'very or extremely interested in yoga'. Over the years, thousands of researches on *yoga* and meditation have been conducted (Murphy & Donovan, 1997; Walsh & Shapiro, 2006), but according to the latter, this research is as yet rather imbalanced. Most research is conducted with beginning practitioners, and the vast majority of researches have been carried out with not more than three basic techniques—*haṭhayoga, vipassana* and Transcendental Meditation (TM). Almost all research is, moreover, in a mode that cultural anthropologists would call *etic,* rather than *emic*. In other words, the research is done from an outsider's, rather than from an insider's perspective; the techniques are decontextualized, and their effectiveness is measured in terms that belong to the theoretical framework of mainstream psychology. This is in itself not surprising, for measurement involves the use of standards, and in science these standards have to come from previously conducted research. But the result is that the effects of *yoga* and meditation have been measured almost exclusively on variables like blood pressure, anxiety, depression and extroversion, which have little to do with what would have been considered relevant in the culture of origin, such as equanimity, compassion, wisdom and detachment.

While reflecting on the scope of existing research on *yoga* and meditation, there is another issue that warrants careful consideration. It is true that India has developed an astounding variety of structured methods to 'do' *yoga* and meditation. There can also be no doubt that it is worth studying these techniques, and that one should not do this only by etic, but also, or even especially, by emic approaches. The methods of *yoga* should be understood on their own terms, and ideally not only in their gross 'effectiveness' but in terms of the underlying spiritual and psychological processes. But even a sympathetic, insider's look at these techniques will not give us the whole story. Amongst the Indian psychological practices that could benefit humanity, there are not only such formalised methods and techniques, but there is also an implicit, informal know-how that is orally transmitted from teacher to student within the *guru–śiṣya paramparā* (the master–disciple relationship), or passed down from generation to generation in the form of social institutions, customs, and culturally prescribed—but individually adopted and adapted—attitudes and inner gestures. When we look at *yoga* not only as a way to find the Divine but also as a way to bring our entire life more in harmony with the highest we can conceive and experientially 'realize', then it becomes clear why these informal, implicit aspects of *yoga* play such a big role in the Indian civilization, and why they are so interesting for modern psychology. An anecdote from E. Richard Sorenson (2008) may illustrate the point. Sorensen relates an experience he had in a Tibetan monastery where most of the monks were young, and where he had noticed earlier that the novices were always 'eagerly rushing to share whatever special tidbit [*sic*] might have come their way (whether material or ideational)' (p. 46). As he relates:

> One day, while having lunch with a group of novices, a burst of mirth snared my attention. An adolescent novice had just selected, as if solely for himself, the largest apple off a plate. Bursts of laughter from the others, no verbal comment, just hilarity, as several then did much the same, usually with some special fillip or perspective of their own. There was no obligation to be either different or the same ... they were just nuzzling at a trait all had seen outside.

The interesting part is that amongst these youngsters, there were no pejorative remarks or outbursts of self-righteous indignation. Egoism was for them not something natural and tempting, yet socially unacceptable, but an utterly hilarious trait they had so far noticed only in the behaviour of people outside their own community. Presuming there is no major genetic difference in such matters, it is clearly worthwhile to study what it is exactly that made sharing the natural baseline for these children. It seems extremely unlikely that such a fundamental difference can be brought about by formal exercises or explicit instructions.

Regarding the spiritual core of the Indian psychological tradition, there is amongst professional psychologists a similar tendency to focus on formal practices and specialised techniques. Yet, in the *Yoga Sūtras* of Patañjali, the undisputed authority on *rājayoga*, only one of its many *ślokas* deals with *āsanas* (*yogic* postures), and the *Bhagavad Gītā* hardly mentions strongly structured practices at all. Even in our times, some of the greatest sages of modern India, like Ramakrishna Paramahansa, Sai Baba of Shirdi, Ramana Maharshi and Sri Aurobindo, did not advocate the use of highly structured and formalized techniques at all. They worked instead through a focussed, specialized application of—in itself quite simple—psychological processes and powers. There is an enormous variety of those, and even though all the great gurus had their own favourites—for example, Ramakrishna's absolute devotion to the Divine Mother, or Ramana's sustained and unremitting focus on the question, 'Who am I?'—they typically adjusted their method of teaching to the needs of each disciple at any given moment.

The literature contains many different lists of desirable inner attitudes and gestures. Typical examples might be: a silent, non-judgemental self-observation; a growing surrender to the highest one can conceive; a sustained aspiration towards the Divine (whether in terms of knowledge, work, love, or oneness); a systematic development of traits like equanimity, calm, patience, vigilance, kindness, compassion, love, joy, harmony, oneness, wideness; small inner gestures of self-giving, consecration, openness, silence, surrender; the relocation of the centre of one's consciousness inwards and upwards. As yet, it is hard to say with certainty, whether such non-sectarian, informal 'paths' will dominate the future of Indian psychology, or the more formalized 'techniques' that have played such a big role in the preservation of the tradition into the present. What seems clear to us is that there is an urgent need for research in both.

Psychological theories

Indian psychology has dealt with most areas in which mainstream psychology is interested, and in many of them it has something unique to add. As we will see, there is a special, common quality to the contributions it can make to all these different fields. If we start with the structure of the personality then we find that the Indian tradition has developed the concept of *ahaṁkāra*, which stands somewhere in between the Western concepts of ego and self-concept. But besides this egoic centre, which belongs to the ordinary waking consciousness, the Indian tradition has also developed a detailed nomenclature for many other, more subtle and non-egoic centres of consciousness;

and it has even worked out, especially in certain Buddhist schools, how a consciousness can exist without any centre whatsoever. Similarly, the Indian tradition has found below the surface of our waking consciousness not only the dark 'unconscious' that depth psychology has explored, but a whole range of subtle *kośas* or layers of consciousness, that each have their own characteristic nature. It has even worked out many different ways of 'realizing' in one's experience (or perhaps one should rather say, in one's being) a Transcendent beyond all nature. It has found that all these inner layers, types, and centres of conscious existence have their specific influences on the surface personality, and that a direct access to them can, with sufficient training, enable levels of freedom, peace, joy, compassion, and understanding much beyond what is possible in the ordinary waking state.

In the field of cognition, we see a similar pattern. On the one hand, there is a detailed theoretical understanding of ordinary, sense-based cognition, mostly described as a system of *pramāṇa*, or knowledge-producing events. Different schools developed somewhat different theories about these matters—and they made much of their differences—but there is actually quite a large common base. It is noteworthy that the philosophical school of the Nyāya-Vaiśeṣika, which specialised in issues of epistemology and methodology, came to conclusions that are similar to modern thought in many respects. However, just as we saw in the field of Self and Personality, the ordinary sense-based cognition was not enough for the Indian tradition, and it developed besides a detailed understanding of intuition, inspiration, revelation, and various other types of 'intuitive knowledge' for which there are not always equivalent terms in English. The sheer complexity of the terminology, the subtle but significant differences between the various terms, and the stress on concrete methods to develop and refine these various forms of intuitive knowledge may give an idea not only of the enthusiasm and energy with which these possibilities have been explored, but also of the rigour, precision and attention for detail with which this work was undertaken. The study, cultivation and perfection of these subtle, not sense-based forms of cognition, might well deserve to become one of the major thrust areas of Indian psychology, as their development may lead to the creation of appropriate research methodologies for a whole new field of psychology.

Another major area of interest in psychology is that of emotion and motivation. To fully understand the various Indian theories of emotion, one has to go back to what should perhaps count as one of the greatest discoveries of the Indian tradition—the idea that the nature of ultimate reality can be described as an indivisible unity of *Sat, Cit* and *Ānanda,* or Existence, Consciousness, and Delight. While in mainstream psychology, it is generally presumed that happiness is dependent on the satisfaction of individual needs and desires, this theory asserts that delight is inherent in existence, even though it can be clouded in humans by their 'ignorance' (*avidyā*). In other words, suffering is attributed to ego-bound deformations and limitations of the over-individualized human consciousness. Seen from this angle, the satisfaction of desires may give temporary relief, but the road to lasting and unconditional happiness and wisdom runs through detachment from the ego, and a rediscovery of one's knowledge of, love for, and oneness with the ultimate reality. With the ideal of perfect detachment and complete equanimity, a series of intriguing questions arises, which have occupied some of the best minds in Indian history, regarding the possibility of action for someone who has completely overcome all desire, preference and attachment. If such 'unmotivated' action is possible—and most schools of Indian thought agree that it is—then what kind of action can that be?

In the field of emotion, a special place deserves to be given to the ideas of Bharata (400–200 BCE) on aesthetic enjoyment. Bharata starts with the fascinating question, why people enjoy watching tragic plays in spite of the fact that they already know beforehand that watching such plays will make them cry. Considering the emotions that spectators and actors suffer and savour, he arrives at the subtle theory of *rasa*, the basic 'taste', which triggers the original delight hidden in all things.

It is commonly held, especially amongst American authors (for example, Walsh & Shapiro, 2006) that there are several areas of psychology where the Indian tradition has little to contribute. Though this is in itself perfectly plausible, it does not hold for the most commonly quoted examples. In all four areas where Walsh and Shapiro, for example, think that 'the meditative traditions' have little to contribute—child-development, psychodynamics, psychopathology and psycho-pharmacology—there is in fact detailed theoretical knowledge available within Āyurvedic and Siddha literature. In all four fields, the Indian tradition has paid attention to very similar social and physical factors as are taken into account in Western psychology; but there is, besides, an additional interest in influences on more subtle planes. In child-development, for example, influences from previous lives and the unique 'soul-quality' of the child, the *svabhāva*, are acknowledged as major contributors to the child's character and development. A similar multilevel understanding is part of the Indian way of looking at psychopathology, and the developmental stages later in life—the four *āśramas*. The misconception that there is no Indian contribution to any of these fields, is in all likelihood due to the same peculiar way in which Western psychology has studied the Indian tradition that we mentioned earlier. Mainstream academics have either looked at the decontextualized techniques of *yoga* and meditation, or at the other extreme, at equally decontextualized philosophical systems. The surrounding culture, as actually practiced, and the mediating theories—which are both very well developed in India—have so far not received the attention they deserve.

Indian psychology applied

Psychology is very much an applied science; and fields like pedagogy, education, social work, human resource development, organisational behaviour and therapy can all be looked at as specialized fields of applied psychology. At present, practitioners in these fields often experience a certain tension between the official theory, which prescribes well-defined, explicit methods and procedures, and experience, which tells them that a more personalized, eclectic and intuitive approach works better. The informal experience seems to come closer to reality than the formal theory. Interestingly, there is substantial statistical evidence to support this view. Bruce Wampold (2001), for example, has collected massive meta-analytical data to show that hardly any of the efficacy in psychotherapy can be ascribed to specific methods and theories. According to his findings, the efficacy in therapy is almost entirely determined by factors that either belong to the environment in which the therapy takes place or that are internal to the therapist and the client. While this is hard to understand from within the medical model that is used in most mainstream therapy research, it is in full harmony with Indian psychology, where the focus is on the work people have to do on themselves. The guide—whether he plays the role of pedagogue, teacher, human resource professional or therapist—guides by example, and perhaps even by direct influence. He shows that growing up is both worthwhile and feasible; that difficult material can be learned; that it is possible to master complex social situations in a constructive manner; and that life's problems can be solved. In a very deep sense, the guide guides mainly by sharing who he is in the essence of his being and what matters is how he expresses that essence in his life. In many forms of therapy-training this is recognized, and undergoing therapy oneself is then an essential part of the training-process. But in Indian psychology, which is built on self-knowledge rather than on knowledge of statistically generalized others, the demand for self-work, for understanding and mastering one's own self, goes further—both in breadth and in depth. In breadth, because it extends to all fields of applied psychology, and in depth because a good guide is supposed to show that it is possible, in the words of Sri Aurobindo, to 'transcend and integrate': A good guide should be able to show that it is possible to go beyond one's limitations; to live from a higher consciousness; to act from less selfish motives; to work more in harmony with the whole.

The practical application of Indian psychology differs from present-day mainstream psychology in a manner that parallels the differences we found in the various areas of theory formation. There is on the one hand the same constant attention to the multidimensional nature of the personality—a multidimensionality that is not limited to the physical and the social, but that extends to, or rather starts with, the spiritual. And there is on the other hand, a constant awareness that each individual is ultimately unique. Both attention points come together in the important concepts of *svabhāva* and *svadharma*—the recognition that individuals have not only their own true nature, their own unique set of qualities, but also their own truth of action, their own rules of conduct. Both concepts are based on the underlying sense that the individual is not just a cluster of self-concepts and tendencies to behave according to pre-established patterns, but a spiritual being, a soul who has taken birth for a definite purpose, a purpose which it has to find and fulfil.

Concluding remarks

Indian psychology as such is as old as history; and in a technical sense, even older than written history, given that there are indications of a long oral tradition before the first texts were ever written down. But Indian psychology as a branch of modern science is a new field, which is as yet truly in its infancy. Our attempt to use the treasures of the Indian tradition for contemporary problems is relatively new and in that sense we are pioneering a new effort. The editors and contributors to this book make no claims on being accomplished *yogis*; they are ordinary scholars and professionals who have tried to see what various ideas and practices from the Indian tradition can contribute to some major issues in contemporary psychology. The different chapters are records of such attempts; most are exploratory in nature and not the outcome of a long, well-established tradition of research. What is more, this book looks at the Indian tradition as a knowledge system in its own right, and tries to see whether its ideas and its practices have the potential to complement and enrich modern science not only in terms of content, theory-construction and practical application, but even in basic research methodology. As said in the beginning of this introduction, this book would like to open up issues like these to a wider discussion.

The lay of the book

The first edition of *Foundations and Applications of Indian Psychology,* was published in two volumes under the title *Foundations of Indian Psychology*. The first of these volumes had as subtitle *Theories and concepts* and contained 22 chapters. The second volume had as subtitle, *Practical applications*, and contained 17 chapters.

The present, second edition comes out as a single volume under the title, *Foundations and Applications of Indian Psychology*. It includes 24 chapters from the first edition, and two new ones, the first by Anand Paranjpe, the second by Ashish Pandey and Rajen K. Gupta. The first 13 chapters of *Foundations and Applications of Indian Psychology* are about the basic theories and concepts of Indian psychology. The remaining 13 deal with its application in the fields of health, education and society.

A short guide to the individual chapters

The first chapter, 'Indian psychology: Implications and applications', gives an overview of what Indian psychology is and what it can contribute. K. Ramakrishna Rao argues that unlike Western psychology which does not have an overarching theory encompassing the entire discipline, Indian psychology's approach is synthetic and holistic, so that it becomes possible to overcome dichotomies such as science and spirituality, the sacred and the secular, theory and practice, individual and society. At the same time, Indian psychology, broadly speaking, has applications ranging from individual transformation to conflict resolution at the societal level. Rao takes centrality of consciousness as the defining characteristic of Indian psychology, and goes on to delineate twelve principles which provide the outline for a model of Indian psychology. The realm of extra-ordinary human experience (including telepathy and the direct action of mind over matter), Rao elucidates, can be researched most thoroughly using the concepts, methods and models of Indian spiritual psychology.

Ajit K. Dalal's chapter deals with the development of academic psychology in India. The title, 'A journey back to the roots: Psychology in India', alludes to the recent and renewed interest in models of psychology that have originated and developed in India over millennia. Dalal's chapter offers a comprehensive history of academic psychology in India, from its inception in 1905 at Calcutta University as part of the Philosophy Department, to the contemporary emergence of the Indian psychology movement. The chapter is accurate and informative in that it provides details of academic psychology in India, in terms of the number of psychologists, universities and colleges offering psychology, details of associations formed by psychologists over the years, and a chronology of events of direct significance to academic psychology. But more than that, Dalal has been able to pin-point that the main reason why psychology has failed to develop as a discipline of national importance is that it is largely a Western import. Right from the beginning, psychologists have led a double life, in the sense that they subscribe to one kind of psychology in their professional lives (Western), but to another when it comes to their personal lives—for which they lean on the Indian textual tradition, and the psychology contained therein (for example, the *Bhagavad Gītā*). As Dalal points out, academic psychology in India became more useful and relevant from the 1970s onwards, with a shift in focus to social problems, and more so in the 1980s when it was acknowledged that culture played a dominant role in the shaping of the psyche. Academic psychology in India is becoming increasingly more culture-sensitive and culturally rooted; and at the same time, the emergence of the Indian psychology movement, with its emphasis on the global relevance of systems such as Vedānta, Buddhism, Yoga and the more recent Integral Psychology of Sri Aurobindo, is also witnessed.

In 'Beyond mind: The future of psychology as a science', Kundan Singh places Indian Psychology in the wider, global context of an increasingly post-modern understanding of reality. He argues that true knowledge is attainable only by a shift in consciousness from a lower to a higher level, and not by clever manipulations of concepts located in the mind. Kundan begins by exposing the limits of induction, the mainstay of the scientific method, and challenges the possibility of any true 'objectivity', largely on the ground that our most basic tool of research, language, not only describes events, but also creates a cosmology, a worldview that influences the thought, behaviour and perception of the user. Leaning towards Eastern wisdom traditions, and basing his arguments largely on Mādhyamika, Advaita Vedānta and Integral Yoga, Kundan then offers the view that mind is not the knower of things, but an object of knowledge. He holds that the truth of one's existence can only be found by identifying oneself with a higher consciousness beyond the mind.

The next four chapters deal with epistemology, methodology, and cognition from different angles. In 'Indian psychology and the scientific method', Peter Sedlmeier explores how the Indian tradition can be used as a source for specific psychological hypotheses that can be tested within the formal parameters of mainstream science. Sedlmeier first outlines the standards of the scientific method and then introduces his own conception of what genuine Indian psychology is all about, including a 'metatheory' of Indian psychology. From this metatheory (and to a certain extent also from theories that are included in the metatheory), he derives several classes of testable hypotheses and exemplifies these with the help of some specific hypotheses or questions. Subsequently, Sedlmeier comes back to the topic of methods with an emphasis on the special methods needed to examine some of the hypotheses that deal with different aspects of consciousness. The chapter ends with an exploration of possible 'interfaces' between Indian and Western academic psychology.

In the next chapter, William Braud makes an attempt at 'Integrating *yoga* epistemology and ontology into an expanded integral approach to research'; on the basis of his work on 'Integral Inquiry' at what at the time was called the Institute of Transpersonal Psychology. Braud is of the view that Indian psychology and *yogic* epistemology and ontology can contribute much to enrich research aimed at bridging the gap between science and the spiritual/wisdom traditions. He describes ways in which *yogic* principles, and processes closely related to these, already have been usefully introduced into research praxis, and suggests additional ways in which aspects of *yoga* might be integrated into research in the future and how this might enliven and transform the research enterprise.

Matthijs Cornelissen makes in 'What is knowledge? A reflection based on the work of Sri Aurobindo' a case for the existence of essentially different modes of knowing. Cornelissen notes that Aurobindo identified four forms of knowing—knowledge by identity, knowledge by intimate direct contact, knowledge by separative direct contact and wholly separative knowledge by indirect contact. Cornelissen goes on to elaborate these four types of knowledge as follows: (1) knowledge by indirect separative contact includes scientific knowledge of the outer reality; (2) knowledge by direct separative contact is the semi-objective introspection of inner processes; (3) knowledge by direct intimate contact is the experiential knowledge of inner processes; and (4) knowledge by identity is the *Vedic* knowledge in which knower, knowledge and known are one. In Aurobindo's view, direct, intuitive knowledge by identity forms the essential core of all our knowledge. The author offers some arguments why such unconstructed, intuitive knowledge might actually exist, and then outlines some of the ways by which the Indian tradition has tried to make self-observation and intuition more accurate and reliable.

In 'Knowing in the Indian tradition', Girishwar Misra gives an account of Indian theories of cognition. Indian theories of cognition emphasize universal concepts, and view reality as a unified whole. The process of knowing begins with doubt, and the desire to know. In general, Misra points out, two domains of knowledge are differentiated in the Indian view—the transcendental (*pāramārthika*) and the empirical (*vyāvahārika*). Transcendental reality is considered as non-changing and universal. The major issues that have been discussed are mind, consciousness, and reality. Misra notes that there is a certain degree of similarity between the Indian and the Western mode of intellectual inquiry. In the Indian view, mind is conceptualized as an internal sense organ. Misra concludes that the Indian perspective on knowing holds contemporary relevance and has practical utility.

The next five chapters offer perspectives on the self, the structure of the personality, the human condition and the aim of life according to five quite different traditions. Vladimir Iatsenko opens the series with a short treatise 'On the *Vedic* Symbolism in the light of Sri Aurobindo'. He attempts to recover as the true meaning of the *Veda* the possibility of realising heaven on earth, that is, to possess and live in the highest Divine consciousness here on earth. He stresses that the *Vedic* view was one of transformation—invoking the higher powers by aspiration, surrendering to them, inviting them to come down and bring about transformation. This was the *Vedic* Sacrifice: its aim was transformation of terrestrial existence.

Priya Ananda and Ajith Prasad point out that Buddhist psychology has formulated various ways of analysing personality which may be termed as 'The models of personality in Buddhist psychology'. These psychological models are valuable in studying a variety of experiences—of the conventional involvement of ordinary beings, of those in the stages of the path to awakening, and the qualities of the fully awakened state. The authors indicate that these models are useful in analysing experiences related to sleep, dream, death, after-death state, etc. In this chapter, various models of personality available in Buddhist psychology are explored. The application of these models in understanding various psychological states and afflictions are also briefly touched upon.

The chapter by Kiran Kumar K. Salagame, 'Ego and *ahaṁkāra*: Self and identity in modern psychology and Indian thought', examines the concepts of 'ego' and '*ahaṁkāra*'. These terms have been used synonymously, and ego has been used as a translation of *ahaṁkāra*. Kiran Kumar points to the conceptual similarities and dissimilarities between the two terms, and outlines their implications for human development and well-being. The author carried out a series of empirical studies at the University of Mysore to study the concept of *ahaṁkāra*. The findings suggest that *ahaṁkāra* can serve as a meta-construct which can embrace many of the modern psychological concepts related to self and identity.

In the next chapter, Bahman Shirazi provides an outline of 'The Sufi path of self-transformation'. Beginning with a brief introduction to Islam (which means 'peaceful surrender' to the Divine Will), Shirazi notes that the process of spiritual transformation involves seven classical stages—awakening, abstinence, non-attachment, spiritual poverty, patience, God-reliance, and joyous certitude. The spiritual journey in Sufism begins with the *sharia* which is a collection of principles and practices that govern the day-to-day life of Muslims. The next level involves *tarigha*, which literally means a path which requires the expert knowledge of a guide (*sheikh*) to traverse. The third level of the spiritual journey brings the aspirant to a higher spiritual consciousness called *haghighat* (Truth-consciousness). The fourth and final level of Sufism is known as *ma'rifa* (Gnosis), which refers to direct knowledge and love of the Divine. The author points out that only persistence, patience and absolute purity of the heart and soul and total sincerity can bring the seeker into direct union with God consciousness.

Suneet Varma's chapter, 'Integral psychology: A new science of self, personality, and psychology', outlines a theory of personality based on Sri Aurobindo's conceptualization of the human being. Starting with the basic notion of self and personhood in various schools of contemporary academic psychology that are largely located in the lower levels of psychological functioning, the field of Transpersonal Psychology is used as a stepping stone to access the higher reaches of humanity. A brief outline of the Advaita Vedāntic perspectives on personality then paves the way for Sri Aurobindo's neo-Vedāntic depiction of the person. Varma then indicates the potential of Integral Psychology in bringing about human unity. In the last section, the author outlines an approach to the transformation of emotions, and its role in psychotherapy.

In the last chapter with a primarily theoretical focus, 'Psychology of emotions: Some cultural perspectives', Girishwar Misra begins with a summary of findings on the study of emotions in mainstream psychology. Whereas early studies on emotions searched for universals, the author notes that studies across cultures do indicate differences in the experience of emotions, in their recognition, and variations in their intensity. Misra builds on this and concludes that emotions are culturally shaped. The Indian contribution of *rasa* theory is then outlined. Misra is of the view that the concept of *rasa* as meta-emotion and *bhāva* as emotion, present a new dimension of aesthetic creativity that goes beyond the established views on emotion and widens their scope. The Indian idea of *rasa* draws our attention to a refined subjective mental state, and in relation to aesthetic experience, the person as dancer/poet and spectator/audience gets transported to an altered state, which may not be in congruence with mundane experience. Misra holds that in the Indian view, emotion can be a transcendental cognition, and *rasa* involves experiencing the universal self.

The second half of *Foundations and Applications of Indian Psychology* has five chapters on health, counselling and therapy, five on education and three on social and organisational issues.

'Philosophy of healing in Indian medicine', is a theoretical overview of Āyurveda, in which Kapil Kapoor first points out that in the Indian intellectual traditions, knowledge is an integrated whole, and Āyurveda is a good example of this. The aims of Āyurveda are two-fold—(*i*) freedom from illness, and (*ii*) protection of good health through prevention. Kapoor then notes that this science of medicine recognizes that there is a deep connection between the body and the mind, and that for good health, the mind must be at peace with itself. This peace of mind is born of moral cognition and conduct.

In the next chapter, 'Healing and counselling in a traditional spiritual setting', Anand Paranjpe describes a typical "neighbourhood guru": not very well-known, living an utterly simple, non-ostentatious life, but highly regarded, deeply respected and much loved by the small circle of people who visit him for guidance and solace. Paranjpe gives his lineage and belief-system, but in many ways more importantly, focuses on the pragmatics: what questions people come with, the type of advice he gives, and the rational behind his responses. It is a type of study we hope to see many more of, as they could provide us with invaluable guidance for the development of more integral, inclusive methods of therapy.

In 'Concept and scope of *pratyāhāra* in the management of mental health', K. M. Tripathi describes how *yoga* can be conceptualized as a system of self-healing. Tripathi notes that following the technical definition of *yoga*, derived from Patañjali's *Yoga-Sūtras*, one could consider *vipāssanā*, Transcendental Meditation, and *śavāsana* as techniques of *pratyāhāra*, the control of the senses. The author further points out that through *pratyāhāra*, one can attain complete isolation from internal as well as external stimuli. Thus, the practice of *pratyāhāra* can help in managing the stresses of personal life and in regaining composure. Tripathi holds that *pratyāhāra* is sense-control, leading to self-control. It is one's sensations, perceptions, notions, imagination, and other mental activities that become the subject matter of study when the mind turns inwards for introspection. Introspection helps in regulating and modulating these mental activities by understanding their nature and field of operation, and is a means of redirecting their energy. Thus, perfection in *pratyāhāra* brings about a deep mental relaxation.

In his chapter on 'Psychotherapy and Indian thought', Alok Pandey provides a broad overview of the many ways in which Indian psychological concepts and practices can be used in all aspects of counselling and psychiatric care. In general, the Indian view of existence is that of the journey of the divine in a person. All struggles and suffering represent a movement from an infra-rational (animal) existence to a more rational (human) existence, and further towards an even greater supra-rational (divine) existence and an end-state of Truth, Bliss, Peace and Beatitude. This is the human journey: from obscure beginnings in a half-lit animal-human consciousness to an increasingly divine humanity. The counsellor or therapist who can assist us in this journey is but a fellow traveller who has walked ahead of us from a life of relative darkness to a life of increasing Light. Only one who has mastered swimming to a high degree can save the one who is drowning; so is the case with therapy.

In 'Psychotherapy and Integral Yoga Psychology', Michael Miovic explores some of the concerns of clinical psychology with special reference to the areas of overlap between psychotherapy and Sri Aurobindo's model of Integral Yoga Psychology. Miovic utilizes Integral Yoga Psychology as an organizing framework because Sri Aurobindo interpreted *yoga* as being primarily a *psychological* process of self-cultivation and ego-transformation, and expressed his insights in modern English. Like psychotherapists, Sri Aurobindo was deeply interested in the problem of how to change character structure and behaviour, the only difference being that he felt the key to this change was ultimately spiritual. Miovic notes that Sri Aurobindo developed a complex understanding of human psychology, including concepts of the ego, the importance of childhood development, defence mechanisms, the unconscious, the significance of dreams, resistance, and the importance of biology. However, where Sri Aurobindo diverges from Western psychology and psychiatry is in his spiritual realism. The practical consequence of this is that he recommends that people find their souls *before* trying to work through the unconscious, because the psychic being is a more powerful agent of knowledge and action than the observing ego.

In 'Integral education: An application of Indian psychology', Neeltje Huppes explores how the basic understanding of life and its purpose which one finds in ancient Indian texts, could revolutionize modern education. In the Indian view, some aspect of the supreme consciousness, though often concealed, pervades each and everything. In our daily consciousness, this supreme consciousness is mostly covered up, yet each of us carries a spark of the Supreme deep within, called the *caitya puruṣa* or soul. Huppes emphasizes that if the soul is allowed to come to the foreground, it can influence the mental, affective, volitional and physical surface consciousness to act more in harmony with this universal consciousness. The psychological process of human development is thus seen as a progressive development: a development balanced between the innermost part of the being—the soul—and the outer life. Huppes notes that the ideal of integral education combines two lines of development: the revealing and unfolding of the soul, and the development of the mental, affective and physical domains as instruments for expressing that soul in daily life.

In 'The blending of healing and pedagogy in Āyurveda', P. Ram Manohar highlights how the medical tradition of Āyurveda has preserved a rather unique concept of education that blends principles of healing with those of pedagogy. With its intense focus on the promotion of positive health and well-being, Āyurveda has discovered that elevated levels of health can be achieved only by a subtle transformation of the inner personality. While diseases can be cured, managed or prevented by medical intervention and other physical means, higher states of health can be achieved only through self-awakening. Manohar thus emphasizes that the process of self-education is essentially an educative development, a psycho-spiritual transformation that enables the individual to not only live with awareness, but also with health. The meeting point of the most refined methods of pedagogy and healing result in the notion of the physician par excellence as the *vaidya*, the one who knows the essentials and helps the individual through education to reach a state of heightened awareness, a state most conducive to the acquisition of both knowledge and health.

In 'Situating teacher education in the Indian context: A paradigm shift', Bharati Baveja indicates how teacher training could be made more responsive to the actual needs of children using theories derived from the Indian tradition. Baveja points out that discourse in education, particularly teacher education, has its origins in pragmatic concerns overridden by social pressures in the late nineteenth century, concerns that are largely, if not entirely, irrelevant today. At the same time, educators in India have consistently failed to acknowledge the richer and more convincing concepts that exist in the Indian traditions since time immemorial. Basing herself on ideas given in the *Bhagavad Gītā,* Baveja notes that teaching is not a collection of skills but an ongoing process of contemplation; a continuous search for truth; an ongoing quest to understand the learner, the processes of learning, the ways of providing learning experiences and inspiration to help students embark on their inner journey. Thus, a teacher has to be a true *karma yogī* who engages in enjoined actions in the pursuit of knowledge, and is committed to the development of her self and her students.

In 'Education for life: The Mirambika experience', Anjum Sibia utilizes the ethnographic method to examine the teaching-learning process in Mirambika, a centre of learning based on Free Progress Education, as outlined by Sri Aurobindo and The Mother. Sibia explicates the pedagogic processes occurring in the classroom in order to understand the relationship between the school philosophy, activities and student outcomes. Sri Aurobindo emphasizes that, 'The chief aim of education should be to help the growing soul to draw out that in itself which is best and make it perfect for a noble cause'. Sibia notes that Free Progress Education is based on the assumption that a person is good in him/herself, and that positive freedom is a pre-requisite to help children by allowing them space to experiment, and by providing them with opportunities for growth.

In 'Krishnamurti and value education', Vinita Kaushik Kapoor notes that the aim of education must be to awaken an intelligence through which thought and knowledge find their right place. Such a perception may be seen as a religious perception. Kapoor further emphasizes that it is only when the truly religious mind informs the values on which we build our daily existence that there is a possibility of a sane and orderly world, free from conflict and sorrow. Krishnamurti emphasizes the importance of understanding oneself first, and the role of the educator here is to help the child observe the ways in which thought creates its own prison. Krishnamurti also stresses the relationship of the child with nature as an essential part of education. Finally, Kapoor notes that Krishnamurti initiates a strong and consistent thrust towards establishing values rooted in the sacred, the truly religious.

'Broadening of consciousness: A healing process among the survivors of the Kachchh earthquake' is an ethnographic study carried out by Kumar Ravi Priya. The study utilizes a cultural psychological perspective on health and illness to understand the phenomena of suffering and healing which took place in the crisis faced by Kachchh during the post-earthquake period. In the chapter, Priya illustrates how the villagers' belief in *karma* (taken here as an internalized notion of duty towards family, community and nature) facilitated the healing process, as it allowed them to transcend the notion of a limited 'I' or ego and broaden their consciousness to experience themselves as part of a pure and absolute consciousness, as one with the Eternal. Priya also provides a poignant account of how the research process contributed to his own growth as a person.

In 'Resolution of social conflicts: An Indian model', R.S. Pirta explores the features, dynamics and outcome of the Chipko (hug-the-tree) movement, a people's non-violent struggle for justice and sustainability in the Garhwal Himalayas. Pirta notes that Chipko had its origins in the environmental desecration of the Garhwal Himalayas, characterized by large-scale logging operations managed by private contractors. The villagers revolted against the logging policies of the forest department as it made their lives much more difficult and complicated. A hawk and dove conflict ensued, in which the doves (native Garhwalis) won. This later transformed into a broad-based Himalaya Bachao Andolan (Save the Himalayas Movement). Pirta provides a unique social-psychological analysis of the movement, while exploring the role played by the local deities and their relation to the mental health of the people.

In the last chapter, 'Spiritual Climate of business organizations and its impact on customers' experience', Ashish Pandey and Rajen K. Gupta come down from the Himalayan villages to the corporate world and offer a good example of what a well-worked-out quantitative study in Indian psychology can offer. After noting how according to the Indian tradition, every aspect of society should be permeated with spirituality, the authors look at various concepts used for the study of spirituality in the corporate domain. They then settle on the following main thesis for their study: "spirituality of employees is reflected in the work climate. This may in turn affect the employees' service to the customers." The study confirms the main thesis, though the effect found is not very large, and apparently just one amongst several others.

With this, we have reached the end of our introduction to *Foundations and Applications of Indian Psychology*. We hope—and actually expect—that *Foundations* will provide an inspiring read. Each chapter has something unique and valuable to contribute and together, its 26 chapters form a harmonious and representative whole.

Obviously, a book of this size cannot be complete. For every issue we have touched upon, and for many that we haven't even mentioned, there exists somewhere a treasury of more detailed knowledge. Unfortunately most of this knowledge and psychological know-how is at present only available outside the borders of academic science. We hope that this book will encourage an increasing stream of rigorous work bringing the two worlds of outer, scientific, and inner spiritual knowledge closer together. Humanity needs both.

Foundations and Applications

of

Indian Psychology

1

Indian psychology: Implications and applications

K. Ramakrishna Rao

Over the years, I have used two metaphors to describe the psychological content in classical Indian thought. Psychological insights in the Indian tradition are rich diamonds in the raw, buried deep in the ravines worn by philosophical streams and covered by issues and concerns extraneous to academic psychology. So they need to be mined and recovered by modern investigative tools, cut into contemporary categories, polished by concepts currently in vogue, and displayed dressed in fashionable discourse. Only then can we see their radiating natural brilliance and their many-sided splendour. In the second metaphor, classical Indian thought is a treasure trove of psychological thought, hidden in the thick forests of philosophical and religious texts, waiting to be harvested.

In a significant sense, the analytic approach of Western psychology is piecemeal. It is said that psychology, with some exceptions, has bits of theories relevant to specific areas such as perception and learning, but not an overarching theory encompassing the entire field. In the Indian tradition, however, the approach is synthetic and holistic. Its metatheoretical postulates help to overcome dichotomies such as the sacred and the secular, spirituality and science, theory and practice, society and individual, reason and experience. They help to build models for studying human nature in its totality and formulate comprehensive theories that apply to a wide variety of topics and issues. Therefore, I believe, Indian psychology has implications that are in a sense broader than psychology itself. It has potential for application to areas, which current Western approaches appear unable to address effectively. These include such vital concerns as conflict resolution at a social level, transformation at a personal level, and the widely held beliefs in spirituality and paranormal phenomena.

With the backdrop of classical Indian thought, it becomes possible to develop a meta-theory and unified models for psychological research. We hope that this exercise will contribute to the growth of the discipline appropriately called spiritual psychology, which has implications for bridging the science–spirituality divide. Science and religion are generally considered to be disparate and inconsistent, if not conflicting, attempts at understanding reality. Our contention is that science and spirituality need not be so considered. In this chapter, I will present an outline of what I consider to be the major assumptions of a meta-theory of science and religion, important conceptual and methodological issues in studies of spirituality, the relevant implications of these assumptions for psychological theory and research, and possible areas of application.

Religion and spirituality

Spirituality and religion have gained a measure of respectability in recent years in academic discussions, thanks to the substantial literature that appears to connect them to health (George et al., 2002; Koenig et al., 2001).

However, what the concepts 'spirituality' and 'religion' precisely mean is a matter of considerable controversy. For example, Koenig et al. (2001), in their *Handbook of Religion and Health*, call our attention to the difficulties involved in finding acceptable definitions for religion and spirituality. Pointing out the inadequacy of their dictionary definitions, they list several distinguishing characteristics of religion and spirituality (Table 1.1, p. 18). These include, first, that religion is community-focused, observable, measurable and objective, whereas spirituality is individualistic, less visible and measurable, and more subjective. Second, that religion is organized, behaviour-oriented, and involves outward practices. Spirituality, however, is less formal and systematic, and more inward directed. Characterizing religion as 'an organized system of beliefs, practices, rituals, and symbols', Koenig et al. (2001) regard spirituality as 'the personal quest for understanding answers to ultimate questions about life, about meaning, and about relationship to the sacred or transcendent...' (p. 18). They depict spirituality as the outer circle which includes various religions as inner circles (Figure 1.1, p. 19).

Others, like Teresa Woods and Gail Ironson (1999), also emphasize the public and private aspects of religion and spirituality. However, it is well known that William James (1902), among others, emphasized the private aspects of religion as well. It is suggested, therefore, that religion and spirituality are overlapping constructs. They exhibit some common characteristics and some non-shared features (Miller & Thoresen, 1999). According to Miller and Thoresen (1999), 'the field of religion is to spirituality as the field of medicine is to health' (p. 28). This view suggests that spirituality is an inner circle within the wider circle of religions, a view somewhat different from the one expressed by Koenig et al. (2001). Empirical studies of spirituality and religion have rarely made operational distinctions between the two. Again, to quote Miller and Thoresen (1999), 'almost all empirical studies to date have not recognized the distinctions ... but instead have treated religiousness, religion, and spirituality as the same general concept' (p. 29). Further, they point out that 'with rare exceptions, the available literature has measured religious ... rather than spiritual variables' (ibid.). The latter assertion may be an oversimplification, once we acknowledge that spirituality and religion are not sufficiently well distinguished for operational purposes.

Peter Hill and Kenneth Pargament (2003) point to the dangers of bifurcating religion and spirituality. They list four such dangers. (1) Manifestation of spirituality in all its forms occurs in a social context, and all organized religions address personal affairs. Therefore, the view that one addresses issues at the social and the other at a personal level is untenable. (2) There is a growing tendency to think that spirituality is good and religion is bad. There is no justification for such attributions as both have potentially beneficial and harmful sides. (3) For most people, the distinction between religion and spirituality does not exist. They have spiritual experiences in an organized religious context. (4) The polarization of the two concepts, spirituality and religion, 'may lead to needless duplication in concepts and measures' (p. 65). Hill and Pargament suggest that the sacred, which includes the divine and the transcendent, is 'the common denominator of religious and spiritual life' and spirituality is 'a search for the sacred, a process through which people seek to discover, hold on to, and, when necessary, transform whatever they hold sacred in their lives' (ibid.).

The definitional and operational ambiguities of religion and spirituality constructs spill over into the science–religion dialogue. Without a certain degree of clarity of the core concepts 'religion' and 'spirituality', the science–religion dialogue would be a non-starter. We believe that the spiritual traditions of India have something to offer in this context. There is a general consensus between the Indian and Western perspectives that the common ground between religion and spirituality is the sacred. The sacred may refer to different things such as god, divinity, ultimate reality and so on. The common denominator of all of them, it would seem, is transcendence. Transcendence implies going beyond what is given in one's normal sensory experience. In the spiritual traditions of India, whether Hindu or Buddhist, there is an overwhelming emphasis on transcendence as a state of being that goes well beyond sensory awareness. Spiritual pursuit is an exercise for transformation of the human condition to achieve transcendence. Spiritual psychology is dedicated to understanding this process. Thus, in the Indic traditions, spirituality is the quest and religions are the tools and technologies—first, to aid in that quest and, second, to apply the discoveries of the spiritual quest to life and living. *Spirituality is to religion what science is to technology*. Seen in this light, science and spirituality are two truth-seeking activities that seem to run parallel to each other.

Science and spirituality

From time immemorial, science and spirituality have been two important avenues of human endeavour. Search for truth is the goal of science as well as of spirituality. Their discoveries have had enormous influence on people across cultures and around the world. However, their relative roles and dominance have varied over time. It would seem that spiritual quest was the dominant force first. Today science clearly has the upper hand, even though spirituality does seem to play a major role in the personal lives of a majority of people. Again, the application of science and spirituality has profoundly influenced human life all along. The discovery of truth, whether in the area of science or spirituality, quite often leads to development of technologies that affect our lives in a variety of ways. Technological development is not the exclusive province of science. Analogous developments take place in the sphere of spirituality as well. In a significant sense, religious practices are the offshoots of the application of spiritual discoveries.

Most of the time, science and spirituality have run as parallel quests. We are concerned at a given time with one or the other. Consequently, they are compartmentalized, considered in isolation, and pursued independently. However, when there is a simultaneous focus on the two for their unified understanding, problems arise in the form of truth conflicts. This in turn leads to the perception of one in opposition to the other. One then tends to pronounce a verdict from one perspective, however disconcerting it may be from another. The option of convenience is to keep science and spirituality as separate as possible and limit them to pre-circumscribed domains with impregnable walls built between them. Alternatively the tendency is to reject outright one in favour of the other. This is an unnatural arrangement, because both science and spirituality continue to affect our being and behaviour, whether or not we acknowledge it. An obvious casualty in the process is a meaningful dialogue between science and spirituality.

If the effects of science and spirituality on humans are genuine as believed, a dialogue between the two is not merely warranted, but necessary. This calls for a meta-theory aimed at the unification of science and spirituality, because a theory of science or spirituality alone is unlikely to facilitate a meaningful dialogue between them. The underlying perspective of such a theory should be one that does not pit science against spirituality, or vice versa, one that does not conceive either in opposition to the other, but postulates unity and complementarity between them, at perhaps a more profound level than is obvious to commonsense. In this context, spiritual psychology, which attempts to gain unified understanding of the transcendental and empirical domains of our existence and experience, appears to be the discipline that holds the key.

The basic postulates of a meta-theory embracing science and spirituality include the following. First, science and spirituality are two knowledge streams that spring from the human mind. The two streams are marked by their distinct epistemological contours. They travel through different terrains, but finally merge into the mother sea of consciousness. Second, emancipation of the human condition from the limiting constraints of ignorance and suffering to a state of happiness and well-being are the goals of both science and spirituality. These goals are pursued by different strategies and methodologies with varying degrees of success. However, success or failure is not confined to one domain or one methodological stance. Rather science is applicable to some areas of human concern, and spirituality appears to matter in some others. Scientific habit of the mind and spiritual outlook are not opposed to each other; they serve different functions. However, together they hold the best hope of achieving the highest happiness, with fewer risks. Third, there is no intrinsic opposition between science and spirituality. There are, of course, epistemic differences between them. They follow different methodological strategies which are valid in their respective domains. Problems arise and mistakes are made when there is conflation of the two, and when transgression of the paths takes place, such as the attempts to prove the existence of God by science or the denigration of evolutionary theories by assertions of creation by some religious sects.

It would not be correct to say that science alone leads to truth. Perhaps it can be said that science leads us more reliably to understand the physical world. The same may be said about spirituality as being more appropriate in dealing with non-physical matters such as values. There may be areas where both approaches are appropriate and a unified approach more fruitful.

In the Indian tradition, both science and spirituality have the same goal, which is *liberation* (*mokṣa*). The goal of science is enriching the human condition by freeing it from constraints of hunger, disease and deprivation; and creating physical conditions for comfort, convenience and need gratification. With their exponential growth during our lifetime, we have come to expect science and its offshoot technologies to provide plenty for all. The growth is not without its problems, however. The explosive growth of science with unpredictable consequences threatens to subvert and distort life itself on this planet. Nuclear energy and genetic engineering, for example, which have extra-ordinary potential to transform the human condition, are more feared today than loved. The promise of science to satisfy human needs has not helped to reduce the needs. Rather, it spurred the insatiable desire for more. Indiscriminate exploitation of resources and ingenious destruction of the environment followed. Also, the belief that satisfying the physical needs of food and shelter, and the psychological concerns of security and stability, will lead humans to devote themselves to finer aspects of life—such as pursuing art and promoting values of love, compassion and altruism—is belied. Economic prosperity and happiness appear to be unrelated beyond a point. Thus science as a liberating influence appears to have serious limits.

The goal of spirituality, like that of science, is also liberation. It is the liberation of the inner spirit. Spirituality could be seen as a complementary force that gives a positive direction to science and acts as an antidote to the latter's use for destructive purposes. In the least, it provides coping mechanisms to deal with psychologically debilitating anxiety, stress, fear and helplessness. At its best, spirituality is known to free humans from all kinds of suffering born out of dysfunctional egos with insatiable desires, and consequent personal frustration and externally directed aggression. *Spirituality could be a soothing syrup to congested minds that cough conflict and abuse.* At the same time, it may also be seen as a blinding influence that shuns reason, spurts superstitious behaviour and stifles ambition and achievement. Instead of liberating, it could exile the human spirit to the dark recesses of ignorance, disease and deprivation. Thus both science and spirituality are double-edged. They could be used to emancipate or to enslave. However, working in tandem, they could help enhance human potential, limiting each other's adverse effects.

A dialogue between science and spirituality would help to clarify their relative roles. In this context, exploring areas in which spiritual matters, such as whether prayer affects measurable empirical variables like health, is of considerable importance. Spiritual psychology is the discipline of relevance here.

Spiritual psychology

Science has methods that work well in their legitimate domains of application. It would be a category mistake, however, to ask of science the proof for the existence of God. It would be equally inappropriate to ask for a spiritual explanation of the structure of the atom. Does it follow then that science is science and spirituality is spirituality and the two shall never meet? Not necessarily so. If it were, the question of dialogue between the two would not arise. Inasmuch as the human mind is the source from which science and spirituality spring and merge back in consciousness, as postulated in the unified theory—despite the distinctly parallel tracks on which they run—there is obvious interaction between the two in our lives. The science–spirituality dialogue is predicated on such interactions. Spiritual psychology focuses on them as its subject matter.

We said that science and spirituality spring from the human mind. However, they manifest as two distinct epistemic modes. One is the rational mode. It is mediated by the senses, the nervous system, and the brain. The other, the intuitive mode, is the revelational component of spiritual experience. It is the so-called transcendental aspect of our being that is not mediated but directly experienced. It processes consciousness-as-such. It is *knowing* by *being*. As William James puts it: 'Mystical experiences are as direct perceptions of fact for those who have them as any sensations ever were for us' (1902/1914, pp. 423–424). The existence of the intuitive/revelational mode is fundamental for spiritual experiences, just as the brain and sensory processing are essential for scientific understanding. Science is based on cognitive processing of information. In the Indian tradition, spirituality is considered transcognitive. Consciousness is believed to manifest in humans at the cognitive as well as transcognitive (transcendental) levels. Spiritual psychology explores the two together in the phenomena that are a joint manifestation of sense and reason on the one hand, and intuition and experience on the other.

Without miracles and mystical experiences, the sacred texts of most religions would be left with little credible substance. The miracles and revelational experiences may have a spiritual source. For this reason, they are labelled as non-natural or supernatural phenomena and are seen as conflicting with the basic limiting principles of science. For some, that is a sufficient justification for their rejection as genuine phenomena. Such a rejection would be comforting if one were to live in the domain of natural science alone. That would leave out, however, a great deal in our beliefs and practices. Exploring the spiritual component in our beliefs and behaviour is the business of spiritual psychology.

Science is based on reason and observation. Spiritual truths are born of revelations and are anchored in experience. Science in general is third-person oriented, whereas spirituality is first-person practised. Thus science and religion enjoy two diametrically different perspectives. Their validity essentially depends on the validity of the sources from which their respective claims emerge. If revelations are delusional experiences of maladjusted messiahs, religious beliefs tend to be false and detrimental. On the contrary, if they are indeed non-rational forms of knowing the truth, then there must be a non-rational source or pathway to truth. If there are thus two diametrically different sources of truth seeking, in which scientific discoveries and technologies on the one hand and religious beliefs and practices on the other are based, it is enormously important that we study the authenticity of religious experiences as we do the validity of scientific discoveries. It is the business of spiritual psychology to do just that. Since the mind is the seat/base of all knowledge, spiritual psychology attempts to study the mind as the interfacing instrumentality between science and religion. In an important sense, it is an attempt to apply spirituality underlying religious behaviour to psychology in general, and to its transpersonal and transcognitive aspects in particular.

Spiritual psychology is both a branch of psychology, like child psychology and social psychology, and a system of psychology, like psychoanalysis. It has a set of basic postulates that provide an overarching theoretical orientation. The basic postulate in this case is the primacy of spirit defined as the principle or centre of consciousness in the embodied human condition. Spiritual psychology, acknowledging the primacy of the spirit, explores its relation to the mind and the body in the person. Spiritual psychology explores the unity of the spirit, the mind and the body as they manifest in the human context. It serves as the bridge to connect the otherwise disparate realms of personal and transpersonal, the secular and the sacred, the cognitive and the transcognitive processes.

Spiritual psychology shares a great deal with religious psychology and yet is very different from it. Religious psychology, as the Cambridge psychologist R. H. Thouless (1972) defined it, seeks 'to understand religious behaviour by applying to it the psychological principles derived from the study of non-religious behaviour'. Spiritual psychology goes well beyond this. It seeks to understand human nature itself from the study of the spiritual aspects in our beliefs and behaviour. Postulation of the primacy of the spirit is the defining characteristic of spiritual psychology. Spirit (*ātman)*, in the Indian tradition, is consciousness-as-such. Consequently, the study of consciousness-as-such in its relation to the thinking-mind and the sensing-brain constitutes the subject matter of spiritual psychology.

Theoretical base

Indian psychology has much to offer for a foundational base to build the edifice of spiritual psychology. Psychology in the Indian tradition is an 'inner' discipline in search of realizing truth and perfection in the human condition. The goal is to find oneself in an unconditioned and unmasked state. While assuming that consciousness is the ground condition of all knowledge, Indian psychology studies consciousness in its multifaceted manifestations and seeks to explore the experience of its true nature in one's being. Indian psychology is not only a body of generalizable principles, but it is also a set of practices that can be used for the transformation of the human condition towards perfection. It has its own methods appropriate to its subject matter and objectives. The methods are observational, but they are different from the externally oriented observations of 'outer' sciences. They are a peculiar blend of first-second- and third-person perspectives. They provide for personal, subjective, and non-relational authenticity and in-group inter-subject validity (Rao, 2002). The strength of Indian psychology consists in the potential it offers for transformation through successive stages and processes of deconditioning the person to a state of freedom and perfection. The following twelve points/principles provide the outline of a model based on classical Indian psychological thought:

1. Psychology is the study of the *person* (*jīva*).
2. The *person* is consciousness embodied.
3. The *person* is not an isolated and disconnected entity in that the *jīva* is transpersonal and interconnected by transcognitive states.
4. Consciousness-as-such is irreducibly distinct from material objects, including the brain and the mind.
5. The mind is different from consciousness as well as the body/brain machine. Unlike consciousness, the mind is material, albeit subtle. Unlike the brain, the mind has non-local characteristics, that is, it is not constrained by time and space variables, as gross material objects are. Thus the mind is the facilitating principle and function that interfaces consciousness at one end and the brain processes at the other.
6. Consciousness in the human context, that is, consciousness embodied, appears circumscribed, conditioned and clouded by a vortex of forces generated by the mind–body connection. Consequently, the conditioned person becomes an isolated instrument of individualized thought, passion and action.
7. From individuation arise, on the one hand, subjectivity, rational thinking and relativity of truth and values. On the other hand, there arises the ego as the organizing principle.
8. With the ego, come attachment and craving which lead the person in turn to experience anxiety, insecurity, stress, distress, disease and consequent suffering.
9. Situated in such an existential predicament of ignorance and suffering, the goal of the person is self-realization.
10. Self-realization consists in achieving a state of *freedom* and *liberation (mokṣa)* by a process of deconditioning training and consequent transformation of the person to achieve higher states of awareness and achievement. This is accomplished

by accessing consciousness-as-such in transcognitive states.

11. Endowed with consciousness, mind and body, the person is capable of brain-processed *learning* (*śravaṇa*), mind-generated *understanding* (*manana*) and consciousness-accessed *realization* (*nididhyāsana*).
12. *Yoga* is a method of liberation via realization of transcognitive states. Realization takes different forms relative to the different dispositions of the seekers. These include knowledge-focussed *jñāna yoga* to meet the thought needs, devotion-filled *bhakti yoga* to deal with one's passionate nature, and action oriented *karma yoga* for those dominated by the impulse to act. Thus *wisdom*, *worship* and *work* are three distinct routes for self-realization.

This model makes a fundamental distinction between 'consciousness/spirit' and 'mind', and a secondary distinction between 'mind' and 'brain'. Consciousness is the knowledge side of the universe. It is the ground condition for all awareness. Consciousness is not a part or aspect of the mind, which, unlike consciousness, is physical. Consciousness does not interact with the mind or any other objects or processes of the physical universe. However, in association with consciousness, mental phenomena become subjective and are revealed to and realized by the person.

In this view, the mind is the interfacing instrumentality that faces consciousness/spirit on one side and the brain and the physical world on the other. The mind thus gives the impression of having two faces—the physical side in its relation to the brain and other physical systems, and the subjective side facing consciousness/spirit. From the physical side, the mind collects information by processing the inputs it receives. This is normal cognitive processing. When the information thus processed is exposed to consciousness at the other end, that is, when the light of consciousness is reflected on it, there is conscious experience of the phenomenal data. In a reflexive situation, where the reflection of consciousness reflects back in consciousness (*pratibimba*), one has subjective awareness.

The mind, though physical like the brain, is different from it. The mind is closely connected to different systems of the brain. It influences and is influenced by events in the brain. Most Indian traditions assert that the mind is comprised of subtler forms of matter than the brain. Consequently, it has different characteristics such as non-locality. Its subtle character makes it possible to receive the light of consciousness/spirit to reflect its contents. By virtue of its implicit non-local nature, it is possible for the mind to act on systems beyond the body complex with which it is associated. Such a conception of the mind leaves open the possibility that the mind may survive the destruction and cessation of the associated body at a given time.

The mind thus enjoys dual citizenship in the physical world as well as in the realm of consciousness. As a material form, the mind's citizenship in the material world is by birth as it were. Its naturalization in the domain of consciousness/spirit is a matter of choice and an outcome of significant effort. Its citizenship in the material realm bestows on it the right to process information through its sensory channels and neural connections. The mind also has involuntary and passive access to consciousness in that the light of consciousness shines on it to illumine its critically poised contents, which become subjectively revealed. The mind also has within its reach the possibility of partaking in consciousness-as-such by disciplined practice so that it may have direct and unmediated knowledge. This possibility is otherwise remote because of the mind's habitual involvement with the sensory and cortical processes.

In the dual roles of the mind, two distinct processes—the cognitive and the transcognitive—aid the mind. The former involves sensory-motor processes; while the transpersonal processes involve accessing consciousness-as-such and achieving pure conscious states. In normal cognitive processes, consciousness is *reflected* in the mind. Awareness consists in those reflections. In transcognitive processes, consciousness is *realized* in the mind. Awareness in such a state consists in a relationship of identity with consciousness.

The main concern of psychology, in general, is with the normal processes of the mind.

Therefore, the spotlight is on the brain and the sensory processes that give us information. Observational techniques from the third-person perspective are appropriately employed to study mental phenomena. Consciousness-as-such, which is not accessible to third-person observation, is lost sight of in scientific discussions. The consequence is a physical paradigm of the mind functioning in a mechanical universe. Functions of the mind, it is assumed, are best understood by identifying the correlated brain states. Significant shortcomings of this approach include: (a) consciousness-as-such is routinely ignored; (b) higher states of consciousness generally remain outside the scope of consciousness studies; and (c) the interest in studying consciousness is confined to the theoretical side, with little appreciation of its practical implications for developing higher states of awareness. The goal has been one of maintaining normality rather than seeking to transcend it.

Theory to testing

So far we have attempted to model a perspective for studying spirituality in the context of doing psychology. If psychology is considered a scientific pursuit to understand human nature, spiritual psychology is an area in which science and spirituality do not go their separate ways; they are not compartmentalized. Rather they are seen as complementing each other. What happens then to the basic issue of incompatibility of science and spirituality? We are told that science essentially deals with observable and tangible things. Its methods require operationalization of variables and replication of results. It is argued that the methods of science make philosophical commitments inconsistent, if not incompatible, with the conceptual foundations of spirituality (Slife, Hope & Nebeker, 1996). Psychology made a commitment to strictly adhere to the methods of natural science. Is it possible then for psychology to study spirituality which stems from altogether different theoretical assumptions? If the hallmark of spirituality is transcendence, can transcendence be studied by methods developed within the sensory framework? Does this necessitate a reinterpretation of spirituality and altering of spiritual conceptions to fit the requirements of science and its methods? Slife, Hope and Nebeker (1996), for example, raised these questions as worthy of formal discussions as they observed that the recent work of researchers in spirituality 'has the potential, at least, to undermine the very conceptions these researchers are attempting to test' (p. 78).

Such concerns are largely an outcome of the prevailing positivist mindset in the Western psychological tradition. In the Indian tradition, for example, there is no such limitation or narrowing of science to observable and tangible phenomena. In fact, there is no clear-cut incompatibility or conflict between science and spirituality. Transcendence is the goal of spirituality; and is achieved through a process of transformation. Transformation takes place in the physical plane by gaining control over normal psychological processes. Meditation, for example, is a method suggested to bring about the transformation of the person and achieve a state of transcendence. Psychology in the Indian tradition has a workable blueprint for erecting the edifice of spiritual psychology by sidestepping the science-spirituality dichotomy. Consciousness is the common denominator of science as well as spirituality.

Spiritual psychology and general psychology represent two distinct conceptual streams that flow in two different directions. The spirituality stream deals with states of pure consciousness and their role in human condition. The general psychology stream touches only the periphery of consciousness and thus leaves out the spiritual and transcendental experiences. Together the two streams appear to cover the entire spectrum of mental phenomena. Therefore, if there were a confluence between the two, we may be in a better position to understand the unity and nexus between mind, body and consciousness. Spiritual psychology is an exercise toward that end. Spirituality per se may not be empirically tested; but, I believe, its effects can be observed and measured.

Implications and applications

Socio-political implications

Spiritual psychology has important implications and some possible applications. M. K.

Gandhi's thought and experiments in political action may be seen as grounded in spiritual psychology. The concept of *satyāgraha* and the nonviolent action themes for social change and moral reconstruction are landmark experiments in spiritual psychology. Gandhi spoke of 'spiritual force'. He referred to an 'inner voice' guiding him. His emphasis on truth, nonviolence, love, compassion, and altruism are hallmarks of spiritual psychology applied to life and social action (Gandhi, 1938, 1958). Thus spiritual psychology has socio-political relevance; and research in this area, which is lagging, is truly warranted.

Therapeutic implications

As mentioned, the primacy of the spirit is basic to spiritual psychology. The concept of spirit has diverse connotations. In Indian psychology, *ātman* (Vedānta) or *puruṣa* (Sāṁkhya-Yoga), come close to the English word 'spirit'. *Ātman* is consciousness-as-such, unclouded by and free from the polluting accretions emanating from the sensory processes. Sri Aurobindo (1992) called the embodied, incarnate portion or aspect of the *ātman* the 'psychic being' of the person. In Western psychology—especially in its applied therapeutic aspects—the ego occupies the centre stage, taking the place of the spirit. It is the functioning of the ego that is of primary concern. Understanding the problems of adjustment of the ego, and dysfunctions of the ego caused by factors such as chemical imbalances, childhood trauma, or problems of sex, has been the saga of much of Western clinical psychology and psychotherapeutic practices.

The ego in the Indian psychological tradition is a manifestation of the mind and not of consciousness. It masks the spirit, the self. Shrouded by ignorance, the ego masquerades as the self. Therefore, tearing down the veil of ignorance, taming the ego, transcending the limiting adjuncts of the mind to allow the true light of the spirit to shine and reflect on the mind of the person, become the focus of spiritual psychology. This is what is involved in the process of transformation of the person. *Yoga*, for example, is a method of training for such transformation. According to Sri Aurobindo, there are three intra-psychic processes involved in ego-transformation. They are aspiration, surrender and rejection. *Aspiration* is the motivating factor, the driving force to feel the presence of the divine spirit. If spirit is consciousness-as-such, aspiration is the desire to access consciousness-as-such. *Surrender* refers to the openness to witness consciousness-as-such with no prior notions, attitudes and expectations. *Rejection* is the throwing out of all those ego accretions that cloud consciousness-as-such, so as to allow the unencumbered play of the psychic being. The function of the psychic being is accessing consciousness-as-such to guide and transform both our individual and collective life (Sri Aurobindo, 1992).

Western psychology pays more attention to ego-adjustment than ego-transformation. For example, the discussions often revolve around the defence mechanisms. G. E. Vaillant (1993) in *The Wisdom of the Ego* provides a brilliant classification of the varieties of defence mechanisms and styles of functioning, ranging from psychotic delusions to mature altruism and humour. All these styles, whether normal or aberrational, are attempts at adjustment and not transformation of the ego. Transformation involves tracing the route back from existential suffering, controlling craving and attachment, and transcending the limiting adjuncts of the mind so that the clouds of ignorance hovering around the person are dispelled and the person experiences states of pure consciousness. Such experiences are the transformational resource and gateway to realization, the discovery of the spirit within. Spiritual psychology in the Indian tradition is positive psychology that promotes health, happiness and joy in a non-ego binding manner. It is the joy of the spirit and not of the ego that the transformed person experiences. The general psychotherapeutic approach is horizontal, travelling across the existential contours of the ego. The spirituality way is vertical, elevating the person from the tangled ego to the sublime heights of the spirit, that is, states of pure conscious experience.

In the Western tradition, consciousness and the mind are conflated. By considering intentionality as the defining characteristic of consciousness, the possibility of the existence of pure conscious states, that is, consciousness without sensory content, is pre-empted. Consequently consciousness is either denied and reduced to processes in the brain or left completely unfathomable as in radical dualist postulations with an unbridgeable chasm between mind and body.

Understanding extra-ordinary human experience

Extra-ordinary human experiences such as telepathy and the direct action of mind over matter, which is technically labelled as psychokinesis (PK) pose severe explanatory challenges within the Western paradigm of science. They refer to events that cannot simply occur in the physical universe as we know it. The basic limiting principles, as C. D. Broad (1953) labelled them, governing the assumptive base of science rule out the possibility of mind-to-mind communication that does not involve meaningful transformation of energy between minds. Similarly non-inferential precognition is an absurdity. All attempts to naturalize the supernatural—that is what parapsychology hopes to do—result in the paradox of demolishing the very assumptive base of science by science itself. The attempts to find a naturalistic explanation of extrasensory perception (ESP), which is the ability to communicate without any sensory channel, and PK have not been successful. These include observational theories based on quantum mechanics (Irwin, 1999).

I am inclined to argue that research in the area of extra-ordinary human experience is unlikely to make much headway if the research continues to employ the disjunctive Western conceptual categories. The most that could be established within the Western paradigm is to provide extensive and even compelling evidence for the existence of cognitive anomalies. Beyond this, I venture to hazard, few insights into the nature of the phenomena themselves could be gained by methods that basically assume their non-existence.

In this context, spiritual psychology has much to offer and may give a new direction and a fresh impetus to parapsychological research. In Indian spiritual psychology, for example, there are concepts, methods and models that could make a difference. In the classical Indian tradition, no sharp distinction is made between the natural and the supernatural, the scientific and the spiritual. At some level of awareness, even the subject–object dichotomy disappears. Consequently, neither the paradox of naturalizing the supernormal nor the perplexities of parapsychological research pose any serious threat for an understanding of the psychic process within the paradigm of spiritual psychology.

Implications for health and wellness

The recent investigations in the area of epidemiology of religion, and clinical studies of the effect of religious and spiritual beliefs and practices on health and wellness, belong to the domain of spiritual psychology. There are now many researchers actively engaged researching in this area. Koenig, McCullough and Larson (2001) review in their *Handbook of Religion and Health* 1,200 research reports and 400 reviews.

Religion of one kind or another has existed in all societies; and it has had profound effects on the lives of those who practice it. Prayer is central to all religious practices. It is universal and ubiquitous, crossing cultural and geographical boundaries. It encompasses all religions, even those that do not specifically acknowledge an entity like God, as in Buddhism. Although the form and object of worship may vary, offering prayers is a pervasive phenomenon that is considered neither unusual nor abnormal. According to a survey published in 1996 by Princeton Religion Research Center, 96% of the US population believed in God or a supernormal power. Despite the universally prevalent and largely shared religious behaviour and the belief that prayer is a means of propitiating gods or invoking supernatural forces/abilities to help improve human condition, it remained a largely unexplored area until recently for contemporary social scientists. However, during the past fifteen years, there are literally hundreds of research reports published in refereed journals.

There are several significant studies that explored the relationship between religiosity and a variety of health conditions. In about 150 studies on alcohol and drug abuse and religious involvement, most of the studies 'suggest less substance abuse and drug abuse and more successful rehabilitation among the more religious' (Koenig, McCullough & Larson, 2001). Also, numerous studies investigated the effect of religion on mental health, delinquency, depression, heart disease, immune system dysfunction, cancer and physical disability. (For a comprehensive review of research in these areas, see Koenig, McCullough & Larson, 2001).

Surveys of literature and meta-analysis of published research seem to confirm the claims of individual researchers linking religious practices with better health outcomes. For example, in a systematic and comprehensive review, Townsend, Kladder, Ayele and Mulligan (2002) assessed the impact of religion on health outcomes. They reviewed all experiments involving randomized controlled trials, published between 1996 and 1999, that assessed the relationship between religious practices and measurable health variables. The review revealed that 'religious involvement and spirituality are associated with better health outcomes, including greater longevity, coping skills, and health related quality of life and less anxiety'. In a meta-analytic review of 29 independent samples, McCullough et al. (2000, p. 1) report that religious involvement has a strong positive influence of increased survival.

If religious involvement does have beneficial health outcomes, as many of the published reports in the West seem to suggest, then we may ask: How does this relationship work? What is its modus operandi, the process that underlies the presumed effect? What is the channel? Who is the source? These important, though often tricky, questions have no easy answers. The favoured explanation is a secular one. Religious beliefs and practices may have psychological effects, which in turn bring about somatic changes. If indeed religious beliefs and activities help to reduce anxiety, stress and depression, they could also help to shield their negative effects on general health and well-being.

As Koenig, Larson and Larson (2001) surmise, when people become physically ill, many rely heavily on religious beliefs and practices to relieve stress, retain a sense of control, and maintain hope and sense of meaning and purpose in life. It is suggested that religion (a) acts as a social support system, (b) reduces the sense of loss of control and helplessness, (c) provides a cognitive framework that reduces suffering and enhances self-esteem, (d) gives confidence that one, with the help of God, could influence the health condition, and (e) creates a mindset that enables the patient to relax and allow the body to heal itself. Again, the values engendered by religious involvement such as love, compassion, charity, benevolence, and altruism may help to successfully cope with debilitating anxiety, stress and depression. All this may be true. Yet, there are issues that go beyond these explanations. For example, if the observed effects of distant intercessory prayer on the health of patients, who did not even know that some one was praying for them, are genuine, as they seem to be, the above secular explanations become clearly inadequate. We need more than a healthy mindset on the part of the patient to recover from illness because someone, unknown to him, had prayed for his recovery. There may be more to religion than being a social and psychological support system. Consider, for example, the case of remote intercessory prayer and its ramifications for future research in the area that explores the effects of religious activities on health and well-being.

Distant (remote) intercessory prayer

A number of studies provide positive evidence linking intercessory prayer with beneficial health outcomes. Intercessory prayer involves praying for others' benefit. In some of these studies, the patients did not know that someone was praying for them. Yet, their condition seemed to have improved compared to the controlled group of patients who did not have the benefit of someone praying for them. Michael Miovic (2004) referred to two cases published recently in the journal *Alternate Therapies,* which document the effects of healing at a distance and 'how an "energy" healer used intention-at-a-distance to cure a girl of glioblastoma multiforme, a very aggressive brain tumour. In this case, the diagnosis and cure were so convincingly established with contemporary medical technology (biopsies and serial brain scans), and the disease itself is known to be so uniformly fatal that it is difficult to ascribe the healer's results to pure chance' (p. 58).

In a double blind study involving 393 coronary care patients, Randolph Byrd (1988) divided his subjects into two randomized groups. One group is the intercessory prayer group and the other is the control group. Neither the physicians attending on them nor the patients themselves knew which patients were being prayed for. Also, those who actually offered prayers did not know the patients for whose recovery they were praying. Results showed that the patients in the intercessory prayer group experienced significantly fewer episodes of congestive heart failures ($p < .05$), fewer cardiac arrests ($p < .05$), received fewer antibiotics ($p < .005$) and required less respirator support and medication ($p < .0001$). W. S. Harris et al. (1999) conducted a double blind study of distant intercessory prayer with 990 patients in the cardiac care unit. In this study with randomized controlled trials, it was observed that the experimental group (the prayed for patients) recovered better than the control group of patients. The results are statistically significant, even after correction for multiple analyses. In a meta-analysis of published studies, Mueller, Plevak and Rummans (2001) found that randomized controlled trials had shown a significant positive effect between intercessory prayer and recovery from coronary disease. They observed that addressing the spiritual needs of the patient may enhance recovery from illness.

If these effects of distant intercessory prayer are genuine, as they seem to be, how do we explain them? The secular explanations of the sort considered earlier are clearly inadequate. What is the mechanism involved? Who is the source? What is the channel? It was clearly understood by those who offered the prayers that it was God who was involved, responding to the prayer to influence the health outcome of the patients. Are we then experimenting with God? Can science go beyond itself and deal with spirituality and the divine? This could be scary and frightening to those who assume the essential incompatibility of science and spirituality.

Impressed with the extensive publications in the area, Chibnall, Jeral and Cerullo (2001) toiled for a couple of years to do a methodologically sophisticated and conceptually unambiguous study to test the influence of distant intercessory prayer on health. They found themselves unable to proceed beyond a critical review of the published reports. Their paper, 'Experiments on Distant Intercessory Prayer: God, Science, and the Lesson of Messiah', turned out to be more a debunking exercise rather than a constructive contribution. They conclude that this area of research is simply unproductive. They argue, among other things, that the notion of intervention by supernatural beings does not simply meet the basic testability and explanatory requirements of science. They write: 'Science does not deny God, miracles, and the like, it merely neglects them.... Science cannot actualize spirituality, so why do we ask this of it?' This paper became quite influential among health professionals in the West for the reason that its rationale is quite consistent with the mindset that makes a clear separation between science and spirituality, between what is believed to be natural as distinguished from the supernatural, which is considered ex-hypothesis as beyond the scope of science. Such separation of the natural and the supernatural engenders among scientists the fear of trespassing into the sacred, which, it would seem, is one of the powerful reasons behind the efforts to fault researches in this and similar areas.

Comforting the critics of the studies reporting significant positive influence of intercessory prayer on health in humans are the results of a recent multi-million dollar study (Benson et al., 2006) funded by John Templeton Foundation in USA. This study of the therapeutic effects of intercessory prayer in cardiac bypass patients, carried out by a team of sixteen researchers, involved three groups of randomly assigned patients in six US hospitals. One group numbering 604 patients received intercessory prayer after being informed that they may or may not receive prayer. The second group of 597 patients did not receive the prayer after similar information that they may or may not receive the prayer. The third group of 601 subjects received intercessory prayer after they were told that they would receive such a prayer.

The subjects in the two prayed-for groups received 14 days of prayer for uncomplicated recovery after the bypass surgery. The primary measure of outcome is the presence of any complication within thirty days of surgery.

The results showed no significant benefit to the patients in the prayed-for groups over the control group of patients who did not receive any prayers. On the contrary, it was found that the patients in group three, who were told that they would receive and did in fact receive prayers, fared significantly worse compared to the other two groups. From this the authors conclude that intercessory prayer itself 'had no effect on complication-free recovery' from the bypass surgery.

The publication of this study by Benson et al. (2006) was considered by several commentators as the final word on the efficacy of intercessory prayer, even though Benson himself leaves room for more studies. I believe this study should not be considered alone. It is in the nature of studies in areas like this that you do not expect replication each time one conducts a study. It is the cumulative results of a number of studies evaluated by an appropriate meta-analysis that should guide our generalizations. Therefore, the Benson et al. study should be seen not only in relation to other studies involving intercessory prayer but also along with a significant amount of literature available in related areas like studies of direct action of mind over matter or psychokinetic effects. Then, one realizes why these effects are not replicable on demand and why occasionally the observed effect is opposite of the one expected, which is technically known as psi-missing. Also, it would not be correct to say that there was no significant influence of intercessory prayer on health outcome in the study by Benson and associates, because the observed difference between the non-prayed for and prayed for groups in this study is statistically significant. Parapsychological literature is replete with such effects (Rhine, 1952; Rao, 1965). Rather it was a negative or psi-missing effect, the one opposite of expectation. This is not that unusual as Rao's (1965) reviews have shown.

Such attempts to scientifically test the effects of spirituality on life show why the argument that researches in the religion–health area do not meet the testability requirements of science is unconvincing, if not false. In addition, there is no intrinsic reason to bring in God or supernatural beings as the source of observed effects of distant intercessory prayer on health. Consider, for example, the wealth of studies that show similar effects of the influence of direct mental influence on remote biological systems. There is a large empirical database accumulated over the years by William Braud and associates that provides strong evidence suggestive of the possibility of influencing the physiology of a remotely situated person by sheer mental intention of another person. Braud and Schlitz (1991) review eight separate experiments in which the subjects attempted to influence remote biological systems by simply wishing such a change. The crucial difference between prayer and such wishing is that no supernatural being is invoked in the wish phenomenon, unlike in the prayer, which is generally directed at seeking the help of God to grant the wish. The results of the experiments by Braud and associates show that a subject by mental intention alone could influence in the desired direction (a) the autonomic nervous system activity of a remotely situated person, (b) the muscular tremor and ideo-motor reactions, (c) mental imagery of another person, and (d) the rate of haemolysis of human red blood cells in vitro. There is no reference in these studies to supernatural beings or non-testable entities. As Braud points out, based on the over all statistical results, the distant mental influence effects are relatively reliable and robust. The magnitude of the effects is not trivial and is comparable to self-regulation effects. The ability to mentally influence is apparently widely distributed. Thus, these experiments not only show the feasibility of scientifically studying such phenomena as healing through distant intercessory prayer, but they suggest also that the source of the effect may be a living person and not necessarily a supernatural entity like God.

Conclusion

I am convinced that spiritual psychology is a viable discipline and that Indian psychology may be seen as providing the foundational base for it. It should be mentioned, however, that spiritual psychology is different from the psychology of religion, and that religion and spirituality are distinct and different in some important aspects, even though the two are often used interchangeably by researchers exploring the effects of religion on health and well-being. It is necessary to underscore the distinction. Religion is doctrinaire and denominational, having specific behavioural and social consequences. Therefore, being religious implies more than being spiritual. Spirituality is not circumscribed within the bounds of any one religion. Rather it is guided by a belief in what may be called the transcendental aspect of being. While all religions aim at promoting spirituality, there is the distinct possibility that the manifest forms of religious worship and participation in religious activities may be dissociated from intrinsic spirituality. Therefore, a measure of religiosity need not be a measure of spirituality. Researchers are now becoming increasingly aware of this possibility. The Fetzer scale of 'Multidimensional Measurement of Religiousness/Spirituality' explicitly recognizes the distinction between religiosity and spirituality.

The Indian social scientists will have an advantage over their Western colleagues in carrying out research at the explanatory level of this area. At the outset, they would be less encumbered and constrained by what I consider a regressive notion that involves the dichotomy of spirituality and science. In Indian psychology, we have appropriate concepts and viable research strategies to meaningfully deal with phenomena that appear anomalous on the surface. In my encounters with theoretical issues in psychology, I find Indian models very helpful. The concept of pure consciousness, the possibility of knowing by being, and the numerous mind-transforming techniques traditionally practised in India, such as *yoga*, would be useful in modelling process-oriented research in this area.

Centrality of consciousness is the defining characteristic of Indian psychology (Rao, 2004). In the classical Indian tradition, consciousness is not conceived as an epiphenomenon or as a quality of experience. Rather consciousness is an autonomous principle, the ground condition of all knowing. However, not all knowing is of the sensory kind, which gives us only representational knowledge. There is another kind of knowing, knowing by being, which arises when we access consciousness-as-such. In a state of pure consciousness, we are told, one has non-representational direct awareness. In such a state, there is no possibility of dissociation between knowing and being, cognition and conduct, and thought and action. As the *Upaniṣadic* statement proclaims, 'to know *Brahman* is to be *Brahman*'. If sensory awareness gives one understanding of the phenomena, knowing by being results in the realization of the phenomena in his/her being. The lives of true saints and those who have had genuine 'peak' experiences are instances of those who achieved realization in various degrees. Realization, on the one hand, removes any gap between belief and behaviour. On the other, it has important transformational consequences to the person and his well-being. It is important to recognize that the notion of pure consciousness is not an armchair metaphysical postulate. It is an empirical claim embedded in Indian tradition. We will do well to understand it and study its implications to psychological research. Spiritual psychology is the discipline that could unravel the many mysteries that shroud the several layers of higher consciousness.

References

Aurobindo, Sri (1992). *Letters on yoga*. Pondicherry: Sri Aurobindo Ashram.

Benson, H., Dusek, J. A., Sherwood, J. B., Lam, P., Bethea, C. F., Carpenter, W., Levitsky, S., Hill, P. C., Clem, D. W. Jr., Jain, M. K., Drumel, D., Kopecky, S. L., Mueller, P. S., Marek, D., Rollins, S., Hibberd, P. L. (2006). Study of the therapeutic effects of intercessory prayer (STEP) in cardiac bypass patients: A multicenter randomized trial of uncertainty and certainty of receiving intercessory prayer. *American Heart Journal, 15*(4), 934–942.

Braud, W., & Schiltz, M. J. (1991). Conscious interactions with remote biological systems: Anomalous intentionality effects. *Subtle Energies, 2*, 1–46.

Broad, C. D. (1953). *Religion, philosophy and psychical research*. New York: Harcourt Brace.

Byrd, R. C. (1988). Positive therapeutic effects of intercessory prayer in a coronary care unit population. *Southern Medical Journal, 81*, 826–829.

Chibnall, J. T., Jeral, J. M., & Cerullo, M. A. (2001). Experiments in distant intercessor prayer: God, science, and the lesson of Massah. *Archives of Internal Medicine, 161*, 2529–2536.

Gandhi, M. K. (1938). *Hind swaraj or Indian home rule*. Ahmedabad: Navjivan Publishing House.

Gandhi, M. K. (1958). *An autobiography or the story of my experiments with truth*. Ahmedabad: Navjivan Publishing House.

George, I. K., Ellison, C. G., & Larson, D. B. (2002). Exploring the relationships between religious involvement and health. *Psychological Inquiry, 13*, 190–200.

Harris, W. S., Gowda, M., Kolb, J. W., Strychacz, C. P., Vacek, J. L., Jones, P. G., Forker, A., O'Keefe, J. H., & McCallister, B. D. (1999). A randomized, controlled trial of the effects of remote, intercessory prayer on outcomes in patients admitted to the coronary care unit. *Archives of Internal Medicine 159*(19), 2273–2278.

Hill, P. C., & Pargament, K. I. (2003). Advances in the conceptualization and measurement of religion and spirituality: Implications for physical and mental health research. *American Psychologist, 58*, 64–74.

Irwin, H. J. (1999). *An introduction to parapsychology* (3rd ed.). Jefferson, NC: McFarland & Company.

James, W. (1902). *The varieties of religious experience*. New York: New American Library.

Koenig, H. G., Larson D. B., & Larson S. S. (2001). Religion and coping with serious medical illness. *Annals of Pharmacotherapy, 35*, 352–359.

Koeing, H. G., McCullough, M. E., & Larson, D. B. (2001). *Handbook of religion and health*. New York: Oxford University Press.

Miller, W. R., & Thoreson, C. E. (1999). Spirituality and health. In W. R. Miller (Ed.), *Integrating spirituality in treatment*. Washington, DC: American Psychological Association.

Miovic, M. (2004). Spirituality, human health and wellness: Overview of the field. Paper presented at the conference, 'Spirituality, Human Health and Wellness' (26 January 2004), Institute for Human Science and Service, 26th January 2004,Visakhapatnam, India.

Mueller, P. S., Plevak, D. J., & Rummans, T. A. (2001). Religious involvement, spirituality, and medicine: Implications for clinical practice. *Mayo Clinic Proceedings, 76*, 1189–1191.

Rao, K. R. (2002). *Consciousness studies: Cross-cultural perspectives*. Jefferson, NC: McFarland & Company.

Rao, K. R. (1965). The bidirectionality of psi. *Journal of Parapsychology, 29*, 230–250.

Rao, K. R. (2004). Centrality of consciousness in Indian psychology. In K. Joshi & M. Cornelissen (Eds.), *Consciousness, Indian psychology and Yoga* (pp. 53–75). New Delhi: Centre for Studies of Civilizations.

Rhine, J. B. (1952). The problem of psi-missing. *Journal of Parapsychology, 16*, 90–129.

Slife, B. D., Nebeker, S. R., & Hope, C. (1996). *Modernism, antimodernism, and postmodernism in conceptions of spirituality*. Paper presented at the meeting of American Psychological Association, Toronto, Canada.

Thouless, R. H. (1972). *An introduction to the psychology of religion*. Cambridge: Cambridge University Press.

Townsend, M., Kladder, V., Ayele, H., & Mulligan, T. (2002). Systematic review of clinical trials examining the effects of religion on health. *South Medical Journal, 95*(12), 1429–1434.

Vaillant, G. E. (1993). *The wisdom of the ego*. Cambridge, MA: Cambridge University Press.

Woods, T. E., & Ironson, G. H. (1999). Religion and spirituality in the face of illness: How cancer, cardiac, and HIV patients describe their spirituality and religiosity. *Special issue: Spirituality and health. Journal of Health Psychology, 4*(3), 393–412.

2

A journey back to the roots: Psychology in India

Ajit K. Dalal

For almost a century, academic psychology in India has continued to be an alien discipline. In the beginning of the last century, psychology was imported lock, stock, and barrel from the West, and was first implanted in 1916 at Calcutta University. The Western model of research and teaching provided the basis on which Indian research grew for a long period. For Indian psychologists trained in the Western traditions, it has been a long journey to turn towards their own heritage and take Indian concepts and theories germane to understanding Indian social reality. Indeed, in this long history, concerns have been voiced from time to time to align psychology with contemporary social issues, so as to meet the challenges of rapid socio-economic and global changes. Looking back, one gets an impression that psychology in India has come a long way to find its roots in its own native wisdom, though it still has to cover much ground to become a science of Indian origin.

Throughout its existence as an alien implant, psychology has been struggling to ground itself in the Indian soil and adapt to local conditions. Over the years this implant has grown, with branches spreading all over the country. However, it has not borne fruits as expected and has largely remained a sterile academic pursuit, as far as the real issues of national development are concerned. The non-visibility of psychologists in various national forums gives rise to serious concerns about its relevance and future. What kind of psychology we aspire to have in the twenty-first century is contingent on a better understanding of the present state-of-the-art. This chapter aims to examine the status of psychology in India as a scientific discipline, identifying the factors responsible for its retarded growth. It also discusses the parallel movement now underway to rediscover the knowledge rooted in scriptures and folk practices, and explores its relevance in the present times.

Three sets of arguments are put forward to explain the retarded growth of academic psychology in India. One, which is more charitable, is the lack of a supportive intellectual climate. In a country where a vast population lives in a condition of subhuman poverty, and decisions about social developmental programmes are politically motivated, any scholarly pursuit is considered peripheral. The academic institutions plagued by a rising student population, political manipulations and lack of funds have gradually become non-performers. There is no premium placed on excellence in teaching and research. Adair, Pandey, Begam, Puhan and Vora (1995) conducted a study on sixty-four Indian psychologists through a mailed questionnaire. The survey revealed three major impediments to research productivity: (a) lack of supportive intellectual climate, (b) poor professional support, and (c) inadequate research funding. Ostensibly, the lack of an academic culture and a non-supportive socio-political environment are greatly responsible for the prevailing state of affairs. It does explain the overall decline in the academic standards in the country. It, however, throws no light on 'why is psychology in India lagging behind other sisterly disciplines, such as sociology, anthropology and economics?' It brings forth the second line of argument that there are some inherent limitations in psychology as a scientific discipline. Its excessive conformity to empiricist-positivist methodologies and confining to micro-level problems have restricted the scope of its psycho-social inquiry.

This methodological approach is insufficient to take up more applied macro-level problems (Dalal, 2010). The restricted boundaries of the discipline obviate the need to work in applied settings, or to work with governmental or non-governmental agencies. The third set of arguments focus on the personal and professional background of Indian psychologists. Psychologists in the first half of this century were a product of the colonial domination of Indian society, greatly influenced by Western scholarly traditions. The first generation psychologists after India's Independence were predominantly converts from the philosophy background. This combined with their elitist-urban background; fewer job openings and self-serving research orientation gave Indian psychologists an identity distinct from those who belonged to other sister disciplines. This chapter examines the progress of psychology in India against the backdrop of these arguments. It endeavours to explore the possibilities of psychology becoming a more vibrant science, accepting the challenges of a rapidly changing Indian society. We need a psychology which is a positive discipline conducive to self-growth and social harmony.

Indian psychology has come a long way in the hundred years of its existence. Today, there are a large number of teaching and research institutions offering wide range of courses in psychology. It is not known how many colleges and universities offer psychology courses and how many psychologists are professionally active. There is no data which official agencies, like the University Grants Commission (UGC), the Indian Council of Social Science Research (ICSSR), or the Department of Science and Technology, can furnish. One estimate (A. K. Jain, 2005) suggests that there are more than 15,000 psychologists in India. In any case, India has the largest number of psychologists outside the Western block, and is considered a 'publication giant' among all developing countries (Gilgin & Gilgin, 1987). This rapid expansion of the discipline has aroused many hopes and expectations about its possible contribution to the success of nation-building projects. The problems of poverty, illiteracy, urban decay and disease control cannot be handled on the basis of sound economic planning only, but also require changes in the attitudes and beliefs of people, and their motivations for collective action. This calls for a realistic appraisal of the impediments which psychology in India is currently experiencing. Psychology needs to break its present disciplinary shackles to join hands with other social sciences. Currently, much soul-searching is going on within the discipline; and it is realized that psychology in India needs to be rooted in its own history and heritage.

In recent years there have been several good publications which enable a critical evaluation of the development of psychology in India. Some of these writings (Dalal, 1990, 1996, 2002; Misra & Gergen, 1993; D. Sinha, 1986, 1996; J. B. P. Sinha, 1993) have critically evaluated the progress of psychology. The five surveys of research in psychology (Mitra, 1972; Pareek, 1980, 1981; J. Pandey, 1988, 2001, 2004) cover important research contributions since the beginning of the last century. Pareek and Rao (1974a), Pestonjee (1986), and NCERT (1981) compiled psychological measures developed in India. Reports prepared by the University Grants Commission (UGC, 1968, 1982, 1999) deal with teaching and research programmes in universities. Some empirical studies (Adair, 1989) have examined the professional status of the discipline of psychology. More recently, Misra (2010), Salagame (2005, 2008), Pandey and Singh (2005), Paranjpe (2006) and Varma (2004) have provided incisive understanding of the current status of psychology in India. These publications have formed the basis of preparing this review chapter.

In brief, this chapter traces the genesis of scientific psychology in India in the beginning of the last century. It examines the constraints and creative pursuits of Indian psychologists in seeking a disciplinary identity. The present chapter is, in a way, an updated and completely revised version of the article initially published (Dalal, 1996). The major focus in this version is on the long and circuitous journey towards indigenization and on the emerging concern to root psychology in Indian traditions. Lastly, some conjectures are made about the possible directions in which psychology is likely to tread in the twenty-first century.

Twentieth century psychology in India: A Western implant

Indian scriptures dating back thousands of years extensively dealt with the analysis of states of consciousness and contents of mental activities. The important feature of this early exposition is that it is mostly experiential and is a culmination of centuries-old tradition of self-verification. In the ancient Indian scriptures no rigid distinction among religion, philosophy and psychology was maintained. The overriding consideration was to help individuals in their pursuit of self-realization and liberation from the miseries of life. In this world-view, the source of all suffering was presumed to be within the person, and thus the emphasis was on exploring the 'world within', to alleviate suffering. The goal was to seek enduring harmony of spirit, mind and body for everlasting happiness. The *yoga* system evolved very sophisticated mind-control techniques in this pursuit. In contemporary literature, this broad field of inquiry is referred to as 'Indian Psychology'.

These rich traditions, however, had little bearing on academic psychology implanted in India as a Western science during the British colonial rule. Scientific psychology with laboratory work was a novel approach, not having any parallel in traditional Indian psychology. Psychology was first introduced as a subject in the Philosophy Department at Calcutta University. Brojendra Nath Seal, who was the then King George V Professor of Mental and Moral Philosophy, drafted the first syllabus for experimental psychology and established a laboratory for demonstration purposes in 1905. Eleven years later this laboratory was upgraded as the first psychology department, the Department of Experimental Psychology. Narendra Nath Sengupta, who chaired this department, had his education at Harvard University with Hugo Munsterberg, a student of William Wundt. Laboratory research in Calcutta in the areas of depth perception, psychophysics and attention inspired early work at other centres. Recognizing the scientific nature of research, psychology was included as a separate section in the Indian Science Congress in 1923. Thus, psychology in India at an early stage acquired the status of a science along with physical and biological sciences, something which Western psychology achieved only after a long struggle. The Indian Psychological Association was founded in 1924; and the *Indian Journal of Psychology*, the first psychology journal in India, appeared the very next year.

Before these experimental traditions could consolidate, Sengupta left Calcutta. He was succeeded by Girindra Shekhar Bose. Being a medical doctor and a psychiatrist who was in close contact with Sigmund Freud, Bose showed much enthusiasm to promote psychoanalysis. In 1922 he founded the Indian Psychoanalytic Society, which two years later was affiliated with the International Psychoanalytic Society. Bose received his Ph.D. from Calcutta on the 'concept of repression'—the first Ph.D. from any Indian University in psychology. He established the Lumbini Park Mental Hospital in Calcutta in 1940; and in 1947 brought out a journal, *Samiksha*. The Department started an Applied Psychology Wing in 1938, when Jung, Meyers and Spearman were invited to the Silver Jubilee Session of the Indian Science Congress.

Prior to India's Independence from the British rule, other departments were established at Mysore and Patna. M. V. Gopalswami, who headed the Department at Mysore, was trained at London University with Spearman in the mental testing tradition. He developed Indian adaptations of Western intelligence tests and applied psychological principles in the field of education. Gopalswami was the first to set up an animal laboratory in India. The Department at Patna began in 1946, along with the Institute of Psychological Research and Services, headed by H. P. Maiti.

Vocational guidance and counselling was provided to a large number of students and to the general public. Since Maiti was trained with Girindra Shekhar Bose, the orientation was psychoanalytic and clinical. In a short time, Patna emerged as a major centre for teaching, research and counselling services.

Research during this period was mainly in the areas of sensation, perception, psychophysics and reaction time, influenced by the work of Wundt and Titchner. Fascination for laboratory work and value-free research, based on the natural science model, sustained the interest of Indian psychologists in these areas. Western research in these areas could easily be replicated without considering the cultural factors. In the area of social psychology, early work focussed on repeating Allport's experiments on social facilitation on Indian samples. An important work of this period was the rumour study by Prasad (1935). Prasad content-analysed the rumours doing the rounds during a major earthquake in northern India. He found that most rumours were anxiety-inducing, thereby justifying the fear experienced by earthquake victims. Festinger acknowledged that this work inspired his formulation of the cognitive dissonance theory (Cohen & Cohen, 1977).

Two worlds of Indian psychologists

The concepts and theories in Western psychology have their genesis in the social upheavals of Europe in the nineteenth century, with its metamorphosis from an agrarian to an industrial society. The discipline evolved to comprehend the complex social realities and the problems of industrialization. With the imperial expansion of modern capitalism, the influence of Western knowledge in the colonized societies was inevitable. The popularity of English-medium education made writings of Western thinkers accessible to Indian scholars. A large body of this knowledge was alien, even in contradiction to that which was prevalent in the colonized traditional societies. The contradictions were more glaring in colonies, like India, having a strong sense of cultural identity and a rich heritage of scholarly work.

In the West, psychology had moved away from theology and philosophy, and had developed its own methods of inquiry based on the natural science models. Indian psychologists saw that in applying Western psychology there was an opportunity of developing a secular identity distinct from that of religion and philosophy, which was not possible within indigenous intellectual traditions integrating philosophy, spirituality and psychology. Moreover, due to the neglect of many centuries, Indian psychology was not well equipped to examine the contemporary world and did not have tools to explain the existing social and moral decay of the Indian society. There were no new concepts, theories and methods in Indian psychology applicable to the changing individual and social order.

Alignment with Western positivism gave Indian psychologists an opportunity to make a fresh beginning. The emerging scientific discipline of psychology gave rise to some hope of generating radically different explanations of the prolonged colonial rule. There were exciting possibilities of making important discoveries about Indian people and society. Also, one could hope that the explanations of positive science would provide the much needed respectability to Indian cultural practices and rituals. At the personal level, it gave a new respectability to the upwardly mobile psychology professionals who mostly hailed from the upper-class, Western-educated elite. Although, as Nandy (1995) stated in the context of Girindra Shekhar Bose, there was an awareness that the sectoral and uni-dimensional approach of academic psychology cannot yield in-depth analysis of the socio-psychological problems of Indian society, it could also not establish durable links with Indian traditions and belief systems.

Nandy (1995) further stated: 'As a result, the usual encounter between an ancient culture with its distinctive culture of science and an exogenous science with its own distinctive culture fractured the self-definition not only of Bose but of many others involved in the similar enterprise' (p. 83). Caught between the two worlds, Indian psychologists always had a problem in balancing between a number of polarities: metaphysical versus empirical; clinical versus experimental; intuitive versus objective. The Indian mind, even if trained to be a scientist, often finds it difficult to ruthlessly pursue the objective reality, something which comes perhaps naturally to a Westerner. Thus, conflicting elements are resolved into a suspension rather than a solution. 'The aesthetic satisfaction of a Hindu myth resides in full savoring of both the extremes rather than seeking a synthesis' (Kakar, 1982, p. 11). Indian psychologists compartmentalized their work in the Western psychological tradition from other scholarly and personally satisfying creative pursuits. They simultaneously lived in two different worlds without any significant overlap.

How Indian psychologists before Independence lived in two different worlds can be illustrated with some examples. Sir Brojendra Nath Seal, who established the first psychology laboratory in the country to promote experimental psychology, was a great historian of ancient Indian science and the inspiration for Jadunath Sinha to bring out his monumental work on Indian psychology. N. N. Sengupta, who was trained to be an experimental psychologist, had a large number of non-empirical papers in scientific journals. His writings covered the whole range from the psychology of mysticism to the psychology of Western dance. Sengupta did not stay in Calcutta for long and joined the Philosophy Department at Lucknow University. There he co-authored a book, *Introduction to Social Psychology*, with an eminent sociologist, Radhakamal Mukherjee, in 1928. The orientation of this book was more sociological than psychological. As Rajanarayan (1983) wrote in his biographical note, he turned religious and got interested in mystical traditions and published work in this area. Girindra Shekhar Bose had, along with his important work in the area of psychoanalysis, serialized an interpretation of the *Bhagavad Gītā* in the prestigious Bengali magazine, *Pravasi*, without any direct reference to psychoanalytic concepts (Nandy, 1995). Bose also wrote a long commentary on sacred Indian texts in Bengali, titled *Purana Pravesa*. Gopalswami, who was at Mysore, came from an affluent background and maintained interest in two diverse fields—intelligence testing and animal laboratory work; besides, he also had his own private radio station and was involved in various cultural activities.

These illustrations are cited to give some clues about how Indian psychologists managed to live simultaneously in two worlds with little overlap. Thus it is no surprise that Indian psychologists remained apolitical all along. There is no reflection in their work of the predominant social and political movements, even that of the freedom movement. Indian psychologists remained on the edge of the society, as far as their professional activities were concerned. Their research lacked continuity, commitment and conviction. The situation changed only marginally after Independence.

Durganand Sinha, who may be considered as one of the architects of modern Indian psychology has observed in his prolific writings that early attempts at formulation of Indian Psychology were rejected by psychologists in India who were trained in the empirical tradition, because of such notions like rebirth, transmigration of souls and supernatural powers. It was considered as 'glib talk', 'revivalism' and 'uncritical worship of the past', and the term Indian Psychology acquired a 'pejorative connotation'. So what is 'spiritual psychology' for Western academicians becomes 'revivalism' for Indian academicians! Reasons for such resistance and rejection of psychology grounded in traditional ideas is primarily due to the negative attitude that we have inherited from our colonial past on the one hand and the influence of the scientific worldview on the other (Dalal, 2002; Paranjpe, 2002).

It may be argued that a vast majority of Indian psychologists have shied away from Indian psychological perspectives because of this attitude, and the religio-philosophical context in which those perspectives are embedded. But, paradoxically, a majority of them share the same socio-cultural context with the rest of the Indian population, and are guided by the same religio-philosophical perspectives which have shaped the attitudes, emotions, motivations, morals and values of the Indian masses in their day-to-day living! As K. Kiran Kumar Salagame (2008) observed, this situation has created some kind of a split in the personality—psychologist as a professional vs. psychologist as a person—and it has contributed to a lack of creativity and originality and draining of personal resources and energy resulting in 'burn out' among many. A psychologist in his role as a scientist conducts the professional activities with one set of assumptions and beliefs and as a person lives and acts with another set of assumptions and beliefs among fellow humans.

One reason why Indian psychologists could live in two parallel worlds was probably because the colonial rulers did not see much utility of psychology in consolidating their empire. This, for example, was not true in the case of sociology and social anthropology, which had much to contribute to the smooth functioning of the colonial administration in India (Dhanangare, 1985). Indian culture and society was totally unfamiliar to the colonial officials when they first arrived. The unique systems of caste, religion, tribal and rural communities, rituals, beliefs, traditions were all baffling to an Englishman. These had no parallel in the experiences of the Western societies. Thus, in the absence of proper understanding of Indian social realities the colonial administrators were facing many problems in their smooth functioning. There was much urgency and support for research on these topics. Neither Indian psychology nor Western psychological research held any such promise and were largely ignored. It is understandable why the British did not promote psychology in India in the same way they did sociology and social anthropology, for instance.

In fact, Indian culture with its liberal and multiple traditions did not offer resistance to this new emerging science. In the West, Descartean philosophy had to face opposition from theology for a long time. Psychoanalysis had a very controversial entry into Western society; many of the books by Freud were initially banned. In India psychoanalysis was accepted without anyone raising an eyebrow. The three main streams of academic psychology in India—experimental psychology, psychoanalysis and intelligence testing—were viewed as culture-free, justifying uncritical borrowing from the West.

The fact that psychologists in India lived in two worlds did not change much after Independence, but rather became more pronounced. In most universities, psychology departments were established by splitting the departments of philosophy. As a result, a large number of philosophy faculty moved to the newly formed psychology departments; many who opted for psychology were those who saw better career opportunities in the new departments. This movement from philosophy to psychology was so pervasive that by the end of the 1960s a majority of the chairpersons in psychology departments had a philosophy background. In the normal course this could have given a strong philosophical knowledge base to psychology, making it richer in terms of indigenous concepts and theories. But this did not happen. In their enthusiasm to establish a new identity as scientists, these faculty members with a background in philosophy completely dissociated themselves from their parent discipline. They were more fascinated by the idea of value-free and culturally-neutral experimental work. The areas they showed interest in were areas such as memory, psychophysics, perception, learning and pattern recognition, which could be studied without bringing in the cultural context. These faculty members from philosophy had little training in research methodology. Their major quest, therefore, was to acquire methodological sophistication and mastery over statistical techniques. In the process they became ardent adherents of Western research methods. Thus, despite their firm moorings in ancient Indian psychology, psychology in India did not reap the fruits of this unique advantage. Indian psychologists were still coexisting in two different worlds. As professionals they were engaged in scientific research based on Western models but to satisfy their creative urges they would engage in other activities. This Indian experience was not an exception in this respect. In neighbouring Pakistan (Ansari, 1990) and Bangladesh (Hamida Begam, 1990) it was the same story, as in many other former European colonies.

Living in two different worlds had at least two major implications for the growth of psychology. One, psychologists did not engage in thematic research over a long period of time. They kept hopping from one area to another and did not sustain their interest in one theme. Often extrinsic factors—such as funds or opportunities—became more decisive factors for conducting research, than any intrinsic interest in the topic. Even a cursory glance at their published works would reveal that most of the Indian psychologists had covered a wide range of topics. It could be baffling to a Western researcher, but in India it is a normal practice. Researchers did not cultivate any theoretical interest, or adhere to a particular theoretical position in their research. There are few Indian researchers whose work has a cumulative effect. Two, the professional bodies of Indian psychologists rarely took any stand on vital national issues. They were more interested in holding annual conferences and meetings, where rarely substantive issues were passionately debated. Most of the conflicts that weakened these professional organizations were of an interpersonal nature. There was no larger vision of the psychology to be.

Initiatives towards socially relevant research

India's Independence from the colonial rule in 1947 did bring changes in the content and concerns of psychological research. The National Government recognized the importance of social science teaching and research in attaining the objectives of national reconstruction and social development. There was much hope and expectation about the role that the social sciences could play in this endeavour. Psychologists began to realize that they have a responsibility to engage in socially relevant research.

As an example, psychologists responded to the human tragedy of the partition of India. In its aftermath, thousands were killed in communal riots, followed by a massive influx of refugees from across the border. Many psychological studies of that period evidenced this concern in the rioting behaviour of the masses. Realizing the urgent need of research in this area, the Ministry of Education procured the services of Gardner Murphy through UNESCO in 1950 to develop a research programme to investigate the causes of communal violence. Many Indian psychologists collaborated on this project which culminated in the book, *In the Minds of Men*, edited by Murphy in 1953. They continued working in this area in later years.

Another area which emerged during this period, but was not sustained in the later decades, is counselling and guidance. The guidance bureau at Patna inspired the establishment of similar bureaus in other states. The UP Psychological Bureau was among the first ones, established in 1947. This bureau, under the leadership of Sohan Lal and thereafter of C. M. Bhatia and S. N. Mehrotra, adapted many intelligence and aptitude tests in Hindi, and provided counselling services to the public. The Bihar Psychological Bureau, under the guidance of Mohsin, worked on similar lines. In Bombay, the Parsi Panchayat Vocational Guidance Bureau provided services to students, as well as to referred cases. The Bureau also brought out the *Journal of Vocational and Educational Guidance*. This journal played an important role in furthering the guidance movement in this country. However, the social and political conditions were just not ripe for the expansion of this movement; and not enough of a research base was built up to sustain this movement. Consequently, instead of growing, the movement lost its momentum (D. Sinha, 1986). The first two ICSSR surveys of research in psychology are testimony to the fact that this area did not yield much research in later years.

A new development after Independence was the growth of psychology outside the university system. The Ahmedabad Textile Industries Research Association (ATIRA) was established in 1950, where Kamla Chowdhury conducted large-scale surveys to study motivational problems in the textile industries. Erikson and McClelland were frequent visitors to this Institute. In the clinical field, advanced training programmes were introduced at the All India Institute of Mental Health (now known as the National Institute of Mental Health and Neuro-Sciences, NIMHANS) in 1955, followed by the Hospital for Mental Diseases in Ranchi (1962). The Indian armed forces also showed interest in using psychological tests in personnel selection. For this, the Psychological Research Wing of the Defence Science Organization was set up in 1949. The aim of this wing was not only to help in the selection of army personnel, but also to do research on the whole range of defence-related problems, such as motivation and morale of the armed forces, leadership, mental health, stress, rehabilitation of disabled war veterans and development of psychological tests. Later on, this wing was elevated as the Defence Institute of Psychological Research, employing a large number of psychologists.

These efforts and opportunities signify the contribution which psychology could make in different domains of national life. Psychology as a discipline was somehow not prepared to seize these initiatives. The poor training and replicative nature of research did not prepare them to confront real life problems. A few psychologists did participate in developmental programmes, but overall the discipline remained on the margin. It was the time when other social scientists, for example, sociologists and economists had already started making their presence felt.

Rapid but unplanned expansion

In the 1950s and 1960s, the growth of psychology in Indian universities was phenomenal. In 1956 the University Grants Commission (UGC) was constituted and it provided funds to various universities to start psychology departments. As a result, the number of psychology departments increased to thirty-two by the end of the 1960s.

This rapid expansion of psychology, though impressive, was quite unplanned. In the absence of any definite educational policy of the government, these departments were often created as a part of the general expansion of higher education and at times without any particular academic considerations. No serious thinking preceded in establishing these departments in terms of their need-based specialization. Nevertheless, in the course of their growth many departments developed a distinct identity (R. E. Pandey, 1969). For example, departments became known for their research in the areas of rural and social psychology (Allahabad), test construction (Mysore), industrial psychology (Osmania), measurement and guidance (Patna) or verbal learning (Poona). Most departments developed around one dominant scholar, usually the person heading the department. His interest and training were decisive factors in the specialization of that department. Psychology during those days (this is more or less true even today) developed around personalities, and when those scholars departed, many centres collapsed, or showed shifts in specialization.

In the late 1960s, concerned about the declining standards of university departments and to facilitate research programmes, the UGC started a new scheme of Centres for Advanced Studies and Centres for Special Assistance. Under these schemes two psychology departments (at Utkal and Allahabad) were elevated to the status of Centres of Advanced Studies in Psychology. The idea was to develop some departments as research centres at par with the best in the world, with the help of liberal government support. Departments at Delhi, Gorakhpur and Tirupati were also elevated to the status of Centres of Special Assistance, a penultimate stage to receiving Advanced Centre status. These departments were expected to provide leadership in the areas of research, teaching and professional activities.

Though the practice of going abroad for higher education was there since long, a significant development after Independence was the beginning of a number of educational exchange programmes. The most sought after were the fellowships of Commonwealth, Fulbright and Ford Foundation. A number of bilateral academic exchange programmes were commissioned by UGC and the Ministry of Education, Government of India. Under these schemes a large number of Indian scholars went to Britain, Canada, and the United States for doctoral and post-doctoral training in the 1960s and 1970s. When they returned to occupy academic positions, they not only had better training in research techniques but also brought along contemporary research ideas, and continued academic collaboration with their seminal professors abroad. This brought qualitative changes in teaching and research. Under these exchange programmes many Western scholars also visited Indian universities. Psychology in India was dominated by the scholars trained abroad for another two decades. Equipped with freshly acquired expertise in Western theories and methods, they exhibited much interest in applying their knowledge to understand and solve Indian social problems.

Another new development was the expansion of teaching of psychology in various professional courses in the fields of engineering, agriculture, management and medical sciences. All Indian Institutes of Technology (IITs) have departments of Humanities and Social Sciences, of which psychology is a constituent subject with Ph.D. programmes. All Indian Institutes of Management (IIMs) have departments of Organizational Behaviour. Psychology is taught in undergraduate classes, particularly in Home Science and Extension Education departments in twenty-six agricultural universities and twenty-eight agriculture institutes. In medical colleges, psychology is part of a course on Preventive and Social Medicine. But as noted by Atal (1976), most of these courses in agriculture and medicine are taught by the junior staff, research assistants and demonstrators, and have low priority. The situation has not changed much till date.

Expansion of psychology departments within the university system continued in the 1970s. However, it became increasingly difficult to conduct research in the university departments. In a bureaucratic university set up, there was little organizational support for pursuing research projects. Again, due to the mass entry of students in higher education and chronic campus unrest for political reasons, the academic environment was on the decline. Heavy teaching, and no incentive for research had a telling effect on the research output of the universities. As a result, research in psychology started growing outside the university system. Psychologists having research inclinations preferred to join various research institutes. A. N. S. Institute of Social Studies, Patna, the Centre for the Study of Developing Societies, New Delhi, and the National Institute of Community Development, Hyderabad, are some examples of prominent institutes which became centres of research in psychology.

Many governmental and autonomous institutions, such as the National Council of Educational Research and Training (NCERT), National Institute of Educational Policy and Administration (NIEPA), National Institute of Public Cooperation and Child Development (NIPCCD), National Institute of Health and Family Welfare (NIHFW) (all in Delhi), Indian Institute of Science, Bangalore, Academic Staff College, Hyderabad, Indian Statistical Institute, Calcutta, have become centres of applied research in different fields of psychology. There are a large number of national and international voluntary agencies which seek the services of psychologists to carry out their research and field projects.

The consolidation of Western research

Two major streams of research, experimental and testing, continued to grow after Independence. The experimental work in the areas of perception, learning and memory was primarily replications of Western studies. There are some good examples of long-term research programmes. Chatterjee (1954) conducted experiments for almost two decades on the role of intensity, time interval and distance between stimuli in producing an optimal apparent movement. Tayal (1970) proposed a broad unifying model through which a number of related visual phenomena could be explained by a new set of principles, challenging the theoretical basis of Fechner's law. In the area of verbal conditioning, J. P. Das (1962) proposed that semantic satiation is a direct function of attentional decrement rather than of inhibition of meaning. Kothurkar (1972) did a series of studies on verbal learning and memory processes. Experimental work in comparative psychology was pioneered by S. D. Singh (1963) who studied the social behaviour of rhesus monkeys. Though M. Singh at Mysore and S. K. Misra at Bhubaneshwar continued working in this area, comparative psychology did not take off at other centres of higher learning.

Research in the area of psychological testing made a quantum leap after Independence. The orientation was still predominantly British. Those who could go abroad for graduate training generally went to London and Edinburgh (Barnett, 1955). They were trained in the mental testing traditions of Spearman and Thomson. On their return, these psychologists were preoccupied with the assessment of intelligence by preparing Indian adaptations of Spearman, Binet-Simon, Stanford-Binet and Terman-Merrill scales in Indian languages. A large number of Christian missionaries were also involved in the construction and validation of psychological tests for their mission schools (Mitra, 1972). Puhan (1994), in his presidential address to the 5th Annual Convention of National Academy of Psychology, critically reviewed the history of the personality test movement in India.

Work at early stages in this area dealt with construction and standardization of achievement and intelligence tests, aptitude scales and personality inventories. Many popular Western tests were adapted into Indian languages. The National Council of Educational Research and Training reviewed all the tests that had been prepared up to 1961 (NCERT, 1966). A large number of these tests were adaptations of Western tests. In the directory compiled by Pareek and Rao (1974a), of the 503 tests, 218 were in the section of personality. Within personality, one out of five tests was related to motivational variables. Even among those classified within the general category, a large number were multidimensional personality tests, or measures of one or more motivational variables. The motivational tests were primarily in the domains of achievement motivation, anxiety, level of aspiration and self-concept.

A few general observations hold for the majority of these tests. First, most of the tests require certain language skills and thus are appropriate only for urban, educated samples. Half of the tests listed in Pareek and Rao's (1974a) directory were for school- and college-level students. Second, classical psychometric theory guided the construction of almost all of these tests which, owing to sub-cultural and language differences merit a fresh look at their usefulness. Third, there has been a general neglect in establishing the validity of these tests. More than 85% of the tests included in the *Handbook* had indeed no information regarding test validity. Thus, though a large number of tests were developed in India, their quality left much to be desired. The *Second Handbook* of tests by Pestonjee (1986) showed considerable improvement. The 326 tests developed in the preceding decade showed the similar trend as in the first *Handbook* with two differences. First, more than 60% of the tests were reported with validity data, and secondly, there were more Indian tests after adaptations of Western tests.

Using these tests, a large number of surveys were undertaken to investigate the prevalence of mental health problems by Sethi and his associates (Sethi, Gupta, & Kumar, 1967; Sethi, Gupta, Kumar, & Promilla, 1972) in Lucknow, by Dube (1970) in Agra, by Elnager, Mitra and Rao (1971) in rural Bengal, and by Verghese (1973) in Vellore. There were very few in-depth studies of the problem areas. Research work in the areas of epidemiology of mental illness, phenomenology of depressive behaviour, drug abuse, *yoga* and health, psychosocial aspects of family planning, and mental retardation was slowly gathering momentum by the seventies (see G. G. Prabhu, 1980). In the area of clinical psychology, most of the research activities were confined to diagnosis and prognosis of mental diseases. Wig and Akhtar (1974) have reviewed the important psychiatric research in India conducted during 1947–1972. Murthy (1980) observed that Western influence was significant in the use of clinical techniques, such as sensitization, aversion therapy, feedback therapy, and classical and operant conditioning techniques in treatment of psychogenic illnesses. Behavioural therapies were quite popular and though psychoanalysis was still practiced, its popularity was on the decline. Recently, interest has grown in examining traditional healing practices in the treatment of mental illnesses (for example, Swami Rama, S. Ballentine, & Swami Ajay, 1976; Kakar, 1982). The area which has emerged more recently is health psychology (Dalal, 2001)—to study the role of psychological and cultural factors in affecting health behaviour.

An applied field that began to grow after Independence was industrial psychology. Rapid industrialization in the 1950s and 1960s created a need for better understanding of the labour–management relationship and organizational efficiency. Psychological research projects on job attitude, work incentive, absenteeism and job satisfaction were quite popular till the 1970s. Ganguli's (1961) book, *Industrial Productivity and Motivation*, is an example of the concerns of that period. With the launching of many self-employment schemes by the Central Government in the 1960s, the research focus shifted to developing training programmes for inculcating entrepreneurship. McClelland's theory of achievement motivation (1961) provided the basis for launching a unique experiment to impart training for achievement at the Small Industries Extension Training Institute, Hyderabad. The findings of this innovative training were not conclusive, and eventually Indian psychologists lost interest in such experimentation.

With the shift in research from industrial to organizational behaviour, the interest grew in studying all spheres of organized work activities. Research on the influence of socioeconomic factors and traditional culture on organizational functioning started attracting Indian psychologists. The two chapters—by Padaki on job attitudes and by Khandawala on organizational effectiveness—in the *Third Survey* (Pareek,1988) cover a large number of Indian work in these areas.

Communal and caste conflicts being perennial problems in India, social prejudice, intergroup relations and socialization of the Indian child emerged as major research interest. Rath and Sircar (1960) and Anant (1970) studied caste stereotypes. Paranjpe's (1970) book *Caste Prejudice and the Individual*, was based on a survey of college students' prejudice against low-caste members. The studies of attitude towards the Chinese (A. K. P. Sinha & Upadhyaya, 1960) are oft-quoted studies of change in attitude as a result of historical events (border dispute with China which led to war). A. K. Singh (1981) examined development of religious identity and prejudice in children, and more recently, Deridder and Tripathi (1992) studied social consequences of norm violation by different ethnic groups. Work in the field of socialization and child rearing practices in India has also been substantial. Two field studies that inspired many studies of the early period are by Carstairs (1957), and by Minturn and Hitchcock (1966). Work on similar lines has been carried out by Anandlakshmy (1975, 1982) and others. Kakar (1978) examined socialization and child rearing in light of the elaborate system of rituals and practices prevalent in Hindu culture. Saraswathi (1987) brought out an annotated bibliography of the work done in India in the preceding decade.

To take stock of the state of research, Ganguli (1971) reviewed about 2,000 research publications of the period 1920 to 1967. He found that the five most important areas of work in order of importance were social (15.9%), experimental (13.7%), mental testing (13.0%), general (10.6%) and industrial (3.6%). An analysis of the publications by Mitra (1972) showed that areas of clinical, social, personality and experimental psychology accounted for half of the total number of publications examined. In a similar analysis, twenty-two years later, J. B. P. Sinha (1993) reported that clinical, social, personality and industrial-organizational psychology accounted for 70% of all the publications. The overall growth rate of research publications was 5.57% in the 1950s, 14.28% in the 1960s and 46.22% in the 1970s. Dalal and Sharma (1990) examined the growth pattern of research for the period 1972–1986 by content-analysing the abstracts included in 'Indian Psychological Abstracts' in the areas of social psychology and personality. It is interesting to note that in personality research, in the initial period (1972–1976), one-fourth of the studies used the experimental method, the use of which declined in later years. In social psychology, only 13% of the studies employed the experimental method, which remained the same in the following years. In personality research, there were an increasingly large number of theoretical papers, whereas in social research, questionnaire method became more popular over the years. The use of student population in this research was much less than that found in Western research.

A crisis of identity

In the 1970s and 1980s, a number of review papers were published to take stock of the contributions made by Indian psychologists, and of the emerging trends. Interestingly, these appraisals of research publications brought home this realization that psychology in India is mostly a poor imitation of Western research and does not lead to understanding Indian social reality. A crisis was perceptible in the discipline in the mid-1970s, as many felt that Indian psychology was going nowhere. The following passages present a brief account of this crisis of direction and progress.

By the mid-1970s, the enthusiasm with which the Western-educated Indian psychologists were conducting research was waning. Indian scholars were getting restive, as Western psychology was failing to throw light on Indian social issues. Sixty years of Western psychology in India had not yielded any significant discoveries. Nandy (1974) argued: 'Indian psychology has become not merely imitative and subservient but also dull and replicative' (p. 5). K. G. Agrawal (1973) called psychology in India as 'adoptology'. There was growing disillusionment about the applicability of Western theories and their mindless testing in India. The failure to resolve inner conflicts of cherishing Indian cultural values at the personal level and maintaining high standards of objectivity at the professional level was reflected in methodologically sophisticated but socially irrelevant research. As a result, Indian psychologists were increasingly marginalized in the society. A strong need was felt to return to the cultural roots. D. Sinha (1977) urged that the scientific understanding of Indian social reality should benefit from its vast treasure of traditional psychological knowledge accumulated over centuries. He called for the development of an indigenous psychology with its own paradigms to understand developmental problems of the region. In short, psychology in India was seeking its own identity.

What will make psychology more relevant in the Indian context? In the concluding chapter of the *Second Survey of Research in Psychology*, Pareek (1981) considered psychology in India as standing at the 'crossroads'. He discussed many referents of relevance, namely, conceptual, methodological, professional, and socio-cultural, in order to build the capability of the discipline to respond to the needs of the society. There are not many pointers that the situation had changed since then. D. Sinha (1986) also stressed on finding appropriate theoretical framework and research methodologies to make the subject 'socially relevant to meet the needs of a changing society' (p. 63). J. Pandey (1988), in the *Third Survey of Research in Psychology*, responding to Pareek's comment, concluded that psychology is outgrowing the alien models and 'probably psychology is not strictly standing at the cross-roads' (p. 354). In the *Fourth Survey*, J. Pandey (2001, 2002, 2004) reported the progress of indigenous psychology by citing important publications. However, as Pandey (2004) noted, '[t]hough these examples of indigenous efforts are laudable, the question remains whether this emerging trend has succeeded in influencing mainstream psychology (bulk of psychology) in terms of academic programmes of teaching and research' (pp. 347–348).

The ongoing debate did result in some noticeable change in the content and quality of Indian research. Indian psychologists were showing more interest in studying problems relevant to the country using Indian concepts and theories. Neki (1973), for example, suggested a teacher–pupil model in clinical counselling to break cultural and social barriers. J. B. P. Sinha (1980) proposed a new leadership style—nurturant task-master, which is more likely to succeed in Indian work organizations. Kakar (1982, 1991) studied the role of traditional healers in maintaining mental health in Indian society. Ramchandra Rao (1983), and Palsane, Bhavasari, Goswami and Evans (1986) developed a concept of stress based on ancient scriptures. Pande and Naidu (1992) developed a measure to study the concept of detachment and its mental health consequences.

However, this crisis of the discipline's identity was of concern for only a handful of psychologists. J. B. P. Sinha (1993) made a distinction between the bulk and the front of psychological research. Not much has changed in the mass-produced bulk of the research which is still replicative and imitative. However, as a response to a long debate and changing global scenario, the front-runners have started taking indigenous psychology more seriously. As argued by Manasi Kumar (2006), the inertia and lackadaisical stance of Indian psychologists towards attending to relevant social problems continued, and their rigidities in exploring new epistemologies and cross-fertilizations within and outside the discipline led to further replication of outdated and a-contextual Western psychological researches. Sitting rather too comfortably in the pigeon holes of the University departments, which do not mirror socio-cultural realities of the common man in India, psychologists have increasingly chosen to remain insular and self-absorbed. Even during the times when social sciences were revamping and scrutinizing their colonial baggage, essentially during the seventies and early eighties, Indian psychologists remained far from this self-reflexive, deconstructive enterprise that was in many ways deeply political in character and calling.

Again, the efforts to investigate indigenous concepts and theories were fragmented and did not show any long-term research commitment. It is heartening to find research articles employing Indian concepts, but these are mostly one-time affairs lacking in in-depth analysis. The best examples of thematic research over a long period have still employed Western models (for example, Kanekar, 1988; R. Singh, 1986). Relevant in this context is the fact that major funding agencies play an important role in setting the priority areas of research endeavours. The UGC, NCERT and ICSSR particularly, have shaped the nature and direction of research in the past four decades. A perusal of the research projects sanctioned by the ICSSR shows that whereas between 1969 and 1972 no research project on tribal communities was funded, between 1982 and 1985, 27% of the projects financed were tribal studies. This explains the spurt of research in this area in the last decade.

A journey toward indigenous psychology

The core of indigenization is the belief that all knowledge, including that of psychology, is rooted in the prevalent world-view of a community and is conditioned by historical and socio-cultural factors. D. Sinha (1994) discussed in detail the indigenization of psychology in India. He refers to two facets of indigenization. The first is purely the product of culture, the concepts and categories which are culture-bound. The second is the product of the interaction of cultural variables with concepts, theories and methods introduced from outside. J. B. P. Sinha (2002) has referred to these two as endogenous and exogenous indigenization. He further expanded the domain by referring to two variants of each kind of indigenization. The first one is a relatively more purist one, having more proximity either to the psycho-spiritual Indian thought system, or to the positivistic mainstream Western psychology. The second variant accepts the salience of the traditions, but maintains greater flexibility in choosing concepts, theories and methods. They differ mainly in terms of their allegiance to either Indian systems of thought, or to Western psychology. Taken together they can encompass the whole range of indigenization in Indian psychological research. Misra and Mohanty's (2002) edited book, *Perspectives on Indigenous Psychology*, is a good anthology of research in this area.

Taking the lead from the above discussion, it is argued in this chapter that indigenous research has moved along two different streams. One considers indigenization as a gradual process. A majority of psychologists in India are trained in Western models, and for them it is not feasible to make any sudden shift towards indigenously developed theories and methods. It is but natural for them to continue using concepts and tests borrowed from the West, albeit with increasing sensitivity to the cultural context. The same trend is observable in many other developing countries as well (Marriott, 1992).

The Canadian psychologist, John Adair, saw indigenization as a gradual process, and, in collaboration with his Indian colleagues, developed a scale to measure the degree of indigenization. Adair (1989) operationalized indigenization in terms of: (a) cultural sensitivity of researcher in designing a study and discussing its findings, (b) citation from one's own culture, (c) problem orientation, (d) development of culture-based concepts, theories and methods, (e) culturally anchored tests, and (f) cross-cultural comparisons. Adair and colleagues concluded on the basis of content analysis of a sample of over 300 journal articles that there was progress in indigenization of psychology in India, albeit at a slow pace (Adair, Puhan & Vohra, 1993). It is important to note in this context that, as Adair and others clarify, their focus is on the indigenization of an 'imported discipline', and not on 'endogenous development' of psychology based on indigenous sources.

Viewing retrospectively, this line of thinking led to the development of three streams of research: problem-oriented research, cross-cultural psychology and Indian psychology. In the 1970s and later too, there was excitement about Western theories, which held promises of dealing with the problems in the Indian setting. The main argument was that psychological knowledge should contribute to solving the problems of developing societies. Reviewing relevant Indian work, J. B. P. Sinha (1973) examined the methodological challenges in conducting problem-oriented research. Studies of political behaviour (Mehta, 1975), developmental norms for pre-school children (Murlidharan, 1971), change in level of aspiration and motivation of farmers (D. Sinha, 1969), prolonged deprivation (Misra & Tripathi, 1980), health modernity (A. K. Singh, 1983) are examples of such research. Pareek and Rao (1974b) reviewed researches in the field of family planning and presented a conceptual model of fertility-regulating behaviour. This concern of studying Indian problems is visible in a number of later studies. It was also realized that Western theories and methods could not be fruitfully applied to study Indian social problems. In the absence of any cumulative knowledge based on cultural understanding and field-testing, these studies did not yield any real insight and solutions of the Indian social problems needed for theoretical and methodological breakthroughs.

A parallel development was cross-cultural testing of psychological concepts and theories. For Indian psychologists who always showed an international orientation, it was an opportunity to operate on a wider plane and to influence developments in mainstream psychology. The cross-cultural movement found natural patronage in India and a large number of Indian psychologists joined this international movement. They occupied important positions in the International Association of Cross-Cultural Psychology, and played a prominent role in augmenting this movement. However, as noted by D. Sinha (1997), the cross-cultural work only led to testing of Western theories on Indian samples. Very rarely studies originated from the needs of the Indian society or tested Indian concepts in other cultures. Indiscriminate search for cultural differences and similarities made such ventures superficial, without providing much understanding of the culture or the contemporary problems of Indian society. To a large extent cross-cultural psychology remained a methodological enterprise and culture remained a peripheral concern (Misra & Gergen, 1993). In recent years, cross-cultural psychology itself is going through a crisis and the classical conception of culture, that was the basis of most research in this area, is being seriously questioned (Miller, 1998).

The third stream is that of indigenous psychology. At the core of indigenization is the belief that all psychological knowledge is rooted in the prevalent worldview of a society and is conditioned by its historical and metatheoretical considerations. D. Sinha (1994) has talked about two types of indigenization. The first is an outcome of adaptation of the mainstream (Western) psychology in a different cultural setup. This adaptation is along the lines argued by John Adair. A large body of research in India can be included in this kind of indigenization in which cultural concepts and practices are examined, employing Western theories and approaches. The other kind of indigenization is that which is based on a systematic analysis of the culture-bound concepts and categories. Such indigenization focuses on the contemporary relevance of cultural heritage and native theories, and is termed 'Indian Psychology'. This stream has primarily relied on the rich storehouse of knowledge found in Indian scriptures and philosophical texts of the last two to three millennia. The work of Kakar (1991, 2003, 2008) can be cited as a good example of research which finely blends these two streams of indigenization.

Indian psychology has developed around the existential quest to overcome human suffering and in the process to raise the person to higher levels of awareness and achievement. Thus, Indian psychology endeavours not only to provide an understanding of the nature of a person, the causes and consequences of his conduct, but also to explore the methods and means of transforming the person in pursuit of perfection in being, certainty in knowing and happiness in feeling. Indian psychology focuses on the inner self, which is accessible through subjective methods of self-verification. The beginning of Indian psychology can be traced in the writings of many eminent thinkers, such as Swami Vivekananda and Sri Aurobindo, in the early part of the last century. The monumental work of Jadunath Sinha (1934/1958; 1961) on Indian psychology can be considered as a landmark in formally establishing it as an independent discipline. The books of Ramachandra Rao (1962) and Ragunath Safaya (1975) gave it further impetus during the early years. These efforts to rejuvenate psychology in the ancient texts intensified in the 1980s and 1990s. Some notable publications of this period are by Paranjpe (1984, 1998), Chakraborty (1995), Saraswathi (1999) and K. Ramakrishna Rao (1988, 2002, 2005). There is a rich and growing body of research in this area and many excellent reviews are available. This stream has built not only on the interpretation of traditional concepts and theories in contemporary idiom, but also on their integration within a broader, global perspective. Cornelissen (2000, 2005) has pleaded that psychological knowledge from the Indian spiritual tradition needs to be integrated in the teaching programmes. According to him, the core of the curriculum could be Indian theories of self and consciousness.

Psychology in the new millennium

Clearly, by the turn of this new millennium, the academic scenario is changing in India. The scientific community is better prepared now than in the past to accept a psychology rooted in native wisdom and philosophical traditions. Psychologists in India are increasingly aware of the wide gap between their academic pursuits and the real-life problems of people. The replicative nature of research endeavours, antiquated and obsolete teaching programmes, and lack of applied orientation have devoid the discipline of any professional momentum. Indian psychologists want to break free from the theoretical and methodological constraints of the discipline to grapple with the real issues of development and to act as social catalysts in the change process. Indian psychologists are also aware that if they fail to take up the challenge, they are likely to be completely marginalized.

The concern over the dominance of American psychology and attempts to develop psychology appropriate to indigenous cultures and societies is common not only to the third world countries but also to the second world countries of Europe (Moghaddam, 1987). The need for developing indigenous perspectives of one's culture has been felt by psychologists in many countries in all the continents. Thus it is not a culture-specific phenomenon, limited to a few Asian societies. Indian psychology is indigenous psychology in that it is a psychology derived from indigenous thought systems and therefore is clearly best suited to address India's specific psychological issues and problems. It is, however, more than indigenous psychology for the reason that it offers psychological models and theories appropriate to address problems of social conflicts, violence and mental health in other societies also.

Four factors have contributed to this change of attitudes and perceptions of Indian psychology. First, is the failure of Western psychology to deal with its own societal problems. It has increasingly been realized that positivistic psychology only provides a fragmented and superficial understanding of human feelings and behaviour. Growing problems such as social and family violence, mental health and moral decay have brought out the gross limitations of mainstream Western psychology. Humanistic and transpersonal movements in the 1960s have been the protest movements against brute empiricism in psychological research. A need was felt to bring back spirituality and religiosity in psychological research, which were banished from psychology for almost 150 years (see special issue of the *American Psychologist*, January 2004). All these contemporary developments are in response to the acutely felt limitations of psychology developed within the framework of modern science, which led to new ways of thinking in terms of feminism, social constructionism, postmodernism and the like, which are much closer to Eastern philosophies. The movement toward positive psychology (Snyder

& Lopez, 2002) also has many ingredients of Indian psychology.

Second, is the growing popularity of *yoga* and other spiritual systems of India in the West. In the past few decades more and more people with spiritual training and experiences from India have been visiting other countries and have acquired a large following. They have been responsible for disseminating the Indian spiritual tradition. Among them, Maharishi Mahesh Yogi and Swami Rama are some prominent *gurus* who have been able to draw the attention of academic psychologists. Sri Aurobindo's Integral Yoga and Integral Psychology attracted worldwide attention. Mahesh Yogi's Transcendental Meditation went through rigorous experimental testing at Harvard and many other universities. Swami Rama offered himself to extensive medical testing at the Meninger Foundation Laboratory, New York, where he demonstrated many yogic feats. These Indian masters were able to demonstrate convincingly the power of mind over body and have contributed significantly towards evoking interest in the Indian psychological perspectives. Publications of the Sri Aurobindo Ashram in Puducherry, and the Himalayan International Institute for Yoga Sciences, Philosophy, and Religion in Honesdale, Pennsylvania, founded by Swami Rama, are valuable for their significant contributions in expounding the psychological insights of the *Vedānta, Yoga, Saṁkhyā* and other Indian systems. These and many other accomplished spiritual masters of the Indian tradition have played an important role in popularizing Indian psychology in the world (Paranjpe, 2005).

Third, is the secular nature of Indian psychology. It is gradually acknowledged that Indian psychology of consciousness has more to offer in terms of self-growth than as religious traditions. Interest in the study of altered state phenomena since the 1960s and the founding of transpersonal psychology as a sub-discipline, encouraged psychologists involved in them to examine the indigenous perspectives available in many religious traditions of the East. It was clearly recognized that modern psychology has nothing to offer regarding the spiritual/transcendental dimension of human nature whether to understand others or for personal growth (Tart, 1975). Unfortunately, most academic psychologists in India have not appreciated this fact, and consider Indian psychology as part of the revivalistic movement.

Fourth, with India emerging as a major economic power in the world, there is a renewed interest in Indian values, philosophies and practices, as well as in the strength and resilience of Indian society. The very Indian culture and philosophy which was debunked for India's poverty and backwardness by many Western Indologists (Max Muller, for example) is now seen behind India's success stories. Indian research is now taken more seriously by Western psychologists, and as a consequence (ironically), by Indian psychologists themselves.

The newly emerging psychology is rooted in traditional Indian thought and practices. As stated in the Pondicherry Manifesto (2002), 'Rich in content, sophisticated in its methods and valuable in its applied aspects, Indian psychology is pregnant with possibilities for the birth of new models in psychology that would have relevance not only for India but also to psychology in general'. The plurality of the Indian tradition and an ethos of accommodating diverse thought systems provide a rich gold mine for creatively building a new psychology. However, despite all diversity and distinctiveness there are some features common across all systems and schools relevant to Indian psychology. Some of these common features which give Indian Psychology a distinct identity are briefly discussed here.

Indian psychology can be deemed as *universal*. It cannot be subsumed under indigenous or cultural psychology if that implies delimiting the scope of psychological inquiry. Indian psychology deals with the perennial issues of human existence which are not bound by any geographical region or time period. Centuries back the sages and thinkers were raising the same questions and dealing with the same problems that are pertinent today, and in this sense Indian psychology is both ancient and contemporary at the same time. Indeed, the use of the term 'Indian psychology' is more of a convenience; maybe a more appropriate term is 'psychology of Indian origin'. While the roots of Indian psychology are decidedly Indian, it was never proposed as the psychology of

Indian people. For instance, Buddhist psychology, which is an integral part of Indian psychology, was developed in Sri Lanka, Tibet and Japan, among other countries. Most of these theories are propounded as trans-historical, dealing with the essential human nature and ways to harness human potential.

Another important feature of Indian psychology is that it primarily deals with the *inner state* of a person, taking consciousness as the primary subject matter of study. Consciousness as a state of being is not an object but is conceived as undifferentiated subjectivity without any content. It can be studied only indirectly through its various manifestations. Buddhism refers to a stream of consciousness as the basis of the subjective feeling of continuity and identity which affects all our perceptions, thoughts, actions and emotions. Human consciousness is considered hierarchical, the highest state being of pure consciousness, bliss and truth. Distortions in consciousness are due to active interference of mind and body which limits our awareness, obscures our knowledge and feelings and cause suffering. The goal of life is to attain this state of pure consciousness where the knowledge is direct, immediate and intuitive, and not mediated by sensory inputs. *Yoga* and meditation are the tools to attain this transcendental state of pure consciousness.

It, however, should not be misconstrued that Indian psychology is not concerned about human conditions of poverty, injustice and pain. Indian psychology does not dismiss the empirical research in these areas but provides a broader perspective within which their findings should make sense. The theories and practices of Āyurveda are fine examples of how the mundane can be blended with the transcendental.

Indian psychology is *spiritual* in its orientation. Spiritual does not mean otherworldly, nor does it mean being religious or dogmatic. Spirituality hereby implies taking into consideration the whole range of human progression, without making a distinction between natural and supernatural. It connotes faith in the existence of higher powers and the possibility of relating to them to seek the higher-order truth of life. Spirituality has opened up the possibilities of developing broader theories of human existence to understand paranormal powers, creativity and intuitive thinking, which many people exhibit. It can be stated that spiritual and sacred go together, though in Indian thought no dichotomy is maintained between science and spirituality. Transcendence and a state of pure consciousness are held as empirical facts in Indian psychology grounded in the experiences of many and attainable for anyone who follows systematic procedures and practices. Though spirituality is at the core of most of the Indian theories it is not bound by any particular faith or 'ism' and serves to provide a secular account of human nature.

Indian psychology is based on *veridical* methods. It should be clear that as a human science of consciousness its methods ought to be different from the methods of physical sciences. However it does not permit it to be a less stringent science. Methods of observation and experimentation are evolved to study the inner functioning of a person. In these methods of self-observation no distinction is made between experience and observation, where true knowledge is not considered as abstract and impersonal but as realization of one's being. There are methods of direct observation (for example, intuition) in contrast to those methods which rely on sensory and mental mediation. These methods rely on the blending of first-person and second-person perspectives. Taken together, these two perspectives provide personal, subjective and non-relational verification and in-group inter-subjective validity. These methods work well within the *guru*–pupil (second person–first person) tradition. Methods of *yoga* and meditation have been used for centuries to test, experiment and empirically validate higher mental states.

Indian psychology is *applied*. It is not just concerned about testing the existing theories and developing generalizable propositions, but more importantly, about the practices that can be used for the transformation of human conditions towards perfection. That is, transformation of the person to higher levels of achievement and well-being. The goal of Indian psychology is to help the person transcend from a conditional state (mechanical and habitual thinking) to an unconditional state of freedom and liberation. This transformation, in more mundane terms, implies becoming more objective, discretionary, equi-poised and knowing about the sources of distortion. Indian psychology extensively deals with ways to deal with human suffering and lead one on the path of personal growth. The techniques of *yoga* and meditation have contributed in a significant way to controlling the mind and feelings.

This newly emerging science of Indian origin calls for a paradigm shift in psychological research. A dominant view is that the Western and the Indian paradigms are irreconcilable and cannot have a meeting ground. Indian concepts and theories are grounded in different notions of human nature, epistemology, values and worldview, than the Western ones. The point is that we need both the paradigms to cover the whole range of human possibilities. Whereas the methodology of Western psychology focuses on the study of the 'other' person, Indian psychology (like other Eastern psychologies) focuses on the study of one's 'own-self'. We need both the first-person, and the third-person approach to research to bring about desired changes in human societies. The experiential basis of knowledge generation is common to theories and practices of many other Eastern philosophies, including Zen, Tao and Buddhism. The proponents of this position posit that building a more harmonious and conflict-free world order where people are able to actualize their inner potential can be a valid goal of research endeavours.

In more recent times, efforts to build Indian psychology as a vibrant discipline have intensified. Several conferences (Puducherry, 2001, 2002, 2004; Kollam, 2001; Delhi, 2002, 2003, 2007; Vishakhapatnam, 2002, 2003, 2006; Bengaluru, 2007) in recent times have given impetus to this movement of Indian psychology. A number of publications on Indian psychology, such as Kuppuswami's *Elements of Ancient Indian Psychology* (1985), Sen's *Integral Psychology* (1986), Misra and Mohanty's *Perspectives on Indigenous Psychology* (2002) have the potential of serving as textbooks. More recently, Joshi and Cornelissen's edited volume, *Consciousness, Indian Psychology and Yoga* (2004); Rao and Marwaha's *Towards a Spiritual Psychology* (2006); Rao, Paranjpe and Dalal's *Handbook of Indian Psychology* (2008), and the present volume, provide rich resource material for teaching and research in this area. It needs to be made clear that the purpose of testing ancient Indian theories and knowledge is not to prove their superiority. It is a movement toward contemporarizing Indian theories and testing their relevance for enhancing human competencies and well-being. It is against this backdrop that Indian psychology is gearing itself to usher in a new era of many exciting possibilities.

References

Adair, J. G. (1989). *Indigenous developments in Indian psychology: A quantitative assessment.* Paper presented at the Annual Meeting of the Canadian Psychological Association, Halifax, Nova Scotia.

Adair, J. G., Puhan, B. N., & Vora, N. (1993). Indigenization of psychology: Empirical assessment of progress in Indian research. *International Journal of Psychology, 29*, 149–169.

Adair, J. G., Pandey, J., Begam, H. A., Puhan, B. N., & Vora, N. (1995). Indigenization and development of the discipline: Perceptions and opinions of Indian and Bangladeshi Psychologists. *Journal of Cross-Cultural Psychology, 26*, 392–407.

Agrawal, K. G. (1973). Psychology or adoptology. *Social Scientist, 1*, 1–4.

Anandlakshmy, S. (1975). Socialization for competence. In J. W. Berry, & W. J. Lonner (Eds.), *Applied cross-cultural psychology*. Amsterdam: Swets and Zeitlinger.

Anandlakshmy, S. (1982). Growing up in Varanasi. *Seminar, 27*, 2–25.

Anant, S. S. (1970). Caste prejudices and its perception by Harijans. *Journal of Social Psychology, 82*, 271–278.

Ansari, Z. A. (1990). Pakistan. In G. Shouksmith & E. A. Shouksmith (Eds.), *Psychology in Asia and the Pacific*. Bangkok: UNESCO.

Atal, Y. (1976). *Social sciences: The Indian scene.* New Delhi: Abhinav Prakashan.

Barnett, W. L. (1955). Survey of research with psychological tests in India. *Psychological Bulletin, 52*, 105–121.

Begam, H. (1990). Bangladesh. In G. Shouksmith & E. A. Shouksmith (Eds.), *Psychology in Asia and the Pacific*. Bangkok: UNESCO.

Carstairs, G. M. (1957). *The twice born*. London: Hogarth Press.

Chakraborty, S. K. (1995). *Ethics in management: Vedantic perspectives*. New Delhi: Oxford University Press.

Chatterjee, R. G. (1954). An investigation on the perceptual side of repression. *Indian Journal of Psychology, 29*, 191–193.

Cohen, D., & Cohen, S. (1977). *Psychologists on psychology*. London: Routledge & Kegan Paul.

Cornelissen, M. (2000). The integration of psychological knowledge from the spiritual traditions into the psychology curriculum. *Consciousness and Experiential Psychology, 4*(1), 1–4.

Cornelissen, M. (2002). Towards an integral epistemology of consciousness: A radical proposal based on Sri Aurobindo. In S. Menon, A. Sinha, & B. V. Sreekantan (Eds.), *A discussion on consciousness and genetics*. Bangalore: National Institute of Advanced Studies.

Dalal, A. K. (1990). India. In G. Shouksmith & E. A. Shouksmith (Eds.), *Psychology in Asia and the Pacific*. Bangkok: UNESCO.

Dalal, A. K. (1996). A science in search of its identity: Twentieth Century psychology in India. *Indian Psychological Abstracts and Reviews, 4*, 1–41.

Dalal, A. K. (2001). Health psychology. In J. Pandey (Ed.), *Psychology in India revisited: Development in the discipline* (pp. 356–411). New Delhi: Sage.

Dalal, A. K. (2002). Psychology in India: A historical introduction. In G. Misra & A. K. Mohanty (Eds.), *Perspectives on indigenous psychology*. New Delhi: Concept.

Dalal, A. K. (2010). Psychosocial interventions in community development. In G. Misra (Ed.), *Fifth survey of research in psychology*. New Delhi: Pearson.

Dalal, A. K., & Sharma, R. (1990). *Sample and method in social and personality research: Content analysis of psychological abstracts*. Unpublished manuscript, University of Allahabad, Allahabad.

Das, J. P. (1962). Learning under conditions of hypnotically induced anxiety and non-anxiety. *International Journal of Clinical and Experimental Hypnosis, 10*, 163–168.

DeRidder, R., & Tripathi, R. C. (Eds.) (1992). *Norm violation and intergroup relations*. Oxford: Clarendon Press.

Dhanagare, D. N. (1985). India. In Y. Atal (Ed.), *UNESCO reports: Sociology and social anthropology in the Asia and Pacific*. New Delhi: Wiley Eastern.

Dube, S. C. (1984). India. In Y. Atal (Ed.), *Social Sciences in Asia and the Pacific*. Paris: UNESCO.

Elnagar, M. M., Mitra, P., & Rao, M. N. (1971). Mental health in an Indian rural community. *British Journal of Psychiatry, 118*, 499–504.

Ganguli, H. C. (1961). *Industrial productivity and motivation*. Bombay: Asia Publishing House.

Ganguli, H. C. (1971). Psychological research in India: 1920–1967. *International Journal of Psychology, 6*, 165–177.

Gilgin, A. R., & Gilgin, C. K. (Eds.) (1987). *Psychology in world perspective: International handbook of psychology*. Westport, C.T.: Greenwood Press.

Jain, A. K. (2005). Psychology in India. *British Psychologist, 24*, 16–24.

Joshi, K., & Cornelissen, M. (Eds.) (2004). *Consciousness, Indian psychology and yoga*. New Delhi: Centre for Studies in Civilizations.

Kakar, S. (1978). *The inner experience*. Delhi: Oxford University Press.

Kakar, S. (1982). *Shamans, mystics and doctors: A psychological inquiry into India and its healing traditions*. Bombay: Oxford University Press.

Kakar, S. (1991). *The analyst and the mystic*. London: Penguin.

Kakar, S. (2003). Psychoanalysis and Eastern Spiritual Traditions. *Journal of Analytic Psychology, 48*, 659–678.

Kakar, S. (2008). *Mad and divine*. New Delhi: Penguin.

Kanekar, S. (1988). Attribution of causal and moral responsibility: The case of a rape victim. In A. K. Dalal (Ed.), *Attribution theory and research*. New Delhi: Wiley Eastern.

Kothurkar, V. K. (1972). Experimental psychology. In S. K. Mitra (Ed.), *A survey of research in psychology*. Mumbai: Popular Prakashan.

Kumar, M. (2006). Rethinking psychology in India: Debating pasts and futures. *Annual Review of Critical Psychology, 5*, Retrieved from: http://www.discourseunit.com/arcp/5.

Kuppuswami, B. (1985). *Elements of ancient Indian psychology*. New Delhi: Vikas Publishing House.

McClelland, D. C. (1961). *The achieving society*. Princeton: Van Nostrand.

Mehta, P. (1973). *Election campaign*. New Delhi: National Publishing House.

Miller, J. G. (1998). Theoretical issues in cultural psychology and social constructionism. In J. W. Berry, Y. Poortinga, & J. Pandey (Eds.), *Handbook of cross-cultural psychology: Theoretical and methodological perspectives* (Vol. 1). Boston: Allyn & Bacon.

Minturn, A., & Hitchock, P. (1966). Rajputs of Khalapur. In R. Whiting (Ed.), *Six cultures*. Cambridge, Mass.: Harvard University Press.

Misra, G. (Ed.) (2010). *Fifth Survey of Research in Psychology* (Vol. 3). New Delhi: Pearson.

Misra, G., & Gergen, K. J. (1993). On the place of culture in psychological science. *International Journal of Psychology, 28*, 225–243.

Misra, G., & Mohanty, A. (2002). *Perspectives on indigenous psychology*. New Delhi: Concept.

Misra, G., & Tripathi, L. B. (1980). *Psychological consequences of prolonged deprivation*. Agra: National Psychological Corporation.

Mitra, S. K. (1972). Psychological research in India. In S. K. Mitra (Ed.), *A survey of research in psychology*. Bombay: Popular Prakashan.

Moghaddam, F. M. (1987). Psychology in the three worlds. *American Psychologist, 42*, 912–920.

Muralidharan, R. (1971). *Developmental norms of Indian children—2 years to 5 years*. New Delhi: NCERT.

Murphy, G. (1953). *In the minds of men*. New York: Basic Books.

Murthy, H. N. (1980). Counseling and psychotherapy. In U. Pareek (Ed.), *A survey of research in psychotherapy: 1971-1976* (Part 1). Mumbai: Popular Prakashan.

Nandy, A. (1974). The non-paradigmatic crisis in Indian psychology: Reflection on a recipient culture of science. *Indian Journal of Psychology, 49*, 1–20.

Nandy, A. (1995). The savage Freud: The first non-Western psychoanalysts and the politics of secret-selves in colonial India. In A. Nandy (Ed.), *The Savage Freud and other essays on possible and retrievable selves* (pp. 81–144). New Delhi: Oxford University Press.

NCERT (1968). *The third Indian yearbook of education*. New Delhi: National Council of Educational Research and Training.

NCERT (1981). *Psychological tests in India*. New Delhi: National Council of Educational Research and Training.

Neki, J. S. (1973). Guru–chela relationship: The possibility of a therapeutic paradigm. *American Journal of Orthopsychiatry, 43*, 755–766.

Palsane, M. N., Bhavsagar, S. N., Goswami, R. P., & Evans, G. W. (1986). The concept of stress in the Indian tradition. *Journal of Indian Psychology, 5*, 1–12.

Pande, N., & Naidu, R. K. (1992). Anasakti and Health: A Study of Non-attachment. *Psychology and Developing Societies, 4*(1), 89–104.

Pandey, J. (2004). Psychology in India enters the 21st Century: Movement toward an indigenous discipline. In J. Pandey (Ed.), *Psychology in India revisited*, (Vol. 3, pp. 342–370). New Delhi: Sage.

Pandey, J. (Ed.) (1988). *Psychology in India: The state-of-the-art* (Vols. 1, 2, 3). New Delhi: Sage.

Pandey, J. (Ed.) (2001). *Psychology in India revisited* (Vol. 1). New Delhi: Sage.

Pandey, J. (Ed.) (2002). *Psychology in India revisited* (Vol. 2). New Delhi: Sage.

Pandey, J. (Ed.) (2004). *Psychology in India revisited* (Vol. 3). New Delhi: Sage.

Pandey, J., & Singh, P. (2005). Social psychology in India: Social roots and development. *International Journal of Psychology, 40*, 239–253.

Pandey, R. E. (1969). Psychology in India. *American Psychologist, 24*, 936–939.

Paranjpe, A. C. (1970). *Caste prejudice and individual*. Mumbai: Lalvani.

Paranjpe, A. C. (1984). *Theoretical psychology: The meeting of east and west*. New York: Plenum Press.

Paranjpe, A. C. (2002). Problems and prospects for an indigenous psychology in India. In G. Misra & A. K. Mohanty (Eds.), *Perspectives on indigenous psychology*. New Delhi: Concept.

Paranjpe, A. C. (2006). From tradition through colonialism to globalization: Reflections on the history of psychology in India. In A. C. Brock (Ed.), *Internationalizing the history of psychology*. New York: New York University Press.

Pareek, U. (1980). *A survey of research in psychology: 1971–1976* (Part 1). Bombay: Popular Prakashan.

Pareek, U. (1981). *A survey of research in psychology: 1971–1976* (Part 2). Bombay: Popular Prakashan.

Pareek, U., & Rao, T. V. (1974a). *Handbook of psychological and social instruments*. Baroda: Samashti.

Pareek, U., & Rao, T. V. (1974b). *A status study of population research in India: Behavioural science*. New Delhi: McGraw-Hill.

Pestonjee, D. M. (1986). *Handbook of psychological tests*. Bombay: Popular Prakashan.

Prabhu, G. G. (1983). Clinical psychology then and now. *Indian Journal of Clinical Psychology, 10*, 1–16.

Prasad, J. (1935). The psychology of rumour: A study relating to the great Indian earthquake of 1934. *British Journal of Psychology, 26*, 1–15.

Puhan, B. (1994). *Psychological testing in India*. Presidential address to the 5th Annual Convention of National Academy of Psychology (21–23 December), at Allahabad University, Allahabad.

Rajanarayan, A. (1983). Narendra Nath Sengupta 1889–1944. *Manovigyan Bharati, 2*(2), 1–12.

Rama, Swami, Ballentine, S., & Ajay, Swami (1976). *Yoga and psychotherapy*. Honesdale, PA: Himalayan Institute.

Rao, K. R. (1988). Psychology of transcendence: A study in early Buddhist psychology. In A. C. Paranjpe, D. Y. F. Ho, & R. W. Rieber (Eds.), *Asian contributions to psychology*. New York: Praeger.

Rao, K. R. (2002). Consciousness studies: A survey of perspectives and research. In J. Pandey (Ed.), *Psychology in India revisited* (Vol. 2, pp. 19–162). New Delhi: Sage.

Rao, K. R. (2005). Scope and substance of Indian psychology. In K. R. Rao & S. B. Marwaha (Eds.), *Towards a spiritual psychology: Essays on Indian psychology*. New Delhi: Samvad India Foundation.

Rao, K. R., Paranjpe, A. C., & Dalal, A. K. (Eds.) (2008). *Handbook of Indian psychology*. New Delhi: Cambridge University Press.

Rao, K. R., & Paranjpe, A. C. (2008). Yoga psychology: Theory and application. In K. R. Rao, A. Paranjpe, & A. K. Dalal (Eds.), *Handbook of Indian psychology*. New Delhi: Cambridge University Press.

Rao, R. (1962). *Development of psychological thought in India*. Mysore: Kavyalaya.

Rao, R. (1983). The conception of stress in Indian thought: I. The theoretical aspects of stress in Samkhya and Yoga systems II. The practical involvement in Gita and Ayurveda. *NIMHANS Journal, 1*, 115–131.

Rath, R., & Sircar, N. C. (1960). Intercaste relationships as reflected in the study of attitudes and opinion of six Hindu caste groups. *Journal of Social Psychology, 51*, 3–25.

Safaya, R. (1975). *Indian psychology: A critical and historical analysis of psychological speculation in Indian philosophical literature*. New Delhi: Munshiram Manoharlal.

Salagame, K. K. K. (2010). Development of indigenous Indian perspective. In G. Misra (Ed.), *Fifth survey of research in psychology*, Vol. 1. New Delhi: Sage.

Salagame, K. K. K. (2008). Indian thought and tradition: A psychohistorical perspective. In K. R. Rao, A. Paranjpe, & A. K. Dalal (Eds.), *Handbook of Indian psychology*. New Delhi: Cambridge University Press.

Saraswathi, T. S. (1987). *Developmental psychology in India (1975-86): An annotated bibliography*. New Delhi: Sage.

Saraswathi, T. S. (1999). *Culture, socialization and human development: Theory, research and applications in India*. New Delhi: Sage.

Sen, I. (1986). *Integral psychology: The psychological system of Sri Aurobindo*. Pondicherry: Sri Aurobindo International Centre for Education.

Sethi, B. B., Gupta, S. C., & Kumar, R. (1967). 300 urban families. *Indian Journal of Psychiatry, 9*, 280–302.

Sethi, B. B., Gupta, S .C., Kumar, R., & Promilla, L. (1972). A psychiatric survey of 500 rural families. *Indian Journal of Psychiatry, 14*, 183–196.

Singh, A. K. (1981). Development of religious identity and prejudice in Indian children. In D. Sinha (Ed.), *Socialization of the Indian child* (pp. 87–100). New Delhi: Concept.

Singh, R. (1986). Two problems in cognitive algebra: Imputation and averaging versus multiplying. In N. H. Anderson (Ed.), *Contributions to information integration theory*. New York: Academic Press.

Singh, S. D. (1963). Effects of dexidine ephedrine phenobarbitone and chlorpromazine on the latency of autokinetic movement. *Psychological Studies, 8*, 7–14.

Sinha, A. K. P., & Upadhyay, O. P. (1960). Change and persistence in stereotypes of university students towards different ethnic groups during Sino-Indian border dispute. *Journal of Social Psychology, 52*, 31–39.

Sinha, D. (1969). *Indian villages in transition: A motivational analysis*. New Delhi: Associated Publishing House.

Sinha, D. (1977). Scientist professional model in problem-oriented applied social psychology research. *Journal of Social and Economic Studies, 5*, 219–233.

Sinha, D. (1986). *Psychology in a third world country: An Indian experience*. New Delhi: Sage.

Sinha, D. (1996). Culturally rooted psychology in India: Dangers and developments. *International Journal of Psychology, 30*, 99–110.

Sinha, D. (1997). Indigenizing psychology. In J. W. Berry, Y. Poortinga, & J. Pandey (Eds.), *Handbook of cross-cultural psychology: Theoretical and methodological perspectives*, Vol. 1. Boston: Allyn & Bacon.

Sinha, J. (1958). *Indian psychology*, Vol. 1 & 2. Calcutta: Jadunath Sinha Foundation.

Sinha, J. B. P. (1973). Methodology of problem-oriented research in India. *Journal of Social and Economic Studies, 1*, 93–110.

Sinha, J. B. P. (1980). *Nurturant task leader*. New Delhi: Concept.

Sinha, J. B. P. (1993). The front and the bulk of Indian psychology. *Psychology and Developing Societies, 5*, 135–150.

Sinha, J. B. P. (2002). Towards indigenization of psychology in India. In G. Misra & A. K. Mohanty (Eds.), *Perspectives on indigenous psychology* (pp. 440–457). New Delhi: Concept.

Snyder, C. R., & Lopez, S. (2002). *Handbook of positive psychology*. New York: Academic Press.

Tart, C. (1975). *Transpersonal psychologies*. San Francisco: Harper & Row.

Tayal, O. P. (1970). Visual processing: General principles for an interpretation of geometrical illusions. *Journal of General Psychology, 86*, 93–115.

Tripathi, R. C. (1988). Aligning development to values in India. In D. Sinha & H. S. R. Kao (Eds.), *Social values and development: Asian perspectives* (pp. 315–333). New Delhi: Sage.

UGC (1968). *Psychology in Indian universities*. New Delhi: University Grants Commission.

UGC (1982). *Status of psychology in Indian universities*. New Delhi: University Grants Commission.

UGC (1999). *Curriculum in psychology*. New Delhi: University Grants Commission.

Varma, S. (2004). Psychology in India: Past trends and future possibilities. In K. Joshi & M. Cornelissen (Eds.), *Consciousness, Indian psychology and yoga* (Vol. 11, part 3, pp. 224–236). New Delhi: Centre for Studies in Civilizations.

Verghese, A. (1973). A social and psychiatric study of a representative group of families in Vellore town. *Indian Journal of Medical Research, 61*, 609–620.

Wig, N. N., & Akhatar, S. (1974). Twenty-five years of psychiatric research in India. *Indian Journal of Psychiatry, 16*, 48–64.

3

Beyond mind: The future of psychology as a science

Kundan Singh

Introduction

Impressed by the apparent potential of physics to explain, predict and control natural phenomena, Western psychology, rooted in a Newtonian-reductionist framework and guided by the philosophy of naïve Realism, embraced a methodology identical to the one employed by the natural sciences, to generate universal, rational, objective and value-free laws of human behaviour. This gave Western psychology the much-coveted status of science. However, as far as the current status of psychology as a discipline goes, there are numerous psychological schools, all claiming scientific 'objectivity'. Trying to find the reason why there are so many different 'objective' psychological truths, this chapter critically examines the methodological and epistemological assumptions behind mainstream psychological research. It narrates the problems associated with the objectivity of psychological knowledge largely by drawing from the critique of science by Thomas Kuhn, Paul Feyerabend and Karl Popper which emerged from their analysis of the history of science. Kuhn's view leads one to identify the crucial role that paradigm plays in scientific research. An extension of his arguments suggests that psychological knowledge is relative with respect to person, time, culture and paradigm. A meta-analysis of the epistemological conclusion gives birth to a peculiar situation where opposite categories like relative and absolute, objectivity and subjectivity, the truth and falsity of facts co-exist.

The second half of the chapter examines the future of psychology as a science against this impasse generated by the recognition of relativism and the aforementioned paradox, and what should be the true foundation for Indian psychology. Vedānta and Mahayana Buddhism have long ago recognized that the intellectual, logical and discursive pursuit of human knowledge ends in such kinds of *cul-de-sac* and impasse, and that such a recognition should necessitate a shift towards changing the *modus operandi* of our pursuit of knowledge. Mind is not the final summit in the evolution of mankind. There can be faculties other than mind which can be used to uncover nature's truths, and it is not in the spirit of science to fall prey to scientism. Furthermore, this chapter, which draws substantially from the writings of Sri Aurobindo, discusses the possibility of a psychology which will be made possible by making a mystical exploration into the nature of Reality where forces invisible to the ordinary human eye, which nevertheless determine human behaviour, will be observed and known. Such psychology has been our Indian legacy. It is time that we recognize it and introduce its epistemological, metaphysical, and ontological underpinnings in academia.

Scientific concerns of modern psychology

Psychology's identification with science is apparent from even a cursory glance at its textbooks, teaching programmes and emphasis on quantitative methods and objective stance toward psychological processes. Interestingly, throughout its disciplinary history, psychology has been defined in myriad ways. The early psychologists defined it as the study of consciousness, mind and mental activity. With the advent of Behaviourism at the turn of the century, due to its central concern with studying only the phenomena that could be objectively measured, psychology came to be described as the study of behaviour. This definition has featured in most psychology textbooks of the 1930s through the 1960s. The cycle has come full circle with the development of cognitive and humanistic/transpersonal psychology, as most current definitions of psychology make references to both behaviour and mental processes (Henley, Johnson & Jones, 1989; Ciccarelli & Mayer, 2006). Despite little variations, most definitions of psychology emphatically maintain and make it explicit that it is a science.

In the late nineteenth century, physics rooted in the Newtonian framework was solving puzzle after puzzle, and this led philosophers like J. S. Mill to believe that by subjecting human beings to a similar kind of experimentation, one could isolate cause and effect relationships in quantitative terms, which would then allow them to generate universal laws of human behaviour. However, more than a hundred years have elapsed since the first experimental lab was established by Wundt in 1879, and the outcome of this approach has been thousands of theories, mostly at variance with one another—all trying to explain behaviour and behavioural problems scientifically.

The crucial question, however, is how we can have so many theories of human nature—all claiming scientific objectivity—and yet be unable to explain anything conclusively. For none of the theorists claimed that their laws were not scientific—on the contrary they all claimed and documented that these laws were derived from an objective and an unbiased observation. Therefore, it becomes increasingly pertinent to review the central tenets of the methodology that have guided psychological research generating these theories, and consequently the pitfalls of this approach before we talk about a new paradigm of psychology—a paradigm which not only explains the cause of numerous 'objective' truths but also proposes an epistemology that does not contain the problems of the current and existent one.

Science was formalized by Francis Bacon in the seventeenth century. He gave two fundamental laws of science: induction and deduction, which form the basic tenets of positivism, a school of thought which has dictated the conduct of psychology from the past to the present. Positivism later developed into logical positivism, and together they are called the 'received view of science'. Also, the birth of science was buttressed by a philosophy that has been called naïve Realism, which contends that there is an objective reality independent of the observer and that it can be understood by wresting out its secrets by a rational, unbiased and value-free observer. Consequently, the philosophy of realism created dualism such as subject and object, fact and value and sharp divisions like objective reality and subjective feelings.

The problem with induction, and challenges to objectivity

Induction starts with observation, stemming from an unprejudiced mind. The observations lead to singular statements—referring to a particular state of affairs at a particular time—that form the body of facts from which the laws and theories that constitute scientific knowledge can be derived. For the singular statements to culminate in universal laws, an important condition that needs to be met is that the number of observation statements forming the basis of generalization must be large (Chalmers, 1999). Following this, a finite set of singular statements would lead to a universal law. This was designated as inductive reasoning. Once the inductive laws are established, they can be tested at a different place and time. This is the process of deduction. The essential condition for the methodology of science is that the observation has to be value free, detached and objective.

As stated before, an important premise of induction is that the number of observations must be large. However, despite a large number of cases showing consistency, it is not guaranteed that the next event would not be contrary to it. Hence repeated observation cannot ultimately justify induction. For example, no matter how many white swans we may have encountered, it does not imply that all swans are white; the next that we encounter may be black (Popper, 1992). The inductive principle is considered as the mainstay of science by positivists. They maintain that if it is removed from the canon of science, science will loose its power to determine the nature of Truth. But how does one logically prove that the principle of induction is true in the first place and not an assumption. In other words, how does one ascertain that the inductive principle helps uncover the truth? It is argued that since it seems to operate well in a large number of cases, the premise is correct. This implies that one uses induction to justify induction and thus the argument assumes circularity. This is called the *problem of induction* (Popper, 1992).

The most serious drawback with induction is, however, with respect to its claim of objectivity in observation. It is a common experience that no two individuals register the same thing even if the respective images on their retinas are the same. One does not require much knowledge of psychology to know that the observer's perception is determined by her expectations, belief, knowledge, inner state and psychological make-up.

The contention of an inductivist, that the true basis of scientific knowledge should proceed from an unbiased and unprejudiced mind, is further rendered absurd by the practice of the scientist to consider only those data that are relevant to her research. Since the idea of relevant and irrelevant is always present during the course of investigation, the possibility of an unbiased and unprejudiced observer takes a back seat. The investigator or scientist cannot but be an integral part of the research work and her subjectivity is bound to play an instrumental role in the outcome of the research. Thus, it can be safely said that the data do not have an independent existence; rather they are constructed within the confines and boundaries of a theory. In other words, data are theory-laden and objectivity is the last thing that scientists should claim. Expressing similar concerns, Feyerabend (1993, p. 12) writes:

> The history of science, after all, does not consist of fact and conclusions drawn from facts. It also contains ideas, interpretation of facts, problems created by conflicting interpretations, mistakes, and so on. On closer analysis, we find that science knows no "bare facts" at all but the "facts" that enter our knowledge are already viewed in a certain way and are, therefore, essentially ideational.

For any meaningful research—or for that matter any research—to take place it is imperative that the researcher has some sort of a framework, otherwise how is she going to collect, organize and interpret the data. Data are essentially neutral and meaning needs to be ascribed to them. It is the paradigm with all its presuppositions, and, as previously acknowledged, the predispositions of the researcher—her psychology, her cosmological world-view, her language, her inner states, her beliefs, her expectations, and her previous knowledge of the world—help interpret the data. The mainstream discourse on science presumes that facts and values are separate. Feyerabend (1993, p. 51), however, using countless examples from the history of science, states that this is a myth:

> The material which a scientist *actually* has at his disposal, his laws, his experimental results, his mathematical techniques, his epistemological prejudices, his attitude towards the absurd consequences of the theories which he accepts, is indeterminate in many ways, ambiguous, *and never fully separate from the historical background*. It is contaminated by principles which he does not know, and which, if known, would be extremely hard to test. Questionable views on cognition, such as the view that our senses, used in normal circumstances, give reliable information about the world, may invade the observation language itself, constituting the observation terms as well as the distinction between veridical and illusory appearance. As a result, observation languages

> may become tied to older layers of speculation which affect, in a roundabout fashion, even the most progressive methodology. (Italics in original)

The problem of objectivity is further compounded by the fact that 'we speak more about our observation of the world rather than of the world, and we do this through a less than fully adequate language system. The linguistic limitation, by itself causes problems even if we could overcome other limitations' (Baker, 1991, p. 12). This happens because language not only describes events but also creates a cosmology, a worldview that influences the thought, behaviour and perception of the user. When a child begins to learn a language, the worldview of her ancestors is passed onto her. The human mind begins to take many facts of life as givens, and the entire process may be totally unconscious. Her worldview begins to create what she may observe. Also, in order to be unprejudiced, one will have to abandon language itself, which will remove all ability to think, as a consequence of which the practice of science will stop before it begins. Writes Edward Sapir:

> Human beings do not live in the objective world alone, nor alone in the world of social activity as ordinarily understood, but are very much at the mercy of the particular language that has become the medium of expression of that society. It is quite an illusion to imagine that one adjusts to reality essentially without the use of language and that language is merely an incidental means of solving specific problems of communication or reflection. The fact of the matter is that the "real world" is to a large extent unconsciously built up on the language habits of the group.... We see and hear and otherwise experience very largely as we do because the language habits of our community predispose certain choices of interpretation. (Cited in Whorf, 1962, p. 134)

In the study of high-energy particles, it has been found that particles cannot be understood as isolated entities but only in the context of their preparation and measurement. This means that the Aristotelian or the Newtonian idea of fundamental basic building blocks does not hold water anymore. Further, the classical distinction between subject and object—which was a natural outcome of the philosophy of naive Realism—has become vague as the observer has been found to be an integral part of the experiment. How an experimenter has set up an experiment and the measurement that she has decided to undertake determine the result of an experiment to a large extent. The observer is an inseparable part of the observation being made, or in other words, reality is not independent of the observer. Capra (1992, p. 78) observes:

> The human observer constitutes the final link in the chain of observational process, and the properties of any atomic object can only be understood in terms of object's interaction with the observer. This means that the classical ideal of objective description of nature is no longer valid.

With the advent of the Relativity theory of Einstein, space and time, which appear to us as absolutes in our everyday experience, have been rendered relative with respect to the observer. The claim of the realists that objects like tables, chairs, bags, stones, and statues have absolute existence also does not hold true in the light of the theory of relativity, for it has been shown that the length of an object—consequently its shape too—is dependent on its motion with respect to the observer. The length of a rod shortens as its motion increases with respect to the observer. Modern physics has also exploded the myth of an absolute linearity of time. Time in the theory of relativity has a meaning only with respect to a frame of reference, for as the velocity relative to the observer increases, time intervals increase. In other words, time for two individuals moving at different velocities presents a different meaning.

To sum up, the preceding arguments indicate that for an individual to be without a bias or a value, she has to come from nowhere. Values and biases are implicit to the human condition and dichotomies like subject-object, and fact-value are a myth.

Sociology of knowledge: Objectivity demystified

Apart from values, inner expectations, knowledge, social position and observer's bias, science embraces other dynamics as well, which can constrain an objective approach to reality. The spirit of science is to question, but science can easily lose its tenor by falling prey to scientism, a kind of dogmatism comparable to the fundamentalist aspect of any organized religion. Imbued with the spirit of questioning, Kuhn (1970) questioned the notion of science itself. His work is significant in that he has made it abundantly clear that science, like any other human activity, is a social activity which affects and is affected by the milieu in which it is embedded, and is guided by the sociological, economic, historical and political forces. According to him, science is practised by the communities of scientists and not by isolated men and women. To understand the workings of science, it is therefore imperative to understand the scientific community, its accepted and shared norms and beliefs. The complex nature of sociological factors that operate when any research is conducted can be appreciated with the help of Figure 3.1.

Figure 3.1. The sociological matrix of scientific research (Adapted from Danziger, 1990)

The innermost circle represents the immediate social condition in which research is conducted. The next circle represents the research community that has to accept the data as scientific knowledge. The outermost circle denotes the wider social context that embraces the research community. The investigators, the research community and the society are interconnected in a complex web of affairs, which has many dimensions.

If we analyse the dynamics of the inner circle—the immediate research conducted for generation of psychological knowledge—we find that the objectivity of psychological knowledge and the rationale of the Newtonian framework for psychology are seriously challenged. The experiments that are conducted are done by human beings on human beings, in sharp contrast to physical sciences where experiments are conducted on inanimate objects. With the recognition of 'experimenter expectancy effects' and 'demand characteristics', it can be inferred that the experimental results are co-determined by the social relationship between the experimenter and the subjects (Danziger, 1990).

As far as the research community is concerned, Kuhn (1970) points out that scientific practice is shaped by deep assumptions of the worldview of which the scientist may be unaware. For research to take place, the community must agree upon the goals, the methodologies and the valid subject matter in the context of research. The agreement on all these issues would constitute a framework or a paradigm. The paradigm has two components—*disciplinary matrix* and *shared exemplars*. The *disciplinary matrix* consists of a certain fundamental set of assumptions that are often unstated and not subject to empirical test. These assumptions form the basis for testing specific hypotheses. For example, reductionism states that the world can be understood by breaking it into smaller units until we arrive at a set of fundamental units. This is an assumption that is not subjected to any kind of an empirical test, and thus constitutes a portion of the *disciplinary matrix* of scientists who adhere to this belief. The other component of a paradigm is *shared exemplars*—the models for investigating new problems which include the methodology for pursuing the research. Kuhn (1970, p. 109) explains:

> [Paradigm] functions by telling the

> scientist about the entities that nature does or does not contain and about the ways in which those entities behave. That information provides a map whose details are elucidated by mature scientific research. And since nature is too complex and varied to be explored at random, that map is as essential as observation and experiment to science's continuing development. Through the theories they embody, paradigms prove to be constitutive of research activity.... In learning a paradigm the scientist acquires theory, methods, and standards together, usually in an inextricable mixture.

The *disciplinary matrix* and *shared exemplars*, by constituting the paradigm, unconsciously trains a researcher to approach a problem in a specific way which gradually becomes her natural way. In this vein, Leahey (1991, p. 14) writes:

> Neither source of data is comprehensible without training, yet once the scientist learns to interpret them, he or she will see them in those ways and no others. Thus training can act as a set of blinders, keeping the scientist from seeing in new ways. All observation and perception—whether scientific or not—is a matter of interpretation as numerous psychological examples have shown.

Thus, the generation and interpretation of data is contingent upon the paradigm in which the research is being conducted. Essentially data are neutral; they become facts when they are interpreted against a theory comprising a priori categories. For example, the measurements made with the Atwood machine would have meant nothing in the absence of Newton's *Principia*. The meaning and interpretation of data change with a change in paradigm. For instance, with a change in electrical paradigm, what was a Leyden jar became a condenser. Kuhn has also shown that science is not as rational and objective as it is supposed. Indeed, scientific rationality is a matter of consensus. It involves unexamined biases and social interests like fame, fortune, love, loyalty and power of the investigator. More often than not, scientists following the same norms of disinterestedness, objectivity and rationality arrive at different conclusions. The history of science reveals that many competing theories exist before one paradigm becomes dominant even if all of them had arisen from experimentation and 'disinterested' observation.

Lyotard (1984) states that this is essentially a problem of legitimization. The question of good research and bad research is contingent upon the community of scholars deciding whether it is in harmony with the criteria of truth, of justice, of beauty—though these criteria are held to be universal to all humanity, they are specific to the larger culture or country to which the community belongs. Since research is a social activity, it is not free from politics. Feyerabend (1993, p. 163) puts this most beautifully:

> Scientists are not content with running their own playpens in accordance with what they regard as the rules of the scientific method, they want to universalize their rules, they want them to become part of society at large and they use every means at their disposal—argument, propaganda, pressure tactics, intimidation, lobbying—to achieve their aims.

The history of science also demonstrates that scientific knowledge is temporally relative. What was considered once as science has been later rejected as superstition. By the same token, what constitutes scientific knowledge today, which has been extracted from nature by subjecting it to repeated investigation, may turn out to be error tomorrow under the influence of a different paradigm.[1]

A committed believer in science would say that this phenomenon has taken place because science is cumulative, and scientists have refined their theories in an effort to come closer to a truer and more accurate interpretation and description of nature. Kuhn disagrees and contends that instead of science being cumulative, it is revolutionary. A change in the paradigm changes the worldview of the scientist. Kuhn holds that it is difficult to demonstrate the superiority of one paradigm over another purely on 'logical' argument. The primary reason is that the proponents of the rival paradigms subscribe to a different set of standards and metaphysical assumptions. The rival paradigms are so incommensurable that no appeal to 'rationality' can settle the issue.

To complete this discussion let us quickly comment on the outermost circle depicted in Figure 3.1. The pursuit of knowledge is also intimately connected with the society in which it develops. It is being increasingly realized that each society has its own vision of reality that shapes the perception and thoughts of its inhabitants. This helps them to negotiate their life with different images, symbols, metaphors and institutions in a unique way that may be incommensurable with that of another society—all of these determine the subject matter of psychology or any discipline for that matter. Sociology of knowledge aptly discusses the social and historical forces that play a major role in the development of a subject. The antitheistic ideas of scientific psychology are a case in point. Science, in order to establish its identity in post-medieval Europe, had to struggle against the Church which had usurped all powers to arbitrate every activity of humankind. It had restricted the freedom of inquiry and held courts of Inquisition to prosecute men like Galileo and Descartes and all those who differed from the scriptures. Moreover, it had waged holy wars in the name of religion and caused much bloodshed. Against this backdrop, science dissociated itself from anything that had to do with God or with supernatural forms of existence, resulting in a bias and dichotomous divide between religion and science which has not been plugged till date in the mainstream scientific circles (see Danziger 1990; Leahey 1991, for details).

Relativism and the paradox of self-referentiality

The line of argument discussed in the previous section very clearly explains why we have as many theories as we have psychologies. Psychologists are human beings as well, and they are very much grounded or caged in their own perspectives which determine the way they approach the problem of solving the enigmas of human behaviour. Psychologists see different facts because they ascribe different meta-structures of biases, theories, paradigms, cosmological worldviews, beliefs, culture, expectations, etc. to the raw data in order to interpret them. In other words, their individual humanness makes them see psychological issues differently. The aforementioned arguments also indicate that psychology and all forms of knowledge—there is an intimate connection between psychology and knowledge—are relative with respect to individuals, time, culture and paradigms. But incidentally, this is a statement suggesting an absolute truth. *Paradoxically the conclusion, 'Truth is relative', harbours in it an absolute truth.* Similarly, experimental psychology has devised experiments (for example, Joseph Jastrow's famous duck–rabbit experiment), the results of which show that the perception of reality is necessarily subjective. But while stating this, it also makes a statement which embodies an objective validity. So a fact discovered by psychology becomes subjective and objective at the same time leading to a paradoxical and a peculiar situation. In other words, the pursuit of knowledge or Truth—which is the basis of any scientific investigation—becomes absolute and relative simultaneously.

A meta-analysis of Kuhn's arguments culminates in a situation that is not different. One of the chief themes of his theses is that paradigms guide research in terms of observation and interpretation of data. If his premise is true—he has, of course supported it with a lot of evidence—then, by extension, it can be said that he has culled out data from the body of the history of science to support his theory that paradigms guide research. In other words, the data was collected with the theory—paradigm guides research—already in his mind. As soon as we recognize this, Kuhn's arguments turn on themselves, thus assuming circularity. *A paradoxical situation emerges again: Kuhn's arguments are true and false at the same time.* True because there is evidence to support his claim, and false because he contradicts himself by inviting his arguments on himself. Alternatively, his arguments have been designated as self-referential by his critics, and have been termed as self-refuting.

Secondly, Kuhn has cited evidence to show that facts and data have no meaning in themselves; they acquire meaning when interpreted against a theory or framework. There is an implicit circularity and paradox here too. By force of Kuhn's arguments, it can be argued that the evidence that he has used to demonstrate the truth of his arguments is meaningful only against his contention that evidence has no meaning in the absence of a framework. Evidence lend support to his theory whereas a similar kind of contradiction as described above, and the fact of being oblivious to his own subjectivity, while attributing the crucial role of the scientist's subjectivity in guiding research, renders Kuhn's theory problematic. If the evidences of the other scientists are not sacrosanct, it can as well be said that Kuhn's are not either.

In view of relativism, self-referentiality, circularities and paradoxes, does this mean that the pursuit of knowledge and psychology approaches a dead end? For the mainstream approach of finding the truths of human behaviour or psychology based in the classical distinction of subject and object, fact and value, and relative and absolute has come to a *cul-de-sac*. Does this mean that the impasse cannot be resolved? The answer is a resounding no if we begin to analyse the Indian spiritual traditions. Let us examine how these traditions offer an alternative paradigm to psychology research that goes beyond mind.

Beyond mind: Towards a new paradigm for psychology

The simultaneous existence of right and wrong, true and false, and relative and absolute that produces a paradox poses no problem for the Mādhyamika philosophers. In this section, we will examine how these paradoxes can be resolved, paving the way for intuitive knowing or for the study of psychology with consciousness as its subject matter.

Nāgārjuna, a second century Mādhyamika philosopher, stated that concepts, events and entities do not exist in isolation but exist in relation to one another. He further contends that concepts, events and entities called *svabhāva,* actually lack any intrinsic existence, and that any attempt to reduce them to having an independent status will lead to absurdity. According to Nāgārjuna, nothing exists in-itself and of-itself, and no concept has any meaning independent of a relation. This is the principle of *pratītya samutpāda* or dependent origination, and the main philosophy under which this is discussed is called *śūnyavāda* or *śūnyatā* or the doctrine of emptiness. Black and white, good and evil, valleys and mountains, friends and enemies are co-implicates. All contradictions and oppositions, seen from a slightly different perspective reveal that they are one and essentially whole. The opposites are not against each other but complement each other. Darkness is born out of light and day is born out of night. Nāgārjuna writes:

> How, indeed, will disappearance exist at all without origination? [How could there be] death without birth? There is no disappearance without [prior] origination.
>
> It does not obtain that origination and disappearance are the same thing. It does not obtain that origination and disappearance are different (McCagney, 1997, p. 59, insertions in original).

McCagney (1997, p. 60) citing from Nāgārjuna's work *Śūnyatāsaptatikārikā,* writes:

> Without one [*eka*] there are not many [*aneka*]. Without many [*aneka*] one [*eka*] is not possible.
>
> The father is not the son, the son is not the father. Neither exists without being correlative. (Insertions in original)

Employing the principle of *pratītya samutpāda* or dependent origination and his dialectical skills, he refutes the contention of the realists that a thing exists in-itself or of-itself. The subject does not exist independent of the object; neither does the cause exist without the effect. These dichotomous pairs—like all that we use in everyday life—have no meaning beyond their relationship with each other.

Thus, the rigid dichotomy between the subject and the object crumbles down, for the Mādhyamika critique shows that the act of knowing is a product of the interaction between the observer/knower and the observed/known. Any dichotomized way of thinking results in *avidyā,* loosely translated as ignorance, which motivates the mind to grasp thoughts as things to be grasped by the individual ego. The solution to the enigma of our existence or the knowledge of the ultimate is gained by the transcendence of all the reified and rigid thoughts through a way of 'seeing' and 'being' called *prajñā*. The search for knowledge is grounded in our language, presuppositions and all those concepts and entities that we hold on to as givens in our everyday life. We attach transcendental and eternal value to them, which Mādhyamika deconstructs by placing them in a sociolinguistic and historical context, thus paving the way for a spiritual seeker to transcend the rationalistic tendency to make sense of the truth through any epistemological or ontological suppositions. Huntington (1989, p. 121) explains this most beautifully:

> According to the Mādhyamika, a ... convoluted and subtle relationship holds between any two dichotomies of conceptual thought, whether expressed in ontological, epistemological, ethical or any other terms: Cause/effect, subject/object, substrate/predicate, absolute/relative, truth/error, good/evil, and all other dualistic concepts find their meaning in the context of their elusive relationship with each other and with an interrelated network of other such concepts. The structure that they give to all experience—a structure that seems "to emerge from the things themselves"—is also dependent on an illusion similar to the Necker cube where each image finds its meaning and existence only in the context of its relationship to partners that must always remain out of sight.

The crucial difference is that whereas illusion in Necker cube is simple, the regular life situations are much more complex. Huntington (1989, p. 121) continues:

> The critical difference is only that the context of everyday life in which these other relationships are embedded is infinitely more complex, for it embodies an indeterminate number of historical and circumstantial factors shared by the sociolinguistic community in which this vocabulary is used and thought and perception take place.

Similarly, Advaita Vedānta posits that this world consists of dualities, and that the Ultimate Reality, which is the source of all that exists, is beyond all these dualities. True knowledge can only be gained when one transcends the dual world. Swami Satprakashananda (1977, pp. 96–97) writes:

> It is maya that brings about the relativity of subject and object, the knower and the known. The two are dissimilar, yet inseparable. One does not exist without the other. The universe is a conglomeration of pairs of opposites, such as life and death, light and darkness, joy and sorrow, knowledge and ignorance, plenty and want, beauty and ugliness, kindness and misery, love and hatred, good and evil, in which the antitheses are correlated; yet either factor appears to be an independent element and in vain we try our utmost to have one of the pair to the exclusion of the other. This is the effect of the maya. There is no elevation without depression, no construction without destruction, no addition without subtraction. In each case they the contraries form a single process. They are inseparable; yet they appear disparate. This is the effect of maya.

Having addressed how the subject–object dichotomy can be transcended, let us examine the cause of underlying relativism, though generally not acknowledged in the discipline of Western psychology. This is because, as supported by many mystical traditions, mind—with reason, logic and intellect as its instruments—cannot arrive at the truths of our existence. Intellectual activity, discursive thinking and logical analysis alone are not capable of solving the final enigmas of our existence—it cannot unravel all the mysteries. According to Sri Aurobindo—one of the greatest mystics of the last century—mind and its instruments cannot perceive the reality as a whole as its very nature is to classify, divide, compare and measure. It creates dualities such as absolute/relative and subject/object. It tries to understand things through categories, concepts and formulas. This is perhaps why in the intellectual history of mankind there have been scores of such formulas and theories but nothing definitive can be said about the fundamentals of our existence despite that most psychological theories have almost equal intellectual appeal, and have evidence to support their claim even if they contradict one another. What we have today are thousand and one schools of psychology each claiming an exclusive monopoly on the truth of human behaviour. Sri Aurobindo (1997, pp. 162–163), who has written extensively on the limitation of the mind on numerous occasions throughout his writings, puts it most succinctly:

> Mind in its essence is a consciousness which measures, limits, cuts out forms of things from the indivisible whole and contains them as if each were a separate integer. Even with what exists only as obvious parts and fractions, Mind establishes this fiction of its ordinary commerce that they are things with which it can deal separately and not merely as aspects of a whole. For, even when it knows that they are not things in themselves, it is obliged to deal with them as if they were things in themselves; otherwise it could not subject them to its own characteristic activity. It is this essential characteristic of Mind which conditions the workings of all its operative powers, whether conception, perception, sensation or the dealings of creative thought. It conceives, perceives, senses things as if rigidly cut out from a background or a mass and employs them as fixed units of the material given to it for creation or possession. All its action and enjoyment deal thus with wholes that form part of a greater whole, and these subordinate wholes again are broken up into parts which are also treated as wholes for the particular purposes they serve. Mind may divide, multiply, add, subtract, but it cannot get beyond the limits of this mathematics. If it goes beyond and tries to conceive a real whole, it loses itself in a foreign element; it falls from its own firm ground into the ocean of the intangible, into the abysms of the infinite where it can neither perceive, conceive, sense nor deal with its subject for creation and enjoyment.

Western psychology—due to the spirit of the times—has mainly been inspired by an intellectual and cognitive activity with a heavy reliance on the logical and discursive mind to find out the truths of human behaviour, for the West has considered intellect with its purified reason to be the ultimate instrument for exploring the nature of human existence. Consequently, it embraced a methodology that operated in strict dualities and dichotomies like subject/object, absolute/relative, and universal/local. But the reason of individuals varies according to their belief, upbringing, culture, attitude, language and perspective. Also the reason that has money and power to back its claim becomes the right reason. Recognizing the relativity of reason, which also explains the presence of relativism in psychology with respect to theories, Sri Aurobindo (1995, pp. 164-165) states:

> You believe according to your faith, which is quite natural, he believes according to his opinion, which is natural also, but no better so far as the likelihood of getting at the true truth of things is in question. His opinion is according to his reason.... How is reasoning to show which is right? The opposite parties can argue till they are blue in the face—they won't be anywhere nearer a decision.... But who can look at the world as it is and say that the trend of things is always (or ever) according to the right reason—whatever this thing called right reason may be? As a matter of fact there is no universal infallible reason which can decide and be the umpire between conflicting opinions; there is only my reason, your reason, X's reason, Y's reason multiplied up to the discordant innumerable. Each reasons according to his view of things, his opinion, that is his mental constitution and mental preference.

Similarly, according to Advaita Vedānta, mind is not the knower of things but an object of knowledge. Just as physical objects—such as a chair, for instance—can be observed, mind also can be observed, which makes it an object of knowledge rather than a knower. Hence the knowledge of our existence cannot be grasped by the mind—it is something else that is the knower. That according to Vedānta is the Self, which is the self-intelligent, self-aware, self-evident, self-illuminating consciousness.

It is only by consciously identifying oneself with the consciousness beyond the mind that one finds the truths of one's existence. That Self is the self of all selves, and by knowing that one not only gains the knowledge of one's own self but also the knowledge of the selves of all others. According to Advaita Vedānta and Sri Aurobindo, all the things that we call our real self like mind and body are not the self at all—these are external aspects of personality put forth by the Nature for the play of life. The real Self is within and above all that we usually identify as our self. The identification with the real Self reveals to us the knowledge of all the mysteries that the universe has concealed from us, which includes the truth that lies behind the psychology of every human being. Sri Aurobindo (1996, pp. 374–375) comments:

> Since the Self which we come to realise by the path of knowledge is not only the reality which lies behind and supports the states and movements of our psychological being, but also that transcendent and universal Existence which has manifested itself in all the movements of the universal, the knowledge of the Self includes also the knowledge of the principles of Being, its fundamental modes and its relations with the principles of the phenomenal universe. This was what was meant by the Upanishad when it spoke of the Brahman as that which being known all is known. It has to be realised first as the pure principle of Existence, afterwards, says the Upanishad, its essential modes become clear to the soul which realises it. We may indeed, before realisation, try to analyse by the metaphysical reason and even understand intellectually what Being is and what the world is, but such metaphysical understanding is not the Knowledge. Moreover, we may have the realisation in knowledge and vision, but this is incomplete without realisation in the entire soul-experience and the unity of all our being with that which we realise. It is the science of Yoga to know and the art of Yoga to be unified with the Highest so that we may live in the Self and act from that supreme poise, becoming one not only in the conscious essence but in the conscious law of our being with the transcendent Divine whom all things and creatures, whether ignorantly or with partial knowledge and experience, seek to express through the lower law of their members.

Consequently, psychology needs to be a science of consciousness as opposed to a science of mind and behaviour. This new paradigm of psychology can be made possible by transcending our mind, and by implication its various created dualities, by attaining *prajñā* or by realization of the Self.[2] This paradigm of psychology warrants the transcendence of mind, logic, intellect and reason by using our mind to the hilt to see how logic, reason and intellect are inferior instruments in the pursuit of the truths of our existence. The mystics claim that the deeper truths of our existence unravel themselves on a silent mind, compared metaphorically to an ocean that is absolutely calm. In other words, stillness of the mind is the necessary condition for accessing knowledge that lies beyond the domain of intellect. It is this region that holds the key to the secrets of mind and consciousness. A complete silence of the mind and a change of ordinary human consciousness hold the promise of accessing knowledge of the fields not available to the physical eye.

A change of ordinary human consciousness becomes a necessary condition for undertaking such a pursuit of psychology. It is not by looking outside of us that we can find answers to the enigmas that shroud us, but by looking within. In this research the researcher and the researched become one; the subject becomes the object and vice versa, leading to the transcendence of the strict dichotomy of subject–object that psychology has practised so far. *Yoga*, which actually means a union with the Divine or with the essential ground of all beings—whichever way one may want to see it according to one's preference—is the key through which a change of human consciousness—and hence a transcendence of mind—is possible. The Indian mystics have practised this art for centuries together, and have left behind a rich source of literature for all kinds of aspirants who want to take this path. Many of them have always stated that there is no one right way to take; that is the reason why there is a plethora of paths leading to the oneness that underlies this universe, based on the different constitutions and psychological make-up that humans have. However, when I talk about the distinctiveness of India in this field, I do not mean to suggest that such experiments have not been conducted anywhere else in the world—what I definitely mean is that they have been fewer in other parts of the world limiting the many possibilities of approaching the consciousness that humans have in their repertoire.

From the spiritual literature, and the written accounts of mystics it is found that there are layers and layers of consciousness, and forces that are invisible to the ordinary human eyes that are constantly impinging on human beings that determine their behaviour. These forces and levels of consciousness can only be discovered if we undertake an enquiry which involves a direct and intuitive experience with the nature of things. Sri Aurobindo (1994, pp. 333–334) states:

> It is not enough to observe and know the movements of our surface nature and the superficial nature of other living creatures just as it [is] not enough for Science to observe and know as electricity only the movements of lightning in the clouds or for the astronomer to observe and know only those movements and properties of the stars that are visible to the unaided eye. Here as there a whole world of occult phenomena have to be laid bare and brought under control before the psychologist can hope to be master of his province.
>
> Our observable consciousness, that which we call ourselves, is only the little visible part of our being. It is a small field below which are depths and farther depths and widths and ever wider widths which support and supply it but to which it has no visible access. All that is our self, our being,—what we see at the top is only our ego and its visible nature.
>
> Even the movements of this little surface nature cannot be understood nor its true law discovered until we know all that is below or behind and supplies it—and know too all that is around it and above. (Insertion in original)

Conclusion

To sum up, psychology needs to base itself on the foundation of a sure knowledge—on having a first hand knowledge of the hidden layers and layers of consciousness, which means mastering the subtle realms of human existence that are not visible to the ordinary human eye. It needs to go into the trans-mental and trans-intellectual realm through purification of mind and body, by transcending logical and intellectual thought, by stilling the mind within all internal and external chaos and flux so that the knowledge of the subtle and the invisible becomes known. Within the Indian tradition, it means seeing things with the 'third eye'. The future psychology as a science or the psychology that I envision, primarily based on the insights of Sri Aurobindo, is one in which such knowledge of 'psychology by identity' becomes a legitimate field of enquiry in academia, and is taken up by large numbers of people. For centuries together in India, the exploration of the deeper truths of our existence has taken place by the mystics—*Ṛṣis*, *Munis* and *Sufis*. Under the destruction brought about by colonization and the dominance of Western heuristics in academia since then, a legitimate field of enquiry into the nature of human existence was systematically decimated and discredited. In modern times the pursuit of knowledge has come a full circle, and the time has come to pursue the ancient science once again, and in its light evaluate the findings of Western psychology. Within the Indian context, the time has come for us to bestow legitimacy to the age-old tradition of ours, and inspire the younger generation of psychologists to become mystics who can determine the psychological laws and the psychology of individuals based on knowledge by identity, and we need to make a quantum jump by exploring the mystical and the invisible realm of Nature who carries in herself all the secrets that govern human behaviour.

Endnotes

1 In a post-script to the *Structure of Scientific Revolutions* in its second edition, Kuhn distanced himself from the relativistic claims. But experts are of the opinion that his claims are relativistic given the way he has advocated the process of change and switch in paradigms, sometimes comparing them to religious and political conversions where not much of reason and logic are involved (for details see Chalmers, 1999, pp. 122-123).

2 I do not suggest that the realizations of Self and *prajñā* result in the same spiritual state. If that were the case, the Vedāntins and Buddhists would not have had such vigorous debates as they did in the past. I am of the view that they result in different spiritual states; however, there is a commonality to both in that they for their respective realizations require the transcendence of logical and discursive faculty.

References

Aurobindo, Sri (1994). *Essays divine and human with thoughts and aphorisms*. Pondicherry: Sri Aurobindo Ashram.

Aurobindo, Sri (1995). *Letters on yoga* (3rd ed., Vols. 1–3). Pondicherry: Sri Aurobindo Ashram. (Original work published 1958).

Aurobindo, Sri (1994). *The synthesis of yoga*. Pondicherry: Sri Aurobindo Ashram. (Original work published 1955).

Aurobindo, Sri (1997). *The life divine* (5th ed.). Pondicherry: Sri Aurobindo Ashram. (Original work published 1940).

Baker, W. J. (1991). Positivism versus people: What should psychology be about? In C. W. Tolman (Ed.), *Positivism in psychology: Historical and contemporary problems* (pp. 9–16). London: Springer Verlag.

Capra, F. (1992). *The tao of physics: An exploration of parallels between modern physics and eastern mysticism* (3rd ed.). London: Flamingo.

Chalmers, A. F. (1999). *What is this thing called science? An assessment of the nature and status of science and its method* (3rd ed.). Queensland, Australia: University of Queensland Press.

Ciccarelli, S. K., & Meyer, G. E. (2006). *Psychology*. Upper Saddle River, NJ: Prentice Hall.

Danziger, K. (1990). *Constructing the subject: Historical origins of psychological research*. Cambridge, United Kingdom: Cambridge University Press.

Feyerabend, P. (1993). *Against method* (3rd ed.). New York: Verso.

Henley, T. B., Johnson, M. G., & Jones, E. M. (1989). Definition of psychology. *The Psychological Record, 39,* 143–152.

Huntington, C. W. (1989). *The emptiness of emptiness: An introduction to early Indian Mādhyamika*. Honolulu, HI: University of Hawaii Press.

Kuhn, T. S. (1970). *The structure of scientific revolutions* (2nd ed.). Chicago: University of Chicago Press.

Leahey, T. H. (1991). *A history of modern psychology. Main currents in psychological thought*. Upper Saddle River, NJ: Prentice Hall.

Lyotard, J. F. (1984). *The postmodern condition: A report on knowledge* (G. Bennington & B. Massumi, Trans.). Minneapolis: University of Minnesota Press. (Original work published 1979).

McCagney, N. (1997). *Nāgārjuna and the philosophy of openness*. Boulder, CO: Rowman & Littlefield Publishers.

Popper, K. R. (1992). *The logic of scientific discovery*. New York: Routledge. (Original work published 1959).

Satprakashananda, S. (1977). *The universe, God, and God-realization: From the viewpoint of Vedanta*. St. Louis, MO: Vedanta Society of St. Louis.

Whorf, B. L. (1962). *Language, thought and reality: Selected writings of Benjamin Lee Whorf.* Cambridge, MA: MIT Press.

4

Indian psychology and the scientific method

Peter Sedlmeier

Introduction

Can Western academic psychology and Indian psychology come together? Although there are some sceptical voices, most of the Indian authors who have written about the topic indicate possibilities to build up connections between the two approaches (for example, Auluck, 2002; Mathew, 2004; Paranjpe, 2004; Krishna Rao, 1997). On the Western side, postulates to consider Indian psychological approaches came mainly from practitioners working with some school of depth psychology (for example, Cortright, 2004; Coster, 1998) or scholars trying to connect Western therapeutic approaches with Indian meditative disciplines (Hayes, Barnes-Holmes, & Roche, 2001; Wallace & Shapiro, 2006). To date, Western academic psychologists outside (and inside) the clinical area seem to be largely unaware of the richness of the Indian approach, whereas proponents of Indian psychology (who are not always psychologists by training) frequently seem to lack knowledge about the vast array of research topics and the fruitful findings in Western academic psychology that have been accumulated in the last some 130 years since Wilhelm Wundt established the first psychology laboratory in Leipzig in 1879.

Apart from mutual ignorance, there might indeed be serious problems in the attempt to bridge the gap between the two approaches. However, I think that, because of the immense potential benefits for psychology as a whole, one should give the endeavour a serious try before being content with two isolated approaches. In my view, one of the conditions for Indian psychology to be acknowledged in the West is that relevant research adheres to the methodological standards postulated in Western academia as expressed in the *scientific method*. In this chapter, I will, for the sake of the argument, first outline what these standards are and why I think that they are important. Then I will introduce my conception of what genuine Indian psychology is all about, including a 'metatheory' of Indian psychology. From this metatheory (and to a certain extent also from theories that are included in the metatheory) I will try to derive several classes of testable hypotheses and exemplify these with the help of some specific hypotheses or questions, some of which are already under scrutiny since long. After that, I will come back to the topic of methods with an emphasis on the special methods needed to examine some of the hypotheses that deal with different aspects of consciousness. The chapter ends with some ideas about possible 'interfaces' between Indian and Western academic psychology.

The scientific method, Western style

Although there might be some disagreement about the exact nature of specific steps—depending on particularities of the research questions—the procedure sketched out in Figure 4.1 is commonly taken to be the way science works. This pragmatic scientific method stems from the natural sciences and was adopted more or less unchanged by Western academic psychology (for example, Bunge & Ardila, 1990).

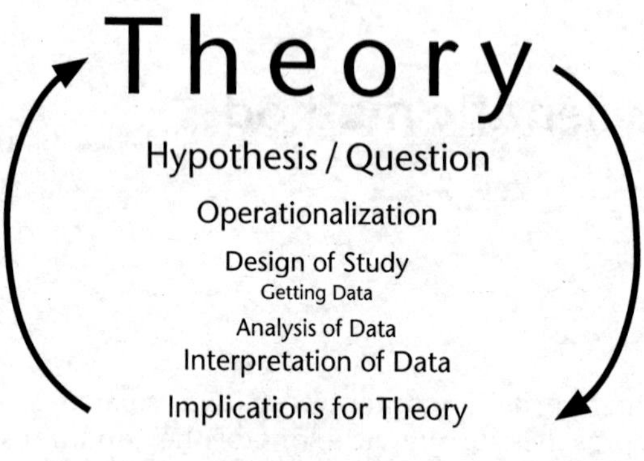

Figure 4.1. Scientific method, as commonly applied in academic psychology (adapted from Sedlmeier & Renkewitz, 2013)

Theories and hypotheses

The starting point of the scientific method is a *theory*. However, the scientific method does not cover the question of where theories come from. A well-known answer to that question is 'bed, bath, and bicycle', meaning that theories or good ideas can arise all of a sudden in states usually not connected to work. But also highly intuitive processes such as brainstorming, day-dreaming or mental imagination have been the basis for theories (Shepard, 1978). On a more systematic level, one can perform guided observations, look over theories and data which are already there or conduct pilot studies after having a first idea, often using qualitative methods. Finally, theories are often connected to metaphors such as the steam engine (Sigmund Freud's model of the id, ego and superego), the computer (many models in cognitive psychology) or the methods themselves (theories modelled after statistical procedures; see Gigerenzer, 1991). Basically there is no single systematic method to arrive at good theories because there is no deductive way to do that, and there is nothing to say against theories that have been 'revealed' to somebody as we will see is claimed to be true for the metatheory of Indian psychology.

It is desirable to start out with a full-fledged theory, that is, a, model that covers a substantial amount of human experience and behaviour (including all kinds of cognitions and emotions) in considerable depth, but basically there are no limitations about what can be a theory: In the extreme, for instance, if a new path of enquiry is undertaken, which is actually quite rare these days, it might be just a rich idea.

The theory is most important (and therefore also written in the biggest font in Figure 4.1), because it—in the ideal case—determines the rest of the procedure. Usually, theories cannot be tested per se due to their complexities. That is why one derives from the theory simpler testable research hypotheses or questions and examines these.

Making hypotheses precise and testable

Usually the hypotheses themselves have to be further elaborated—the operations or procedures to make them testable, that is, observable in some way, have to be specified. This step is often termed *operationalization* and should lead to objective measurement. However, psychologists have produced convincing evidence that true objectivity is hard to achieve, because all our perceptions are to a certain extent determined by what we know or expect (Goldstein, 1999). It is even worse when we 'make measurements' from memory (for example, Loftus, 1979). Even the wording of questions and the specific scales used can elicit systematic expectations or yield biases (Schwarz, 1999; Sedlmeier, 2006). Nonetheless, the amount of intersubjective agreement can be systematically varied: The more precise one can be in the process of operationalization both for measuring outcomes and for creating the conditions and procedures for the study, the higher this agreement will be. The conditions and procedures for a study are usually summarized by the term *design*.

The design of the study specifies, for instance, when and how observations are to be made, or whether single persons or groups of persons should be looked at. Moreover, the design should allow the researcher to achieve high levels of external and internal validity. High external validity means that the results found can be generalized well to other persons and situations. The best way to ensure that is to take a random sample of the population for which generalizations should be made because then every member of the population has the same chance to be in the sample. A high internal validity is necessary when one wants to draw justifiable causal conclusions. The *via regia* to achieve a high internal validity is to conduct a (true) experiment. In the simplest case of a psychological experiment, two groups are compared that differ in the so-called *independent variable* (for example, in the independent variable *training* with the values '*yoga*-training' and 'no *yoga*-training'). If one now finds that the training group does better in some *dependent variable* (for example, a measure of happiness), one needs to rule out other possible causes for the difference found, as, for instance, differences in intelligence, motivation, teachers, or a priori happiness. This is usually done by randomizing, that is dividing the participants in the experiment randomly between the training group and the control group. Randomizing ensures that all the possible moderator variables (alternative explanations, including those the experimenter has not thought of before) have comparable levels across groups. If randomizing is not possible, there is still a huge arsenal of techniques that allows one to control moderator variables at least to a certain extent.

When the design of a study is fixed (and sound), meaningful data can be collected. Note that there is no a priori restriction on which data are admissible to scientific scrutiny. There are, however, restrictions on what one can do with these data later on (for example, with which statistical procedures they can be analysed—see below). These data are then analysed and interpreted in the light of the theory. This interpretation in turn is used to make inferences about the theory.

The logic of testing hypotheses

There is still something missing in the above sketch of the scientific method. How, for instance, are hypotheses derived from theories? And how does one decide upon the value of the research outcome for the theory? Meanwhile, no serious scientist claims that theories can be proven or verified. This is made visible in Figure 4.1 by the loop structure of the process—theories are always 'provisional truths' that should be improved or abandoned according to empirical results. The most widely accepted principle that guides (or at least should guide, according to a common consensus among contemporary researchers) the selection of hypotheses and the interpretation or research outcomes is the *falsification principle*, which plays a central role in Popper's (1969) *critical rationalism*. Somewhat simplified, the falsification principle follows *modus tollens* (*H* for 'hypothesis', *O* for 'observation'):

$$\frac{\begin{array}{c} H \rightarrow O \\ \neg O \end{array}}{\neg H}$$

In plain words: if a theory H predicts that observation O will be made and if O is not observed, then one should conclude that H is wrong. There are, however, two problems with this simple version. First, recall that all variables involved have to be operationalized. To do this, one needs additional assumptions (for example, that an IQ-test really measures intelligence; or that some special attributes of the participants do not have an influence on the results). If we call these n additional assumptions $A_1, A_2, \ldots, A_n$, then modus tollens yields ('$\wedge$' stands for 'and' and '$\vee$' stands for 'or'):

$$\frac{\begin{array}{c} H \wedge A_1 \wedge A_2 \wedge \ldots \wedge A_n \rightarrow O \\ \neg O \end{array}}{\neg H \vee \neg A_1 \vee \neg A_2 \vee \ldots \vee \neg A_n}$$

That means that strict falsification of a hypothesis is only possible if one can be sure that all additional assumptions hold (otherwise, not having observed O could be due to any (or all) of the assumptions A_1 to A_n being wrong). One can, of course, almost never be sure about that in psychological research. The second problem is that data in psychology (and also in the natural sciences) are fallible, due to random error or due to the influence of overlooked variables. This means that in practice, one discrepant observation is not enough evidence to reject a theory. To take care of this problem, Popper (1969) introduced the notion of 'probabilistic falsification': a theory is practically falsifiable if strongly deviating evidence is found repeatedly. Building on the critical rationalism, Lakatos (1970) argues that theories are embedded in a broader research programme. Such programmes have a theoretical kernel and a 'protecting belt'. According to Lakatos, the theoretical kernel cannot be falsified whereas hypotheses derived from the protecting belt can. A given research programme should, according to Lakatos, only be abandoned if a) it stagnates, and b) there is a rival research programme, that can explain all the phenomena explained by the first programme and that in addition allows to derive additional hypotheses. Note that this does not exclude formerly abandoned research programmes to revive again if there have been new insights that overcome stagnation. Also, Lakatos suggests that new theories should be given special protection so as not to run the risk of prematurely abandoning a promising research programme after one negative result.

However, in the daily scientific practice, pragmatic constraints also play important roles (Kuhn, 1970). Doing science means to work in a scientific community—whether one likes the views of the other members or not. Usually, there is intensive communication among the members, most often high consensus about the main issues, and a common or at least very similar education for students and young scholars. The commonly accepted theoretical assumptions, empirical generalizations and applications regarded as successful, as well as the methodology, technology and the scientific language used lead to what Kuhn (1970) called a *paradigm*. A paradigm has a strong resistance to change. If there is evidence that contradicts a theory, the research community first tries to explain these *anomalies* within the paradigm. If more anomalies arise, usually different groups of researchers try to modify the paradigm. But finally, if no good solution is found, a 'revolution' takes place, yielding a new theory with higher precision that is more specialized and able to account for more facts. However, such a revolution—leading to a new paradigm—might sometimes only take place after the death of some influential researcher, and it does not necessarily incorporate all the earlier knowledge.

In sum, one could argue that science does not exactly work like it should according to eminent philosophers of science such as Popper and Lakatos. Is this a sufficient reason to reduce the impact of philosophy of science to Feyerabend's 'anything goes' (1975, p. 4)? I do not think so. We probably have to accept that science does not yield absolute truths and that the best one can do about a theory is to try to reach informed consent in a community of researchers that are most knowledgeable about the theory in question. This informed consent is, however, always open to modification depending on convincing empirically and logically based argument, or in other words: scientific theories are open to falsification.

Alternatives to the scientific method?

The provisional nature of scientific truth as well as the falsification principle may not look so attractive, but what are the alternatives? How can we arrive at knowledge? How do ordinary people arrive at their own 'theories' about how the world works? They say, for instance: 'I feel that this is right, it cannot be wrong' or they say that such and such (preferably an actor or noble-prize winner in chemistry who comes up with a psychological theory in a TV show) also holds this view. Another valued method to argue that something is true is to find half a dozen examples for a contention; and in general, looking for evidence is restricted to confirmatory search. It should be immediately clear, that neither a 'guts feeling', nor the opinion of 'authorities', nor examples provide good evidence. But why are these 'methods' used so commonly? One reason is that also wrong theories can by coincidence yield right predictions. Another reason is that our perception is usually quite selective and we tend to see what we want to see and overlook the rest. Moreover, explanations often come post hoc, that is, the theory comes after the data in some 'intuitive' way. But sometimes, theories also influence actions, which again yield respective reactions as, for instance, in the case of self-fulfilling prophecies (see Dawes, 1988, 2001, for ample evidence about all the above). For the advancement of knowledge, unsatisfying as it may be, there is, in my opinion, at present no alternative to using the scientific method.

Western scientific method and Indian orthodox systems

One might suspect that the Western scientific method is totally alien to the Indian orthodox systems, but Indian scholars might actually have applied it before the West did so. While the scientific method seems to have a lot in common with the methods of enquiry proposed in the Nyāya school, one of the six Indian orthodox systems of philosophy (see section on "What is Indian psychology?"), the falsification principle has evidently already been used by Advaitic philosophers in the sixteenth century (Paranjpe, 2004). However, this ancient tradition seems to have been taken up rarely in contemporary Indian psychology (Ramakrishna Rao, 2004, p. 58):

> The most serious of the lacunae shared by many writers on Indian psychology is the failure to build models and draw out the implications of Indian thought for generating new research programmes that could advance the science of psychology.

One possible starting point for building up new research programmes might be to see how far one comes with applying the scientific method as sketched out above. This is what I am trying to explore in this chapter.

Indian psychology

For Western psychologists, at least those in academia, it might come as a surprise that there is something such as a genuine 'Indian psychology'. Indeed, Indian psychology in the sense meant here is not just a little modification of Western academic psychology, but a quite different view.

What is Indian psychology?

By 'Indian psychology' I do not mean 'psychology done in India', nor 'psychology done by Indian people', although all three of these may coincide. A glance through Indian psychology journals (with the notable exception of the *Indian Journal of Psychology*) and scholarly books (for example, Ramalingam, 2002) indicates that the methods used in work which could be classified under the latter two headings are usually not much different from what psychologists in the West do. This is no wonder, because the curricula in the Indian universities are mostly taken from mainstream Western psychology (Bhatia, 2002; Huppes, 2002; Petzold, 1989; Ramakrishna Rao, 1988), with a slow change to observe in recent years (Misra & Mohanty, 2002). So what then is Indian psychology? Indian psychology is 'the psychology that has grown out of Indian thought and ethos' (Ramakrishna Rao, 1988, p. 38). This thought and ethos is concentrated in the *Vedic* literature that originated between 1500 BCE and 500 CE (Sharma, 2003; Hiriyanna, 2000), although the exact time estimates differ.[1]

The *Vedic* scriptures are generally regarded as revealed to seers, that is, having a supernatural origin. These scriptures consist of four collections. The term *veda* (knowledge) stands sometimes only for the first or the first two collections, the *mantras* and the *Brāhmaṇas*, but sometimes it is also used to refer to all four parts (for example, Sharma, 2003). The last part, the *Upaniṣads* or Vedānta (= end of the *Vedas*) is often regarded as being the most relevant for psychology, although some authors also give great importance to the *mantras*, and especially the oldest one, the *Ṛg Veda* (for example, Sri Aurobindo, 1995; Singh, 2004).

The discussions in the *Upaniṣads* centre around four questions dealing with 'pure consciousness' or the 'supreme principle': the explanation of its nature, the prevalence of general ignorance about it, the necessity of having its knowledge, and the methods to achieve it (Kulkarni, 1978, p. 27). One could say that the concept of pure consciousness, which leads to a view of the world quite different from that of Western psychology, is the central contribution of Indian psychology (see also Cornelissen, 2003; 2004). What is this pure consciousness? A 'super-normal clarity of inward vision or intuition untroubled by either discursive intellection or hedonistic affection' (Sinha, 1958, p. 359). Attaining pure consciousness means—according to most authors—to enter a state of totally different consciousness and of knowledge that, according to all sources, cannot be compared with the status quo of the large majority of mankind (those who have not attained it). However, pure consciousness cannot be recognized by the normal mind, which according to most accounts only mirrors it. To achieve pure consciousness, one has to practise specified methods,[2] which are also part of Indian psychology.

The original *Vedic* scriptures gave rise to several schools of thought which interpreted the contents of these scriptures sometimes quite differently. There are six 'orthodox' systems—orthodox in the sense, that they are based on different parts of the *Vedic* scriptures—that deal with different aspects. These six systems are usually seen as consisting of pairs: Sāṁkhya and Yoga, Nyāya and Vaiśeṣika, and Mīmāṁsā and Vedānta. These six systems have authors who not only acted as receivers of truth but put in their own ideas. The same holds for several 'heterodox systems' that developed in opposition to the then dominating Brahmanical tradition, whose rigid system of sacrificial ritual and social hierarchy was seen as oppressive and unsatisfactory (Hamilton, 2001). Examples of the heterodox systems are Jainism and the many forms of Buddhism. All these systems, orthodox and heterodox alike, deal with the question of how we can recognize our true Self and this true Self is nothing but pure consciousness; and all these systems—with the exception of Cārvāka, an early form of materialism in Indian thought—hold some common assumptions (for example, Hamilton, 2001; Raju, 1962; Shukla, 2004) which I term the *metatheory of Indian psychology*.

Indian psychology: A metatheory

The metatheory of Indian psychology, closely following the lines of thought advanced by Ramakrishna Rao (1997; 2004), is shown in Figures 4.2 and 4.3. It can be regarded as having three components—a description of the status quo of a 'normal person', a methodology to overcome the status quo, and a description of the result after having successfully applied that methodology.[3] So basically, the metatheory is a theory about change or, more exactly, transformation. According to the metatheory, ordinary persons are not aware of their true Self, which is nothing but pure consciousness. They live with a conception of self that arises from the interaction of mind, senses and external world (left part of Figure 4.2). In contrast to the prevalent Western view (for example, Farthing, 1992), consciousness in the Indian tradition is not identical to the mind or contained in it. Rather it is *reflected* in the mind—which is considered to be a very subtle form of matter—and enables it to make conscious contact with the internal and external world. This contact is, however, error

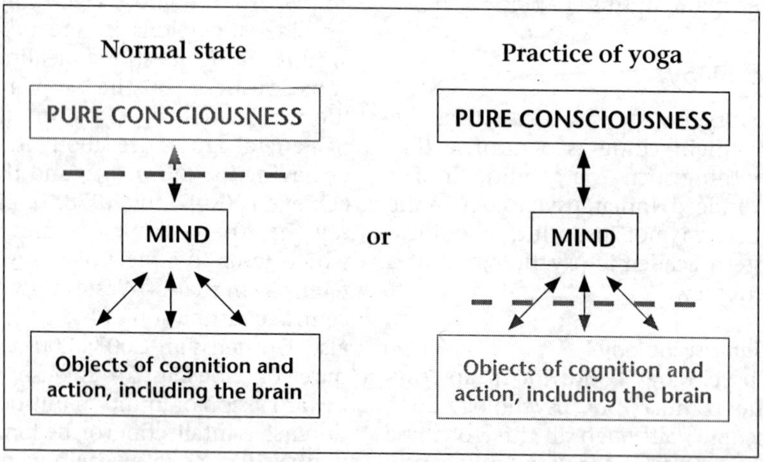

Figure 4.2. The first two stages of the metatheory

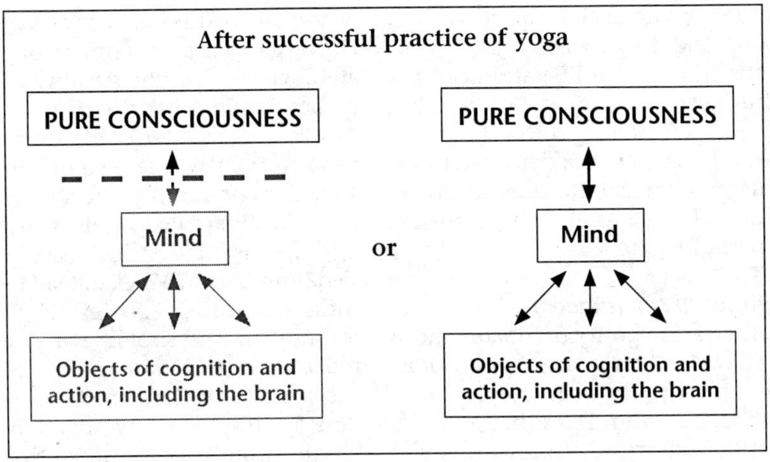

Figure 4.3. Third stage of the metatheory, two accounts

prone and does not allow a person to know the true reality. The way out of this containment and into liberation is to apply a practical method out of a collection of methods, subsumed under the name of *yoga* (Sri Aurobindo, 1996, p. 3):

> All methods grouped under the common name of Yoga are special psychological processes founded on a fixed truth of Nature and developing, out of normal functions, powers and results which were always latent but which her ordinary movements do not easily or do not often manifest.

The methods of *yoga* are very diverse (for example, Eliade, 1970; Sri Aurobindo, 1996; see also Part II in Joshi & Cornelissen, 2004), but the goal is the same: establishing the connection with pure consciousness and attaining liberation from a limited experience of the world. This conception of *yoga* can also be found in theories that originally stem from Indian approaches such as Zen and Tibetan Buddhism (Shukla, 2004; Chang, 1959). In contrast to the concept of consciousness as used in Western thought, which always is of or about something, pure consciousness has no qualities or characteristics of its own, but it underlies all our being and knowing.

The general method to attain pure consciousness is to free the mind from the senses and the objective world (right part of Figure 4.2). The experiences through the senses, which are also considered to consist of matter, although not as subtle as the mind, and—according to most accounts (for an exception, see AMA Samy, 2005, p. 22)—the influence of prior lives leads the mind to a wrong perception of the self and the ego. In many systems, liberation is achieved only at the expense of giving up normal life and choosing an ascetic life. Usually, this does not mean that the whole life should be ascetic. To the contrary, traditional systems found it helpful to first lead a normal life, before renouncing worldly affairs (for example, Raju, 1962). After liberation, however, the *yogī*, that is, the person who has successfully practiced *yoga* dwells in pure consciousness and gives up the contact to worldly affairs (see left part of Figure 4.3) because works will destroy his knowledge and bring him back to a life of bondage (see Jayashanmugam, 2002). This is, however, not true for Zen, where compassion with all other creatures in everyday life plays a central role in the life of enlightened persons as, for instance, expressed in the last of the famous 10 *ox-herding pictures* (for example, AMA Samy, 2005; Kapleau, 1989). Also, more recent *Vedāntin* philosophers and *yogīs* such as Swami Vivekananda and Rama Tirtha have questioned the renunciation of the social aspects of life (Srinivas, 2004); and Sri Aurobindo's Integral Yoga claims that the goal of liberation can be reached within everyday life (Sri Aurobindo, 1996; 2001; see also Maitra, 2001). In these systems the lower levels are not detached from the upper ones as soon as pure consciousness is acquired but become transformed themselves (right part of Figure 4.3).

Scientific status of the metatheory

According to the vast majority of Indian scholars, ancient (Cārvāka being an exception) as well as contemporary, the metatheory itself is not open to falsification. Does that exclude it from scientific inquiry? I do not think so. The metatheory might be given a similar status as the (Darwinian) theory of evolution, or its aspect more relevant here—evolutionary psychology (for example, Barkow, Cosmides, & Tooby, 1988). Evolutionary theory per se cannot currently be falsified and as in the metatheory of Indian psychology, there are different approaches that, for instance, differ in the unit to which selection processes apply—the individual, the group, or the single gene (for example, Dawkins, 1990). Although, according to the lines of thought advanced by Lakatos (1970), if a better theory will be found, evolutionary theory should eventually be replaced by that theory. The same might be expected for the metatheory of Indian psychology, if after considerable unsuccessful attempts to find evidence for the predictions derived from it, another theory came up with better explanations—although that seems to be practically impossible, because many of the passages in the *Vedic* scriptures are quite ambiguous.

Can the more specific theories, such as the six orthodox systems, variations thereof, and the heterodox systems be falsified? That should actually be possible, because they are usually much more specific than the *Vedic* scriptures and they—at least in part—make different statements and predictions about the same or similar issues.[4] One might expect divided opinions here, though. Whereas adherents of a given system might not allow the possibility of its falsification, adherents of other systems might. This, too, is quite reminiscent of the way mainstream science works (Kuhn, 1970). However, in the long run, wrong theories that are open to scientific scrutiny will either have to be changed or will be dismissed (or will simply be forgotten) because of the pressure towards the advancement of knowledge in the scientific community. But should the scientific method be applied at all to Indian psychology? Let us look at the answer of the famous Vedāntin Swami Vivekananada who, as many Indian scholars, equates religion with philosophy and psychology: 'In my opinion this must be so, and I am also of the opinion that the sooner it is done the better. If a religion is destroyed by such investigations, it was then all the time useless, unworthy superstition; and the sooner it goes the better.' (cited after Swami Jitatmananda, 2004, p. 171). In sum, although there might be opposition to this view, depending on which theory is under scrutiny, the theoretical approaches of Indian psychology are in principle falsifiable and can therefore be tested by using the scientific method.

Indian psychology: Possible hypotheses

According to the scientific method, theories and hypotheses or questions derived from them are the basis of the scientific enterprise. In the ideal case, methods should be custom-tailored to a given hypothesis. This ideal will seldom be reached but there exists a panacea of methods in psychology from which suitable tools can be selected. Even if at first glance there were no such suitable methods to examine a given hypothesis at the moment, this is no reason at all to stop the scientific endeavour at this point because history has shown again and again, that if there are good theories, good methodological instruments will follow eventually. So even if it seems that hypotheses derived from Indian psychology currently lack adequate methodological tools to examine them, this should be no hindrance to think about possible hypotheses without any restrictions. On the other side, if there is no theory, the best tools are worthless. In fact, all the kinds of hypotheses discussed below are—in my opinion—at least partly open to examination by currently available methods (see paragraph on 'Methodological issues').

Throughout the paragraph the hypotheses are formulated as questions, because questions are more general than hypotheses (for example, the hypothesis 'god exists' is fully dealt with in the question 'does god exist?' but the question also includes the hypothesis 'god does not exist'). Whenever I was aware of any, I included evidence accumulated for specific hypotheses. The collection of hypotheses is certainly far from complete and I might have missed some very interesting ones. Also, the hypotheses are not ordered according to importance because different scholars may have quite different rankings in this respect. The main purpose is to open up (and also to make suggestions for summarizing) possibilities for meaningful research on Indian psychology. I will begin with 'existential' hypotheses about the metatheory. Most hypotheses are, however, related to *yoga*, the collection of methods that is part of the metatheory, and most of these hypotheses deal with intermediate states on the way. In addition, I have also included examples of hypotheses that are derived from specific theories of Indian psychology. In some cases, these hypotheses allow a test of one theory against another, if they differ in their predictions. This is followed by some examples of hypotheses about differences between the Western and the Indian approaches.

Basic existential hypotheses

For Indian scholars, the following two hypotheses might sound ridiculous, but for many Western academic scientists it will not be easy to accept the corresponding claims a priori, that is, without some systematic empirical evidence.

Does pure consciousness exist at all? The best evidence to answer that question in the affirmative would be to show that some persons exist or existed that really reached the state of pure consciousness. In Indian texts, usually several examples for persons that have attained pure consciousness are cited, very prominently among them Buddha, Ramakrishna Paramahamsa and Sri Ramana Maharshi. Zen Buddhist texts list many historic Zen masters and usually, becoming an authorized Zen master means to have attained enlightenment (see Kapleau, 1989), although sometimes there remains doubt about whether some persons who claim to be enlightened really have attained that state (AMA Samy, 2002, p. 17). There are also Western texts that have collected evidence. For instance, Bucke (1961) lists several historical personalities (among them some Americans whom he knew personally—the book was originally published in 1901) for having reached 'cosmic consciousness', and he himself also claimed to have had an experience of that sort. His criteria for what an experience of cosmic conscience is seem to be largely based on his own experience, because there is no systematic discussion of these criteria in the short biographies his book mainly consists of. However, although the experience Bucke describes was certainly very remarkable, it cannot be equated with pure consciousness, because there is still duality in the state he describes (d'Aquili & Newberg, 2000), but some of the persons whose life he describes might be generally regarded as having attained liberation. So one interesting question might be: 'What is common among the experiences of persons that claim (or whose followers claim for them) to have achieved pure consciousness?' If one cannot find such common characteristics, several conclusions are possible. There is, of course the—rather implausible—conclusion, that there is no such state. Second, whereas some of these persons might have acquired pure consciousness, others might not, or not to the end. Third, there might be different ways in which an experience of pure consciousness shows itself. This conclusion is logically difficult, because pure consciousness is usually defined as the absence of all attributes and so there cannot be different kinds of it, but that does not exclude that the same experience is communicated in different ways. One could also argue that the issue is not really decidable, so why take the troubles? In any case, a systematic collection of criteria and characteristics might help to come closer to the truth than the mostly anecdotal evidence available so far. It might also make possible to construct a common 'vertical structure'—the steps that have to be passed in order to obtain the state of pure consciousness—in spiritual experiences described in different systems.

Is pure consciousness just a special brain state, selected for by evolution? An answer to the affirmative is hinted at in the works of d'Aquili and Newberg (for example, d'Aquili & Newberg, 1993; 1998; 2000; Newberg, d'Aquili, & Rause, 2002). These authors argue, similar to many theories included in the metatheory, that there is a progression of spiritual states culminating in the state of absolute unitary experience (AUB). They suggest that the progressive blocking of neural input to the posterior superior parietal lobe and adjacent areas (especially on the non-dominant side) leads to a decreased sense of self and other, a decreased sense of space and time, and to an increased sense of unity among discrete objects. If input is totally blocked, AUB, that is, a sense of pure consciousness arises. They present some evidence for their case in showing increased blood flow after meditation in certain brain areas for highly experienced meditators, that is, Tibetan Buddhists (Newberg et al., 1997) and Franciscan nuns (Newberg et al., 2003). In Newberg et al. (2002) they offer an evolutionary explanation: Persons who reached the AUB state by blocking the respective neural input (for example, after fasting and staying alone in solitude for a prolonged period) were instrumental in the creation of religions. The religion, in turn, enforced the bonds of the respective clan, thus providing a selection advantage for the respective group. So their evolutionary argument focuses on groups—groups with individuals who have achieved AUB have a selection advantage. According to Newberg et al. (2002, p. 125) the 'neurological machinery of transcendence', that is, the respective brain mechanisms, might not have evolved for the purpose of experiencing AUB per se but might have arisen from the neural circuitry that evolved for mating and sexual experiences. This argument rests on the analogy between words with which sexual experiences and experiences by mystics are described: *bliss*, *rapture*, *ecstasy*, and *exaltation*. However, in the end they remain somewhat indecisive and do not really make a strong commitment for their view that pure consciousness is just a special brain state, selected for by evolution. One way to test their hypothesis would be—if that is possible without side effects—to induce a blocking of the respective brain regions and examine whether a subjective state consistent with AUB is experienced. It would be especially fortunate if persons could be found who have experienced that state—they could compare their experiences found the 'natural way' (for example, by meditation) with what they experienced the 'artificial way' (by the induced blocking of the neural pathways). Another possibility to test the hypothesis about 'why god won't go away' (the title of the Newberg et al. 2002 book) is to look for evidence outside the individual, because according to this hypothesis, everything happens inside the individual's brain. If, as many theories postulate, supernormal phenomena that include other persons are connected with higher mind-states, then showing a single convincing evidence of such paranormal states would refute the most extreme version of this 'pure-consciousness-is-in-the-brain' hypothesis.

Hypotheses about the impact of yoga

Which effects does the practice of *yoga* have on a person? As almost all varieties of *yoga*, including Buddhist meditation practices, refer in some way to Patañjali's *Yoga-Sūtras* (for example, Shukla, 2004) one might use the *Yoga-Sūtras* as a basis for predictions or questions.[5] All these predictions are about change or transformation and there are basically two ways about going to examine change. One is a one-shot method where one compares persons with a different amount of practice (or some other relevant difference), and the other is to conduct a long-term-study within a given person. The first option is much more convenient and that may be the reason why most studies I am aware of used that way. In the simplest case, one would compare two groups, one group that practices *yoga* and another (control-) group that does not. The main methodological problem here is that of controlling alternative explanations—the problem of internal validity mentioned above. The second way is much more difficult, for practical reasons (the collaboration between *yoga*-practitioner and researcher may have to last many years) and for methodological reasons (see the paragraph on 'Methodological issues'). However, in the long run, insights will be very limited if only the first approach will be followed. As spelled out in the metatheory, the main effect of *yoga* is to cut off or transform the connections between mind and sensory stimulation. So, for instance, negative emotions or 'thinking errors' should have less and less influence on the mind, and the weakening connection between mind and senses should also be observable in physiological measures.

Can the senses be shut out by practitioners of yoga? As the main aim of *yoga* in the traditional sense is the separation of the mind from the senses, even adverse stimuli should have less and less effect on the mind. Several studies have been conducted to examine this hypothesis. For instance, Anand et al. (1961, cited in R. J. Mathew, 2001, p. 227) administered strong stimuli (strong light, loud banging noise, contact with a hot glass tube, ice-cold water, and a tuning fork) to experienced *rāja yogīs*. They found only minimal changes in EEG despite the adverseness of the stimuli, and the pattern was also quite different from the EEG-patterns obtained during sleep. Also, in a study with Zen monks, it was found that they lack the usual EEG-responses to sensory stimulation: they did not habituate to repeated exposures of the stimuli, which could mean that they did not process them in the usual way (Kasamatsu & Hirai, 1966).

Are bodily functions drastically altered? Patañjali and several later sources from Zen and Advaita Vedānta postulate that in the course of successfully practicing *yoga* techniques, breathing slows down and becomes imperceptible when the mind is in the state of pure consciousness (Shear & Jevning, 1999, p. 196). This hypothesis also entails that metabolic activity should decrease considerably when meditators come close to separating the mind from the senses. Indeed, several studies have found that in advanced meditation, the pulse, as well as the metabolic rate are markedly reduced and respiration becomes basically imperceptible (Badawi et al., 1984; Farrow & Hebert, 1982; Travis & Wallace, 1997). As there have been numerous studies done already on this topic (for a comprehensive summary see Murphy, Donovan, & Taylor, 1997; see also Austin, 1998; Delmonte, 1985; Murray, 1982), a systematic summary of everything around—if possible in the form of one or several meta-analyses (for example, Hunter & Schmidt, 1990)—might be a good idea before conducting further studies on open or undecided questions.

Do the five kleśas *(hindrances, difficulties) become less pronounced?* According to the *yoga* philosophy, the five *kleśas* are the causes of misery (see second book of *Yoga-Sūtras*, for example, Woods, 1998; Raju, 1983, pp. 593-594). The hindrances are ignorance (*avidyā*), the feeling that one is so-and-so (*asmitā*), attachment (*rāga*), hate (*dveṣa*), and the desire to continue to be what one is (*abhiniveṣa*). With increasing *yoga* practice, these five hindrances should lose more and more weight. Similar claims are made by Buddhist contemplatives. They would, for instance, expect that with progressing practice in meditation, afflictive emotional states such as aggression and craving occur less frequently and are of briefer duration (Wallace, 1999, p. 185). Many hypotheses referring to the receding of negative attitudes or emotions can be derived from these very general hypotheses. A recent meta-analysis (Sedlmeier et al., 2012; see also Eberth & Sedlmeier, 2012) found overwhelming evidence for positive effects of meditation. This is consistent with the hypothesis that the five *kleśas* indeed become less pronounced when people practice *yoga* with meditation as the core element.

Do practitioners of yoga attain paranormal abilities? The third book of the *Yoga-Sūtras* deals in detail with the attainment of supernormal power (for example, Woods, 1998). Upon mastery of fixed-attention, contemplation and concentration, practitioners of the *yoga* method can be expected to have many such abilities, among them to be able to see into the future, read the thoughts of other persons, and make their bodies indiscernible (see also Paranjpe, 1982). Again, similar claims are made for Tibetan Buddhists who have attained the state of pure consciousness. Apart from the above, the abilities postulated include various forms of extrasensory perception, recalling one's previous lifetimes, moving through solid objects, walking on water, or multiplying one's own forms (Wallace, 1999, p. 185). There seems to be already some preliminary evidence in favour of the general hypothesis (and also against it) from systematic studies, but the empirical basis, at least as systematic research attempts are concerned is still rather scarce (Ramakrishna Rao, 1982; Ramakrishna Rao, Dukhan & Krishna Rao, 1978). However, recent meta-analyses provide convincing evidence for small but highly replicable effects (see Storm, Tressoldi & Di Risio, 2010; Utts, 1991).

Can yoga be successfully used in the treatment of drug addicts? Certain drugs seem to induce states of consciousness similar to those obtained with *yoga* practices. Since early times, people are susceptible to these effects of drugs, and drugs such as *sura* or *bhāng* are already mentioned in the *Vedas* (R. J. Mathew, 2001). Drugs may primarily have sedative, stimulating, or dissociative effects, but all can arouse some kind of euphoria. These euphoric states can be linked with altered states of consciousness (R. J. Mathew, 2001)—sedative drugs (for example, alcohol) release consciousness from inhibition, stimulating drugs (for example, cocaine) stimulate consciousness directly by expanding and enlarging it, and dissociative drugs (for example, ayahuasca, marijuana, peyote, or LSD) can produce a variety of 'religious feelings' connected with depersonalization and unification, among others (Schultes & Hoffmann, 1992; Shanon, 2001). One might see all these effects as weakening the connection between the mind and the objects of reality similar to what the practice of *yoga* is supposed to yield (see Figure 4.2). This similarity between the effects of drugs and those of *yoga* suggests the hypothesis that the practice of *yoga* might turn out to be a very potent therapy for drug addicts.

Does the practice of yoga have social implications? *Yoga* is a method for the individual, and not for the society. Therefore, one would not expect much impact for society from the practice of *yoga*. And in fact, the common tendency in India to neglect everyday life in favour of spirituality (except in the school of Mīmāṁsā) is commonly deplored (for example, Raju, 1962; Sri Aurobindo, 2001, chapter III). However, this is not totally consistent even with what the proponents of Advaita Vedānta, the most dominant school of Indian thought (and also the one which is commonly seen as rejecting the world most) taught. Already according to Śaṅkara, Advaita stands for both social welfare (*abhyudaya*) and spiritual progress (*niśreyas*) and Neo-Vedāntins such as Swami Vivekananda make an even stronger case: He derived the ideal of universal brotherhood from the Advaitic view that *Brahman* and individual are basically the same, irrespective of the individuals' differences, demographic or otherwise (Srinivas, 2004). Similar views are also held by Zen Buddhists (for example, AMA Samy, 2002). However, the most radical and explicit view about social consequences of *yoga* is held by Sri Aurobindo's Integral Yoga. According to this school, 'the liberated individual has one occupation and this is to deliver God in his fellow beings, and all else is secondary to him' (Jayashanmugam, 2002, p. 38). It seems, however, hard to derive precise hypotheses from these accounts, except that society will somehow profit from an increasing number of people who practice *yoga*. Also here, a systematic collection of the schools' social impacts would—if not already done with me not being aware of it—be very helpful for doing systematic research on the issues.

Which method for whom? As there are many varieties of *yoga*, it might be helpful for beginners to find out quickly which method suits them best. This question would become especially important if Indian psychology would be successfully accepted by the West, because the practical consequence then would probably be a strongly increased demand for education in *yoga*. One hypothesis already elaborated in the *Dharma-Śāstras* is a connection between predominance of one of the three *guṇas*—the three aspects of temperament postulated in the Sāṁkhya school—in a person and the kind of *yoga* method that is best suited for that person. According to that source, persons high in *sattva* (knowledge) should chose *jñāna yoga*, those high in *rajas* (action) *karma yoga* and those high in *tamas* (inertia), *bhakti yoga* (Raju, 1985). There are already several existing scales that allow the measurement of the three *guṇas'* relative strength (Daftuar & Anjali, 1997; V. G. Mathew, 2001; Sitamma, Sridevi, & Krishna Rao, 1995; Wolf, 1998); and a summary of the research on the three gunas is given by Puta & Sedlmeier (in press).

Hypotheses derived from specific Indian theories

To adherents of a given theory of Indian psychology, that theory is probably much more relevant than the metatheory outlined above, and there is, of course, the possibility that the 'best' theory already exists. However, at the moment, it cannot be expected that all informed experts would agree on such a best theory (adherents of different theories might not even agree on who is an 'expert'). One way to recommend a theory to potential practitioners would be to actually test hypotheses derived from that specific theory and thereby try to corroborate that theory. The six orthodox (as well as the heterodox) systems differ in a multitude of ways, but the differences are partly due to their relying on different parts of the *Vedic* scriptures (Raju, 1962; Sharma, 2003). However, there are also some differences on the same topics. For instance, schools differ in whether they assume that cause and effect are the same or different in nature, whether there is one or many Selves, or whether liberation can be attained while alive or only after death. In the following, I give just three arbitrary examples out of potentially very many hypotheses that can be derived from specific theories of Indian psychology. The third hypothesis given below is one that compares two different theories.

Do the stages postulated by Tibetan Buddhist psychology accord with the experience of practitioners? Wallace (1999) lists nine quite clearly defined attentional states that according to Buddhist psychology are attained successively in the *samatā* training. For each of the nine states, specific achievements are specified. One could now examine, whether the successive attainment of the stages is common for all practitioners or whether there are shortcuts for some and not for others, or whether there are pronounced differences in the time practitioners need to attain these states and whether these differences can be linked to differences in personality or other variables (see Dubs, 1987 for an attempt to do so for Soto-Zen meditators).

Does meditation on certain cakras produce the postulated effects? In Tantra and *kuṇḍalinī yoga*, concentration on one of the nine major *cakras* plays an important role. These *cakras* are said to be connected to different bodily, emotional, and spiritual effects. For instance, it is postulated that meditation on the *lalanā cakra* (forehead *cakra*) helps to cure neurotic and psychotic disorders and is therefore of great importance to psychologists (Mukhopadhyay & Renukadevi, 2004, p. 133). Analogously hypotheses can be specified for the other *cakras*.

Is analogy recognized by inference or associatively? This question could be from one of the mainstream psychology journals in the West, but actually it is an example of how systems of Indian psychology can hold different views about aspects of cognition. Whereas the Sāṁkhya school holds that analogical judgments use inference mechanisms, the Nyāya school contends that analogies can be recognized immediately in a way we would term associative (Raju, 1983; Sharma, 2003). A test of this differential hypothesis could be pursued by using methods from mainstream psychology, resorting, for instance, to reaction time measures.

Differential hypotheses between Indian and Western psychology

The most important difference between the Indian and the Western approach seems to be about the existence of pure consciousness as postulated by the former. However, as far as 'normal life' is concerned, ancient Indian psychology, especially as expressed in the systems of Nyāya and Vaiśeṣika have astonishingly parallel views with modern Western psychology (for example, Raju, 1983; Sharma, 2003). But there are also some striking differences. For instance, in contemporary Western cognitive psychology, the relationship between brain and mind is seldom explicitly spelled out, but if one would press researchers to make a statement, most would probably resort to the view that cognitive processes co-vary with brain processes, and if pressed still harder, some might say that essentially brain processes produce cognitions and emotions (for example, Damasio, 1999). The Indian view is just the opposite: the brain is used as an instrument by the mind (for example, Raju, 1983).

Does the mind use the brain or is the reverse true? This is a very interesting question, which cannot easily be tested. One might, however, try to find evidence for whether mind exists independently from brain. If the brain is the basis for the mind, there should be no mind if the brain is dead. So a good starting point to examine the hypothesis might be to look for evidence on near-death experiences or on reincarnation (for some attempts do to so see Cook, Greyson, & Stevenson, 1998; Stevenson, 1987).

Do the senses connect to their 'sense-objects'? In Indian psychology, at least in the systems of Nyāya and Vaiśeṣika, Sāṁkhya, and Mīmāṁsā, it is assumed that the senses go out to their objects and contact them or even 'become' the objects (for example, Raju, 1983). Therefore, sense-organs such as the eye or the nose that do not really touch their objects seem to be not the whole story according to the Indian view. So one might, for instance, hypothesize that even if the visual sense in the Western understanding does not work any longer, the remaining part of the visual sense in the Indian understanding might still be functioning and an (incomplete) perception might be the result. This hypothesis might open up some interesting links to phenomena such as 'blindsight' (for example, Cowey, 2004).

Can several senses produce cognitions simultaneously? The schools of Indian psychology hold that sense-organs can only work in connection with the mind. The mind, however, at least according to the Nyāya school, can only serve one sense organ at a time (Raju, 1983, p. 601). At a first glance, this is contradicted by synaesthetic experiences reported in the psychological literature. It might, however, be worthwhile to have a closer look at these reports and check whether the simultaneousness of experiences reported there could be explained by a rapid succession of different experiences (see Srinivas & Krishna Mohan, 2004).

Is yoga more efficient than Western psychotherapy, are there differential effects? This hypothesis is only marginal from the standpoint of the metatheory (the main aim of *yoga* is to attain pure consciousness and not to heal psychological or mental disorders), but it has probably received the highest amount of attention among Westerners, and also among Indian psychologists (Krishna Rao, 1995). Early on, psychoanalysts were interested in *yoga* as, for instance, a means to increase happiness in life (Coster, 1998). The interest in *yoga* and derivates such as Zen meditation is nowadays widespread in the therapeutic community, but it seems that only a few systematic studies have been conducted to find out more about the differential beneficial effects of *yoga* as compared to traditional Western approaches (Shapiro & Zifferblatt, 1976). For instance, a few studies compared the effects of Zen meditation with conventional relaxation techniques in the reduction of anxiety and found no differential effects with a week-long treatment (Goldman, Domitor, & Murray, 1979), but marked effects for both approaches already after 6 weeks with an advantage of Zen meditation over relaxation training in a scale that measured participants' degree of interpersonal problems (Tloczinki & Tantiella, 1998; see also Dubs, 1987). Finding out more about differential effects and conditions for effectiveness of different approaches should be in the interest of the probably very many therapists who already practice a combination of approaches (and in the interest of the public, of course).

Status of the hypotheses

Due to my rather scarce knowledge about the topic, I might have omitted substantial bodies of evidence for some of the hypotheses discussed above, but still, it seems that the existing evidence is quite insufficient or at least has to be analysed and summarized systematically for most of the hypotheses. An exception might be the hypotheses on the physiological correlates of states of concentration and meditation. But here also, a systematic summary would have a much higher impact on the scientific community than the scattered evidence in a wide variety of sometimes rather obscure journals. One reason why some of the hypotheses outlined above—especially those dealing with specific states of consciousness—have received so little interest from academic psychologists might also be due to a perceived lack of suitable methods. In the next paragraph I will argue that there are indeed methodological problems that, however, can be solved in principle by putting in additional effort.

Methodological issues

Now that some hypotheses from Indian psychology have been derived, the next steps according to the scientific method (Figure 4.1) are the operationalization of the variables involved, the design of the study, data collection, and data analysis. I have already dealt with issues of operationalization and design above, but the operationalization of the dependent variables (the variables by which the effect of the causal variables is determined) needs some more comment. These variables are operationalized by some measure of behaviour which can also be a subjective experience.[6] Often, researchers are not so much interested in the behaviour or experience itself but in the underlying constructs such as memory functions, emotions, cognitions. So the biggest difficulty in the operationalization of dependent variables is to establish a sound connection between behavioural or experiential measures (for example, some measure of blood flow in the brain, or some measure of emotionality) and the underlying suspected 'real' variable (for example, attention, or happiness). Academic psychology has developed several tools to ensure that measurement makes sense, among them *measurement theory*, which defines what a meaningful measurement is (for example, Steyer & Eid, 1993), *test theory*, which specifies criteria for constructing sound psychological tests and questionnaires (for example, Lienert & Raatz, 1994), and a variety of *multidimensional procedures* that seek to connect observable behaviour to the underlying constructs or 'latent variables' (for example, Backhaus et al., 2000). All these procedures can be applied to both quantitative and qualitative data. Although in mainstream research, the dominating design involves the comparison of groups, single-case designs, which are probably needed for many of the hypotheses outlined above, are by no means uncommon, especially with populations whose members are hard to get (for example, people with rare diseases, CEOs, *yogīs*). If the design is fixed, also the data collection stage is basically fixed, although in real research modifications may be necessary in between (for example, if participants do not show up or get sick, if instruments break down, or if new insights arise in the course of the study). The analysis of the data and the interpretation of the results are, of course, also determined by the hypothesis. But for data analysis, there are many possibilities, with a major distinction being between quantitative and qualitative methods, which are concerned both with measurement and data analysis.

Quantitative versus qualitative methods

In the methods literature, quantitative and qualitative approaches in psychological research are sometimes treated as totally separate, and this view is often expressed already in the titles of textbooks (with a strong dominance of the word 'quantitative'). However, if one looks at what researchers really do or have done, qualitative and quantitative methods co-existed all the time (for example, Pope & Mays, 1995) and the distinction is to a certain extent artificial (Stoppard, 2002). Academic psychology in Germany actually started with what one would today call qualitative research. Interestingly, in many studies in which the method of introspection was used, the 'subject' was the professor and the interviewer was often his assistant (for example, Bühler, 1907; Lück & Miller, 2002). It was thought that the introspectionist had to be more highly skilled than the interviewer, to make the subjective data he produced meaningful. In contrast to the views of some critics of Western psychology, subjective experiences still play an important role even in mainstream psychology. Especially if a new line of research is introduced, explorative interviews dominate the beginning phase and all considerate experimenters ask their participants to explain their impressions, experiences, and motivations in experiments in their own words. Interviews of different types also play an important role in developmental and organizational, as well as in clinical research. But often, what persons say is not left as is, but is restructured or quantified. This involves elaborating adequate categories and scales. So quantification is rather the end product of a data analysis that might begin qualitatively. Data, be they utterances, observations, counts, etc., often do not speak for themselves—they only make sense in the light of an idea or a theory. Even verbal data do not come out of the void, but are usually responses to questions which, in turn, are motivated by at least a rudimentary form of 'theory' or idea.

Qualitative methods do not always yield numbers in the end. There are also qualitative researchers who shy away from quantification on principle, because they feel that the analysis of experiences, attitudes, and views of the research participants may not yield any meaningful numbers. In some cases, such as when little is known about a given topic or when the aim of the research is to generate new hypotheses or theories, quantification does indeed not make much sense. It is true, however, that qualitative data analysis is often done more or less ad hoc, because scholars lack adequate training. This led to an emphasis on 'the old methods' (Aiken, West, Sechrest, & Reno, 1990), which are not so seldom applied ritualistically, without much thought (Salsburg, 1985). This state of affairs seems to be slowly changing, especially in applied settings and in domains that rely heavily on verbal protocols; but systematic qualitative approaches such as discourse analysis, grounded theory, or content analysis (see Richardson, 1996; Smith, 2003; Wood & Kroger, 2000) still play a marginal role in the journals considered most important by mainstream psychologists (Rennie, Watson, & Monteiro, 2002). Apart from the lack of knowledge about suitable qualitative methods, another reason for the reluctance of mainstream researchers to use qualitative methods is probably the emphasis of some qualitative researchers on a 'social constructionist' position, that is, the assumption, that reality is, at least in part, socially constructed and does not exist independently of culture and social environment (Stoppard, 2002). But even with a social constructivist approach, the scientific method (Figure 4.1) still holds, irrespective of whether a quantitative or a qualitative approach to measurement and data analysis is used. Meanwhile, qualitative methods are also regularly taught in universities in UK and Canada (Stoppard, 2002) and I personally know of several programmes in Germany and Austria. In sum: although qualitative methods—which often use highly subjective data—currently do not play a dominant role in mainstream psychological research, they are a widely accepted part of psychology's methods arsenal. Whether these methods will thrive more in the future depends on whether they show some advantage in the examination of specific questions or hypotheses. The hypotheses derived from Indian psychology may be a case in point.

First-, second-, and third-person methods

In a sense, all our perception is subjective, irrespective of whether one takes the Eastern view in which the mind reaches out towards the objects via the senses, or the prevalent Western view, in which a stimulation of the sense organs has to be processed by the brain—a direct or really objective perception is impossible according to both accounts. Both accounts have also extensively dealt with possible errors arising from the subjectivity of our perception (for example, Sharma, 2003; Goldstein, 1999). The problem can be minimized if perception is 'externalized' to a measurement device such as scales, meters or other indicators of physical properties as usually done in the natural sciences. A person outside the physical process or phenomenon to be observed (for example, voltage, duration, weight), a 'third person' is able to make quite accurate judgments. This 'third person' could in principle be any observer, but in practice, especially if some theoretical knowledge is required to understand what is going on, third persons have to undergo substantial training. Third-person methods, as taken from the natural sciences, are also quite widespread in psychology. For instance, two of the main criteria of goodness in constructing psychological tests are *objectivity* (it should not matter who conducts the test, who evaluates the test results, and irrelevant information should not play any role), and *reliability* (for example, if the test is administered again, the same outcome should be observed, given an unchanged state of affairs). Also, all possible influences of the experimenter in psychological research are usually regarded as 'nuisance variables' and should be strictly controlled. This makes sense for examining a wide variety of psychological hypotheses, and often, the possible values of nuisance variables (for example demographic variables of experimenter, information about participants) are systematically varied to see how they influence research outcomes. More recently, a new approach to nuisance variables has been developed. Nuisance variables are now increasingly incorporated into computer models that simulate how humans think, feel, and act (for example, McLeod, Plunkett, & Rolls, 1998) or—to give a specific example—how a sense of self might come about (Nowak et al., 2000).

However, third-person methods have their limitations in psychology because, as Velmans (2001) has argued nicely, experimenters and 'subjects' or observers and observed persons can in principle exchange roles, in contrast to the situation in physics or chemistry. This is the more a problem, the less strictly meaningful measurements can be defined a priori. For instance, when more 'technical' hypotheses about the impact of meditation are examined, measures such as blood flow, respiration, or EEG patterns can be well defined and third-person methods are quite adequate. A similar argument would hold for studies in which the therapeutic effectiveness of *yoga* is compared to a different approach. If, however, one wants to find out about changes in consciousness, third-person methods do not make much sense for at least three reasons. First, if the interrogation procedure is fixed a priori, very likely, important information will be missed. Second, the role of a detached observer does not work in this case: there has to be a good 'rapport' between the persons involved in this kind of research, otherwise again, important information may not be disclosed (Vermersch, 1999). And finally, it will not do to have an arbitrary researcher do the interviewing. Even if the relationship among the person observed and the observer is good, if the interviewer does not have adequate experiences and knowledge herself, chances are that important information will be missed or misunderstood. One could now argue that all these problems are solved if the observer is identical with the observed, that is, by applying 'first-person methods'. This may work in some exceptionally well-trained individuals, but already directing one's attention to one's own mental states usually changes these (Velmans, 2001). Moreover, expectations, belief systems and personal views, as well as social and cultural factors add many more problems to the first-person approach. This leaves as a third option a kind of compromise between third- and first-persons methods: 'second-person methods'.[7] The 'second person' must be experienced, knowledgeable, on good personal terms with the 'first person' and, last not least, well trained in a suitable method—in the words of Varela and Shear (1999, p. 10), 'an empathic resonator with experiences that are familiar to him and which find in himself a resonant chord'. Such second-person methods have, at least sometimes, been applied in the beginning of academic psychology in Germany, where highly educated post-docs observed the professors' verbal associations (Lück & Miller, 2002). However, in the course of time, the expert participants were replaced by 'naïve' participants with the college student as the prototypical 'subject'. In recent times, there seems to be a revival of the approach, largely motivated by research having to do with different aspects of consciousness (see the Feb/March issue of *Volume 6*, of the *Journal of Consciousness Studies*, 1999). Well-founded second-person approaches to study consciousness are proposed by Depraz (1999), Petitmengin-Peugot (1999), and Vermersch (1999); and a detailed account of one way of doing second person interviews is suggested by Petitmengin (2006). Common to all these approaches is the necessity of a substantial amount of practice as a pre-requisite to apply the method. All of these methods fulfill the two conditions postulated by Varela & Shear (1999, p. 6):

1. Providing a clear *procedure* for accessing some phenomenal domain.
2. Providing a clear means for an *expression and validation* within a community of observers who have familiarity with procedures as in the previous point.

Validation can either be done by having several 'second persons' interact with the same participant, having one 'second person' interact with several participants, or a combination of the two. Who can be a second person in research on suitable hypotheses derived from Indian psychology? Certainly the *guru* as suggested by Ramakrishna Rao (2004), which would also include Zen masters, who often use meditators' attempted solutions for *Koans* as diagnostic yardsticks for progress. However, the most common case for a second person in this kind of research will probably be the interested researcher, trained in a suitable second-person method and experienced in at least some practice of *yoga* (see Wallace, 1999).

Potential problems with second-person methods

There are at least three potential problems with the use of second-person methods. The first concerns the potential participants. There should be no problem finding interested practitioners of *yoga* in the beginning or even intermediate stages, but it may be hard to find really advanced *yogīs*. And even if such persons can be located, they might not be willing to be subjected to a second-person kind of enquiry. In addition, samples might be highly selective and therefore the results might not be representative. However, there are some indications that at least practitioners of Zen, Tibetan Buddhist meditators, and adherents of *Transcendental meditation* based on Advaita Vedānta are generally willing to participate, irrespective of the status they have reached (Brown & Engler, 1980; Dubs, 1987; Gillani & Smith, 2001; Shear & Jevning, 1999; Wallace, 1999). After all, practitioners, especially if they have been socialized in a Western culture might want to seek some confirmation that a method they have invested considerable time and effort in, really works according to their expectations. Others might be interested in propagating their own method, which is—at least in the West—much easier to propagate, if it is backed by scientific evidence; and—the best case—some practitioners might be intrinsically motivated.

The second problem concerns the method itself. Nisbett and Wilson (1977) published a highly influential article on the accuracy of verbal reports in studies that examined social judgment tasks. After reviewing the evidence, they claimed to have shown that introspectionists may not have access to higher order cognitive processes, and that the accuracy of subjective verbal reports is generally very poor. Some 10 years later, White (1988) published another (much less influential) review in which he showed that Nisbett and Wilson's analysis was methodologically flawed; and he also presented some positive evidence, concluding that the issue is far from closed. A similar conclusion is also drawn by Ericsson and Simon (1984), who discuss several factors that can be expected to have an impact on the validity of verbal reports. The studies analysed by Nisbett and Wilson (1977) as well as White (1988) used naïve participants and observers not especially trained in assisting in the introspectionist process. So, one might not expect tremendously good results anyway. But what about the attempts to introspection in early German psychology as, for instance, practiced in the Würzburg school, some of which might justifiably be called 'second-person method'? Why were these attempts given up afterwards? Vermersch (1999) argues that the main reason may have been that the theories held were too weak for the data. He also discusses other objections to introspection but argues that although the method is rarely used in academia, practitioners in psychology still use it for teaching, remedial action, re-education, training, coaching, therapy, etc., which should be an indicator of its usefulness. The crucial point, according to Vermersch (1999) is that a solid second-person introspectionist procedure needs considerable training on the side of the second person. Overall, the evidence against the method of introspection is not convincing; and for the kind of introspection-studies needed to examine some of the hypotheses of Indian psychology, there is just no evidence yet. But anyway, 'nothing is gained by refusing the entire enterprise because of some a priori argument.' (Varela & Shear, 1999, p. 14).

Also the third problem is such an a priori argument. Second-person methods are embedded in the scientific method (Figure 4.1). This method works on the intellectual level but at least some of the hypotheses listed above are concerned with the level of pure consciousness which, according to all theories considered here, is not thoroughly understandable by the ordinary mind. So the problem is whether a methodology that is based on the mind can reach beyond the mind. A possible solution to this problem might be seen in Figures 4.2 and 4.3—according to the metatheory, there is always the possibility to connect the mind to pure consciousness; and this connection grows stronger with an increasing practice of *yoga*. So if both the interviewer and the interviewee using a second-person method have reached a higher state of consciousness, the interviewer could use the mind to express his or her (possibly intuitive) experiences, could analyse them systematically and finally communicate them. If the interviewer has not reached that higher state but the interviewee has, the 'data' might be less perfect but still very useful to further scientific knowledge about states of higher consciousness.[8] It seems to me that the limitations lie not so much in the interviewer as a deficient 'measurement device' but in the translation of the interviewer's experiences (and, of course, also the interviewee's utterances) into an apt language for the communication of the results. Science, however, depends on some kind of language, be it natural language or a more formalized one. This dependence on language is certainly a limitation of the scientific method when used to study higher states of consciousness, but it is the only means available. Unless a substantial part of humankind learns to communicate in an efficient nonverbal way, language is the only general way to pass on information, be it scientific or otherwise.

Appreciation of Indian psychology in the West

Indian psychology was early on recognized by analytical theory (for example, Coster, 1998) but it has never played a substantial role in Western academic psychology so far. There have always been a few researchers that tried to link the Western and the Indian view, though. For instance, already James (1898) mentioned a state of 'superconsciousness' (*samādhi*) but did not advance a really good explanation for it. Later on, James's work was not much taken up until the 1960s and 1970s, and Indian psychology only gained some more interest through some physiologically oriented studies that connected aspects of consciousness with physiological measures (Peters, 1998).

In recent times, there has been increased interest, however, which might have at least two causes. One could be the wide dissemination of *yoga* and meditation techniques, by which chances have risen that academics might collect some first hand experiences. For instance, in the U.S., Buddhist meditation and Transcendental meditation seem to have been able to attract special attention recently (Pickering, 1997; Shear & Jevning, 1999). A second cause for the increased interest could be that even mainstream researchers are discontent with the current state of affairs in academic psychology. Discontent arises because psychologists—often out of quite practical reasons, such as the availability of grant money and tenure considerations—are too occupied with small fragmented questions which have the potential of alienating them from larger intellectual and human concerns (Bevan & Kessel, 1994). Also, there is a tendency of the scientist's role away from value-neutral research to being a participant in natural events (Bevan, 1991). This increased interest in practically oriented daily life matters can be seen in a renewed interest of academic psychology in the effects of religious practice and in at least three lines of research that have gained quite a lot of popularity recently. First, materialist values as the main cause for well-being are being questioned more and more by prominent mainstream psychologists (for example, Diener & Seligman, 2004,

Kahneman, Diener, & Schwarz, 1999). Second, the central role of happiness in life and how it can be achieved found an expression in a new line of research termed *positive psychology*, which is 'an attempt to urge psychologists to adopt a more open and appreciative perspective regarding human potentials, motives, and capacities' (Sheldon & King, 2001, p. 216; see also the other articles in the March issue, 2001 of the *American Psychologist*). And a third topic that finds increasing interest among psychologists is wisdom research (for example, Ardelt, 2004; Baltes & Kunzman, 2004). To the best of my knowledge, none of these new developments in the West takes yet account of Indian psychology but all these topics could be good interfaces for bringing together Indian and Western approaches (for example, Misra, Suvasini, & Srivastava, 2000), and they might serve as a starting point for a process which could eventually lead to a redefinition of psychology that appreciates the meditative mode of knowing and being (Rosch, 1997).

Conclusion

In this chapter, I have put a heavy emphasis on methods, because a sound methodology is what makes the difference between lay psychology and the scientific approach to psychology. A rigorous test of the hypotheses derivable from Indian psychology is all the more necessary because of the abundance of publications on *yoga* and related issues in the West that do not meet even minimal scientific standards. The low quality of many of these publications (and of some institutions and private practices that propagate them) is certainly an important reason why Indian psychology is not regarded as scientific by most academic psychologists who usually do not know much about its real background. In academic psychology there prevails a strong sentiment against 'theories' that rely heavily on authority and 'good stories'. This sentiment can, for instance, be witnessed in the fate of psychoanalysis, which is quite marginalized in academic psychology because it (still) is only partly open to falsification. If a system of thought is not in principle open to falsification it can—according to the view taken in this chapter—not be treated as a scientific theory. However, this must not be equated with a judgment about the value of the respective system—psychoanalysis has helped many people and also the practice of religion is increasingly recognized as helpful in daily life. Note that this recognition is due to research results *about* psychoanalysis and religion. Here the research was not concerned with testing the 'theories' as such but it was about effects, which, at least in the case of religion, were not predicted from the 'theory' itself but from a theory about the 'theory'.[9] In contrast, hypotheses derived from Indian psychology can in principle be examined rigorously, as has already been done to a limited extent (see examples cited earlier). Apart from holding up high methodological standards, I think it would speed up the dissemination of research results considerably if Indian psychologists tried more to publish their results in high ranking international journals or with well known publishing houses. These outlets are highly selective but guarantee high methodological standards; and therefore they are the main source of information for academic psychologists. The issue about where to publish research results is just a practicality and may not be to the taste of everybody. However, it would greatly enhance the perception of these results among a large group of researchers. Many scientists in the West who are (in the beginning) only marginally interested in a topic do not search actively for it—because of the time pressure in academia (publish or perish)—they do, however, routinely scan major journals and new books of renowned publishing houses. This all said, let me come back to the question implied in the title: How far can Western scientific methods and Indian psychology go together? In principle: all the way through; in practice: let us try our best!

Author's note

I would like to thank AMA Samy, Matthijs Cornelissen, as well as Anita Hewer, Udo Rudolph, Isabell Winkler and Maria Wirth for their helpful comments on a first version of this chapter.

Endnotes

1 So when one is looking for genuine Indian psychology, one finds more experts in the philosophy departments than in the psychology departments. In ancient India (as in ancient Europe by the way), there was no division between philosophy, psychology (and religion).

2 Note that the term 'method' has a different meaning here—*yoga* is a collection of methods to *achieve some ends* (liberation) whereas research methods are used to *find out about something* (for example, about the specific effects of *yoga*).

3 As all meta-models, the above meta-theory of Indian psychology is heavily simplified and leaves out specific details that adherents of a given theory, which might be subsumed under the meta-model, think of as most important. Just one example: In Sri Aurobindo's Integral Yoga, the division would be between the several gradations of mind and the *supermind*, which, in the vertical scale of that specific system precedes the three-leveled *saccidānanda* (Aurobindo 2001, p. 280).

4 Although here one might object that at least some of the six orthodox systems deal with different parts of the *Vedic* scriptures.

5 There is even evidence that the *Yoga-Sutras* might have been heavily influenced by Buddhism (Whiteman, 1993).

6 In fact, in German textbooks, the definitions of what psychology is about still often contain both the terms 'observations' and 'experiences' (Ponkratz, 1984). If one looks at its usage in the literature, the term 'observation' mostly used in American textbooks does meanwhile cover subjective experiences as well.

7 Note that while there is some correspondence between quantitative vs. qualitative and third-person vs. first- and second-person methods, third-person methods can also be applied to qualitative data and first- as well as second-person methods can in principle be used for quantitative data.

8 As outlined above, one prerequisite for the interviewer is at least some experience in the practice of *yoga*.

9 In the case of psychoanalysis, the question behind the research that established its effectiveness was motivated by the question whether psychotherapy was effective at all and whether different approaches differed in their effectiveness (for example, Smith & Glass, 1977).

References

Aiken, L. S., West, S. G., Sechrest, L., & Reno, R. R. (1990). Graduate training in statistics, methodology, and measurement in psychology: A survey of Ph.D. programs in North America. *American Psychologist, 45*, 721–734.

AMA Samy (2002). *Zen-heart, Zen-mind: The teachings of Zen master AMA Samy*. Sridevi Rao, (Ed.). Chennai: Cre-A:.

AMA Samy (2005). *Zen: Awakening to your original face*. Chennai: Cre-A:.

Anand, B. K., Chhina, G. S., & Singh, B. (1961). Some aspects of EEG studies in Yogis. *EEG and Clinical Neurophysiology, 13*, 452–456.

Ardelt, M. (2004). Wisdom as expert knowledge system: A critical review of a contemporary operationalization of an ancient concept. *Human Development, 47*, 257–285.

Auluck, S. (2002). Psychology in Indian philosophical thought. *Journal of Indian Psychology, 20*, 13–22.

Aurobindo, Sri (1995). *The secret of the Veda*. Twin Lakes: Lotus Light Publications.

Aurobindo, Sri (1996). *The synthesis of yoga*. Twin Lakes, WI: Lotus Light Publications.

Austin, J. H. (1998). *Zen and the brain*. Cambridge: MIT Press.

Backhaus, K., Erichson, B., Wulff, P., & Weiber, R. (2000). *Multivariate Analysemethoden: Eine anwendungsorientierte Einführung*. (9. Aufl.). Berlin: Springer.

Badawi, K., Wallace, R., Orme-Johnson, D. et al. (1984). Electrophysiologic characteristics of respiratory suspension periods occurring during the practice of the transcendental meditation program. *Psychosomatic Medicine, 46*, 267–276.

Baltes, P. B., & Kunzmann, U. (2004). The two faces of wisdom: Wisdom as a general theory of knowledge and judgment about excellence in mind and virtue vs. wisdom as everyday realization in people and products. *Human Development, 47*, 290–299.

Barkow, J., Cosmides, L., & Tooby, J. (Eds.) (1992). *The adapted mind.* New York: Oxford University Press.

Bevan, W. (1991). Contemporary psychology: A tour inside the onion. *American Psychologist, 46*, 475–483.

Bevan, W., & Kessel, F. (1994). Plain truths and home cooking: Thoughts on the making and remaking of psychology. *American Psychologist, 49*, 505–509.

Bhatia, S. (2002). Orientalism in Euro-American and Indian psychology: Historical representations of "Natives" in colonial and postcolonial contexts. *History of Psychology, 5*, 376–398.

Brown, D., & Engler, J. (1980). The states of mindfulness meditation: A validation study. *Journal of Transpersonal Psychology, 12*, 143–192.

Bucke, R. M. (1961). *Cosmic consciousness.* Secaucus, N. J.: Citadel Press. (Original work published 1901).

Bühler, H. (1907). Tatsachen und Probleme zu einer Psychologie der Denkvorgänge. 1. Über Gedanken. *Archiv für die gesamte Psychologie, 9*, 297–365.

Bunge, M., & Ardila, R. (1990). *Philosophie der Psychologie.* Tübingen: Mohr.

Chang, Garma, C. C. (1959). *The practice of Zen.* New York: Harper & Row.

Cook, E. W., Greyson, B., & Stevenson, I. (1998). Do any near-death experiences provide evidence for the survival of human personality after death? Relevant features and illustrative case reports. *Journal of Scientific Exploration, 12*, 377–406.

Cornelissen, M. (2003). The need for the Indian tradition. *Psychological Studies, 48*, 38–52.

Cornelissen, M. (2004). Sri Aurobindo's evolutionary ontology of consciousness. In K. Joshi & M. Cornelissen (Eds.), *Consciousness, Indian psychology and yoga* (pp. 11-52). New Delhi: Centre for Studies in Civilizations.

Cortright, B. (2004). The meeting of East and West: The fusion of Vedanta and Western psychology in Integral Psychology. In K. Joshi & M. Cornelissen (Eds.), *Consciousness, Indian psychology and yoga* (pp. 342–352). New Delhi: Centre for Studies in Civilizations.

Coster, G. (1998). *Yoga and Western psychology: A comparison.* Delhi: Motilal Banarsidass. (Original work published 1932 by Oxford University Press, London).

Cowey, A. (2004). The 30th Sir Frederick Bartlett lecture: Fact, artefact, and myth about blindsight. *Quarterly Journal of Experimental Psychology A, 57*(4), 577–609.

Daftuar, C. N., & Anjali. (1997). Occupational stress, organizational commitment and job involvement in sattva, rajas and tamas personality types. *Journal of Indian Psychology, 15*, 44–52.

Damasio, A. (1999). *The feeling of what happens: Body and emotion in the making of consciousness.* San Diego: Harcourt.

d'Aquili, E. G., & Newberg, A. B. (1993). Mystical states and the experience of god: A model of the neuropsychological substrate. *Zygon: Journal of Religion and Science, 28*, 177–200.

d'Aquili, E. G., & Newberg, A. B. (1998). The neuropsychological basis of religion: Or why god won't go away. *Zygon: Journal of Religion and Science, 33*, 187–201.

d'Aquili, E. G., & Newberg, A. B. (2000). The neuropsychology of aesthetic, spiritual, and mystical states. *Zygon: Journal of Religion and Science, 35*, 39–51.

Dawes, R. M. (1988). *Rational choice in an uncertain world.* San Diego, CA: Harcourt Brace Jovanovich.

Dawes, R. M. (2001). *Everyday irrationality.* Boulder: Westview Press.

Dawkins, R. (1990). *The selfish gene* (2nd ed.). Oxford: Oxford University Press.

Delmonte, M. M. (1985). Response to meditation in terms of physiological, behavioral and self-report measures: A brief summary. *Psychological Reports, 56*, 9–10.

Depraz, N. (1999). The phenomenological reduction as praxis. *Journal of Consciousness Studies, 6*, 95–110.

Diener, E., & Seligman, M. E. P. (2004). Beyond money: Toward an economy of well-being. *Psychological Science in the Public Interest, 5*, 1–31.

Dubs, G. (1987). Psycho-spiritual development in Zen Buddhism: A study of resistance in meditation. *The Journal of Transpersonal Psychology, 19*, 19–86.

Eberth, J., & Sedlmeier, P. (2012). The effects of mindfulness meditation: a meta-analysis. *Mindfulness*, 3, 174-189.

Eliade, M. (1970). *Yoga: Immortality and freedom.* Princeton, NJ: Princeton University Press.

Ericsson, K. A., & Simon, H. S. (1984). *Protocol analysis: Verbal protocols as data.* Cambridge, MA: MIT Press.

Farrow, J. T., & Hebert, R. (1982). Breath suspension during the transcendental meditation technique. *Psychosomatic Medicine, 44*, 133–153.

Farthing, G. W. (1992). *The psychology of consciousness.* Englewood Cliffs, NJ: Prentice Hall.

Feyerabend, P. K. (1975). *Against method: Outline of an anarchistic theory of knowledge.* London: New Left Books.

Gigerenzer, G. (1991). From tools to theories: A heuristic of discovery in cognitive psychology. *Psychological Review, 98*, 254–267.

Gillani, N. B., & Smith, J. C. (2001). Zen meditation and ABC relaxation theory: An exploration of relaxation states, beliefs, dispositions, and motivations. *Journal of Clinical Psychology, 57*, 839–846.

Goldman, B. L., Domitor, P. J., & Murray, E. J. (1979). Effects of Zen meditation on anxiety reduction and perceptual functioning. *Journal of Consulting and Clinical Psychology, 47*, 551–556.

Goldstein, E. G. (1999). *Sensation & perception* (5th ed.). Pacific Grove, CA: Brooks/Cole.

Hamilton, S. (2001). *Indian philosophy: A very short introduction.* Oxford: Oxford University Press.

Hayes, S. C., Barnes-Holmes, D., & Roche, B. (Eds.) (2001). *Relational frame theory: A post-Skinnerian account of human learning.* New York: Kluwer/Plenum.

Hiriyanna, M. (2000). *Outlines of Indian philosophy.* Delhi: Motilal Banarsidass. (Original work published 1932).

Hunter, J. E., & Schmidt, F. L. (1990). *Methods of meta-analysis.* Newbury Park: Sage.

Huppes, N. (2001). *Psychic education, a workbook.* New Delhi: Sri Aurobindo Education Society.

Huppes, N. (2002). Workshop teaching psychology: The methodology of an integrated approach. In P. Ramalingam (Ed.), *Applied psychology for world peace and prosperity* (pp. 74-92). New Delhi: PR Books.

James, W. (1898). *Varieties of religious experience.* New York: Collier.

Jayashanmugam, N. (2002). Sri Aurobindo and traditionalism. *Pondicherry University Journal of Social Sciences and Humanities, 3*, 37–49.

Joshi, K., & Cornelissen, M. (Eds.) (2004). *Consciousness, Indian psychology and yoga.* New Delhi: Centre for Studies in Civilizations.

Kapleau. P. (1989). *The three pillars of Zen.* New York: Anchor books.

Kasamatsu, A., & Hirai, T. (1966). En electroencephalographic study of the Zen meditation (Zazen). *Folia Psychiatrica Neurologica Japonica, 20*, 315–316.

Kahneman, D., Diener, E., & Schwarz, N. (Eds.) (1999). *Well-being: The foundations of hedonic psychology.* New York: Russel Sage Foundation.

Krishna Rao, P. V. (1995). Yoga: Its scientific and applied aspects. *Journal of Indian Psychology, 13*, 1–12.

Krishna Rao, P. V. (1997). Indian philosophical psychology in the context of contemporary psychology: A general appraisal. *Journal of Indian Psychology, 15*, 25–30.

Kuhn, T. (1970). *The structure of scientific revolutions* (2nd ed.). Chicago: University of Chicago Press.

Kulkarni, T. R. (1978). Psychology: The Indian point of view. *Journal of Indian Psychology, 18*, 22–39.

Lakatos, I. (1970). Falsification and the methodology of scientific research programs. In I. Lakatos, & A. Musgrave (Eds.), *Criticism and the growth of knowledge* (pp. 91-196). Cambridge, England: Cambridge University Press.

Lienert, G. A., & Raatz, U. (1994). *Testaufbau und Testanalyse* (5. Aufl.). Psychologie Verlags Union: Beltz.

Loftus, E. E. (1979). *Eyewitness testimony*. Cambridge, MA: Harvard University Press.

Lück, H. E., & Miller, R. (2002). *Illustrierte Geschichte der Psychologie*. Stuttgart: Beltz.

Maitra, S. K. (2001). *An introduction to the philosophy of Sri Aurobindo*. Pondicherry: Sri Aurobindo Ashram. (Original work published 1941).

Mathew, R. J. (2001). *The true path: Western science and the quest for Yoga*. Cambridge, MA: Perseus Publishing.

Mathew, V. G. (2001). Models of consciousness and its transformation. In M. Cornelissen (Ed.), *Consciousness and its transformation* (pp. 188-198). Pondicherry: Sri Aurobindo International Centre of Education.

Mathew, V. G. (2004). Personal growth and psychology in India. In K. Joshi & M. Cornelissen (Eds.), *Consciousness, Indian psychology and yoga* (pp. 248-256). New Delhi: Centre for Studies in Civilizations.

McLeod, P., Plunkett, K., & Rolls, E. T. (1998). *Introduction to connectionist modelling of cognitive Processes*. Oxford: Oxford University Press.

Misra, G., & Mohanty, A. K. (2002). Introduction. In G. Misra, & A. K. Mohanty (Eds.), *Perspectives on indigenous psychology* (pp. 13-33). New Delhi: Concept Publishing.

Misra, G., Suvasini, C., & Srivastava, A. K. (2000). Psychology of wisdom: Western and Eastern perspectives. *Journal of Indian Psychology, 18*, 1–32.

Mukhopadhya, B., & Renukadevi. (2004). Cakra meditation in achieving altered states of consciousness. In K. Joshi & M. Cornelissen (Eds.), *Consciousness, Indian psychology and yoga* (pp. 130–136). New Delhi: Centre for Studies in Civilizations.

Murphy, M., Donovan, S., & Taylor, E. (1997). *The physical and psychological effects of meditation: A review of contemporary research with a comprehensive bibliography 1931-1996* (2nd ed.). Sausalito, CA: Institute of Noetic Sciences.

Murray, J. B. (1982). What is meditation? Does it help? *Genetic Psychology Monograph, 106*, 85–115.

Newberg, A. B., Alavi, A., Baime, M., Mozley, P. D., & d'Aquili, E. G. (1997). The measurement of cerebral blood flow during the complex cognitive task of meditation using HMPAS-SPCET Imaging. *Journal of Nuclear Medicine, 38*, 95.

Newberg, A., d'Aquili, E., & Rause, V. (2002). *Why God won't go away: Brain science & the biology of belief*. New York: Ballantine Books.

Newberg, A., Pourdehnad, M., Alavi, A., & d'Aquili, E. G. (2003). Cerebral blood flow during meditative prayer: Preliminary findings and methodological issues. *Perceptual and Motor Skills, 97*, 625–630.

Nisbett, R. E., & Wilson, T. D. (1977). Telling more than we can know: Verbal reports on mental processes. *Psychological Review, 84*, 231–259.

Nowak, A., Tesser, A., Vallacher, R. R., & Borkowsky, W. (2000). Society of self: The emergence of collective properties in self-structure. *Psychological Review, 107*, 39–61.

Paranjpe, A. C. (1982). Parapsychology and Patanjali's Yoga. *Journal of Indian Psychology, 4*, 13–20.

Paranjpe, A. C. (2004). Challenges and opportunities for Indian psychology in a rapidly globalizing post-modern world. In K. Joshi & M. Cornelissen (Eds.), *Consciousness, Indian psychology and yoga* (pp. 205-237). New Delhi: Centre for Studies in Civilizations.

Peters, F. (1998). Lucid consciousness in traditional Indian psychology and contemporary neuro-psychology. *Journal of Indian Psychology, 16*, 1–25.

Petitmengin-Peugot, C. (1999). The intuitive experience. *Journal of Consciousness Studies, 6*, 43–77.

Petitmengin, C. (2006). Describing one's subjective experience in the second person: an interview method for the science of consciousness. *Phenomenology and the Cognitive Sciences*, 5, 229-269.

Petzold, M. (1989). The heritage of India: Yoga psychology in East and West. *Psychologia, 32*, 275–280.

Pickering, J. (Ed.) (1997). *The authority of experience: Essays on Buddhism and psychology*. Surrey: Curzon Press.

Ponkratz, L. J. (1984). *Problemgeschichte der Psychologie (2. Aufl.)*. München: Francke Verlag.

Pope, C., & Mays, N. (1995). Qualitative research: Reaching the parts other methods cannot reach: An introduction to qualitative methods in health and health services research. *BMJ, 311*, 42–45.

Popper, K. R. (1969). *Logik der Forschung*. Tübingen: Mohr.

Puta, M. & Sedlmeier, P. (in press). The concept of Tri-Guna: A working model . In S. Schmidt, & H. Walach, (Eds.) *Meditation: Neuroscientific approaches and philosophical implications*. Berlin: Springer.

Raju, P. T. (1962). *Introduction to comparative philosophy* (Part 3: Indian philosophy and explication of inwardness, pp. 170–248). Lincoln: University of Nebraska Press.

Raju, P. T. (1983). Indian psychology. In H. Bhattacharyya (Ed.), *The cultural heritage of India*, (Vol. III, pp. 581–607). Calcutta: The Ramakrishna Mission Institute of Calcutta.

Raju, P. T. (1985). *Structural depths of Indian thought*. New Delhi: South Asian Publishers.

Ramakrishna Rao, K. (1982). A priori and theoretical objections to Psi. *Journal of Indian Psychology*, *4*, 3–12.

Ramakrishna Rao, K. (1988). What is Indian psychology? *Journal of Indian Psychology*, *7*, 37–57.

Ramakrishna Rao, K. (1997). Two faces of consciousness: A look at Eastern and Western perspectives. *Journal of Indian Psychology*, *15*, 1–24.

Ramakrishna Rao, K. (2004). Centrality of consciousness in Indian psychology. In K. Joshi & M. Cornelissen (Eds.), *Consciousness, Indian psychology and yoga* (pp. 53-75). New Delhi: Centre for Studies in Civilizations.

Ramakrishna Rao, K., Dukhan, H., & Krishna Rao, P. V. (1978). Yogic meditation and Psi scoring in forced-choice and free-response tests. *Journal of Indian Psychology*, *1*, 160–175.

Ramalingam, P. (2002). *Applied psychology for world peace and prosperity*. New Delhi: PR Books.

Rennie, D. L., Watson, K. D., & Monteiro, A. M. (2002). The rise of qualitative research in psychology. *Canadian Psychology*, *43*, 179–189.

Richardson, J. T. E. (1996). *Handbook of qualitative research methods for psychology and the social sciences*. Leicester, UK: BPS Books (The British Psychological Society).

Rosch, E. (1997). Transformation of the Wolf Man. In J. Pickering (Ed.), *The authority of experience: Essays on Buddhism and psychology*. Surrey: Curzon Press.

Salsburg, D. S. (1985). The religion of statistics as practiced in medical journals. *The American Statistician*, *39*, 220–223.

Schultes, R. E., & Hofmann, A. (1992). *Plants of the gods: Their sacred, healing, and hallucinogenic powers*. Rochester, NY: Healing Arts Press.

Schwarz, N. (1999). Self-reports: How the questions shape the answers. *American Psychologist, 54*, 93–105.

Sedlmeier, P. (2006). The role of scales in student ratings. *Learning and Instruction*, *16*, 401–415.

Sedlmeier, P., Eberth, J., Schwarz, M., Zimmermann, D., Haarig, F., Jaeger, S., & Kunze, S. (2012). The psychological effects of meditation: A meta-analysis. *Psychological Bulletin*, 138, 1139-1171.

Sedlmeier, P. & Renkewitz, F. (2013). *Forschungsmethoden und Statistik: Ein Lehrbuch für Psychologen und Sozialwissenschaftler* (2. überarbeitete und erweiterte Auflage). [*Research methods and statistics: a textbook for psychologists and social scientists* (2nd revised edition)]. München: Pearson.

Shanon, B. (2001). Altered temporality. *Journal of Consciousness Studies, 8*, 35–58.

Shapiro, D. H. Jr., & Zifferblatt, S. M. (1976). Zen meditation and behavioral self-control. *American Psychologist, 31*, 519–532.

Sharma, C. (2003). *A critical survey of Indian philosophy*. Delhi: Motilal Banarsidass. (Original work published 1960).

Shear, J., & Jevning, R. (1999). Pure consciousness. *Journal of Consciousness Studies, 6*, 189–209.

Sheldon, K. M., & King, L. (2001). Why positive psychology is necessary. *American Psychologist, 56*, 216–217.

Shepard, R. N. (1978). Externalization of mental images and the act of creation. In B. S. Randhawa & W. E. Coffman (Eds.), *Visual learning, thinking, and communication*. New York: Academic Press.

Shukla, K. (2004). The tradition of the Buddhist Yoga. In K. Joshi & M. Cornelissen (Eds.), *Consciousness, Indian psychology and yoga* (pp. 104-116). New Delhi: Centre for Studies in Civilizations.

Singh, S. P. (2004). The Vedic seers quest for the supramental consciousness. In K. Joshi & M. Cornelissen (Eds.), *Consciousness, Indian psychology and yoga* (pp. 91–103). New Delhi: Centre for Studies in Civilizations.

Sinha, J. (1958). *Indian psychology* (Vol. 3). Calcutta: Sinha Publishing House.

Sitamma, M., Sridevi, K., & Krishna Rao, P. V. (1995). Three gunas and cognitive characteristics: A study of field dependence—independence and perceptual acuity. *Journal of Indian Psychology, 13*, 13–20.

Smith, J. A. (Ed.) (2003). *Qualitative psychology*. London: Sage.

Smith, M. L., & Glass, G. V. (1977). Meta-analysis of psychotherapy outcome studies. *American Psychologist, 32*, 752–760.

Srinivas, K. (2004). The social significance of Advaita Vedānta. *The Voice of Śaṅkara, 29*(1), 179–193.

Srinivas, K., & Krishna Mohan, K. (2004). The concept of mind in orthodox Indian thought: Its implications for modern psychology. In K. Joshi & M. Cornelissen (Eds.), *Consciousness, Indian psychology and yoga* (pp. 296–306). New Delhi: Centre for Studies in Civilizations.

Stevenson, I. (1987). *Children who remember previous lives: A question of reincarnation*. Charlottesville: University Press of Virginia.

Steyer, R., & Eid, M. (1993). *Messen und Testen*. Berlin: Springer.

Stoppard, J. M. (2002). Navigating the hazards of orthodoxy: Introducing a graduate course on qualitative methods into the psychology curriculum. *Canadian Psychology, 43*, 143–153.

Storm, L., Tressoldi, P. E., & Di Risio, L. (2010). Meta-analysis of free-response studies, 1992-2008: Assessing the noise reduction model in parapsychology. *Psychological Bulletin, 136*, 471-485.

Swami Jitatmananda. (2004). Spiritual experiences of Ramakrishna – Vivekananda. In K. Joshi & M. Cornelissen (Eds.), *Consciousness, Indian psychology and yoga* (pp. 145-176). New Delhi: Centre for Studies in Civilizations.

Tloczynski, J., & Tantiella, M. (1998). A comparison of the effects of Zen breath meditation or relaxation on college adjustment. *Psychologia, 41*, 32–43.

Travis, F., & Wallace, R. (1997). Autonomic markers during respiratory suspensions; possible markers of transcendental consciousness. *Psychophysiology, 34*, 39–46.

Utts, J. (1991). Replication and meta-analysis in parapsychology. *Statistical Science, 6*, 363-403.

Varela, F. J., & Shear, J. (1999). First-person methodologies: What, why, how? *Journal of Consciousness Studies, 6*, 1–14.

Velmans, M. (2001). A map of consciousness studies. In M. Cornelissen (Ed.), *Consciousness and its transformation* (pp. 257–282). Pondicherry: Sri Aurobindo International Centre of Education.

Vermersch, P. (1999). Introspection as practice. *Journal of Consciousness Studies, 6*, 17–42.

Wallace, B. A. (1999). The Buddhist tradition of *Samatha*. *Journal of Consciousness Studies, 6*, 175–187.

Wallace, B. A. & Shapiro, S. L. (2006). Mental balance and well-being: Building bridges between Buddhism and Western Psychology. *American Psychologist, 61*, 660–701.

Walsh, R. & Shapiro, S. L. (2006). The meeting of meditative disciplines and Western psychology: A mutually enriching dialogue. *American Psychologist, 61*, 227–239.

White, P. A. (1988). Knowing more about what we can tell: 'Introspective access' and causal report accuracy 10 years later. *British Journal of Psychology, 79*, 13–45.

Whiteman, J. H. M. (1993). *Aphorisms on spiritual method: The "Yoga Sutras of Patanjali" in the light of mystical experience*. Gerrards Cross: Colin Smythe.

Wolf, D. B. (1998). The Vedic personality inventory: A study of the gunas. *Journal of Indian Psychology, 16*, 26–43.

Wood, L. A., & Kroger, R. O. (2000). *Doing discourse analysis: Methods for studying action in talk and text*. Thousand Oaks, CA: Sage.

Woods, J. H. (1998). *The Yoga-System of Patanjali*. Delhi: Motilal Banarsidass. (Original work published 1914).

5

Integrating *yoga* epistemology and ontology into an expanded integral approach to research

William Braud

> This new psychology looks to me very much like children learning some summary and not very adequate alphabet... and imagining that their first book of obscure beginnings...is the very heart of the real knowledge. They look from down up and explain the higher lights by the lower obscurities; but the foundation of these things is above and not below... The superconscient, not the subconscient, is the true foundation of things. The significance of the lotus is not to be found by analysing the secrets of the mud from which it grows here; its secret is to be found in the heavenly archetype of the lotus that blooms for ever in the Light above. ... [You] must know the whole before you can know the part and the highest before you can truly understand the lowest. That is the promise of the greater psychology awaiting its hour ...
>
> (Sri Aurobindo, 1993, p. 97)

This chapter addresses ways in which *yogic* (and related) principles and practices can be introduced more fully into psychological research, in order to allow that research—and psychology itself—to be more inclusive, integrated, and relevant to human psychospiritual concerns. Much of the chapter takes the form of an illustrative case study of how this approach already is being implemented in the curriculum of one graduate psychology programme—that of the Institute of Transpersonal Psychology in Palo Alto, CA.

For students who initially encounter research courses in their graduate psychology training, *research* and *empirical* are thought to be synonymous with *quantitative* and *experimental*. In the research courses of the Institute of Transpersonal Psychology, however, they soon come to appreciate that there is more to quantitative research than experiments—that this form of research also includes less restrictive causal-comparative and correlational approaches. More important, they also quickly learn that research legitimately includes even less restrictive *qualitative* approaches, and that *empirical* can be understood in its original meaning of being based on *experience*. This growth of students' understanding of the nature of research mimics the ongoing extension and expansion of research and disciplined inquiry approaches in psychology at large.

Although still enthralled by positivistic and cognitive behavioural assumptions and practices, researchers in psychology now are employing an increasing variety of qualitative methods and inquiry approaches. These include forms of research with names such as cooperative inquiry, grounded theory, hermeneutics, heuristic research, multiple case studies, narrative research, participatory action research, and phenomenological research (see Braud & Anderson, 1998). Virtually all of these acknowledge the crucial importance of the researcher as the chief instrument of knowing and also emphasize human lived experiences as their primary subject matter.

Along with this felicitous extension and expansion of research approaches, there has been a corresponding growth in the recognition of alternative and complementary modes of knowing. Within psychology, some of these have been identified with different intelligences (multiple intelligences, somatic intelligence, emotional intelligence, spiritual intelligence), feminine ways of knowing, forms of knowing associated with different states of consciousness, intuition, tacit knowing, and different forms of learning and memory (see Braud, 2006a).

Contemporary psychologists now recognize an expanded range of what might be known. They study observable behaviours and actions of individuals, groups, societies, and cultures, but they also have developed technologies that allow them to explore covert processes such as physiological reactions and the concomitants of imagery, thinking, memories, and volition. They now investigate intangibles such as 'qualia', meanings, imaginings, symbolic and even unconscious processes.

These developments have been useful and fruitful, yet they remain unnecessarily limited. Despite these extensions and expansions, much still has been left out, and much remains undone. There is a need for even more inclusive forms of research and disciplined inquiry—forms that provide greater opportunities for synergistic interactions of knowledge gain, clinical and other practical applications, and the personal and psychospiritual growth, development, and even possible transformation of the researcher. There is a need for effective bridging of science and the various spiritual and wisdom traditions. Growth in areas of morality, scholarship, depth and subtlety of thought, care, and wisdom seems not to have kept pace with the growth of knowledge. Although we have experienced great advances in technology, today we appear to know more and more about less and less, and know less and less about truly important matters—matters of ultimate concern.

Indian psychology and *yogic* epistemology and ontology can contribute much to enrich research and help satisfy the needs mentioned above. The aim of this chapter is to describe ways in which *yogic* principles, and processes closely related to these, already have been usefully introduced into research praxis, and to suggest additional ways in which aspects of *yoga* might be integrated into research in the future and how this might enliven and transform the research enterprise. Before treating these contributions, some additional background will be useful.

A pluralistic epistemology

Above, there was an allusion to the increasing recognition, in Western psychology, of alternative modes of knowing. Different forms of knowing have received equal or greater attention outside of Western psychology—in philosophy and in the great spiritual and wisdom traditions, particularly in the Indian tradition.

Virtually all traditions have distinguished forms of knowing that are *intellectual* and *of the head* from those that are *experiential* and *of the heart.* In intellectual knowing, the knower is removed from what is to be known; the knowing is mediated, and it tends to be academic, abstract, and cognitive. Experiential knowing is fully and deeply lived, immediate, and embodied; it tends to be particular and concrete.

In the West, these major complementary forms of knowing have been variously described and named. In early Greek philosophy, they appear as *dianoia* (the discursive, conceptualizing, and logical faculty) and *nous* (the largest manifestation of mind, the deepest core of one's being that could know the inner essences or principles of things by means of direct apprehension or perception). *Dianoia* was only part of *nous* (see Palmer, Sherrard & Ware, 1995, pp. 427–437). *Nous* possessed qualities 'more spiritual than mind, more intellectual than spirit' (Underhill, 1960, p. 121). In the well-known opening passage of *Ennead* 4.8.1, Plotinus (1988) mentioned descending from Intellect (*nous*) to discursive reasoning (*dianoia*).

In the Middle Ages, the different forms of knowing often were described as different *eyes*—the *eye of the flesh* (sensory knowing), the *eye of reason* (mental knowing), and the *eye of contemplation* (spiritual knowing). These ways of knowing were elaborated, for example, by Boethius, by Hugh of St. Victor and other Victorine mystics (Richard of St. Victor, Thomas of St. Victor), by Bonaventure, and by Thomas Aquinas (see Boethius, 524/1980; Bonaventure, 1259/1953; McGinn, 1996, 1998; Thomas Aquinas, 1267-1273/1971).

Roger Bacon (1268/1928) distinguished two modes of acquiring knowledge: by *reasoning* [*argument*] and by *experience*. For Bacon, nothing could be sufficiently known without experience; when one has had an actual experience, one's mind was made certain and rested in the full light of truth.

William James, in the *Principles of Psychology* (1890/1950, pp. 221–222), distinguished two kinds of knowledge: *knowledge-about* (which might also be called representative knowledge, and of which thoughts, conceptions, and judgments are the vehicles) and *knowledge of [or by] acquaintance* (of which feelings, emotions, and sensations are the vehicles). The former can be imparted to others; the latter, because it is a direct and immediate experience, cannot be so imparted—through conventional means—but must be partaken of, directly, by another, in order to be appreciated.

Similar distinctions have been made in the various streams of the Sufism tradition:

> Knowledge is empty unless it is connected internally with what is known. Reason always means knowledge at a distance, across the mediation of language and concepts; but wisdom presupposes something like the intimacy of becoming what one knows. "What a difference there is," al-Ghazali writes in his autobiography, "between *knowing* the definition of health and satiety, together with their causes and presuppositions, and *being* healthy and satisfied!" (p. 55). Only the mystics can raise knowledge to the level of *gnosis* (*ma'rifa*), in which one experiences what one knows with all the intimacy of being... (Bruns, 1992, p. 127).

Within the Naqshbandi tradition of Sufism, in using experiences with fruit as metaphors for knowing the Divine, the forms of knowing are elaborated further:

> Three 'kinds of knowledge'...have to be separated, and the difference has to be felt:
>
> - The description of something—as in the words used to convey the idea of a fruit;
> - The feeling of something, as when one can see, feel, and smell a fruit;
> - The perceptive connection with something, as when one takes and tastes, eats and absorbs a fruit.

These three departments of cognition are described in more technical language as:

> - Certain knowledge *(Ilm-al-Yaqin)*, which comes from the intellect, which tells us that there is a fruit;
> - Eye of certainty *(Ayn-al-Yaqin)*, which is from the 'inner eye', and operates like the senses but in relation to deeper things; the 'assessment of a fruit';
> - Perfect truth (*Haqq-al-Yaqin*), which is the experience of 'union with Truth' (Schneck, 1980, pp. 32–33).

Additional forms of knowing that have been treated in the West include Dilthey's concepts of *Erlebnis* ('intentional experience'), *Verstehen* ('empathetic understanding'), and *Nachleben* ('re-experiencing' or 'reliving'; see Hargiss, 2001); *tacit knowing* and *personal knowledge* (Polanyi, 1964); a form of knowing called *mimesis*, in which a member of the audience of a performance comes to know through imitation, personal identification, and sympathetic resonance with a performer (Havelock, 1963; Simon, 1978); and *ritual knowing*, in which participation in a ritual can allow one to know in a more direct personal manner and embody what is being addressed in the ritual and can facilitate transformative change (Deslauriers, 1992), especially in liminal contexts (McMahon, 1998). To these may be added knowing through affect, compassion, and love; through being and becoming what is to be known; through direct knowing and intuition; through sympathetic resonance and empathy; through *unknowing*; and through *pure consciousness* (see Braud & Anderson, 1998; Forman, 1997, 1999). The varieties of paranormal knowing—processes identified as telepathy, clairvoyance, and precognition—also can be added to this listing (see, for example, Braud, 2006a; Rammohan, 2002).

Within the *yogic* and Indian psychology traditions, the means of knowing have been described with great subtlety and precision. Three aspects of knowing, in particular, can be highlighted here: the refinement of knowing within the training system of the Patañjali *Yoga-Sūtras*, Sri Aurobindo's views of the four types of knowledge, and Sri Aurobindo's views of the process of intuition.

The eight limbs described in the Patañjali *Yoga-Sūtras* (see, for example, Woods, 1927) provide ways of readying and purifying the body, emotions, and mind for a form of knowing through being or identifying with what is to be known, achieved through *saṁyama*, the intensive and conjoint practice of the last three limbs of *dhāraṇā* (concentration), *dhyāna* (contemplation or meditation), and *samādhi* (absorption). The several limbs of Patañjali *Rājayoga—yama, niyama, āsana, prāṇāyāma, pratyāhāra, dhāraṇā, dhyāna, samādhi*—provide methods for systematically reducing the possible environmental, social, bodily, sensory, emotional, and cognitive sources of 'noise' or distraction that might serve as impediments to, or distortions of, accurate and sensitive knowing.

Sri Aurobindo (1972, p. 524) identified and described four forms of knowing that occur in our ordinary waking consciousness:

> Our surface cognition, our limited and restricted mental way of looking at our self, at our inner movements and at the world outside us and its objects and happenings, is so constituted that it derives in different degrees from a fourfold order of knowledge... A knowledge by identity, a knowledge by intimate direct contact, a knowledge by separative direct contact, a wholly separative knowledge by indirect contact are the four cognitive methods of Nature.

These four types of knowledge have been clearly elaborated by Matthijs Cornelissen (see this volume, pp. 99–104).

Sri Aurobindo (1972, pp. 946–947, 949) described a special form of knowing that he called *intuition*. Intuition, of course, has meant many different things to different people. For Sri Aurobindo, it has a special meaning, as follows:

> Intuition is a power of consciousness nearer and more intimate to the original knowledge by identity; for it is always something that leaps out direct from a concealed identity. It is when the consciousness of the subject meets with the consciousness in the object, penetrates it and sees, feels or vibrates with the truth of what it contacts, that the intuition leaps out like a spark or lightning-flash from the shock of the meeting; or when the consciousness, even without any such meeting, looks into itself and feels directly and intimately the truth or the truths that are there or so contacts the hidden forces behind appearances, then also there is the outbreak of an intuitive light; or, again, when the consciousness meets the Supreme Reality or the spiritual reality of things and beings and has a contactual union with it, then the spark, the flash or the blaze of intimate truth-perception is lit in its depths. This close perception is more than sight, more than conception: it is the result of a penetrating and revealing touch which carries in it sight and conception as part of itself or as its natural consequence. A concealed or slumbering identity, not yet recovering itself, still remembers or conveys by the intuition its own contents and the intimacy of its self-feeling and self-vision of things, its light of truth, its overwhelming and automatic certitude....
>
> Intuition has a fourfold power. A power of revelatory truth-seeing, a power of inspiration or truth-hearing, a power of truth-touch or immediate

> seizing of significance, which is akin to the ordinary nature of its intervention in our mental intelligence, a power of true and automatic discrimination of the orderly and exact relation of truth to truth, — these are the fourfold potencies of Intuition. Intuition can therefore perform all the action of reason, — including the function of logical intelligence, which is to work out the right relation of things and the right relation of idea with idea, — but by its own superior process and with steps that do not fail or falter.

Don Salmon (2001, pp. 31–33) has provided a useful treatment of Sri Aurobindo's views on intuition, elaborating the concept, identifying it with Sri Aurobindo's conception of the faculty of supramental consciousness (Sri Aurobindo's *vijñāna*), distinguishing it from other processes, indicating how it underlies all other forms of knowing, and suggesting ways in which intuition might be developed. The latter is treated later in this chapter.

> The simplest description of intuition is the direct knowledge of Reality, a knowledge in which the knower is not separate from either the process of knowing or the object which is known... It is the consciousness of the subject (the percipient for which the brain constructs the image) meeting up with the consciousness in the object (the apparently separate perceived object — a chair, tree, rock, etc.) that is united by means of an intuition which is rooted in the same Self common to both... In using intuition one has to become involved in what one knows, but without getting lost in it... Intuition underlies virtually all forms of knowing, whether instinctive, aesthetic, imaginative or intellectual.

An additional form of knowing, described in certain Indian traditions, is that of *śaktipatha*, which involves the direct transmission of experiential knowledge or 'spiritual energy' from one person to another (usually from *guru* to *celā*), which may influence a dramatic change in being in the recipient of such a transmission.

The various Western and Indian views presented above suggest a pluralistic epistemology involving a *spectrum of ways of knowing*. The range and varieties of what might be known in these different ways also suggests a pluralistic ontology—a *spectrum of knowables*, with each aspect of that spectrum having its distinctive reality.

A pluralistic ontology

Near the beginning of this chapter, the variety of 'objects of knowing' that are being explored in contemporary Western psychology—the 'big three' being affects, behaviours, and cognitions—was mentioned. This could be expanded to include a wide range of physical, physiological, somatic, emotional, mental, imaginal, societal, and cultural processes and contents, which can be addressed by a combination of first-person, second-person, and third-person approaches that are being applied to the study of consciousness (e.g., Varela & Shear, 2002) and by means of the four major perspectives described by Ken Wilber (2000) in his popular 'all quadrants, all levels' (AQAL) model (which addresses objects of knowing and corresponding ways of knowing that can focus on interior or exterior aspects of individuals or collectives). This spectrum of what might be known can be filled out and extended by adding sensations, perceptions, feelings, memories, meanings, symbolic appreciations, and other 'qualia'.

However, these additions are not sufficiently bold. To be true to human experience, we should add more *subtle qualities* of things, others, and ourselves—characteristics that might be perceived not in more conventional ways, but through less familiar forms of inner knowing, direct knowing, intuition, and gnosis. Some of these would include subtle fields and subtle energies around or within objects, plants, animals, and persons; perceived 'presences' of various sorts; experiential encounters with other realms or beings, with the Self, with the Divine, with the One.

The perceptions and knowings of the types of subtle qualities just mentioned can be treated in conventional science, psychology, and phenomenology simply as *experiences*, without confronting the issue of the ontological status of the objects or elicitors of the experiences. The question of the reality of these objects/elicitors receives much greater attention in parapsychology and psychical research, transpersonal psychology, mystical studies, and in the great wisdom and spiritual traditions. These objects or elicitors are just as 'real' as are the more familiar objects of our experience, but that they partake of different forms of reality that usually are not available to our conventional senses in ordinary conditions of consciousness but can become available to faculties that are understood as unconscious or superconscious, in other states of consciousness. In the terminology of the three eyes of knowing, these objects and elicitors may not be 'seen' by the eye of flesh, but may be seen by the eyes of the mind, of the heart, of the spirit. An even bolder suggestion would be that each object of knowing possesses its own form of consciousness with which the consciousness of the knower can connect and thus know directly, in an 'internal' manner. Such a suggestion is consistent with Sri Aurobindo's (1970, pp. 2, 234–237) view that consciousness and inherent intuition are present throughout existence—both above and below the human range, even in 'inanimate' matter, where it may appear nonexistent—but variable in its status, condition, and operation.

Mentioning the three eyes raises the issue of matching the appropriate eye to the nature of what is to be seen. Ken Wilber (1990) has warned of the risk of *category error*, when one eye attempts 'to usurp the roles of the other two' (p. 7). There would appear to be three positions with respect to this issue. First, one can contend that each eye (each mode of knowing) is adapted and specialized (prepared, adequate) for one set of 'data' (objects, elicitors); each eye can see only in its own realm, and it makes no sense to expect one eye to look into the realm of another eye. Second, one can agree that each eye is optimized for a particular realm, but some seepage or crosstalk (generalization, transfer) can occur; one eye may, under special conditions, see imperfect glimpses, or glimpses of only certain aspects, of what usually is available only to another eye. Third, perhaps the eyes have different fields of view; some eyes may see only very narrowly (their own realms), whereas others might have much broader and deeper vision and might see all or nearly all of what might be seen (in all or nearly all realms).

In agreement with this first position, one might imagine a spectrum of modes of knowing perfectly aligned with a spectrum of knowables, with very narrow correspondences and limitations of what each mode is able to know. This is perhaps the most commonly accepted view of science and of disciplined inquiry. According to the second position, category errors could be defeated in that some features of some knowables could be available to all modes of knowing. Examples of this possibility are the empirical findings within the field of parapsychology (psi research) that the thoughts and intentions of one person may be associated with traces that can influence other persons or even physical measuring devices; other examples would be observations of certain parapsychological resemblances or analogs of mystical and revelatory experiences, or observations of brain activity patterns associated with forms of meditation, contemplation, and prayer. Here, it might be more accurate to speak of *varieties*, rather than *spectra*, of knowings and knowables, with various degrees of overlaps among them.

A more detailed example, presented elsewhere (Braud, 1994, p. 30), may further clarify the nature of this second position:

> Imagine a three-dimensional cube constructed of twelve sticks, and imagine a light source projecting the shadow of this cube frame onto a two-dimensional sheet of paper. Viewed only as a two-dimensional projection, the cube has lost its third dimension, and its reality has been "stepped down." Imagine, further, that the light source begins to move and that the cube begins to move and to rotate. The cube's two-dimensional projection will change dramatically. If one is limited to a study of the two-dimensional surface, what one can say about the cube itself will be limited and necessarily incomplete. The constantly

> changing, and sometimes apparently contradictory, patterns of the projections may lead to confusion and seeming paradoxes about the source of these shadows. To attempt to draw final conclusions about the nature of the cube from any one shadow-pattern would be unwise. To build up a conception of the cube gradually, and by considering all of the projections and their possible interrelationships, would provide a truer picture of the cube's nature. Although each projection is incomplete, it is nonetheless true to a particular aspect of the cube. Invariant relationships of aspects of the cube in three-space will be reflected in similarly invariant relationships within the two-space shadow projections. *The projections never tell us anything false about the cube.* Their lessons are merely incomplete and relative.

In this cube-and-shadows example, the 'eye' of the two-dimensional paper can capture at least certain aspects of the cube that would be available to an 'eye' capable of seeing the cube, clearly and directly, in three-dimensional space.

According to the third position, a certain form of knowing might be able to access the essential qualities of all knowables. This would seem to be the contention of Sri Aurobindo, when he argues that knowledge by identity (*Vedic* knowledge) or by intuition can know all that is essential about the Many because of the underlying oneness shared by the knower and the multiple knowns. Relevant here are the *Upaniṣadic* avowal, 'When That is known, all is known' (cited in Cornelissen, 2001, p. 8), as well as Sri Aurobindo's (1981) statement about knowing 'the entire universe in one of its frontal appearances' (p. 30).

Another issue that arises in the context of the plurality of knowing modes and the manifold objects of knowing is the question of whether there might be hierarchies of efficacy, power, or quality for the various ways of knowing and of value, worth, or importance for the many objects of knowing. Such hierarchies (or holarchies) are implied by the spectrum conceptualization. Inequalities among forms of knowing and among what might be known are implied by Kurt Gödel's and Gregory Chaitin's theorems and theories that certain things are not knowable within a given system and that no system can explain any other system that is more complex than itself (Gödel, 1962; Nagel & Newman, 1958; Rucker, 1987), as well as by Huston Smith's (1992, pp. 119, 151, 200) contention that a form of knowing might not be capable of understanding anything that is superior to itself in qualities of intelligence, awareness, compassion, value, or worth. These views suggest that there are certain things that we might never truly know. However, this position might be countered by the understanding of *tat tvam asi* (that thou art)—that in an essential and profound manner we *are* all things and therefore are able to know all things, through a knowledge by identity.

Given these contextualizations of the ranges and limits of knowings and knowables, we are ready to move on to a consideration of practical ways in which *yogic* principles and techniques have been or might be introduced into research praxis.

Initial integrations of *yogic* principles and practices into research

This section provides descriptions of ways in which *yogic* and related principles and practices already are being implemented into the forms of research conducted at the Institute of Transpersonal Psychology.

The Institute's general atmosphere. Because of the Institute's emphasis on transpersonal psychology, its general ambiance already is one that is favourable to the aims, values, and principles of *yoga* and Indian Psychology. Most of the faculty and students already have backgrounds, interests, and experiences relevant to spirituality and to psychospiritual growth and transformation. In addition, the Institute's pedagogy emphasizes experiential and whole-person teaching and learning, and this fits well with the general emphases of *yoga*. A subset of the faculty and students are engaged more specifically and actively in the spiritual and wisdom traditions of Hinduism, Buddhism, Advaita Vedānta, and various forms of *yoga*, per se, and these persons already are integrating *yogic* and *yogic*-like principles and practices into their lives and work, including their research endeavours. All of this provides a very hospitable context for the implementation of the ways of Indian Psychology into the research conducted at the Institute. However, the presence of this special conducive atmosphere, to the extent that it is not available elsewhere, suggests caution in generalizing what may or may not be possible or successful in other research contexts.

Inclusions in Integral Inquiry. The research approach of Integral Inquiry (Braud, 1994, 1998a, 1998b) includes several principles and practices that are directly or indirectly related to *yoga* and to Indian psychology more generally. The naming of this approach had nothing to do with the Integral Yoga and Integral Yoga Psychology of Sri Aurobindo (1948/2000) and The Mother, the integral structure of consciousness described by Jean Gebser (1949/1986), or the Integral Psychology of Ken Wilber (2000). However, the approach has considerable overlaps with these views. With Integral Yoga, the approach shares the aim of being as inclusive and integrative as possible, in both its epistemology and its ontology. The approach acknowledges the legitimacy of a great variety of ways of knowing (endorsing William James' [1912/1976] *radical empiricism*) and levels of what is to be known (levels of reality). The following are additional areas of overlap and correspondence between Integral Inquiry and the emphases of Integral Yoga and Indian psychology at large:

- Emphasis on experience as disciplined inquiry's primary subject matter
- Research may be transformative for the researcher, the research participants, and the audience of a research report
- Inclusion of bodily, emotional, aesthetic, and intellectual facets in research and as validity indicators
- Recognition of the limitations of purely intellectual or exclusively sensory approaches to research
- The importance of the processes of intention, attention, and intuition in research
- The possibility of direct knowing and knowing through being or becoming what is to be known
- Stressing the importance of the adequacy or preparedness of the researcher
- Clearing and optimizing researcher-as-instrument through reduction of psychological impedance and sources of distraction, bias, and 'noise'
- Patañjali's *saṁyama* as a way of knowing
- Acknowledging the research-relevant contributions of many disciplines (natural sciences, social and human sciences, humanities, arts, spiritual and wisdom traditions)

Preparation of the researcher. It is well recognized that a researcher's knowledge, skills, and characteristics are of the utmost importance in research. The researcher's own qualities inform all aspects of a research project. These qualities help determine the subjects and topics to be investigated; how projects are framed; the nature of research hypotheses or questions; how research participants are treated; how data are collected, analyzed, and reported; and where and how one looks for inspiration and support throughout the research process. Researcher characteristics are especially important in *qualitative* research, in which the researcher is the major 'instrument' in the research project, and in which all materials are collected, processed, and interpreted through the filters that are the researcher's personal qualities. This aspect of research has been recognized in the qualitative approach of grounded theory in its treatment of *theoretical sensitivity*, in which the investigator's prior familiarity with what is studied and her or his observational and interpretative experiences and skills help inform the theories that are being developed along with data interactions throughout a research project (Glaser, 1978). Investigator qualities also have been treated by Skolimowski (1994) in terms of the various *sensitivities* of the knower, and by Schumacher (1978) as the knower's *adaequatio* (adequateness) with respect to that which is to be known. The essence of these and other related treatments is that a researcher can know only that for which his or her being has been adequately prepared. Some of this preparation may be influenced by preexisting dispositions (perhaps genetically or *karmically*-informed), and other aspects may be developed through appropriate *training*. The important role that *yoga* might play in such training has been expressed well by Cornelissen (2001, p. 11):

> A considerable purification of one's inner instrument, or *antahkarana* is essential. The ... yogic traditions ... all have ... methods to improve the range, ... "resolution" and ... reliability of inner perception. These ... can be grouped into those that aim at greater concentration, at freedom from the sense-mind leading to an ability to penetrate the deeper and higher layers of consciousness, and at freedom from partial identifications, that is from the body, ... vital drives and emotions, ... thoughts and ... ego-sense. These techniques are ... considered to lead to a free consciousness, capable of watching the movements of *Prakriti*, nature, as a completely independent witness, making it possible to observe inner events ... with a greater precision, ... perfect "objectivity" and ... reliability. The inner disciplines of Yoga can thus play exactly the same role for a science of the inner realities as modern technology is playing for the material sciences.

Although, in this comment, Cornelissen was addressing the use of *yogic* preparation in developing more accurate introspection, in refining the observation of inner experience, the same techniques can be applied in preparing and purifying the researcher's *antaḥkaraṇa* (internal organ of knowing) for a deeper, more accurate, and more satisfying study of any object of inquiry. This purification process can allow the researcher to reduce various distractions and biases that might distort what is to be known. This is similar to, but much more profound than, the role played by the so-called *bracketing* process in phenomenological research (see Polkinghorne, 1989), in which one attempts to set aside preconceptions and pre-understandings of what is studied. The *yogic* preparation and purification is more profound in that it addresses a much wider and deeper range of possible distractors or impediments to knowing that can exist not only at the cognitive level, but at sensory, bodily, emotional, and more subtle levels, as well. Besides reducing possibly interfering 'noise' or distractions, these same preparatory and purifying techniques—in the form, for example, of practicing the eight limbs of Patañjali's *Aṣṭāṅgayoga*—can help the researcher adjust his or her very being in ways that can allow more direct forms of knowing the object of research (that is, forms of knowing through being or becoming what is to be known).

At the Institute, Olga Louchakova (2005) has been developing a training programme for enhancing the researcher's preparedness, 'fitness' (*adaequatio*), 'clear mind' or 'clear internal instrument' (*antaḥkaraṇa śuddhi*), and capacity for 'knowledge by presence', based on principles and practices from the traditions of Vedānta, Śākta-Vedānta, Sufism, and Hesychasm (the early mystical tradition within Christianity).

This researcher training was intended to develop the following qualities, as understood in the Indian and related traditions, and as summarized in Louchakova's report (2005, paraphrased from p. 98):

- Discrimination (*viveka*)—the capacity of discernment of real and unreal, that is, between cognitions of constant and changing elements of the mind, and eventually between pure awareness and phenomenal awareness
- Dispassion (*vairāgya*)—due to cessation of resolved or satisfied desires, as a precondition for knowledge of the Self, to be followed by control of the mind and senses, cessation of social activity, control of passions and endurance, settling down to reflect on the nature of consciousness, and faith
- Passionate desire for liberation (*mumukṣutvam*)
- Qualities of humility, modesty, nonviolence, endurance, simplicity, purity, persistence, and self-control (from the Śākta-Vedānta tradition)
- Removal of the 'veils' of the mind, in its natural condition, through persistence in study, contemplation, spiritual discipline

and exercise, in the quest to develop a 'mind of the heart', that is, direct intuition, rather than knowledge via logical processes (from the Sufism tradition)

- Purifying the heart through watchfulness, curtailing passions, resisting temptation to the external senses, and developing detachment, mindfulness, and inwardly deployed attention (from the Hesychasm tradition)

Developing the qualities noted above can help correct mental and character structures and processes that ordinarily interfere with the clarity of direct perception and direct knowing.

The actual training exercises involved practice of mindfulness in identifying, recognizing, and naming forms of internal awareness (sensing, feeling, imagining, and thinking); reflecting on the type of research paradigm (for example, positivism/postpositivism, critical theory, constructivism) that best fitted the researcher's project and aims; and developing knowledge through presence (developing 'mind of the heart') through a technique of focused introspection on the sense of self, localizing awareness in the inner space of the (right side of the) chest.

Louchakova (2005, pp. 106–107) described outcomes of the training as follows:

> Students described the layers of introspective experiences as emerging in the following succession: (a) sense of personal self of the right side of the chest; (b) sensory experiences; (c) ... rising emotions, subtler sensations of energy, and breath; (d) ... 'talking' mind; (e) ... images; (f) stillness, nothing, unknowing, like in a deep sleep ... (g) ... sheer intellect, meanings, and vast space and subtle mental states, archetypes, and essential relations, ... (h) absorption of awareness in pure subjective consciousness .... Students ... learn to differentiate between the various manifestations of consciousness ... This direct knowledge of the structures of the psyche provides a very tangible help in learning the skills of phenomenological analysis, by correlating the maxims of phenomenology and one's own inner experience. Phenomenology stops being perceived as an abstract philosophical system and becomes a practical guide to self-understanding and interior transformation.

The exercises mentioned above focused upon the preparation of the researcher for phenomenological research; however, their use may be generalized to other forms of qualitative research and, indeed, to research in general. Like these exercises, the practice of the eight limbs of Patañjali *yoga* and of the integral research skills described below also can foster a greater preparedness and adequacy of the researcher.

Integral research skills. 'Integral Research Skills' is the name of the first in a sequence of research courses offered at the Institute. This course is placed first because it provides a very accessible introduction to research. In this course, students learn how personal and spiritual practices can be translated into skills that can be used in the service of research. The skills can play three roles in research—they can help increase the sensitivities and preparedness of the researcher, they can provide vehicles for multiple modalities of knowing, and they can allow access to a greater range of what might be known in any research project. The skills are relevant to Indian Psychology and to *yoga* in that they can help researchers experience more expanded aspects of themselves and of their potentials, they can help establish preconditions for direct knowing, and some of them closely resemble actual *yogic* techniques. The skills are called integral research skills because when used together they can help provide a complete and integrated (integral) appreciation of the topic being studied.

Table 5.1 indicates the skills covered in this course, along with brief descriptions of how each skill is practiced and used. Students identify and practice these skills through experiential exercises presented by the course instructor. They then indicate how they might use the skills, in themselves—as researchers—in the three major phases of any quantitative or qualitative research project (planning and collecting data, working with data, presenting data). They also are encouraged to introduce the skills more fully into their professional

The skills	Their description, practice, and use
Working with intention	Awareness of, and deliberate framing of, intentions for all phases of a research project
Quieting and slowing	Sets stage for use of other skills, relaxes and quiets, reduces distractions and 'noise' at many levels, reduces structures and constraints, allows change, allows fuller observations and appreciation of more subtle aspects of what is studied
Playing	Fosters curiosity, creativity, and insight; encourages beginner's mind; provides novelty, new combinations; encourages excitement, enthusiasm, exploration
Working with attention	Practice in deploying, focusing, and shifting attention; deautomatizing attention; attending to different forms and channels of information; changing focal plane or magnification of attention; developing witnessing consciousness
Auditory skills	Practice in devoting more complete attention to external and internal sounds and to sound memories and sound imagination
Visual skills, imagery, visualization, imagination	Practice in devoting more complete attention to outer and inner sights and images; use of memory images, visualization, spontaneous and guided imagery; active imagination; empowered imagination
Kinesthetic skills	Practice in knowing, remembering, and expressing knowing and being through gross and subtle movements
Proprioceptive skills	Practice in identifying and attending to subtle visceral and muscular sensations; working with felt senses, feelings, affective knowing
Direct knowing, intuition, empathic identification	Identifying with the object of knowing; knowing through presence, empathy, sympathy, compassion, love, being, becoming, participation; sympathetic resonance; empathic identification; parapsychological processes
Accessing unconscious processes and materials	Reducing egoic control; tacit knowing; liminal and transitional conditions; incubation; attention to vehicles that carry previously unconscious information; identifying unconscious tendencies
Mindfulness	Being present in time, capacity to identify and disidentify appropriately, self-awareness, skills of self-observation
Discernment	Mature judgment, integrity, capacity to know the sources and natures of events that arise in consciousness
Compassion	Empathy, service, personal presence, caring and love for others, understanding the feelings and experiences of others
Appreciation of differences	Openness to new information, assumptions, and other ways of being, knowing, and doing; openness to change; flexibility, inclusiveness, and tolerance; honouring of differences and others

Table 5.1. Integral research skills and how they are practised and used

work and into their lives, in the service of their personal growth and development.

In addition to working with these skills, themselves, as researchers, students are encouraged to consider ways in which they might request the research participants in their future studies to use similar skills—for purposes of remembering, reliving, and communicating past or present experiences to the researcher, in ways that might be more complete, detailed, and accurate than what might be possible without the use of such techniques. Also, students are asked to consider how they might ask the audiences/readers of their research reports to use similar skills, in order to more fully receive the findings that are being presented to them.

Some of the integral research skills mentioned above are closely related to principles and practices of Indian Psychology and, especially, to certain of the eight limbs of Patañjali *yoga*. None of the skills are closely related to the first two limbs *yama* (restraints) and *niyama* (observances). Quieting and slowing are somewhat related to the third and fourth limbs of *āsana* (postures) and *prāṇāyāma* (vital energy/breath control). The auditory, visual, kinesthetic, and proprioceptive skills, to the extent that these involve shifts away from the outer world and toward inner experience, are somewhat aligned with the fifth limb of *pratyāhāra* (sensory withdrawal). The skills of attention, direct knowing, intuition, empathic identification — and, to some extent, slowing and quieting as well — share certain features with the sixth, seventh, and eighth limbs of *dhāraṇā* (concentration), *dhyāna* (meditation), and *samādhi* (absorption). Direct knowing itself, as a form of knowing through being or becoming or by identity, is related most closely to the intensive and conjoint practice of *dhāraṇā*, *dhyāna*, and *samādhi*, treated as *saṁyama* in the *Yoga-Sūtras* of Patañjali. The skill of playing, of course, resonates with the Hindu concept of *līlā*, cosmic play.

Yogic principles and practices in psi research. The important roles that Indian thought and *yogic* principles and practices have played in psi research (the scientific and scholarly study of paranormal processes of telepathy, clairvoyance, precognition, psychokinesis, and related phenomena) have been treated extensively elsewhere (for example, Braud, 2006b; Rammohan, 2002; Rao, 2002). *Yogic* applications in psi research have emphasized both theory (for example, the relevance of the *guṇas* and the *siddhis*) and technique (particularly the relevance of some of the limbs of Patañjali's *Aṣṭāṅgayoga* for the somatic and psychological preparation of research participants in psi experiments). Here is a summary, in tabular form, of how researchers have used practices related to those of several of the limbs of *Aṣṭāṅgayoga* in conducting experiments and exploring relationships in various areas of psi research. Table 5.2 is organized simply to indicate concentrations and patterns of research—four *clusters* of research areas that correspond to four *clusters* of *yogic* techniques—rather than precise one-to-one correspondences; it is recognized that the various *yogic* practices are interrelated, as are the processes at work in the various psi research areas. The reader is referred to Braud (2006b) for detailed treatments of this material. It may be of interest to note that virtually all of these applications have been in psi research projects that have been carried out in a *quantitative* research fashion.

The use of techniques similar to the *yogic* practices in experimental psi research not only indicates the relevance of the Indian practices to research, but to the extent that their practice is associated with accurate psi functioning in the experiments, the experiment outcomes provide empirical support for the existence of the *siddhi*-like processes that are believed, in Indian thought, to be associated with the extensive practice of the *yogic* techniques in more natural settings. These empirical confirmations of certain *yogic* claims increase the possibility that future research will support the validity of other *yogic* epistemological and ontological claims as well.

Further possibilities

The foregoing section outlined the beginnings of attempts to introduce *yogic* principles and practices into quantitative and (especially) qualitative research. There are several ways in which such introductions and integrations might be increased in the future:

Psi research areas	*Yogic* practices
—	*Yama* (restraints) *Niyama* (observances)
Relaxation research Hypnosis research Physiological research	*Āsana* (postures) *Prāṇāyāma* (vital energy/breath control)
Dream telepathy research Ganzfeld research	*Pratyāhāra* (sensory withdrawal)
Concentration/visualization in receptive psi Concentration/visualization in active psi Meditation research Absorption research	*Dhāraṇā* (concentration) *Dhyāna* (meditation) *Samādhi* (absorption)

Table 5.2. Areas of psi research and corresponding 'limbs' of *yogic* practice

- Practices associated with each of the limbs of *Aṣṭāṅgayoga* could be introduced more fully and more formally into research praxis. Presently, practices associated with the first two limbs — *yama* (restraints) and *niyama* (observances) — are conspicuously absent. The relevance of these two limbs not only to research dealing with psycho-spiritual topics but to research at large would seem to be an especially fruitful arena for future exploration. The practice of these two limbs should be especially useful for enhancing the preparedness (adequacy) of the researcher.
- In order to introduce forms of inner knowing (direct knowing, knowledge by identity, intuition) into research, ways of training and development of these forms can be investigated more fully. An obvious first approach to developing direct knowing is the practice of the eight limbs of *Aṣṭāṅgayoga.*
- Several practices that might facilitate the development of intuition have been identified. Salmon (2001) has described a number of these: making ourselves more receptive to intuitional knowing; working with symbolism, metaphors, and dreams; attending more fully to conscience or 'ethical intuition'; preparing ourselves for intuitive knowing by learning more effective ways of quieting the mind, emotions, and body; and by practicing detachment and honesty. These could be pursued personally, as well as in formal research contexts.
- Salmon (2001, pp. 33–34) suggests that intuition might be developed by engaging in *analytic meditation*:

> Analytic meditation ... involves an alternation between purely discursive reasoning and stable, one-pointed concentration on intuitive realizations as they arise. One takes an idea or theme, such as the impermanence of all things that can be perceived or conceived. One then engages in careful intellectual reasoning, and calls up images and memories from personal experience, bringing the central theme to mind with great vividness, clarity and aliveness. When this process is pursued with sufficient concentration, there will come moments in which a sudden inspiration flashes into the mind. ... When such a moment arises, active thought should be temporarily suspended, and all one's concentration focused with great energy on the intuition. ... If this practice is followed with diligence, a change may gradually occur in which the discursive reasoning takes on a more intuitive and global quality, while the intuitions that emerge gain in acuteness of perception and discernment.

- Mentioning 'intuitive and global quality' calls to mind a fascinating and potentially powerful research tool—the *projective differential*, developed by Peter Raynolds (1997). The projective differential (PD) is a standardized, holistic and intuitive procedure that can be used to qualitatively and quantitatively assess a person's salient integration of cognitive and affective reactions to a particular topic that is being assessed. The PD uses choice responses to very briefly presented pairs of carefully designed, abstract images in order to register holistic, intuitive, affective (nonverbal, 'unconscious') reactions, preferences, and attitudes. It has features similar to those of the more familiar *semantic differential* (Osgood, Suci, & Tannenbaum, 1957). It resembles a tachistoscopic Rorschach presentation. The rapid and projective nature of the procedure serves to minimize deliberate, conscious distortions, and, therefore, the PD results may have greater validity than do many deliberate, verbal assessments. The PD procedures also include built-in indicators of the discrepancy or incongruence between its own novel (imagistic, intuitive, affective) measures and more traditional (verbal, consciously and deliberately considered) measures. The PD is recommended as a very specific way in which to study a form of intuitive knowing and its accompaniments and outcomes in formal research settings.
- Future researchers may profitably explore methods described by Sri Aurobindo and The Mother (Das, 1997), in writings on education, for developing and refining the major mental faculties. In his section of that book, Sri Aurobindo described these functions as the four layers of the inner instrument (*antaḥkaraṇa*): basic mental consciousness and memory (*citta*); sense-mind (*manas*); intelligence (*buddhi*); supermind (*vijñāna*). In the context of these functions, he addressed simultaneous and successive teaching methods and suggested ways of removing obstacles and obstructions to knowing and ways of training the accuracy and sensitivity of the senses, the mental faculties generally, and the logical faculty specifically. He also addressed the imagination as a most important and indispensable instrument, and its proper exercise as being as important as the training of the faculties that observe and compare outward things. Many of the methods and procedures described in a previous section of this chapter, on Integral Research Skills, are very closely aligned with Sri Aurobindo's suggestions for useful educational training.
- The approach of Insight Dialogue, developed by Greg Kramer and Terri O'Fallon could be explored as a way not only of accessing inner knowing but also of communicating that knowing with someone else.

The approach was described by Salmon (2001, p. 24) as follows:

> Greg Kramer ... in collaboration with Terri O'Fallon, has developed a meditative practice he calls "Insight Dialogue." In its simplest terms, the practice involves meditating while engaged in interpersonal interaction; in other words, speaking while meditating ... Kramer developed a research methodology which applies this practice to scientific research. The methodology has each individual, on their own, attempt first to enter into a meditative state of deep tranquillity and equanimity. From this state, they each engage in a process of intellectual and intuitive exploration regarding an inner object of study such as a particular mind state, feeling, pattern of sensations, sequence of ideas, memory, worldview, etc. After a period of individual investigation, they would come together. Engaging in an insight dialogue session, they would communicate—while remaining in a state of tranquillity and equanimity, always mindful of and receptive to flashes of intuitive knowing—the results of their respective investigations, inquiring more deeply of each other, checking for biases, unquestioned assumptions, etc. Perhaps other such approaches will evolve in coming years.

This dialogic inquiry approach is described in detail in an unusual joint dissertation by Kramer and O'Fallon (1998).

- The dialogic inquiry approach could be extended to develop ways of sharing one's inner knowing with others, in a manner that might help establish the validity and reliability of such knowledge. This would be a step in the direction of what Charles Tart (1972) has advocated as 'state specific science'.
- Forms of paranormal knowing (telepathy, clairvoyance, precognition) might be introduced more fully into the research enterprise, not only as objects of study but as techniques to be used in the actual conduct of research. The Integral Research Skills course mentioned earlier already includes some of these techniques in the context of the direct knowing, intuition, and empathic identification skills.
- In connection with paranormal knowing, the use of exercises related to *Aṣṭāṅgayoga*, mentioned in Table 5.2 above, could be extended from quantitative studies, in which they typically have been used, to qualitative investigations of psi.
- At the Institute, Rosemarie Anderson (2004) has been developing a research approach, Intuitive Inquiry, that substantially honours intuition as a research tool. She has identified five modes of intuition: unconscious processes, psychic or parapsychological experiences, sensory modes of intuition, empathetic identification, and through our wounds, along with a blended form of these modes. Although only some of these modes closely resemble intuition as it is considered in the present chapter, a greater emphasis on the modes described by Anderson, along with greater practice of ways of fostering those respective modes, may be helpful in establishing some of the preconditions necessary for the emergence of the more direct, knowing-by-identity, form of intuition discussed here.
- Typically, one attempts to *express* one's inner knowing through linear prose. Alternative means could be tried—for example, poetry, artwork, movement, and various nonlinear, nonverbal means—and these might be able to communicate sympathetic understandings to others that are not possible via linear prose. Anderson (2001) has taken steps in this direction through developing what she calls *embodied writing,* in which one attempts to 'presence' an inner experience while writing, in order to invite the same experience in a reader, through sympathetic resonance. The practices mentioned here—which one usually thinks of only in connection with the fine arts and the humanities—could be introduced more fully into research and disciplined inquiry in order to communicate one's findings more effectively to the audience of one's work. In India, there is a long tradition of using poetry to express inner knowing, as in the *Vedas*, in the *Upaniṣads*, and in various forms of mystical poetry.

Additional considerations

The foregoing sections addressed some of the ways in which specific aspects of *yogic* practices and principles and some aspects of Indian psychology already have been applied, or might be applied, in the context of research praxis. Along with such applications there arise a number of issues that merit additional consideration. One of these is that care is needed when certain practices developed in one culture are applied in other cultures. The success of such applications may vary widely, depending on the nature of the prior and new contexts and whether the practices are applied in unchanged or in modified forms. This issue may be addressed by paying careful attention to the contexts of origination and application and to how the practices are framed and presented to the new users, along with careful monitoring of the accompaniments and outcomes of the applications.

Another issue relates to how and how much of the principles and practices of one tradition might be wisely applied in another tradition. Salmon (2001) has highlighted the dangers of picking and choosing only selected aspects from a complex and well-integrated

Indian tradition, with the resultant risks of dilutions and distortions. He urged taking Indian psychology seriously—honouring its own understandings, rather than filtering those understandings through other interpretative lenses. As examples of such filtering, he indicated how certain aspects of Indian thought and teachings might be variously interpreted through phenomenological, historical, psychoanalytic, neuroscientific, and postmodernist lenses. In applying *yogic* principles and practices to research, it is important to be alert to the possible losses or distortions that might result through gross or subtle—perhaps even 'unconscious'—framing of the borrowed or translated techniques, influenced by the predispositions of the borrowers. One may address these risks by attempting to deepen one's understanding of the source and nature of what is borrowed as much as possible and by attending as fully as possible to the application itself and to its side effects and outcomes.

In the Indian and *yogic* traditions, in which the principles and practices treated in this chapter have their home, the overarching emphasis is on the psychospiritual growth, development, and transformation of the practitioner. In applying the various techniques to research, in other contexts, it is important that attention be paid not only to how those techniques might facilitate the knowledge gain of the discipline, but also to how well the borrowed or bridging techniques might foster the wisdom, spiritual growth, and transformative change of the researcher, the research participants, the intended receivers of the research findings, and society and culture at large.

In this vein, this chapter ends with a short quotation from the conclusion of a previous paper (Braud, 2006b, p. 22):

> Prior uses of yoga-related processes in psi research might be likened to stealing jewels from temples. A deeper appreciation of these processes might foster a realization of the purposes for which the temples were constructed in the first place.

References

Anderson, R. (2001). Embodied writing and reflections on embodiment. *Journal of Transpersonal Psychology, 33*(2), 83–98. Retrieved December 15, 2006, from http://www.integral-inquiry.com/cybrary.html#embodied

Anderson, R. (2004). Intuitive inquiry: An epistemology of the heart for scientific inquiry. *The Humanistic Psychologist, 32*(4), 307–341.

Aquinas, Thomas. (1971). *Summa theologica* (Vol. I) (Fathers of the English Dominican Province, Trans.). Chicago: Encyclopedia Britannica. (Original work written 1267-1273).

Aurobindo, Sri (1970). *Letters on yoga*. Pondicherry, India: Sri Aurobindo Ashram Press. (Original work published 1947-1951).

Aurobindo, Sri (1972). *The life divine*. Pondicherry, India: Sri Aurobindo Ashram Press. (Original work published serially in the monthly review *Arya* between August 1914 and January 1919 and in book form 1939-1940).

Aurobindo, Sri (1981). *The Upanishads: Texts, translations, and commentaries* (2nd ed.). Pondicherry, India: Sri Aurobindo Ashram Press.

Aurobindo, Sri (1993). *Bases of yoga*. Twin Lakes, WI: Lotus Press.

Aurobindo, Sri (2000). *The synthesis of yoga*. Pondicherry, India: Sri Aurobindo Ashram Press. (Original work published serially in the monthly review *Arya* between 1914-1921 and in book form 1948).

Bacon, R. (1928). *The Opus Majus of Roger Bacon* (2 vols.) (R.B. Burke, Trans.). Philadelphia: University of Pennsylvania Press. (Original work written 1268).

Boethius. (1980). *The consolation of philosophy*. (V.E. Watts, Trans.). New York: Penguin. (Original work written 524).

Bonaventure. (1953). *The mind's road to God* (G. Boas, Trans.). New York: Liberal Arts Press. (Original work written 1259).

Braud, W. (1994). *Toward an integral methodology for transpersonal studies*. Working Paper Number 1994-1 of the William James Centre for Consciousness Studies, Institute of Transpersonal Psychology, Palo Alto, CA. Retrieved December 15, 2006, from http://www.integral-inquiry.com/cybrary.html#toward

Braud, W. (1998a). An expanded view of validity. In W. Braud & R. Anderson (Eds.), *Transpersonal research methods for the social sciences: Honouring human experience* (pp. 213–237). Thousand Oaks, CA: Sage.

Braud, W. (1998b). Integral inquiry: Complementary ways of knowing, being, and expression. In W. Braud & R. Anderson (Eds.), *Transpersonal research methods for the social sciences: Honouring human experience* (pp. 35–68). Thousand Oaks, CA: Sage.

Braud, W. (2006a). Educating the "More" in holistic transpersonal higher education: A 30+ year perspective on the approach of the Institute of Transpersonal Psychology. *Journal of Transpersonal Psychology, 38*(2), 133–158.

Braud, W. (2006b). *Patanjali yoga and siddhis: Their relevance to parapsychological theory and research.* In K. R. Rao, A. C. Paranjpe & A. K. Dalal (Eds.), *Handbook of Indian psychology* (pp. 217–243). Foundation Books: New Delhi. Retrieved December 15, 2006, from http://www.infinityfoundation.com/mandala/h_es/h_es_patanjali_yoga_and_siddhis.htm

Braud, W., & Anderson, R. (1998). *Transpersonal research methods for the social sciences: Honoring human experience.* Thousand Oaks, CA: Sage.

Bruns, G. L. (1992). *Hermeneutics ancient and modern.* New Haven, CT: Yale University Press.

Cornelissen, R. M. M. (2001, June 23). *Towards an integral epistemology of consciousness: A radical proposal based on Sri Aurobindo's work.* Paper presented at the International Seminar on Consciousness and Genetics, National Institute of Advanced Studies, Bangalore, India. Retrieved December 15, 2006, from http://ipi.org.in/TEXTS/Others/Matthijs/NIAS-2001-Epistemology.html

Das, M. (1997). *Sri Aurobindo on education*. Retrieved December 15, 2006, from http://www.ncte-in.org/pub/aurobin/auro_0.htm

Deslauriers, D. (1992). Dimensions of knowing: Narrative, paradigm, and ritual. *ReVision: A Journal of Consciousness and Transformation, 14*(4), 187–193.

Forman, R. K. C. (1997). *The problem of pure consciousness: Mysticism and philosophy*. New York: Oxford University Press.

Forman, R. K. C. (1999). *Mysticism, mind, consciousness*. Albany, NY: State University of New York Press.

Gebser, J. (1986). *The ever-present origin* (N. Barstad & A. Mickunas, Trans.). Athens, Ohio: Ohio University Press. (Original work published in German in1949).

Glaser, B. G. (1978). *Theoretical sensitivity*. Mill Valley, CA: Sociology Press.

Gödel, K. (1962). *On formally undecidable propositions of Principia Mathematica and related systems*. New York: Dover. (Original work published in German in 1931).

Hargiss, D. (2001). Integral phenomenology: A method for the "new psychology," the study of mysticism and the sacred. In M. Cornelissen (Ed.), *Consciousness and its transformation*. Pondicherry, India: Sri Aurobindo International Centre of Education. Retrieved December 15, 2006, from http://www.saccs.org.in/TEXTS/IP2/IP2-5.2-.htm

Havelock, E. A. (1963). *Preface to Plato*. Cambridge, MA: Belknap Press/Harvard University Press.

James, W. (1950). *The principles of psychology* (Vol. 1). New York: Dover. (Original work published 1890).

James, W. (1976). *Essays in radical empiricism*. Cambridge, MA: Harvard University Press. (Original work published 1912).

Kramer, G., & O'Fallon, T. (1998). *Insight dialogue and insight dialogic inquiry*. Unpublished doctoral dissertation, California Institute of Integral Studies, San Francisco, CA.

Louchakova, O. (2005). On advantages of the clear mind: Spiritual practices in the training of a phenomenological researcher. *The Humanistic Psychologist, 33*(2), 87–112.

McGinn, B. (1996). *The growth of mysticism.* New York: Crossroad.

McGinn, B. (1998). *The flowering of mysticism.* New York: Crossroad.

McMahon, J. D. S. (1998). The anatomy of ritual. In B. Batey (Ed.), *Gateways to higher consciousness: 1998 Annual conference proceedings of the Academy of Religion and Psychical Research* (pp. 49–56). Bloomfield, CT: Academy of Religion and Psychical Research.

Nagel, E., & Newman, J. R. (1958). *Gödel's proof.* New York: New York University Press.

Osgood, C. E., Suci, G. J., & Tannenbaum, P. H. (1957). *The measurement of meaning.* Urbana: University of Illinois Press.

Palmer, G. E. H., Sherrard, P., & Ware, K. (Trans. and Eds.) (1995). *The Philokalia: The complete text* (Vol. 4). London: Faber & Faber.

Plotinus (1966-1988). *Enneads* (Vols. 1-7) (A.H. Armstrong, Trans.). Cambridge, MA: Harvard University Press. (Original work written circa 250 CE)

Polanyi, M. (1964). *Personal knowledge: Towards a post-critical philosophy.* New York: Harper Torchbooks.

Polkinghorne, D. E. (1989). Phenomenological research methods. In R. S. Valle & S. Halling (Eds.), *Existential-phenomenological perspectives in psychology* (pp. 41–60). New York: Plenum.

Rammohan, V. G. (Ed.) (2002). *New frontiers of human science.* Jefferson, NC: McFarland.

Rao, K. R. (2002). *Consciousness studies: Cross-cultural perspectives.* Jefferson, NC: McFarland.

Raynolds, P. A. (1997). On taming the evaluation monster: Toward holistic assessments of transformational training effects. *Simulation and Gaming: An International Journal of Theory, Practice and Research, 28*(3), 286–316.

Rucker, R. (1987). *Mindtools: The five levels of mathematical reality.* Boston: Houghton Mifflin.

Salmon, D. (2001, September 8). *What if we took Indian psychology seriously?* Retrieved December 15, 2006, from http://www.infinityfoundation.com/mandala/i_es/i_es_salmo_psych_frameset.htm

Schneck, G. (1980). Three forms of knowledge. In G. Schneck et al. (Eds.), *Visits to Sufi centres: Some recent research papers on Sufis and Sufism* (pp. 32–35). London: Society for Sufi Studies.

Schumacher, E. F. (1978). *A guide for the perplexed.* New York: Harper & Row.

Simon, B. (1978). *Mind and madness in ancient Greece: The classical roots of modern psychiatry.* Ithaca, NY: Cornell University Press.

Skolimowski, H. (1994). *The participatory mind: A new theory of knowledge and of the universe.* New York: Penguin Arcana.

Smith, H. (1992). *Beyond the post-modern mind.* Wheaton, IL: Theosophical Publishing House.

Tart, C. T. (1972). States of consciousness and state-specific sciences. *Science, 176,* 1203–1210.

Underhill, E. (1960). *The essentials of mysticism and other essays.* New York: E. P. Dutton. (Original work published 1920).

Varela, F., & Shear, J. (Eds.) (2002). *The view from within: First-person approaches to the study of consciousness.* Bowling Green, OH: Imprint Academic.

Wilber, K. (1990). *Eye to eye: The quest for the new paradigm* (Expanded ed.). Boston: Shambhala.

Wilber, K. (2000). *Integral psychology: Consciousness, spirit, psychology, therapy.* Boston: Shambhala.

Woods, J. H. (1927). *The yoga system of Patanjali.* Cambridge, MA: Harvard University Press.

6

What is knowledge? A reflection based on the work of Sri Aurobindo

R. M. Matthijs Cornelissen

Introduction

The scientific and technological developments of the twentieth century have expanded our understanding of the workings of the nervous system beyond anything previous generations would have thought possible, but at the same time the concentration on the biological correlates of mental processes seems to have led us away from a deeper understanding of the amazing miracle that is human knowledge as a subjective phenomenon. While an enormous collective effort has gone into the refinement of physical and mathematical instruments with which we can measure the outer physical reality, there is no comparable systematic collective effort to improve our own inner instruments of knowledge. This is true even for research on meditation. The vast majority of such researches focus exclusively on the physiological states and processes that occur in the physical bodies of those who meditate; the remainder is almost entirely limited to those psychological variables that are conveniently measured objectively (Murphy & Donovan, 1997). As such they are about physiological and psychological side-effects of meditation, ignoring the aims and objectives of meditation in the culture of origin.[1] Even in research which ostensibly deals with the subjective side of life, the type of experience addressed tends to be limited to what naïve subjects can report about themselves, and in much of modern psychology it is not experience itself but statistically processed reports about experience that are taken as the actual data. As these reports are almost always based on unsophisticated self-observations by representative members of a larger population, all such studies can provide is thus a kind of social demography of surface mental self-perceptions. Though this has its uses, it is not sufficient for the development of deeper insight in human nature. What is strikingly missing in contemporary psychology is a systematic effort to hone and perfect our inner perception, our sensitivity to what is going on deep within ourselves. Any science that wants to make cumulative progress must look below surface appearances. We have done this with astounding results in the objective domain, but as a civilization, we have neglected the inner side of the equation. Cataloguing and correlating phenomena that are either visible right on the surface (behaviour) or directly below it (through surveys based on naïve introspection) is not enough to develop a really meaningful and effective psychology.

Limitations of the explicit representational mode of knowing

The demand for objectivity has gone hand in hand with a tendency to think of explicit representational knowledge of the outer world as the only type of knowledge that can be cultivated systematically, reliably, and profitably. This tendency seems to have been reinforced by the ease with which such representational knowledge can be rendered symbolically and, more recently, stored, manipulated and redistributed digitally. This is so much part of our everyday experience that many people are under the impression that computers can actually think. Though the extent to which the working of the mind differs from the way computers work is well-known, the workings of the mind are commonly described in the language of computer science, even amongst cognitive scientists. The basic principle behind all this is not new. Freud thought of the human mind as a steam engine ready to explode, and when clocks were cutting-edge technology, humans were commonly depicted as fancy clockworks driven by a *homunculus*, a tiny man lodged somewhere deep inside the machine. Mechanical clocks and homunculi have fallen from grace, but we still model our own nature on our latest technology.[2] There is no doubt that the use of such metaphors has its positive side. Our understanding of clockworks has helped us to understand the mechanical forces active in our musculoskeletal system, and computer science is telling us valuable things about the way the brain processes nervous stimuli. But we should not forget that, in the end, they are no more than metaphors. At best, they can help to model certain aspects of a limited group of mental processes, but they do not tell the whole story. In fact, they light up only a tiny corner of the wonder that is human knowledge.

Diverse ways of knowing

For many of us, the most important and memorable experiences in life are those that connect us to deep, inner realities. They need not necessarily be of a spiritual or religious type. Such experiences occur even in the midst of a completely ordinary life—there is something extremely beautiful and deeply intriguing in simple things like our ability to hear a song in the distance, to see a tree swaying in the wind, to feel the warmth of the first sun rays on our skin in the morning, to look into the eyes of a child. These are cognitive events, but not of the ordinary representative type. How do we study these subtler moments of knowledge? How do we explore the utter miracle that is our subjective experience of ourselves and the world? These may seem questions suitable only for poets and dreamers, best left for Sundays, and unfit for practical men, but they may actually be crucial to our survival—psychology will fail the coming generations if it does not help us to develop a deeper insight into the more subtle aspects of human nature and the love and oneness that sustain us. Way back, in 1915, Sri Aurobindo wrote about this: 'The safety of Europe has to be sought in the recognition of the spiritual aim of human existence, otherwise she will be crushed by the weight of her own unillumined knowledge and soulless organisation'. In his next sentence he stressed the need for balance. There he said: 'The safety of Asia lies in the recognition of the material mould and mental conditions in which that aim has to be worked out, otherwise she will sink deeper into the slough of despond of a mental and physical incompetence to deal with the facts of life and the shocks of a rapidly changing movement'. Now, in the beginning of the twenty-first century, Asia is clearly waking up, but the danger of insufficient respect for the spirit is still real, and this time that danger looms not only in Europe.

It is in this area of subtle, subjective enquiry that the Indian tradition has perhaps made its greatest contribution to our collective understanding, and the rest of this chapter will be mainly about the type of inner knowledge that the Indian civilization has cultivated over thousands of years—why it must be there, how it can be found, and how it can be made more accurate and reliable. For my interpretation of the Indian tradition I base myself on the work of Sri Aurobindo (Arvind A. Ghose, 1872–1950) who made a comprehensive synthesis of the Indian tradition in order 'to feel out for the thought of the future, to help in shaping its foundations and to link it to the best and most vital thought of the past' (1998, p. 103). His unique combination of spiritual depth, intellectual rigour and clarity of exposition, combined with the astounding detail and precision with which he describes the psychological processes that help or mar our individual and collective evolution, make his writings an exceedingly rich store-house of insights in human nature and its development.

1. Four types of knowledge in the ordinary waking state

Sri Aurobindo locates the secret of human knowledge in depths of our being that may not be directly available to all of us, but there are links between the depths and the surface and at one place in his main philosophical work, *The Life Divine,* Sri Aurobindo distinguishes four types of knowledge that all occur within our ordinary surface awareness: knowledge by identity, knowledge by intimate direct contact, knowledge by separative direct contact, and separative knowledge by indirect contact (Aurobindo, 1990, pp. 524–532). The first of these, knowledge by identity, or *ātmavidyā*[3] plays a central role in the *Vedas* and *Upaniṣads,* but is almost entirely ignored in contemporary science; aspects of the other three are known, respectively, as experiential knowledge, introspection, and the ordinary, sense-based knowledge of the outside physical world. Sri Aurobindo lists them, in harmony with the *Vedic* tradition, from the inside out: he starts with the knowledge of the Self, and ends with the knowledge of the outside world. I'll discuss them here in the modern sequence, starting with the outer world, and moving from there, slowly towards the deeper, inner realities.

1. Separative knowledge by indirect contact is the ordinary, sense-based knowledge that we have of the physical world around us. Sri Aurobindo calls it *separative* because it goes with a clear sense of separation between the observer and the observed. He calls it *indirect,* because it is dependent on the physical senses. A tremendous collective effort goes at present into the development of this type of knowledge, and as it is the bedrock of science and technology, it plays an ever-increasing role in our society. It is this type of knowledge that makes the continuous stream of ever more fancy gadgets possible, and perhaps as a result of this, there is an increasing tendency to think that this is the only type of knowledge that really works and is worth cultivating.

2. Knowledge by separative direct contact has a much lower status both in contemporary science and society. When applied to ourselves, it is known as introspection, the knowledge we acquire when we try to look pseudo-objectively at what is going on inside ourselves. In this type of knowledge, the usual sense-organs are not needed and in that sense it is direct, but it is still separative because we try to look at what is going on inside ourselves 'objectively', that is, as if we were looking at ourselves from the outside. Psychology cannot do very well without introspection, as it is the simplest, and in some areas the only way to find out what is going on inside one's mind, but it is notoriously difficult to make reliable. Classical behaviourism tried for many years to avoid it entirely, but at present psychology is making an extensive use of self-reports based on introspection. We will see later how the Indian tradition tackles the difficulties inherent in introspection and we will discuss some of the methods it uses to enhance introspection's reliability. I am inclined to think that these Indian methods are not only logically impeccable, but also indispensable if we want to take psychology forward.

3. Knowledge by intimate direct contact is the implicit knowledge we have of things in which we are directly involved. When applied to ourselves it is known as experiential knowledge. Sri Aurobindo calls it again *direct* because the sense organs are not required, and *by intimate contact* because one knows the processes that are taking place not by looking at them from the outside, but by being directly with them. When I'm very happy, for example, I need not observe myself to find out whether I am happy or not. If I would look at myself in a (pseudo-) objective manner, through introspection, I would say something like 'Hey, I'm happy', and this would imply a certain distance from the happiness. But I can also stay directly with the happiness, and exclaim, in full identification with my feelings, 'What a great day it is!' If I do the latter, I also know the state I am in, but not in a representative, objective manner. I know then what I am as if from within, through a direct intimacy with the inner state or process.[4] It might appear as if the introspective mode of knowing oneself goes more with the mind, while experiential knowledge, knowledge 'by being with', goes more with one's feelings and body-sense, but this is not always the case: When one fully identifies with one's thoughts, for example, there is a mixture: the thought itself belongs most likely to the realm of 'separative knowledge', while the implicit, pre-reflective self-awareness of 'being busy thinking' belongs to the realm of 'knowledge by intimate direct contact'. Knowledge by intimate direct contact is used in many forms of therapy and all kind of psychological training programmes, but till now it does not seem to have received the theoretical attention it deserves.

4. Knowledge by identity is for Sri Aurobindo the first and most important of these four types of knowledge. In the ordinary waking state it is, however, hardly developed. The only thing we normally know entirely by identity is the sheer fact of our own existence. According to Sri Aurobindo it does play, however, a crucial role in all other types of knowing. In experiential knowledge (type 3) this is clear enough, as here we tend to identify with our experience. In introspection (type 2) it is less immediately apparent, as we do not fully identify with what we see, but try to observe what goes on inside ourselves, in as detached and 'objective' a manner as we can muster. Still, in introspection we recognize that what we look at is happening within our own being. In sense-based knowledge (type 1) the involvement of knowledge by identity is the least obvious, but even here knowledge by identity does play a role in at least two distinct ways: The first is that even though we normally feel a certain distance between ourselves and the things we observe 'outside' of us, we still see them as part of 'our world', we feel some inner, existential connection between ourselves and what we see. The degree of this sense of connectedness may, of course, differ. On one extreme, there are the mystics who feel in a very concrete sense 'one with the world'; on the other extreme, there are forms of schizophrenia, in which hardly any connection is felt between one's self and the world; the ordinary consciousness wavers somewhere between these extremes. The second manner by which knowledge by identity supports all other forms of knowledge is not through this existential sense of connectedness, but through the structural core of their cognitive content. According to Sri Aurobindo, the information the senses provide is far too incomplete and disjointed to create the wonderfully precise and coherent image that we make of the world. He holds that there must be some inner knowledge, some basic 'idea' about how the world should hang together, that helps to create meaning out of the raw impressions, which our senses provide. According to the Indian tradition, knowledge by identity can provide this as it is the core-element of all forms of intuition,[5] and, as such, the source of the deep theories about reality that guide our perception, the fundamental rules of logical thinking, a large part of mathematics, and the ability to discriminate between what is true and false, real and unreal. Once fully developed and purified, Sri Aurobindo considers it the only type of knowledge that can be made completely reliable. Within Indian philosophy it is known as the knowledge of the Self, *ātmavidyā*, which contains the largely subconscious link that exists between our individual consciousness and the cosmic consciousness that sustains the manifestation as a whole.

1. Separative knowledge by indirect contact Sense-based, constructed knowledge of the outer world. *Scientific knowledge*
2. Knowledge by separative direct contact Looking at one's own mental processes, 'as if from outside'. *Introspection*
3. Knowledge by intimate direct contact Awareness of one's own inner states 'by being with them'. *Experiential knowledge*
4. Knowledge by identity Awareness of the simple fact of one's own existence (details of self-concept provided by other three types). *Knowledge inherent in one's existence*

Table 6.1. Four types of knowledge in the ordinary waking state

Mixed patterns

Before we can have a closer look at the possibility of developing true intuitive knowledge, we have to consider a few caveats which Sri Aurobindo himself mentions about this division of four distinct types of knowledge. The first one is that these four types of knowing are not entirely separate or exclusive of each other. There are smooth transitions between them, and in daily life they often occur mixed up together. When I am angry, for example, something in me stands apart and still knows that I am what I am, that the world is what it is, and that deep, deep within, in spite of anything that happens, all is well (type 4, knowledge by identity). And yet, I am also directly involved in getting angry. In fact, to some extent I become the anger (type 3, experiential knowledge). At the same time,[6] part of me watches what is going on in myself semi-objectively. I observe that I do not think clearly, that I have a cramp in my stomach and that there is a nagging fear in me that things are going wrong (type 2, introspection). While all this is going on, I notice that I cannot speak very clearly, that my hands tremble and that the person I am talking to looks nonplussed about what I am so worked-up about (type 1, sense-based knowledge).

Not all knowledge is representational and intentional

A second issue is that of these four modes of knowing, only the first two are representational and intentional in the sense of being 'about something'.[7] To realize that there are types of knowledge that are not representational, one need not rise to any extraordinary state of *samādhi* or to some otherwise non-egoic consciousness. Even in perfectly ordinary states, when we feel happy to be alive, when we love the world, or just one special person in it, we know the state we are in, but the knowledge of this state is not representative, it is a knowledge embedded in our very being. We can subsequently take distance from that direct experience, look at it introspectively, and then describe what we then see in a third person, 'objective' format—the result is then representative knowledge of the introspective type, which is indeed intentional, but the original knowledge was not about something at all, it was simply itself.

Not all knowledge is constructed

A third thing to note is that underlying the four types of knowledge there are three, closely related gradients. The first is the gradient from the surface aspects of the outer world to our own inmost essence. The second is the gradient from gross matter, via mind, to pure spirit. The third is the gradient from knowledge which is constructed with difficulty out of diverse elements, to knowledge which comes directly, spontaneously, simply because it *is*. I will discuss the first two gradients in some more detail in the other sections, but the third gradient deals directly with the very essence of what knowledge actually is, and it needs to be taken up at least tentatively before we can move on.

According to the cognitive sciences, what we know in our ordinary consciousness about our environment is the result of a fantastically complex mental labour combining new sense-impressions with earlier findings. This complexity is supposed to be there equally in the way the individual makes sense of his own life in the world and in the way science builds up our collective knowledge base. But if Sri Aurobindo and the Indian tradition are right, then not all knowledge is 'constructed' in this complicated manner and there is a second type of knowledge that comes to us in the form of ready-made intuitions. This direct, intuitive apprehension of reality is part of what Sri Aurobindo calls knowledge by identity, and he holds that it plays a far greater role in our individual and collective life than we realize. There is fascinating evidence of the amazing extent to which perception is guided by expectations,[8] and according to Sri Aurobindo these expectations are not only informed by past experience and present circumstances but also by a deep intuitive knowledge of how the world should be by its own inherent logic, a logic of which we are aware, however dimly, because in our deepest essence we are one with it. In this chapter I will try to show that this idea is not as far-fetched as it may seem to those who have been brought up with the idea that all knowledge comes from without.

According to the *Vedic* tradition, such inner knowledge can exist because it is a conscious energy *(cit-śakti)* that gives reality its shape and dynamism. Interestingly one can find implicit hints of similar ideas even in the informal language used by scientists. 'Applied' and 'pure' scientists have in their daily practice very different attitudes towards knowledge. Technical people, who work in the field of applied knowledge, typically see themselves as *inventing* new ways to use knowledge; pure scientists do not claim to invent, they claim to *discover* laws that have always been there. The technical man creates a new application; the pure scientist discovers a pre-existing truth and then tries to formulate it in the most elegant and useful manner. The difference between the two is, of course, not absolute, and if we look closely we see that in almost all our cognitive processes, there are elements of both. All formulated knowledge is partly discovery, partly construction. But the core question remains: Where did the knowledge hide before the scientists 'discovered' it? Did it exist only implicitly in the movements and patterns of nature from where the scientist abstracted it while formulating his laws and theoretical models?

The physicalist bias of mainstream Western science makes it hard for it to comprehend the intuitive component of knowledge. Hardcore physicalists like Daniel C. Dennett, for example, presume that this world is built entirely through dumbly mechanical or chance-driven processes (1994)[9] and argue that complex entities can be reduced without losing anything significant to their constituting components ('you are your neurons'). Within such a philosophical framework knowledge is ultimately based on sense-perceptions ('facts'), and there is no place for intuitive knowledge (except for the subconscious pseudo-variety). The Indian tradition, on the other hand, has no real problem with the existence of intuitive knowledge. In fact, the possibility of achieving a direct perception of the knowledge underlying reality is not only one of the ends aimed at by *yoga*, but also its historical and philosophical starting point: All authoritative texts on *yoga*, whether ancient or modern, are supposed to have been received through such a direct perception of truths behind reality, whether through direct vision of truth, *dṛṣṭi*, revelation; or through direct hearing of truth, *śruti*, inspiration. Given the present predominance of Dennett's worldview, it becomes useful to consider how one might move from the narrower materialist's view to the much more comprehensive, and, I would say, more coherent, Indian one.

The knowledge in things

When we say that science has discovered a certain law of physics, the phrase we use implies that the law existed beforehand, but if that is so, where was it before discovery, and what form did it have? It is clear that it cannot have had the same linguistic or mathematical form as it now has in the human mind, but the fabulous beauty, order and lawfulness of nature does suggest that there must be in matter at least some kind of built-in order, which we could look at as a kind of subconscious know-how, not dissimilar to the implicit know-how humans have of complex skills like cycling. To recognize the inner structure of matter as a form of know-how, one might look at the knowledge-constituent of matter as a subconscious habit of form, a tendency to act in harmony with the basic *dharma*[10] of the physical entity in question: an electron 'knows' how to behave like an electron, a hydrogen molecule how to behave like a hydrogen molecule, a rock like a rock, and a river like a river.

Interestingly, the information content needed to do so is not as small as it may appear at first sight. As matter makes no mistakes, every part of it needs to have the 'know-how' required to act perfectly according to the laws that guide its movement. As the laws of physics are supposed to be interrelated and derivable from each other, this might well mean that in some extremely involved way, it has to be aware of all the laws that keep our universe together. What is more, as matter's movements are influenced, to whatever small degree, by everything else that occurs in the universe, each part has to be perfectly aware, in however implicit a manner, of everything else that is going on. Together this amounts to a rather staggering kind of 'subconscient omniscience' which in a fully automatic fashion self-limits itself to the very simple set of dumb but perfect actions that are proper to each little part of reality. One could of course argue that even if this complete knowledge has to be there in every part, it is still far too implicit, far too 'involved' to be extracted. In practice this may be true, at least for the moment, but it does not change the basic principle, and thus the potential.

In the *Vedic* ontology the universe is a manifestation of consciousness, and it holds, like many ancient philosophical systems, that the knowledge that is implicitly embedded in the physical reality, is a reflection from realms of pure knowledge that exist permanently and inalienably, parallel to and in a sense 'far above'[11] the physical world. More interesting for psychology, it holds that since our individual consciousness is in its essence still one with the consciousness that engenders the universe, there arises the possibility of aligning our own individual consciousness to the knowledge that is built-in in the very structure of the universe. In other words there is a possibility of genuine, spontaneous, and perfect intuitive knowledge and action, which can arise in us because the world and all that is in it is in its essence one with the essence of our own being.[12]

As discussed earlier in our discussion of knowledge by identity, the constructed representational knowledge science consists of is in this context seen as a mixture of knowledge and ignorance, an attempt instigated and aided but also limited and distorted by our senses, that in this complex manner can arrive at a progressively more accurate reflection inside our brain-based individual mind-stuff of the basic knowledge structures that underlie the actual workings of the manifestation. Indications of such mixtures of sense-based and direct intuitive knowledge can be found in all fields of human endeavour: in mathematics and logic, in the sudden insights that lead to a new revolution in technology, and in lines of poetry that haunt the reader because of their unearthly perfection, their 'inevitability' as Sri Aurobindo calls it.[13] One could perhaps even find traces of direct, intuitive knowledge in less momentous but highly satisfactory moments of 'right action', when one simply knows from within what is to be done at a given moment.

But before we can proceed to discuss how our access to this intuitive knowledge can be cultivated, we need to get clear on one more essential distinction. This is the distinction between ordinary introspection, in which one looks with one part of one's mind at all the other activities that take place inside one's nature, and the perception that occurs through a pure witness consciousness, *sākṣī*.

Of birds and balconies

There is a common notion, equally widespread, for example, in contemporary consciousness studies as in classical *pramāṇa*-based Buddhist and Indian epistemology, that one cannot at the same time observe the world, and be aware of oneself observing it. The standard logical argument against doing both at the same time is that this would lead to infinite regress: one observes that one observes that one observes, and so on, and on, and on. The simpler, but perhaps even more convincing, symbolical image is that one cannot stand at the same time on a balcony and walk in the street. So it is argued, and in ordinary introspection one can actually observe this, that one switches very quickly between looking at the outside world and looking at the memory of how one looked at the outside world just a moment earlier. One possible reason for the mutual exclusiveness of perception and self-awareness in our ordinary waking consciousness might be that they function through the same inner instrumentation: In the Indian terminology, it is the same *manas*, or sense-mind, which in our ordinary consciousness either looks at the outside world through the outer senses, or at the inner world through the inner senses. The *manas* may simply not be able to do both at the same time.

There is, however, a second way of observing oneself that actually can take place at the same time as any outer or inner action. This second type of self-observation can easily be confused with ordinary introspection, but it has an entirely different character. The main difference is that it is not based on an activity by the mind, but on a direct apprehension of reality by a pure witness consciousness (*sākṣī*). This second type of self-observation is depicted in the ancient Indian image of two birds, good friends, beautiful of feather, who sit in the same tree: one eats the fruit while the other watches (*Ṛg Veda* I. 164. 2). Here what watches is not the separative, ego-centric, and sense-mediated surface mind, but a deep, silent, non-egoic, all-inclusive, pure consciousness that allows the egoic actions (and even the egoic observations) to continue somewhere in its own infinitude without being perturbed by them. As there is no egoic centre and no boundaries to this background awareness, the question of recursion does not arise. The core issue here is that the consciousness that watches must be 'pure' and utterly silent. If for some reason the 'running commentary', which is so typical of the surface mind, intrudes and one notices, 'Hey, look, I'm watching what is going on from my deep silent inner self!', one obviously has lost it, and gone back to the ordinary, ego-based introspection.

Introspection	Pure witness consciousness
looking with one part of the mind at other parts of the mind (and at the rest of one's nature)	observing the workings of one's nature from the position of a pure, silent witness
giving a running commentary; volunteering value judgements; reacting to what it observes	silently watching in perfect equanimity
intrinsically prejudiced	equal to all that comes up
limited to the ordinary waking consciousness	able to penetrate deeper layers of consciousness and being

Table 6.2. Introspection versus pure witness consciousness

In practice, these two different types of inner apprehension are not entirely exclusive of each other, and there is a certain gradient between them. As one becomes only gradually more settled in the deeper, inner silence, it is possible to arrive first at an in-between status of consciousness from which one introspectively observes what one is doing (type 2), and yet retains some intimate contact (of type 3) with a deep inner vastness of silent awareness (of type 4). In this state one is aware of the presence of pure consciousness as a kind of background for the superficial mental activity in which one is involved, but one identifies more with the mental activity on the surface than with the wider consciousness in the background. Only when one goes still deeper within, one begins to centre in that vastness itself. Then one sees, supports and sanctions from deep within the activities of the surface mind without losing in any way one's real 'identity' (if that term still applies) as the all-including vastness. One is then a borderless infinitude in which one is aware through knowledge by identity (type 4) of the entire stream of events, including birds and people, streets and balconies, which peacefully continue to exist somewhere on the surface of one's being. It is this second way of watching in an absolute inner silence, which is claimed to produce knowledge by identity, not only of one's own innermost self, but, potentially, of anything in existence.

It may be noted that in spite of its 3D imagery, the street and balcony simile presumes a 'flat' concept of consciousness in which exclusivity reigns—one can either observe oneself *or* the world, one is either the observing subject *or* the observed world, and so on. The image of the two birds, on the other hand, is based on a totally different multidimensional concept of consciousness and reality. Here the dichotomies that perplex our mind are easily resolved in a higher-order unity. In our interpretation of this ancient image, the tree inhabited by two birds represents the relation between the world and two major aspects or portions of our self. The tree-world of the first bird called *nara* (man) belongs to the ordinary waking consciousness and is exclusive, enmeshed in time and causality. This bird 'eats the fruits': he is fully engrossed in life and suffers the consequences of his actions. The world of the second bird, *nārāyaṇa* (the Supreme), is part of an all-inclusive consciousness, containing all time and all opposites within itself. *Nārāyaṇa* watches in the Vedāntic, non-dual sense of the *sākṣī*, and remains unaffected by *karma*. Interestingly, and typical of the ancient, even-handed love for man and God, the birds are mentioned as good friends, and both as 'beautiful of feather'.[14]

If there is any truth in the distinctions and possibilities mentioned so far, then the next question is, how do we move from the superficial and often erratic knowledge provided by the observation of outer behaviour and ordinary introspection, to a more penetrating and reliable insight in the deeper layers of the mind.

2. Perfecting the inner instruments of knowledge

Sources of error

Over the long history of India's thinking about these issues, many different descriptions of the mind's difficulties have been given and many different solutions have been proposed to overcome them. Ego and desire are probably most frequently mentioned as factors leading to unhappiness, ignorance and distorted knowledge. The factor most commonly indicated as leading to bliss and unbiased knowledge is perfect detachment.

A slightly different perspective is offered by Sri Aurobindo in two interesting passages of *The Synthesis of Yoga*. He describes here the basic defects of the ordinary human mind as essentially of two kinds, *immixture* and *improper functioning* (1999, pp. 298, 618). Both can best be understood in the context of Sri Aurobindo's vision of an ongoing evolution of consciousness.[15] Within this framework of a gradually evolving consciousness, he sees these two basic defects of the mind as essentially due to the stickiness of our evolutionary past.

Immixture. Immixture happens when an earlier and more primitive form of consciousness interferes in a higher or later form. A typical example occurs when two people discuss a theoretical question. Their minds are genuinely interested in finding out what is true, because the quest for truth is part of the basic *dharma* of the mind. But when the vital part of their natures interferes, things go haywire. The vital part of human nature is not concerned with truth. The natural tendency of the life-force, which we have inherited from the animal stage of evolution, is survival, self-assertion, possession. So when the vital part of the nature enters into the debate, the stress is no longer on finding out what is true, but on who will win the argument. If the vital part of our nature is sufficiently purified, it will obey the mind and enjoy whatever it offers—a pure vital nature will be happy if the truth has been found irrespective of who has won the argument. But if an unregenerate part of the vital nature dominates over the mind, it will insist on winning, even to the extent of tempting the mind to bring in false arguments.

Improper functioning. In harmony with the idealistic nature of his *Vedic* philosophy, Sri Aurobindo holds that for each part of our nature there are 'ideal' or proper ways of functioning, as well as improper ways. For the vital nature the proper functioning includes an equal, glad enjoyment of whatever happens. The mixture of happiness, pain and indifference, of desires and fears from which the ordinary waking state suffers, is the result of the gradual and as of now only partially completed evolution of the vital nature out of the totally involved nescience of matter. Similarly the ideal function of the mind is to receive in a complete passivity the knowledge that sustains the world and to express it in the physical life-form it inhabits. What the unregenerate mind does instead, again due to remnants of its slow emergence out of the stupor of matter and the ignorance of the life in which it grows up, is to strive after knowledge, construct it in an ever more complicated, but never fully satisfactory confusion.

One could summarize these two defects of the mind as the 'noisiness' of the ordinary mind. Just as perfect joy can only be received in a heart that is wide, calm, and completely free of desire and attachment, so also true knowledge can only be received in a wide and calm mind that is completely free of mental preferences and distortions. The deeper one tries to enter into the recesses of one's inner nature, the more imperative becomes the need for a complete silence of the observing consciousness. Just as fine physical measurements demand a vibration-free room, so also in psychology, to reach the deepest layers of one's being, a silent mind is essential. To silence the mind is of such importance that Patañjali describes it as nothing less than the central objective of *yoga* and Sri Aurobindo describes it sometimes as an essential step for deeper knowledge and sometimes as the ultimate essence itself.[16] If this is so, then how is it done, how do we purify and ultimately silence the mind?

The purification of the mind

Most people who try to silence their mind soon realize that they have little control over their thoughts and that thoughts seem to come and go on their own. When one looks more closely, one sees that the vast majority of these mechanical thoughts that go on ruminating in one's mind are triggered by sense-impressions, and that they draw their energy from often trivial physical and social needs and desires. The latter issue we have already discussed: an absolute prior condition for silencing the mind is to avoid what Sri Aurobindo calls immixture of the unregenerate vital in the mind's workings. The necessity to overcome desires is mentioned in practically all spiritual traditions and is directly related to the two defects of immixture and improper functioning we mentioned earlier. As we discussed there, desire is itself a deformation of the vital's true nature, and its interference in the mind's workings is the main obstacle to direct and unbiased insight. The most obvious way to achieve silence in the mind is thus either to isolate the mind from the vital part of the nature, or, for a more lasting result, to quieten and purify the vital nature itself. Freeing the mind from negative vital influences is, however, not sufficient as the mind itself has its own defects. Sri Aurobindo mentions three conditions that need to be met if we want to arrive at deeper and more reliable inner knowledge:

Freedom from the senses. The first defect of the ordinary mind is that it is too dependent on the senses, and that it gets triggered too easily by their input. To keep the mind detached from the senses is common enough in ordinary concentration (when you read a book, you do not hear the street noise), but more difficult when there is no obvious focus of attention to keep the mind engaged. Yet, this is needed to create the space for more subtle perceptions to enter our consciousness.

Freedom from the past and future. The second defect of the mind is that it is too anxious. This form of improper functioning is in essence the same as the main defect in the vital. The vital part of our nature is too anxious to be happy, and as a consequence it loses its inherent peace and joy and gets instead lost in a jumble of desires and fears. When the mind is too anxious it first grabs intuitions (or even sense-impressions) too eagerly, then builds all kind of unwarranted extrapolations on them, and finally it sticks too tenaciously to the little it has found. To continue to grow in knowledge, one should always remain quiet, accept what comes, and yet remain open to what comes next (Aurobindo, 1999, pp. 315–316). The solution is thus the same as for the immixture and the clinging to the senses: one should retain a perfect equanimity, detachment and a vast inner calm.

Silence of the mind. Sri Aurobindo describes several methods to silence the mind (e.g. 1999, p. 324). The easiest, most commonly advocated but perhaps not the fastest method, is to let the mind run its own course but to withdraw one's interest and sanction. If one manages to consistently refuse engagement in the thoughts that pass through one's mind, they slowly die out. The stress, however, is on the 'if', and on the 'slowly'. The second method is to enter with the centre of one's consciousness into a realm of silence that pre-exists in an inner space deep within the heart or well above the mind.[17] The third is to call this same pre-existent silence down into one's mind, heart and even body. The fourth is probably the most efficient, but also the most strenuous method. Here one distances oneself again completely from what goes on in one's mind, and then one stays on guard and systematically throws out every thought as soon as it enters into one's awareness. This is effective but it requires the ability to centre oneself in one's mental *puruṣa*, one's real, innermost Self on the level of the mind, and yet remain active. There are many other methods, but the core of most, if not all, is to distance oneself from the activities of the mind and vital and to watch whatever goes on inside one's nature as an absolutely disinterested outsider. This is not an ultimate truth or a stance that can remain: in due time one finds that everything, even outer things, are actually part of oneself, but it is an effective means to get rid of the partial, ego-based identifications. The feelings of 'I'm me and not you', 'I like this and not that', 'I believe this and not that' are the effective cause both of our suffering and of our inability to see reality as it is.

3. Inner knowledge

If one would like to give a label to the ontology that underlies the theory of knowledge that I've tried to present here, then one could call it a strong form of *realistic idealism*. In philosophical texts there is a tendency to view idealism and realism as opposites, but Sri Aurobindo sees no inherent conflict between the two. He writes in *The Life Divine*, 'The world is real precisely because it exists only in consciousness; for it is a Conscious Energy one with Being that creates it' (1940/90, p. 22). In line with the *Vedic* tradition he holds that it is a conscious energy that manifests the world, and thus that knowledge is present throughout creation, even if largely implicitly embedded in the 'habit of form' of material objects. Just as in a rock it is consciousness that gives that rock its particular form and qualities, there is also in man a very close link between our consciousness and the form and functioning of our body—the ordinary human consciousness identifies itself with its material substrate. Seen from this angle, the only difference between the rock and the human is that in case of the human being, the substrate includes an immensely complex nervous system capable of (re)presenting to itself a small stretch of the physical and social world around it. As a result our consciousness tends to identify with the centre of that representation, and especially with our individual memories, body-sense, feelings, desires, ideas, social roles, etc. But, interestingly, in man consciousness need not remain entangled in the workings of the body and the nervous system. It appears that once our little chunk of biologically embedded consciousness is sufficiently individualised and self-aware, it can learn to free itself from its physical encasement.

The Indian tradition has found that once the consciousness emancipates sufficiently from the body, several forms of inner knowledge open up to it, that can be grouped under the last two of the four types of knowledge I discussed in the beginning of this chapter, knowledge by intimate direct contact and knowledge by identity. As discussed earlier, these two are closely related: there is a gradient of intermediate forms of knowing in between them, and an increasing proficiency in one often, though certainly not always, leads to a more frequent occurrence of the other.[18] Still, for the sake of mental clarity it is good to distinguish them, if only because they belong to two entirely different epistemic realms: knowledge by intimate direct contact is still, just as sense-based knowledge and introspection, the result of a contact, however direct and subtle, between the self and something considered not oneself. As a consequence it is, in the radical language of the *Vedic* tradition, still considered to be a form of *avidyā*, no-knowledge or ignorance. Knowledge by identity, on the other hand, is the pure faculty of knowledge, *vidyā*, that is inherent in all being. In humans, it is to be found in its pure form only in the *puruṣa*, our silent, innermost Self. The aspect of knowledge by identity we will discuss in this section is the possibility to know as if from within things that ordinarily are not considered to be part of one's own individual self. According to the Indian tradition this is possible because in its very essence everything is one, is *Brahman*. The condition however is, and this is a difficult condition, that we must have disentangled our consciousness completely from the little chunk of nature we ordinarily identify with, our ego. From that absolute freedom it is considered possible to know everyone, everything, every event, with a total perfection, 'in the way God knows it'.

Two forms of knowledge by identity

I will discuss here two varieties of knowledge by identity. Within the inner realms of our psychological nature, one can distinguish an intriguing system of two intersecting dimensions, one reaching from the surface ego inwards to the soul, and one rising upwards from the subconscient below, via the physical, the vital and the mind in between, to the superconscient spirit and the Self above.[19] Along both dimensions one can find entry-points to the realms of direct inner knowledge, and, interestingly, they lead to different aspects of this knowledge, some primarily personal, others in the first instance impersonal. Before we go into more detail about these two dimensions, it may be useful to come back once more to the difference between constructed and direct knowledge.

Direct and constructed knowledge revisited

There are plenty of indications in ordinary life that direct, intuitive knowledge indeed does exist. A mathematician typically first 'sees' the solution to a problem, and only then works out the logical steps that 'prove' he is right. It is presumed that he has followed, unconsciously, the same steps of the proof to arrive at his first insight, but this is just a conjecture, which is far from certain. Similarly, an inventor, writer, composer typically first 'gets' an idea and only then works it out. According to contemporary cognitive sciences, the idea is actually constructed and only seems to pop-up in one's consciousness as a ready-made product because almost all the processing remains unconscious. But if one learns to quieten one's mind and to attain to a state of sufficient clarity within, one can actually *see* how ideas arise. One discovers then that new insights sometimes do arise in the way modern psychology describes—Sri Aurobindo calls this 'pseudo-intuition' because it imitates the real thing—but occasionally, and especially when the mind is silent, the real thing itself also happens. At such moments, one can observe how an unformed idea drifts into one's mind as if from another realm, and only subsequently gets clad, dressed-up as it were, in words and images that seem to be provided by the individual's outer mind, perhaps from a brain-based stock of material. It even happens sometimes that ideas 'pop-up' completely formed, in 'inevitable' words or images. It appears then as if all knowledge consists of a core of direct, intuitive material, clad in an outer casing provided by the senses, with a gradient in the percentage of direct and constructed knowledge. St. John of the Cross gives a vivid description of the fine distinctions between those different 'degrees' of inspiration and of some possible causes of the variance between the proportion of descending and constructed material (Steele, 1994). He also describes how the descending idea may come direct from the highest and purest layers of consciousness one has access to, or how it may come from intermediary layers or even from active agents that can have distorted the expression to suit their own agenda.

In the surface consciousness that provides the experiential ground for most modern philosophical speculation, it may look as if reality is divided by an absolute, Cartesian dichotomy in gross, inconscient matter on one side, and our thoughts on the other (with, for those who believe in it, an extra-cosmic Divinity beyond both). But inner experience supports rather the idea that there is a smooth gradient between matter and pure spirit. Inner experience confirms the idea, which the *Vedic* tradition has in common with virtually all other spirituality-based schools of thought, that there actually is a whole range of worlds connecting the Absolute with the manifest world we all know. The *Vedic* tradition holds that the physical world is ultimately a condensation of consciousness, and it has worked out the transitions from the subtle to gross levels in great detail, for example in its description of the different worlds (or 'births'), and the various sheets of consciousness. These inner realities and their interconnections are extremely complex, and it is not easy to recognize the underlying structure and even more difficult to place different experiences correctly into the whole. As a result many different ways to bring some order into it all have been suggested, but for our present enquiry in the nature of knowledge, the simple distinction mentioned earlier between an inward horizontal, and an upward vertical dimension is particularly useful, both from a theoretical and from a practical viewpoint.

Knowledge from within

A first approach to inner knowledge is by an inward movement from the surface consciousness that characterizes the ordinary waking state, through the subliminal intermediate layers of our inner nature, to our innermost, true being, the *puruṣa*. Though ultimately there is only one Being, one Consciousness, one Self, the *paramātman* forever one with *Brahman*, transcending, supporting and inhabiting the manifestation in its entirety, the *Vedic* tradition recognizes not only that every individual being also has its own Self, but that even within the complexity of each individual being, there exist different Selves on each of the various planes (*koṣas*) of consciousness on which it exists. On each plane the *puruṣa* is our true Self, the silent witness, the support, and ultimately the master of our nature. Though the *puruṣa* is pure consciousness, and not affected by the *guṇas* (the various qualities that characterize manifest nature) still the characteristic experience of the *puruṣa* differs according to the plane on which it is found. Though everywhere silent, vast, unaffected, on the mental plane it is the aspect of the witness that dominates, in the higher vital that of love and compassion, in the lower vital planes that of joy and strength, and so on. There are two forms or 'instances' of the Self that stand out, one that stays eternally, immutably above the individual manifestation, also called the *jīvātman*, and another, the innermost self that sustains and inhabits the incarnate being as a whole, the *caitya puruṣa*, or *antarātman*. The former I will discuss further in the next section on 'Knowledge from above', about the latter I will discuss a few points here.

The *caitya puruṣa* is found behind the heart *cakra*,[20] where, if one goes deep enough, one finds what has been called the inner oracle, the guide within, one's deepest, innermost soul, *antarātman* or *caitya puruṣa*. Sri Aurobindo calls it the *psychic being*. In its own realm, in the depths of its own being, the psychic being is felt as a centre of true, self-luminous perfection; it is the source in us of our deepest aspirations, of true love, goodwill, compassion and a deep inner joy and gratitude. Sri Aurobindo describes it as a direct expression of the very being of the Divine immanent within us. It is the one part of us that can manage simultaneously to remain perfectly faithful to its own essential nature (*svabhāva*) and yet be in a perfect, dynamic harmony with the manifestation as it unfolds from moment to moment in and around it.

In terms of knowledge, the psychic being is the one part in us that is completely one with truth, and yet, as long as one lives in the surface personality, the guidance which the surface mind receives from the psychic being cannot always be perfect, for it reaches the surface consciousness through the intermediaries of one's heart and mind, and they can easily distort its messages. In terms of force also, deep inside the psychic being has the perfection of power inherent in its truth, but on the surface its strength cannot manifest easily or openly because there it is bound by the limitations of one's instrumental nature. Only to the extent that the inner channels are clear and open, can its guidance be reliable and its action effective. Though it knows whatever one needs to know at any given moment, it is only when one's inner instruments of knowledge are pure enough that its gentle voice can be trusted to give the immediate and perfect guidance for the best possible action.

Knowledge from above

The other entry-point to direct knowledge is reached not by an inward movement, but by a movement of the centre of one's consciousness upwards, through the *sahasrāra*, the highest of the seven *cakras*, the seven centres of consciousness in one's subtle being. Through this *cakra* one opens up into the higher planes of consciousness and being, which, like a ladder, climb up into ranges that are felt as leading to the very origin of creation. These realms of higher knowledge are by their very nature impersonal. According to Sri Aurobindo, for most people the route through the heart is the most easy and natural, but for some people this ascent is the easiest way to move out of the individual mind into the cosmic vastness.

An interesting difference between the inner and higher knowledge is that the knowledge that comes by going inside tends to be situational: it typically gives an indication for 'right action', for what to do or what to say in the here and now. The knowledge one reaches by moving upward, on the other hand, tends to be more abstract and generic. Immediately above the mind there is, for example, a realm where one participates in comprehensive, global patterns of thought. If one concentrates on a philosophical issue while in that world[21] one immediately sees how a wide variety of related ideas hang together. To use a schoolchild's image, it is a bit as if one reads the pages at the end of a dream-quality schoolbook where all the answers are kept together in a perfectly contextualized manner: one sees not only the perfect answer to the question raised, but even the answers to a wide variety of related questions. Sri Aurobindo calls this world the Higher Mind. As it gives such an impression of impersonal, all-comprehensive perfection, it can easily be mistaken for the Gnostic or 'unitary' consciousness, but it is still very far below it: what one experiences here is not the Gnostic consciousness itself but only a more or less luminous shadow of it within the realm of the mind. Immediately above the Higher Mind there are realms where the relations between things and processes are not known in words or thoughts, but seen or felt as luminous images and presences. The higher one goes, the more the sense of perfection, unity and truth increases, but the more difficult it becomes to express what one experiences in words, because our ordinary language consists of words indicating dualities that are far surpassed in those higher realms.

There are two quite different ways in which one can make this upward movement. The first approach is a kind of jump, or at least a very quick climb, by which one moves more or less directly from one's ordinary consciousness to the Absolute by a systematic rejection of all thoughts and feelings that might arise in between. If one manages to do so, this is a very effective process and it can produce dramatic results in an amazingly short time. But the disadvantage is that this procedure leaves a gap between the consciousness in one's ordinary state and the higher state. One reaches the Absolute in some kind of trance or *samādhi* and one cannot carry a detailed memory of either the Supreme Reality or the intermediate layers back to one's ordinary state. What such experiences do leave behind, however, is the certainty of having reached a Truth and Bliss so absolute that compared to it, all the imperfections and sufferings of the ordinary world lose their relevance. The power and felicity of this experience may be one of the reasons why so many great saints and sages, in the West as well as in the East, have looked at the manifestation as a lesser aspect of the Divine or even as an unreal farce that needs to be surpassed and left behind if one wants to reach the Divine in His/Her/Its absolute essence. Given how infinitely (literally!) more perfect the Absolute seems to be than anything in between, it is understandable that many great mystics have advised to forget about all lower experience and concentrate directly and exclusively on the highest.

Sri Aurobindo, however, takes the dynamic unfolding of the world as an aspect of the Divine that has as much importance as the static, absolute essence. He looks at our imperfect world simply as a 'work in progress'. Sri Aurobindo's stress on the value of life in the world is related to his vision of an ongoing evolution of consciousness of which he sees the next stage as the physical embodiment of *vijñāna*[22], the Gnostic, supra-mental plane of truth-consciousness that according to him must be the ultimate origin of the manifest world. It may be clear that an organic embodiment of such an absolute truth-consciousness would require an extremely drastic transformation of human nature. To get a handle on the details of this process of transformation, a comprehensive understanding of all the intermediate layers of consciousness is required, which can only come through a second approach to the higher ranges of consciousness for which Sri Aurobindo found many references in the *Vedas*. In this approach one climbs slowly and meticulously, step by step, a kind of inner stairs that rises from below right up to the highest planes, delivering the detailed knowledge as one goes.[23]

Though this goes beyond the immediate topic of this chapter, it is interesting to note that Sri Aurobindo insists for this approach to knowledge on a double movement, which is mentioned throughout the *Vedas*, but which in later times seems to have been forgotten except in some lesser known *Tantric* schools—one climbing from the ordinary mind, through all the intermediate layers of higher mind, illumined mind, intuition up to the overmind, and one descending, a 'bringing down' of these higher capacities and powers back into oneself. One finds this movement mentioned throughout the *Vedas* as the request for the gods 'to increase' in the person on whose behalf the *Vedic* sacrifice is made. If the *Vedic* gods are taken in their esoteric sense as the higher powers of the human mind, then it becomes clear how closely the *Vedic* image of a material sacrifice matches what Sri Aurobindo describes as a psychological process of ascent and integration: one has first to reach, connect with, and 'realize' the higher faculties of *Indra* (the illumined mind), *Agni* (the will and aspiration), the *Vāyus* (the barrier breakers), and many others, and then make them an integral part of one's nature. Where Sri Aurobindo differs from the *Vedas* is that he seems to expand the range over which this process of ascent and integration can be made to work. At the high end, some of the *Upaniṣads* but especially the later Vedāntic texts seem to jump directly from the Overmental plane of Indra—where there are still fights between gods and *asuras* (mental forces of good and evil)—to the plane of *ānanda*, the plane of perfect bliss and oneness. Sri Aurobindo, on the other hand, focuses on the *vijñāna*, the supra-mental link plane between the lower and higher hemispheres, where there is a simultaneous existence of perfect oneness and variety. At the low end, Sri Aurobindo tries to anchor this Gnostic plane in the physical reality, and to make it an organic part of our evolutionary, biological nature.

4. Yoga as research tool

If there is indeed, as the Indian tradition claims, a knowledge that can be apprehended directly from within without the necessity of mediation by the senses, then this has major consequences for the choice of the optimum methodology in psychological research. There where such direct inner knowledge refers to phenomena in the external world, one can indeed decide on the accuracy of the inner knowledge 'objectively' by comparing the symbolic rendering of that inner knowledge with the symbolic rendering of sense information about the external events. But where the inner knowledge refers to inner states or processes, this may not be the appropriate way of verifying such knowledge. What we need there is not objectivity, but reliable subjectivity.

In our study of the outer world, progress is to a large extent made by using better and better instruments. What 'better' means here depends to some extent on the field: in astronomy 'better' might mean for example higher resolution, higher and more specific sensitivity combined with less noise and distortion. Wherever possible, the results are then corroborated with findings from others with different but equally reliable instruments. Where the quality of the findings cannot be ascertained through comparison with findings made by different observers, instruments and experimental pathways, the inherent logic of the instrument's construction plays a major role in our assessments of their reliability. I suggest that we can apply the same ideas to the inner domain. In the inner domain the instrument of choice is self-observation, which includes knowledge by intimate direct contact, knowledge by identity, and the pure witness consciousness (*sākṣi*). Just as in the physical domain, the quality of the results in the inner domain can be ascertained on the one hand through corroboration by equally or better qualified observers, and on the other hand by the intrinsic quality of the instrument. The latter can in its turn be ascertained to some extent, though never fully, by what that specific instrument delivers in comparatively better known fields of enquiry. The only difference is that in the inner domain, the instrument is not some physical instrument, but the inner instrument of knowledge, the *antaḥkaraṇa*, of the *yogi*-researcher. The quality of this instrument depends on things like the amount of immixture and improper functioning; its freedom from ego, vital desires, mental preferences and physical limitations; its sensitivity, flexibility, and ability to move at will through different inner worlds and centres of consciousness; etc. In other words, *yoga*, in its widest sense of spiritual discipline, is the method of choice to perfect the inner instrument of knowledge. It leads to a more comprehensive, impartial and harmony enhancing understanding of reality not only through the purification of the inner instrument, but also by raising the observing consciousness above its ordinary, corrupting and limiting involvement in the processes and entities that psychology is supposed to study.

That it can indeed deliver is attested to by the incredibly rich Indian heritage in the psychological field.

In short, for the outer periphery of psychology, objective population surveys and behavioural studies may be appropriate, but for the inner core-territory, the legitimate heartland of psychology that consists of the deep movements of consciousness, what we need are reliable subjective methods. For those subjective methods, self-reports are *not* the original data: they are at most part of the reporting. Even introspection, as defined in the beginning of this article, is in itself not the right research method to reach the deeper layers. The actual research consists of the processes that take place in the inner worlds themselves. They can only be ascertained by a silent witness consciousness in a deep inner self-observation. Subsequently this inner knowledge can be brought to the surface and shared with others, as long as we acknowledge that its veracity can only be ascertained by those who have access to the same inner worlds with the help of inner instruments of knowledge that are similar or better in quality. One could, perhaps, look at this as a reprehensible form of occult elitism, but it need not be. The situation might be close to that in physics where one cannot expect results unless one has a good grasp of mathematical and instrumental methods. I'm inclined to think that *yoga* has a very similar role to play in the advancement of Psychology, as mathematics and physical instrumentation have in physics. It can improve the quality of the inner instrument of knowledge and make us more open to sources of direct knowledge. Which of the many entirely different methods and techniques of *yoga* are the most suitable for incorporation into Psychology, is one of the major tasks for Indian Psychology to take up in the coming years.

5. Evaluation and conclusion

When a little girl looks up to us, it is up to us whether we want to see that her dress is untidy, that her English needs correction, or that the heavens from which we all come are visible just behind the surface of these wide, wondering eyes. Even if we consider it our duty to tinker with the details of the outer manifestation of this subtle wonder, it still helps to remain aware of the deeper inner realities, however deeply buried in the background of our consciousness. At the very least, that inner connectedness will help us to avoid the worst forms of cruel insanity to which our human race is so amazingly prone. At its best, it may help to bring about a more harmonious world for future generations to enjoy.

If Sri Aurobindo and the *Vedic* tradition on which he builds are right, then direct, intuitive knowledge by identity forms the essential core of all our knowledge, and especially of our basic sense of truth, beauty, meaning, love, self, and reality. We may doubt whether we as individuals can ever hope to develop intuitive knowledge to the level of detailed perfection that Sri Aurobindo and the *Vedic* tradition assert to be possible. But even if there were only a remote chance that such a type of knowledge actually exists and that it can be cultivated, it would still be worthwhile to give it, both individually and collectively, much more attention than we presently do. The least the methods of *yoga*, especially *jñāna yoga*, can contribute to Psychology are well-developed methods for the study of the subjective side of our psychological nature, methods that work through a systematic removal of the imperfections of introspection, and through a rigorous refinement of the inner instrument of knowledge (*antaḥkaraṇa*) so that it can penetrate the deeper layers of consciousness that are described throughout the Indian tradition but that are not accessible in our ordinary mental states.

There is, however, another, and perhaps more important reason to pursue the systematic development of knowledge by identity and that is simply, that *if* it exists, it is the type of knowledge humanity needs most at the moment. All major human problems are problems of harmony (Aurobindo, 1990, p. 2), and the kind of direct, intuitive knowledge we've discussed in this chapter may well be one of the most direct ways to find that harmony back. After all, the core of the intuitive knowledge Sri Aurobindo speaks about is nothing else than the ancient *ātmavidyā*, the knowledge of the self[24] at a level where the individual self is consciously one with the cosmic Self, and through that, with the individual selves of all others. As such, it is the knowledge that reconnects us to our common source and that supports our communality as well as our essential individuality. As a result, the pursuit of knowledge by identity can provide answers to our deepest need for love and harmony, and it can give humanity the wisdom and power it so desperately needs to heal the many wounds and distortions that now mar both our individual human natures and our collective existence. So even if the chances of finding this knowledge were exceedingly small, the gamble would still be worth it. But, fortunately, the chance of finding this knowledge is not small at all.

Though mainstream science ignores and in her more dogmatic moments even denies its existence, intuitive knowledge has played a major role in all known civilizations. It is true that some cultures have held it to be something of a gift that cannot be cultivated, but there are many other cultures that have worked out methods to develop it, and in India, where spirituality has been the very foundation of the mainstream culture right from the beginning of known history, there are several highly sophisticated and intellectually rigorous systems of ideas on how it can be developed. So actually, collectively, we not only know that this knowledge is there, but we even know how to develop it.

At the end of his wonderfully detailed history of spiritual movements in the U.S.A., Eugene Taylor comes to the conclusion that we can expect over the coming years a growing influence of Indian ideas on the developing global civilization, and especially a major shift in its basic epistemological assumptions, away from materialism and in the direction of Indian spirituality (1999, pp. 289–296). Taylor considers it an open question whether this growing reliance on spiritual knowledge will develop as part of science, or as an independent, parallel knowledge system that will gradually gain in prominence, as people begin to realize how much it can contribute to our understanding of human nature (ibid. p. 285). To what extent spirituality and science can and should merge or collaborate is a complicated issue, but there seems very little inherent reason why they should not join hands at least in some key areas. The almost complete separation of the knowledge systems of spirituality and science that we see at present seems to be little more than a highly unfortunate outcome of the peculiarities of European history. In individuals, the independent co-existence of incompatible knowledge systems is a sign of schizophrenia, and it is hard to conceive how this could be different for society at large. Even if a true integration[25] of spirituality with the presently dominant knowledge system of science will be hard to achieve, the least we should strive for is some form of active cooperation. What form this cooperation should take is again difficult to say. In all likelihood psychology will see for a long time the co-existence of several competing knowledge systems rooted in a wide gamut of ideas and methods, that perhaps could be mapped in a three-dimensional space indicating their relative stress on physiological, social and spiritual factors. In the long run I expect, however, that there will be an increasing awareness of the value of spiritual knowledge, and of the interdependence between psychological insight and spiritual practice. If this is true and if we will indeed see an increasingly widespread recognition that *yoga*, and spiritual practice in general, leads to valid and reliable psychological knowledge of a quality that cannot be obtained otherwise, then we can foresee a time when *yoga* will be considered equally essential for the psychologist as mathematical proficiency for the physicist.

Within the field of psychology, but potentially elsewhere as well, science and spirituality are complementary quests for knowledge in need of each other. Science is by its very nature down-to-earth, progressive and self-critical, and without these three qualities, spirituality tends to become too otherworldly, it gets stifled in the encrustations of religion, or it floats off in some new-age vagueness. On the other hand, science also needs spirituality to complement itself. Till now science has occupied itself mainly with the objective, outer half of reality, but this outer half has no independent existence. Reality-as-we-know-it is a relationship: a relationship between what we see as ourselves and what we see as the world in which we live. To fully understand what happens in this relationship, we need to know both sides of it, the inside as well as the outside. If we concentrate too exclusively on the outside we lose out on the deeper meaning of life, on the treasures of the spirit, and if we concentrate too much inside we get an other-worldly spirituality that doesn't do justice to the love that sustains this beautiful creation. Only when we pay equal attention to both sides of the equation can we develop a knowledge and mastery that are fully in harmony with the marvel of the evolving manifestation. Only then may it finally be said of humanity that its tread shall 'justify the light on Nature's face' (Aurobindo, 1994, p. 344).

Acknowledgement

In this chapter I have tried to give a faithful impression of Sri Aurobindo's ideas on knowledge in a language that is understandable and relevant for those who are engaged with contemporary psychology. In this attempt I have tried to stick as closely as possible to my own experience, and to be explicit about my philosophical presumptions and predilections. I am aware that these different objectives are not fully compatible. The language of modern psychology is not really suitable to deal with the type of experiences on which Sri Aurobindo bases his ideas, and the limited nature of my own experience enables me to see and understand only a small corner of his work. Still, I hope the result will be intriguing enough for the reader to give a serious thought to the ideas expressed in this chapter and to turn for further clarification to Sri Aurobindo's own writings.

Endnotes

1 There are exceptions, but they are few and far between. For an overview see Walsh and Shapiro, 2006.

2 According to Sheldrake (2005, p. 38) a recent exhibition in the Science Museum in London presented the human mind as the flight-deck of an aeroplane, but without a pilot. An unexpected Buddhist influence?

3 In the part of *The Life Divine* on which much of this discussion is based, Sri Aurobindo does not explicitly state that the distinction he makes between 'knowledge by identity' and 'separative knowledge' is equivalent to the traditional distinction between *vidyā* and *avidyā*, but I think it is a safe assumption.

4 There is also a dynamic aspect to this type of knowledge. Sri Aurobindo doesn't mention it in this context, but logically the dynamic side of this type of knowledge should include skills, the 'know-how' to do things.

5 In contemporary psychology it is widely held that intuition is constructed subconsciously and only appears to pop-up ready-made. Sri Aurobindo calls this pseudo-intuition. Intuition is used here in the original sense of true knowledge that is not constructed, but that comes to us at least partially 'ready-made' from some inner or subtle source. Much of this article can be seen as an attempt to show that such direct knowledge actually exists and is worth cultivating systematically.

6 'At the same time' may not be taken too literally. See the subsection entitled 'Of balconies and birds'.

7 In a state of pure consciousness there is evidently no distinction between subject and object, but not everybody agrees that such states are possible (Steven Katz, 1978, pp. 62–63). Even Jung, who is for many an early hero of the transpersonal movement in psychology, seriously thought that a state without ego, and thus without a clear distinction between subject and object, would intrinsically be an unconscious state. This seems to betray a somewhat surprising lack of understanding of the Indian tradition. For a brilliant discussion of Jung's position vis-à-vis Eastern thought, see Coward (1985).

8 In one famous experiment a video-clip is shown of two teams of six players, one team dressed in white, the other in black, who pass two balls on to each other in what looks like informal volleyball training. The observers are asked to count how often a white player manages to pass on a ball to another white player without a black player intercepting it. In the middle of the clip an actor dressed up

as a black gorilla enters the scene, stands still in the middle, waves his two hands at the audience, and then moves out from the other side. Even when one shows this video clip to large audiences, there is hardly ever someone who sees the gorilla. If at the end, one tells the audience to relax and watch the video once more without counting anything, just for the sake of seeing if there is anything special they missed during the first viewing, nobody misses the gorilla, and most people have a hard time believing it is the same movie (see Simons & Chabris, 1999).

9 For a refutal of one of Dennett's main arguments, see Cornelissen (2008).

10 The Sanskrit word *dharma* is difficult to translate. It denotes truth in the realm of agency. As such it is often translated as (moral, social) duty and even as religion, but especially the latter is not satisfactory, as *dharma* has a strong connotation of something that is part of one's essential nature and that as such goes beyond social conventions.

11 Inwardly, subjectively, there is an interesting vertical dimension to our awareness of different types of consciousness: we tend to visualise the heavens above and the dark, subconscious realms below. We will come back to this later.

12 Sri Aurobindo claims that it is actually possible to cultivate intuitive knowledge to such an extent that it can take over all ordinary mental functions and become one's normal way of knowing reality. We know from the diary Sri Aurobindo maintained during a few years of intense *yogic* practice, that he made this amazing claim not on the basis of literary exegesis or philosophical speculation, but on the basis of meticulously carried out experiments, of which he maintained a detailed day-to-day record. The 'laboratory notes' in this *Record of Yoga* (2003) are full of examples of detailed knowledge even about trivial events in the outer, material world, that would be extremely difficult to explain as constructed on the basis of sense-impressions and memories alone. For an interesting study of yogic powers and parapsychology, see Braud (2008).

13 'Inevitable' is the highest 'grade' in Sri Aurobindo's appraisal of lines of poetry in terms of their level of inspiration.

14 This is significant as the *Vedas*, from where this simile hails, are extremely terse; they are like mathematical formulas of the spirit, and there is never a word too many. Each word covers a world of meanings.

15 Sri Aurobindo looks at the Darwinian evolution as gradual emancipation of consciousness. He holds that just as life has developed in matter, and mind has developed in embodied life, still higher forms of consciousness are bound to develop in embodied mind. Sri Aurobindo looks at *yoga* as a concentrated attempt in the individual to achieve in a short period what Nature itself is working out at her own speed on a larger scale.

16 At the end of a passage where he describes several ways to silence the mind, Sri Aurobindo says, 'In a complete silence only is the Silence heard; in a pure peace only is its Being revealed. Therefore to us the name of That is the Silence and the Peace.'

17 The dimensionality of the 'inner' or subtle experience of consciousness is an intriguing phenomenon that one finds mentioned throughout spiritual literature, and that consistently returns in experience. In the 'inner' experience, one can actually centre one's consciousness at different vertical levels, and more or less deeply 'inside'. I will come back to this in the next section.

18 I'm not aware of hard statistical data on this issue, but both tradition and personal experience tell that 'enlightenment', which is closely related to one's capacity for knowledge by identity, tends to bring with it some degree of telepathic capacity, even though clairvoyants are certainly not always enlightened.

19 For more details see Sri Aurobindo's *The Synthesis of Yoga* and *The Life Divine*. A short summary of the system can be found in Cornelissen (2005) and a more detailed account in Dalal (2001).

20 *Cakras*, Sanskrit—centres of different types of consciousness arranged one above the other in the subtle body. Though the idea

that different types of conscious activity take place at different locations in the body has been worked out in much more detail in the Indian tradition, traces of it occur even in the English language, for example, 'use your head' means 'think better'; 'open your heart' means 'feel more compassion'; 'follow your gut-feelings' means 'follow your basic life instincts'. In an interesting example, Matt Frei (2008) wrote for BBC News, '[I]f America votes with its heart, it will elect Obama. If it votes with its gut, it will go for McCain.'

21 I could have written 'in that state' but at the risk of being accused of occultism, I have chosen consciously for 'in that world' as the latter appears more accurate. In many contexts, 'state' and 'world' are interchangeable, but they do not have the same connotations. 'State' stresses that what one describes happens inside the mind of an individual and is dependent on its condition. 'World' stresses the complexity and internal coherence of what one experiences, and it implies some kind of objective existence, though the latter can be apparent only (as in, 'a dream world'). I am inclined to think that what I describe here are indeed worlds, not just states. They seem to pre-exist independent of the human mind, though what one actually experiences is indeed dependent on one's inner condition. According to Sri Aurobindo this is equally true for all worlds, even for the ordinary physical world: all worlds come about in an interaction between *puruṣa* and *prakṛti*, self and nature, conscious being as subject and the same conscious being as object. They differ from each other in the type of consciousness on the subject and on the object side.

22 *Vijñana* is here used in its older sense of the Gnostic link-plane between the upper and lower hemispheres, equivalent to the *Vedic mahas*. In later times the same word was used in the much-diluted sense of intellect. In both cases *vijñana* is the plane above the *manas*. In the *Vedic* sense which Sri Aurobindo uses, it is the plane entirely above the mind as a whole, in the later sense it is used for a plane above the sense-mind, but still within the mind in its more general sense.

23 Sri Aurobindo describes these higher planes of consciousness with an exemplary and, one must add, rather rare intellectual discipline and 'rectitude'. From his diaries and the autobiographical poetry he wrote during the same periods as his published writings, we know that he carefully avoided quoting the sometimes strong claims of classical Sanskrit texts if he had not on the one hand fully understood their implications, and on the other seen them supported by his own experience. This, together with the detailed studies he made of our ordinary human nature as seen from the higher planes of consciousness with an eye on its transformation, make his work so exceedingly interesting for Psychology.

24 With 'self' I mean here the eternal centre of one's consciousness, the *ātman*, or the *puruṣa* of the Indian tradition, not the western 'self-concept', which corresponds in the Indian tradition more closely with the *ahaṁkāra*, the constructed, socially determined egoic centre in the outer nature, with which the real self erroneously identifies.

25 It may be noted that integration is not the same as amalgamation. In amalgamation, the original substances lose their own qualities and get merged into a new, essentially amorphous substance. In integration, the differences of the various parts are carefully maintained and uplifted into a new, and more complex unity (like the various parts of a car, that find the fulfilment of their existence in their cooperation in the workings of the larger unit of which they are the constituents.) True integration is above all not constructed with the mind, but an offering, a taking up in the pre-existing higher oneness of the conscious existence of the Divine.

References

Aurobindo, Sri (2003). A system of national education: Some preliminary ideas. In *Early cultural writings*. Pondicherry: Sri Aurobindo Ashram Publication Department. (Original text published 1910).

Aurobindo, Sri (1998). Our ideal. In *Essays in philosophy and yoga*. Pondicherry: Sri Aurobindo Ashram Publication Department. (Original text published 1915).

Aurobindo, Sri (1990). *The life divine*. Pondicherry: Sri Aurobindo Ashram Publication Department. (Original text published 1914–1920. Extensively revised 1939–1940).

Aurobindo, Sri (1994). *Savitri*. Pondicherry: Sri Aurobindo Ashram Publication Department. (Original text published 1950).

Aurobindo, Sri (1999). *The synthesis of yoga*. Pondicherry: Sri Aurobindo Ashram Publication Department. (Original text published 1914–1920. Extensively revised 1949).

Aurobindo, Sri (2003). *The record of yoga*. Pondicherry: Sri Aurobindo Ashram Publication Department. (Original text written 1910–1927).

Braud, W. (2008). Patanjali yoga and siddhis: Their relevance to parapsychological theory and research. In K. Ramakrishna Rao, A. C. Paranjpe, & A. K. Dalal (Eds.), *Handbook of Indian psychology* (pp. 217–243). Delhi: Foundation Books.

Cornelissen, M. (2005). Self and personality in Sri Aurobindo's yoga: An overview of his terminology. In K. Ramakrishna Rao & Sonali Bhatt Marwaha (Eds.), *Towards a spiritual psychology* (pp. 157–168). Delhi: Samvad India Foundation.

Cornelissen, M. (2007). In defence of rigorous subjectivity. *Transpersonal Psychology Review, 11*(1), 8–18.

Cornelissen, M. (2008). The evolution of consciousness in Sri Aurobindo's Cosmo-Psychology. In Helmut Wautischer (Ed.), *Ontology of consciousness: Percipient action* (pp. 399–427). Boston: The MIT Press.

Coward, H. (1985). *Jung and Eastern thought*. New York: State University of New York Press.

Dalal, A. S. (2001). *A greater psychology*. New York, NY: Jeremy P. Tarcher and Putnam.

Dennett, Daniel C. (1994). *Darwin's dangerous idea*. New York, NY: Simon and Schuster.

Frei, M. (2008). Obama now has a mountain to climb. Washington: BBC News, 4 June 2008. Retrieved on 4 June, 2008 from http://news.bbc.co.uk/2/hi/americas/7434740.stm

Guzeldere, G. (1995). Consciousness, what it is, how to study it, what to learn from its history. *Journal of Consciousness Studies, 2*(1), 30–51.

Katz, S. T. (1978). Language, epistemology and mysticism. In Steven T. Katz (Ed.), *Mysticism and philosophical analysis*. New York, NY: Oxford University Press.

Murphy, M., & Donovan, S. (1997). *The physical and psychological effects of meditation*. Sausalito, CA: Institute of Noetic Sciences.

Petitmengin-Peugot, C. (1999). The intuitive experience. *Journal of Consciousness Studies, 6*(2/3), 43–77.

Sheldrake, R. (2005). The sense of being stared at. *Journal of Consciousness Studies, 12*(6), 10–49.

Simons, D. J., & Chabris, C. F. (1999). Gorillas in our midst: Sustained inattentional blindness for dynamic events. *Perception, 28*, 1059–1074.

Skinner, B. F. (1953). *Science and human behavior*. New York: Macmillan.

Steele, S. (1994). The multistate paradigm and the spiritual path of John of the Cross. *The Journal of Transpersonal Psychology, 26*(1), 55-80.

Taylor, E. (1999). *Shadow culture, psychology and spirituality in America*. Washington DC: Counterpoint.

Tart, C. (1972). States of consciousness and state-specific sciences. *Science, 176*, 1203–1210.

Tolman, E. C. (1938). The determiners of behavior at a choice point. *Psychological Review, 45*, 1–41.

Walsh, R., & Shapiro, S. (2006). The meeting of meditative disciplines and western psychology: A mutually enriching dialogue. *American Psychologist, 61*(3), pp. 227–239.

Wampold, Bruce E. (2001). *The great psychotherapy debate: Models, methods and findings*. Mahwah, NJ & London: Lawrence Erlbaum Associates.

Watson, J. B. (1929). *Behaviorism*. New York: W.W. Norton.

7

Knowing in the Indian tradition

Girishwar Misra

> The intellect acquires critical acumen by familiarity with different traditions. How much does one really understand by merely following one's own reasoning only?
>
> —Bhartṛhari (*Vākyapadīya* 2.484)

The quest for knowledge in social sciences has largely emulated and adopted the natural scientific mode of knowing under the assumption that the crux of scientific understanding lies in the set procedures irrespective of the domain of study. A close scrutiny of the repertoire of the empirical methods and techniques makes it amply clear that such an approach was based on the premises of unity of science, observer-independent reality, static and fixed nature of reality and possibility of valid and value-free method of knowledge generation. The promise was to offer unequivocal evidence and certainty. With this kind of conviction effort was made to develop theories and principles of various phenomena. In fact, the emphasis on manifested empirical world has yielded increasingly greater amount of data regarding variables of various kinds supposed to unravel principles stating invariances. In this kind of knowledge-generation, an object is observed by the scientist with the explicit goal of control and prediction. In this context, empiricism informed the scientific effort towards understanding any phenomenon and constituted a prototypical approach for modern social sciences including psychology. Until recently it unquestioningly enjoyed the status of the most respectable and authoritative means of knowledge. The tradition of modern psychological study of learning/knowing was framed in the context of sensory experiences. The cognitive and computer-based information theoretic models of learning too are ultimately rooted in the empiricist tradition. Now it is clear that both top-down and bottom-up processes are required for explaining the vast range of cognitive processes. Contrary to empiricism, the roots of rationalism lie in reason. It assumes that mind must be integral to the experiencing self. It is not something that follows or processes experience. It is quite clear that the sensory experiences and mental operations cannot be meaningfully separated and appreciated.

However, the success story of the physical sciences has impressed the social scientists, particularly psychologists, in such a way that research modeled after physical sciences standardized the pursuit of knowledge. It was treated as secular, real, trustworthy, universal and rational. However, adoption of the same in the case of human beings has proved not only problematic but also the primacy of the method started dictating the terms and conditions of the whole inquiry. It was a matter of methodological discretion whether a given phenomenon would be admitted for the purposes of study. This assumption was based on the strong belief that the scientific procedure is equipped with in-built mechanisms of generating unambiguous and flawless data, and could provide dependable and generalizable knowledge. The most damaging consequence was that the subject matter was appropriated and a number of tactics were employed to preserve and sustain the scientific spirit at any cost.

The developments in the sociology of science and the philosophy of science, however, tend to suggest that scientific activity is a human social activity. Also, the limitations of positivist-empiricist mode of knowing are becoming apparent and new meta theories of understanding are emerging from diverse areas such as critical theory, hermeneutics, phenomenology and literary criticism, which are opening new ways of looking at the problem of knowledge. The interpretive turn is challenging the foundationist views and favors multiplicity of truth and understanding. Empiricism as only epistemology is being questioned and alternative epistemologies are being sought. Rationalism is one alternative. However, post modernists object to empiricism and rationalism and go for social constructionism and modes of hermeneutic engagement as better options. Both of them situate knowing in the social domain. The social constructionist scholarship has illustrated that understandings of various phenomena do vary across societies, cultures and eras. The conventional understandings in Western psychological scholarship are different from what we find in non-Western cultures. This has been demonstrated in the domains of self, emotions, values, motivation and personality. In the Western world the process of knowing as well as values attached to it have been largely linked with the idea of progress. To a large extent the practice of the discipline of psychology has subscribed to this view and has become ethnocentric. This has resulted in depicting cultural differences as deficits. In recent analyses the applicability of the imported knowledge systems has been found quite constrained and efforts are directed toward exploring alternative perspectives on knowing available in the disparate traditions.

Against this backdrop, this chapter explores the process of knowing in the Indian tradition. In particular it provides a sample of thoughts the content and characteristics of which are worthy of investigation by cognitive, cultural and cross-cultural psychologists.

Indian perspectives on knowledge

A close perusal of the Indian philosophical texts reveals that in this tradition, the existence of human beings is usually conceptualized as but a constituent part of a broader field encompassing the whole universe. Unlike in the Western tradition, man is not at the centre of the universe. The manifest diversity of the experienced or phenomenal world is grasped and often conceived in terms of a non-individualistic and a predominantly cosmic world-view. While Western thinking is characterized by dynamics 'which continually expresses itself in setting problems, and approaches the single object as static entity; India utilizes the fundamental notions of statics in stating the leading questions, but at the same moment conceives the actual object dynamically as passing from its origin to decay, without becoming clearly recognized and distinguished as a static existent, separated from other cosmic phenomena' (Heimann, 1937, p. 19). Thus Indian thought treats reality as a unified whole as opposed to a collection of discrete objects or events. Within a relational world view everything present in the universe is treated as a part of an interconnected whole. This implies that all the constituents share the essential properties of the whole (*yat piṇḍe tad brahmāṇḍe*). It implies interdependence and connectivity. Ramanujan (1990) has termed it context sensitivity.

Another related feature of the Indian way of thinking is its emphasis on abstract concepts and universals. Thus, as Nakamura (1964, p. 47) states 'most of the Indian thinkers are apt to emphasize universal concepts and to subordinate the concrete individual and the particular perception to the universal. The individual soul, for instance, was given the metaphysical status of a permanent substance co-eternal with God.' This implies that the essence of the individual or the particular is not greater than the universal which becomes a basis for realizing the particular.

While the above characterization holds true for many systems of Indian thought it would be incorrect to argue for complete homogeneity in the Indian perspectives. The Indian tradition is very rich and consists of many schools of thought, which have grown and addressed the issues of reality and methods of knowing in diverse ways. Even a brief introduction to these systems and their nuances is beyond the scope of this presentation. There are twelve major schools of Indian philosophy. They constitute two main groups, that is, the *Vedic*—those who accept the authority of the *Vedas* are called *āstika* (orthodox) and the Non-*Vedic*—those who deny the authority of the *Vedas* are called *nāstika* (heterodox). The six orthodox schools can be arranged in three sets that are akin to each other:

1. Nyāya and Vaiśeṣika,
2. Sāṁkhya and Yoga, and
3. Mīmāṁsā and Vedānta.

The six heterodox schools come under the following three heads:

1. Materialism known as Cārvāka or Lokāyata,
2. Jainism,
3. Buddhism, which has four sub-divisions:
   (a) Vaibhāṣika (direct realism),
   (b) Sautāntrika (indirect realism),
   (c) Yogācāra (idealism), and
   (d) Madhyamika (nihilism)

(See for details Akhilanand, 1948; Bijalwan, 1977; Coomaraswamy, 1943; Dasgupta, 1922; Dutta, 1960; Goward & Kunjunni Raja, 1990; Hiriyanna, 1932; Larson & Bhattacharya, 1987; Matilal, 1990; Paranjpe, 1984, 1998; Potter, 1977; Radhakrishnan, 1952; Raju, 1985; Safaya, 1975).

The present attempt is limited to providing a selective overview of the major perspectives on knowledge available in the Indian tradition.

The nature of knowledge and knowing

The notion of knowledge has been approached by Indian thinkers in diverse ways. It has been conceptualized as 'relation', 'act', 'quality', and 'self-subsistence'. However, all these terms are interlinked and do not refer to exclusive categories. In the philosophical literature, *jñāna* (cognition), *upalabdhi* (attainment) and *buddhi* (intellect) are often used independently as well as interchangeably to refer to knowledge. The Sāṁkhya theory proposes that knowledge is a mode of *buddhi*, which is an evolute of *prakṛti* (matter). As an activity, knowing is characterized as a process of consciousness. We use a number of measures/means (*pramāṇa*) as instruments (*karaṇa*) to obtain valid cognition (*pramā*). A valid cognition is one which is 'free from doubt' (*saṃśaya*), indefiniteness (*anadhyavasāya*), and error (*bhrama*), and which, therefore, reveals things as they are (*yathārtha*), furnishes the basis of successful activities (*samvādi-pravṛttyanukūla*) and is not contradicted (*abādhita*) by any other experience (Dutta, 1967, p. 119).

The process of knowing involves four factors, that is, subject (*pramātā*), object (*prameya*), method (*pramāṇa*) and the resulting knowledge (*pramā*). True or valid knowledge is not possible in the absence of any one of these. However, the operative cause of knowledge is *pramāṇa*. It is also subject to various types of errors. However, the validity of knowledge may be determined by focusing on the functional aspects of reality. This empirical world is treated as a field of action (*karmamayam jagat*). Everything, therefore, is meant for some action and every action has an end. We can test when a given object serves the end for which it is meant (*arthakriyākārin*). It is believed that novelty is the major feature of knowledge.

According to Gautama, the founder of Nyāya School, the beginnings of any inquiry lie in doubt (*saṁśaya*) and the desire to know (*jijñāsā*). At this point the utility for human good is explicitly stated and a careful analysis of the pros and cons of the issue (*pakṣa pratipakṣa*) is done and an attempt is made to ascertain true knowledge. The terms are accurately defined (*lakṣaṇa*) and their indications are stated. The seeker of knowledge is advised to observe the following steps of rigorous critical inquiry:

- Use all valid sources of knowledge;
- Use (and avoid conflict with) established theories;
- Use examples acceptable to all;
- Use the five-step method of discovery and proof;

- Use the indirect hypothetical/postulation method to strengthen the argument;
- Avoid material fallacy (*hetvābhāsa*),
- Avoid quibbles (*cala*),
- Avoid false analogies (*jāti*), and
- Avoid self-satisfying steps which may cause defeat in debates.

The inquiry is rooted in multiple sources including direct experience, introspection, knowledge obtained from other valid sources, current linguistic usage and knowledge of previously established theories. The inquiry is disciplined by certain norms. It is stated that the suppositions should be parsimonious (*laghavaḥ*) and if perception is sufficient nothing unperceived should be supposed. Alternative suppositions have to be eliminated. Defects in the process of reasoning such as self-dependence (*ātmāśraya*), mutual dependence (*anyonyāśraya*), circular reasoning (*cakraka*) and infinite regress (*anavastha*) have to be checked and eliminated. The validity of knowledge is regarded natural by some (for example, Mīmāṁsā and Vedānta) who think that the conditions of validity lie within the very conditions that generate the knowledge. Thus knowledge is known from the knowledge itself (*svataḥ-pramāṇa*). Contrary to this other thinkers (e.g., Nyāya Vaiśeṣika) hold the position that knowledge is not self-manifest and needs external validity (*parataḥ pramāṇa*). Buddhists think that validity is nothing but practical efficiency. Knowledge of knowledge has also been explained in diverse ways. Some consider knowledge as self-manifest (*svataḥ-prakāśa*) (for example, Sāṁkhya, Vedānta, Prabhākara, Jain) while others consider it as based on introspection (Nyāya) or inference (Bhaṭṭa). True knowledge (*vidyā*) leads to the awareness of the unity incorporating all the manifestations. On the other hand, ignorance (*avidyā*) denotes an understanding which leads to the view that all things are separate and diverse.

Types of knowledge and systems of studies

The pursuits in the realm of knowledge were classified in two broad categories, that is spiritual knowledge (*parā vidyā*) and empirical knowledge (*aparā vidyā*). Spiritual knowledge is concerned with the experience of universal reality and empirical knowledge is bound to specific objects. It deals with the name (*nāma*) and form (*rūpa*) of ultimate reality in its diverse manifestations. The knowledge of supreme reality was supposed to lead to liberation (*mokṣa*). Empirical knowledge is of practical significance and deals with the ordinary world. It is pragmatic. In this context, it may be mentioned that the two types of knowledge are used to support the whole range of existential concerns and, therefore, are complementary. Both have a significant place in realizing the life goals (*puruṣārthas*). Liberation is accessible by multiple means and does not necessarily imply renunciation of the world. Rather, it involves liberation from the false ego boundaries which make a person self-centered.

It is interesting to note that the term *vidyā* was used for science as well as philosophy. *Vidyās* were classified in four major categories, that is, *ānvīkṣikī*, *trayī*, *vārttā*, and *daṇḍanīti*. They dealt with philosophy, *vedic* knowledge, and economic and political studies, respectively. *Ānvīkṣikī* is 'philosophizing' rather than 'philosophy'. Thus the Buddhist, the Jain, the Cārvāka together with (the *veda*-believing) Sāṁkhya, Nyāya, Vaiśeṣika are recognized as divisions of *ānvīkṣikī*. The development of these *vidyās* demonstrates a dialectic of two perspectives, the orthodox and the heterodox. As Pandey (1984, p. 220) says,

> The former stressed authority and tended to be conservative while the latter relied on reason and experience alone. In the course of their interaction the orthodox stream sought to reconcile tradition with reason and introduced modifications through commentarial interpretations and even interpolations.

The development of knowledge systems is conceptualized in the form of *śāstras*. As Pandey (1984) says,

> [A *śāstra* consisted] of a system of rules with its own techniques and concepts. It was required to define itself with respect to its subject matter, purpose, relevance, and the class of inquirer who was eligible

for its study (*anubandha-catustaya*). The knowledge which the sastras embody is discursive, rational and practical. Being discursive it is different from intuitive spiritual wisdom which is timeless and unchanging. Its rational and practical aspects are complementary. Reason is not conceived here as an independent source of knowledge. It is integrally connected with experience and faith but differs from these in being self-critical and indirect.

The treatises on erotics (*kāmaśāstra*), wealth/economy (*arthaśāstra*) and ethics (*dharmaśāstra*) were very systematically developed and exemplify the idea of *śāstra*.

Attitude towards knowledge

Knowing involves relating to the different aspects of our Reality such as persons, events, objects and ideas. The Indian attitude towards knowing is grounded in a set of premises as stated below.

1. *Ignorance is the cause of suffering.* The pursuit of knowledge in general is oriented towards removal of suffering (*sā vidyāyā vimuktaye ṛte jñānān na muktiḥ/ vidyayāmṛtam aśnute*) experienced in one's life. It is not considered as a pure intellectual exercise.
2. *Knowledge of any kind is inseparable from the human goals and values.* Human life has been traditionally conceived as the pursuit of four related goals (*puruṣārthas*), that is, *dharma* (ethical merit), *artha* (wealth), *kāma* (enjoyment) and *mokṣa* (salvation). The pursuit of these goals has to take place in the context of the four life stages or divisions of life, that is, student (*brahmacarya*), householder (*gṛhastha*), forest dweller (*vānaprastha*) and renouncer (*sannyāsa*). These stages are preparatory to the life goals. It may be noted that *mokṣa* (liberation) as a goal has been a later addition to the goal structure and is not a compulsion. Similarly, forest dwelling is also optional. One may decide to remain a householder and continue in the community life and instead of becoming a renouncer may try to pursue *dharma* as a *gṛhastha*.
3. *The philosophical discourse,* although it has intellectual and academic focus on the problems of human existence, *is intimately linked to the life of action in society.* A motive towards the search for an ideal life and a deeper sense of life is always present. The quest for being itself (ontological being), which encompasses both being and becoming is central to the process of knowing.
4. *Knowledge is characterized more in terms of modifications, structuring and reorganization of the knower.* It changes the knower or the person engaged in the pursuit of knowledge more than changing or controlling the object or the thing being known. In fact, knowledge was supposed to transform the whole person by introducing changes in mental, linguistic and behavioural functioning of the person.
5. The *relationship between dharma and knowledge in the Indian tradition is congenial.* As Paranjpe (1984) has rightly indicated, in the Indian context of *Adhyātma*, there is no conflict between science and religion, which has resulted in an avoidant attitude towards religion in the West. As a result, Indian science developed in close relationship with *dharma*.
6. The Indian view assumes that the universe is lawful and there is continuity within the entire animate kingdom. Similarly, man's relationship with nature is also construed in different ways. The Western view emphasizes a conflict between man and nature because man is placed over nature. In the Indian tradition, man and nature are interdependent and share coexistence. As V. N. Misra (1984) has remarked, man does not stand on the top of the universe nor is the rest of existence subservient to him. There is an inherent correspondence of macrocosm and microcosm. The man in Indian thought is operating on two planes, one operating along the dimension of time and space, while the other transcends time through its projection in its progeny and transcends space through its identity not only with the nature around, but with all the beings.

Mind: Its nature, states and functions

Most of the schools of Indian philosophy consider that mind (*manas*) cannot be equated with self (*ātman*) who is the knower. It is considered as a substance and an instrument of knowledge. The materiality of mind has been very strongly emphasized by the Sāṁkhya system. Some schools consider mind as an internal sense organ responsible for the experiences of pleasure, pain, and other internal states (Chennakesavan, 1980).

It is held that knowledge constitutes the nature or quality of self (*ātman*) acting through mind, reaching out to the objects and making them known to the self. An early reference to the functions of mind in *Aitareya Upaniṣad* includes the following: *samjñāna* (awareness), *ājñāna* (perception), *vijñāna* (discrimination), *prajñāna* (intelligence), *medhā* (wisdom), *dṛṣṭi* (insight), *dhṛti* (steadfastness), *mati* (thought), *manīṣā* (thoughtfulness), *smṛti* (memory), *saṃkalpa* (conception), *kratu* (purpose), *asu* (life), *kāma* (desire for a thing), and *vaśa* (desire for possession). *Chāndogya Upaniṣad* also gives a list of mind's functions which incorporates some additional functions such as *citta* (intelligence and thought), *dhyāna* (concentrated reflection), and *smara* (remembrance). Finally, the *Bṛhadāraṇyaka Upaniṣad* considers *kāma* (desire), *vicikitsā* (doubt), *śraddhā* (belief), *aśradhā* (disbelief), *dhṛti* and *adhṛti* (steadiness and unsteadiness), *hrī* (shame), *dhī* (meditation) and *bhī* (fear) as the mind's activity.

The Yoga system delineates five modes or states of mental activity consisting of *kṣipta* (wandering), *mūḍha* (forgetful), *vikṣipta* (distracted), *ekāgra* (one-pointed) and *niruddha* (restrained). In terms of discriminating power, mental activities are classified as *kliṣṭa* (hindered) and *akliṣṭa* (unhindered). The *akliṣṭa* has discrimination for the objects and consists of *vṛtti pramāṇa* (valid knowledge), *viparyaya* (illusion), *vikalpa* (predicate relation), *nidrā* (sleep), and *smṛti* (memory). Perception depends on mental modification or *citta vṛtti* and contact between the target object and *manas* through sense organs. Self (*puruṣa*) is considered as the real cognizer. The *citta vṛttis* are illuminated by *puruṣa's* reflection in *buddhi*. Knowledge is illumination of a thing not already presented and is caused by the operation of the self. Illusion (*viparyaya*) means knowing of the unreal possessing a form not of its *own*. It is incorrect cognition (*mithya jñāna*). Such knowledge is contradicted or sublated by a subsequent cognition. The realization of the true self is also blocked by misconceptions (*kleśa*) such as *avidyā* (ignorance), *asmitā* (egoism), *rāga* (attachment or passion), *dveṣa* (aversion) and *abhiniveśa* (clinging to life). *Vikalpa* (predicate relation) is considered by *Yoga sūtra* as a way of knowing. It involves imagination without any corresponding perceptible object. It is the result of verbal expressions of knowledge. Recognition (*pratyabhijñā*) is considered as a form of perception by the Nyāya school of Indian philosophy. It occurs because of many factors such as attention (*praṇidhāna*), association (*nibandha*), practice (*abhyāsa*), indicative (*liṅga*), distinguishing features (*lakṣaṇa*), likeness (*sādṛśya*), ownership or possession (*parigraha*), support (*sambandha*), sequence (*anantarya*), separation (*viyoga*), similar employment (*ekakārya*), enmity (*virodha*), superiority (*atiśaya*), acquisition (*prāpti*), cover (*avadhāna*), pleasure and pain (*sukha* and *duḥkha*), desire and aversion (*icchā* and *dveṣa*), fear (*bhaya*), need (*arthitva*), profession (*kriyā*), affection (*rāga*), and merit and demerit (*dharma* and *adharma*). These causes of recognition are not mutually exclusive. They refer to the characteristics of objects and events, their contexts and relationships. In this conceptualization recognition is considered as recollective cognition. Some thinkers emphasize its perceptual aspects and directness of experience, while others emphasize its memory component.

Memory (*smṛti*) refers to the activation of residual impressions or traces of the past experiences (*saṁskāras*). Memory is a function of the contact of these *saṁskāras* with mind (*manas*). It has been distinguished from recollection on the basis of presence/absence of objects. Some scholars have considered that being dependent on past experience (*anubhava*) memory is only a mediate knowledge. Others argue that memory is an indicator of the continuity of life and experiences. Memory is importantly related to *ākāra* (configuration) while perception involves *rūpa* (form). The *saṁskāras* gradually become stronger with their repeated manifestations in actions. This has implications for the practice of *Yoga*. For instance, bad and painful *saṁskāras* have to be substituted by good and pleasant *saṁskāras*. The stored up experiences have tendencies for actualization (*vāsanas*). The *saṁskāras* are often present at the unconscious level.

Thus, while knowledge is a quality of the self it is manifested by the mind through its contact with the objects. It should be noted that if the self has to attain knowledge, the mind has to be active and regulate the entire process. Mind is matter but has *sattva guṇa* (luminosity) and, therefore, has the capacity to reflect. The objects being largely *tāmasic* (quality of darkness and heaviness) are incapable of luminosity. In the Nyāya-Vaiśeṣika, there are nine kinds of matter (or rather elements), namely, earth, water, fire, air, space, time, direction, mind, and self.

Consciousness

The meaning of consciousness in the Indian tradition has gradually evolved. The initial realization of the principle of oneness of the universe gradually led to the view that consciousness is transcendental and entirely unlike any known object of the empirical world. The absolute consciousness is empirically non-characterisable. It is yet not unknown, and its nature is *'jñā'* or pure intelligence. Its nature is of the constant, unchanging and basic consciousness. This provides a background and support for the empirically experienced consciousness. In fact the coalition of the changing and unchanging consciousness forms the basis of experience within which the distinctions of subject and object are made. Once we attain perfect harmony between our vital, mental and psychical beings and *sādhanā* has purified our being, we get the intuition of the transcendental. In the western tradition the psychological complex (for example, sensation, thoughts, feelings) is held to be mental. Contrary to this, Indian thinkers have considered the mental world also as part of matter. The difference between the two is only of subtlety (*sūkṣmata*) and fineness retained in the process of modification.

Causality

The problem of causality has been analyzed in different ways in the various philosophical systems. In *Vedic* thought, causation is looked at from the cosmic point of view and the question considered is about the 'making' or 'creating' of the whole cosmos. According to one view the creator is *Brahman* or *Ātman* (Self) who creates the entire world out of itself and remains present in it. Another theory holds that the world evolved out of a primordial chaos or non-being. As Heimann (1937) says, *Upaniṣadic* cosmology teaches that the world originated by *sṛṣṭi* or *sarga*— seminal emission from the supreme body.

However, the idea of universal causality was questioned by subsequent thinkers. For instance Dignag argued that 'events alone are perceived substances and relations are constructed in judgment (*vikalpa*). The world that is directly perceived is only a flux of instantaneous events, but the world that is constructed by rational knowledge is an ordered whole of substances and relations. The constructed world is superimposed on the perceptual world as its relevant description in verbal conceptual terms and this "systematic" or "transcendental" illusion is the basis of all thought and action' (Pandey, 1984, p. 228). Thus in this tradition causality is related to the nature of the mind and justified on the ground of its indispensability.

Buddhists have argued that the joint use of observation and inference and non-observation under certain conditions should be employed to ascertain causal relationships. The logicians (*naiyayikas*) view 'cause' in terms of 'activity of making'. In this sense causation stands for the whole process comprising of 'some agency producing some entity by acting on something else as its material'. Thus we have three causes, that is, the agent as efficient cause (*nimitta kāraṇa*), the material (*samavāyi kāraṇa*) and the joining/contributing factors (*asamavāyi kāraṇa*). In this framework, a cause is different from the emerging effect. The causes are considered as regular antecedents for the effects. In contrast, the Sāṁkhya theorists advanced the view that the effect pre-exists in the creation in some latent fashion. In other words, causation is really a manifestation of continuous evolution.

Reality

Reality is dealt within a general sense by

reference to the notion of *padārtha* or *tattva*, the ultimate category. Different systems of thought identify different numbers of such categories. The ultimate principles are often put forward as distinct intuitable essences. They are conceptualized in terms of distinctive features (*lakṣaṇas*). Let us briefly examine the conceptualization of reality in the historical perspective.

In the early *Ṛg Veda* we find Varuṇa, a deity of universal character who was thought of as pervading nature, and influencing everything including sun, stars, water, the human mind and animal life. Varuṇa is referred to as the representation of *ṛta*—the cosmic order, or inner balance of the cosmic manifestations. It is a remarkable fact that the majority of texts emphasize cosmic plurality and cosmic interchangeability, involving alternation of even divine forms. As Heimann (1964, p. 39) says, 'to the Indian mind ... beasts are just as worthy an expression of divine Nature as is man. In India, then, not singleness, but plurality and manifoldness of form and type have been emphasized during every period... From the very beginning... matter is on an equal footing with spirit or mind...there is equal valuation of matter and spirit.'

It is very important to note that matter and spirit—eternal primeval essences share similar status. Also, the cosmic and specific faculties are derived from matter including intellect. The spiritual principle is often viewed as 'inactive'. Heimann (1937) has referred to three metaphors to illustrate the status of Spirit in the Indian tradition:

- Spirit riding as a mere passenger in the chariot of the cosmic urge.
- Spirit as the owner of a bedstead without active participation in supplying the material. He is only the customer for whom the bed has been manufactured so that he may sleep in it.
- Spirit as the magnet attracting matter, thus causing it to move and influencing its direction while himself remaining static.

The principles of reincarnation and *karma* are universal. They, however, are not pre-existent to the cosmic happenings, but come into existence together with these. There is no pre-eminent ultimate, unique principle. It has often been argued that the doctrine of *Māyā* is illusory and *Nirvāṇa* indicates annihilation of existence. As Heimann (1937) observes that *māyā refers* to measurable empirical things. They are smaller than the unmanifest (*avyaktam*) and being constructions are subject to destruction. The empirical reality is definite. The objects of empirical world do not share the transcendental reality of the 'indefinite'. Thus Indian thought recognizes an eternity of 'transcendental statics', and the 'continuity of an empirical dynamics'. Similarly, *Nirvāṇa* does not mean nullity. It refers to 'not thing', that is the indefinite thing.

The Indian ontology postulates two major planes (*satta*) of reality—transcendental (*pāramārthika*) and empirical (*vyavahārika*). The transcendental reality is considered to be non-changing and universal. It can be experienced under certain conditions like *samādhi*. In addition a category of apparent reality (*pratibhāsika*) has also been proposed (for example, the silver seen in the glittering conch-shell). It exists only for the duration of the cognition itself. It is not the matter alone but matter and spirit combined which forms the basis for activity. Also, there is the fundamental notion of an after-life for every existing entity. This world (*saṁsāra*) is supposed to be a continuous stream of active lives. The same cannot be interpreted as 'cycle of rebirths' since the individual in its rebirth never returns to the same point, but always to a more developed stage of incarnation, in accord with the growth of its own inherent tendency.

Thus, objects do not have only static existence. Rather, they are subject to continuous changes both in themselves as well as in their relationship with other existing objects. Heimann (1937, pp. 61-62) designates it as transcendental materialism which 'postulates the transformation of one empirical form into another, and finally all these into a static shapelessness which is beyond all empirical experience...It has an outlook tending towards ultimate oneness—the real *universe*—that is towards the primal and final *sat*, static being, which can nevertheless be grasped only in its derived forms of transient "becoming" in the empirical *Bhavas*.' In this framework human beings are not considered to be endowed with some great power because they have the capacity to reason, as Descartes postulated. Instead, as Heimann (1937, p. 97) says, 'India's conclusion is: In spite of my reasoning I exist just as do all other accidental manifestations of the primeval unity.'

The means of knowledge

Apprehending reality (*tattvajñāna*) and becoming aware of it requires some measure (*pramāṇa*) or means. In Western philosophy perception and inference are two sources of knowledge. The various schools of thought have proposed diverse sources of knowledge and have various orders of preference. The major means of knowledge include the following: *pratyakṣa* (perception), *anumāna* (inference), *upamāna* (comparison), *śabda* (verbal testimony), *arthāpatti* (postulation) and *anupalabdhi* (non-cognition) are accepted as auxiliary sources of knowledge. In addition, *pratibhā* (intuitive knowledge), *aitihya* (unbroken tradition) and *sambhava* (possible inclusion) have been considered by some schools as sources of knowledge.

Perception (Pratyakṣa)

Perceptual knowledge is viewed as direct knowledge of objects, dealing with both external as well as internal (bodily) objects and states. It is an achievement of coordination among sense organs, self (*ātman*) and mind (*antaḥkaraṇa/manas*). In this process knowledge occurs in the form of 'consciousness' or awareness when mind and self come into contact. Thus it may be considered as an objective action based on the contact between sense-organ and dynamically active sense object. The internal objects (for example, feelings, states, etc.) are known through mind (*antaḥkaraṇa*) coming directly into contact with self. We perceive attributes of things or substances and experience their identities. It is assumed that individual characteristics as well as generic attributes are both perceived. It is held that knowledge requires modification of mind corresponding to the object. In this sense knowledge becomes a manifestation of consciousness through an appropriate mental mode. For instance Vedānta considers four states or functions (*vṛtti*) of mind, that is, deliberation (*manas*), determination (*buddhi*), egoism (*ahaṁkāra*) and recollection (*citta*).

A distinction has been made between indeterminate (*nirvikalpaka*) and determinate (*savikalpaka*) perception. Indeterminate perception is perception of the mere being. In determinate perception the identity is also included. The sensory experience is considered to be definite and assuring because the objects are directly presented to the knowing self by the activity of the sense-organs and the mind. Thus united with the sense-organs, mind contacts the objects. Mind plays an active role in this process. Perceptual knowledge, therefore, is a broader concept than what is usually understood by sensory experience. It subsumes the whole range of common sensory perception, introspection, as well as intellectual and mystical intuition.

Inference (Anumāna)

Inference is treated as knowledge of the invariable concomitant relation between what is perceived and what is deduced. The *Sanskrit* term *anumāna* means 'knowing after' or knowledge derived from some other knowledge. It also refers to 'measure along' using other measures. Thus, it involves deductive inference which follows from the already existing knowledge. In this framework, the significance of inference depends on what is available from direct perception. The syllogistic reasoning which illustrates the inference as conceived in the Indian tradition consists of five steps as follows:

- Proposition to be proved (*pratijñā*): The hill has fire.
- Reason for this (*hetu* or *liṅga*): Because it has smoke.
- Universal proposition supported by an instance (*udāharaṇa* or *nidarśana*): Whatever has smoke has fire, such as a kitchen.
- Application of the universal proposition (*upanaya* or *anusandhāna*): Hill has smoke, such as is always accompanied by fire.
- Conclusion proved (*nigamana*): Therefore hill has fire.

It is evident that this kind of reasoning combines deductive as well as inductive processes. It involves formal validity with material truth through inductive generalization and deductive particularization. The use of example supplies a basis for enumeration and empirical induction enabling verification for sensible prediction. It shows that the major premise is really based upon an actual instance. This whole process is termed as comprehension (*parāmarśa*) which establishes a link in the entire process of inference.

Thus inference relies on the understanding of invariable concomitance deduced from observation of agreement in presence, absence, and non-observation of the contrary. Some scholars have talked about three types of inference based on a priori (*pūrvavat*) (inferring effect from cause), a posteriory (*śeṣavat*) (inferring cause from effect), and analogical (*sāmānyatodṛṣṭa*) (inference from something perceived as similar). A distinction between inference for self (*svārthānumāna*) and inference for other (*parārthānumāna*) has also been made. The major difference between the two is that in the latter all the premises have to be stated while the same is not necessary in the case of the former.

On the whole, the Indian syllogism exemplifies a novel way to approach the problem of inference. As Heimann (1937, p. 87) has observed, it 'is not ... an affair of pure deduction, but a sequence of inductions, and it is characteristic of India's practical outlook and its practical conception of proof'. It presents a 'paradigm of the union of diverse epistemic principles'. Pandey (1984, p. 221) states that in this paradigm 'reason examines a principle given in tradition in terms of its logical ground, empirical evidence and analogy. If reasons were unguided by tradition it would lead to endlessly changing conclusions. Although it is admitted that doubt requires reasoning and reasoning proceeds till one reaches a contradiction, it was realized that merely hypothetical reasoning or *tarka* can only have a subordinate role within the broader sweep of syllogistic reasoning or *anumān*.' He further notes that, 'by its working within the framework of tradition this conception of reason tends to be scholastic and conservative but by its working within a context of practical inquiry and experience, it has a pragmatic or *vyavahārika* character'.

Comparison (Upamāna)

Comparison is a spontaneous cognitive process to be called by the observance of similarity or analogy. This may be viewed as a way of knowing A's similarity to B from the perception of B's similarity to A which has been perceived elsewhere. Thus, it involves an empirical association of two similar observations. For instance, the relationship between *Brahman* and *Ātman* is viewed as all-pervading and unrelated like *ākāśa* (space, sky). This source of knowledge is based on sensory facts but inference transcends the senses and helps in exploring the unseen. It is mediate and general in nature and shows that when perception is not sufficient the immediate cognition is used. It is important to note that the role of memory in this process is secondary. The cognition of similarity leads to recollection and not vice versa. The observed similarity leads to the past experience. It seems that mind is considered to possess some special process leading to the observance of similarity. Unlike western thinkers Indians do not consider comparison as a form of inference.

Postulation (Arthāpatti)

This source of knowledge involves supposition or presumption of some fact. When in our experience some unit of cognition is incomplete, we posit something to make it a structured whole. In such a situation we often engage in assuming some unknown fact in order to account for a known fact that is otherwise inexplicable. A famous example often referred to in the Indian treatises goes like this: Suppose we found 'a stout person A who does not eat in the day'. Now, 'stoutness' is not possible without eating. The person, therefore, 'must be eating' and if he is not eating in the day then he must be eating in the night. Thus, in order to explain 'stoutness' we posit the fact of 'eating in the night'. Postulation is distinguished from inference on the basis of the absence of a major premise. It is also different from induction. A distinction has been made between postulation to explain something seen and postulation of a meaning for making words intelligible.

Verbal testimony (Śabda)

Most of the facts in everyday life are made known to us by means of words. In addition, under certain circumstances words can even serve as a means of immediate knowledge. They often supplement perception and inference. Not only this, in the Indian tradition they are viewed as the only vehicle of supra sensuous knowledge. Words are assumed to precede intuitive perception. This kind of knowledge is based on the comprehension of the meanings of the pertinent words and their interrelations. The words of trustworthy people who have attained knowledge (*āpta*) are important sources of knowledge. *Veda* or *Śruti* (scriptural authority) has been consistently considered as the only source of knowing *Brahman*—the absolute reality. *Vedas* are viewed as divine revelation representing indisputable truth. They are known as *nigama*. *Āgama* is actually a divine text different from *nigama or Veda*. The various tantric texts are *āgama* or 'the word that has become', the *Brahman* itself in the word-form. This is to be contrasted with 'the word that has come', a report on what God has said. The meaning of words (*śabda bodha*) works as a source of knowledge. It involves constructive combination of ideas. In this process the cognition of words is the instrument, recollection of meaning is the operation, and verbal comprehension is the outcome. However, scriptural authority is not the ultimate source of knowledge of *Brahman*. It is, rather, *anubhava* (intuitive experience), which leads to realization of *Brahman*. *Śruti* only clears the ignorance.

The words signify objects, actions, and attributes which have universal (for example 'cow' to refer to all cows) and particular (for example, 'cow' to refer to one particular individual cow) aspects. Usually the implied meaning is secondary but it is sought when primary meaning does not work. The primary meaning is related to saying (*abhidhāna*) and secondary meaning involves pointing or indicating (*lakṣaṇa*). Thus, metaphors employ secondary meaning and point to something and have a suggestive power (*lakṣyārtha*). It is generally accepted that words have meaning only when they exist in the sentence. A sentence has four important features; that is, word order (*ākāṅkṣa*)—each word expects something from other words, coordination of meaning of a word with another (*yogyatā*), continuity in time and space (*sannidhi*) and intention (*tātparya*). The denotative meaning can be of four types, namely derivative (*yaugika*), conventional (*rūḍha*), derivatively conventional (*yogarūḍha*), and derivative and conventional (*yaugika-rūḍha*).

In the determination of meaning the context under reference plays a crucial role. The context involves several types of relationships (for example, association, dissociation, mutual association, hostility, opposition, purpose, context, situation, indicator sign, proximity, capacity, propriety, place, time, gender and accent). According to Patañjali, a great exponent of grammar, the meaning is learned from the behaviour of people. The convention (*samaya*) is viewed as the primary determinant of the meaning because the speaker and hearer are both members of a linguistic community. According to Prabhākara, words have no meaning apart from the action they lead to and the meaning of a word is the action to which they lead.

The importance of language as an activity, as languaging (*śabdana vyāpāra*) was clearly recognized by the Sanskrit grammarians. Language makes the human transactions possible. It is held that linguistic expressions have evolved out of one principle—word essence (*śabda tattva*)—eternal verbum. It refers to the ever extending consciousness of the sentient. Word as *Brahman* and alphabets as *akṣara* (undestroyable) convey an important sense. Matilal (1990) finds a significant link: 'our perceived world is also an interpreted world'. The act of interpretation is nothing but languaging. Language is inseparably related to awareness. All cognitive awareness appears in the form of interpretations through language.

It is interesting to note that Indian grammar (*vyākaraṇa*) which dealt with the systematic study of language also developed as a philosophical system. Being aware of the significant contributions of language to human experience and consciousness, not only the phenomenal aspects of language were taken into account but also contemplation about its metaphysical foundations was done. It was realized that knowledge is grounded in language. In the Indian tradition, the normative aspect of language focused on the oral or spoken form of language because the written form of language was considered inadequate to comprehensively encompass all aspects of linguistic reality. Words were treated as constituents of consciousness in the act of speaking.

Bhartṛhari, one of the most important grammarians, postulated that there is no cognition without the operation of words; all cognition is shot through and through by the word. All knowledge is illumined through the word (*sarvaṃ śabdena bhāsate*). It is through the meaning conveyed by words that all knowledge is experienced. This is true because we understand and communicate our thoughts only through the expressed words. Here, the word is not identified with sound only. The understanding regarding objects (*sampratyaya*) is also included in it. The relationship between word and meaning is eternal and impersonal. Bhartṛhari observes that language operates at two levels. At first an idea comes as an inner flash (*sphoṭa*). This is the first level which is termed as *paśyantī vāc*. This is reflected in the intuitive flash of idea, sentence, or poem as a whole. Its manifested or uttered form is *vaikharī vāc*. Between these two levels there is a middle level known as *madhyamā vāc* in which the intuitive holistic idea is separated in sequence. This scheme covers the entire-range of linguistic operations.

Non-cognition (Anupalabdhi)

This is a means to the knowledge of non-existence (*abhava*). The underlying assumption is that if a thing is known by a particular sense-organ, its opposite will also be known by the same sense-organ. It is argued that non-existence of a thing is apprehended by its non-perception. The remarkable fact is that here the emphasis is on 'non-apprehension of presence' rather than non-perception of non-existence. Thus both existence and non-existence are facts of cognition. We say that 'there is no pen on the table'. Here the sense contact is with the *locus* of non-existence and not with the non-existence. Thus, only appropriate non-apprehension can cause valid cognition of non-existence. Indian logicians have identified several types of non-existence, such as those caused by destruction, absolute non-cognition and mutual non-cognition.

Knowing pleasure and pain

Manas (mind) as an internal sense-organ has been considered responsible for emotional experiences. The different schools of thought have explained these experiences in different ways. According to the Nyāya system, pleasure and pain (*sukha* and *duḥkha*), desire and aversion (*icchā* and *dveṣa*), cognition (*jñāna*) and volition (*prayatna*) are the qualities of the self (*ātman*). But they are known to self only when *manas* comes into contact with the self as possessed of these qualities. Pain occurs when the pressure from a want becomes extreme. When the want is satisfied, the person feels pleasure. Obstruction is the characteristic of pain (*bādhana-lakṣaṇam duḥkham*). On the other hand, agreeableness (*anukūla*) is pleasure.

According to Vaiśeṣika *sūtras*, pleasure and pain are different as they have diverse causes and effects. Pleasure leads to a feeling of pleasantness (*anugraha*), attraction (*abhiṣvaṅga*) and brightness of the eyes and face, etc. (*nayanādi prasāda*). In contrast, pain's effects include anger, ideas of harm doing and depression. Both, pleasure and pain can be with reference to past and future. In these cases, they are based on recollection and reflection, respectively. Also, they are immediate perceptions, unlike cognition (*jñāna*) which involves doubt and assurance (*saṁśaya* and *nirṇaya*). Pleasure and pain cause desire and aversion (*icchā* and *dveṣa*). Desire is the source of effort, remembrance, virtue and vice. Some major types of desires are: lust, hunger, affection, aspiration, compassion, disinclination, disposition (to impose or deceive others) and inclination (unexpressed desire). Aversion leads to anger (*krodha*), ill-will (*droha*), resentment (*manyu*), jealousy (*akṣamā*), and indignation (*amarṣa*). The knowledge of pleasurable things leads one to put incessant effort to obtain it. All other emotional experiences emerge out of pleasure and pain.

Realization of supreme knowledge

The learning processes for higher order knowledge (*parā vidyā*) require a Guru. It involves *sādhanā* (spiritual praxis) in the supervision of a *ṛṣi* or *draṣṭā* (seer). As Pandey (1984, p. 1) argues,

> Ultimate authority in India is in practice held to belong not to ancient books, nor their learned expositions, but to those who are believed to have personal experience of spiritual truth. It is a living vision which transforms the inner life, faculties and powers of the person who attains it. The process of seeking and attaining spiritual vision and inner transformation has been variously called, the commonest expressions being sadhana, or *yoga*.

In its broadest sense *sādhanā* involves perfection in work for every person in his or her respective pursuit and performance of duties. *Sādhanā* also denotes 'making', and thus implicates transformation of self. It involves detached truth seeking (*jijñāsā*), sensitiveness (*ākṣiptakalpatā*), earnestness (*saṃvega*), maturity and wisdom (*viveka*), and realization of the constraints and limitations emanating from egoism and acquisitiveness.

In general, three ways (*mārga*) *of* spiritual realization have been practiced. They consist of knowledge, action and devotion (*jñāna*, *karma* and *bhakti*). The *yogic* system of Patañjali prescribes the practice of *yoga* consisting of eight limbs: restraints (*yama*), observances (*niyama*), postures (*āsana*), breathing exercises (*prāṇāyāma*), withdrawal of senses from its objects (*pratyāhāra*), concentration (*dhāraṇā*), contemplation (*dhyāna*), and *samādhi* (a trance like state). The *samādhi* state also has several hierarchically arranged levels or stages as listed below:

- *Savitarka*: In this stage words and their denotative and connotative meanings remain mixed together.
- *Nirvitarka*: This stage involves consciousness devoid of meanings and association originating from social conventions.
- *Savicāra*: This is characterized by a focus on space, time, and causal context of the object of cognition.
- *Nirvicāra*: This is a state uncharacterized by past, present, or future characteristics of object.
- *Sānanda*: This is focused on means of cognition.
- *Sāsmitā*: This is focused on the sense of self.
- *Asamprajñāta*: This state is the highest state devoid of all objects of cognition. The *yogī* attains final liberation, which is complete aloofness or isolation of *puruṣa* from *prakṛti*. The experiencing subject is completely withdrawn into himself so that he is no longer conscious of anything. This condition emerges when all varieties of the processes of consciousness are completely restrained. It is usually achieved for short periods of time. Its practitioner experiences a superior form of direct perception, an essence-envisioning perspective on objects, a truth-bearing insight, and an experience of bliss (Paranjpe, 1984). Also, its effects/consequences do not impel a person to seek various objects of desire. This trans-cognitive state is a qualitatively different type of experience.

Vedānta also suggests that *nirvikalpaka samādhi* leads to the attainment of a superior state of being. This requires (a) correct discrimination between the everlasting and the impermanent, (b) maintaining mind (*sama*), withholding the senses from the objects of their pleasure (*dama*), preventing the mind from modifying itself (*uparati*), enduring hardships and pain (*titikṣā*), (c) adopting a conviction about faith in scripture and teacher (*śraddhā*) and resting mind (*samādhāna*), and (d) intense desire for liberation from the bonds created by egoism and ignorance. In addition, three broad strategies have been suggested, that is, learning/listening (*śravana*), intellectual training (*manana*) and ethical training (*nididhyāsana*).

Devotion (*bhakti*) is the second mode of spiritual realization. Devotion requires recognition of a personal God, who is omnipresent, omniscient and omnipotent, and who confers his grace on the devotee when he surrenders himself unreservedly to God. The *Bhagavad Gītā* states that meditation of God and offerings with devotion and dedication make people free from the fruits which constitute the bondage of action. God is even-minded to everybody. However, those who worship him with devotion, they abide in God and God also in them. In the *Bhagavad Gītā*, Krishna says to Arjuna, 'On Me fix your mind, become My devotee, My worshipper; render homage unto Me. Thus having attached yourself to Me, with Me as your goal, you shall come to Me.' Giving up all action to God, full devotion, lodging all the understanding in God, removal of egoism (I-ness and my-ness), friendship and pity for all beings, tranquil, equality to pleasure and pain, patient, and forgiving have been enumerated as important characteristics of a *bhakta* (devotee).

Yoga of action (*karma*) is the third way to approach the supreme being and the transcendental reality. It is said that doing the assigned work without attachment leads to the highest goals. Work is also necessary for the solidarity of the society (*loka saṃgraha*). Thus in order to fulfill one's social obligations, one has inevitably to perform the assigned work. Thus one should engage in work and remain uninvolved in its consequences. The *Bhagavad Gītā* says that actions of all sorts are actually performed by the dispositions of matter (*Prakṛti*). However, due to egoism, a person thinks that 'I am the doer'. A person who knows that self, matter and action are different does not become attached to the results of actions. On the other hand, those who are attached to the dispositions and actions are attached to the outcomes. Actions do not cling to the person if there is no yearning for their fruit. Such an action is non-action. A person steadfast in *yoga* engages in action and abandons attachment. He becomes even-minded in success and failure. These approaches have been developed in detail by the different schools of thought and its subsystems have emerged. However, the existence of a reality which transcends the phenomenal world and has no beginning or end has been accepted by almost all the orthodox systems of Indian thought. This reality is treated in popular Hinduism as God.

Concluding comments

The preceding account of knowing in the Indian context reveals a very rich and complex metatheoretical framework which has the potential to offer insights into the intricate processes of human understanding. The diversity in Indian thought is remarkable; it shows considerable similarity with the Western mode of intellectual inquiry up to a point. It is more rigorous and inclusive than western empirical approach as currently practiced in psychological science. Also, it goes beyond the Western approach in many ways. Belief in multiple but interdependent worlds, use of discursive practices, significance of language, perception, reason and *sādhanā* to obtain empirical truth on the one hand and a realization of transcendental reality on the other, are very important for a holistic understanding.

In terms of knowing, a comprehensive methodology has to respect the first person perspective also. Psychology as an inner discipline seeks to locate and find oneself in its true and unconditioned form. The empirical manifestations of the inner do not constitute the essence. The observations at the surface level are but expressions. The experiencing person has exclusive accessibility to and ownership of a state of awareness. Knowing, which incorporates both—understanding and realization of truth in one's being, is the goal. In this formulation the identity of subject and object opens up a new possibility of experience beyond the confines of the observation of surface manifestations. Realizing truth or experiencing reality in an unmediated mode through participation or conscious experience makes truth a part of being. The processes of *śravana*, *manana* and *nididhyāsana* relate to learning, understanding and realization, respectively. They emphasize sense mediated learning, reasoning and meditative knowing. Movement across these three levels involves third, second and first orders of knowledge in which externally observable, interpersonal or inter-subjectively shared and personally experienced self-transformation take place. It may have intrinsic authenticity. In this case validity is reflexive. It involves direct experience and a state of consciousness. It differs from the third person accounts prevailing in psychology which are framed within the context where subject-object duality is maintained and where interpersonal consensual validation is achieved. Ego remains at the centre. Contrary to this the Indian pursuit of knowledge moves in the direction of ego annihilation as it is an illusion. The egoless experiencing person is a mere witness—a *sākṣī*. Reducing the first person experience to third person observation is problematic. The existing approach in psychology is limited in its scope as it hardly touches consciousness as such—a reality in its own right. The Indian perspective takes a qualitative and spiritual position and warrants inner development that may enable direct experience. It calls for a consciousness based paradigm with the scope of direct and experiential knowledge. Such a move is a matter of contemporary relevance and practical utility. It generates new, different and a more comprehensive theoretical perspective, and concepts in which emancipatory values are central and pursuit for knowledge is more engaging.

References

Akhilananda, S. (1948). *Hindu psychology*. London: Allen & Unwin.

Bijalwan, C. D. (1977). *Indian theory of knowledge based upon Jayant's Nyayamanjari*. New Delhi: Heritage Publishers.

Chennakesavan, S. (1980). *Concept of mind in Indian philosophy*. Delhi: Motilal Banarasidass.

Coomaraswamy, A. K. (1943). *Hinduism and Buddhism*. Wespot Con: Greenwood Press.

Dasgupta, S. N. (1922). *History of Indian philosophy*. Delhi: Motilal Banarasidass.

Dutta, D. M. (1960). *The six ways of knowing*. Calcutta: Calcutta University Press.

Dutta, D. M. (1967). Epistemological methods in Indian philosophy. In C. E. Moore (Ed.), *The Indian mind: Essentials of Indian philosophy and culture* (pp. 48-135). Honolulu: East West Center Press.

Goward, H. G., & Kunjunni Raja, K. (Eds.) (1990). *Encyclopedia of Indian philosophies* (Vol. V): *The philosophy of the grammarians*. New Delhi: Motilal Banarasidass.

Heimann, B. (1937). *Indian and western philosophy: A study in contrasts*. London: Allen & Unwin.

Heimann, B. (1964). *Facets of Indian thought*. New York: Shirken Books.

Hiriyanna, M. (1932). *The essentials of Indian philosophy*. London: Allen & Unwin

Larson, G. J., & Bhattacharya, R. S. (Eds.) (1987). *Encyclopedia of Indian philosophies* (Vol. IV): *Samkhya*. New Delhi: Motilal Banarasidass.

Matilal, B. M. (1990). *The word and world*. Delhi: Oxford University Press.

Misra, V. N. (1984). *The image of man in Indian literature*. Personal communication.

Nakamura, H. (1964). *Ways of thinking of eastern people: India-China-Tibet-Japan*. Honolulu: East-West Center Press.

Pandey, G. C. (1984). *Foundations of Indian culture: Spiritual vision and symbolic forms in ancient India*. New Delhi: Books & Books.

Paranjpe, A. C. (1984). *Theoretical psychology: The meeting of east and west*. New York: Plenum Press.

Paranjpe, A. C. (1998). *Self and identity in modern psychology and Indian thought*. New York: Plenum Press.

Potter, K. H. (Ed.) (1977). *Encyclopedia of Indian philosophies: Indian metaphysics and epistemology: The traditions of Nyaya-Vaisesika up to Ganesh*. New Delhi: Motilal Banarasidass.

Radhakrishnan, S. (1952). *History of philosophy: Eastern and western*, 2 vols. London: Allen & Unwin.

Raju, P. T. (1985). *Structural depths of Indian thought*. Albany: State University of New York.

Ramanujan, A. K. (1990). Is there an Indian way of thinking? An informal essay. In M. Marriott (Ed.), *India through Hindu categories* (pp. 41-58). New Delhi: Sage.

Safaya, R. (1975). *Indian psychology: A critical and historical analysis of the psychological speculation in Indian philosophical literature*. New Delhi: Munshiram Manoharlal.

8

On the *Vedic* symbolism in the light of Sri Aurobindo

Vladimir Iatsenko

Ādityas and other gods

The faculties of Consciousness in the *Veda* are seen as projected from the Divine Mother, Aditi, Infinite Consciousness-Force. The supreme emanations of that Consciousness-Force are called *Ādityas*, the Sons of Aditi. There are seven of them—Varuṇa, Mitra, Aryaman, Bhaga, Dakṣa, Amśa and Sūrya.

There are different classes of gods mentioned in the *Veda*: *Ādityas, Vasus, Viśve-devās, Māruta-gaṇa, Raudra-gaṇa*, etc. Although they differ from each other they also share many features and powers in the process of manifesting the Divine, which makes it difficult for the mind not used to distinguish the subtle differences in the commonly shared features. Ordinary mind would only see the crowded common imagery assigned to all of them. The ability to distinguish the particularities in the commonly shared features Sri Aurobindo attributes to the higher mind. He writes (1998, pp. 497–498):

> Yet as all these things form one in the realised godhead, as each element ... contains the others in itself and none of them can exist separately from the rest, therefore each of the Four (Ādityas) also possesses by force of his own essential quality every general attribute of his brothers. For this reason if we do not read the *Veda* as carefully as it was written, we shall miss its distinctions and see only the indistinguishable common functions of these luminous Kings, — as indeed throughout the hymns the unity in difference of all the gods makes it difficult for the mind not accustomed to the subtleties of psychological truth to find in the Vedic divinities anything but a confused mass of common or interchangeable attributes. But the distinctions are there.... Each god contains in himself all the others, but remains still himself in his peculiar function.

Āditya-gaṇa is a class of deities, which distinctly differ from other types of gods such as *Viśve-devās*, for instance, who are the Universal Gods, operating already in the created Universe, whereas *Ādityas* are still representing the transcendental and supramental levels. In their original status they also differ from the *Vasu* class, though many times they are called upon to be identified with the status of *Vasus*, especially when they are to rise in the consciousness of man.

Vasu literally means a 'luminous dweller within the substance'; Agni is often invoked by this name. And since Agni represents all the gods and godheads here and is their gate to the manifested consciousness of man, as it were, this word is also applied to all of them when used in this particular meaning of rising to the higher status from within. Thus *Ādityas, Maruts, Aśvins,* Indra, Uṣas, Rudra, Vāyu, Viṣṇu, Śiva and Kubera are invoked as *Vasus* then. In post-*Vedic* literature, the class of *Vasu, vasu-gaṇa*, consists of eight *Vasus*, the eighth one was born as Bhīṣma in the epic *Mahābhārata*.

There is also a clear distinction between

the *Ādityas* and the *Maruts*, or the class of *Rudras*, though again they may be called upon to be identified with *Rudras* for a particular purpose, in the same way as Agni can take any of the features of other gods on himself. *Rudras* is a class of gods, especially when they are mentioned in plural, indicating the sons of Rudra (sometimes identified with or distinguished from the *Maruts*, who are 11 or 33 in number). In the *Brāhmaṇas* and *Āraṇyakas* 11 *Rudras* are mentioned together with their female energies, *Rudrāṇīs*. The number of *Ādityas* also changes and grows up to 12, which seem to represent symbolically the 12 months of the Sun, *Āditya*.

The eighth son of Aditi

Sūrya or Savitṛ is the Creator, representing the Supramental Manifestation in all its glory of all the godheads, embodying all his brothers. He, by projecting himself into the darkness of the Inconscient, becomes Vivasvat of Mārtāṇḍa, Mortal Embryo, or Mortal Universe. It is this dark Sun, who is hidden by the Titans in the Subconscious cave of Darkness, which has to be recovered by the Sacrifice.

So Vivasvat is a Creator of the Universe, who thus carries within himself all the potentialities of his seven brothers from whom they are to rise to their high throne, from where they could see both the Supreme realms of Existence and the Lower Nature.[1] It is only then they may arrive at a supreme perception of the Lord. We can find a similar approach to the concept of Puruṣottama of the *Bhagavad Gītā*, or of Īś of the *Īśopaniṣad*.

The four transcendental godheads

The four transcendental godheads, or the Guardians of Light, are:

1. Varuṇa represents the Vastness of Infinite Being, *sat*.
2. Mitra represents the luminosity and harmony of the Divine Consciousness, *cit*.
3. Aryaman is the power of the Divine *tapas*.
4. Bhaga is the Bliss of the Divine Fulfillment, *ānanda*.

Sri Aurobindo calls the first four *Ādityas* the Guardians of Light, for they are guarding the Transcendental Light from one side and from another introducing it into the lower hemisphere. He writes in *The Secret of the Veda* (1998, p. 475), 'Aditi is the infinite Light of which the divine world is a formation and the gods, children of the infinite Light, born of her in the Ritam, manifested in that active truth of her movement guard it against Chaos and Ignorance'. Sri Aurobindo (1998, p. 497) defines the characteristics of the first four *Ādityas* in this way:

> The Divine is existence all-embracing, infinite and pure; Varuna brings to us the infinite oceanic space of the divine soul and its ethereal, elemental purity.
>
> The Divine is boundless consciousness, perfect in knowledge, pure and therefore luminously right in its discernment of things, perfectly harmonious and happy in its concordance of their law and nature; Mitra brings us this light and harmony, this right distinction and relation and friendly concord, the happy laws of the liberated soul concordant with itself and the Truth in all its rich thought, shining actions and thousand-fold enjoyment.
>
> The Divine is in its own being pure and perfect power and in us the eternal upward tendency in things to their source and truth; Aryaman brings to us this mighty strength and perfectly-guided happy inner upsurging.
>
> The Divine is the pure, the faultless, the all-embracing, the untroubled ecstasy that enjoys its own infinite being and enjoys equally all that it creates within itself; Bhaga gives us sovereignly that ecstasy of the liberated soul, its free and unfallen possession of itself and the world.
>
> This quaternary is practically the later essential trinity of Sachchidananda, — Existence, Consciousness, Bliss with self-awareness and self-force, Chit and Tapas, for double terms of Consciousness; but it is here translated into its cosmic terms and equivalents.

The triple status of the Supermind

Sri Aurobindo described the triple status of the Supermind in various ways. First we will use his description in philosophical terms. It is important for us to identify the faculties of the next three *Ādityas* and their functions, which will be directly connected with the triple status of the Supermind.

1. Unity.
2. Many in One and One in Many.
3. Many.

In the chapter, 'The Triple Status of the Supermind', Sri Aurobindo (1972, pp. 145-146) writes about these three levels: 'The first founds the inalienable unity of things, the second modifies that unity so as to support the manifestation of the Many in One and One in Many; the third further modifies it so as to support the evolution of a diversified individuality which, by the action of Ignorance, becomes in us at a lower level the illusion of the separate ego.'

This vision will be then projected into all the structure of the lower manifestation on all its levels. We may always find these three elements in the life of every creature: (a) the unifying oneness dominating over the individual elements, (b) the harmonizing diversity and its relation with oneness, and (c) the diversifying individual elements, deviating from the oneness as far as possible. These three will become the major grades in the hierarchy of the mental-vital-physical structure of consciousness, maintaining their approaches to the reality as a whole and to each other in particular.

Sri Aurobindo (1971, p. 26) also depicts the three layers of the Supermind in psychological terms, in relation to three activities of the intuitive mind—for Intuition is a flash of the Supramental light reaching out to the lower levels of consciousness. It is interesting to compare the two—the philosophical and the psychological descriptions. Here is the psychological one:

1. Interpretative Supermind ... corresponding to *Intuition*. I call it interpretative, because what is a possibility on the mental plane becomes a potentiality on the supramental plane and the *Interpretative puts all the potentialities* before you. It shows the root cause of events that may become true on the physical plane. When *Intuition* is changed into its supramental value, it becomes Interpretative Supermind.
2. Representative Supermind ... represents the actual movements of potentialities and shows what is in operation. When *Inspiration* is changed into its supramental value, then it becomes this Representative Supermind. Even this is not the highest. There you know certain potentialities in thought and action working and you can in many cases say what would happen or how a certain thing happened if it does.
3. Imperative Supermind ... which corresponds to *Revelation*. That is always true. Nothing can stand against it. It is knowledge fulfilling itself by its own inherent power.

The three godheads of the Supermind

The three godheads of the Supermind are:

1. Dakṣa represents the power of Thought, the All-discerning and All-distributing Power of Supramental Consciousness.
2. Aṃśa represents the diversity in Oneness supported by that Unifying Power of Dakṣa.
3. Sūrya or Savitṛ represents all the seven *Ādityas* and projects them into a lower Creation. His rays represent the diversity in the domains of *Svar*.

Dakṣa is the Father of all the *Ādityas* born for manifesting the Divine in the material Universe. Even Aditi is born to him as his daughter, the cosmic universal Cow, supporting with her milk all the creation. It is in Dakṣa that the triple conception by the Lord within his Consciousness is taking place,[2] which creates the triple status of the Supermind. Sri Aurobindo speaks of Dakṣa in this way (1998, pp. 473–474):

> Aditi is originally the pure consciousness

> of infinite existence one and self-luminous; she is the Light that is Mother of all things. As the infinite she gives birth to Daksha, the discriminating and distributing Thought of the divine Mind, and is herself born to Daksha as the cosmic infinite, the mystic Cow whose udders feed all the worlds.
>
> It is this divine daughter of Daksha who is the mother of the gods. In the cosmos Aditi is the undivided infinite unity of things, free from the duality, *advaya*, and has Diti the separative dualising consciousness for the obverse side of her cosmic creation, — her sister and a rival wife in the later myth.

Aṃśa literally means a 'portion', which implies two meanings simultaneously—oneness and separateness. It is in this *aṃśa* that the *jīvātman* is being shaped, projecting itself as the Psychic being into the lower hemisphere of the Sūrya Savitṛ, the Creator.

Sri Aurobindo speaks of the second status of the Supermind in this way (1972, p. 146):

> In the second poise of the Supermind the Divine Consciousness stands back in the idea from the movement which it contains[3], realising it by a sort of apprehending consciousness, following it, occupying and inhabiting its works, seeming to distribute itself in its forms.[4] In each name and form it would realise itself as the stable Conscious-Self, the same in all; but also it would realise itself as a concentration of Conscious-Self following and supporting the individual play of movement and upholding its differentiation from other play of movement, — the same everywhere in soul-essence, but varying in soul-form. This concentration supporting the soul-form would be the individual Divine or Jivatman as distinguished from the universal Divine or one all-constituting self.

The seven sons of Aditi

The seven sons of Aditi, the Divine Mother, are:

1. Varuṇa, *sat*;
2. Mitra, *cit*;
3. Aryaman, *tapas*;
4. Bhaga, *ānanda*;
5. Dakṣa, Supramental Knowledge-Force;
6. Aṃśa, Supramental Many in Oneness and Oneness in Many;
7. Sūrya Savitṛ, Supramental Manifestation.

So we can see that the whole range of the powers and consciousness is already prepared in the Supermind as a Creator before the manifestation of Cosmos can take place physically. Sūrya is the Creator of this Universe and at the same time he is the Supreme Lord, who gathered all his power, consciousness and bliss to create himself anew, to become many, *bahu syām iti*.[5]

<table>
<tr><th colspan="2">World</th><th>Svar
(a link to the World)</th><th>Supermind
(triple status)</th></tr>
<tr><td>Mental Mind
Vital Mind
Physical Mind</td><td>Mind</td><td rowspan="3">trī rocanā
(three luminous realms)</td><td rowspan="3">Unity

Many in One &
One in Many

Many</td></tr>
<tr><td>Mental Vital
Vital Vital
Physical Vital</td><td>Vital</td></tr>
<tr><td>Mental Physical
Vital Physical
Physical Physical</td><td>Physical</td></tr>
</table>

Figure 8.1. The triple worlds

Aditi thus reflects through her sons the higher status of the Divine in the lower hemisphere. Then she is called in the *Veda* Diti.

So there are all the equivalents of the Seven *Ādityas* within the lower Creation, there is the presence of the All-embracing Infinity of Varuṇa, there is a creative and harmonizing *Māyā* of Mitra, there is a powerful presence of Aryaman, and the delight of Bhaga on all the levels of Creation. It is because of the Sacrifice of the Divine Mother, Aditi, that the higher states of Consciousness are projected into and present in the lower creation. It is these who manifest the world.

This duality is created by the Supramental Consciousness-Force which thus maintains the double process of the One—its diversity and its oneness. The Consciousness of the Supreme is thus including both, and exceeding them both. To rise to his Supreme perception one must maintain both states simultaneously, as the *Īśopaniṣad* says: *vidyāṃ cāvidyāṃ ca yas tad vedobhayaṃ saha avidyayā mṛtyuṃ tīrtvā vidyayāmṛtam aśnute* (The one who knows both simultaneously, Knowledge and Ignorance, indeed by Ignorance passes through Death (as the field of constant change in Time and Space) and by Knowledge enjoys Immortality (as the all-knowing state of Being)).

It is a description of the Supreme Consciousness partaking in both, and infinitely manifesting itself in time and beyond time, being essentially one.

The Lord experiences the state of his Immortality within the transitory situation, within the time and space continuum, being infinitely free from them. It is only when man can perceive both that he may rise to the highest consciousness of the Lord and see the two poises of Diti and Aditi. And that is what these godheads are doing through man's consciousness, rising to their highest realization.

Sūrya Savitṛ: The Lord of Creation

The Rays of the Sun thus build up the luminous planes, called in the *Vedas, Svar*. It has three luminous realms, called *trī rocanā,* which thus project the higher three realms of the Cosmic Mind, called *tisro dyāvaḥ*, sustaining the three spaces of the Vital realms, called *trī rajāṃsi,* supported by the three foundations of the Physical, called *tisro bhūmīḥ.*[6]

Sri Aurobindo (1972, p. 142) translated *trī rocanā* as 'three luminous worlds divine': 'three powers of Light uphold three luminous worlds divine', *trī aryamā manuṣo devatātā trī rocanā divyā dhārayanta*. These three powers of Light as the triple status of the Supermind uphold the three luminous worlds of the *Svar, trī rocanā*, supporting then the three heavens *trīn uta dyūn*, and the three spaces of the midworlds, *trīṇi rajāṃsi.*

So the three luminous realms are projected into the three heavens of our mentality and the three spaces of our vitality; and all of them are supported by Mitra and Varuṇa. It is as if they penetrate through it from the beyond, influencing them with their presence, consciousness, and power.

The *Ṛg Veda* (2. 27.8) also mentions the three earths, *bhūmīs*:

> *tisro bhūmīr dhārayan trīn uta dyūn trīṇi*
> *vratā vidathe antar eṣām*
> *ṛtenādityā mahi vo mahitvaṃ tad aryaman*
> *varuṇa mitra cāru*
> (They [*Ādityas*] support the three earths, and the three heavens. Three are the laws within the sacrificial gathering (inside the *antarikṣa*). By the Truth the sons of Infinity have their greatness here great, and that is Beautiful, O Aryaman, Varuṇa and Mitra.)

The triple worlds

> There are three earths, three levels in the vital and three levels in the mind: *tisro bhūmīḥ, trīṇi rajāṃsi* and *tisro dyāvaḥ*, projected, as it were, from three worlds of *Svar, trī rocanā*, as the Rays of the Sun of the Supramental Consciousness-Force.

The Mental Mind is what Sri Aurobindo calls in *Savitri* the Self of Mind, the Cosmic or Universal Mind. The Vital Mind is the Universal Life's Mind and the Physical Mind is the one which manifests the physicality of the Universe. Human mind is also built on the material ground, dependent on the physical brain, dealing with the physical reality of the Cosmos.

And these are the three heavens mentioned in the *Ṛg Veda* (1.35.6) as *tisro dyāvaḥ* of Savitṛ; two are his own realms and one is in the realm of *Yama—tisro dyāvaḥ savitur dvā upastāṃ ekā yamasya bhuvane virāṣāṭ*. So it is the Mind of the physical universe, which is in the world of Yama, and the Universal Vital Mind and the Universal Mental Mind are in the realms of Savitṛ, which Sri Aurobindo calls in his system of Knowledge: Higher Mind and Illumined Mind.

If we were to compare Sri Aurobindo's terms with the *Vedic* terminology we would see a picture as in Figure 8.2.

Supramental Overmind	*trī rocanā*, 'three luminous worlds divine'
Overmind	
Intuitive Mind	

Illumined Mind	*tisro dyāvaḥ*, three heavens
Higher Mind	
Mind	

Figure 8.2. A comparison of Sri Aurobindo's and *Vedic* terminologies

We have already mentioned *tisro dyāvaḥ*, the three realms of the Universal Mind—Mental, Vital and Physical, which in Sri Aurobindo's terminology are identified as Illumined Mind, Higher Mind and Mind—but we did not speak about the three *rocanas* yet, the three luminous realms of *Svar*. The particularity of *Svar* is that it begins in the Supermind and extends itself into the Overmind and then to the Intuitive Mind. It is here that the major difficulty of understanding of *Svar* lies. Sri Aurobindo speaks of *Svar* differently in different contexts—sometimes he identifies it with the Supermind and sometimes he underlines the difference between the two. It is the world of the Rays of the Sun, which in its first stage, before going out, is still a part of the Sun and is Sun itself. It is only later that the Rays disperse into the groupings of flashes in the Overmental realms and finally become separate in the Intuitive Mind.

Sri Aurobindo describes this phenomenon in a letter speaking of the levels of the Overmind (1970, p. 261):

> There are different planes of the overmind. One is mental, directly creative of all the formations that manifest below in the mental world—that is the mental overmind. Above is the overmind intuition. Still above are the planes of overmind that are more and more connected with the supermind and have a partly supramental character. Highest in the overmind ranges is the supramental overmind or overmind gnosis.

Commenting on the hymn to Mitra and Varuṇa, Sri Aurobindo speaks about the three *rocanas* as 'the three luminous worlds in which the triple mental, the triple vital, the triple physical find the light of their truth and the divine law of their powers' (1998, p. 538).

There is another fundamental difficulty in the understanding of *Svar*, for, according to the *Veda*, it was created last, after Heaven and Earth and *Antarikṣa* came into existence. It is as if it requires a feedback, or a field of application. If the lower creation were not there, *Svar* would not come into being. It is because of Agni being born in the lower creation, calling for the light from above, that *Svar* finally manifests.

> *gīrṇam bhuvanaṃ tamasāpagūḍham/ āviḥ svar abhavaj jāte agnau* / (*RV*, 10.88.2)
> ([First] Being was swallowed by the Darkness and hidden within it. Then, when Agni was born, *Svar* became manifest.)

The Hymn of Creation (*RV*, 10.190) also speaks of *Svar* as being created last:

> *ṛtaṃ ca satyaṃ cābhīddhāt tapaso 'dhi ajāyata* /
> *tato rātrī ajāyata tataḥ samudro arṇavaḥ*
> (The Law and the Truth were born from the kindled Power of *Tapas*.
> From that the Night was born, from the Night—the Ocean of Inconscient Waters.)
>
> *samudrād arṇavād adhi saṃvatsaro ajāyata/*
> *ahorātrāṇi vidadhad viśvasya miṣato vaśī*
> (From the Ocean the Year was born,

distributing Days and Nights, the Master of All that changes.)

sūryācandramasau dhātā yathāpūrvam akalpayat /
divaṃ ca pṛthiviṃ ca antarikṣam atho svaḥ
(The Sun and Moon, the Establisher fashioned as before. Heaven and Earth and Space in-between, and then—*Svar*!)

The explanation for this phenomenon we can find in the understanding of the fact that there is a fundamental difference between the Illumined Mind and the higher realms of the Intuitive Mind and the Overmind. Sri Aurobindo writes about it in a letter (1970, p. 264):

> Intuition is above Illumined Mind which is simply higher Mind raised to a great luminosity and more open to modified forms of intuition and inspiration.... The Intuition is the first plane in which there is a real opening to the full possibility of realisation—it is through it that one goes farther—first to overmind and then to supermind.

He also defines the difference between the Illumined Mind and Intuitive Mind in *Savitri,* in the Canto, 'The Self of Mind', where Intuitive Mind can be reached only through the higher action of Intuition itself, coming down from above to the Illumined Mind. It is through the overflooding directness of the Overmind via Intuition that the Illumined Mind can come into contact with the Supramental consciousness, says Sri Aurobindo in one of his letters (1970, p. 365):

> [T]he thousand-petalled lotus—*sahasradala*—above commands the higher thinking mind, houses the still higher illumined mind and at the highest opens to the intuition through which or else by an overflooding directness the overmind can have with the rest communication or an immediate contact.

The *trī rajāṃsi*, the three realms of the Vital are the levels of (a) the Higher Universal Life, (b) the Universal Life, as such, with an entrance (*antarikṣa*) to the Infinite Darkness, and (c) the Universal Life as it is known to us projected into the creation of material Universe.

Mental Vital	*trī rajāṃsi,* three vital realms
Vital	
Physical Vital	

Mental Physical	*tisro bhūmīḥ,* three earths
Vital Physical	
Physical	

Figure 8.3. The two lower triple realms

So, the Mental Vital corresponds to the plane which Sri Aurobindo describes in the *Second Book of the Traveller of the Worlds*, in the Ninth Canto, 'The Paradise of the Life-Gods'. It is the Life Force which is on the other shore of material Creation, beyond the darkness, as it were. To reach that shore Aswapati must cross the regions of the Eternal Night, which are described in the previous two Cantos, seventh and eighth, 'The Descent into Night' and 'The World of Falsehood, The Mother of Evil and the Sons of Darkness'.

It is only after crossing those regions of Infinite Darkness and Evil that he moves to the realms of the Mental Vital and then to the Mind levels in the following Cantos, first to 'The Kingdoms and Godheads of the Little Mind', which corresponds to the Cosmic Physical Mind, depicted in the *Veda* as Heaven of *Yama*, ruling over men, *yamasya bhuvane virāṣāṭ* (*RV*, 1.35.6), which is our human mind in its highest potential; and then to the 'Kingdoms and Godheads of the Greater Mind', to the Cosmic Higher Mind's regions.

Thus the realms of Life are the place where all the troubles begin, where the dark forces enter into our system of mental-physical existence. It is here in the Vital, *antarikṣa*, that the bridge is to be made by the Sacrifice to the higher domains of consciousness, seeking their direct and effective influence. It is here that the whole battle is going on between the

Sons of Light and the Sons of Darkness, in the field of our Life.

The *tisro bhūmīḥ* are the three realms of the Universal Physical, determined by:

1. the Mind, which makes it self-conscious in manifesting and maintaining its form,
2. the Life, which makes it dynamic in its own movement;
3. the proper Physical, as a faculty housing all other forces and levels of consciousness, taking their part in the material manifestation of the Divine.

Without the physical being fully prepared there cannot be any direct Supramental influence in the material Nature, for it is, as it is clear now, dragging down the vital and the mind inherent in it, not allowing them to realize freely their full potential. And there is a reason for it, for all of them are here only to manifest the Divine in matter, and not for any other reason. Sri Aurobindo says in his letter to a *sādhak* (1970, pp. 1228–1229):

> There can be no conquest of the other planes by the supermind but only an influence, so long as the physical is not ready.... And how is it possible to perfect the mind and vital unless the physical is prepared—for there is such a thing as the mental and vital physical and mind and vital cannot be said to be perfectly prepared until these are ready.

Body as a Supramental creation

The triple conception by the Creator, depicted in the *Veda*, within his own Consciousness creates the Supermind. The very physical consciousness is a result of this conception and a part of its realization.

The physical and mental consciousness are seen in the *Veda* as two luminous firmaments, *rodasī*, supporting the growing Soul in this Creation.

The body itself is seen as the outcome of a Supramental Creation, which at first glance is not easy to understand, but which explains why in the post-*Vedic* spiritual traditions, together with the disappearance of the concepts of *Svar* and the Supermind, the body also lost its proper meaning and got reduced to be seen as an imprisonment and even as a problem in finding our true self rather than a solution in manifesting the Divine in matter.

Sri Aurobindo writes in a letter, 'The supramental is necessary for the transformation of terrestrial life and being, not for reaching the Self. One must realise the Self first, only afterwards can one realise the supermind' (1970, p. 105).

In the *Vedas*, the Heaven and Earth, our mental and physical consciousness, was considered to be pure and conscious of the Divine. The body was seen as a fortress and refuge for the soul of man against the forces of Darkness. It was referred to as 'well-made', a dwelling place for the Spirit. The treatment of the physical body underwent a fundamental change in the later *Māyāvāda*-oriented spiritual traditions; it was seen as an obstacle and hindrance on the path to the spiritual realization, rather than the supporter of, or the field of, realization. It fell off into the domain of a lower consciousness and was blamed for keeping the soul here, bound to suffering against its will to be free.

The seven Suns of the Supermind

Sri Aurobindo reconsidered the usual *yogic* practices, oriented towards Liberation alone—which came in the post-*Vedic* period when the transformation of earthly life and physical body was considered impossible—and turned towards the *Vedic* view of transformative practice: invoking the higher powers by the means of aspiration in the heart and surrendering to them for the transformation. He introduces the ancient *Vedic* methods of a Descent of a Higher Consciousness and Power into our mental, vital and even subtle physical and physical bodies for transformation.

It is as if he is looking from above at the physical body, seeing it from the Supramental point of view. He writes about the seven centres in the body as the manifestation of the Seven Suns of the Supermind in this way (2001, p. 1342):

1. The Sun of Supramental Truth, Knowledge-Power, originating the supramental creation.

   Descent into the *sahasradala*.

2. The Sun of Supramental Light and Will-Power, transmitting the Knowledge-Power as dynamic vision and command to create, found and organize the supramental creation.

   Descent into *ājñā cakra*, between the eyes.
3. The Sun of Supramental Word, embodying the Knowledge-Power, empowered to express and arrange the supramental creation.

   Descent into the throat centre.
4. The Sun of Supramental Love, Beauty, and Bliss, releasing the Soul of the Knowledge-Power to vivify and harmonise the supramental creation.

   Descent into the heart-lotus.
5. The Sun of Supramental Force dynamised as a power and source of life to support the supramental creation.

   Descent into the navel centre.
6. The Sun of Life-Radiances (Power-Rays) distributing the dynamis and pouring it into concrete formations.

   Descent into the penultimate centre.
7. The Sun of Supramental Substance-Energy and Form-Energy empowered to embody the supramental life and stabilize the creation.

   Descent into the *mūlādhāra*.

The concept of Sacrifice

Heaven and Earth, the mental and physical consciousness, are housing souls here, as the eternal *aṃśas* of the Divine, to perform the Sacrifice; that is, to invoke and bring down the higher forces of Consciousness. Heaven and Earth, meanwhile are supporting and nourishing them, protecting them from *abhva*, the Inconscient, which they have descended to convert and to save.

Agni, the Divine Will, the spiritual Father of all the evolving souls of men, is thus a growing Lord in the Darkness, taking all of it onto Himself and changing it into the Divine nature.

Heaven and Earth, our Father and Mother, Mental and Physical Consciousness, were seen as projected from the Supermind into the darkness of the Inconscient as the Golden Embryo, the *hiraṇya garbha*. Then they got separated into two halves. The upper one became Heaven and the lower Earth. The Space in-between became *antarikṣa*, introducing into our system through its opening the powers of the beyond, of the superconscient and subconscient realms, from the Abyss of *abhva*, to meet and to fight in this space. It is a window to the Infinite Light and the Infinite Darkness. It is a place of Sacrifice.

And in this space the soul of man is growing, supported by our physical and mental consciousness. Sri Aurobindo (1998, pp. 383–384), speaking about the *Vedic* symbolism of the Sacrifice, says:

> Thus the soul is a battlefield full of helpers and hurters, friends and enemies. All this lives, teems, is personal, is conscious, is active. We create for ourselves by the sacrifice and by the word shining seers, heroes to fight for us, children of our works. ...
>
> The soul of man is a world full of beings, a kingdom in which armies clash to help or hinder a supreme conquest, a house where the gods are our guests and which the demons strive to possess; the fullness of its energies and wideness of its being make a seat of sacrifice spread, arranged and purified for a celestial session.
>
> Such are some of the principal images of the Veda and a very brief and insufficient outline of the teaching of the Forefathers. So understood the Rig Veda ceases to be an obscure, confused and barbarous hymnal; it becomes the high-aspiring Song of Humanity; its chants are episodes of the lyrical epic of the soul in its immortal ascension.
>
> This at least; what more there may be in the Veda of ancient science, lost knowledge, old psycho-physical tradition remains yet to be discovered.

Sacrifice as a way to transformation

Agni is a summoner, *hotṛ*, and a messenger, *dūta*, to the Gods from above and from within the depth of his own Consciousness-Force, introducing them and their transcendental presence here in the earthly consciousness of man.

In the depth of his being he has access to all the Godheads, for he himself represents all of them here in the realms of the fallen Self.

It is by the Sacrifice performed by men in himself that these transcendental Godheads, *Ādityas*, are rising to their highest Throne, from which they can see both the Infinite and the Finite Creation.

Agni invokes and brings them here from the luminous realms of *Svar, rocanād,* into the earthly mind, life and body of men. Thus we see in the *Ṛg Veda* (1.14.9):

> *ākīṃ sūryasya rocanād viśvān devān uṣarbudhaḥ /*
> *vipro hoteha vakṣati*
> (May the Invoker, the Ecstatic Priest, (Agni) bring here to us the Gods, who awake with the Dawn, from the luminous world of the Sun, *rocanād.*)

Indra and Agni: The two poles of the Sacrifice

As Agni is building it from within, from the depth of the Inconscient, Indra is coming from above, from the beyond of our mentality, striking it with his Lightning, illumining all the enemies hiding there and destroying them. Sri Aurobindo writes in the *Secret of the Veda*:

> Indra, the Puissant next, who is the power of pure Existence self-manifested as the Divine Mind. As Agni is one pole of Force instinct with knowledge that sends its current upward from earth to heaven, so Indra is the other pole of Light instinct with force which descends from heaven to earth. He comes down into our world as the Hero with the shining horses and slays darkness and division with his lightnings, pours down the life-giving heavenly waters, finds in the trace of the hound, Intuition, the lost or hidden illuminations, makes the Sun of Truth mount high in the heaven of our mentality (1998, p. 30).

The illumination which Indra brings is the light of the Sun.

> Surya... is the master of that supreme Truth,—truth of being, truth of knowledge, truth of process and act and movement and functioning. He is therefore the creator or rather the manifester of all things—for creation is outbringing, expression by the Truth and Will—and the father, fosterer, enlightener of our souls. The illuminations we seek are the herds of this Sun who comes to us in the track of the divine Dawn and releases and reveals in us night-hidden world after world up to the highest Beatitude. (1998, p. 380)

The aim of the Sacrifice

The union of the three levels of the physical consciousness with the three spaces of the vital and three heavens of the mental consciousness is the aim of the *Vedic* Sacrifice.

For thus it effectuates the ascent to *Svar*'s three luminous realms, *trī rocanā,* introducing the Supramental consciousness into the lower hemisphere.

The union of Agni, Vāyu and Sūrya, was considered to be the aim of the *Vedic* Sacrifice, where Agni was seen as the essence of Earth, *pṛthivī;* Vāyu as the essence of the Space inbetween, *antarikṣa;* and Sūrya the essence of Heaven, *dyaus*. So if these three fires are united into one Fire, then the aim of the Sacrifice is realized. For it recreates the Oneness of the triple status of the Supermind here in the lower hemisphere by completing it on all the levels of Consciousness.

Planes of consciousness in *Savitri*

There is a wonderful description in *Savitri* of all the levels starting from the Higher Mind and ending with the Supermind (1997, pp. 659–662):

> A few have dared the last supreme ascent
> And break through borders of blinding light above,
> And feel a breath around of mightier air,
> Receive a vaster being's messages
> And bathe in its immense intuitive Ray.
> On summit Mind are radiant altitudes
> Exposed to the lustre of Infinity,
> Outskirts and dependencies of the house of Truth,
> Upraised estates of Mind and measureless
> There man can visit but there he cannot live.

[Higher Mind]
A cosmic Thought spreads out its vastitudes;
Its smallest parts are here philosophies
Challenging with their detailed immensity,
Each figuring an omniscient scheme of things.

[Illumined Mind]
But higher still can climb the ascending light;
There are vasts of vision and eternal suns,
Oceans of an immortal luminousness,
Flame-hills assaulting heaven with their peaks,
There dwelling all becomes a blaze of sight;
A burning head of vision leads the mind,
Thought trails behind it its long comet tail;
The heart glows, an illuminate and seer,
And sense is kindled into identity.

[Intuitive Mind]
A highest flight climbs to a deepest view:
In a wide opening of its native sky
Intuition's lightnings range in a bright pack
Hunting all hidden truths out of their lairs,
Its fiery edge of seeing absolute
Cleaves into locked unknown retreats of self,
Rummages the sky-recesses of the brain,
Lights up the occult chambers of the heart;
Its spear-point ictus of discovery
Pressed on the cover of name, the screen of form,
Strips bare the secret soul of all that is.
Thought there has revelation's sun-bright eyes;
The Word, a mighty and inspiring Voice,
Enters Truth's inmost cabin of privacy
And tears away the veil from God and life.

[Overmind]
Then stretches the boundless finite's last expanse,
The cosmic empire of the Overmind,
Time's buffer state bordering Eternity,
Too vast for the experience of man's soul:
All here gathers beneath one golden sky:
The Powers that build the cosmos station take
In its house of infinite possibility;
Each god from there builds his own nature's world;
Ideas are phalanxed like a group of suns,
Each marshalling his company of rays.
Thought crowds in masses seized by one regard;
All Time is one body, Space a single look:
There is the Godhead's universal gaze
And there the boundaries of immortal Mind:
The line that parts and joins the hemispheres
Closes in on the labour of the Gods
Fencing eternity from the toil of Time.

[Supermind]
In her glorious kingdom of eternal light
All-ruler, ruled by none, the Truth supreme,
Omnipotent, omniscient and alone,
In a golden country keeps her measureless house;
In its corridor she hears the tread that comes
Out of the Unmanifest never to return
Till the Unknown is known and seen by men.
Above the stretch and blaze of cosmic Sight,
Above the silence of the wordless Thought,
Formless creator of immortal forms,
Nameless, investitured with the name divine,
Transcending Time's hours, transcending Timelessness,
The Mighty Mother sits in lucent calm
And holds the eternal Child upon her knees
Attending the day when he shall speak to Fate.[7]
There is the image of our future's hope;
There is the sun for which all darkness waits,
There is the imperishable harmony;
The world's contradictions climb to her and are one:
There is the Truth of which the world's truths are shreds,
The Light of which the world's ignorance is the shade
Till Truth draws back the shade that it has cast,
The Love our hearts call down to heal all strife,
The Bliss for which the world's derelict sorrows yearn:
Thence comes the glory sometimes seen on earth,
The visits of Godhead to the human soul,
The Beauty and the dream on Nature's face.
There the perfection born from eternity
Calls to it the perfection born in Time,
The truth of God surprising human life,
The image of God overtaking finite shapes.
There in a world of everlasting Light,
In the realms of the immortal Supermind
Truth who hides here her head in mystery,
Her riddle deemed by reason impossible
In the stark structure of material form,
Unenigmaed lives, unmasked her face and there
Is Nature and the common law of things.
There in a body made of spirit stuff,
The hearth-stone of the everliving Fire,
Action translates the movements of the soul,
Thought steps infallible and absolute

And life is a continual worship's rite,
A sacrifice of rapture to the One.
A cosmic vision, a spiritual sense
Feels all the Infinite lodged in finite form
And seen through a quivering ecstasy of light
Discovers the bright face of the Bodiless,
In the truth of a moment, in the moment's soul
Can sip the honey-wine of Eternity.
A Spirit who is no one and innumerable,
The one mystic infinite Person of his world
Multiplies his myriad personality,
On all his bodies seals his divinity's stamp
And sits in each immortal and unique.[8]

Endnotes

1 *RV*, 5.62.8: *ā rohatho varuṇa mitra gartam ataś cakṣāthe aditiṃ ditiṃ ca /*
(O Varuṇa, O Mitra, you two are ascending to your throne from where you see Aditi and Diti, Infinite and Finite Consciousness).

2 *RV*, 5.69.2: *trayas tasthur vṛṣabhāsas tisṝṇāṃ dhiṣaṇānāṃ retodhā vi dyumantaḥ /*
(There stand wide three luminous Bulls and cast their seed into the three Thoughts).

3 Reference to *saṃjñāna, vijnāna, ājñāna, prajñāna*

4 Reference to *Aṃśa Āditya*

5 *Taittirīya Upaniṣad*, 2.10.

6 *RV*, 5.69.1: *trī rocanā varuṇa trīn uta dyūn trīṇi mitra dhārayatho rajāṃsi*
(Three worlds of the Light you two uphold, O Varuṇa, three heavens, three mid-worlds, O Mitra!'
The three luminous worlds *trī rocanā* (from root *ruc*, to shine) are the three levels of *Svar*).

7 *RV*, 5.69.3: *prātar devīm aditiṃ johavīmi madhyaṃdina uditā sūryasya /*
rāye mitrāvaruṇā sarvatātā īḷe tokāya tanayāya śaṃ yoḥ
(In the Dawn I call constantly to the Divine Mother Aditi, and in the midday and in the rising of the Sun. For the shining wealth for all I seek her with adoration, O Mitra and Varuṇa, for peace and for creation and for the birth of her Son.)
It is a culmination and the meaning of this creation, the birth of the Son of Aditi, the Supreme in the physical body of man.

8 *RV*, 7.52.1: *ādityāso aditayaḥ syāma pūr devatrā vasavo martiyatrā /*
(May we become Ādityas in their infinite qualities, which they all share in the Supreme Mother Aditi, and at the same time remain unique, stay like a fortress among the Gods and among the Mortals, O Luminous Dwellers in the substance!)

References

Aurobindo, Sri (1970). *Letters on yoga*. Pondicherry: Sri Aurobindo Ashram Press.

Aurobindo, Sri (1971). *The hour of God and other writings*. Pondicherry: Sri Aurobindo Ashram Press.

Aurobindo, Sri (1972). *The life divine*. Pondicherry: Sri Aurobindo Ashram Press.

Aurobindo, Sri (1997). *Savitri—A legend and a symbol*. Pondicherry: Sri Aurobindo Ashram Publication Department.

Aurobindo, Sri (1998). *The secret of the Veda*. Pondicherry: Sri Aurobindo Ashram Publication Department

Aurobindo, Sri (2001). *The record of yoga*. Pondicherry: Sri Aurobindo Ashram Publication Department.

9

Models of personality in Buddhist psychology

Priya Ananda & Ajith Prasad

Introduction

A comprehensive framework for psychology should address a wide spectrum of applications. At one end, it should identify the limiting factors of the ordinary psyche and the scope of the perfected state that humans can realize. In this regard, it should also comprehend the profound mystical experiences of the practitioners of various spiritual traditions. At the other end, it should cover the pathological experiences of those struggling to cope with the travails of the mundane world. In the middle, it should also be applicable in the analysis of psychological tendencies and developmental opportunities of conventionally 'normal' individuals. Buddhist psychology, with its balanced approach combining structured rational analysis and first person accounts of direct *yogic* experience, is of great relevance in contributing toward the formation of a comprehensive framework for psychology.

Buddhist psychology is both a psychology of transformation and a theory of cognition. As a psychology of transformation, it aims to develop the innate psychic potential of every being to its perfection. The ordinary state of being is 'flawed' or pathological in the sense that one works with limited perceptions of the world and undergoes cycles of suffering and psychological tension in ceaseless attempts to cope with and respond to the world. These attempts fail to produce ever-lasting happiness because the perceptions about oneself and the world, which one formulates as the basis for action, are discordant with one's true nature. Buddhist psychology aims to transcend this entrapment. It begins the endeavour by analyzing the root cause behind this pathology. In the absence of such an understanding, one might go after an enlightenment ideal with the same pathological tendencies that tie one to the miseries of ordinary being; and thus remain contented with an intermediate state of blissful experience, where the tendencies leading to future suffering may still be dormant.

The goal of the Buddhist psychology of transformation can be viewed as triple-fold, corresponding to the three scopes of motivation on the Buddhist path.[1] The lower goal is about coping with the ordinary state of being while minimizing suffering. The middle goal is the ever-lasting liberation (*vimukti*) from suffering by eliminating afflictive tendencies. The higher goal is to achieve complete and perfect awakening (*saṃbodhi*).[2] The process of awakening involves the attainment of total perfection in all dimensions of being, with their transformation into pristine wisdom (*jñāna*). The ultimate spiritual attainment on the Buddhist path, as described in the Great Perfection (*mahā-sandhi-yoga*, Tibetan: *rdzogs chen*) teachings, is to realize the primordial purity and spontaneous perfection of all appearances. This realization is inseparably coalesced (*yuganaddha*) with a display of unceasing compassion. This is a state completely transcending ordinary psyche, without grounding in or clinging to its distorted projections and being able to appreciate the truth 'as it is'.

Buddhist psychology is also a theory of cognition. This is an inevitable part of Buddhist exploration since the higher goal of Buddhist training is the attainment of *saṃbodhi* that eliminates all cognitive 'errors'.[3] The view of cognition that evolves through Buddhist psychology is that of the co-emergence of the person and the world. The distinction between inner and outer vanishes on deep analysis of the process of experiencing. Thus the scope of 'personality' in Buddhist studies includes the entire sphere of experience covering not only the person, but also the world as perceived by the person. The study of the dynamics of this co-emergence equips Buddhist psychology with ways of altering the person and the world thus brought forth. This knowledge is applied in eliminating the cognitive 'errors' of the ordinary state of being, and thus in relating to appearances in a whole new way as the person progresses on the path to omniscience.

An important theme running throughout Buddhist psychology is the five dimensions of underlying capabilities in which various aspects of personality and the awakened state are understood. At the mundane level, the manifestation of these capabilities in its distorted forms appears as the five aggregates (*skandha*) of personality. The aggravation of these distortions leads to five afflictions (*kleśa*), and to various psychological realms of experience. Through perfect awakening, clarified aspects of these capabilities manifest as the five aspects of the fully awakened omniscient wisdom (*buddha-jñāna*). These five clarified aspects are:

1. Seeing reality 'as it is',
2. Unperturbed clarity in knowing all phenomena,
3. Perfect distinction of all details of phenomena,
4. Sensing the happiness and suffering of all beings with the experience of one-taste, transcending ordinary pleasure and pain, and
5. The creativity of spontaneously-accomplishing actions.[4]

Buddhist psychology has formulated various ways of analyzing personality. These could be termed as 'the models of personality'. These psychological models are valuable in studying a variety of experiences like the conventional experience of ordinary beings, of those in the stages of the path to awakening, and the qualities of the fully awakened state. These models are also useful in analyzing experiences related to sleep, dream, death, after-death state, etc. In this chapter, various models of personality in Buddhist psychology are explored. The application of these models in understanding various psychological states and afflictions are also briefly touched upon.

The three turnings of the Buddhist view

These psychological models are presented with their own specific scopes of application in various phases of Buddhist teaching. The opinion among various Buddhist schools differs regarding how to view these phases together. A brief introduction to the three phases of Buddhist philosophy and the position taken in this chapter regarding an integral view is necessary before delving into the details of the models.

The evolution of Buddhist philosophy took place in three distinct periods renowned in Mahāyāna literature as 'the three turnings of the wheel of dharma'.[5] The first turning comprises the Buddha's teachings (as present in the Pali canon) that he gave to a wide audience. The second and third turning teachings were delivered to disciples who had already made progress on the path to awakening. The second turning, which became widely known around the second century, is centred on the *Prajñā-pāramita-sūtras* of the Buddha. Madhyamaka philosophy was developed by Nāgārjuna based on these *sūtras*, and was further established through the treatises of scholars like Āryadeva, Śāntideva, Candrakīrti and Śāntarakṣita (2nd–8th century CE). The third turning is based on a vast array of *sūtras* such as the *Tathāgatagarbha-sūtra*, *Sandhinirmocana-sūtra*, *Laṅkāvatāra-sūtra* and the *Avatāmsaka-sūtra*. Maitreya, Asanga, Vasubandhu and others (4th century CE onwards), developed the third turning views further, through their treatises (*śāstra*) and commentaries. The second and third turning views were extended further in the teachings of Buddhist *tantrās* (*Vajrayāna*).

In the first turning, focus is on the most immediate problem of the individual—the suffering nature of ordinary existence and the possibility of going beyond. The suffering in this context is not just the apparent forms of suffering like those due to physical pain, emotional turmoil and boredom. Suffering in its broader context is the underlying psychological tension that pervades even happy states of mind. It is the struggle to cling to mistaken identities which keep drifting away like a mirage. Like the ecstatic experience of a narcotic addict while dipping into deeper agony, one expends enormous energy to create an island of happiness along with an ocean of underlying suffering. One sinks into deeper anguish as the island of ecstasy drifts away. The first turning teaches the recognition of the true nature of a person, as the way to freedom (*vimukti*) out of this mistaken struggle. In this context, the conventional personality is analyzed in great detail. The psychological models presented in this turning, analyze the constituents and operational dynamics of a person, in terms of underlying building blocks. This phase of Buddhist psychology is already finding applications in the modern context. The dialogues between Buddhist scholars, modern psychologists and cognitive scientists, as documented by Goleman (1997, 2004), shed light on this topic. Parallels between the decentralized view of mind developed in cognitive science, and the decentralized experience of personality emerging through mindfulness meditation in Buddhist traditions, were investigated by Varela, Thompson and Rosch (1993).

The second turning focuses on the ultimate nature of all phenomena including the building blocks of personality. The aim here is to remove the veil of knowables (*jñeyāraṇa*) toward perfect awakening (*saṃbodhi*), in addition to the removal of the veil of afflictions (*kḷeśāvaraṇa*) which aid in the movement towards liberation, from suffering (*vimukti*). The psyche exists not in isolation but is interwoven with the rest of the phenomenal world. An understanding of the true nature of all phenomena is necessary to realize omniscience. The separation between psychology and ontology disappears as one transcends objectivism and subjectivism, in this view of dependent co-arising of psyche and the world. The Madhyamaka view establishes the profound groundlessness (*śūnyatā*) where no phenomenon can be self-arising or self-sustaining in isolation with the rest of the world. While drawing parallels between the Madhyamaka view and their work on enactive cognitive science, Varela et al. (1993, p. 253) state:

> There is a profound discovery of groundlessness in our culture — in science, in the humanities, in society, and in the uncertainties of people's daily lives. ... Taking groundlessness as negative, as a loss, leads to a sense of alienation, despair, loss of heart, and nihilism. The cure that is generally espoused in our culture is to find a new grounding (or a return to older grounds).... In Buddhism, we have a case study showing that when groundlessness is embraced and followed through to its ultimate conclusions, the outcome is an unconditional sense of intrinsic goodness that manifests itself in the world as spontaneous compassion.

The third turning of the Buddhist view shows how the realization of the most profound truth of groundlessness becomes the experience of ultimate purity of appearances, with its spontaneously accomplishing nature manifesting as the all-encompassing display of compassion. If the second turning does not generate such an experience, one has not reached the correct understanding of groundlessness (*śūnyatā*). One mistakenly falls to either the shades of nihilism—with resulting fear, dullness or indifference; or to the shades of absolutism—with resulting ego-centric aggression, despair, or anesthetic complacence. The third turning guides the practitioner towards perfecting the profound realization of groundlessness, through stages of progressively pure experiences. A phenomenological description of stages in the path (*bodhisattva-bhūmi*) to *saṃbodhi* is given as far as words can capture it. It describes the potential for full awakening (*Tathāgatagarbha*) as innate to every being. An elaborate and sophisticated model of psychology is developed in this turning. This may be termed as the psychology of spiritual awakening. The third turning has not yet been significantly put to use in modern psychology. However, there is tremendous value in studying the third turning model of personality, while developing a modern psychology of spiritual transformation. In this chapter, the model of eight-fold collection deals with the third turning psychology.

Reification of the building blocks of the first turning led to the realist schools of Buddhist philosophy like Vaibhāṣika and Sautrāntika. Reification of certain elements of the psychological model of the third turning led to idealist interpretations to schools like Vijñānavāda and Yogācāra. If one is careful not to make such reifications, the three turnings together provide a consistent and comprehensive view. Many scholars of the Prajñā-pāramita tradition[6] of Indo-Tibetan Buddhism embrace such a view and accept all the three turnings. According to this view the three turnings are three phases of understanding. The first turning provides the phenomenology and psychology of mundane existence. The second turning presents the profound view of groundlessness that provides the ontological perspective. The third turning is the culmination where phenomenology and psychology of both mundane and enlightened experiences are seen in inseparable union with the ontological insight of the second turning. The approach taken in this chapter is such an integral perspective, with the philosophical basis of Madhyamaka. Influences of the second and third turning can be found in this chapter, even while discussing the first turning. This is intentional, and aims at bringing clarity to the whole theme from an integral perspective. With this approach, the models of personality from the first and third turnings become useful psychological tools, with varying subtlety and applications.

Model 1: The aggregate model of personality

The first turning presents two models for studying personality. The first is a schema of analyzing personality into its building blocks. According to this model, all experiences that arise as the continuum[7] of a person[8] are analyzed and categorized into five aggregates (*skandha*). The original aim of this model is to arrive at the realization of the ultimate nature of a person through direct observation of experiences in mindfulness meditation (*smṛti upastāna*, known popularly through the Pali term *sati-patthana*). This is the means to go beyond suffering produced by ego-clinging. The simplicity of this model along with the ease of direct observation makes it a good starting point to formulate the structure of personality. It also leads to the identification of five dimensions of capabilities that fuel the five categories of experiences. The aggregates are:

1. Form (*rūpa*): This is an experience that arises as a concretized and objectified view of phenomena. Form is not just the physical body of a person. According to Vasbandhu's *Abhidharma-kośa*,[9] all forms, including the perceived external environment, belong to this aggregate. The objects of all five sense consciousnesses are considered to be forms—for example, shape and colour for the visual consciousness, and sound for the auditory consciousness. It also includes sense faculties. Asanga's *Abhidharma-samuccaya*[10] also categorizes the mental objects of perception like concepts and mental images into form.
2. Feeling (*vedanā*): This is an experience of a sensation that lies on the scale of painful (*duḥkha*), neutral and pleasurable (*sukha*). It is the subjective appreciation that senses suffering and happiness. It includes both sensual and mental feelings. The feeling aggregate only covers the basic feeling that comes as part and parcel of an experience. The process of building up additional emotional states and observable reactions is not in itself a part of feeling. However, such build-ups also result in feeling. For example, becoming anxious is not a feeling, but anxiousness is experienced with its associated feeling of pain.
3. Perception (*saṃjña*): This is an experience of recognizing something within the field of cognition. This recognition is due to predispositions and familiarity, and is not

a process of inference. However, the process of inference can lead to a generalized image corresponding to the direct experience under investigation. The experience of recognizing the generalized image would belong to the aggregate of perception. Perception could be about labelling a form to be a specific object, viewing a situation to be either desirable or threatening, perceiving a quality in an object, etc.

4. Formation (*saṃskāra*): This is an experience additionally fabricated in the continuum of a person in response to other experiences. Thus, the aggregate of formation is the reactive and responsive aspect of personality. The process of intellectualization (*buddhi*) through which one analyzes and infers is part of this aggregate. Emotional build-ups and behavioural aspects are also formations of various mental episodes (*caitta*, also known as *caitasika*) arising in dependence upon each other. In addition, through conditioning, the context of experiencing and directing attention into or away from specific aspects in the sphere of experience, formations alter future experiences.
5. Consciousness (*vijñāna*): It is the experience of being conscious of an object of experience. *Vijñāna* literally means 'qualified knowing' in which there are three spheres—the knower, the object of knowledge, and the process of knowing. In the first turning model, *vijñāna* is of six kinds—the mental consciousness and the five sense consciousnesses. Buddhist psychology treats these six as different types of *vijñāna*, since they know their objects through their uncommon aspects—for example, knowing the aspect of shape and colour for eye consciousness, and sound for ear consciousness. The experience of mental consciousness is about being conscious of concepts, mental images, recognitions, feelings, emotions, etc.

Vijñāna is to be contrasted with pristine wisdom (*jñāna*) knowing reality 'as it is'. Unlike *jñāna*, *vijñāna* is qualified and it remains specific through its entangled nature, where the prior experiences in the continuum colours the way knowledge arises. The field of knowing and the specific ways of 'seeing' are continually perturbed and modified in the process of knowing. So are the modifications of other aggregates too. The aggregates of feelings, perceptions and formations arise as the subjective aspects, and the aggregate of forms arises as the objective aspect, in the context of experience provided by *vijñāna*.

The aggregates are momentary experiences arising in an interdependent way and a person is none other than a continuum of such experiences. Each of the aggregates is closely related to and contains other aggregates. For example, the aggregate of perception could arise as the recognition of either an aggregate of form, feeling, formation or *vijñāna*. There could be a perception of feeling or vice-versa, a feeling of perception. Similarly, experience of form need not always correspond to the appearances of material forms. It can also arise as the objectification of feeling, perception, formation or *vijñāna*. This corresponds to the objectification of mind (*citta*) as the agent behind experiences. Thus, *citta* can be viewed as the objective view of the subjective aspect of experience.

Model 2: The network model of mental continuum

The model presented above analyzes personhood as a continuum of experiences belonging to five dimensions. The second model from the first turning scriptures is that of main-mind (*citta*) and mental episodes (*caitta*, also known as *caitasika*). The cognitive and behavioural dynamics of a person are looked upon in this model as the interplay of mental episodes in an ever-changing continuum of the complex of *citta* and *caitta*. Personality traits evolve through this complex. This complex of *citta-caitta* corresponds closely to the meaning of the English word 'mind'.

The notion of *vijñāna* in the aggregate model and *citta* in this model, are synonymous to the extent that *vijñāna*—with its triple-fold division of the agent of knowing, the object of knowledge, and the knowing itself—and *citta* including its content, are mutually inclusive. The entity being studied by various terms like *vijñāna, citta* and *manas*[11] is the same. However, the perspectives from which they are looked upon are different. While *vijñāna* emphasizes experiences, *citta* emphasizes the apprehension of experiences as if through an agent.

In the *citta-caitta* model, the main-mind (*citta*) is the bare apprehension.[12] The stream of *citta* changes continuously as various objects, along with the apprehension of them, arise and vanish. The mental episodes are further apprehensions and reactions through the aggregates of feeling, perception and formation. In this model, the aggregate of form is considered as the content of *citta* and hence does not become an explicit element in the model.[13]

The actual types of mental episodes are numerous, while various scriptures enumerate around fifty. These are grouped into six categories. The first category is that of ever-present mental episodes accompanying each and every experience. These include contact (*sparśa*) between mind and its object, feeling (*vedanā*), perception (*saṃjña*), volition (*cetana*) and mental engagement (*manaskāra*).[14] *Manaskāra* is the mental episode that keeps the person attentive to any given object of appearance, and helps in engaging deeper into the object. The second category is the mental episodes that are essential in ascertaining the characteristics of the object being engaged with. These include interest (*chanda*), determination (*adhimokṣa*), mindfulness (*smṛti*), one-pointedness (*samādhi*)[15] and insight (*prajñā*). The third category is of wholesome mental episodes. These are desirable and indicative of a healthy personality. The fourth and fifth categories include the primary and secondary unwholesome mental episodes which are undesirable for a healthy personality. Unwholesome mental episodes have the potential to produce suffering. The sixth category consists of changeable mental episodes for which the wholesomeness depends upon the context.

As a person engages with an object, various mental episodes ripen, based on specific *karmic* tendencies. The manifestations of various mental episodes condition the mental continuum, making it either fertile or sterile for other mental episodes. For example, the unwholesome mental episode of bewilderment (*moha*) would weaken one-pointedness, and thus make the mental episode of insight shallower. As another example, there is less likelihood of the mental episode of anger arising in a mental continuum in which the mental episodes of patience are strengthened.

This model is considered important for mind training through meditation. Varying modes of using it are available, depending on the nature of the vehicle (Hīnayāna, Mahāyāna and Vajrayāna) that a person trains on. For example, the approach in Hinayāna, in general, is to apply mindfulness meditation to find and remove the causes that lead to unhealthy mental episodes. The approach in Mahāyāna is to cultivate an opposing mental episode as an antidote, such that the ground is sterile for unwholesome mental episodes. Such an approach works through understanding how the presence and strength of various mental episodes affect the enriching or diminishing of others.

Selflessness and emptiness

Due to their ever-changing nature, neither can phenomenal experiences on their own be a source of happiness or suffering, nor can they form a basis for permanent identity for the person. Clinging to experiences in this ever-changing continuum is the cause of suffering. As Asanga points out in *Abhidharma-samuccaya* (Trans. 2001), clinging could arise as a mistaken identification of self with experiences belonging to any of the five aggregates. It is a notion of 'I' around which other experiences are related as either favourable or threatening. Clinging to such notions provides mistaken frames of reference for actions, and binds the person to the cycle of suffering through discordant actions, causing undesired results.

Clinging to an experience of form arises with the mistaken notion of self as the body. Clinging to an experience of feeling (as in the bliss of *samādhi*) arises from the mistaken notion of self as the enjoyer experiencing its innate bliss. The perception of the label 'I' (as in 'I am') can be the basis for mistaken notion of a self as the perceiver at its own bare recognition (as in *asmitā samādhi*). The aggregate of formation is the basis for the mistaken notion of self as the agent behind action. A non-dual appearance of *vijñāna*, where no object of knowing is distinctly present, can be confused as the self experiencing its innate nature. Since all these experiences are constructed on the basis of various causes and conditions, attempts to cling to these experiences as self-nature lead to psychological tension and suffering. For example, the very attempt to cling to the bliss of meditation leads to anger and mental turbulence, when a disturbing stimulus shakes the person out of *samādhi*. Happiness is ever-lasting only when the basis is transformed (*āśraya-parāvṛtti*), leading to the co-emergence (*sahaja*) of peace with every sprout of experience.

In the first turning philosophy, various notions of self (*ātma*) are refuted through the view of not-self (*anātma*) to thoroughly eliminate all modes of clinging. The arising and subsiding of aggregates (including the subtler experiences in meditation) are observed to study their causes and conditions[16]. Direct recognition of the momentary nature of all aggregates leads to the realization of the lack of a permanent abiding ground for the person in aggregates. It also leads to the realization of how futile constructions around an impossible notion of self leads to suffering. This realization of not-self (*anātma*) leads to abandonment of all clinging and discordant actions arising out of mistaken identity, and thus to liberation from suffering. Experiences are no more in the nature of suffering, as the conditions for suffering cease through the cessation of mistaken impulses. The peace one reaches is no more the constructed bliss of a specific state of being, but an unconditional one that is co-emergent with every sprout of experience. Once the mental continuum undergoes such a transformation, the experience of the phenomenal world can no more be the cause of suffering.

Refutation of the above notions of self is not a total denial of conventional experiences of a person. The emphasis is on removing the root-ignorance that confusedly identifies and clings to some of these experiences in the continuum (including the so-called transcendental experiences), as the essential nature of a person.

The removal of mistaken notions about the self of a person is sufficient for freedom from suffering, but not for omniscience. The insight into the true nature of reality is essential for this. The Madhyamaka view based on the second turning explores the true nature of all phenomena and asserts the lack of inherent existence (*niḥsvabhāva*). Madhyamaka recognizes that no phenomenon (including the notion of person and the constituent aggregates) can exist from its own side. Nāgārjuna invokes arguments of pure reason to establish the lack of inherent existence, the emptiness of all phenomena. Even the notions of causation, time, space, etc., cannot be established from their own side (*Mūla-madhyamaka-kārika*, Trans. 1995). A general idea about the doctrine of emptiness may be generated through an example. The existence of a table can be spotted neither in any of its parts like the platform or legs, nor as a separate and independent entity. A collection of all its parts does not become the table either, unless it is organized in a specific way that does a specific function to a perceiver. Hence, the collection of parts in itself does not contain any essential identity for the table. Many causes and conditions like the parts of the table, the designer, the carpenter and the user together give rise to the phenomenal experience of a table. Thus, the experience of table is a phenomenal appearance whose essence cannot be traced down to its components. The same argument could be extended deeper into its constituents like the platform and the legs to see that no object exists on its own. Even the perceiver that imputes a name to the object does not exist on its own, because the *citta* arises in dependence upon objects of experience.

The nature of appearances can be understood in terms of three concepts. These are emptiness (*śūnyatā*), conditional arising (*pratītya-samutpāda*) and dependent imputation (*upādāya-prajñāpti*). The first is the lack of inherent existence of phenomenal experiences from their own side. The second is about how the experiences of phenomena still arise through various causes and conditions based on other phenomena that are equally empty. Phenomenal experiences arise and vanish interdependently without any inherent self-support anywhere. Empty appearances of phenomena support each other. The third is about the phenomenal appearance of *citta* as an imputation of conceptual notions to the ever-changing flux of conditional arising, based on suitability. This leads to a contextual view of truth. An example may clarify this. When one recognizes the constant flow of water, one imputes the concept of river. Though the water in the river flows by continuously and there is no river other than the flowing water, through conceptual imputation one cognizes a river that does not flow away with every drop of water.

When all such imputations are pacified, it leads to the direct realization of the truth 'as it is' (*tathātā*) that is non-elaborated (*niṣprapañca*). It is the inseparable coalescence of phenomenal experiences with their ultimate essencelessness. This is also termed the void sphere of reality (*dharmadhātu*). The scholar-yogi of Tibet, Longchen Rabjampa explains:

> The appearance of all things of *saṃsāra* and *nirvāṇa* is based on the causal process of interdependent origination. These appearances are undeniable. They are the unceasing natural play of voidness (*śūnyatā*) [emptiness], like the play of light, the play of eddies and waves on the water and the rustling of the leaves. All things of relative reality are this way. Thus because appearances are irrefutable, there is the relative [conventional] level of truth. On the ultimate level there are no validly cognized objects other than the one taste of the absence of all mental fabrications (*prapañca*). Ultimate reality transcends the division of subject and object. It is the underlying stratum, the unborn, pure mode of existence of the appearances of the relative level. Thus the two levels of truth are inseparable. (Trans. 1979, p. 15)

Longchen Rabjampa describes this coalesced nature of the void sphere of reality further in these poetic verses:

> Ultimate reality is the mandala [the sphere of experience] of the perfectly pure expanse of voidness. It is like a 'magic' mirror. What unimpededly appear on it are all phenomena (*dharma*) of relative reality, your mind included. These things appear naturally on this 'magic' mirror, through and to your mind. There is no third reality of a truly existing mind or objects juxtaposed to the ultimate reality of the mirror and the relative reality of the images in it. (Trans. 1979, p. 18)

Dynamics of experience

The sphere of experience of a person is a conditioned view arising through imputations into this void sphere of reality. This appears as the mind (*citta*) and its objects. This limited sphere of experience is conditioned by the specific context in which a person's mental continuum evolved. Experiences and reactions continuously modify this context. New appearances of objects and *citta* arise in this ever-changing context. Detailed understanding about this dynamics can be derived from the third turning and *vajrayāna* teachings.

This ever-changing context of experience is related to imprints (*vāsana*). Imprint is like a thin fragrance left behind after the scent has evaporated, or like a stain still left behind on a cloth after many washes. The stains left by various experiences blend together in forming the context for newer experiences. *Vāsana* acts like a filter that constraints the breadth and depth to which a *citta* penetrates reality. It leads to the formation of a conceptually projected view of reality that prevents further penetration into the true nature. This results in certain grounding of the awareness (*vidyā*), making the experience specific to a frame of reference. This specific frame of reference results in distorted contextual knowing (*vijñāna*) as opposed to the pristine wisdom (*jñāna*) that an ungrounded awareness with its omniscient expanse and unhindered penetration can achieve. A few examples would help in making this clear. A room might be pleasant for a person, too hot for another, and too cold for yet another—all at the same time. Past experiences and expectations lead to this difference. Depending on *vāsana*, one penetrates reality differently and sees either a river that is unchanging or the flowing water. There can be similarities in *vāsana* for an entire species of beings. Thus, humans experience a lawn to be beautiful to watch, and soft to touch. A dog might not appreciate the beauty, though it still finds it soft to roll on. A cow might find the same lawn tasty! The structure of the human eye that constrains the visual consciousness to objects of certain dimensionality (not seeing microscopic structures for example), may be said to be a bodily *vāsana* that humans carry by being embodied into a certain cognitive structure. Removing all *vāsana* is essential as part of breaking the veil of knowables (*jñeyāvaraṇa*) towards omniscience. This is called the veil of knowables since the conceptually projected images of knowables obstruct the knowledge of the truth as it is.

Another stream of modification in the mental continuum of a person is the urge for action that arises as the ripening of *karmic* tendencies (*karma-bīja*). The distinction between *vāsana* and *karma-bīja* is thin, since the very appearance of an experience involves an imputation which is an implicit action. In addition, actions lead to modification of the context of experience. Similarly, the very urge to act arises in the context of experiencing. However, it may be termed that *vāsana* predominantly deals with how experiences arise and *karma-bīja* about how a person reacts to experiences.

Karmic tendencies are habitual associations made in the mental continuum between situations, actions and results from the past. For example, having responded many times in the past in a certain style creates a seemingly automatic urge to respond in a similar style when such situations arise again. Similarly, having experienced immediate happiness due to a particular action many times in the past, creates an urge to act in such a way again. For example, venting out anger might give immediate relief to a person, though it leads to unhappy after-effects like a disturbed state of mind and angry retaliations from others. This might lead to the development of a habitual association between venting out of anger and the experience of immediate relief, further leading to similar urges in future. Once a person habituates with letting out anger whenever the urge arises, the mental continuum turns into a fertile ground for the mental episodes of anger to arise often with little provocation. *Karmic* tendencies from a multitude of experiences reinforce each other. This may be viewed as a non-linear dynamics that sustains and reinforces a tendency till it drives the person into experiencing a *karmic* result.[17] The aggregate of formation arises from the ripening of *karmic* tendencies based on situational conditions.

Every moment of awareness arises with an innate creative potential. However, the *karmic* tendencies severely condition and narrow down the way this creativity manifests. *Karmic* tendencies mixed with root-ignorance about selflessness lead to afflictive obscurations (*kleśāvaraṇa*) that bond a person to the experiences of suffering.

Model 3: The eight-fold collection

In the third turning philosophy, personality is analyzed in terms of the context and the structure of experiences, by focusing on the experience of knowing (*vijñāna*). The formation of personality is explained as the dynamic interplay of:

1. The ever-changing continuum of the context of experience,
2. The basic structuring of experiences in that context,
3. The formation of the sense of self, and
4. The arising and vanishing of specific experiences.

In this model, personality is viewed as an eight-fold collection consisting of seven consciousnesses (*vijñāna*) and the defiled mentality (*kḷṣṭa-manas*). The seven are the all-ground consciousness (*ālaya-vijñāna*) along with its projections, through the mental and sense consciousnesses. According to the *Yogācārabhūmi-śāstra* (Asanga, Trans. 2006), the mental and sense consciousnesses are also known as functional consciousnesses (*pravṛtti-vijñāna*). The dynamics of the eight-fold collection is described in the *Laṅkāvatāra-sūtra*:

> Like waves that rise on the ocean stirred by the wind, dancing and without interruption, the *ālaya*-ocean in a similar manner is constantly stirred by the winds

> of objectivity, and is seen dancing about with the *vijñānas* which are the waves of multiplicity. (Trans. 1999, p. 42)

The eight-fold collection is as explained below:

(1) All-ground consciousness (*ālaya-vijñāna*): This is the limited sphere of experience of a person that arises as a distorted view of the void sphere of reality (*dharmadhātu*) through dependent imputation. *Ālaya-vijñāna* forms the foundation for embodied cognition and defines the basic structure of all experiences. The *vāsana* and *karmic* tendencies (*karma-bīja*) lead to a biased perspective and structuring, and thus provide a context for all experiences in this eight-fold collection. Thus, *ālaya-vijñāna* is also regarded as the store house of *vāsanas* and *karmic* tendencies (*vāsanāparibhāvita* and *sarvabījaka*). However, it is neither the permanent identity of a person nor a form of collective unconscious. Continuous build-up and discharge of *karmic* tendencies cause the ever-changing nature of *ālaya-vijñāna*. Though *ālaya-vijñāna* always provides the context to all experiences, a person in ordinary states of awareness does not become conscious of the subtle and direct experience of *ālaya-vijñāna* because the gross nature of functional consciousnesses dominates in such states.

(2) Defiled mentality (*kḷṣṭa-manas*): The mentality (*manas*) is the subjective aspect experienced as the enjoyer (or as perceiver, knower, actor) of objects. The mentality is defiled because it is constantly conceited with the idea of 'I am'. From the sphere of experience presented by *ālaya-vijñāna*, the defiled mentality arises as an experience of 'I'. Ācārya Mañjuśrīmitra, a renowned master in the lineage of *Mahāsandhi-yoga* teachings, explains:

> Depending on the power (*prabhāva*) of various *vāsanas* from the manifold formative forces of *karma*, the potential for experience appears forth as objects and subjective being (*ātma-bhāva*)... By taking the continuum of accumulating *vāsana* as the basis, mentality (*manas*) arises as an experience of *ātma* that does not exist. (Trans. 2001, p. 117)

As Asanga explains in *Abhidharma-samuccaya* (Trans. 2001), the notion of 'I' is conceited with the four defilements of—the perception of self (*ātma-dṛṣṭi*), self-love (*ātma-sneha*), the feeling of 'I am' (*asmimāna*) and the ignorance about the true nature of self (*avidyā*). The defiled mentality conceives a limited identity within the sphere of experience as 'mine' and provides a basis for emotional afflictions to arise trying to protect and enrich that identity. The thoughts of defiled mentality are subtle and do not become gross objects of knowing in ordinary experiences. However, it forms the subjective reference around which the six functional consciousnesses project and construct ordinary gross experiences. These projections in turn affirm the defiled sense of 'I'.

(3-8) Functional consciousness (*pravṛtti-vijñāna*): Mental consciousness (*mano-vijñāna*) and the five sense consciousnesses constitute the six functional consciousnesses. These consciousnesses arise as projections from the sphere of experience of *ālaya-vijñāna*. Ācārya Mañjuśrīmitra explains:

> By the power of formations (*saṃskāra*), the subtle (*ālaya-vijñāna*) is obscured and does not appear vividly, which gives rise to specific cognitive projections (*vijñāpti*). (Trans. 2001, p. 117)

These projections are ways of differentiating and knowing specific aspects from the sphere of experience that remains largely obscured. The examples for these specific aspects are forms and colours for eye consciousness, or images and concepts for mental consciousness. The ripening of *karmic* tendencies (*karma-bīja*) leads a person to project and follow specific aspects. *Karma* causes one to develop interest (due to afflictive emotions like attachment, aversion and closed minded ignorance) towards a specific aspect of this projection, which in turn leads one to modify the projection. *Karmic* tendencies lead to these afflictive emotions with the intent to protect or enrich the identity established by the defiled mind. One fabricates the ordinary realm of experience (*saṃsāra*) by following after and concretizing various projections. The sphere of experience of *ālaya-vijñāna* with its accumulation of *vāsana* and *karmic* tendencies provides the basis for such functional projections to arise continuously. The functional consciousnesses are so called because they are entangled with and work towards bringing forth an objectified world. They are localized in the sense that one makes objectified projections of specific aspects, while no more remaining conscious of the rest of the sphere of experience. Thus one remains unaware of the experience of *ālaya-vijñāna* when functional consciousnesses dominate.

The *ālaya-vijñāna* and defiled mentality are regarded as stable because their ever-changing continuum is present at all times. The functional consciousnesses are unstable because they arise and subside contextually. For example, the six consciousnesses are dormant during dreamless deep-sleep. The coordination between the six functional consciousnesses is established through the *vāsana* and *karmic* tendencies that continually modify the basis of projections—that is, the *ālaya-vijñāna*.

It may be noted that the six functional consciousnesses are always dualistic in nature. These cognitive projections arise with the three spheres of knower, known and knowing. In contrast, *ālaya-vijñāna* is non-dualistic from the point of view of the object-subject division. Depending on the context of experience, *ālaya-vijñāna* appears with the multiplicity of phenomenal distinctions. It can also fade out into an appearance of a unified stratum in certain states of experience.

In the *Precious Treasury of the Meaning of Words* (Trans. 1989) Longchen Rabjampa clarifies the distinction between various terms like *ālaya-vijñāna*, *ālaya* and *dharmadhātu* appearing in scriptures of *sūtra* and *tantra*. He reveals the structure of personality more deeply. *Dharmadhātu* is the term for reality 'as it is' (*tathātā*) or the 'void sphere of reality'. All-ground (*ālaya*) is the unawakened (unenlightened) nature of a person and forms the foundational stratum for the continuity of *vāsana* and *karmic* tendencies. *Ālaya* arises when a person has root-ignorance (*avidyā*) of not comprehending the true nature of all phenomena. It modifies itself through the accumulation of *vāsana* and *karmic* tendencies. Longchen Rabjampa further divides *ālaya* into four aspects to illuminate its structure. These include (i) the all-ground of primordial nature (of root-ignorance) (Tibetan: *ye don gyi kun gzhi*) (ii) the all-ground of application (Tibetan: *sbyor ba don gyi kun gzhi*), (iii) the all-ground of various *vāsana* (Tibetan: *bag chags sna tshogs pa'i kun gzhi*) and (iv) the all-ground of bodily *vāsana* (Tibetan: *bag chags lus-kyi kun gzhi*). Of these, the first is about the co-emergence of root-ignorance with any sprout of awareness. The second and third are related to how the *karmic* tendencies and *vāsana* further shape up the structure of personality. A person associates with the sense organs and bodily structure to form a stable reference to experience, from birth to death. The stable structure of *vāsana* that forms one's specific cognitive structure from birth to death is the fourth category. *Ālaya-vijñāna* is the aspect of being conscious of the sphere of experience constrained by *ālaya*. According to Longchen Rabjampa, if *ālaya* is like a mirror, *ālaya-vijñāna* is like the luminous clarity of the mirror, and the functional consciousnesses are like the arising of reflections in the mirror (Trans. 2002).

Afflictions and psychological states

The constraints of the ordinary psyche and the resulting psychological traits are studied in terms of the five root afflictions (*kleśa*) and their derivatives. The combinations of these afflictions result in various limiting psychological states. In Buddhism, the primary perspective to afflictions is not social ethics, but their potential to produce a state of suffering in a person. The root afflictions have a correspondence with the five aggregates. These afflictions are aggravated forms of distortions in relating to the world through the underlying capabilities of the aggregates.

The affliction related to the aggregate of form is bewilderment (*moha*), which makes one unable to engage with an object with single pointed concentration. One gets disinterested through distractions, becomes satisfied with a certain depth of knowing, gets confused through the multiplicity of appearances or remains afraid of deeper levels of truth. Thus one keeps wavering away from one object to another, without penetrating the appearances. Bewilderment can also be in relation to the mental objects of concepts, when one is unable to penetrate into the deeper layers of understanding.

The affliction of pride (*māna*) is related to the aggregate of feeling. Pride is an ego-centred approach where one looks for an enriching pleasurable sensation within the ego-boundary. One remains contented with ego-centric pleasures and fails to develop an appreciation of the interdependence of the entire sphere of experience. Attempts to enrich the pleasurable feeling within the ego-boundary as an isolate—without an overall enrichment of the entire sphere of experience—are not sustainable due to its interdependent nature. Intoxication (*mada*) is a related affliction, where one is overwhelmed with pleasure and remains too complacent to produce conditions for the sustenance of that pleasure.

The aggregate of perception has its associated affliction as attachment (*rāga*). In Buddhist terminology, attachment is differentiated from love and likeness. Attachment is the clinging to an object of experience with an exaggerated perception of its qualities. While focusing on a quality of the object, if one fails to discern the numerous supporting conditions that bring about its attractiveness, one mistakenly clings to the object as if it possesses the quality from its own side. One also fails to see the many alternate conditions that would have made the same object repulsive. This leads to clinging to the object for what it is not. One cultivates undue expectations and thus undergoes suffering due to attachment.

The root affliction of jealousy (*īrṣya*) is associated with the aggregate of formation. It arises as the result of aggressive pushes of *karmically* driven actions. With the mistaken notions of ego-boundary the person begins to compare the immediate results of actions with those of others, leading to jealousy. Thus the person loses focus on the basic intent behind the action, that is, the intent to move away from suffering towards happiness. It also leads to competitiveness (*mātsarya*) as the focus shifts to comparison of narrowly created concepts of results instead of genuine happiness. Thus one constructs greater suffering through narrow-sighted actions.

The affliction of hatred (*dveṣa*) is associated with the aggregate of *vijñāna*. Hatred is the aggravation of mental turbulences that distorts and clouds the faculty of knowing. This is the result of the perturbed nature of contextual knowing (*vijñāna*), undergoing turbulent changes in its context. When the ego-identity is threatened in the face of an experience, the attempt to protect that identity arises strongly. It leads to unwholesome action and suffering. An unperturbed knowing may be compared with the surface of a still pond that reflects objects like a mirror. If a stone falls into the still pond, ripples appear at the surface and the sediments float up, turning the water muddy. The perturbed pond reflects the objects with distortion and lack of clarity along with added colours. Similar distortions happen to the process of knowing, when inflicted with hatred.

Buddhist psychology categorizes all ordinary modes of existence with their gross afflictions, into a psychological realm called the desire realm (*kāma-dhātu*—sphere of experience of desires). It is possible to cultivate states free of such gross afflictions through one-pointed meditation that calms the mind. However, such states of meditative absorption (*samādhi*) do not irreversibly transform the mental continuum. It still remains a fertile ground for afflictions which arise once the person comes out of the meditative absorption. The psychological realms corresponding to these states of *samādhi* are the form-realm (*rūpa-dhātu*—sphere of experience of forms free from gross projections) and the formless-realm (*arūpa-dhātu*—sphere of experience devoid of forms).

The desire realm is further classified into six sub-realms of psychological traits, based on relative dominance of one or the other affliction. One way of understanding the sub-realms is to consider them as six personality types among humans. In this categorization, the ordinary human psyche with a more or less balanced mixture of the five afflictions is one of the types. When any one of the afflictions dominates strongly over the others, the person belongs to the other five types. Over time, one could change the habitual tendencies and drift from one type to another.

However, these variations are limited because of the stability provided by the all-ground of bodily *vāsana*.

A grosser shift in the psychological attitude comes up during rebirth. The continuum of a person during rebirth can undergo drastic changes in the way one relates to the world. This is because the stability provided by the all-ground of bodily *vāsana* is affected during death. The re-structuring of the all-ground of bodily *vāsana* happens in accordance with the psychological type acquired through the specific mixture of the five afflictions. This can lead the mental continuum to a sphere of experience completely different from human experience. The Buddhist scriptures mention five other sub-realms of being, namely, *sura-loka*, *asura-loka*, animal-realm (*paśu-loka*), *preta-loka* and *naraka-loka* in addition to human-realm (*nara-loka*). These correspond to the aggravated levels of pride, jealousy, bewilderment, attachment and hatred respectively. These depict the many different ways in which a person (a sentient being[18]) can bring-forth and relate to the world. These realms are experiences of the same sphere of reality with differing *vāsanas* and *karmic* tendencies of the beings.

The *ālaya* provides an ever-changing, but stable context for a person to relate to the world consistently in one of these realms. The defiled mentality and functional consciousnesses work in tandem with *ālaya-vijñāna* to provide this stability, by concretizing the sphere of experience. This stability is disturbed during death. The structure of *ālaya* and the eight collections dissolves during the process of dying, resulting in the dissolution of the structure of experience. The experiential states in the intermediate state between death and rebirth are narrated by Guru Padmasambhava (Trans. 1975). This corresponds to the process of the restructuring of the *ālaya* and the eight collections; and thus the emergence of a new structure of experience for the continuum of the person. The defiled mentality, with its clinging to the idea of self, plays a vital role in the process of rebirth. The defiled mentality undergoes a struggle to re-establish one's identity. This struggle leads to an identification of the self with certain experiences that arise in the person's continuum. This leads to the process of concretization and re-stabilization of the *ālaya* centred around such experiences. This centring is usually by habitual identification, rather than through any conscious choice. This process has a striking similarity in its dynamics with the concept of attractors in the theory of non-linear dynamics.

Psychology of transformation

The models of personality introduced above, can be applied in studying the psychology of transformation. Distinctions between the subtler experiential states of *samādhi*, liberation (*vimukti*), stages on the path to full awakening (*saṃbodhi*), etc., can be understood with the help of these models. Buddhism does not consider *samādhi* states as liberation from suffering, because these do not result in the irreversible transformation of the basis of suffering. Such a transformation is possible only through cultivating insight (*prajñā*) about the actual mode of existence of a person.

A person accesses the states of meditative absorption (*samādhi*) through subduing the five afflictions and cultivating the mental episodes of one-pointed concentration (*ekāgratā*). Eight major levels of *samādhi* states are identified, of which the first four are categorized as form-realm and the remaining as formless-realm. The *Surangama-samādhi-sūtra* is one of the sources with detailed descriptions of these realms and their sub-realms (*Surangama-samādhi-sūtra,* 2003). In summary, the form-realm presents the experience of vivid appearances of ephemeral forms with reducing levels of grasping, and an absence of explicit suffering.[19] *Ālaya-vijñāna* becomes the dominant level of consciousness as the person progresses through various form-realms. The functional consciousnesses and the *ālaya* are secondary.

In the formless-realm states, *ālaya-vijñāna* and the functional consciousnesses tend to become increasingly dormant and *ālaya* dominates. In these states, distinctions and comprehension weaken. The experiences are like a vast undifferentiated space (*ākāśa-ananta-āyatana*), like a vast consciousness devoid of even the objective perception of space (*vijñāna-ananta-āyatana*), a perception of the lack of any perceivable phenomena (*akincana-āyatana*) and a complete subsiding of consciousness as 'neither perception, nor non-perception' (*naiva-saṃjñā na-asaṃjña-āyatanam*). In the last of the above, *ālaya-vijñāna* and the functional consciousnesses are completely dormant, while the person continues with all the *vāsana* and *karmic* tendencies dormant and intact in the *ālaya*. In Buddhism, the formless states are not regarded as desired results of spiritual practice. They lack both the omniscient quality of the enlightened state and the limited distinctions of ordinary beings. As the functional consciousnesses that help in getting down to specific aspects are dormant, cultivating insight is difficult in formless realm.

One who is liberated from suffering is called an Arhat. One progresses to the state of Arhat through the union of insight meditation (*vipaśyana*) and calm-abiding (*samatā*), by cultivating wisdom regarding the true nature of a person—*anātma*. An Arhat's *ālaya-vijñāna* undergoes a level of irreversible transformation that no more supports the sprouting of defiled mentality (*kḷṣṭa-manas*). The accomplishment is irreversible, since a mental continuum ripened with wisdom does not provide a suitable condition for the arousal of ignorance (*avidyā*). In the light of wisdom of *anātma*, an Arhat is no more pushed around by the winds of *karma*. This is to be contrasted with the reminiscent effect of *samādhi* that continues after meditation, but fades away over time. Though an Arhat has achieved freedom from the veil of afflictions (*kleśāvaraṇa*), the veil of knowables (*jñeyāvaraṇa*) is still present. Thus an Arhat's sphere of experience is still limited.

A person (*Bodhisattva*) on the path to complete awakening (*saṃbodhi*) needs to remove the veil of knowables in addition to veil of afflictions. Removal of all the stains of *vāsana* is essential for this. This can be achieved only through working with the projections of functional consciousness to actively modify *vāsana*. Thus the path of progress of a Bodhisattva is different from that of an Arhat. It requires compassionate engagement (*upāya*) with the world along with insight (*prajñā*) into the true nature of all phenomena. These two necessarily need to go hand-in-hand, since the realization of subtler levels of interdependence and enriched levels of compassion through post-meditational periods, and the realization of deeper levels of emptiness through meditation, support each other. Through gradual coalescing of meditative and post-meditative experiences, one completely wipes out stains of *vāsana*. This results in the irreversible abandonment of *ālaya* that structures experiences through past habits, and in a direct experience of truth 'as it is'. Then there is wisdom co-emergent with every sprout of experience. The eight-fold collection of the ordinary personality transforms into the pristine wisdom that is ever-fresh. Detailed descriptions of the stages on the path to liberation and complete awakening, and their relations with the models of personality, as described above, can be found in scriptures such as the *Abhisamayālaṃkāra* and the *Yogācārabhūmi-śāstra*.

Going beyond 'confusion'

The absence of recognition of the truth 'as it is', leads to the 'confusion' (*bhrānti*—the cognitive error) of seeing truth from a perspective—distorting and concretizing certain aspects, failing to see the rest, imputing layers of concepts, etc. The colouring of the sphere of experience is the first level of embodiment or grounding of awareness—in the form of *ālaya*. This is also the beginning of 'confusion'. The grounded perspective of a person does not remain the same over time. It undergoes change within a limited scope within a life-span, and restructures significantly between death and rebirth. The suffering and limited pleasures one undergoes are the result of this confusion. Confusion is the only basis for suffering. However, the ultimate nature of confusion is none other than that of awareness. It is merely a distortion of awareness resulting from the lack of recognition of the truth 'as it is'.

When one progresses in the path by working to eliminate the veils (*kleśāvaraṇa* and *jñeyāvaraṇa*), one recognizes the true nature of reality. *Ālaya* loses its support through this recognition (because *avidyā* is its necessary support). Aspects of pristine wisdom (*jñāna*) shine forth after this recognition. In the absence of conditioning through past experiences in the form of *vāsana* and *karmic* tendencies, this pristine wisdom is an ever-fresh awareness comprehending truth 'as it is'. There is nothing essentially pure and impure, except for confused perspectives making such distinctions through exaggerations. The five aggregates, the five root afflictions and the eight-fold collection are distorted perspectives to pristine wisdom. The five inseparable aspects of pristine wisdom are:

1. Pristine wisdom of discrimination (*pratyavekṣaṇa jñāna*),
2. Pristine wisdom that is mirror-like (*ādarśa jñāna*),
3. Pristine wisdom of equality (*samatā jñāna*),
4. Pristine wisdom of all-accomplishment (*kṛtyānuṣṭhāna jñāna*), and
5. Pristine wisdom of the void sphere of reality (*dharmadhātu jñāna*).

The 'pristine wisdom of discrimination' differentiates and understands all details of phenomena. It engages with the entire sphere of experience to distinguish details. It is the capability behind the aggregate of perception. In the absence of the confusion of grounded perspectives, the power of attachment is transformed into its purified form as correct discernment, through unbiased engagement without exclusions and exaggerations. Thus the aggregate of imputed perceptions dissolves in this pristine wisdom.

The 'pristine wisdom that is mirror-like' reflects the void sphere of reality (*dharmadhātu*) in its fullness, without getting perturbed into disturbing emotional states (through *karmic* tendencies) and habitual colouring (through *vāsana*). This is the aspect of unwavering clarity. This is the capability behind the aggregate of *vijñāna*. The grounded context that formulates *vijñāna* (qualified knowing) dissolves by the recognition free from confusion. The power that drives the affliction of hatred is transformed into its purified form as the power for unperturbed clear experience.

The 'pristine wisdom of equality' is the wisdom sensing the happiness and suffering of all beings with one-taste, transcending beyond the ego-centric feelings of suffering and limited pleasures. Due to the absence of confused identities with suffering and pleasure, this leads to an even-minded quality of compassionate all-rounded enrichment. The aggregate of feeling dissolves into the realization of this pristine wisdom. The power that drives the affliction of pride (*māna*), and the ego-clinging nature of enriching one's happiness, is transformed into an all-enriching attitude.

The 'pristine wisdom of all-accomplishment' is the creative wisdom of a fully awakened being. It represents the power for spontaneous accomplishments (*anabhoga*) instead of being bound to *karma*-driven actions. With the dawn of recognition, the aggregate of formation dissolves into this naturally accomplishing wisdom. The power that drives the afflictions of jealousy and competitiveness is released from its confused journey of aggression into that of effortless accomplishment.

The 'pristine wisdom of the void sphere of reality' is the experience of truth 'as it is'. The confused perspectives lead from this wisdom to concretized aspects as the aggregate of form. It is the same power of this wisdom that drives the affliction of bewilderment, when one diverts from the deeper investigation of the nature of truth, into confused identification with appearances. The comprehension of certain unchanging patterns within the ever-changing flux of appearances results in seemingly permanent forms. If one perfectly transcends bewilderment with insight (*prajñā*) and one-pointed concentration, one cuts through all appearances into the true nature of reality.

Similarly, the eight-fold collection of *ālaya-vijñāna*, and so forth, are confused presentations of pristine wisdom. The sense consciousnesses with its power to relate to the world through *karma*-driven projections are nothing but the power of the pristine wisdom of all-accomplishment, applied within the limited perspective of grounded cognition. The mental consciousness, with its power to conceptually analyse its object, is the distortion of the pristine wisdom of discrimination operating within the constraints of grounded perspectives. The defiled mentality with its subjective formulations is the confused display of the power behind the pristine wisdom of equality, trying to set a limited scope for moving from suffering to happiness. The *ālaya-vijñāna* is the confused display of luminous clarity of the mirror-like pristine wisdom, being coloured and perturbed by experiences of the past. The *ālaya* itself is the confused colouring of the pristine wisdom of the void sphere of reality, displaying forth as the limited sphere of experience.

On recognizing the true nature, confusion ceases. Various dimensions of awareness-potentials and capabilities are amalgamated into the ever fresh display of pristine wisdom of complete awakening. Nothing is abandoned—neither the experience of distinctions, nor the experience of wholeness; neither the experience of sensation, nor the creative potential of action. All these are coalesced into inseparable aspects of omniscient wisdom in the void sphere of reality. Going beyond 'confusion' (*bhrānti*), through developing the irreversible foundation of insight (*prajñā*), one transcends beyond the ordinary to this perfect and completely awakened state.

Conclusion

The three models presented above cover different ways of analyzing personality—in terms of the categories of experiences, the dynamics of mental continuum, and the context and structure of experiences. The five dimensions of capabilities show how all these models are connected together, and how the same faculties can manifest either as the distorted demonstrations of afflictions or as the purified presence of pristine wisdom. It reveals the ineffable potential pent up in every being, which can be unleashed to its spontaneous perfection by developing recognition. This recognition has to be cultivated through the focused application of method (*upāya*) and wisdom (*prajñā*) in its initial stages, and through spontaneous perfection of the inseparability of method and wisdom in its advanced stages. Buddhist psychology primarily addresses how to progress systematically from the ordinary state of being into the state of perfect recognition.

Elements from Buddhist psychology can also be studied and utilized for application in other facets of psychology. The network model of mental continuum and the view of Madhyamaka have already found their places in the research topics of psychology and cognitive science. The rest of the models remain largely untapped. The model of eight-fold collection presents a good psychological description of the process of sleeping, dreaming and dying. This can potentially be studied in correlation with scientific observations. This model also provides a suitable framework to study the psychology of transformation, and to map and correlate the experiences of practitioners from various spiritual traditions. The five dimensions of capability can provide a useful template for studying psychological afflictions in the scientific context. This would help in root-cause analysis of various psychological disorders, and in integrating that knowledge for the holistic transformation of a person.

Endnotes

1 The three scopes of motivation for Buddhist practice were pointed out by the sage and scholar Atīsa Dīpānkara Srijñāna in 'The Lamp to the Path to Enlightenment' (*Bodhipatha-pradīpa*). These include the lower motivation of good rebirths (that of relatively low levels of suffering), the middle motivation of liberation from cyclical existence and the higher motivation of complete and perfect awakening as an omniscient knower.

2 The Buddhist term *nirvāṇa* is used in two contexts. Its lower scope is freedom from suffering (*vimukti*) and the higher is perfect and complete awakening (*saṃbodhi*). Commonality is that both of these states are free from *saṃsāra*.

3 The distortions that arise when experiencing the truth from various frames of reference may be termed in modern terms as 'cognitive errors'. This concept is further explored in later sections of this chapter in relation to terms like obscuration to omniscience (*jñeyāvaraṇa*) and confusion.

4 The five aspects of pristine wisdom are mentioned by the Buddha in *kāyatraya-avatāra-sūtra*. The theme of these five aspects is detailed out further in *vajrayāna* teachings.

5 Mahāyāna (higher vehicle) refers to schools that focus on the higher scope of motivation—that of *saṃbodhi*. Many schools (like Theravāda) that primarily focus on the middle scope of lower *nirvāṇa*—that of *vimukti*—accepts only the first turning *sūtras*.

6 Prajna-pāramita tradition refers to the scholastic tradition followed in the ancient universities of India like Nālandā, Vikramaśila and Odanḍapuri. This is also the tradition followed by Tibetan Buddhism. Vajrayāna, the Tantric tradition of Buddhism is regarded to be part of this.

7 The phrase 'continuum (*santāna*) of a person' is used in Buddhism to refer to the person as an ever-changing stream of various aggregates. It also makes it explicit that person does not refer to a monolithic entity. A related term is mental continuum (*citta-santāna*) that refers to mind as an ever-changing stream of various mental episodes.

8 The Sanskrit word used for person is *pudgala*, meaning embodied being. In the Buddhist context, the discussions on psychological models apply not only to human beings, but also to all other sentient beings. Also see endnote 18.

9 *Abhidharma-kośa* (Treasury of higher knowledge) is an ancient text by the Buddhist scholar Vasubandhu detailing Buddhist teachings as understood by the Sarvāstivādin school of Sanskrit Hinayāna tradition.

10 *Abhidharma-samuccaya* (Compendium of higher knowledge) is an ancient text by the Buddhist yogi-scholar Asanga detailing *Abhidharma* teachings from a Yogācāra perspective.

11 *Manas* is introduced and discussed in the section, 'Model 3: The eight-fold collection'.

12 Asanga in his treatise named *Bodhisattvabhūmi* (part of *Yogācārabhūmi-śāstra*) states 'the appearance of objects is known as *vijñāna*' and 'the first conceptualization of these [appearances] is known as *citta*'. The conceptualization (*vikalpa*) in this context relates to the basic imputation of the object of cognition through *vāsana* as explained later in this chapter in connection with emptiness and the context of experience. This is not the grosser conceptualization that forms various additional ideas about the object through the aggregate of formation.

13 This is clarified in the third turning through the phrase '*svacitta-dṛśya-vikalpa*' (conceptualized appearances to the mind) in the *Laṅkāvatāra-sūtra*. It does not mean that there is no basis to appearances other than mind. Such an interpretation leads to the mistaken view of the third turning as subjective idealism. It rather means, whatever 'appears' to mind is not truly existent outside mind. The truth 'as it is' that is beyond all conceptual elaboration is apprehended through limitations of *citta* as something else.

14 It may be noted that the three aggregates presenting subjective aspects, viz., feeling, perception and formations contribute to the mental episodes.

15 In this context, *samādhi* does not refer to its usual meaning associated with meditative absorption. It refers to the basic stability in mental engagement needed for ascertaining the qualities of an object correctly.

16 Insight meditation (*vipaṣyāna*) is an integral part of Buddhist practice along with calm-abiding meditation (*śamata*).

17 The non-linear dynamics of a collection of similar *karmic* tendencies leading a person into pleasurable and painful states of experience are termed *puṅya* and *pāpa*. Such collections can build up exponentially due to mutual reinforcement and due to the fuel that the mind-stream provides to the tendencies continuously.

18 Sentient being refers to a being with mind that can sense suffering and happiness. Also see endnote 8.

19 The Buddha pointed out that all-pervasive suffering of construction (*saṃskāra-dukhata*) is present even in the realms of form and formless experiences even though the explicit and gross suffering is absent. This is because these realms of experiences are constructed through many conditions. The struggle for construction is an implicit suffering that one may remain unaware of. In constructed states, one has to constantly struggle to generate supporting conditions. Or else,

the state fades away upon exhaustion of supporting conditions like meritorious *karma* (as like a lamp going off on exhausting oil).

References

Asanga (2001). *Abhidharma-samuccaya* (W. Rahula & S. Boin-Webb, Trans.), *Abhidharma-samuccaya: The compendium of the higher teaching*. Fremont: Asian Humanities Press (Original text 5th century CE).

Asanga (2006). The Alaya treatise: Pravṛtti and nivṛtti portions, Viniścaya-samgrahaṇi, *Yogācārabhūmi-śāstra* (W. S. Waldron, Trans.), *The Buddhist unconscious: The ālaya-vijñāna in the context of Indian Buddhist thought*. New York: Routledge (Original text 5th century CE).

Goleman, D. (1997). *Healing emotions: Conversations with the Dalai Lama on mindfulness, emotions and health*. Massachusetts: Shambhala Publications.

Goleman. D. (2004). *Destructive emotions: A scientific dialogue with the Dalai Lama*. New York: The Bantam Dell Publishing Group.

Laṅkāvatāra-sūtra (1999). (D. T. Suzuki, Trans.) *The Lankāvatāra sūtra: A Mahayana text*. New Delhi: Motilal Banarasidass (Date of original text uncertain. Original translation 1932).

Longchen, Rabjampa. (1979). *The precious garland of four Dharmas* (Tibetan: *chos bzhi rinpochei phreng ba*) (A. Berzin, Sharpa, Tulku & M. Kapstein, Trans.), *The four-themed precious garland: An introduction to Dzogchen, the great completeness*. Dharamsala: Library of Tibetan Works and Archives (Original text 14th century CE).

Longchen, Rabjampa. (1989). *Precious treasury of the meaning of words* (Tibetan: *tshig don rin po che'i mdzod*) (Tulku Thondup, H. Talbott, Trans.), as translated in the chapter 'How Saṃsāra and Nirvāṇa Originated' in *The practice of Dzogchen*. Colorado: Snow Lion Publications (Original text 14th century CE).

Longchen, Rabjampa. (2002). *The great chariot* (Tibetan: *shing rta chen po*) (Rime Lodro Waldo, & Lama Ugyen Shenpen, Trans.), *The commentary on 'The great perfection: The nature of mind, the easer of weariness' called 'The great chariot'*, retrieved January 2008 from http://sacred-texts.com/bud/tib/chariot.htm

Mañjuśrīmitra (2001). *Bodhicittabhāvana* (Namkhai Norbu & K. Lipman, Trans.), *Primordial experience: An introduction to rDzogs-chen meditation*. Massachusetts: Shambala Publications Inc (Original text 2nd century BCE). (The English translation in this chapter is modified by the authors based on the Tibetan translation that appears in the aforementioned book).

Nāgārjuna (2008). *Mūla-madhyamaka-kārika* (Padmakara Translation Group, Trans.), *Root stanzas on the middle way: Mūlamadhyamakakārika*. France: Edition Padmakara (Original text 2nd century CE).

Padmasambhava (1975). *Liberation through hearing in the intermediate state* (Tibetan: *bardo thos grol*) (Chogyam Trungpa & F. Fremantle, Trans.), *The Tibetan book of the dead: The great liberation through hearing in the Bardo*. Massachusetts: Shambhala Publications (Original text estimated 8th century CE, revealed by Karma Lingpa in 14th century CE).

Surangama-samādhi-sūtra (2003). (E. Lamotte & S. Boin-Webb, Trans.) *Surangamasamādhi Sūtra: The concentration of heroic progress*. New Delhi: Motilal Banarasidass (Date of original text uncertain).

Varela, J. V., Thompson, E., & Rosch, E. (1993). *The embodied mind: Cognitive science and human experience*. Massachusetts: The MIT Press.

10

Ego and *ahaṁkāra*: Self and identity in modern psychology and Indian thought

Kiran Kumar K. Salagame

'Know thy self' and *'ko'ham'* (who am I?) probably epitomize the Western and Indian approaches to the problem of human identity from ancient times. While the dictum, 'know thy self', is an injunction from the 'other', *ko'ham,* is an inquiry from 'within'. Though both of them aim at realizing the nature of one's true identity, they may be considered as representing the second person and first person or objective and subjective perspectives, and have formed the foundations of two different types of self—psychologies offering different perspectives on human nature *per se*. Ego and *ahaṁkāra* are representative concepts from Western and Indian traditions, which refer to human identity at a psychological level. They have been used synonymously and often *ahaṁkāra* is translated as ego. However, there are certain conceptual similarities and dissimilarities between the two. The purpose of this chapter is to examine these two concepts and their implications for human development and well-being.

In contemporary psychological discourse, the formulations related to psychological functioning in almost all domains are egocentred. For example, psychodynamic theory uses a language that is replete with terms such as 'ego-strength', 'ego-weakness', 'egoboundary', 'ego-loss', 'strengthening of ego' and 'ego-functions'. Similarly, Piaget, in his theory of cognitive development, identified 'egocentrism' as one of the characteristics of the stage of pre-operational thinking. Egocentrism is difficulty in seeing the world from another's outlook. 'Ego resilience' is another concept recently used in life span developmental context, which refers to 'powerful personality resource that enables people to handle midlife changes' (Kail & Cavanaugh, 2004, p. 514).

Similarly, the goals of psychotherapy are conceptualized as 'promoting autonomy', 'enhancing self-esteem', 'increasing self-regulation', 'achieving self-efficacy', 'facilitating self-actualization', and so on. It is observed that in general, the Western conception of the self is of an individual who is separate, autonomous and atomized (that is, made up of a set of discrete traits, abilities, values and motives), seeking separateness and independence from others (Markus & Kitayama, 1991).

Prevalence of ego related constructs in modern psychology can be understood, both as a cultural phenomenon and as a matter of the range and depth of human consciousness studied. As a cultural phenomenon, these constructs gain importance because the psychological theories and methods developed in the West in general, and in the United States in particular, adopted the *individual* as the basic unit of analysis, affirming the individualistic bias of Western culture (Kim & Berry, 1993). Berry et al. (1992) observe that the notion that a person is a bounded individual has been central to the discipline of psychology in general, and to personality psychology in particular (Much, 1995). Since psychodynamic and other theories are rooted in Western culture, the formulations of psychopathology and therapy as well as the mental health profession per se, are guided by the Western ethos.

The Western view of the relation between ego and consciousness is spelt out clearly by Carl Jung, who does not admit consciousness without ego at its centre (Jung, 1971). The Indian tradition agrees that in the ordinary waking state the ego seems to be the centre of one's consciousness, but it does not limit consciousness to the ordinary waking state. It considers the ego too limited a construct to encompass the entire range of consciousness and human identity, and asserts that there also exists a type of pure consciousness, beyond all the dualities, called *cetanā* in its awareness aspect, and *caitanya* in its energy aspect. It is in this pure consciousness that it locates the real/true identity of a person, his *puruṣa*. From this perspective, the altered states of consciousness can be considered more appropriately as altered states of mind, pure consciousness being the substratum which remains changeless (Salagame, 1988). The distinction between pure consciousness and mind is crucial in the Indian tradition and has far-reaching implications for understanding human self and identity.

It is only in the last four decades, with the emergence of transpersonal psychology, that Western researchers have paid attention to the distinction between pure consciousness and mind, and the corresponding identity sense. In Eastern cultures the conception of a transcendental 'Self' is more prevalent than in Western cultures. It should be noted that Abraham Maslow in his last days recognized that human beings have a 'need for transcendence' and spoke of 'Being-Needs' (or 'B-Needs' for short), 'Meta-Needs' and 'meta-motivations' (Maslow, 1971). He was responsible for the establishment of Transpersonal Psychology.

Transpersonal psychology emphasizes the spiritual dimension of human nature. It considers man as divine and spiritual in addition to being an animal and uniquely human. Sigmund Freud, a physician by profession, boldly postulated a theory of unconscious mental process out of necessity to account for certain disorders. In a similar way, some Western psychologists and psychiatrists took the bold step of establishing Transpersonal Psychology (Sutich, 1969; Tart, 1975) and Transpersonal Psychiatry and Psychotherapy (Cortright, 1997; Scotton, Chinen & Battista, 1996) when they encountered 'peak experiences' and altered state phenomena. Within the discipline of psychology, psychoanalysis and transpersonal perspectives may be considered as marking a distinct shift from body to mind, and from mind to spirit. They have turned towards Eastern traditions, such as Buddhism and Hinduism, in their attempt to formulate new theories and models. Thus psychology has completed a full circle, recovering the soul/spirit that was lost on its way (Salagame, 2006).

Identity and self in Indian thought

The Indian perspective views human beings as bio-psycho-social-spiritual organisms. Hence, there are many concepts related to identity and self, referring to different aspects. Among them are: *ātman, puruṣa, jīva, dehī, kṣetrajña, ahaṁkāra, ahambhāva, asmitā, jñātā, bhoktā*, and *kartā*, which are used in different contexts with specific meaning and significance. They represent transcendental, empirical (physical) and psychosocial dimensions of human nature.

On the transcendental level, identity refers to *ātman* in Vedānta and *puruṣa* in Sāṁkhya. Since the *Upaniṣads* declare that the transcendent Self, *ātman*, is identical with the highest principle of the universe, *Brahman*, (*ayam ātmā brahma*), the *Upaniṣads* also declare that this self is *Brahman* or 'I am *Brahman*' (*ahaṃ brahmāsmi*). The notion of a transcendent Self, *ātman*, requires further elaboration because it is said to be beyond the distinction of subject-object. Viewed in this context, transcendence is really *not* an 'experience' in the ordinary sense because, transcendence implies no experiencer or experienced. The transcendent state of consciousness, if it can be called a state at all, is itself called Self, *ātman*. Hence, the idea of self here is not the same as the idea of self-sense on the empirical level or its psychological referent, and it is cogently articulated in *Māṇḍūkya Upaniṣad* as follows:

> The Fourth (*turīya*), the wise say, is not inwardly cognitive, nor outwardly cognitive, nor cognitive both-wise; neither is it an indefinite mass of cognition, nor collective cognition, nor non-cognition. It is unseen, unrelated, inconceivable, un-inferable, unimaginable, indescribable. It is the essence of the one self-cognition common to all states of consciousness. All phenomena cease in it. It is peace. It is bliss, it is non-duality. This is the Self, and it is to be realized (MU, 7, Trans. Swami Sarvananda, 1976).

Thus *turīya* or the so-called fourth state of consciousness, vis-à-vis the other three—*jāgrat* (waking), *svapna* (dream) and *suṣupti* (deep sleep)—is the substratum of all phenomenal experience, irrespective of the state. Hence, as one follower of Vedānta put it (personal communication), *turīya* is the original condition and the real state; and all other phenomenal states of consciousness, including waking, are altered states from the *Upaniṣadic* point of view (Salagame, 1988). Thus, *turīya* is the 'ground' of awareness, on which waking, dream, deep sleep, and other experiences happen with a 'subject-object/self-other' duality as 'figure'. Therefore, *turīya* was considered as the essence of the one self-cognition common to all the other states, and was regarded as the Self to be realized—*sa ātmā sa vijñeyaḥ*.

This 'subject/self' of phenomenal experience is termed as *jīva* or *dehin* in the Indian tradition, and they are incorporated into the linguistic structures of many regions. The person who undergoes the cycle of birth and death is *jīva* and it is at the empirical plane. It is also referred to as *dehī* in the *Bhagavad Gītā* (II. 22).

> *vāsāṁsi jīrṇāni yathā vihāya navāni gṛhṇāti naroparāṇi |*
> *tathā śarīrāṇi vihāya jīrṇānyanyāni saṁyāti navāni dehī ||*
>
> Just as a human being casts off worn-out clothes and takes on a new one, similarly, the owner of this body *(dehī)* gives up worn-out bodies and takes on new ones. (Author's translation).

The term *puruṣa* is also used in a pluralistic sense to refer to *jīva*. Thus the concept of person or individual or self or subject is represented by three terms—*jīva, dehin*, and *puruṣa*—in the Indian tradition. Padmapāda, the foremost disciple of Śaṅkara, gives a definition of *jīva* as follows:

> And that Jiva—of the nature of 'not this', conditioned as ego in the waking and dream state, and conditioned in sleep by avidya which has within it traces of the impressions (that the inner sense has left behind) which is the opposition of Jnana and which obstructs the light (of Atma)—keeps going forwards and backwards and as such is termed in Sruti, Smrti in common parlance as Samasari (the worldly person), Jiva, vijnanaghana, vijnanatma, prajna, sariri, sarirah, atma, samprasadha, purusa, pratyagatma, karta, bhokta, and ksetrajna.
> (*Panchapadika of Padmapada*, XXXIV 135, pp. 100–101. Quoted in Safaya, 1976, p. 213.)

In the preceding definition, we find that different terms have been used to represent the different aspects of the self in a conditioned existence. Their connotations are as follows:[1]

- *Sansārin*—involved in worldly enjoyment and activity;
- *Jīva*—soul;
- *Vijñānaghana*—embodiment of discriminatory knowledge with a spiritual dimension;
- *Vijñānātman*—prime mover of discriminatory knowledge;
- *Prajñā*—self as cognizer;
- *Śārīrin*—one who is embodied;
- *Śarīra*—the equipment which enables the *jīva* to function in the phenomenal world;
- *Samprasāda*—the self-sense present in dream;
- *Puruṣa*—human being;
- *Pratyagātman*—self as *Brahman*;
- *Kartā*—self as agent;
- *Bhoktā*—self as experiencer/enjoyer/sufferer;
- *Kṣetrajña*—knower of the field.

It is the identification with the *jīva* that is called *avidyā* (ignorance of one's true nature) or *ājñāna* (lack of transcendental Self-knowledge). Therefore, the tradition emphasizes on delinking the self-sense from *jīva*. All phenomenal experiences are attributed to *jīva* or *dehin*, while *ātman* is 'experience-less', as the term experience is understood with reference to an empirical subject.

Ahaṁkāra is derived from the word *aham*. *Aham* simply means a feeling of 'I', as in the question 'who am I?' (*ko'ham*). The Sanskrit term '*aham*' is a nominative singular of the term *asmad*, a pronominal base from which several cases of the first personal pronoun are derived. *Asmad* refers to individual soul or embodied soul (Apte, 1988). *Ahaṁkāra* represents the sense of doership and ownership, thus serving as a generic term representing the cognition and the feelings associated with me and mine. In the Vedānta tradition, *ahaṁkāra* along with *buddhi*, *citta* and *manas* constitute what is called the *antaḥkaraṇa catuṣṭaya*, the quartet of the internal organ. In its technical sense *ahaṁkāra* refers to that aspect of the *antaḥkaraṇa* which provides a subjective frame of reference to experience (Rao, 1962). Rama et al. (1976, p. 70) illustrate it thus: '... when a sensory-motor mind functions, a rose is seen. But when *ahaṁkāra* adds its influence, I see a rose.' Thus *ahaṁkāra* appropriates the experience to itself, leading to an affirmation of the sense of an objective world as perceived by the subject—resulting in increasing differentiation between subject and object serving as the principle of individuation. *Ahaṁkāra* also refers to the feeling of individuality/uniqueness, one's identifications and the sense of differentiation of oneself from the other, the 'I' from the 'not-I'. Thus, the term *ahaṁkāra* refers to the subject in the subject-object duality in the realm of mind/psyche, and therefore it is more appropriate to translate it as 'self-sense'. On the other hand, scholars often translate the term *ahaṁkāra* in English as 'ego', 'egoism', 'egotism', etc. (Salagame & Raj, 1999).

In the ontological sense, *aham* represents 'being'. Hence, when the question is asked as to who this being is, in the first person as 'who am I?' (*ko'ham*), it has different referents, depending on the level at which it is understood—transcendental, empirical and psychological. For example, one may say *ahaṁ ātmā* (I am *ātman*), *ahaṁ puruṣaḥ* (I am *puruṣa*), *ahaṁ jīvaḥ* (I am the embodied soul), *ahaṁ bhoktā* (I am the experiencer) and *ahaṁ kartā* (I am the doer). A layperson's understanding from his/her daily experiences is that whoever is that 'experiencer' or the 'subject' who participates in all experiences during *jāgrat* (waking state) is the real self. This includes our body, our mental states and our social relationships. So we incorporate most experiences of *jāgrat* as part of our identity or self-sense, and deny some of them into our self-structure, which constitutes the Freudian unconscious. Hence, a layperson's identity is largely bio-psycho-social (Salagame et al., 2005).

A layperson also usually treats experiences that occur during *svapna* (dream state) as not part of reality (exceptions being certain tribal people—Tart, 1969), though at the time of dreaming their reality is no less than those of the *jāgrat* experience. Similarly, many other types of experiences that may happen to people are rejected as figments of the imagination, dreams, hallucinations, delusions, far-fetched ideas and so on. In other words, they are treated as non-real. Thus, whatever one tends to identify with, becomes part of reality; and whatever one denies, becomes unreal. Hence a vast domain of possible human experiencing is declared unreal.

In the Indian tradition, all experiential phenomena which involve a subject-object (*vyakti-viṣaya*) duality, like the experiencer (*bhoktā*) and the experienced (*bhogya*), the observer (*dṛk*) and the observed (*dṛṣya*), the knower (*jñātā*) and the known (*jñeya*), are considered to be in the realm of *manas*, or mind[2] in its broadest sense. From the Indian perspective, all types of human experiences involving subject-object duality—be it normal, abnormal, pathological, paranormal, religious or mystical—are all mental phenomena (*manovyāpāra*), however extraordinary they may be. There is a vast domain of possible human experiences which we now call paranormal and mystical, and Indian texts provided detailed descriptions of such experiences. They also discussed dreams, illusions, hallucinations and delusions (Sinha, 1985).

However, they went a step ahead of the laity and modern psychologists in their analysis of the real and unreal. They declared that even the commonly understood self of *jāgrat* is actually non-real and declared that the only true self is that 'ground awareness', or *ātman*. This is the unique contribution of the *Veda* and the *Upaniṣads*.

Thus, the difference between most modern psychologists and the Indian view can be summarized as follows. The former affirm a narrow range of human experience as real and self, and they deny a vast domain as unreal. The latter declare all human experiences involving a subject-object/self-other dichotomy as not more than relatively real and as only 'figures' against the backdrop of a 'ground awareness' that is the only fully true reality; and the only real Self while the rest is seen as non-real and non-self. Hence, for them *jīva* (soul) or *dehin* (owner of the body) is also non-self and it is a wrong understanding to treat non-self as Self. This is *ājñāna* (lack of transcendental Self-knowledge), and leads to wrong identification with the non-self—*jīva* or *dehin* instead of Self—*ātman*, and this is seen as the root of all human problems and suffering. The solution lies in first obtaining the right understanding of the distinction between the non-self and the Self, called *viveka* (discrimination), through the process of listening (*śravaṇa*) (in modern times includes other means of acquiring information) and reflection (*manana*). The next step involves making a conscious attempt to overcome the wrong identification through a process of meditation (*nididhyāsana*). It is only then that a person becomes *jñānī* (Self-realized). Therefore, in the Indian scheme of understanding the self and identity, two processes play a crucial role. One is *viveka* or discrimination, and the other is *vairāgya*, or the process of dis-identification or detachment.

The question is who identifies with the non-self, who has to make the discrimination between the non-self and the Self, and who has to make the conscious attempt to dis-identify with the non-self? *Ahaṁkāra* is regarded as one of the *antaḥkaraṇa* ('inner instrument', mind) as the one involved in this process. Safaya (1976, pp. 221–222) observes that different schools have used different terminologies to refer to what is called the Mind, 'Sāṁkhya named it *antaḥkaraṇa*, Yoga named it *citta* and Nyāya named it *manas* (*buddhi* etc., included in the same). Vedānta calls it *antaḥkaraṇa*, but enumerates distinctly the four aspects viz., *buddhi, manas, citta* and *ahaṁkāra*.' However, it is debatable whether the term *antaḥkaraṇa* as used in Sāṁkhya and Vedānta is generic in its meaning, or refers exclusively to the cognitive aspect, requiring further research. On the other hand, *citta* of Yoga and *manas* of Nyāya are more generic in nature.

As Rao (1966) has clarified, according to Sāṁkhya the *buddhi* is only the *adhyavasaya* or discriminating principle in general. It does not have any 'individual' or 'egoistic' touch about it. So at this level the *puruṣa* does not even feel that he is the enjoyer or sufferer. It happens to be the function or contribution of *ahaṁkāra* to make the *puruṣa* strictly 'personal'. Further, Rao (1966) notes that self-consciousness or a feeling of personal identity cannot arise if the mental organ does not present something determinate to it. Though it is generally believed that it is a Sāṁkhya concept, references to *ahaṁkāra* are also found in the *Chāndogya* and *Praśna Upaniṣad*. In the *Praśna Upaniṣad* (IV, 8, Trans. Subramanya Sharma, 1947), *ahaṁkāra* is listed along with *buddhi, manas,* and *citta*. *Chāndogya Upaniṣad* (VII, 25, 1 & 2, Trans. Sachhidananda Saraswathi Swami, 1956) speaks about *ahaṁkāra* as self-sense, and points out that those who fail to discriminate between *ātman* and body will confound the self-sense with the body.

Elucidation of the nature and function of *ahaṁkāra* can be found in the *ślokas* related to *antaḥkaraṇa, aham-padārtha-nirūpaṇa*, and *ahaṁkāra nindā* in the *Viveka Cūḍāmaṇi* of Śaṅkarācārya. In *śloka* 103, Śaṅkara defines *ahaṁkāra* by stating that the *antaḥkaraṇa* dwells in the sensory and motor organs and in the body as *aham* with *abhimāna* (*ahamityabhimānena*) in the reflected brightness of *ātman*. In *śloka* 104, he states that it is to be understood as *ahaṁkāra*, which due to *abhimāna* (identification) becomes *kartā* (doer) and *bhoktā* (enjoyer), and also due to its association with *sattva* and other *guṇas*, will have *avasthātraya* (three states—waking, dream and sleep states). It is made clear that *ahaṁkāra* experiences happiness and sadness in relation to favourable and unfavourable circumstances, and therefore *sukha* (happiness) and *duḥkha* (sorrow) are its *dharma,* and not the *dharma* of the *ātman* which is *sadānanda* (forever blissful).

Śaṅkara further makes a distinction between *ahaṁkāra* and *aham-padārtha* (*Viveka Cūḍāmaṇi, ślokas*: 292–296). He equates *aham-padārtha* with *ātman* and elucidates it as the self-sense which remains even in deep sleep, and which is the witness even for *ahaṁkāra* and other functions. Therefore, he exhorts giving up *abhimāna* (identification) with *māṁsapiṇḍa* (body made of flesh), as well as with that *ahaṁkāra* which has *dehābhimāna* (bodily identification), and is fashioned out of *mūḍha buddhi* (dull intellect). Further, Śaṅkara exhorts giving up *abhimāna* (identification) with *kula* (caste), *gotra* (clan), *nāma* (name), *rūpa* (form) and *āśrama* (stage of life), which are dependent on the 'living corpse' (*ardhaśava aśriteṣu*). He also exhorts giving up *abhimāna* with the doer and enjoyer of the *linga śarīra* (subtle body). Thus, in modern terms, Śaṅkara is exhorting one to give up one's sense of identity with bio-psycho-social and even psychical aspects of human nature—all of which constitutes *ahaṁkāra*—in order to realize the *ātman,* attain *śānti* and to realize *akhaṇḍa ānanda*—inseparable bliss, itself.

Thus, it appears that *abhimāna* is the essence of *ahaṁkāra*. Apte (1988) has listed different meanings of the term *abhimāna,* one of which is 'referring all objects to self, the act of *ahaṁkāra*, personality'. As mentioned earlier, Swami Rama illustrates this with a very lucid example—'when sensory-motor mind functions, a "rose is seen". But when *ahaṁkāra* adds its influence, this becomes "I see a rose"' (Rama et al., 1976, p. 70). To see a rose, therefore, an 'I' is not essential. Similarly, to experience life, a sense of self is not essential.

According to the *Upaniṣads* and Vedānta, all problems start when this non-essential factor adds its influence in our lives. Therefore, *ahaṁkāra* is considered negative, and we find many *ślokas* denigrating *ahaṁkāra* (*ahaṁkāra nindā*) (14 as against 3 describing its nature) in the *Viveka Cūḍāmaṇi*. *Ahaṁkāra* is looked down upon with the following metaphors and descriptions (*ślokas* 297–310). It is *vikāra, duḥkha, rāhu,* powerful wild serpent, residue of poison in the body even after it is purged from a body, a thorn in the throat of a person taking food, an enemy to be slain with the sword of *vijñāna,* and fashioned out of *mūḍha buddhi* (dull intellect). Even after it is completely rooted out, if its thought is left for a while, it sprouts hundreds of *vṛttis* (mental modes, movements, and disturbances). Even after it is completely controlled, it should not be given scope through sense objects. If it is given any such leeway, it is like watering a withering lemon plant that will come into life.

Some Indian psychologists and philosophers have described the nature of *ahaṁkāra* in modern terms. Rao states: 'The general consciousness which is undifferentiated and rudimentary in course of time gets individuated. It acquires a subjective frame of reference and the process of individuation is afoot. This state, a further development of the capacity to be conscious of objects may be designated as self-consciousness. The Sāmkhya theory has brought into currency the expression "*ahaṁkāra*" to denote this. This is a word which superficially signifies "I making"' (1962, p. 41).

Srinivasan (1967, p. 199), interpreting the views of the Viśiṣṭādvaita Vedānta of Rāmānuja, states thus, '*Ahaṁkāra* is characterized by the contracted consciousness of the individual whereby he imposes on himself artificial and ego-centric "separative" limitation, conceives himself as divided from "God" and opposed to other individuals and lands himself in a state of struggle and suffering in the pursuit of selfish desires. This is the state of human bondage or inauthentic existence. Only by transcending this state of *ahaṁkāra* can the true status of the individual soul be realized.'

Safaya (1976) notes that according to Sāṁkhya, with the development of *ahaṁkāra,* the subject-object differentiation in living beings takes place. Joshi (1979) observes that through this process a false centre is created, around which one moves, and becomes a subject of constant friction and irritation. Rama et al. (1976, p. 70) observe that the I-ness inherent in *ahaṁkāra* 'provides a sense of separateness from the rest of the world, a feeling of distinction and uniqueness. It is the agency, which defines what of the sensory data and memories is "I". It is the property of subjectivity.' Ajaya (1983, p. 128) notes that as the distinction between 'not-I' and 'I' rigidify, the human being comes increasingly under the illusion that this distinction is real rather than an artificial creation of the mind. This illusion limits the human being from experiencing the 'holistic substratum of existence'.

Ahaṁkāra and ego: Some conceptual issues

In modern psychology, due to non-recognition of a transcendent Self, all discussions on the self terminate at the level of one's bio-psycho-social identity. Neither *ātman* nor *jīva* is accepted as real. Therefore, notions like life after death, reincarnation and transcendence are suspect. Engler (1986) notes that a classically trained psychoanalyst will have difficulty in appreciating the possibility of transcendence because it involves going beyond the personal identity or ego, which is the basis of healthy human functioning. This idea is reinforced by some studies on meditation, which show that those who have not achieved a reasonable amount of ego-integration are likely to break down due to meditative experiences (Boorstein, 1997). Hence, Engler (1986) made the famous statement that 'you have to be somebody before you can become nobody'.

An issue of far reaching clinical significance that is debated in this context is whether attempts at transcendence lead to psychopathology. The position postulated here is that such issues are semantic in nature and they arise due to incorrect translation of concepts from one language to another. For example, the exhortation in the *Upaniṣads* is only to lose *ahaṁkāra* in the sense of false identity in order to realize *ātman* the true identity, but not to lose *vijñāna* or *buddhi*, the discriminating principle, which is very much required to understand the difference between *ātman* and *anātman* (non-Self). What is emphasized in general in the spiritual traditions is to go beyond the limited identifications, *but certainly not to lose those ego-functions, which keep a person sane.*

Freud and other early psychoanalysts used the concept of ego to include both the identity sense and many other functions collectively referred to as secondary process thinking (Bellak et al., 1973). Bellak et al. (1973) consider the sense of identity or self-sense (*ahaṁkāra* in the Indian context) as one of the twelve ego-functions. It was only later that self-psychologists used the term 'self' to refer to the identity sense and retained the term ego-functions for many of the secondary process functioning (St. Clair, 1986). Hence, there is a need to understand and articulate the Indian and Western concepts more sharply. Thus, the contention here is that the concept of *ahaṁkāra* and the concept of self of self-psychologists are nearer to each other than *ahaṁkāra* and the psychoanalytic concept of ego-functions.

Understanding *ahaṁkāra:* An empirical approach

To examine some of these issues, this author initiated a series of studies in the Department of Psychology, University of Mysore. Archana Raj (1993), Shireen Gaur (1994), Rekha (1995), Pannaga K. Murthy (1999) and Parimala (2001) worked on this topic for their post-graduate dissertation. In 2001 and 2002, Kiran Kumar collected data on large samples of students from the University of Mysore and the Makrere University in Uganda. The findings of the first study are reported elsewhere (Salagame & Raj, 1999), while findings from the other studies are detailed in Salagame et al. (2005). A summary of the findings of all these studies is provided here.

From the findings and the trends emerging from the analysis of different sets of data the following inferences were drawn. *Ahaṁkāra* is a different construct than ego as defined by psychoanalysts and the functions of the latter appears to be conceptually more similar to the functions of the *buddhi*. The four main components of *ahaṁkāra* derived theoretically, are vindicated from factor analysis. They are Identification, Individuality, Agency and Separation. The Identification component of *ahaṁkāra* as measured in this study in terms of one's associations, attachments (*mamakāra*) and attractions (*moha*) may represent the most important aspect of *abhimāna* and thus validates the theoretical analysis of Śaṅkara, with regard to the essence of *ahaṁkāra*. The concept *abhimāna* and Identification as measured here seem to be similar to Otto Kernberg's concept of internalization in his synthesized model of object relations theory and Freudian instinctual theory. Kernberg's process of internalization has three levels: introjection, identification, and ego-identity which are progressively more conscious in operation (St. Clair, 1986). *Abhimāna* seems to encompass all the three levels.

The factors Separation (*dvaita bhāva*) and Individuality (*vaiśiṣṭya*) of *ahaṁkāra* appear to be conceptually near to Margaret Mahler's concepts of Separation and Individuation. 'Separation and individuation have two intertwined and complementary tracks. The track of individuation involves the evolution of intrapsychic autonomy, by which the child assumes the characteristics of being his or her own individual. The track of separation involves the child's emergence from the symbiotic fusion with mother, and therefore a differentiation and disengagement from her...' (Mahler et al., 1975, p. 63 cf. St. Clair, 1986, pp. 106–107).

The findings show that there is a lack of uniformity in the number and composition of the factor structure which may suggest that people differ in terms of the composition of *ahaṁkāra*. It could also be due to variations in the number of items, their wording, response alternatives in different versions used and the different samples on which the data is collected. Nevertheless, it is possible to speculate that individuals may be differentially predominated by one or more components of *ahaṁkāra*. One person may have a greater *ahaṁkāra* in terms of uniqueness and Individuality, another in terms of Agency, a third in terms of one's attachments and Identifications and a fourth in terms of the extent to which one feels separated from the others. In other words, to use Sanskrit equivalents, one may be seeking *vaiśiṣṭya* (uniqueness and individuality); another may feel a strong self-sense as *kartā* and *bhoktā* (I am the doer and enjoyer); a third may seek self-sense in terms of associations, attachments, and attractions, *saṅga*, *mamakāra* and *moha*; a fourth may feel a strong sense of boundary in *dvaita bhāva*, separation in terms of self-other, with strong in-group-out-group feelings, strong likes and dislikes, etc. However, this can only be confirmed after ruling out the other possible psychometric reasons for the obtained differences (Salagame et al., 2005).[3]

Speculations and conclusion

The findings have the following implications for the development of a theory of self and personality, psychopathology, psychotherapy, mental health and positive psychology from an Indian perspective. With the different components discussed above, the concept of *ahaṁkāra* can serve as a meta-construct that can embrace many of the modern psychological concepts related to self and identity, such as locus of control, self-efficacy, self-esteem, individuality, relational self, individualism-collectivism, ego-boundary and autonomy. The *ahaṁkāra concept with its components delineated here appears to be parsimonious* and it is possible to understand several contemporary theories of self and identity with reference to this meta construct.

It is possible to speculate that certain mental problems, particularly neurotic and personality disorders, can be seen as manifestations of under or over emphasis of one or the other component of *ahaṁkāra*. For example, a Type A person who may have problems, may be speculated to have the agency component, *kartṛtva*, overemphasized. Similarly, its under-emphasis may result in the sense of loss of control that is associated with many disorders. While over-emphasis on identification, *mamakāra, moha, saṅga,* results in all kinds of emotional problems and conflicts, under-identification may lead to psychopathic and antisocial tendencies. Similarly, the lack of *dvaita bhāva*, or feeling of self-other separation, except in transcendent phenomena, may lead to an undifferentiated psychotic state; and its rigidification may lead to obsessions, insulation, withdrawal, and the like. Hence, *there is here scope to build an indigenous theory of psychopathology and psychotherapy from an Indian perspective.* On the healthy side is the emphasis on *vaiśiṣṭya*, or uniqueness and individuality, which is required for self-actualization.

However, from an *Indian psychological point of view*, experiencing any of the above four components in greater degree is dangerous. All of them reinforce one's bio-psycho-social identity. *Kartṛtva, vaiśiṣṭya, dvaita bhāva, mamakāra, moha* and *saṅga*—all of them have personal involvement and investment, feeling of me and mine, which is *abhimāna*. While it is necessary to some extent for normal functioning, it cannot be the *ultimate ideal of growth from an Indian point of view*. While modern psychotherapeutic methods emphasize their development, the Indian tradition stresses that for further spiritual development, involvement in all of them is to be refrained from. For example, Sri Aurobindo says in one of his aphorisms, 'When we have passed beyond individualising, then we shall be real Persons. Ego was the helper; Ego is the bar' (1915/1998, p. 199). Hence the need for detachment from all of them. Only then can one experience true identity. Viewed from this perspective, the modern psychological attempt is to increase *abhimāna*, and thus *ahaṁkāra*, in the name of therapy and growth. Here is the difference between growth and self-actualization of modern psychology, and the Self-realization of Indian psychology.

Endnotes

1 Author is grateful to Sri M. A. Narasimhan, Sanskrit scholar, for helping to distinguish these terminologies.

2 The word *manas* is also used in a much narrower sense to specifically denote the sense-mind.

3 In a recent study we have found that the factors of *kartrtva* and *dvaita bhava* are positively and negatively correlated with the task oriented and people oriented leadership styles respectively (Archana and Salagame, manuscript under preparation). This lends some support to the observations made above.

References

Ajaya, Swami (1983). *Psychotherapy east and west: A unifying paradigm*. Honesdale, PA: Himalayan Institute.

Apte, V. S. (1988). *The student's Sanskrit English dictionary*. Delhi: Motilal Banarasidass.

Aurobindo, Sri (1915/1998). *Essays in philosophy and yoga*. Pondicherry: Sri Aurobindo Ashram Publication Department.

Bellak, L., Hurvich, M., Gediman, H. K., Crawford, P., & Jacobs, D. (1973). *Ego functions in schizophrenics, neurotics, and normals: A systematic study of conceptual, diagnostic and therapeutic aspects*. New York, USA: John Wiley & Sons.

Berry, J. W., Poortinga, Y. H., Segal, M., & Dasen, P. R. (1992). *Cross-cultural psychology: Research and applications*. Cambridge, UK: Cambridge University Press.

Boorstein, S. (1997). *Clinical studies in transpersonal psychotherapy*. Albany, NY: State University of New York Press.

Cortright, B. (1997). *Psychotherapy and spirit: Theory and practice in transpersonal psychotherapy*. Albany, NY: State University of New York Press.

Engler, J. (1986). Therapeutic aims in psychotherapy and meditation: Developmental stages in the representation of self. In K. Wilber, J. Engler, & D. P. Brown (Eds.), *Transformation of consciousness: Conventional and contemplative perspectives on development*. Boston and London: Shambhala, New Science Library.

Gaur, S. M. (1994). *A study of the concepts of ahamkara and ego functions in males and females*. Unpublished Master's Dissertation. University of Mysore. Department of Psychology.

Joshi, R. V. (1979). *Studies in Indian logic and metaphysics*. Delhi: Bharatiya Vidya Prakashan.

Jung, C. G. (1971). *The portable Jung*. New York: The Viking Press (Penguin Paperback, 1977).

Kail, R., & Cavanaugh, J. C. (2004). *Human development: A life-span view* (3rd ed.). Belmont, CA: Wadsworth/Thomson Learning.

Kim, U., & Berry, J. W. (1993). *Indigenous psychologies*. New Delhi: Sage.

Markus, H. R., & Kitayama, S. (1991). Culture and the self: Implications for cognition, emotion, and motivation. *Psychological Review, 98*(2), 224–253.

Maslow, A. H. (1971). *Farther reaches of human nature*. New York: Penguin Books.

Much, N. (1995). Cultural psychology. In J.A. Smith, R. Harre, & L. V. Langenhove (Eds.), *Rethinking psychology*. New Delhi: Sage.

Pannaga, K. M. (1999). *Study of the concepts ahamkara and ego functions*. Unpublished Master's Dissertation. University of Mysore. Department of Psychology.

Parimala, N. (2001). *Ahamkara and ego functions among short term meditators and long term meditators*. Unpublished Master's Dissertation. University of Mysore. Department of Psychology.

Raj, A. (1993). *Meditation: Transcendence of ahamkara or disintegration of ego functions?—An empirical investigation on the concepts of ahamkara and ego functions*. Master's Dissertation. University of Mysore. Department of Psychology.

Rama, Swami, Ballentine, R., & Ajaya, Swami (1976). *Yoga and psychotherapy*. Honesdale, PA: Himalayan Institute.

Ramachandra Rao, S. K. (1962). *Development of Indian psychological thought*. Mysore, India: Kavyalaya Publishers.

Ramakrishna Rao, K. B. (1966). *Theism of preclassical Samkhya*. Mysore, India: Prasaranga, University of Mysore.

Rekha, K. (1995). *Ahamkara and ego functions among neurotics and general population*. Unpublished Master's Dissertation. University of Mysore. Department of Psychology.

Sachhidananda Saraswathi, Swami (1956). *Chhandogya Upanishad*. Kannada translation with commentary of Sri Shankaracharya. Holenarsipura, Karnataka, India: Adhyatma Prakasha Karyalaya.

Safaya, R. (1976). *Indian psychology: A critical and historical analysis of the psychological speculations in Indian philosophical literature*. Delhi: Munshiram Manoharlal Publishers Private Limited.

Salagame, K. K. K. (1988). States of consciousness: Perspectives from modern psychology. In M. A. S. Rajan (Ed.), *Consciousness: Proceedings of the workshop*. Melkote, India: The Academy of Sanskrit Research.

Salagame, K. K. K. (2006). *Concepts of self and identity in Indian thought and their implications for mental health profession*. Psycho award oration delivered at the 32nd Annual Conference of the Indian Association of Clinical Psychologists, Jaipur.

Salagame, K. K. K., & Raj, A. (1999). Ahamkara and ego functions among meditators and normals. *Journal of Indian Psychology, 17*(1), 46–55.

Salagame, K. K. K., Raj, A., Murthy, K. P., Parimala, N., Rekha, K., & Gaur, S. (2005). Concept ahamkara: Theoretical and empirical analysis. In K. R. Rao & S. B. Marwaha (Eds.), *Towards a spiritual psychology: Essays on Indian psychology*. New Delhi: Samvad India Foundation.

Sarvananda, Swami (1976). *Mandukya Upanishad*. English translation with a summary of Gaudapada's Karika. Madras: Sri Ramakrishna Math.

Scotton, B. W., Chinen, A. B., & Battista, J. R. (1996). *Textbook of transpersonal psychiatry and psychology*. New York: Basic books.

Sharma, S. (1947). *Prasna Upanishad*. Kannada translation with commentary of Sri Shankaracharya. Holenarsipura, Karnataka, India: Adhyatma Prakasha Karyalaya.

Sinha, J. (1996). *Indian psychology—Volume 1, Cognition*, (2nd ed.). Delhi: Motilal Banarsidass.

Srinivasan, G. (1967). *The existential concepts and the Hindu philosophical systems*. Allahabad, India: Udayana Publishing.

St. Clair, M. (1986). *Object relations and self-psychology*. Monterey, CA: Brooks/Cole Publishing Company.

Sutich, A. J. (1969). Some considerations regarding transpersonal psychology. *Journal of Transpersonal Psychology, 1*(1), 15–16.

Tart, C. T. (1969). *Altered states of consciousness: Book of readings*. New York: John Wiley & Sons.

Tart, C. T. (1975). *Transpersonal psychologies: Perspectives on the mind from seven great spiritual traditions*. San Francisco: Harper Collins.

11

The Sufi path of self-transformation

Bahman A. K. Shirazi

Islam: A brief introduction

Islam is one of the largest and fastest growing world religions. It began with the prophetic vision of Mohammad approximately 1,400 years ago in the Arabian Peninsula and spread at an astonishing rate throughout the Old World. It spread north to Syria, Anatolia, and to the Caucus Mountains and beyond into southeastern Europe. It moved south and west through Egypt and North Africa into Andalusia in Spain. In the northeasterly direction, it spread into Persia and Central Asia and western China, and east into northern India. By sea it spread to the west coast of India and as far as Indonesia and other Southeast Asian island nations.

Islam has thus become an important force not only in terms of religious principles and practices, but also as a vehicle for cultural exchange worldwide. Although some aspects of the original Arab culture such as language, art and architecture greatly influenced other cultures, wherever Islam spread, in turn, local cultures contributed to the fabric of Islam with their own cultural heritage to create a unique expression as well as distinct forms of religious practice and rituals. Today there is a tremendous range of cultural forms unified by the same set of Islamic religious principles and beliefs.

Islam teaches that there's only one God/Ultimate Reality (*Allah*) and nothing is ultimately real but God. God is neither born nor gives birth, that is, it is not a sentient being. It is self-existent and self-sufficient, and all creation depends on God. It permeates all creation, but no single sentient being can be equal to God in entirety. God is both without and within all beings, and thus can be found at the innermost centre of all human beings. In this way, all humans are equal with respect to God. Human beings are uniquely positioned with special potential to consciously experience their unity with the creator. However, many human beings live in a state of sleep-like ignorance (*gheflat*) and are unconscious of their essential oneness with God. Most are born in this state of ignorance, live and die in such a state. However, human beings can exercise their free will and perfect themselves through a process of psychospiritual transformation with distinct stages through which they first use their free will to purify themselves, and surrender themselves to God's will and ultimately experience God's power, knowledge and beauty directly.

Islam literally means 'peaceful surrender' in Arabic. This refers to the process of yielding of human will to the Divine Will, and ultimately the reconciliation and the unification of the two. The agency of human will is called the *nafs* (self) which is the principle of embodiment of spirit and the immediate experience of the ordinary human being in the world; the *nafs* is of this material world. *Nafs-al-ammarah* (the commanding self) is the human agency of organization, control, volition and action in the world. The human *nafs* is the product of the evolutionary process on Earth and is composed of several evolutionary sub-layers—the inorganic/mineral, the organic/vegetable and the animal layers. However, the journey of the soul does not stop here. When an individual is ready and with God's grace, the journey of spiritual transformation begins and the *nafs* continues to transform first into the 'regretful self', before turning into the 'inspired self', and finally the 'serene/secure self'. The process of spiritual transformation involves seven classical stages—awakening, abstinence, non-attachment, spiritual poverty, patience, God-reliance and joyous certitude.

Islam: Exoteric and esoteric

Sufism has often been referred to as the heart or soul of Islam, or in other words, it is the esoteric dimension or inner territory of Islam. According to Ibn Al-Arabi, the great Andalusian Sufi master, Islam consists of four dimensions or layers. The exoteric dimension, or the outer layer, is known as *sharia* (literally meaning a road). *Sharia* is a set of relatively fixed rules and guidelines for the average Muslim. The *sharia* is a collection of principles and practices that govern the day-to-day life of Muslims. The ordinary Muslim is expected to follow the rules of *sharia* as a driver follows a road without deviating. The basic requirements for all Muslims are—belief in unity of Allah and prophecy of Mohammad as God's messenger, daily prayer, fasting during the month of Ramadhan, charitable acts, and if possible pilgrimage to Mecca at least once in a lifetime.

The *sharia* is analogous to the crust of the earth or the surface terrain which is solid. Below this terrain is the esoteric realm, or the inner terrain. The next layer is *tarigha*, which literally means a path, like a trail in the forest or in the desert, which is not pre-established and requires the expert knowledge of a guide to traverse. When one enters the *tarigha*, he or she is initiated into a Sufi order with a help of a teacher (*sheikh*) who has experience and knowledge of the path. At this part of the journey the heart of the seeker is full of fiery passions and the journey full of trials and tribulations and involves the purification of the base nature of the *nafs* (embodied self) through the opening of the spiritual heart and the alchemy of transformation. It results in purification and removal of idiosyncratic illusions and development of truth consciousness. The *tarigha* may be likened to the hot magma layer beneath the earth's crust, which is hot and fluid as is the fire in the heart of the seeker.

The third layer is that of a higher spiritual consciousness called *haghighat* (Truth-consciousness). Like the huge solid mantle of the earth, *haghighat* is stable and unshakable faith and perfection of Truth-consciousness. The innermost core of Islam is known as *ma'rifa* (Gnosis), which refers to direct knowledge and love of the Divine. Just as little is known about the core of the Earth, to the seeker this part of the journey is a mere mystery, the secret of all secrets. Only persistence, patience and absolute purity of the heart and soul and total sincerity could bring the seeker into direct union with God consciousness.

Sufism in India

Sufism is the esoteric or inner dimension of Islam, and not a branch of exoteric Islam. Scholars trace the root of the term Sufi to *suf*, a woollen garment worn by some early Sufis. Some argue that the term is related to the Arabic word '*saafi*', meaning purity. Various Sufi orders do not differ with the exoteric traditions, and with one another, in terms of the basic tenets and practices of Islam. Origins of Sufism go back to the 8th century CE, when the first known Sufis lived. Sufi orders began to be established by 12th and 13th centuries, and historically developed more or less as a matter of geographic location as Islam spread throughout the world. Many of the orders were further sub-divided into branches, but most trace their background to the following orders (discussed below)—all of whom trace their heritage ultimately to Prophet Mohammad.

The *Ahmadi* (*Badawi*) and *Burhani* orders were both founded in Egypt. The *Shadhili*, *Sanusi*, and *Tijjani* orders have followers in North Africa, Arabia and Syria. The *Yasawi*, *Mawlawi*, *Jerrahi* and *Bektashi* orders are centred in Turkey. The *Rifai*, *Kubrawi* and *Qadiri* (known as the first Sufi order) orders originate in Mesopotamia. The *Ni'matullahi* and *Owaysi* orders were founded in Iran. The *Suhrawardi* order originated in Iran and spread to India, where it gained more prominence and split into a number of branches. The *Naqshabandi* is a major Sufi order, which became popular in Central Asia, Kurdistan and the Indian subcontinent. The *Chisti* order was founded in India by Khawja Mu'in al-Din Hassan Chisti (1142–1236 CE), whose shrine is visited by millions of people every year. Sufism was brought to Europe and America by the great Indian Sufi master, Hazrat Inayat Khan, in the 1910s and 1920s from the *Chisti* tradition, bringing the message of 'love, harmony, and beauty' to the West.

Islam spread to India as Arabs began settling on the Indian west coast of Kerala as early as the eighth century, which is much earlier than the time of the invasion of India from the north by Mahmud Ghazni in 1001 CE. The development of Sufism in India has a highly distinctive feature, in that Islamic mysticism has been influenced by Indian mysticism throughout the centuries. This amalgamation was so deep that, according to Peter Hardy (1983, p. 41), 'After the death of a great Sufi shaikh, his tomb could become a place of pilgrimage for both Muslims and non-Muslims alike.' The greatest confluence of Sufism and Hinduism can be found in the teachings of Meher Baba, who was initiated by five spiritual masters—two of whom, Hazrat Babajan and Tajuddin Baba, were Sufi masters. In the book, *God Speaks*, Meher Baba (2001), who attempted to unite all the major religions, brings together a comprehensive comparative presentation of Sufism and Hinduism, demonstrating the essential oneness of these two and other major world spiritual traditions.

Essentials of Sufi psychology: *Nafs*, heart and soul

Sufism offers a comprehensive approach to sacred psychology with the ultimate aim of self-knowledge and self-acceptance. The collective experience and knowledge from Sufi practice makes available to us today a thorough understanding of who we are as human beings and what the purpose of our embodied existence here on Earth is. It reveals to us the principal aspects of our nature and a way to transform our selves to become true instruments of manifestation of Divine love, Divine consciousness and Divine action.

Based on the experiences of numerous seekers and masters, Sufism offers one of the most complete road maps for the stages of transformation of consciousness. Each seeker (*salek*) travels a unique path suited to his/her unique personality characteristics and spiritual potential. It is possible, however, to speak of general stages of the transformation of consciousness in terms of the stations of the *nafs* and key challenges and attainments of each stage. The journey from our mundane surface awareness to the depths and heights of self-consciousness involves a process of transformation of personality and consciousness that may be described in terms of seven stages of psychospiritual transformation.

In the context of spiritual growth and development the term transformation may refer to a shift in locus of consciousness, emotional patterns, sense of identity, or an aspect or total configuration of personality, and even physical nature or characteristics. As form expresses essence or function, transformation allows for expression of a truer essence and a new level of functionality. The term 'psychospiritual transformation' highlights the importance of the psychological dimension in the overall process of spiritual transformation. It refers to transformation of consciousness by means of psychological insight. Insight into our emotional nature may help purify our emotions and emotional attachments. This may result in our increased ability to identify with higher spheres of consciousness. Insight into the nature of our phenomenal self or *nafs* is essential in the process of psycho-spiritual transformation.

Three principal aspects of the human being and their relationship comprise the triadic foundation of Sufi psychology: the *nafs* (self), *ghalb* (heart) and *ruh* (soul). Sufis believe that the spiritual heart is the agent of reconciliation between the physical and metaphysical dimensions of the human being. The spiritual destiny of each human being depends on whether the soul, or *nafs*, becomes the eventual winner of the inner battle (*jihad*) between the tendencies exercised by the *nafs* and the higher qualities of the soul. If the *nafs* dominates, the heart becomes darkened and weakened and ineffective. If the forces of the soul take over the heart, it becomes transparent and illumined. To know the real depth of the human being means to know intimately and masterfully these three parts and to be able to harmonize and unify them.

Nafs

Nafs is simply the equivalent of the English word 'self'. It has often been translated as 'ego' or 'lower self' both of which are somewhat inaccurate. The term ego, as used in Western psychological discourse, is hardly an equivalent of this term. The ego is generally a hypothetical construct which has a different definition and function in each school of psychology. *Nafs*, however, is not an abstract or theoretical concept—it is a lived, organic reality which could be experienced in day to day life situations. The *nafs* is essentially the embodiment principle and has a unique formation and developmental process in each individual. It is the agency of will in the human being and is the product of bio-psycho-social development. *Nafs* is also not just the lower self, but when qualified, it refers to all stages of self as it undergoes transformation. According to Frager (1999, p. 3), 'in Sufi psychology the self, or *nafs*, is an aspect of the psyche that begins as our worst adversary but can develop into an invaluable tool.'

It is possible to speak of the *nafs* in terms of seven levels. *Nafs al-ammarah*, *nafs-al-lawwamah*, *nafs-al-molhamah* and *nafs-al-motmaenah* refer to the four basic levels of the self. *Nafs-ammarah* (the commanding self), encompasses three levels of the *nafs* prior to the human self in evolutionary terms. These are:

- The mineral/inorganic self (*nafs al-jamaadi*),
- The vegetable/organic self (*nafs-al-nabaati*), and
- The animal self (*nafs-al-haywaani*)

As the principle of embodiment, the human self is the crown of the evolutionary process, presiding over the animal self, vegetable self and the mineral self.

Table 11.1 summarizes in one glance, the triune nature of human consciousness—the *nafs*, the heart, and the soul in correspondence

State of Consciousness	Self (*Nafs*)	Heart (*Ghalb*)	Soul (*Ruh*)
inorganic	mineral (*nafs aj-jamaadi*)		mineral
vital+inorganic	vegetable (*nafs al-nabaati*)		vegetable
mental+vital+ inorganic	animal (*nafs al-haywaani*)		animal
rational+mental+ vital+inorganic (intelligence/passions)	personal (*nafs a-ammarah*)	physical heart	human
heart/intuition/ intellect	regretful (*nafs al-lawwamah*)	spiritual heart	individual
truth/inner consciousness	inspired (*nafs al-molhamah*)	inner heart	secret
unity/gnosis/innermost consciousness	secure/certain (*nafs al-motma-ennah*)	innermost heart	secret of secrets

Table 11.1. Seven planes of consciousness and the corresponding stations of the self, heart and soul

to seven universal planes of consciousness. These are, in order of higher to lower density—inorganic, vital, mental, rational, intuitive, Truth Consciousness (*Haggh*) and Unitary Consciousness (*Tawheed*). The self (*nafs*) finds multiple expressions corresponding to all of these planes.

The commanding self (*nafs-al-ammarah*), though intelligent in worldly ways, generally lacks spiritual wisdom. According to Shafii (1985, p. 49), 'indulgence in animal desires... and enslavement in habits are the core of ignorance and veiling'. Desires operate at the various sub-levels of self. The mineral-self generates inertia; the vegetative-self creates desires for food and inactivity; and the animal-self is the source of both sexual and destructive tendencies. *Nafs-al-ammarah* seeks material objects, power, and is plagued with various other ego-desires and narcissistic tendencies.

The *nafs* often craves worldly objects and ignores the wisdom of the heart which is the medium of transmission of the knowledge of the soul. The *nafs* needs spiritual guidance to awaken to its spiritual potential from the state of sleep-like ignorance (*gheflat*). In Sufi practice, it has long been known that spiritual transformation necessitates opening of the heart as the first order of the work. Through the wisdom of an open heart, an individual is capable of self-love and self-compassion, qualities that are crucial to a non-judgmental approach to self-knowledge.

Heart

Sufism has frequently been referred to as the path of the heart. This is true, and a distinctive way of referring to this great tradition, but it is not the whole truth. Sufism has also developed one of the most complete teachings and practices for understanding and knowing the self, its growth and evolution in the context of the human psychospiritual developmental process. While focusing on the *nafs* and its relationship to the heart, Sufism never loses sight of the presence of the soul and its ultimate role in the human destiny. To make real progress in self-knowledge, one must encounter and discover the *nafs*, but the *nafs*, being extremely intelligent, is never capable of the kind of sincerity needed to see through its own makeup. The heart is the wisest place to start. Javad Nurbakhsh (1992, p. 71) writes:

> The heart is a city between the domain of Unity (spirit, *ruh*) and the land of multiplicity (*nafs*). If the heart snaps the cord linking it with the *nafs*, it falls under the sway of the spirit; that is to say, it becomes heart in the true sense of the word, polished clean of the corrosion of multiplicity. On the other hand, if the heart becomes dominated by the *nafs*, it becomes darkened by the tarnish of the *nafs'* multiplicity, taking on its hue.

Four stations of the heart have been identified by the Sufi master Tirmidhi—the breast or physical heart, the spiritual heart, the inner heart and the innermost heart (see Table 11.1). The breast or the physical heart corresponds to the commanding self (*nafs al-ammarah*), and its function is to purify the physical body by constantly circulating and purifying the blood. It is also known as the seat of duality of good and evil; and the moral conflict between the two. The spiritual heart, which is on a subtle plane, corresponds to the regretful self (*nafs al-lawwamah*). Its function is to purify unwholesome states of mind and emotions by providing their antidote (such as loving-kindness for anger). Opening of the spiritual heart is paramount to spiritual progress as ignorance of the *nafs* perpetually generates negative energies that can darken our consciousness.

It is a priority for Sufis to awaken their spiritual heart which needs to be integrated with the *nafs*. An open heart provides a loving and forgiving platform from which one can contemplate and discover the nature of our *nafs*. It will facilitate the transition from *nafs al-ammarah* to *nafs al-lawwamah* (the regretful *nafs*). As the *nafs* transitions to the stage of *nafs al-molhamah* (the inspired *nafs*), the heart arrives at another more subtle station, the inner heart. Finally, the heart is experienced at the deepest level of consciousness, the innermost heart, as the *nafs* transitions to its final station, the certain, serene and secure *nafs* (*nafs-al-motma'ennah*). Meher Baba (2000, p. 14) asserts:

> Open your heart by weeding out all desires and by harbouring only one longing—the longing for union with the ultimate Reality. The ultimate Reality is not to be sought in the changing things of the external environment but in one's own being. Every time your soul intends to enter your human heart, it finds the door locked and the inside too full of desires. Do not keep the doors of your heart closed. Everywhere there is the source of abiding bliss, and yet all are miserable because of desires born of ignorance. The goal of lasting happiness shines forth fully only when the limited ego, with all its desires, finds its complete and final extinction.

The role of the heart in the overall process of psychospiritual transformation is cardinal, as the heart is the reconciler of material and spiritual realities, and the gateway to the soul and to the final stations of consciousness. In Sufi practice the initial goal is to open the seeker's heart. The open heart first helps to transcend, and then, transform the *nafs*. As the *nafs* transforms, it no longer acts as a separative agent, but rather cooperates with further transformation of consciousness. Desires of the *nafs* give way to the desires of the heart, and finally there remains only one desire—desire to know God.

Soul

Hazrat Inayat Khan (1972b, p. 153) wrote, 'It is the coming of the soul from its original place to manifestation and its returning again from manifestation to its original condition that makes life's journey.' According to Prophet Mohammad, human beings are the highest of creation. Each human being is a microcosmic expression of the macrocosm.

> It does not require a large eye to see a large mountain. The reason is that though the eye is small, the soul which sees through it is greater and vaster than all the things which it perceives. In fact it is so great that it includes all objects, however large or numerous, within itself. Or it is not so much that you are within the cosmos as that the cosmos is within you. (Meher Baba, 1974, p. 43)

The human soul (*ruh*) is the innermost dimension (*baatin*) of the human being and is hidden to the immediate consciousness of the ordinary individual as our surface consciousness (*zaaher*) is dominated by the activities of the *nafs*. All souls are formless and seek experience and expression as they enter the various planes of consciousness (Table 11.1). Hazrat Inayat Khan (1972a, p. 127) reveals that 'the soul is a current, yet one unlike the electric current we know on this physical plane, different from its power and phenomena; a current which is beyond time and space; a current which runs through all the planes of life.' Different souls, though identical in origin, are different in their experience and their state of consciousness. The ascent of the soul through various planes of consciousness is called transmigration or metempsychosis (*tanaasukh*).

When the soul is experiencing the inorganic state of consciousness (stone or metal), it is referred to as the mineral-soul or state of mineral selfhood and so on, as detailed in Table1. In the fourth stage after mineral, vegetable and animal stages, the human form is accomplished, which is the end result of the evolutionary process. The commanding self (*nafs-al-ammarah*) associated with this level is not yet spiritually awakened and is full of blemishes, impurities and unwholesome traits such as hypocrisy, selfishness, delusions, spite, envy and cruelty. The behaviours committed by the *nafs* stem from its own many layers of identity and identification—physical, emotional, mental, familial, social, professional, racial, national and historical dimensions of identity. All of the pre-human and human layers of *nafs* are considered veils or covers of the true self. Self-realization requires a gradual disidentification with, or unveiling of, all these conditioned identities to reveal the innermost layer, the true Divine Self.

It is at the next level when the spiritual heart is opened that the soul experiences wholeness and true individuality. The next two stations of the soul are referred to as the 'secret', and the 'secret of secrets', which are unknowable to the ordinary mind and are marked by oneness with Ultimate Truth and Unity with God or the over-soul, respectively. In its origin the individual soul is part of the over-soul or God, yet it is not conscious of its identity with God. Through its journey the soul moves through the various states of consciousness and experiences its identity with the various states.

> The homeward journey of the soul consists in freeing itself from the illusion of being identical with its bodies—gross, subtle, and mental. When the attention of the soul turns toward Self-knowledge and Self-realization, there is a gradual loosening and disappearance of the *sanskaras* that keep consciousness turned towards the phenomenal world. Disappearance of the *sanskaras* proceeds side by side with piercing through the veil of cosmic Illusion, and the soul not only begins to transcend the different states of the phenomenal world but also to know itself as different from its bodies. The spiritual path begins when the soul tries to find itself and turns its full consciousness toward Truth (God). (Meher Baba, 2000, pp. 225–226)

The term *saṁskāra* refers to mental impressions that are acquired through the mind and the senses associated with *nafs* and embodied existence. These impressions create numerous veils of illusion that keep human beings in the state of *gheflat* or sleep-like ignorance and unconsciousness. According to a traditional saying, 'there are seventy veils between the human being and God, yet none between God and the human being'. In Sufi practice the goal is to open the seeker's heart, which is the gateway to the soul. The open heart first helps to transcend and then transform the *nafs*. As the *nafs* transforms, it no longer acts as a divisive agent, but rather cooperates with further transformation of consciousness.

The journey

Understanding the nature of the *nafs* and the modifications it undergoes in the process of psychospiritual transformation into the cosmic self, is at the core of the teachings in the Sufi tradition. Sufi practice begins with the first stage of psychospiritual transformation, spiritual awakening. Once the first stage is perfected (as demonstrated by a lack of recourse to the previous tendencies of the *nafs*), *nafs-al-ammarah* undergoes a gradual process of transformation known as *fana*, which means ego-annihilation or loss of self-centred personality characteristics.

As *nafs-al-ammarah* becomes modified and transformed, a new self is experienced. This is called *nafs-al-lawwama*. The term '*lawwama*' literally means 'blaming' or 'accusing'. *Nafs-al-lawwama* is perhaps best described (in functional terms) as self-in-transition, or regretful self. Regret is the result of the new consciousness, which reveals the imperfections of the *nafs* and the futility of its unconscious ways of being in the world. Many refined and mature human beings, whether Sufis or not, manifest the characteristics of *nafs-al-lawwama*, both in their inner life and outward behaviour. Such persons are decreasingly influenced by the tendencies of *nafs-al-ammarah*, and increasingly show the signs of higher emotions and subtler behaviours. A Sufi practitioner in the second stage, characterized by 'abstinence', actively avoids all forms of inferior impulses and tendencies by observing the ethical codes of the discipline (*adab*) until eventually the third stage, or 'non-attachment', is mastered.

It is crucial to distinguish abstinence (detachment) from non-attachment. While abstinence is required as an initial step, it does not automatically lead to non-attachment as the roots of craving still persist. Over-emphasis on abstinence may result in lopsided development, extreme asceticism and the development of a pious self which becomes judgmental and critical of others, which further separates one from the others. Sufism prescribes modesty in abstinence only with the goal of de-conditioning the *nafs* from its original habits and addictions.

By means of successive passages into the next two stages, 'spiritual poverty', during which the heart is perfectly purified and 'patience', longing for Divine grace, the practitioner attains the sixth stage, referred to as 'self-surrender', or 'reliance on God', through completion of which all tendencies of *nafs-al-ammarah* are eradicated at the root. Completion of the sixth stage also marks the cessation of all effort on the part of the individual. Beyond this point experiences of cosmic self and universal consciousness occur spontaneously, or by Divine grace. At the seventh and last stage, called 'contentment', the self takes on its final mode, *nafs-al-motma'enna*, which is characterized by joyful satisfaction and removal of all doubts.

Fana, or ego-annihilation, is also described in terms of a parallel process for an initiated seeker—annihilation of the ego first in the *sheikh* or teacher, and then in the Prophet Mohammad, and eventually in God or cosmic consciousness. At first a disciple undergoes a process of loss of self-identity through identification with the qualities of his or her teacher. Sufi practice, like those of other traditions, is best mastered under the guidance of a teacher. Just as ordinarily a lover at first loses his or her identity in that of the beloved, a sincere disciple is so impressed by the love and characteristics of a teacher that through observation and identification with the *sheikh* he or she becomes immersed in the virtues of the teacher. The *sheikh*, in the beginning, acts as a mirror through which the disciple gains insight into his or her characteristics of personality. Slowly the disciple observes the many virtuous qualities of the teacher and cultivates them.

If the teacher happens to be a Perfect Master, then he or she reflects the ninety-nine attributes of the Prophet Mohammad, who is known to the Sufis as a perfected human being (*ensan-al-kaamel*). The attributes of the Prophet are themselves nothing but the reflection of the ninety-nine attributes of Allah, or God. These ninety-nine perfections are the object of contemplation by Sufis at various stages of the practice. The practices of contemplation are generally called *zikar* (*dhikr*), and they take the form of chanting, movement or mediation exercises. Nurbakhsh (1990, p. 5) summarized the relationship between *dhikr* and self-development in the following way:

> ... *dhikr* is considered to be like a torrent which in addition to eliminating the undesirable qualities of the disciple and substituting Divine Attributes for them, in the final analysis effaces the individual ego in such a way that not a trace of the 'I' remains. This is the end of the Tarigha and the beginning of the sea of annihilation or *fana*.

According to Nurbakhsh (1990, p. 5), '...the goal of Sufism is knowledge of absolute reality, not as learned men explain it to us through logic and demonstrations but as it is in itself. This knowledge can be attained only by the "eye of the heart", that is, by means of illumination and contemplation'. Contemplation on Divine attributes is the final means of self-purification. From the Sufi point of view a perfected individual is one who has escaped the domination of *nafs-al-ammarah*.

As one approaches perfection, the *nafs* makes its final attempts to take control of the psyche. These re-appearances, despite their decreasing frequency, may be immensely difficult to withstand. That is why, until the final illumination, a certain degree of doubt as to the full annihilation of *nafs-al-ammarah* remains in the mind of the (by now) saint undergoing final transformation.

With the eventual disappearance of doubt the sixth stage of Sufi practice (self-surrender) is completed, and the last stage (contentment/joy) is attained. At this point the individual free-will is replaced by Divine Will. As mentioned earlier, the process of annihilation of the ego is known as *fana*. It takes place through successive stages of annihilation of the ego in the teacher (*fana-fe'sheikh*), in the Prophet (*fana-fe'rasul*), and in God (*fana-fe'llah*). However, *fana* has another process complementary to it, *baqa*. As Nurbakhsh (1990, p. 10) explained:

> Baqa consists of subsistence in God and is realized when God gives a new will to the disciple directly from himself, in order to replace that which had become annihilated in the course of the path... At this very advanced stage God does not veil the world from the Sufi, nor does the world veil God; no sort of separation exists any longer and duality is transformed into Unity.

Conclusion

This chapter was an attempt to provide a brief overview of Islam and its mystical dimension, Sufism. Emphasis was given to the psychological aspects of the process of spiritual transformation and the associated processes and stages of self-transformation merely in an outline fashion. There is much more that can be said about all the issues that were raised in this limited space. It is important to remember, however, that all that can be said in this manner makes only a map; the territory is the actual experience of the seeker and is always a unique process that cannot be moulded into any model or description however sophisticated. It is hoped that the map will simply provide an inspiration for the seeker of God.

References

Frager, R. (1999). *Heart, self & soul: The Sufi psychology of growth, balance, and harmony.* Wheaton, Il: Quest Publishing.

Hardy, P. (1983). Islam and Muslims in South India. In R. Israeli (Ed.), *The crescent in the East.* Great Brittan: Curzon Press.

Khan, Hazrat Inayat. (1972a). *The Sufi message of Hazrat Inayat Khan* (Vol. I). London: Barrie and Jenkins.

Khan, Hazrat Inayat. (1972b). *The Sufi message of Hazrat Inayat Khan* (Vol. XI). London: Barrie and Jenkins.

Meher Baba. (1974). *Life at its best.* (Ivy O. Duce, Ed.). Walnut Creek, CA: Sufism Reoriented.

Meher Baba. (2000). *Discourses.* Ahmednagar, India: Adi K. Irani.

Meher Baba (2001). *God speaks.* Hyderabad, India: Meher Mownavani Publications.

Nurbakhsh, J. (1992). *The psychology of Sufism.* London: Khaniqahi-Nimatullahi Publications.

Nurbakhsh, J. (1990). Sufism and psychoanalysis. *Sufi, 5*, 5–10.

Shafii, M. (1985). *Freedom from the Self.* New York: Human Sciences Press.

12

Integral Psychology: A new science of self, personality, and psychology

Suneet Varma

This chapter outlines a theory of personality based on Sri Aurobindo's conceptualization of the human being. Starting with the basic notion of self and personhood in contemporary academic psychology, largely located in the lower levels of psychological functioning, the field of Transpersonal Psychology is used as a stepping stone to access the higher reaches of humanity. A brief outline of the Advaita Vedāntic perspective on personality then paves the way for Sri Aurobindo's neo-Vedāntic depiction of the person. The contribution of the integral approach to the transformation of emotions, and its role in psychotherapy is then outlined. It is the author's contention that Sri Aurobindo's system contains a comprehensive framework of psychology, which allows for both Western as well as Indian conceptualization of the psyche and provides a synthesis, which is more than a mere sum of parts, giving a vision for an optimistic and glorious future of humankind, paving the way for divine life to manifest upon earth.

Introduction

Over the last ten years, I have increasingly been exposed to the writings of Sri Aurobindo, which seem to synthesize the best of what the Western as well as the Indian traditions have to offer by depicting existence from a consciousness perspective within an evolutionary framework. It is in the works of Sri Aurobindo that I get satisfactory answers to some of the most profound questions, which have haunted me for over two decades. The focus in this account is conceptualizations of the person, that is, personality in psychology, and how a deeper understanding of the psyche and its workings provides the key to human unity and world peace. Being situated in academic psychology, I delineate those perspectives in the mainstream of the discipline which demonstrate clear links with the larger Indian perspective and to which I have personally been able to relate to. This includes Psychoanalysis, Behaviourism, Humanistic Psychology, and finally Transpersonal Psychology, which is used as a stepping stone towards the higher reaches of the Indian perspective, which—in my judgement—finds complete and perfected form within the framework outlined by Sri Aurobindo.

Western perspectives

In the Western intellectual/philosophical tradition, the term person refers to human beings as entities who have certain rights and duties, whereas the term personality refers to individuality. Both meanings derive etymologically from the Latin *persona* denoting mask, and thus refer to outer appearance and behaviour only. 'Self' and 'ego' are two other terms, more or less equivalent, referring to a particular person distinct from others. In the Indian context, the nature of the self, and the nature of reality as a whole are the two central topics of enquiry in the *Upaniṣads*. The *Upaniṣadic* sages conceived of an ultimate principle of reality, or existence itself, and called it *Brahman*. A major conclusion of their enquiry is that the Self is identical with *Brahman*.

I came to academic psychology to understand aspects of my self as well as that of the larger reality, in relation to problems encountered in my life. Now this goal is closer to the *Upaniṣadic* approach, but somewhat distant from the concerns of most of the conceptualizations available in the exclusively Western viewpoints in psychology. But it was much later that I became aware of the Indian perspective. The first major viewpoint on psyche and the nature of the person that I was exposed to was Psychoanalysis, the framework of Sigmund Freud. Freud pointed out—based on his observations of mentally disturbed persons who came to him for help—that our normal waking consciousness, termed as 'ego', is only a small part of the larger psychological reality and was but a 'tip of the iceberg' of the deeper aspects of consciousness which were hidden from our awareness. The hidden part he referred to as the unconscious, which comprised instinctual energies inherited from our evolutionary past, including our animal heritage. The two instincts which Freud largely focused on were those supporting sexuality and aggression, both of which had a survival function. The instincts resided in the domain called the *id*. As a human infant developed over time, she was socialized to channelize her instinctual impulses in socially accepted ways. The domain of the societal codes of conduct was the 'super-ego'. Thus the major role of the personality or ego was to allow, under close supervision, the expression of the *id* impulses in ways which did not violate the rules of the super-ego. Growth and maturity in the Freudian system thus consisted in the emergence of a strong ego, which worked towards striking a balance between the contrary demands of the *id* on the one hand, and the super-ego on the other; and going by Freud's final analysis after he had witnessed the two world wars, it was a losing battle—for the dark forces residing in the unconscious ultimately succeeded in having their way. Freud was pessimistic about the future of humankind.

When I first encountered Psychoanalysis, I found it extremely difficult to locate my own existence, my experience, in this framework. Sexuality and aggression played a minimal role in my life; nor did social rules pose much of an obstacle for me. The experiences which I cherished such as happiness, harmony, peace, love—none of these were the goals of Psychoanalysis; nor did the quest for the ultimate meaning of existence have any place in Freud's system. Michel Foucault (1988, p. 18) referred to practices aiming at improving the human condition, resulting in growth as 'technologies of the self' which 'permits individuals to effect by their own means or with the help of others a certain number of operations on their own bodies and souls, thoughts, conduct and way of being, so as to transform themselves in order to attain a certain state of happiness, purity, wisdom, perfection, or immortality'. I find the description given by Foucault a useful criteria for assessing the effectiveness of different systems of psychology; and I am unable to rate Psychoanalysis as effective in this regard.

The second major system of psychology that I was exposed to was Behaviourism. The behaviourists assumed that all aspects of human functioning can be accounted for via the mechanism of learning, based on an analysis of a person's interactions with the external environment; and that the human organism to begin with is a *tabula rasa*—a blank slate upon which anything can be written, in the form of stimuli impinging from the outside. The behaviourists thus sought laws of learning valid for at least all mammals, and assumed the extension of animal findings to human psychology. J. B. Watson stood at the head of this tradition and his conception of psychology is clearly stated in his 1913 paper, 'Psychology as a behaviorist views it':

> Psychology as a behaviorist views it is a purely objective branch of natural science. Its theoretical goal is the prediction and control of behavior.... The behaviorist in his efforts to get a unitary scheme of animal response recognizes no dividing line between man and brute. (Leahey, 1991, p. 190)

It was Watson's ambition to raise the status of psychology to that of an objective natural science. To do so, he adhered as closely as possible to the methodology and principles of

Newtonian mechanics, the eminent example of scientific rigour and objectivity. To subject psychological experiments to the criteria used in physics required that psychologists focus exclusively on phenomena that can be registered and described objectively by independent observers. Thus in the behaviourist view, living organisms were complex machines reacting to external stimuli, and this stimulus-response (S-R) mechanism was of course modelled after Newtonian physics. It implied a rigorous causal relation that would enable psychologists to predict the response for a given stimulus, and conversely to specify the stimulus for a given response. A logical consequence of the S-R model was a tendency to look for the determinants of psychological phenomena in the external world rather than within the organism.

It appears to me that Behaviourism can account for many of my habits and other superficial characteristics of my personality which have obviously been learnt, but it tells me little about the nature of self, what it means to be a person, leave alone the complex issues of growth, fulfilment, happiness, love or the purpose of existence. The strength of Behaviourism lies in its description of the process of how the immediate external environment shapes certain bodily aspects of behaviour, but not much more than that. Of course, it was a system of knowledge generated by strict adherence to a rigorous 'scientific' procedure which relied exclusively on tangible observables, which ended up ignoring significant aspects of human existence located in lived experience within conscious awareness—in fact, conscious awareness finds no place in the behaviourist scheme of things. In terms of 'technologies of self', the behaviourists have nothing to offer.

So far, in my journey on the pathways outlined in academic psychology, I found no clue as to who I really was, why I had come into existence and what I was to do with my life. The third major system I was exposed to, one which I found addressing some of my concerns and also optimistic in outlook, was that of Humanistic Psychology and the major proponents of this school of thought were Abraham Maslow and Carl Rogers. These psychologists were critical of the limited views of human nature offered by Psychoanalysis and Behaviourism, where we are seen, in the case of the former as victims of unconscious forces, and in the latter as passive responders to external stimuli. While most humanists acknowledge the influence of external stimuli and instincts, they do not believe that human beings are unchangeable victims of these forces. We can and must rise above our past, our lower unconscious nature, the features of our environment, and develop and grow beyond these potentially inhibiting forces. The humanist psychologists' image of human nature is optimistic and hopeful for they believe in our capacity for expanding, enriching, developing, and fulfilling ourselves to become all that we are capable of becoming.

The humanists were thus the first within academic psychology to point to our capacity for growth which, as Rogers emphasized, is the urge which is evident in all organic and human life—to expand, extend, become autonomous, develop, mature—the tendency to express and activate all the capacities of the organism or the self. As a plant attempts to become a healthy plant, as a seed contains within it the drive to become a tree, so a person is impelled to become a whole, complete and self-actualized person. Now this formulation of a person was helpful for me, personally, for it outlined a positive goal of existence—growth. But at the same time it was incomplete for it did not exactly tell me what the end point of growth was, nor did it outline any precise or systematic 'technology of the self' to help me in transforming myself. In the humanist view, my existence was to be understood on my own terms, within my own narrow individual experience. There was no mention in this system of my connection with other aspects of the world and the cosmos at large; and thus there was no way of addressing who or what I ultimately am, and for what purpose I have come into existence.

It was only in Transpersonal Psychology that I got a glimpse of what I was searching for. Transpersonal Psychology is concerned with the study of humanity's highest potential and with the recognition, understanding and realization of unitive, spiritual and transcendental experiences. Transpersonal experiences refer to experiences in which the sense of identity or self extends beyond (*trans*) the individual or personal to encompass wider aspects of humankind, life, psyche and the cosmos. The underlying concept of human nature in Transpersonal Psychology is not a new one. It has always existed in human culture, and includes the following four basic premises (Fadiman & Frager, 2002):

- There is a transcendent reality or unity that binds together all (apparently separate) phenomena.
- The ego or individual self is but a reflection of a greater, transpersonal Self or oneness. We come from and are grounded in that Self. However, we have become estranged from our origins and we need to return to them in order to become fully healthy and whole human beings.
- The fact that individuals can directly experience this reality or greater Self is at the core of the spiritual dimension of life.
- The experience involves a qualitative shift in experiencing oneself and the larger world. It is a powerful, self-validating experience.

Transpersonal growth as the transformation of human consciousness has been described with the help of various metaphors such as the transforming of the caterpillar into a butterfly; awakening from a dream to reality; moving from captivity to liberation; going from darkness to light; being purified by inner fire; going from fragmentation to wholeness; journeying to a place of vision and power; returning to the source; and dying and being reborn.

In summary, whereas Humanistic Psychology focuses on personal growth and full development of the personality, the transpersonal approach focuses on expansion of the boundaries of the self, which, as we shall see shortly, is the central concern in the Indian traditions on psychological functioning and the nature of self. Angyal describes each of these viewpoints:

> Viewed from one of these vantage points (the full development of personality) the human being seems to be striving basically to assert and to expand his self-determination. He is an autonomous being, a self-growing entity that asserts itself actively instead of reacting passively like a physical body to the impacts of the surrounding world.... This tendency—which I have termed "the trend towards increased autonomy"—expresses itself in spontaneity, self-assertiveness, striving for freedom and mastery.
>
> Seen from another vantage point, human life reveals a very different pattern from the one described above. From this point of view the person appears to seek a place for himself in a larger unit of which he strives to become a part... he seems rather to surrender himself willingly to seek a home for himself and to become an organic part of something that he conceives as greater than himself. (Fadiman & Frager, 1984, p. 481)

For the very first time I became aware of a system within academic psychology, though a weak voice located at the fringe of the discipline, which addressed concerns very central and pertinent to questions for which I sought answers. It appeared that if I were to understand my essential nature, I would need to know more about the transcendental unity that binds together all, of which my individual self is a part. I also wished to know more about this for if I had really become separated from my origins, it was essential that I became acquainted with the different facets of this larger canvas of existence. Thus began my exploration of Indian perspectives on existence and psychological functioning.

Indian perspectives

As noted earlier, the two major concerns in the ancient *Upaniṣads* were—the nature of the self, and the nature of reality as a whole. In a story narrated in the *Kaṭha Upaniṣad*, the famous dialogue between Naciketas and Yama reveals certain essential aspects of the nature of Self in the *Upaniṣadic* perspective, which is, of course, transcendental in nature. The story (based on the account given by Paranjpe, 1998) goes as follows: Naciketas, a boy in his teens, is in conversation with Yama, the gatekeeper of heaven and hell. Naciketas finds himself at Yama's gate because his father was renouncing his worldy possessions and the puzzled Naciketas asked his father if he would also give away his son. Angered by his son's query, the angry father in a fit of rage replied in the affirmative. Thus Naciketas finds himself at Yama's gate but cannot enter as Yama is away to earth on a routine assignment of picking up ripe souls.

When Yama returns, he finds Naciketas waiting at his doorstep for the last three days, and thus feels embarrassed that he had been unable to provide hospitality to him. As compensation, Yama tells Naciketas that he may ask for any three wishes, which would be granted to Naciketas. The boy first asks for complete fulfilment of his father's wishes and that he be reunited with a happy father. Naciketas' second wish was that he may secure a place in heaven, based on the esoteric knowledge of the heavenly fire. The first two wishes granted, for his third wish Naciketas asks Yama to reveal to him the knowledge of that which exists beyond life and death. Yama, who had unhesitatingly granted the first two wishes, was most reluctant to grant Naciketas this third and final wish. Instead, he attempts to talk the boy into accepting all sorts of worldly as well as heavenly pleasures and riches. Despite Yama's best efforts, Naciketas refuses to change his last wish and shows no interest in these pleasures and riches, as he knows them to be ephemeral.

Yama is deeply impressed with Naciketas' perseverance, and his ability to distinguish between that which is merely pleasurable (*preyas*) with that which is the Good (*śreyas*); and the fact that the boy opted for the latter. Yama finally agrees to teach Naciketas about the true nature of the Self, the essence in persons that is changeless. The Self can neither be divided nor destroyed, and it is by gaining the knowledge of the Self that one becomes immortal.

> The Knowledge (*vidyā*) of the eternal principle (*akṣara*) is quite different from the knowledge of changeable (*kṣara*) objects in the world. One cannot obtain the knowledge by reaching out to objects in the world; Knowledge of the Self is hidden deep within the innermost self, in the very "heart" of the person. It lies beyond the senses, the mind, and the intellect; its essence cannot be seen with the eyes or captured by the mind or by words, for the Self is not observable and locatable within physical bodies; it is disembodied, and hence everywhere like space. Toward the end of the text, the *Kaṭha* Upaniṣad (6.10–11) explains that the Self is experienced when, through the practice of Yoga, the five senses are held back, the mind is undistracted, and the intellect is stabilized. (Paranjpe, 1998, p. 118)

From the above passage, it is quite clear that the *Upaniṣadic* view describes the true Self as transcendental and this constitutes our essential nature underlying all forms. The true Self can be experienced only upon disengagement from the outer world, which includes our thoughts, feelings and bodily sensations. In other words, we have first to go beyond the boundaries of the narrow ego or the limited self before we can begin to move in the direction of realizing the true Self. Śaṅkara's Advaita Vedāntic system, derived from the *Upaniṣads* (Paranjpe, 1998), emphasizes that there is one single principle that accounts for the ultimate reality—*Brahman*—characterized by the trilogy of terms—Being, Consciousness and Bliss (*sat, cit, ānanda*). The nature of *Brahman* is described with the help of the following adjectives—eternal (*nitya*), pure (*śuddha*), sentient (*buddha*), ever released or emancipated (*mukta*), existent (*satya*), subtle (*sūkṣma*), all-pervasive or ubiquitous (*vibhū*) and 'without a second' or nondual (*advitīya*).

Brahma pervades the entire world and extends even beyond it, and is the transcendent and immanent principle of the entire universe. The true Self is identical with *Brahman*; but in our mundane existence appears to be different, because of the state of ignorance which we are normally trapped in. As long as we remain within the clutches of this distorted view of self and reality, we fail to see the world as it really is. Realization of our true and essential nature which is Self, thus amounts to a union or merging with our original and actual form, from which we find ourselves separated. All suffering arises because we identify and become attached with external transitory aspects of existence which are impermanent and fail to grasp and apprehend that which is permanent, which is our true Self, one with the Cosmos. Thus all attempts to realize or merge with our true Self become a form of *yoga*, in its most general sense. The Advaita Vedāntic system is one amongst many paths—for example, the formal schools of *yoga* (*bhakti*, *jñāna*, *karma*), the Buddhist approach, to name the major—which aim at guiding us in the realization of our true nature and leading us to a greater knowledge, bliss, love, and ultimately a state of oneness with the entirety of existence.

These Indian approaches to *yoga* (in the generic sense), all fall into the category of 'technologies of the self' and are clearly systems which help us in generating insights about our psyche and its relation with existence in general, and through the adoption of various practices lead to a transformation in the experience of our very being. We would then find ourselves aware of higher states of consciousness, be able to elevate ourselves to these higher states at will and at the same time become more effective in those aspects of the out-worldly affairs we choose to engage with and be able to experience far greater levels of joy and love, to mention some of the positive effects attained in the process of *yoga*. Here, I outline the essential aspects of the Advaita Vedāntic perspective on personality. The Advaita system is generally considered to be the one most representative interpretation of the Indian view on reality and existence, and shares many elements in common with most other schools.

Advaita Vedāntic model of personality

The Advaita Vedāntic position on personhood or who we really are, as outlined above, is aligned with the principle of *Brahman*. The core of each individual's being is one with *Brahman*, which is the eternal principle characterized by *Sat*, *Cit* and *Ānanda*. As we are caught up in ignorance (*avidyā*), we are oblivious of this greater truth. In Vedānta, the term *jīva* is used to designate a human being, though literally *jīva* refers to all living beings—the higher and the lower forms—where it is held that a *jīva* has to undergo a process of evolution through manifold life cycles before it takes birth in the form of a human being. The Vedāntic *jīva* (referring to the human form) has been described as a five-layered entity, one enveloping the other similar to the sheaths of an onion.

The outermost layer refers to the body and is termed as *annamaya koṣa*, which literally means 'cereal or food sheath'. The second inner layer bears the name *prāṇamaya koṣa* or 'sheath of vital breath' and refers to breathing as well as other processes of the body, which ensure the functioning of the various organs. The *manomaya koṣa* is the third inner sheath and refers to the processes of the senses and is also considered to be the basis of the ego in terms of 'me' or 'mine' awareness. The fourth inner layer is called the *vijñānamaya koṣa* and refers to the functioning of the intellect—thinking and reasoning, or in general the higher cognitive functions. The *ānandamaya koṣa* or 'bliss sheath' is the fifth and the innermost layer of the *jīva* and is thus the seat of the true Self, the *ātman*, identical with *Brahman*. Since the true Self or *Brahman* is at the core of each and every human being, blissfulness is therefore our essential nature. This state is infinitely more joyful than all the pleasures attainable through wealth and power put together.

Ordinarily, most of us are trapped in a state of ignorance based on a distorted notion of who we are and thus tend to suffer. The goal of Vedānta is the removal of this ignorance through a systematic procedure and restoration of our self-awareness to its original state of the true Self, one with *Brahman*, characterized by *sat*, *cit* and *ānanda*. Vedānta thus promises liberation (*mokṣa*) via the process of attaining self-knowledge and delivers us to a state, where we experience boundless joy devoid of any pain whatsoever. The reason why we suffer and remain in ignorance, unaware of our pure and essential state of blissfulness, is because of the superimposition of the fluctuating attributes of the ego (now happy then unhappy, perplexed or clear, etc.) onto the unchanging and blissful *ātman*. In a reverse manner, the ego which is forever fluctuating, derives a sense of selfsameness by erroneously attributing the *ātman's* permanence, onto itself. It is the mind or *antaḥkaraṇa* (inner instrument) which creates the properties of the ego (e.g. knowing, acting, and suffering). As Paranjpe (1998, pp. 170–171) notes,

> ... it is the ego that doubts and determines, feels clear or confused, agitated or arrested, exhilarated or morose. Yet, such states are attributed to the Ātman, which transcends all such mutations. On the other hand, the fickle ego derives a sense of permanence and the inert body gains consciousness from the unchanging and conscious Ātman. Seen from the Advaita Vedāntic point of view, this is the most fundamental attributional error, whereby the true self is identified with the nonself and vice versa... such misconstrual constitutes the primeval illusion (*ādi māyā*) and is the prime cause of human suffering.... As soon as one discards the erroneous identification with the ever-changing states of the ego, the true nature of the self as Being, Consciousness, and Bliss shines forth, and one sidesteps and thereby "escapes" the miserable chains of action and its consequences.

In essence, the Advaita Vedāntic system aims at a total transformation of a person's life by strict adherence to a highly demanding programme of study which begins with the recognition of one's imperfections, moves through the process of the cultivation of dispassionateness aided by teachings and meditation, and culminates in self-realization. I have deliberately not detailed the 'technology' offered by the Vedāntists for realization of the true Self for that demands a lengthy explanation and discussion of the entire system. The objective in this chapter is to use the transpersonal Advaita Vedāntic notion of self and personhood as a means to introduce the Indian perspective, and then move on to a more detailed coverage of Sri Aurobindo's perspective on the same.

Sri Aurobindo's perspective

The following account of Sri Aurobindo's perspective is based on a preliminary understanding of his works. I consider it tentative, subject to revision and expansion upon greater exposure and comprehension of his Integral view of human existence. As was the concern in the *Upaniṣads*, Sri Aurobindo, too, has dealt with the nature of Self and nature of reality in general. Some three thousand years have elapsed since the *Upaniṣadic* times and both the context of human enquiry as well as the enquirer—the human entity—have changed since that time. Sri Aurobindo was well versed with the *Upaniṣadic* writings and the different systems of *yoga*. Based on his readings of the classical accounts, at the same time relying on his own personal insights, experiences and realizations, Sri Aurobindo outlined a new system of *yoga*—Integral Yoga—appropriate for the present as well as the future.

In this chapter, the focus is on self and personality which I now outline with reference to Sri Aurobindo's integral view. Before doing that, I first refer to Sri Aurobindo's larger vision of the future of humanity, within which we locate individual human existence. Sri Aurobindo held an evolutionary perspective but his focus was on the evolution of consciousness. Consciousness is the original, fundamental and essential stuff of the universe, which has at some point manifested itself in such a way that material form comes into existence. Now this is not a vague or difficult idea to grasp, because when we look at the fundamental building block of matter, the atom, we find that it in turn is composed of more elementary particles, and as we go deeper in the analysis of the sub-parts we reach a point when the distinction between particle (matter) and energy (wave-form) breaks down. Finally we end up dealing with certain forces which are organized in a meaningful and lawful manner, a kind of Consciousness-Force. At this point we may once again refer to the origin—pure Consciousness which has the potential of acting out and manifesting in and as Form. Since the ancient times the term *puruṣa* has been used to denote pure Consciousness, which when acting out from its latency and manifesting in and as Form, is referred to as *prakṛti* or nature. Both are but two sides of the same coin, pure consciousness on one side and pure material form on the other. Thus Sri Aurobindo (1970a, pp. 236–237) notes:

> Consciousness is a fundamental thing, the fundamental thing in existence — it is the energy, the motion, the movement of consciousness that creates the universe and all that is in it — not only the macrocosm but the microcosm is nothing but consciousness arranging itself. For instance, when consciousness in its movement or rather a certain stress of movement forgets itself in the action it becomes an apparently "unconscious" energy; when it forgets itself in the form it becomes the electron, the atom, the material object. In reality it is still consciousness that works in the energy and determines the form and the evolution of form.

The story of existence goes something like this—in the beginning there was One which at some point manifested as the Many in terms of material forms. 'In the creating of the material world there was a plunge of this descending Consciousness into an apparent Inconscience and an emergence of it out of that Inconscience, degree by degree, until it recovers its highest spiritual and supramental summits and manifests their powers here in Matter' (1970a, pp. 1–2). Thus after involution, a process of evolution sets in and as the organization of material form evolves, life-forms emerge and their complexity increases over time. First plants, then the lower animals, then the higher, and finally the human being comes into existence. Simultaneously, consciousness, the inner dimension, is also evolving—in inanimate matter it is inconscient, not aware of itself, but is nevertheless present as Will or forces which sustain the existence of matter in its peculiar form. The electron revolves around the nucleus, but is not aware of itself. Consciousness evolves further in plant and then animal form, but remains hidden and not self-aware, as the driving force behind their acts for sustenance. In humans conscious awareness emerges to a far greater extent, as compared to the animal world. But humans are in the process of evolving further—consciousness grows to its higher forms and ultimately merges with the One or original state of *saccidānanda*. Again, Sri Aurobindo (1970a, pp. 43–44) notes:

> ... the Many exist in the One and by the One, the differences are variations in manifestation of that which is fundamentally ever the same.... The world is a manifestation of the Real and therefore is itself real. The reality is the infinite and eternal Divine, infinite and eternal Being, Consciousness-Force and Bliss. This Divine by his power has created the world or rather manifested it in his own infinite Being. But here in the material world or at its basis he has hidden himself in what seem to be his opposites, Non-Being, Inconscience and Insentience. This is what we nowadays call the Inconscient which seems to have created the material universe by its inconscient Energy, but this is only an appearance, for we find in the end that all the dispositions of the world can only have been arranged by the working of a supreme secret Intelligence. The Being which is hidden in what seems to be an inconscient void emerges in the world first in Matter, then in Life, then in Mind and finally as the Spirit. The apparently inconscient Energy which creates is in fact the Consciousness-Force of the Divine and its aspect of consciousness, secret in Matter, begins to emerge in Life, finds something more of itself in Mind and finds its true self in a spiritual consciousness and finally a supramental Consciousness through which we become aware of the Reality, enter into it and unite ourselves with it. This is what we call evolution which is an evolution of Consciousness and an evolution of the Spirit in things and only outwardly an evolution of species. Thus also, the delight of existence emerges from the original insentience, first in the contrary forms of pleasure and pain, and then has to find itself in the bliss of the Spirit or,

> as it is called in the Upanishads, the bliss of the Brahman.

In the earlier stages of human evolution, withdrawing from the higher planes of consciousness and returning to the lower, worldly planes involved a separation from the higher states, which could not be brought down into waking consciousness. But humanity has evolved further, and today, and more so in the near future it will be possible for a greater number of persons to ascend to higher levels and then upon descending retain something of the higher which would also transform individual functioning on the material plane. Disagreeing with the illusionist *Advaitic* perspective, Sri Aurobindo affirmed a realistic Advaita as noted in the preceding passage. He emphasized the equal importance and significance of the material worldly existence as of the spiritual, and noted that the time has come when the higher spiritual consciousness will inspire and guide our life in the earthly form and thus the possibility of 'The Life Divine'. In his vast writings, numerous illustrations have been given, which substantiate this view as well as evidences of all sorts have been provided that affirm the future vision of humankind. It is beyond the scope of the present writing to explore and outline this larger vision of Sri Aurobindo, and this brief introduction has been provided as a backdrop for the portrayal of personality and self.

Sri Aurobindo's portrayal of the human entity, as of existence in general, retains the Vedāntic flavour in his reference to the nature of the true Self, the demarcation of layers or sheaths that a person is made up of, and the possibility of liberation from ego-boundedness, that is, the state of ignorance. Sri Aurobindo's system refers to these categories, but in a somewhat different, more detailed and expanded form, and the goal and endpoint of liberation and transformation via the process of Integral Yoga is radically different and more difficult to attain. In addition, new categories and distinctions have been added, which make it possible to accommodate Western conceptualizations of psychological functioning and personality in his comprehensive Integral view. In other words, Sri Aurobindo's perspective provides legitimate spaces for the insights gathered on human existence both from the West as well as the East, and allows us to integrate these and seems to go beyond what the previous systems offer in terms of growth and expansion which are possible for the human being.

Sri Aurobindo's model of personality

Sri Aurobindo's description of human functioning begins with the basis of everyday existence as experienced through the mind, feelings/desires and the body. We have thoughts related to the outside world (mental consciousness or *manomaya puruṣa*), positive and negative affect associated with objects and people in the outer world (vital consciousness or *prāṇamaya puruṣa*) as well as experiences of the body (physical consciousness or *annamaya puruṣa*) in its exchanges with the surrounding environment. 'The outer consciousness is that which usually expresses itself in ordinary life. It is the external mental, vital and physical' (1970a, p. 311). This aspect of personality is what Western psychology has largely been preoccupied with. Identification with only the outer aspects of our existence keeps us trapped in a state of ignorance because we remain unaware of that which supports the outer.

> The very first step in getting out of the ignorance is to accept the fact that this outer consciousness is not one's soul, not oneself, not the real person, but only a temporary formation on the surface for the purposes of the surface play. The soul, the person is within, not on the surface — the outer personality is the person only in the first sense of the Latin word *persona* which meant originally a mask. (1970a, pp. 304–305)

> There are always two different consciousnesses in the human being, one outward in which he ordinarily lives, the other inward and concealed of which he knows nothing. When one does *sadhana*, the inner consciousness begins to open and one is able to go inside and have all kinds of experiences there. As the *sadhana* progresses, one begins to

> live more and more in the inner being and the outer ... is felt by many as a dream or delusion, or else as something superficial and external. The inner consciousness begins to be a place of deep peace, light, happiness, love, closeness to the Divine or the presence of the Divine, the Mother. One is then aware of two consciousnesses, the inner one and the outer which has to be changed into its counterpart and instrument — that also must become full of peace, light, union with the Divine. (1970a, p. 307)

The inner being consists of the inner mind, inner vital, inner physical and serves as a connection between the psychic and the outer being. The outer being is capable of experiencing only a narrow range of stimuli and events related to stimuli impinging from the external world. But this is only a fraction of the experiences possible to the person—it is like the dial of a radio restricted to moving between a narrow range of frequencies. While we are asleep and dreaming, a different range of frequencies or realm of consciousness opens up—and we have access to an inner world which is not dependent on stimuli from the external world. Dreams are but one example of the worlds existing apart from the external.

On each level—mental, vital and physical—there is a wider range of experience possible and vaster energies that can be tapped. The inner being is in contact with the universal planes of consciousness. The opening of the *cakras* in the process of the awakening of the *kuṇḍalinī* refers to the expansion of the boundaries of consciousness where a vast range of experience, which could not hitherto be accessed, becomes available to the outer being. Through the process of *sādhanā* the inner being awakens and gets activated and with the opening of the *cakras* the outer being also has access to the universal bands of consciousness. Sri Aurobindo (2005, pp. 442–443) has used the general term subliminal for all parts of the being, which are not on the waking surface, especially those referring to the workings of the inner being:

> Our subliminal self is not, like our surface physical being, an outcome of the energy of the Inconscient; it is a meeting-place of the consciousness that emerges from below by evolution and the consciousness that has descended from above for involution. There is in it an inner mind, an inner vital being of ourselves, an inner or subtle-physical being larger than our outer being and nature... There is here a consciousness which has a power of direct contact with the universal unlike the mostly indirect contacts which our surface being maintains with the universe through the sense-mind and the senses. There are here inner senses, a subliminal sight, touch, hearing; but these subtle senses are rather channels of the inner being's direct consciousness of things than its informants: the subliminal is not dependent on its senses for its knowledge, they only give a form to its direct experience of objects; they do not, so much as in waking mind, convey forms of objects for the mind's documentation or as the starting-point or basis for an indirect constructive experience. The subliminal has the right of entry into the mental and vital and subtle-physical planes of the universal consciousness, it is not confined to the material plane and the physical world; it possesses means of communication with the worlds of being which the descent towards involution created in its passage and with all corresponding planes or worlds that may have arisen or been constructed to serve the purpose of the re-ascent from Inconscience to Superconscience. It is into this large realm of interior existence that our mind and vital being retire when they withdraw from the surface activities whether by sleep or inward-drawn concentration or by the inner plunge of trance... The subliminal is ... the seer of inner things and of supraphysical experiences; the surface subconscious is only a transcriber. It is for this reason that the Upanishad describes the subliminal being as the Dream Self because it is normally in dreams, visions, absorbed states of inner experience that we enter into

> and are part of its experiences, — just as it describes the superconscient as the Sleep Self because normally all mental or sensory experiences cease when we enter this superconscience.

But the essence of human personality is not to be found even in the inner being. Behind the inner being is the inmost or psychic being which is the true centre of the person. The psychic is a portion of the Divine Self or *jīvātman* which manifests in the human being, but is in itself differentiated from the Divine Self. The soul or psychic evolves from birth to birth and survives bodily death. Its evolution over the lifetimes (in human form) in which it manifests is toward the original Oneness or *Brahman*, in other words, a merging with the *jīvātman*. The psychic is a drop of the ocean of cosmic consciousness, which has got separated from its source and longs once again to return to it. This is possible only through evolution, via manifestation in human form, over the course of numerous lifetimes. The true purpose of human existence is a union with the Divine; and this is what the psychic always directs us toward. The psychic is that entity within us that awakens us toward the Good, the True, the Beautiful and Love. The existence of the psychic remains latent (outside of conscious awareness) within most of us, but is responsible for the experience of all that is sublime.

Over lifetimes the psychic evolves. At first we are not aware of its existence but it is the psychic which is secretly guiding the course of our lives and seeks to grow towards the Light. Situations which seem the biggest obstacles in our lives, and which we repeatedly confront, provide us with the lessons we most need to learn. A point comes when the psychic evolves sufficiently to make its presence felt in outward consciousness. This is accompanied by a change in the very 'stuff' of consciousness as experienced by the person. There is a sense of lightness, greater freedom from the external as reflected in the ease with which one is able to withdraw from the 'noise' in the outer world. This is accompanied by an experience of silence, peace, bliss, love—all spontaneous and not a response to anything outside of the person; though at first one may have difficulty in distinguishing between the true psychic response and distractions from the external. From this point onward, as the presence of the psychic is increasingly felt in the waking consciousness, it is possible and necessary through *sādhanā* to progress rapidly, aided by conscious and deliberate effort, towards spiritual awakening—entailing an ascent to the higher planes of consciousness (to be described in the next section). Thus Sri Aurobindo (1970a, pp. 301–302) notes:

> The being of man is composed of these elements — the psychic behind supporting all, the inner mental, vital and physical, and the outer, quite external nature of mind, life and body which is their instrument of expression. But above all is the central being (Jivatma) which uses them all for its manifestation: it is a portion of the Divine Self; but this reality of himself is hidden from the external man who replaces this inmost self and soul of him by the mental and vital ego. It is only those who have begun to know themselves that become aware of their true central being; but still it is always there standing behind the action of mind, life and body and is most directly represented by the psychic which is itself a spark of the Divine. It is by the growth of the psychic element in one's nature that one begins to come into conscious touch with one's central being above. When that happens and the central being uses a conscious will to control and organize the movements of the nature, it is then that one has a real, a spiritual as opposed to a partial and merely mental or moral self-mastery.

In another place, Sri Aurobindo (2005, p. 239) remarks:

> The psychic being can at first exercise only a concealed and partial and indirect action through the mind, the life and the body, since it is these parts of Nature that have to be developed as its instruments of self-expression, and it is long confined by their evolution. Missioned to lead man in the Ignorance towards

> the light of the Divine Consciousness, it takes the essence of all experience in the Ignorance to form a nucleus of soul-growth in the nature; the rest it turns into material for the future growth of the instruments which it has to use until they are ready to be a luminous instrumentation of the Divine. It is this secret psychic entity which is the true original Conscience in us deeper than the constructed and conventional conscience of the moralist, for it is this which points always towards Truth and Right and Beauty, towards Love and Harmony and all that is a divine possibility in us, and persists till these things become the major need of our nature. It is the psychic personality in us that flowers as the saint, the sage, the seer; when it reaches its full strength, it turns the being towards the Knowledge of Self and the Divine, towards the supreme Truth, the supreme Good, the supreme Beauty, Love and Bliss, the divine heights and largenesses, and opens us to the touch of spiritual sympathy, universality, oneness.

The gradients of consciousness: The lower and the higher spiritual planes

As noted above, the story of existence began with the involution of the supreme superconscience in and as gross matter. The lowest form of consciousness is that found in inanimate matter as involved in the workings of the atom with the electrons revolving around the nucleus, and is referred to as the inconscience. 'The Inconscience is an inverse reproduction of the supreme superconscience: it has the same absoluteness of being and automatic action, but in a vast involved trance; it is being lost in itself, plunged in its own abyss of infinity' (2005, p. 572). The next higher level of consciousness is the subconscient, '... that quite submerged part of our being in which there is no wakingly conscious and coherent thought, will or feeling or organized reaction, but which yet receives obscurely the impressions of all things and stores them up in itself and from it too all sorts of stimuli, of persistent habitual movements, crudely repeated or disguised in strange forms can surge up into dream or into the waking nature' (Sri Aurobindo, 1970a, p. 353). Further in the gradient of consciousness is the physical or the body consciousness which is present in animals as well. 'The body ... is a creation of the Inconscient and itself inconscient or at least subconscient in parts of itself and much of its hidden action...' (Sri Aurobindo, 1989, p. 10).

Next in the ladder of consciousness is the vital, '... a thing of desires, impulses, force-pushes, emotions, sensations, seekings after life-fulfillment, possession and enjoyment; these are its functions and its nature; — it is that part of us which seeks after life and its movements for their own sake and it does not want to leave hold of them if they bring it suffering as well as or more than pleasure; it is even capable of luxuriating in tears and suffering as part of the drama of life' (Sri Aurobindo, 1970a, p. 323). The highest that is most commonly found in humans is the level of the mind. 'The "Mind" in the ordinary use of the word covers indiscriminately the whole consciousness, for man is a mental being and mentalises everything; but in the language of this *yoga* the words "mind" and "mental" are used to connote specially the part of the nature which has to do with cognition and intelligence, with ideas, with mental or thought perceptions, the reactions of thought to things, with the truly mental movements and formations, mental vision and will, etc., that are part of his intelligence' (1970a, p. 320). For those human beings who have not gone deeper within themselves, mind and consciousness are synonymous. It is only when one becomes aware of oneself by a growth in consciousness, then one can see different degrees, kinds and powers of consciousness—mental, physical, psychic and spiritual.

With the surfacing of the psychic being, the higher ranges of consciousness above mind become accessible through *sādhanā*. These include—Higher Mind, Illumined Mind, Intuitive Mind, Overmind, and Supermind. Sri Aurobindo's depiction of psychological functioning and development thus refers to a two-tiered system—one horizontal, moving from the outer being to the inner and finally the inmost with the psychic at the centre; and the other

complete picture of the human personality and psychological functioning as compared to the other available perspectives, and goes much beyond a mere sum of the parts which would amount to a simple amalgamation of the above mentioned schools of psychology. Within this view it becomes possible to understand isolated experiences and occurrences in one's life against a wider canvas. It helps us in getting in touch with the most essential and fundamental aspect of our existence. Further, the Integral view has potential applications in the area of psychotherapy, parenting, attitude towards work, human relationships, education, organisational behaviour, social work/development, and in the general sense of understanding Integral Yoga as applied psychology. In this chapter, I examine two closely related applications of the Integral approach—the transformation of emotions, and the place of psychic unfoldment in psychotherapy.

The transformation of emotions

As mentioned earlier, Sri Aurobindo uses the term 'psychic' or 'psychic being', for the soul. What is unique in Sri Aurobindo's depiction is that, though in agreement with the preexisting conception of the soul's immortality and its transmigration from body to body, the psychic is not a static entity, but immensely dynamic in the sense that it continues to evolve from lifetime to lifetime. The psychic is that part of us that responds to the true and the beautiful; joy and love being its essential nature. Perhaps the single most defining characteristic of psychic consciousness is its groundedness in a deep and unconditional love, devotional in essence, accompanied by a state of sincere and total surrender to the Divine.

This brings us to the subject of *bhakti*. In *Bhakti yoga,* the emotional life of the aspirant or seeker undergoes a gradual transformation, and (s)he begins to reside more and more in a state of pure and unconditional love of, and for the Divine. Looking at it from the *rasa* and *bhāva* perspective, the Indian meta-theory of emotions developed by Bharata, the aspirant attempts to reside more and more in the eighth and highest *rasa,* that of love. To enter into this state, the devotee commonly uses the aids of chanting the name of the preferred deity (Rāma, Kṛṣṇa, Durgā, etc.), and singing about his love for the chosen form of divinity. In so doing, the aspirant, or shall we say *rasika*, experiences a dissolution of his/her ego self, wherein everyday connotations and experiences in the mundane human realm around the emotion of love are transcended, and the devotee enters into a state of pure and absolute universal love, devoid of any sense of 'I' or 'mine'.

In general, when we are immersed in an aesthetic experience via exposure to art (for example music or dance), the *bhāvas*, or the experienced emotions are located in a context far removed from one's everyday personal life, and hence we are able to derive *rasa* or a sense of pleasure or delight, even if we are experiencing so called negative emotions like anger and fear. In a sense, the personal or 'I' element melts away, and we find ourselves transported to the realm of pure emotion, devoid of any ego involvement. Now in *Bhakti yoga*, the aspirant as seeker of the Divine, gradually disidentifies with all emotions—except that of love. Thus Rupa Goswami offered a reinterpretation of the original *rasa-bhāva* perspective in terms of major and minor devotional states. In this depiction, love is conceived of as the major *rasa*, the essential emotion state to be sought and attained by the *bhakta*. All other emotions, the minor devotional states, are to be understood as resulting from our seeking of love, which in the early stages of *bhakti* often eludes the devotee, resulting in a state of frustration in our seeking upon encountering failure, or loss of the love we thought we had possessed.

Over time, through continuous and sincere *sādhanā*, the devotee begins to reside more and more in a state of universal love and *ānanda* which is the very nature of the soul and the Spirit. Then out of the sheer joy and sense of completeness of the act, we surrender our entire being to the Divine. In other words, the attempts of the devotee to ground him/her self in universal love leads to the coming forward of the soul or psychic being, our divine essence. The coming forward of the psychic being results in a shift of power in terms of what element of our being exercises control over our life, from the ego to the psychic. This is accompanied by a major affective transformation in our life, as well as profound behavioural change. Our life becomes increasingly characterized by a feeling of goodwill towards all human beings, and we view all and relate to all in terms of unconditional love. And true love is not about taking or getting, only about giving; and thus selfless service becomes part of our very nature. Perceiving our ground in the Divine, and the ground of all other human beings, all of existence for that matter, in the Divine, we at last experience the truth of the ancient tenet *vasudhaiva kuṭumbakam* (the world is one family).

The coming forward of the psychic being has another profound consequence. The search for direction in our life, for which we often seek a *guru*, comes to a close, with the inner *guru*, our psychic, now performing that function completely and perfectly. There is a certain knowingness about psychic consciousness, which acts as a sure guide in matters of truth and the good and the beautiful. In short, our life is transformed from the life human, to the Life Divine.

Being a psychologist, I cannot stop at this point, for I must reflect on the fuller psychological consequences of the emergence of the psychic as the true centre of our being, and its impact on individual and collective well-being. Notably, we become from a seeker to a 'finder'. In general, an individual who resides in a psychic consciousness radiates an aura of 'healthiness' and well-being. For the psychic ever guides us to what is good for our whole being, and the dominant emotion is that of love and joy, which by its very nature is integral and complete.

The place of love in psychotherapy and spiritual healing

Consciousness is contagious. Thus, in my opinion, a psychologist or more accurately a counsellor/psychotherapist who is chiefly concerned with restoring a state of health and well-being in his clients, must him/her self be a relatively permanent member of the abode of well-being, which in itself is a hallmark of psychic existence. In other words, to be an effective therapist, a tremendous amount of self-work/*sādhanā* has to be carried out on the part of the therapist (one who facilitates healing, and thus restores health). More than anything else, it is the consciousness of the therapist interacting with the consciousness of the client that brings about a positive change in the client, from a state of suffering to a state of well-being.

In general, the Indian view of existence is that of the journey of the Divine in a person. All struggles and suffering in life represent a movement from an infra-rational (animal) existence, to a more rational (human) existence, and further, towards a yet greater supra-rational (Divine) existence and end-state of Truth and Bliss and Peace and Beatitude. This is the human journey; from a life of obscure beginnings in a half-lit animal-human consciousness, to an increasingly diviner humanity. And the counsellor/therapist who can assist us in this journey is but a fellow traveller who has walked ahead of us from a life of relative darkness to a life of increasing Light. Only one who has mastered swimming to a high degree can save the one who is drowning, and so is the case with therapy.

For convenience, the process of psychotherapy can be divided into two stages. The first is the movement from a weak ego state (low level of autonomy) to a strong ego state. This is the goal of most psychotherapy in the West. The second, and in my opinion the more important goal is the movement from the ego to the Self, or the shift in government from the ego to the psychic. This is the more common goal in the context of spiritual healing. Thus Sudhir Kakar, the noted psychoanalyst states (in personal communication) that 'Psychoanalysis is undergraduate work, and spirituality is post graduate work'. Freud had stated that the goal of psychoanalysis is 'To make the unconscious, conscious'. In the original German, Freud said, '*Wo es war, soll Ich werden*'—Where it (the impersonal and unconscious) was, let the I (personal and conscious) become. Kabir Das has beautifully expressed the transformation that takes place on the spiritual path, 'When I was, God was not; Now God is, I am not' (*Jab mai tha tab Hari naahi; Ab Hari hai, mai nahi*). Thus from the vantage point of spirituality, the goal of psychotherapy/healing and growth is summarized as such: 'Where I was, let Thou become'.

In general, I can confidently state that the most essential pre-requisite on the part of the therapist/spiritual guide for healing to take place, is a posture of and groundedness in unconditional love. Without this, healing cannot begin, and thus the importance of self- work/*sādhanā*. This has been noted in the western context by the eminent psychotherapist Carl Rogers in his emphasis on the absolute necessity of the attitude of 'unconditional positive regard' on the part of the therapist toward the client, and more explicitly by the eminent psychiatrist M. Scott Peck in his well-known work, *The Road Less Traveled*. A moment's reflection on healing in the traditional Indian context immediately reveals that when individuals in distress approach their guru, the healing process begins with the love and unconditional acceptance of the person in distress, by the guru. Thus, at the risk of overstating, I again underscore the key importance of self-work on the part of the therapist/guru.

Love has an extraordinary transformative power which can heal all breaches and wounds in our consciousness, and eventually liberate us from fear, guilt, and egoism. It is via the showering of love from without that love awakens in our being (psychic consciousness), may it be love in the romantic human sense, or in the spiritual divine sense. One of the greatest discoveries that we can make in our lifetime is that the source of love is within us, and not without. Till some such time, we continue to roam about lost like the musk deer, forever seeking the fragrance of love all about, not realizing that the secret source of love lies within us hid deep in our very bosom, waiting to be discovered. Thus Huston Smith (1997, p. 334) notes:

> It remained for the twentieth century to discover that locked within the atom is the energy of the sun itself. For this energy to be released, however, the atom must be bombarded from without. So too, locked in every human being is the store of love that partakes of the Divine — *the imago dei,* image of God, as it is sometimes called. And it too can be activated only through bombardment, in it's case, love's bombardment. If we too felt loved, not abstractly or in principle but vividly and personally, by one who unites all power and perfection, the experience would melt our fear, guilt, and self-concern permanently. As Kierkegaard said, if at every moment both present and future I were certain that nothing has happened and nothing can ever happen that would separate us from the infinite love of the Infinite, that would be the reason for joy.

An equally or even more profound impact of love is its capacity to transform evil. As a therapist/spiritual healer, one encounters all sorts of individuals, even those who have a chequered past and may best be described as 'bad' or even 'evil'. These are individuals who have no regard for the happiness and well-being of others, and do not hesitate to hurt others, even those who are supposedly close to them. Upon encountering such persons, one feels disgust in their presence, and the first reaction is to distance oneself from them. As a therapist/spiritual healer, one may at times be unable to feel love for these individuals, and is thus unable to help them. In such cases, the person remains unchanged, the world remains the same, and evil continues to exist. Yet, perhaps the only truly effective way to deal with evil is to transform it through love. M. Scott Peck (1990, p. 309) who has deeply reflected on this issue and has worked extensively in this area, points out that:

> The healing of evil—scientifically or otherwise—can be accomplished only by the love of individuals. A willing sacrifice is required. The individual healer must allow his or her soul to become the battleground. He or she must sacrificially absorb the evil. Then what prevents the destruction of that soul? If one takes the evil itself into one's heart like a spear, how can one's goodness still survive. Even if the evil is vanquished, thereby will not the good be also? ...
>
> I do not know how this occurs, but I know that it does. I know that good

> people can deliberately allow themselves to be pierced by the evil of others, to be broken thereby, yet somehow not broken. To be even killed in some sense and yet still survive and not succumb. Whenever this happens, there is a slight shift in the balance of power in the world.

In this way we obtain a glimpse of the extraordinary transformative potential of *bhakti*. To begin with, to reside more and more in a state of love is in itself an extremely positive state of being, one most conducive to health and well-being. And this also has a profound impact on one's dealings with others, as these are characterized by a posture of giving and serving, devoid of any ulterior motives of gaining something. Further, the increasing experience of universal love facilitates the act of complete surrender to the Divine, as a spontaneous and integral process. This is an extraordinarily empowering experience—the shift from a narrow ego-bound consciousness to a psychic consciousness grounded in the true Self.

A groundedness in love is perhaps the most essential quality which must be present in the being of a psychotherapist/spiritual healer. This quality cannot be obtained by any external study or degrees, and can be acquired only through intense self-work/*sādhanā*. The role of love in the healing of psychological wounds and hurts, and the transformative power of love in its encounter with evil, is only beginning to be fully appreciated by psychologists, in India and elsewhere.

Concluding remarks

The future of psychology as a truly useful, emancipating, liberating, and life-giving discipline lies in bringing back soul and Spirit to its rightful place at the centre stage of psychology, and existence at large. To this end, Integral Psychology has a great deal to offer. But most important in the present context are the insights provided by the Mother and Sri Aurobindo, for attaining individual and collective transformation, leading to a lasting human unity and global peace. Guided by their vision, I continue to be astounded by the increasingly clear indications of a new social order—one characterized by a deep unconditional love, joy, peace and harmony. The signs may be dim and indirect at times, but their certain implications are abundantly clear.

References

Aurobindo, Sri (1970a). *Letters on yoga* (Vol. 1). Pondicherry: Sri Aurobindo Ashram Press.

Aurobindo, Sri (1970b). *Social and political thought*. Pondicherry: Sri Aurobindo Ashram Press.

Aurobindo, Sri (1989). *The supramental manifestation and other writings*. Pondicherry: Sri Aurobindo Ashram Press.

Aurobindo, Sri (2005). *The life divine*. Pondicherry: Sri Aurobindo Ashram Press.

Fadiman, J., & Frager, R. (1984). *Personality & personal growth*. NY: Harper & Row.

Foucault, M. (1988). Technologies of the self. In L. H. Martin, H. Gutman, & P. H. Hutton (Eds.), *Technologies of self: A seminar with Michel Foucault*. Amherst: University of Massachusetts Press.

Leahey, T. H. (1991). *A history of modern psychology*. Englewood Cliffs, NJ: Prentice Hall.

Mother, The (2003). *Collected works of The Mother* (Vol. 2). Pondicherry: Sri Aurobindo Ashram Press.

Paranjpe, A. C. (1998). *Self and identity in modern psychology and Indian thought*. NY: Plenum Press.

Peck, M. S. (1990). *People of the lie: The hope for healing human evil*. London: Arrow Books.

Satprem (2000). *Sri Aurobindo or The adventure of consciousness*. Mysore: Mira Aditi.

Smith, H. (1997). *The world's religions*. New Delhi: Harper Collins India.

13

Psychology of emotions: Some cultural perspectives

Girishwar Misra

After a long association with cognition, psychology is now deeply and intensely engaged with affect and emotion. Emotionality may not be liked, but being emotionally competent is often considered a virtue. A moment's reflection makes it clear that our thoughts, actions and interactions are almost always coloured by the emotions which accompany them. Indeed, emotions are ubiquitous in our lives. Interestingly enough while 'being emotional' is intrinsic to human nature, at the same time humans have the capacity to reflect on and regulate their emotions. This implies that emotions vary not only across individuals and groups but also within the same person. As Ekman (2003, p. 213) has remarked, 'we each experience the same emotions, but we all experience them differently.' This chapter tries to examine how emotion experiences are shaped by culture. The overarching goal of this chapter is to explicate and appraise the current state of understanding in this area, and to bring out the indigenous contributions of Indian thought to the centre-stage.

The lived reality of emotions

Emotions such as love, hatred, surprise, excitement, joy, envy and fear are frequently experienced in day-to-day affairs. In fact they supply a lot of information about us and help in regulating our actions and interactions with fellow beings. In common parlance, they are held as triggers of actions as well as goals or end points towards which actions are directed. Emotions are certainly involved in determining the ill-being and well-being of individuals and society. They are inescapably involved in almost all kinds and shades of human activities (for example, violence, helping, altruism, cooperation and competition). In lay theories, therefore, emotions are treated as the real and immediate springs of action. They are used as well as misused in everyday affairs. They are sites of manipulation and subject to arousal, suppression, projection, substitution and elaboration by people. Emotions matter for everybody as they energize us and in a significant sense configure our identities. Our sense of being is unimaginable in the absence of emotional scripts.

Notwithstanding the recognition of emotion in human life by the lay person, the discipline of psychology, particularly the so-called mainstream, has not given emotion the importance it deserved. Perhaps its unpredictability, subjectivity and fluidity have rendered it into a less-scientific theme. Of course, psychologists of other persuasions engaged in the study of personality and motivation-related issues, and understanding the problems of depression, anxiety and stress and pursuing clinical and particularly psychodynamic work did look into the emotional lives of people. In all these endeavours, emotion's image has largely been portrayed as negative, pathological and irrational. In general, it dealt with the darker side of human life. It was considered opposed to reason, logic and rationality. As a result, the meaning of 'emotion' became fuzzy and problematic. It is only during the last one decade or so that the study of positive emotions such as happiness, hope, optimism, and processes such as flourishing, have started gaining attention by the positive psychology movement. One reason for this increased attention is that studies of negative emotions such as anger, depression and anxiety were capturing only a limited part of the affective lives of people and ignored the potentials of growth and positive dispositions. Considering the salience of emotions in our lives, it is not surprising to note a revival of interest in the study of emotions in many sister disciplines such as sociology (Stets, 2003; Williams, 2001), anthropology (Hinton, 1999), social psychology (Forgas & Smith, 2003), philosophy (Roberts, 2003; Wollheim, 1999), political studies (Marcus, 2003), marketing (O'Shaughnessy & O'Shaughnessy, 2003) and neuroscience (Panksepp, 1998; Rolls, 1999).

The changing contours of the emotional world

Literary evidence, ethnographic records and other kinds of evidence suggests that the ideas about emotion and emotional lives of people vary across time and space, and between and within cultures (see Averill & Saundarrajan, 2006; Ray, 2001). Looking at the large-scale changes in social mobility, transportation, social institutions and ideologies, one is bound to think that the future of our emotional lives would be different from the past and the present. Today emotions are often driven by the market forces and are attached to physical objects (Mestrovic, 1997). Contemporary humans, being self-absorbed, seem to have more feelings and pay more attention to them, but seem to have fewer feelings for others and the surroundings, and pay less attention to them. Contrarily, in the traditions of oral cultures emotions happen to be immediate, sensual, inclusive and interactive. People have the capacity to resonate their bodies with other bodies and with the imbedding physical and social contexts. With technological inventions people started disengaging themselves from interactions. Thus the virtual experience of the electronic era has brought back the sensory qualities of direct experience but without the interactive part. It makes emotions detached from action. The unemotional life may not be worth living. The present scenario of emotional life is problematic.

Thus the reality that one has to face is that whether one wants it or not, our emotional lives are bound to change. These changes, however, also imply that emotions are not purely biological or genetically predetermined. Instead they can be shaped in certain directions. We may opt for an emotionally creative life by paying attention to our feelings, cultivating certain habits of thought; practicing to experience certain mental states and encouraging desired emotional positioning of self toward own self and others. The Indian view has addressed this transformative potential of emotions in significant ways. Against this backdrop, this chapter makes an effort to bring out some of the perspectives on emotions in mainstream psychology and explores the Indian perspectives on emotion.

In the Indian context human action is expressive, symbolic, or semiotic. The apparent is not all. Instead, it is a manifestation of something greater which is unmanifest. It is an indicator of our existence and not the existence itself. Understanding indigenous epistemology, aesthetic criteria and sensibility, therefore, offer an alternative perspective on human action. Our emotions not only operate at different levels of being but may help (or hinder) our movement across different levels of consciousness. Contrary to this, modern psychology has treated emotions as predominantly physiological. It has been argued that emotions have an evolutionary history and the expressed commonality across species is used to lend support to the biological primacy of emotional processes and their predetermined form.

Studies across cultures do indicate differences in the experience of emotions, in their recognition and differences in intensity. Building on these it is argued that emotions are culturally shaped. After presenting an overview of the developments in the study of emotions in psychology, the Indian contribution of the *rasa* theory is outlined. The concept of *rasa* as meta-emotion and *bhāva* as emotion, present a new dimension of aesthetic creativity that goes beyond the received view of emotion and widens its scope. Viewing emotional experience in terms of a matrix of meanings, identities and relationships, emotion is treated in a non-physicalist and non-reductionist manner. It is more like a situated performance and narratives with potential for creative transformation and social engagement. The Indian idea of *rasa* draws our attention to a refined subjective mental state. The person as dancer/poet and spectator/audience get transported to an experienced state, which may not be in congruence with the mundane experience. Emotion is transcendental cognition, and *rasa* involves experiencing the universal self. It is especially instructive in the contemporary period. However, before we explore these aspects it would be pertinent to see how emotions have been treated in psychology.

Psychological thoughts on emotions: The Euro-American tradition

The disciplinary journey of psychology to understand emotions is more than a century old. Today it has reached a point where a unitary notion of emotion as a physiological thing has collapsed and it is difficult to offer a precise definition. In an impressive discussion Damasio (1994) has noted that emotions are innate, pre-organized, and relatively inflexible responses to certain combinations of stimuli. Although they provide a quick and efficient set of responses, the next step is the feeling of emotion in connection to the object that excited it. The awareness of connections between the object and certain emotions serves several adaptive functions. Also, significant variations across individuals are found in temperament, emotion regulation, intensity of emotional experience, ability to regulate emotions, or to control, modify and manage aspects of emotional reactivity and expressivity. In fact there is growing convergence on the view that emotions encompass the processes that vary in duration from briefly experienced feelings resulting from conscious or unconscious appraisal, to more enduring affective styles.

Emotions perform motivational, communicative and regulatory functions within and between individuals. In a normative sense they inform about intended or likely behaviours and underlying mental states of others during interpersonal interactions. It is often held that while there is a biologically based substrate of adaptive emotional functioning, learning, experience, and the active socialization of emotions significantly influence the same and may lead to healthy or pathological consequences. Let us examine in some detail the developments in mainstream psychology pertaining to the study of emotions.

The interest of psychologists in emotional phenomena is often traced to Darwin (1872/1965). He argued for phylogenetic and ontogenetic continuity of major expressive patterns of emotions. It was followed by the work of William James (1890), who observed that '*the bodily changes follow directly the perception of the exciting fact, and that our feeling of the same is the emotion*' (Vol. 2, p. 449). Following this view, emotion came to represent the feelings related to physiological changes. People 'have emotions' like other dispositions. Emotions are localized in the body. The psycho-physiological symbolism present in this view has dominated most of the theories of emotions. This view was rooted in Descartes' thinking, and demanded a mechanical view. For instance, Freud considered emotions as safety valves that let off their energy. The physicalist view helped to assume that the basic emotions are universal. Thus emotions came to be known as passive things that happen to people. The next step was the development of a cognitive view in which *appraisal* and *labelling* became central to the conceptualization of emotion (Schachter & Singer, 1962).

The physiological or bodily base of emotion and presumed evolutionary continuities led to a view that there are some primary or basic emotions, which are pre-packaged and pre-wired. As Lazarus (1991) has noted, while emotions are genetically determined, they are altered by social and biological variables. They express personal meanings and experience. The nature and experience of emotions, however, do not take place in a vacuum. Instead, they are organized through and embedded in cultural contexts. As we shall see in the following section, the role of culture vis-a-vis emotions has been diversely explored contributing to varied hypotheses and findings.

Understanding the culture–emotion interface

The relationship between culture and emotion has been approached from many perspectives leading to not only different answers to the same questions but to different questions too. Mesquita (2001) has identified three paradigms which are followed by the researchers in such endeavours. The first paradigm tries to understand *universal* emotions. It asks the question—is emotion *X* present or absent in culture A? The underlying assumption is that emotions come as packages consisting of invariant patterns of emotion specific responses. The second paradigm involves a *componential* approach which has questioned the idea of emotion as a unitary whole. The focus is on understanding invariant configurations of responses. Accordingly, the aspect of emotion that was most and least susceptible to variation was examined. The degree of similarities and differences across cultures was delineated. The third paradigm is the *cultural* one. It proposes cultural differences in emotions and tries to understand how the tendency of people in a culture to respond in certain emotional ways relates to cultural ideas and practices. Let us examine these paradigms in some detail.

The quest for basic emotions

The search for basic emotions (Ekman, 1992; Izard, 1994) is premised on the assumption that there are certain universal emotions that involve unique patterns of responses for each of the universal basic emotions. The evidence in support of this position comes largely from facial recognition studies. They indicated an above chance level recognition of facial expressions from different cultures. The studies suggest certain universal modes of communication of emotion or certain emotion components. However, differences in the rates of recognition of facial expressions, the fact that emotion words associated with facial expressions mean different things in different languages (Wierzbicka, 1986), ambiguity about the question, whether emotions are spontaneously inferred by people across the world (Russell & Fernandez-Dols, 1997), have rendered this approach as problematic.

The study of *vocal expressions* of emotions has revealed that in all cultures the recognition of vocal expression was the best for the same emotion. Cultural differences have also been indicated (Mesquita & Frijda, 1992). The basic emotion approach has difficulty on account of too much emphasis on intra-individual states, rather than processes in context. The focus has been on potential rather than prevalence. The dichotomous approach has many problems. Emotions share many things and differ in many respects. Universality and cultural specificity are treated as mutually exclusive.

Cultural variations in the components of emotions

This perspective views emotions as multicomponential phenomena (Frijda, 1986; Lazarus, 1991; Scherer, 1997). It maintains that an emotion comprises of an antecedent event, appraisal, physiological change, change in action-readiness, change in cognitive readiness, change in cognitive functioning, and change in regulator process. In most of the cases emotions are thought to involve all these components. Thus an emotionally charged event starts the emotion process, yet each component has its particular determinant. The components are thought to change somewhat independently of each other. Of course, mutual influences are also recognized. This approach has led to the study of emotion experiences with a focus on appraisal of emotion antecedents and action-readiness. The appraisals can be conscious or unconscious. This approach has shifted the focus on cross-cultural variability of the different components independently. The work of Scherer and his associates (Scherer, Wallbolt, & Summerfield, 1986) does not show very strong cultural effects. On the whole the evidence supports similarities between appraisal and emotion experience. Similar emotions are characterized by a similar core action-readiness; modes explain a significant part of the variance in emotions. However, emotions in different languages tend to have a culture-specific action-readiness profile. The approach is limited by self-report data and offers a compartmentalized study of emotions. It does not provide any direction to study the cultural differences in emotions.

Culture-specific patterns of emotions

Emotions appear to be a core aspect of the behaviour of conscious beings. They are prominently present in social settings and regulate the same by connecting individuals to their social world within a cultural context. As Kitayama and Markus (1994) propose, the cultural frame or meaning system makes different things to occasion the diverse experiences as providing feelings of sadness or joy. The cultural frames inform what an emotion is and when and why an emotion is experienced. The studies of display rules were proposed to uncover the culture specific proscriptions (who can show which emotion to whom and when). Studies have indicated that there are differences in display rules. The studies of emotion lexicon do not provide evidence for cultural diversity in emotions (see Lutz, 1988; Lynch, 1990; Mesquita & Frijda, 1992; Russell, 1991). Japanese *amae* (Doi, 1973), Illongot's *liget* (Rosaldo, 1980) and Indian *lajja* (Menon, & Shweder, 1994) suggest cultural specificity of emotion experience.

It seems that the awareness of having emotional experiences takes place in the socio-cultural context in which a person is situated. Thus while appraisal as such is a general process common to all cultures, the particular form of appraisal and the processes utilized in it are brought into action by certain implicit theories or notions. In a recent analysis of emotion Averill, Chon and Hahn (2001) have proposed an interesting model of emotion. They suggest that the origins of behaviour lie in a person's biological and social heritage. The sum of a person's biological endowment is his or her genotype. Similarly one may speak of social systems of behaviour or institutionalized patterns of response that help assure the survival of a society. The biological systems are coded in the gene pool of the species. The social systems are encoded in the symbols, artefacts, and customs of society or 'cultgenes' (Lumsden & Wilson, 1983). The sum of a person's cultgenes, acquired during socialization, is his or her sociotype. The genotypes and sociotype, together with experiences unique to the individual, combine to form his or her *emotional traits*. These are long-enduring predispositions to respond in an emotional way; for example, with fear, anger, or sadness. They are different from emotional states. There are some *emotional syndromes* which are theoretical constructs involving cultural beliefs and implicit theories about the nature of emotions. These include *existential beliefs and social rules*. These theories are evaluative. They not only describe what is, but also provide what should be. The manifestation of emotional syndromes in thought, behaviour and feelings, and the relevant rules and beliefs need to be internalized. These internalized beliefs and rules constitute emotional schemes and scripts.

Averill et al. (2001) assert that culture can influence the emotional life of individuals in two main ways: first, through social system of behaviour contributing to a person's sociotype and their influence on emotional traits; and second, through the implicit theories (beliefs and rules) that help constitute emotional syndromes and regulate behaviour. The sociological (Parkinson, 1996; Roberts, 2003; Thoits, 1989; Williams, 2001) and anthropological (Lutz, 1988) works, recent studies of emotional vocabulary and emotional recognition (Elfenbein & Ambady, 2003; Mesquita, & Frijda, 1992; Shaver, Murdaya, & Fraley, 2001) and social constructionist accounts of emotion (Harre, 1986; Averil et al., 2001) suggest that emotional life in terms of categories and processes may take diverse forms in different cultures. The challenge is to develop a genuinely multidisciplinary perspective capable of analysing and theorizing in fresh ways the mutually constituted nature of culture and individual experience (Moore & Mathews, 2001).

Thus we need to learn about subjective, behavioural and embodied aspects of individual experience in their cultural context. Thus an individual's experiences form the basis for shared cultural beliefs and various cultural forms. They in turn shape the perceptions and understandings of individual cultural members. The challenge is to evolve a theoretical and methodological perspective capable of analysing and theorizing in fresh ways the mutually constituted nature of culture and individual experience. Williams (2001, p. 132) has perhaps rightly captured the contemporary scene of emotional understanding by saying '*emotion is a complex, multidimensional, multifaceted human compound, including irreducible biological and cultural components, which arise or emerge in various socio-relational contexts. As a thinking, moving, feeling 'complex'—rather than a static, unidimensional 'thing'—emotion is embodied through and through; the animating principle of sociality and selfhood, conceived in intersubjective, intercorporeal, communicative terms.*' With this in view we may examine the indigenous Indian perspective on emotion experience.

Emotions in the Indian thought

Historically, sage Bharata first conceived the *rasa* theory in the context of theatre which was subsequently extended to all poetry. His treatise entitled *Nāṭyaśāstra* was composed approximately in the third century AD. Of course, reference to *rasa* does exist in *Vedic* hymns in which *rasa* is considered as a stream of consciousness, as illumination and as offering oneself to the universal self. In the subsequent developments in Indian thought, *rasa* has become a core and all-pervasive concept cutting across various domains including literary criticism, dance and visual arts. *Rasa* is abstract and perhaps it is on account of this that it helps in universalizing the experience. *Rasa* is translated into English variously as emotion/meta-emotion/sentiment/mood. The details of the theory have been discussed by many authors in different contexts (for example, Gnoli, 1956; Jain, 1994; Kapur, 1998; Lynch, 1990; Masson & Patwardhan, 1970; Misra, 2004; Pandey, 1959; Paranjpe, 1998; Shweder & Haidt, 2000; Sinha, 1961).

The theory illuminates human emotions by contextualizing them in the reception of creative work (for example, poetry, drama and other acts). Literally *rasa* is the relishable quality inherent in the emotive content of some work of art. In the course of time the concept of *rasa*, which was originally an aesthetic concept referring to the act of relishing or gustation (*rasana*), has evolved and has been interpreted in many ways. Aesthetic experience is the apprehension of the created work as delight. The objects and situational contexts define the feelings present in drama or poetry. Emotion becomes manifested by the object to which the emotion is directed, other exciting conditions, the overt expressions, and other ancillary feelings. A different sense of *rasa* is the relishable experience occasioned by the work in the reader or spectator. Bharata's chief concern was the analysis of the emotion-experience which the spectator (*prekṣaka*) undergoes, while witnessing a dramatic performance on the stage or reading poetry. For Bharata, *nāṭya* or drama is so comprehensive that nothing is excluded from it:

> *Na tat jñānam na tat śilpam na sa vidyā na sa kalā,*
> *Nāsau yogo na tat karma nāṭye'smin na dṛśyate.*
>
> There is no such knowledge, no such craft, no such education, no such art, no such learning, and no such activity, which cannot be seen in drama.
>
> —*Nāṭyaśāstra* (I. 116)

It may be noted that Bharata assigned specific emotional values to musical notes (*svaras*) and melodic patterns (*jātis/rāgas*), when they are used in stage presentation. Thus musical sounds too can be suggestive of *rasa*. In Indian dance the elaborate language of hand gestures, glances, and body movements is designed to enact the mood of the song. The gestures and pure dance movements (foot work, poses) are also involved. The gestures express feelings and various mental states. The *rasas* are expressed in paintings and sculptures too. *Rasa* has also been conceptualized as a blissful state of mind, comparable to the enjoyment of *Brahman*.

Typology of emotions

The *rasa* theory implies that there are a number of specific emotions, each with its distinct tone or flavour, and not an anonymous aesthetic emotion. The theory of *rasa* was posed as the fundamental on which Indian poetics rests. But Indian poetics draws on and in turn influences all other thought-disciplines, so it has a trans-disciplinary character. In particular, it has direct relevance to contemporary psychology of emotions. Bharata lists forty-nine *bhāvas* out of which eight are primary or durable states (*sthāyi bhāvas*), with corresponding *rasas* or aesthetic moods. In addition there are thirty-three transitory states. The basic emotions can be developed into distinct aesthetic moods. Other transient emotions come and go according to their affinity with the durable emotions. The classification proposed by Bharata lists eight *rasas—śṛṅgāra* (love or delight), *hāsa* (amusement, laughter), *karuṇa* (sorrow), *raudra* (anger), *vīra* (perseverance or heroism), *bhayānaka* (fear), *bībhatsa* (disgust), *adbhuta* (wonder, astonishment). There are corresponding *bhāvas*, namely, *rati, hāsya, śoka, krodha, utsāha, bhaya, jugupsā* and *vismaya*. The commentary on *Nāṭyaśāstra* by Abhinavagupta adds a ninth *rasa*—the *śānta* or the mood of total freedom in which neither happiness nor unhappiness occur. Its *bhāva* is *śāma*. Since then, these nine *rasas* have been accepted as the fundamental units. Certain additions like *vātsalya* (love for child) and *bhakti* (love for God) was made by later writers and these also have some acceptance. For practical purposes then, only the nine *rasas* are considered as the established consensus.

It may be worthwhile to note that 'love for child' and 'love for God' are subsumed under 'erotic mood' or the 'mood of love' namely *śṛṅgāra* by those who do not accept their separate existence. Despite this nine fold division, there is an argument that fundamentally there is only one *rasa*. This is important for the contemporary discussions since it posits that there is in fact only one emotion which then manifests itself into many colours assuming distinct identities. Which one of this is the most basic *rasa*, is a matter of debate. Abhinavagupta takes *śānta*, the ninth one which is implicit, as the basic one. But there have been given at least three other choices—*karuṇa, adbhuta* and *śṛṅgāra*. The last, *śṛṅgāra* is the erotic mood, and has been given a strong theoretical support by Bhoj. In his vision, *śṛṅgāra* is the basic force responsible for the creation of the universe. In contrast, the famous Sanskrit poet Bhāvabhuti has stated that *karuṇa* (sorrow) is the only *rasa* and appears in various forms.

The concepts of *bhāva* and *rasa*

The Indian perspective treats emotions in a narrative framework composed of causes, consequences and concomitants of an illusive meta-emotion—a *sui generis* form of consciousness—called *rasa*. The experience of *rasa* is rooted in the concept of *bhāva*. *Bhāva* is that which brings about a condition or which gets established through what happens (*kaver antargataṃ bhāvaṃ bhāvayan bhāva ucyate*). *Bhū* means to be and *bhāva* means that which brings about being. Thus *bhāva* stands for Being or existence, and also the ultimate meaning (*bhavatīti bhāvaḥ; bhāvayantīti bhāvāḥ*). Thus *bhāva* refers to existence as well as the mental state. As Bharata has stated, the dance, poetry or drama works as a catalyst and activates the *bhāva* (emotion) that is already present.

In everyday life we experience a number of *bhāvas* on different occasions. The traces of these experiences stay with us. The *bhāvas* are present in us in the form of *vasanas*. The *sthāyibhāvas* are dispositions or *cittavṛttis*. When we recognize these *bhāvas* by means of enlightened bliss in the self, the very same *bhāvas* are designated as *rasa*. In this way the experience of *rasa* operates in a sequence of transformations in the person. To begin with, a *bhāva* becomes manifest due to someone or something and is to some extent determined by the circumstances. Once such a condition of being appears, the person begins to overtly behave in a given way (*anubhāva*). There may be a dominant *bhāva* in a number of ancillary emotions (*sañcāribhāvas*). Each mental state is correlated with certain forms of physical demeanour and behaviour (*abhinaya*). The *rasa* experience involves the above-mentioned *bhāvas* but is not equal to the sum of them. Instead it has its own quality. The various components are necessary and in totality sufficient cause of *rasa* experience.

When the entire sequence of events is enacted in a text or on a stage, the reader or spectator relishes (*āsvādati*) or experiences a *rasa*. Abhinavagupta, one of the chief exponents of *rasa* theory, locates *rasa* in the viewer's or *sāmājika's cittavṛttis*. The *cittavṛttis* or *sthāyibhāvas* refer to a person's inherent predispositions. They are manifest when they come in contact with a pertinent experience. The same is generalized in a literary representation. In those moments the viewer's separate identity evaporates and consciousness merges in the universal experience of *rasa*. The *rasa* exists only in this apprehension, and once manifest produces *alaukika ānanda* or bliss.

In Vedānta, joy is the affective core of consciousness or existence. The idea of *Saccidānanda* implies that the ultimate reality is inseparable oneness of existence (*sat*), consciousness (*cit*) and joy (*ānanda*). However, at the mundane level of existence pleasure and pain are both present. In fact pain and suffering often dominate our lives. But its meaning varies. Both pain and pleasure are relative. It is human smallness and egoistic feeling that leads us to dislike suffering. When our consciousness enlarges, our capacity for joy and suffering also increases. Sri Aurobindo has proposed that the goal should not be to escape in an absolute of existence, consciousness and bliss but to call them right down in the manifestation. He talks of a biological evolution, which will move from an embodied mind, *manas*, to an embodied super mind, *vijñāna*, through transformation of our nature (see Dalal, 2001). Thus the Indian approach to affect and emotion is signally instructive from the perspective of well-being. It is emphasized that attaining well-being requires that we must understand our true nature or self.

The cognition involved in the *rasa* experience is possible because it forms the object of higher consciousness assuming the witness attitude or *sākṣibhāva*. Differing from other ordinary forms of cognition this experience of bliss or *ānanda* is an enrichment of one's sensibility. At that moment we are endowed with the ability to have the experience of suffering, etc. of another person as our own. The *citta* becomes self-aware. It represents comprehension of the general nature of a *bhāva*, such as grief, from particular instances independent of specific objects and events. It then becomes part of the self. When empathy takes place the self takes the form of *ānanda* and the viewer is totally immersed in it. This state is *rasa*. It is consciousness modified by the awareness. The *rasasvāda* or relish of an emotional state of being occurs when we are educated in our feeling (*sādhāraṇīkaraṇa*). The experience requires that one should be in tune with others (*sahṛdayatā*). Such a person shows communion with the aesthetic experience. A *sahṛdaya* requires a keen and intense recollection and contemplation when there is an aesthetic confrontation.

Thus we find that emotional experience involves a sequence of interrelated events that form a story or a narrative. The *rasa* experience (*rasānubhāva*) starts at the sensory level and moves to the level of imagination, level of *bhāva*, level of *sādhāraṇīkaraṇa*, to a superconscious level that goes beyond the material world. We come in contact with objects of pleasure through sense organs. The objects lead to our imageries. We complete the experience through imagination. At this level the person changes. He is in a different world of his own creation. Thus a *sahṛdaya* viewer identifies with the hero who is acting in the play. He views things from the perspective of the hero and responds accordingly. This is the level of *bhāva*. The intense *bhāva* experience results in the loss of individuality.

The making of *rasa*

According to Bharata, emotions are expressed through the conjunction of their causes and symptoms, and other ancillary feelings that accompany the emotions. It is through the *saṁyoga* (conjunction or union) of *bhāvas* that *rasa* becomes manifest (*vibhāvānubhāva-sañcāri-saṁyogād rasa-niṣpattiḥ*). The four necessary conditions for the manifestation of an emotion include causes (*vibhāva*), symptoms (*anubhāva*), and other ancillary feelings (*sañcāribhāva*) and their conjunction (*saṁyoga*). Here the word cause means those factors which generate or excite the emotions. In drama they become the cause of the knowledge of emotion. This includes all the background information including words, physical gestures, and involuntary psychic symptoms (e.g. sweating, trembling, etc.), settings, events, and action tendencies that might make manifest some state of the world and one's relationship to it. Some of them are primary causes, resting on which the emotions are born (*ālambana vibhāva*). Others are exciting causes (*uddīpana vibhāva*). They reinforce the basic emotion tone. The behavioural expressions of emotions are called *anubhāvas*. They make the feeling apprehensible. Thus, for instance, grief is born out of bereavement due to the death of a dear one, loss of property, experiencing the sorrow of near and dear ones. These are the causes. It is exhibited by shedding tears, weeping, a sinking of limbs, long and heavy breathing, becoming immobilized, etc. These are expressions or symptoms. They express the mental state and are under different degrees of control. The more directly related expressions are called *sāttvikabhāvas*.

Finally, there are some other feelings which normally accompany and are called ancillary feelings. They are known as *vyabhicāri bhāvas*. For instance in love, infatuation, eagerness, pride, gladness are also seen. These are ancillary and transient in nature. They stabilize the principal emotions. They prolong and sustain the relevant mood for some time. Thus emotions are caused by objects, manifested by expressions and nurtured by the ancillary emotions. A listing of the various components of *bhāvas* is given in Appendix 1.

It may be observed that the theory does not indicate that these factors are separately capable of creating *rasa*. For Bharata, *rasa* is an organic unity of the four components. They do not stand in any fixed relationship with one another. The poetic genius harmoniously unites them in such a manner that a given *rasa* is experienced or relished. It should also be remembered that the four constituents are not natural products. They are neither real nor unreal but have an independent existence in their own world.

The analysis of the locus of *rasa* experience and type of knowledge has been interpreted differently. Lollata Bhatta sees *rasa* located in *anukārya*. Also, through *aropa* or imposition in *anukartā*, the actor. The nature of knowledge is both *laukika* and *alaukika*. Sankuk finds *rasa* in *anukārya*—but its relish in the *sāmājika* is by *anumiti* or inference. So, in *sāmājika* as well. It is a kind of *vilakṣaṇa jñāna*. Bhattanayak locates *rasa* in the *sāmājika*. The nature of knowledge is *ātmasākṣātkārarūpa*. Abhinavagupta, the undisputed champion of *rasa* theory, locates *rasa* in *sāmājika's cittavṛttis*. The knowledge is of *ātmabodha* kind. According to this view *cittavṛttis* or the *sthāyibhāvas* are inherent predispositions. They become manifest when they come in contact with pertinent experience, which becomes generalized, in a literary representation. The viewer's separate personality weakens and his consciousness merges in the universal experience and he experiences *rasa*. The *rasa* exists only in this apprehension, and once manifest produces *alaukika ānanda*. Though it exists only in the *āsvādana* or relish, it may be regarded as something to be cognized as it forms the object of super physical consciousness assuming the *sākṣibhāva* and as such differs from perception and other ordinary forms of cognition.

Thus it is clear that the stable and transient, both kinds of *bhāvas*, are articulated in terms of causes and expressions. Some of the mental states like sleep, intoxication, are physical conditions and others may be caused by physical factors. They, however, refer to the mental states that they give rise to. In order to appreciate how specific emotions are treated in the Indian tradition, the following section describes some of the prominent *rasas*.

Śṛṅgāra **(love or delight)**: Its *sthāyibhāva* is *rati*. According to the *Nāṭyaśāstra* it involves intense delight, which arises from the attainment of the object desired. Other authors have considered it as desire characterized by a feeling of pleasure for objects agreeable to the mind. It is also called attachment (*anurāga*) or love (*prema*). It is reciprocally felt by a young couple for each other when desirous of union. Some others expand it to include friendship (*sneha*), reverence (*bhakti*), and affection (*vātsalya*) as varieties of *rati*. *Rati* is colouring of mind with joy and inclines it towards the enjoyment of pleasure. *Śṛṅgāra* is of two types, that is, union or enjoyment (*saṁbhoga*) and separation or privation (*vipralambha*).

In the context of *śṛṅgāra*, union does not mean coexistence at the same place and separation does not indicate existence in different places. Union and separation are conceived as two mental modes. They are in the nature of consciousness. It may be noted that union and privation cannot be divorced from each other. Apprehension of separation and expectation of union are always there. The pain of separation may be blended with the joy of union. Therefore it is possible to relish the union and separation both, which heighten the charm of each other (see Sinha, 1961). This *rasa* is compared with whatever is pure, holy and bright in the world. *Rati*, however, is not the transitory kind of lust, but the permanent disposition of love, which continues till it culminates in a completely joyful experience. Thus a favourable man and a loving young woman are the basic determinant cause (*ālambana vibhāva*) of *śṛṅgāra*. The moon, sandal paste, the spring season, pleasure gardens, the humming of bees, etc. are the excitant causes (*uddīpana vibhāva*). Looking at the face of the beloved person, hearing of his or her qualities, contraction of the eyebrows, sidelong glances, etc., are the ensuant cause (*anubhāva*). All transitory emotions and states are accessory (*vyabhicāri bhāva*).

***Hāsa* (amusement / comic):** This emotion is characterized by the blooming of the mind because it frees the mind from depression and relaxes it. It may be self-centred or other-centred. Its exciting causes (*bibhāvas*) include fun, foolishness, mimicry of other's actions, obtrusiveness, ugly appearance and odd dress, strange conduct and disguise. Its *sthāyibhāva* is *hāsa* (humour). Its *anubhāvas* include blooming and contraction of the eyes, redness of the face, perspiration and throbbing of the nose, the cheeks and lips. Bharata talks about six types of laughter: (1) *Smita*: in which the cheeks brighten up a little, the glances of eyes become graceful, and the teeth are not visible. (2) *Hasita*: in which the face and the eyes brighten up and the teeth are slightly visible. (3) *Vihasita*: in this the eyes contract, the cheeks dimple, the voice becomes sweet and the face becomes red. (4) *Upahasita*: in this the nose is expanded, the eyes squint and the head and the shoulders are bent. (5) *Apahasita*: in this the eyes are filled with tears, and the head and the shoulders swing upwards on inappropriate occasions. (6) *Atihasita*: in it the eyes are expanded and suffused with tears, a loud cry is set up, and the sides are held with hands.

The accessory states (*vyabhicāri bhāvas*) include indolence, apprehension, shyness, sleeping, dreaming, envy, etc. The organic expressions (*sāttvika bhāvas*) include contraction and movement of the eyes, perspiration, trembling, change of colour and shedding of tears.

***Karuṇa* (sorrow):** It involves excess of sorrow on account of bereavement or death of near or dear ones. It involves affliction of all mind, motor and sense organs. It has a paralyzing effect. Its *sthāyibhāva* is *śoka* (grief). Its *vibhāvas* include separation from dear ones or their death, loss of wealth, captivity, misfortune, loss of cherished objects, distress, sickness and poverty. In broad terms they encompass deprivation of cherished objects, bereavement of beloved persons or calamity. Its *anubhāvas* are many. They include repentance, change of voice, inactivity, fainting, dryness of mouth, loss of memory, trembling, sobbing, dejection, misery, anxiety, perplexity, etc. The *vyabhicāri bhāvas* include self-abasement, agitation, terror, deathlike condition, immobility, weeping, and loss of voice. The expressions include shivering due to feeling cold, dryness of mouth and weeping with tears.

***Raudra* (anger):** It is an emotion of fierceness aroused by hostile objects. It is considered as blazing and inflaming of the mind due to contempt, persecution and other such misconduct of the enemy. In it people are possessed by intense heat of the mind which results in hatred and desire to do harm. It is thus roused by hostile objects and opposition. It is different from revenge which is a transitory emotion that is not expressed in immediate action. Its excitatory causes include insult, abuse, false allegations, threat, acts of hostility disobeying orders, ridicule, mischief, disparagement, etc. Its *sthāyibhāva* is *krodha* (anger). Anger is expressed by frowning, grinding of teeth, biting of lips, clenching of fists, thumping them, beating, throwing on the ground, oppression, seizing and cutting, perspiration, trembling, upturned eyes or fierce look. The expression of anger varies depending upon the person whether he or she is an enemy, friend, superior, beloved or subordinate. Its *vyabhicāri bhāvas* include right knowledge, determination, energy, excitement, revenge, instability, fierceness, pride, trembling, stammering, arrogance, intoxication and cruelty. Jealousy, recollection and patience have also been mentioned.

***Bhayānaka* (fear):** It is defined as extreme restlessness and bewilderment or instability of the mind evoked by the power of dreadful objects leading to apprehension of great evil or danger. Its *sthāyibhāva* is *bhaya* (fear or terror). Its excitatory causes, *vibhāvas*, include perception of ferocious beasts, darkness of the night, sounds of animals, offending the preceptor or authority, etc. Its accessory states include inactivity, perspiration, choking voice, trembling, apprehension, dejection, excitement, restlessness, perplexity, terror and death-like condition. The organic expression of fear includes trembling of hands and feet, shaking of the whole body, palpitation of the heart, perspiration, terror, inactivity, dryness of mouth, change of colour, loss of voice, running away, loud cry and search for shelter. These expressions further reinforce the emotion of fear.

***Bībhatsa* (disgust):** It is related to the shrinking of the mind evoked by the perception of loathsome objects (for example, blood, vomiting, wounds). It involves hatred excited by such perceptions. Its *sthāyibhāva* is *jugupsā* (disgust). Thus the sight of loathsome objects or hearing the description of such things causes disgust. It works as *vibhāva*. The expressions of disgust include shrinking of the body, spitting, narrowing of the mouth and the eyes, covering the nose, bending down the head, hurried movement, palpitation of the heart, etc. Its *vyabhicāri bhāva* include anxiety, insanity, despair, intoxication, fear, agitation, sickness, aversion, fainting, anger, sleep, delusion and deathlike condition.

***Adbhuta* (wonder):** It is expansion of the mind at the sight of objects which transcend the boundaries of experience. It is unfolding of the mind produced by the sight of extraordinary or strange objects. Disguise, acts of magic, superhuman feats, learning and skills acts as its *vibhāva*. Its *sthāyibhāva* is *vismaya* (amusement or astonishment).The occurrence of the unusual, unfamiliar, sublime, supernatural and extraordinary excite the emotion of wonder. The expansion of eyes, knitting of the eyebrows, shaking of the head, applause, tremor, choking of voice, and perspiration constitute its *anubhāva*. The accessory states include excitement, quickness, joy, instability of mind, inactivity, fainting and perspiration.

***Vīra* (perseverance or heroism):** It refers to quick action of mind or zeal involving firm endeavour. It works as a mental mode of superiority based on recollection of another's prowess and charity. Its *sthāyibhāva* is *utsāha* (energy). Its *vibhāva* includes absence of dejection, power, patience, heroism, renunciation, absence of wonder, right knowledge, influence, glory, modesty, and power of good counsel. Its *anubhāva* includes patience, charity, skilful diplomacy, valour, gravity, heroism, influence and rebukes. Its accessory states include patience, ascertainment of duty, pride, fierceness, excitement, revenge, recollection, exhilaration, joy and eagerness.

It may also be noted that these emotions also relate to each other in a positive or negative fashion. Thus love, comic, rage and heroic go together. Similarly wonder, rage and heroic go together. The pairs of grief-fear, wonder-quietude, and fear-disgust are compatible. Other combinations seem to be dissonant. In the indigenous literature the emotion of love is central. It is concordant with heroic, wonder, comic and rage. Perhaps this is the reason why it is called the chief *rasa—rasa rājā*. There is another relationship consisting of rage. On the one hand, it is related positively to love, heroic and comic, and on the other it relates to three negative emotions—grief, disgust and fear, which are positively related to each other. Heroic is positively related to rage, love and wonder. Comic is positively related to rage and love. Love is positively related to wonder and wonder is positively related to quietude.

It is also noted that some emotions are discordant and don't go together. Thus disgust, grief, fear and quietude do not go with love. Similarly comic does not go with grief and fear. Grief is discordant with rage, erotic, comic and heroic. The heroic is discordant with fear, disgust, grief and quietude. Fear is discordant with rage, wonder, quietude, heroism and comic. Disgust does not go with wonder, erotic and heroic. Wonder does not go with disgust, fear and grief. Quietude does not go with fear, disgust, grief, love and heroism.

Emotion of *bhakti*

The emotion of *bhakti* or devotion presents an important development in *rasa* theory. The term *bhakti* is derived from the root *bhaj* which means service of the Lord. It reflects passion or love for the infinite. It is pursued in many forms including the image of God as child, master, friend or lover. But it is non-selfish, humble, and leads to sublime joy (*ānanda*). *Bhakti rasa* presents the case of divinization of emotion. *Vallabha Vedānta* considers it a separate emotion with god as object. It is not the desire (*icchā*), attachment (*rati*), or ordinary affection (*sneha*) or volition (*prayatna*). Instead it is a permanent emotion of extraordinary sublime ecstasy for God. The underlying assumption is that man is part of *Brahman*. The visible and manifest plurality is derived from Him. *Bhakti* is often taken as a mental mode. By the practice of listening to the merits of *bhāgavata*, the mind melts and flows towards the supreme Lord. Enjoyment lies in being enjoyed. It is in the nature of intense bliss. The devotion to God occurs in diverse forms, including prayer, meditation, love, being devoid of desire for other objects, and worship of God. Sage Nārada defines it as supreme love for god. It is single-minded devotion. It can be experienced but cannot be described as it is transcendental. It gets manifested in love for God's creatures. It is in the nature of tranquillity and supreme bliss. It is considered as the fruit of all spiritual disciplines. Psychologically it may be characterized as the concrete religious/spiritual consciousness with specific elements of cognition, feeling and conation. Directing emotions toward the divine has significant implications for well-being and personal growth.

The experience of *bhakti rasa* is excited by the image of God, being in the company of *bhaktas* or in the presence of other devotees, etc., which work as determinant causes (*ālambhana vibhāva*). The image is its object while devotees are its abode. God, in such forms as that of Krishna, is considered as the repository of all excellences. His qualities constitute his essence but when meditated upon as different from Him, they become the excitant causes. On the other hand, when they as essence are the object of meditation, they work as basic determinant (*vibhāva*). Its *anubhāva* include various organic manifestations including dancing, rolling on the ground, singing, shouting, deep breathing, laughing loudly, etc. They are both voluntary and involuntary. It is argued that mind affected by the emotion of *bhakti* agitates and that this results in various expressions such as trembling, perspiration, shedding tears, singing, yawning, etc. The innocent love for God works as *sthāyibhāva*. The transitory emotions and states emerge out of and again merge in the basic emotion and develop into *bhakti rasa*. On the whole *bhakti* is a different kind of *rasa*. As Madhusudan Saraswati says:

> *Bhagavān paramānanda-svarupaḥ svayam eva hi*
> *Manogatas tadākāra-rasatām eti puṣkalām*
>
> God, who is the nature of supreme bliss, himself enters into a devotee's mind, is experienced by him, becomes a permanent emotional disposition, and then is transformed into the rasa.
>
> —*Bhakti Rasayan*, I-10

In a classic description of *bhakti* the *Bhāgavata Purāṇa* mentions nine aspects of devotion, that is listening (*śravaṇa*), chanting his names (*kīrtana*), recollection (*smaraṇa*), service (*pādasevana*), worship (*arcanā*), eulogy of him by hymns (*vandanā*), servitude (*dāsya*), friendship (*sākhya*) and self-dedication (*ātmanivedana*). Taken together these steps create an occasion for complete self-transformation. *Nārada Bhakti Sūtra* describes 11 kinds of devotion involving attachment to the qualities and greatness of god (*guṇamāhātmya*), his beauty (*rūpa*), worship (*pūja*), recollection (*smaraṇa*), servitude (*dāsya*), friendship (*sākhya*), wifehood (*kānta*), parenthood (*vātsalya*), self-dedication (*ātma nivedanam*), absorption in him (*tanmayatā*), and separation from him (*paramaviraha*). Rupa Gosvami lists the following features of *bhakti*. It destroys afflictions, offers well-being and belittles the importance of liberation. It is difficult to attain. It attracts God and subjects him to the devotee. A devotee must direct all emotions and passions toward him. When all actions are done for God then they do not bind. Taking refuge in God (*prapatti*) is an essential ingredient of devotion. This involves surrendering the ego to reach greater heights in life.

It may be noted that devotion is a form of love and the key to love is intimate relationship, attachment and affiliation. In this case love is directed to God. The role of love in survival is well documented. It involves empathy and compassion. It also involves self-revelation or disclosure. Affirmation of value and meaning in all humanity for all life, understanding, communication, celebration, empowerment, communion and forgiveness are at the core of love.

In the Indian tradition, self (*ātman*), when united with an appropriate self-object becomes the locus of bliss (*ānanda*). Collins (1991) has drawn attention to the fact that in Indian aesthetics appropriate audience for a performance is called *sahṛdaya*, a person whose heart is one with the aesthetic work or performance, and where the essence of the work is said to be taken in as *rasa* (flavour) by the audience. Similarly the idea of sharing occurs in *bhakti* where the worshippers of the same god are encouraged to be one self through the god, and to reject all distinctions which seem to divide them. As Collins (1991, p. 174) remarks 'satisfaction results from the discovery and maintaining of self objects that mirror the self back to itself, either by extending its sphere of influence or by removing obstacles to its self revelation.'

The system of *bhakti* is considered as a path of emancipation. It is marked by an intense desire to go beyond self-centeredness. It involves identification of the individual self with the cosmic self. Two modes, that is, *saguṇa* and *nirguṇa* are distinguished. The object of intense love is central. An intense longing is crucial for this. In this tradition *bhakti* is of the nature of pure emotion. In the *nirguṇa* tradition it is the self-realization through knowledge that matters. As Śaṅkara terms it, it is an investigation of one's own being (*svasvarūpānusandhāna*). Being *nirguṇa* the ultimate reality is indescribable. It is monistic with the provision of identification of *ātman* and *paramātman*. It is certainly a difficult path to self-realization.

In *Śrīmadbhāgavata* Śrī Kṛṣṇa says that there are four kinds of worshippers—distressed (*ārta*), the seeker of knowledge (*jijñāsu*), devotion of selfish (*arthārthī*) and wise (*jñānī*). The *saguṇa* form of devotion has led to many divine forms. There is the realization that God is both, very much within and outside the being of the devotee. *Jñāna* and *bhakti* are complementary. One needs to have a feeling of oneness with the divinity and establish a bond of love with his whole creation.

Love can have positive or negative consequences depending on its direction. But love always involves dispossession, sharing and ultimately annihilation of ego, and losing one's identity (*tadīyatā*). It does not involve any fear and is a subject of direct experience and perception. It is attained through single-minded supreme devotion (*parā bhakti*). Restraint of sense organs and concentration of mind allows absorption in God and makes the devotee free. *Bhāgavata* also identifies two main forms of *bhakti,* viz.—*saguṇa* and *nirguṇa*. The former is subdivided into *sāttvika, rājasika* and *tāmasika* in which purity, energy and inertia dominate. All of them make a distinction between devotee, God and devotion. *Bhakti,* which is unconditional and spontaneous, is an integral experience and is characterized by service to God and transcends the three *guṇas*. Such a devotee sees God in himself and in all creatures, sees them in God and in himself, and sees the divinity of his self. He loses his identity and does not feel any distinction between himself and others and dedicates all his actions to God.

> *sarvabhūteṣu yaḥ paśyed bhagavadbhāvam*
> *ātmanaḥ*
> *bhūtāni bhagavatyātmanyeṣa*
> *bhāgavatottamaḥ*
>
> —*Bhāgavata*, xi, 2, 45

In a subsequent analysis, the Gosvamies articulate the path along which *bhakti* grows. According to them the beginning is with faith (*śraddhā*) in God. Then one goes for the company of saints (*sādhusaṅga*), acts of devotion (*bhajana kīrtana*), purging of impurities (*anarthanivṛtti*), worship without distraction (*niṣṭhā*), desire for worship (*ruci*), natural attachment (*āsakti*), nascent love (*bhāva*), ardent love (*prema*), *parā bhakti*, affection (*sneha*), sulks (*māna*) , intimacy (*praṇaya*), passionate attachment (*rāga*), transcendent attachment (*anurāga*), transcendent love (*bhāva*), and supreme holy love (*mahābhāva*). On attaining primary devotion a devotee becomes fulfilled (*siddha*), immortal (*amṛta*) and contented (*tṛpta*). The supreme love for God is infinite, absolute and complete in itself.

Conclusion

Human emotions are complex but meaning generating experiences. They are embedded in our lived experiences and have the creative potential to shape the same. The study of emotion in psychology in its received form is ill prepared to the situated and discursive stance of emotion that real life offers. The physical metaphors do not match this complexity and under-represent it. As Averill (1990) noted, emotions are the products of culture and constitute one of the chief ways of cultural distinctiveness. It is more realistic to the modes of our emotional being to locate emotions in the social space and in the happenings in the lives of the people. The narrative form of emotion experience is emerging as a major departure from the received view of emotions (see Sarbin, 1989). It is in the course of happenings and their narrative articulation that emotions are born. It is said that the first poet of Sanskrit, Vālmīki, wrote the epic *Rāmāyaṇa* after witnessing the death of a bird, when grief took the shape of poetry (*śokaḥ ślokatvam āgataḥ*). The Indian approach to emotion as developed in the *rasa* theory clearly demonstrates the narrative form of emotion. As such, *rasa* theory cuts across many domains such as Yoga, Āyurveda, Advaita and Tantra.

Thus, emotion is a whole story. It is a unitary experience of self-transformation in which *rasa* is nothing but the union of three script-like or narrative components. It is the simultaneous experience of all the components or perhaps more accurately the unitary experience of the whole package deal. The *rasa* experience or *rasānubhāva* starts at sensory level and moves to the level of imagination, the level of *bhāva*, the level of *sādhāraṇīkaraṇa*, and to a super-conscious level that goes beyond the material world. We come in contact with objects of pleasure through our sense organs. The objects are the medium of the *rasa* experience. The objects lead to our imageries. We complete the experience through imagination. At this level the person changes. He or she is in a different world of his own creation. Thus a *sahṛdaya* viewer identifies with the hero who is acting in the play. He views things from the perspective of the hero and responds accordingly. This is the level of *bhāva*. The intense *bhāva* experience results in the loss of individuality. He is free from the limitations of time and space. He generalizes. This however is not the end of the journey. Abhinavagupta says that the climax is the experience of bliss, pure bliss. It is the experience of the self. It is *mahārasa*. During this stage the *sthāyibhāva* goes to the unconscious level. The experience of bliss characterizes the *rasa*. It reminds the *Upaniṣadic* statement *raso vai saḥ*. It's the experience of the *ātman*.

The Indian theory of *rasa* also posits a schema in which *rasa* is brought into existence through a joint activity of several elements or processes namely *vibhāva, anubhāva*, and *sañcāribhāva*. This suggests that there are prototypes of specific emotions, which are part of the cultural meaning system. Recently, Misra (2004) empirically examined the antecedents of emotion experiences. He noted that the emotion experience in the Indian context has a remarkable cultural continuity. The specific emotions do share a mode that has considerable degree of consensus. Also, there are multiple pathways through which these emotions are experienced. We notice that collective as well as individual processes both shape the emotions. The antecedents indicate that emotional episodes involve motivational, communicative, and regulatory processes operating within and/or between individuals. It was noted that while some of these processes apply or are potentially applicable more generally, others vary considerably across individuals. From the protocols one can sense the existence of certain normative aspects which perhaps provide information about intended or likely behaviours and underlying the diverse mental states of others. It seems fair to argue that intra psychologically, the emotions perform organizing and motivating functions to facilitate adaptive goal directed behaviour. People will strive for rich emotional experiences that contribute to self-growth. This is why it is often said that unemotional life will not be worth living.

In this context it may be noted that the connection of self and emotion is very deep in Indian thought. Interestingly enough the term *bhāva* is used to denote both, being or self, and mental state. The root *bhū* means to be and *bhāva* means that which brings about Being. The *bhāvas* emerging or emanating from an interaction with persons and events constitute our experience. Experience is reflected in the self in forms of *vṛttis* (movements or actions) through the fourfold cognitive mechanism of *manas, buddhi, citta,* and *antaḥkaraṇa*. The *saṁskāras*, the traces of experiences, shape our selfhood, which both determines and is further shaped by the way they engage with *bhāvas* (or *rasas*). In this way a continuous tension between emotion experience and self occurs. This analysis is frequently applied to the Indian aesthetic experience. It is held that *bhāva* becomes manifest in someone and/or due to someone or a thing and are to some extent determined by the circumstances of the event. Once such a state of being occurs, the person begins to behave in the given ways (*anubhāva*). There may be a dominant *bhāva* in the midst of a number of ancillary emotions (*sañcāribhāva*). This complex mental condition is correlated with certain forms of physical demeanour and behaviour in life (*abhinaya*). The *bhāva* produces certain physical effects. When all these co-occur, they evoke the *sthāyibhāva*. In life the hearer or spectator of the *sthāyibhāva*, given the empathy, experiences the concomitant *rasa* through the attachment of his or her mind to the *sthāyibhāva*. When this complex sequence of events occurs, then one experiences *rasa*.

Until recently, mainstream psychology has been preoccupied with treating the human psyche as a natural structure or entity. In this analysis the person with socio-cultural identity was missing. Also, the relationship between individual and society was treated as mechanical and the individual attained primacy over sociality in most of the accounts of social behaviour. Rooted in a machine metaphor the academic practices were engaged in sustaining the psychological enterprise for a long time. In this framework psychology was chiefly directed towards the scientific study of 'others'. The Indian perspective is unique in recognizing the social roots of being emotional and subjecting this to personal creative endeavour for welfare and emancipation. For a *bhakta*, emotion does not bind or impoverish. Instead it is used creatively to empower self and others. This potential of emotional creativity is yet to be fully examined and nurtured. It is important not only for the alleviation of present day suffering but also for ensuring a sustainable future.

The complex relationship between emotion and culture is often revealed in the lived experiences of active goal directed persons. The constructivist approaches give greater emphasis on cultural diversity and tend to imply that each culture constructs its own unique psychology. The emphasis on local cultural content presents people either as passively absorbing or reflexively resisting such cultural content. How active and creative people meet the challenges of thinking, feeling, remembering, etc. is not taken into account. We need methods to understand the mutually constituted nature of culture and individual experience. We need to forge a cooperative multidisciplinary approach. The individual experience and its relationship with culture needs to be studied from a perspective that maintains that instead of being entirely culturally constructed, individual psychology is also partially explicable in terms of universal patterns of human biological development as well as similar behavioural and psychological adaptations that groups make to common problems.

Appendix: List of *bhāvas*

***Sthāyibhāva* (emotion):** *Sthāyibhāvas* are considered as enduring, persisting, dominant and intense emotional dispositions. They are *sthāyin* or permanent in the sense that they cannot be suppressed or obscured by other emotional dispositions. Also, it is pointed out that a *sthāyibhāva* is produced by many factors. The list of *sthāyibhāvas* includes *rati* (love or delight), *hāsa* (humour), *śoka* (sorrow), *krodha* (anger), *bhaya* (fear or terror), *utsāha* (energy or *heroism*), *jugupsā* (disgust), *vismaya* (amusement or astonishment), and *śama* (serenity or calm). It may be worthwhile to point out that a given *sthāyibhāva*, if it contributes to another emotion, it becomes subsidiary. Thus when anger contributes to heroism and heroism contributes to fear they act as subsidiary or transitory emotions. It has also been indicated that *sthāyibhāva* are innate and present in everyone as they are in the structure of human mind. Their manifestations are visible and they remain in the background.

***Vyabhicāribhāva* (transient emotions):** These mental states are accessory states of the *sthāyibhāva* because they promote or facilitate the *sthāyibhāva*. They appear and disappear in the *sthāyibhāvas*. As subordinates they surrender to the *sthāyibhāvas*. They are also termed as *sañcāribhāva* because they quicken the movement of emotions. There are thirty-three such secondary states including emotions, feelings, and cognitive states. They are: *dhṛti* (contentment), *smṛti* (recollection), *mati* (determining the real nature of an object), *vrīḍā* (shame), *jāḍyam* (inactivity), *viṣāda* (dejection), *mada* (exhilaration and intoxication), *vyādhi* (sickness), *nidrā* (sleep), *supta* (deep sleep), *autsukya* (eagerness), *avahitthā* (concealment of emotional expression), *śaṅkā* (apprehension of harm), *capala* (instability), *ālasya* (apathy), *harṣa* (joy), *garva* (pride), *augrya* (fierceness), *prabodha* (wakefulness), *glāni* (langour), *dainya* (misery), *śrama* (fatigue), *unmāda* (derangement of mind), *moha* (fainting), *cintā* (anxiety), *amarṣa* (revenge), *trāsa* (fright), *apasmāra* (epilepsy), *nirveda* (self-abasement), *āvega* (excitement), *vitarka* (conjecture), *asūyā* (envy), and *mṛti* (death like condition). It may be noted that the same set of transitory emotions works as exciters of some emotions and consequents for some. Also, they can act independently or in a dependent manner. Emotions have a life cycle. They emerge, subside, blend and show friction.

***Vibhāvas* (determinants/eliciting conditions):** This includes all the background information, settings, events, and action tendencies that might make manifest some state of the world and one's relationship to it. Taken together, they define the emotive situation which works as a medium. *Vibhāvas* act as determinant and exciting causes. The *abhinaya* is known by them. They produce *rasa* and make them relishable. It is of two kinds. One is related to the object of *rasālambana*. The *rasa* is based on that. The other is instrumental and stimulates (*uddīpana*) the *rasa* experience.

***Anubhāva* (consequences):** These are physiological changes which are consequent on the rise of emotions and are often considered as effects of emotions. They include eight kinds of voluntary willful expressions of emotions, such as abusing the body and expressive modes (bodily movements, voice tone, facial expression, wailing and tears). They occur after (*anu*) the emotion (*bhāva*). They work as ensuing causes of *rasa* when it is represented in poetry or drama. *Vibhāvas* may also lead to *anubhāvas*.

***Sāttvikabhāvas* (organic manifestations of emotions):** These are involuntary or spontaneous organic expressions. Bharata lists the following eight *sāttvikabhāvas: stambha* (inactivity), *sveda* (perspiration), *romāñca* (bristling of the hairs of the body), *svarabhaṅga* (change of voice), *vepathu* (trembling), *vaivarṇyam* (change of colour), shedding of tears (*aśru*), and *pralaya* (insensibility). These *sāttvikabhāvas* often facilitate each other. They are excited by the *vibhāvas* and intensify emotions. The *sāttvikbhāvas* vary in their intensity.

References

Averill, J. A. (1990). Inner feelings, works of the flesh, the beast within, diseases of the mind, driving force, and putting on a show: Six metaphors of emotion and their theoretical extensions. In D.E. Leary (Ed.), *Metaphors in the history of psychology* (pp. 104–132). Cambridge: Cambridge University Press.

Averill, J. A., Chon, K. K., & Hahn, D.W. (2001). Emotions and creativity: East and West. *Asian Journal of Social Psychology, 4*, 165–183.

Averill, J. A., & Saundarrajan, L. (2006). Passion and Quing: Intellectual histories of emotion, West and East. In K. Pawlik & G. d'Ydewalle (Eds.), *Psychological concepts: An international historical perspective* (pp. 101–139). Hove, England: Psychology Press.

Collins, A. (1991). From Brahma to the blade of grass: Towards an Indian self psychology. *Journal of Indian Philosophy, 19*, 143–189.

Dalal, A. S. (Ed.) (2001). *A greater psychology*. Pondicherry: Sri Aurobindo Ashram Trust.

Damasio, A. R. (1994). *Descartes' error: Emotion, reason, and the human brain*. New York: Avon Books.

Darwin, C. (1965). *The expression of emotions in man and animals*. Chicago: Chicago University Press. (Original work published 1872. London: John Murray).

Doi, T. (1973). *The anatomy of dependence*. Tokyo: Kodansha International.

Ekman, P. (1992). Facial expressions of emotion: An old controversy and new findings. *Philosophical Transactions of the Royal Society of London, Series B, 335*, 63–64

Ekman, P. (2003). *Emotions revealed*. London: Weidenfield & Necolson.

Elfenbein, H. A. & Ambady, N. (2003). Cultural similarity's consequences: A distance perspective on cross-cultural differences in emotion recognition. *Journal of Cross-Cultural Psychology, 34*, 92–110.

Forgas, J. P., & Smith, C. A. (2003). Affect and emotion. In M.A. Hogg & J. Cooper (Eds.), *The Sage handbook of social psychology* (pp. 161–189). London: Sage.

Frijda, N. H. (1986). *The emotions*. Cambridge: Cambridge University Press.

Gnoli, R. (1956). *The aesthetic experience according to Abhinavagupta*. Rome: Instituto Italiano per Il Medio ed Estremo Oriente.

Harre, R. (1986). *The social construction of emotions*. Oxford: Blackwell.

Hinton, A. B. (1999). *Biocultural approaches to the emotions*. Cambridge: Cambridge University Press.

Izard, C. E. (1994). Innate and universal facial expressions: Evidence from development and cross-cultural research. *Psychological Bulletin, 115*, 288–299.

Jain, U. (1994). Socio-cultural construction of emotions. *Psychology and Developing Societies, 6*, 151–168.

James, W. (1890). *The principles of psychology* (Vol. 2). New York: Henry Holt and Company.

Kapur, K. (1998). *Literary theory*. New Delhi: Prentice Hall.

Kitayama, S., & Markus, H. R. (Eds.) (1994). *Emotion and culture*. Washington: American Psychological Association.

Lazarus, R. S. (1991). *Emotion and adaptation*. Oxford: Oxford University Press.

Lumsden, C. J. & Wilson, E. O. (1983). *Promethian fire*. Cambridge, MA.: Harvard University Press.

Lutz, C. (1988). *Unnatural emotions: Everyday sentiments on a Micronesian atoll and their challenge to western theory*. Chicago: Chicago University Press

Lynch, D. M. (1990). *The divine passions: The social construction of emotions in India*. Delhi: Oxford University Press.

Marcus, G. E. (2003). The psychology of emotion and politics. In Sears, L. Huddy & R. Jervis (Eds.), *Political psychology* (pp. 183–221). New York: Oxford University.

Masson, G. & Patwardhan, M. V. (1970). *Aesthetic rapture: The rasadhyaya of the Natyashastra*. Poona: Deccan College

Menon, U., & Shweder, R. A. (1994). Kali's tongue: Cultural psychology and the power of shame in Orissa, India. In S. Kitayama & H. R Markus (Eds.), *Emotion and culture* (pp. 241–284). Washington: American Psychological Association.

Mesquita, B., & Frijda, N. H. (1992). Cultural variations in emotion: A review. *Psychological Bulletin, 112*, 179–204.

Mesquita, B. (2001). Culture and Emotions: Different approaches to the question. In T. J. Mayne & G. A. Bonanno (Eds.), *Emotions: Current issues and future directions* (pp. 214–250). New York: The Guilford Press.

Mestrovic, S. V. (1997). *Postemotional society*. Thousand Oaks: Sage.

Misra, G. (2004). Culture, self and emotions: The case of antecedents of emotion experiences. *Indian Psychological Abstracts and Reviews, 11*(1), 1–27.

Moore, C. C., & Mathews, H. E. (2001). *The psychology of cultural experience*. Cambridge: Cambridge University Press.

O'Shaughnessy, J., & O'Shaughnessy, N. (2003). *The marketing power of emotions*. Oxford: Oxford University Press.

Pandey, K. C. (1959). *Comparative aesthetics* (Vol. 1) *Indian Aesthetics*. Varanasi: Chakhambha Sanskrit Series.

Panksepp, J. (1998). *Affective neuroscience: The foundations of human and animal emotions*. New York: Oxford University Press.

Parkinson, B. (1996). Emotions are social. *British Journal of Psychology, 87*, 663–683.

Paranjpe, A. C. (1998). *Self and identity in modern psychology and Indian thought*. New York: Plenum.

Ray, R. K. (2001). *Exploring emotional history: Gender, mentality and literature in the Indian awakening*. New Delhi: Oxford University Press.

Roberts, R. C. (2003). *Emotions: An essay in aid of moral psychology*. Cambridge: Cambridge University Press.

Rolls, E. T. (1999). *The brain and emotion*. Oxford: Oxford University Press.

Rosaldo, M. Z. (1980). *Knowledge and passion: Ilongot notions of self and social life*. Cambridge: Cambridge University Press

Russell, J. (1991). Culture and the categorization of emotions. *Psychological Bulletin, 110*, 426–450.

Russell, J. A., & Fernandez-Dols, J. M. (Eds.) (1997). *The psychology of facial expression*. Cambridge: Cambridge University Press.

Sarbin, T. R. (1989). Emotions as narrative emplotments. In M. J. Packer & R. B. Addison (Eds.), *Entering the circle: Hermeneutic investigation in psychology* (pp. 185–201). Albany: State University of New York Press.

Schachter, S., & Singer, J. (1962). Cognitive, social and physiological determinants of emotional state. *Psychological Review, 69*, 379–399.

Scherer, K. R. (1997). The role of culture in emotion-antecedent appraisal. *Journal of Personality and Social Psychology, 73*(5), 902–922.

Scherer, K. R., Wallbolt, H. G., & Summerfield, A. B. (Eds.) (1986). *Experiencing emotions: A cross-cultural study*. Cambridge: Cambridge University Press.

Shaver, P. R., Murdaya, U., & Fraley, R. C. (2001). Structure of Indonesian emotion lexicon. *Asian Journal of Social Psychology, 4*, 201–224.

Shweder, R. A., & Haidt, J. (2000). The cultural psychology of emotions: Ancient and new. In M. Lewis & J. Hoviland, (Eds.), *Handbook of emotions* (pp. 397-414). New York: Guilford Press.

Sinha, J. (1961). *Indian psychology: Emotion and will* (Vol. 3). Calcutta: Sinha Publishing House.

Stets, J. E. (2003). Emotions and sentiments. In J. Delamater (Ed.), *Handbook of social psychology* (pp. 309–478). New York: Kluwer Academic.

Thoits, P. A. (1989). The sociology of emotions. *Annual Review of Sociology, 15*, 317–342.

Williams, S. J. (2001). *Emotion and social theory: Corporeal reflections on the (ir)rational*. London: Sage.

Wierzbicka, A. (1986). Human emotions: Universal or culture specific? *American Anthropologist, 88*, 584–594.

Wollheim, R. (1999). *On the emotions*. New Haven: Yale University Press.

14

The philosophy of healing in Indian medicine

Kapil Kapoor

Indian medicine is a good example of how knowledge forms an integrated whole in the intellectual traditions. While major philosophical systems provide the theoretical framework for an analysis of disease, its causes and cure, the world-view enshrined in those systems provides the governing philosophy of health and healing. It is also interesting to note that Āyurveda shares some of those theoretical categories with other disciplines such as Aesthetics.[1] In fact, Āyurveda and Art share the common goal of restoring human beings to good health, both moral and physical.[2]

Āyurveda is a science that enables a man to achieve a full life-span. Good health has to be sustained in order to lead a happy life, and the body has to be freed of the ailments afflicting it. It is towards this end that this system of medicine, with its two aspects of principles and practice, has been established by sages and seers. It has two ends—(*i*) freedom from illness, and (*ii*) protection of good health through prevention.[3] Caraka and Suśruta are two celebrated proponents of this science, one dealing with medicine in his *Carakasaṃhitā* and the other with surgery in his *Suśrutasaṃhitā*.

Texts pertaining to the science of medicine have attested to a history from the 5th century B.C. to modern times and are divided into eight parts—surgery (for bodily pain); illnesses of the throat and above (including ENT); the main body (chest, stomach, heart, etc.); drives and obsessions (including nerves); pregnancy to child-care; poisons; constituents/elements of the body (liquids, blood, fat, flesh, bones); and energy (including reproductive functions). *Carakasaṃhitā* deals comprehensively with all eight and is evidently a text that has emerged at the end of a long tradition of thought.[4] Caraka describes Āyurveda as the science of a happy and useful life. He classifies the ailments of the body into three types (intrinsic to the body, afflictions from external sources, and those of the mind) and says that all ailments are ultimately rooted in what he calls *prajñāparādha*, some failure of one's discriminating intellect, and argues that to rid oneself of illnesses of the body and mind and sustain good health, one must be or become *sadvṛtta*, a person with affirmative, morally correct cognitions. 'Who remains healthy?', he asks and answers, 'One who eats in moderation and carefully, acts with discrimination, is not in bondage of the objects of senses, treats every one alike (*samabuddhi*), is truthful, is of forgiving disposition, and always follows what the elders say' (CS, 4.2.46).

Caraka's theory of medicine is wholly embedded in the six principal *darśanas*,[5] and is founded on the shared conceptions of what constitutes a 'good' life and what the conditions for human happiness are.

Caraka's philosophy and his theory of medicine are based mainly on the Sāṁkhya Yoga framework, although Vaiśeṣika and Nyāya are also drawn upon in the definitions of ontological categories (such as *mana*) (CS, 4.1.16–18). The living human body, its afflictions and their cure form the subject matter of Āyurveda. However, this human body is in its totality much more than just its physical substance—it also comprises the internal organs, their disposition and their functions. This 'totality' is designated by the term *puruṣa*. What constitutes a human being? What forms his totality? This needs to be understood; only then can one study what the ailments are, what part(s) of the body they afflict, what the nature and causes of those afflictions are, and what their cure is. Out of the eight *sthānas*, divisions of *Carakasaṃhitā*, a whole division, *śarīrasthāna*, is devoted to the human body—its constitution, its parts, its conception and growth in the mother's womb, and its sustenance after birth. The first chapter of this division is devoted to the suffering that afflicts *puruṣa*, the questions of *sukha-duḥkha* and *vedanā*, the causes of suffering and the role of the physician.

As noted above, this exposition is primarily based on the Sāṁkhya Yoga system. *Puruṣa* is defined in terms of the 24 Sāṁkhya ontological primitives—the *tattva* (CS, 4.1.16–38, 63). This entire *puruṣa* is the substratum of suffering. The suffering is three-fold—*ādhidaivika*, *ādhibhautika* and *ādhyātmika*,[6] or *nija* (engendered in the body), *āgantuka* (received in the body from outside) and *mānasa* (of the mind) in the Caraka framework (CS, 1.11.45). Suffering is produced by a marked conjunction of six factors: failure of the intellect (*dhī*) to discriminate, of the faculty of restraint (*dhṛti*) to restrain, of memory (*smṛti*) in pertinent recall, of unrighteous experience of objects, of senses, or experience that is inimical for the self (*asātmyārtha āgama*) (CS, 4.1.98). It is recognized that suffering has as its substratum both the self (*ātmā*) and the body (*śarīra*) (CS, 4.1.84–85,136). Mind, *mana*, is of course the cognizer of joy and sorrow[7] regardless of where it is experienced. Further, suffering is not located in the present alone—it has a past and a future, and therefore the physician treats suffering in its three temporal dimensions (CS, 4.1.86).

Caraka says that *cikitsā*[8] is of two kinds, symptomatic (*upadhā cikitsā*) and fundamental (*naishathiki cikitsā*) (CS, 4.1.94–97). The first is directed at the attributes of the ailment and is complete when the external symptoms disappear. The second is directed at the ultimate cause(s) of the ailment, which it seeks to eliminate. The ultimate cure for all suffering, both physical and that of the spirit, is stabilizing one's mind in the *sāttvika guṇa* (CS, 4.1.94), freeing oneself from the objects of senses (CS, 4.1.95) and overcoming desire (*tṛṣṇā*) (CS, 4.1.134). In other words, all *vedanā*, suffering, ceases in the state of *mokṣa*, which is but the *yogic* state of *citta-vṛtti-nirodha* (*Yogasūtra*, 1.1.2) in which mind, *manas*, with all its *vṛttis*, tendencies of the mind, is under the complete control of the Self. Caraka defines *mokṣa* (CS, 4.1.142) as the dissolution (*viyoga*) of attachment (*sambandha*) with all that binds and, hence, torments the Self. In the next four verses (CS, 4.1.143–146, 154), he lays down the rules of conduct that help to attain this state: seek and serve the good and avoid the bad human beings; be happy in the happiness of others; live a life of restraint and discipline (*niyama*); do your duty without attachment; sustain an evenness of the mind and the intellect; and control the 'waves', cognitions, of the mind. These values are ingrained in the ordinary, average Indian mind, which unquestioningly accepts and follows them in the lived life. He sums up these rules—there is no liberation, *mokṣa*, without knowledge. This is right knowledge as it leads to liberation.

This philosophy of health and happiness has over a period of time sedimented into the Indian mind, and programmed it as believing this to be the only means of *ārogya*, a disease-free, state. Āyurveda is the science that deals with life, a life of *ārogya*, freedom from disease, and of good health,[9] so that one is able to perform one's enjoined duties and attain the four ends of life—*dharma* (righteousness), *artha* (material ends), *kāma* (desires) and *mokṣa* (freedom of the self from all pursuit). Āyurveda is thus not concerned merely with *āyu*, a long life. It asks, 'Why must one live a long life, and what kind of a long life should we aspire for?' Āyurveda is not concerned with ensuring a long life, *dirgha āyu*—it seeks to promote *sukha āyu* and *hitāyu* (CS, 1.1.41), a happy life and a useful life. Caraka defines a happy life as one '... free of bodily or mental ailments, able to do all work, endowed with strength and with energy to do [his] duty, possessed of knowledge, able to use and enjoy all his senses, ornamented with virtues, able to fulfil/achieve his tasks, blessed with different *sukha* ...' (CS, 1.30.23).

And *hitāyu*, useful life, is defined as the life of one:

> ... who in all his life-time thinks of the well-being of others, considers others' wealth as *tuccha*, of no consequence, is possessed of acknowledged virtues, *sadguṇa*, such as truth-telling, acts thoughtfully, respects those who are worthy of respect, is indifferent (*udāsīna*) to others, serves devotedly the learned and the aged, controls his passions, is constantly involved in sharing his knowledge, his wealth, sees all beings in his own self, accepts good advice (CS, 1.30.26).

Roga, disease, robs life of both happiness (*sukha*) and usefulness (*hita*). Hence Āyurveda, the science of medicine, enables *cikitsā*, a restoration of the body to its pre-affliction state (CS, 1.16.34). Afflictions are of three kinds, as we noted above, but according to Caraka, it is the third group of ailments, *mānasa vyādhi* (afflictions of mind and spirit), which needs for its treatment *darśana*, philosophy, apart from medicine.

The nature, properties and functions of *manas*, the mind, have been established by Caraka with exactitude and thoroughness with the help of ideas drawn from the six philosophical systems (CS, 1.8.4, 5, 12; 4.1.18–23). Mind is an ontological primitive and has the function of selecting objects for cognitive focus (*saṅkalpa/vikalpa*). In this sense, the mind is the presiding sensory organ. Its functions are identified as:

1. Grasping/cognizing the sense-object contact;
2. Self-regulation for that knowledge;
3. Analysis of and reflection on cognitions.

After this, the intellect, *buddhi*, takes over. It is the intellect presided over by the self (*ātmā*) that programmes the mind to select, control and cognize the sense-object conjunction. Mental ailments have their roots in a deviant programme that sets up extreme, undesirable or inappropriate goals for the mind, which generate, in terms of conduct, acts that Caraka describe as *prajñāparādha* (CS, 4.1.21)—inordinate desire and jealousy (CS, 4.1.102), for example. An inability to get what one desires and a continuing presence of that which one dislikes leads ultimately to illness. Those who are *sāttvika* of disposition, predominantly good (*sattvaguṇa pradhāna*), are not prone to acts, either mental or physical, that violate wise intelligence. Desire and hate are so classified because they harm the one who nurses them more than those towards whom they are directed. As Caraka says elsewhere (CS, 1.7.52), jealousy, grief, fear, anger, pride and rivalry are products of the failure of true intelligence, a failure to see what is bad or good for one's self. *Prajñāparādha* are those volitive acts that are not approved by the intellect (*buddhi*), tolerance faculty (*dhairya*) and memory (*smṛti*). Caraka lists acts (CS, 4.1.103) that may lead to ailments as serious as paralysis—exerting oneself beyond one's capacity, sexual indulgence, abandoning civil behaviour, insulting those worthy of respect, indulging knowingly in wrong-doings, befriending the wrong people, being susceptible to jealousy, fear, anger and greed, indulging in despicable, disgusting acts with one's body—these are all 'crimes of intellect', and show a complete absence of a discriminating faculty (*viveka buddhi*).

These acts are analogous to *vṛttis*, tendencies of the mind. When a person is afflicted by certain ailments, he has to exercise control over his mind. Caraka says:

> In all ailments, the responsibility is of a physician, but in the mental ailment, it is the patients' own responsibility. A wise man keeping in mind his own welfare, acts with great care in respect of *dharma*, *artha* and *kāma*. It is these three that are the cause of internal *sukha* or *duḥkha* .... Such a patient should discipline himself, respect the physician and recognize the truth about himself, the *maryāda* or limits of his family honour and conduct, the nature of time and place and social and economic strength (or weakness) .... (CS, 1.1.46).

It is said that mental ailments can be cured or removed by cultivating *sadvṛttis*, positive or righteous cognition and attitudes. He should not 'seek his own sukha alone ...' (CS 1.8.26). *Sadvṛtti* is the conduct of 'good people' (*sajjana*), those who are at peace, are pure, truthful and guided by righteousness in all their acts. By following their examples, a person regains good health and also conquers his senses. This is considered so crucial for a happy and healthy life that Caraka declares that he is laying down in detail the *sadvṛttis* (CS 1.8.18–25). A study of these shows that great value is placed on cleanliness of the body and of the mind, generosity of spirit, kindness to others, respect for elders, parents, teachers and guests, restraint in speech and movement, control over one's senses, absence of jealousy, worry and fear, possession of humility, faith in God, devotion to those who excel in learning and the arts, thoughtfulness and carefulness. We have listed only some of the properties upheld by Caraka. The whole list is a comprehensive enumeration of what everyone will agree are the virtues of a pious and good man. Evidently, these *sadvṛttis* are the same as the *daivīsampada* elucidated in The *Bhagavad Gītā* (16.1–3). Four of these—*maitrī*, *karuṇā*, *mudita* and *upekṣā* are mentioned in the *Yogasūtra* as the means of purifying the *citta* (1.33).

The science of medicine thus recognizes the deep connection that exists between the body and the mind, and that to ensure good health, the mind must be at peace with itself. This peace of mind is born of moral cognition and conduct. This thought itself emanates from a world-view that considers control of the self the highest conquest, and a deliverance from the limitations of a narrow self as *mokṣa*, the final state in which all suffering ceases. In rigorously analysing the properties and afflictions of both body and mind, Caraka, the celebrated exponent of Āyurveda, not only draws upon the major philosophical systems, the ontology of Sāṁkhya and the epistemology of Yoga, but also transforms their constructs into practical rules of conduct that will ensure people a long, happy and useful life.

Endnotes

1 The categories of *rasa* ('aesthetic experience' and 'chemical or substance') and *ānanda* ('joy' of art, experience and life), for example.

2 In fact, plays such as *Prabodhacandrodaya* and *Jīvanāndanam* had actually been composed, one of them as late as the eighteenth century, to dramatize the whole event of falling ill and recovering, ending with the joy or bliss (*ānanda*) that accompanies good health resulting from the cultivation of moral values.

3 *Suśrutasaṃhitā*, 1.12.

4 It is said that Caraka, an Afghan resident of Gandhara, the kingdom ruled by Nagnajit, was a contemporary of the great Persian King Daryus (Darius) in the 6th century BC, and a teacher at the University of Taxila.

5 In the first chapter of the fourth division of *Carakasaṃhitā*, in the chapter titled *śarīrasthāna*, Caraka seeks to define *duḥkha*, sorrow, and *vedanā*, suffering, and analyse their causes and their cures. Here, we only note that the vocabulary of his discussion is that of the six systems, *ṣaḍa-darśana*: *puruṣa*, *prakṛti*, *ātmā*, *buddhi*, *manaḥ*, *indriya*, *bhoga*, *karma*, *bhāva*, *dhṛti*, *smṛti*, *prajñā*, *tṛṣṇa*, *mokṣa*, terms from Sāṁkhya, Yoga, Nyāya and Vaiśeṣika.

6 *Sāṁkhyasūtra*.

7 See *Vaiśeṣikasūtra*, karikā 85, which is cited as authority.

8 *Cikitsā* is a key concept of Indian thought in grammar, philosophy, medicine and art. The word, made up of the prefix *ci-* and the verb root *ökit*, followed by the *-san* affix, means 'to systematically act almost as an act of devotion to restore or cure or elevate/purify'.

9 It protects and promotes the health of the healthy and cures the ills of the ailing.

Classical texts quoted

Bhagavad Gītā
Carakasaṃhitā
Yogasūtra

15

Healing and counselling in a traditional spiritual setting

Anand C. Paranjpe

Introduction

This essay presents an account of healing I have witnessed in the presence of my *guru*, Shri Ramchandra Bapuji Ambekar (1904-1990). In the first part of this essay I provide a description of the setting in which he sat for several hours three evenings every week listening to, and counselling, a stream of visitors. Then I present an overview of his life history and that of his *guru*, Shri Raosaheb Sahasrabuddhe, based on their published biographies. Shri Ambekar's perspective on his work based on an extensive interview follows, as does an explanation of the principles underlying the healing process as reflected in their biographies. The first part ends with an overview of the historical background of the spiritual tradition of the Dattātreya sect to which both these healers belonged. In the second part I provide a detailed discussion of these healing practices from the perspective of modern psychology. In this discussion attention is provided not only to concepts and major theories of counselling and psychotherapy, but also to the relevant aspects of the wider world view within which contemporary Western psychology is ensconced.

The case study of a traditional Indian form of healing presented here is based on the following sources of data: (a) the author's direct experience of sitting in the presence of the healer for numerous hours over ten years in his early adulthood, (b) an extensive semi-structured interview with the healer for over three hours, (c) two biographies, one of this healer (Sane, 1988) and another one of his *guru* (Deshpande, 1978), and (d) historical accounts of the tradition and lineage of *gurus* to which these two healers belong (Dhere, 1958/1999; Rigopulous, 1998). While the author's observations as a participant, along with the reminiscences of several "clients", offer examples of the varied problems for which cure was sought, the interview and the biography provide useful information about the principles on which interventions were grounded. To help get a sense of the situation in which this traditional form of healing and counselling happens, it would be useful to first describe the scene. This will be followed by a detailed discussion of the healing process first in light of the interview and biographical materials, and then by an examination of the practices and principles in light of contemporary concepts and practices.

The scene

In a middle class locality in the city of Pune in Maharashtra, a man who appears to be in his late fifties sits in the corner of the front room of a two-room apartment. He sits there for three days a week usually from about five in the evening to eleven o'clock in the night, i.e., for about five to six hours each time, as a series of relief seekers keep coming in. The front door is kept open during this period as people, young and old, men and women, walk in and get seated in front of him. Nobody is stopped at the door. The room, which is about 10' by 12' size, is packed wall to wall with people huddled together. The walls are bedecked with pictures of deities and calendars as is common in middle class homes in the area. There is a cot near the entrance of the room, which is used by visitors to sit on during visiting hours, and doubles in the night for family members to sleep. Behind this visiting room there is a smaller room which serves as a kitchen and additional living space for a family composed of the healer, his wife, their two adult children, plus the daughter's two young children. Usually other members of the family are absent during the visiting hours, or confine themselves to the other room. The healer, clad in a clean white shirt and dhoti sits on a small mat in the corner diagonally opposite from the entrance. In a small cabinet behind him there is a statue of his *guru* seated with folded hands. Behind the statue hangs a framed picture of Lord Dattātreya, the three-headed deity worshipped in their tradition. The three heads represent the trinity of Brahmā, the creator, Viṣṇu, the protector, and Śiva, the destroyer of the world. The tradition of the worship of this triune deity is a very old one.[1] In front of the statue of the healer's *guru*, incense sticks keep burning next to some fruit and sweets offered by the day's visitors.

The healer sits there for hours with a smiling face, intently listening to the visitors who take their turn asking for his help in connection with whatever is bothering them at the time. Some thirty to a hundred visitors may drop in each day. Many of the visitors come with some offerings, usually fruit, sweets, and incense sticks, which are given to the healer, who puts them in front of his *guru's* statue. Generally the healer opens the pack of incense sticks, lights one or two of them, and returns the rest to the visitor who offers them. Most of the fruit and some of the sweets are returned to the person offering them, and the rest of the sweets are distributed among those present. As visitors are packed from wall to wall on the floor as well as on the cot, there is no privacy; the visitor may speak in a normal voice or whisper as she or he reveals the nature of suffering that brings her/him there. It is up to the visitor or the "client" to decide what or how much to reveal, since it may not be wise to disclose some of the personal details to the surrounding people. Needless to say, there is no place for a 'case history' or a record made of whatever sort. But despite the veil of secrecy and ambiguities of the conversation, the general nature of the topic of concern often becomes transparent, especially when it is brought to the attention of the healer for the first time. The typical problems include (a) sickness of the visitor or a family member; (b) quarrels or other interpersonal problems within family, co-workers or adversaries in a litigation; (c) students' difficulties with studies or examinations or the parents' concerns about the same; (d) concerns about finding or keeping a job; (e) marital problems such as spousal discord or childlessness; (f) loss of property from misplacing or theft; (g) court cases between business partners, renters and landlords—and the list can go on.

As the visitor sits in front of the healer, he looks straight into the eyes of the visitor. The most common response by the healer is a reassurance that things will turn out positively in the course of time. Sometimes the healer asks questions about the visitor's background if she or he is a first time visitor. It is common that, after a bit of exploration of the visitor's place of residence and some significant events in the life of the visitor, the healer speaks about some aspect of the background—the nature of the house and the place of worship therein, some major event such as death in the family and so on. Most often what he says comes out correct as indicated by the visitor's spontaneous expression of astonishment and positive remarks. A common topic of conversation concerns the visitor's religious background: which deity was commonly worshipped and in what form and so on. A common form of advice or remedial "prescription" is burning incense sticks returned by the healer with an instruction to light one each at the time of the daily prayer or on full moon nights, or some other auspicious days. In some cases, the healer suggests reading of a religious text—a "*pothī*" or a text such as the *Guru-caritra*—or performance of a *vrat*, i.e., following certain self-chosen restrictions such as fasting once a week, or performing periodic rituals as per one's commitment to oneself. The visitor is normally sent away with the offer of a sweet by way of *prasād* with a generous smile and kind words of reassurance.

Background of the healer and his *guru* revealed in their biographies

The healer. According to the biography (Sane, 1988) of the healer, Shri Ramachandra Bapuji Ambekar, was born in 1904 in a middle class family in Maharashtra. After completing his high school education, he started to work, going from one temporary job to another. Most commonly the work involved operating and maintaining machines of various sorts: boilers, engines, pumps, and so on. At one time, for instance, he worked as a driver of a road roller. He got married in his early twenties, and the couple moved from place to place wherever he would find employment. In later years he found a steady job maintaining engines and pumps in a city water supply outfit in a part of Pune city. All through the years he was interested in religious and spiritual pursuits. In his early forties one of Shri Ambekar's friends introduced him and his wife to Shri Raosaheb Sahasrabuddhe at his home in Pune. They hit off on a positive note at the first sight, and thus began a life-long relationship between the *guru* and the two disciples. Shri Raosaheb, often called Baba, or Baba Maharaj, usually spent most of his time alone, lost in deep meditation. He preferred to have tea in the afternoon, which Mrs Ambekar chose to supply every day year after year. A close association between the families provided ample opportunities for spiritual guidance for members of the Ambekar family.

At some point in time Baba asked his disciple—endearingly called Bhau (short of Rambhau)—if he would take over some of his responsibilities (*upādhi*). The obedient disciple immediately acquiesced, although the nature of the work to be done was not specified. Soon after this, Baba started sending some of his "clients" to Bhau with a piece of paper with the latter's name and address written on it. The visitors would ask for help, saying that Baba had assured them that this is where they would get answers to all their questions. Bhau had no clue as to what to do, and was initially quite upset for being placed in an awkward situation. So he went to Baba and bitterly complained about the ordeal of having to face people in difficulty; how on earth could he offer help when he had no idea what to do? Baba immediately put him at ease, saying that he could just give the visitor some holy ash (*aṅgārā* or *bhasma*), and say some soothing words. As Baba continued to send more and more of his "clients" over to him, over a period of time Bhau settled in the role of a healer. Gradually his reputation began to grow, and more and more of his time after work began to be taken up by a steady flow of relief seekers. When the heavy demands of this role started to affect family life, Bhau's wife, son and daughter forced him to limit the time for visitors to three evenings per week. This routine continued till his death in 1990.

The healer's guru. The biography of Shri Ambekar's *guru*, Shri Raosaheb alias Baba Maharaj Sahasrabuddhe, was published by one of his disciples named Deshpande (1978). It includes reminiscences of dozens of his disciples. According to the biography, Shri Sahasrabuddhe was born in a middle class family in 1883. In his late teens, while he was a student at a college of engineering, he was introduced to Ramananda Beedkar Maharaj, a well-recognized saint in the Datta Sampradāya (a tradition of devotees of the deity called Guru Dattātreya), and became his disciple.[2] After being trained as a civil engineer, he started working for the Public Works Department of the government of the Bombay province. In his early twenties Raosaheb got married and eventually became the father of a girl. He kept working diligently and successfully on the job, but began to be known for his whimsical behaviour. As he became more and more deeply involved in his spiritual quest, he started saluting not only images of gods and goddesses here and there, but kept saluting any and every human being or animal he would come across. Finding him engrossed in himself quite often, and given his odd mannerisms like saluting anybody and everybody, his family got him admitted to a mental hospital when he was in his early thirties. After being treated there for several months for a condition diagnosed as "Mental Defect Melancholia", he was discharged from the hospital. Thereafter he started getting government pension as an invalid, and spent time in deep meditation for days on. The pension amount was barely adequate to support a family of three. Gradually, the extraordinary qualities disguised under the veneer of madness began to reveal themselves, and he started attracting an increasing number of people who came for healing and advice.

The biographies of these two gentlemen throw much light on their thinking and modes of healing. More specifically, the biography of Shri Sahasrabuddhe contains reminiscences by dozens of seekers who benefited from his advice—and these provide a perspective on the principles on which his guidance was based.

The interview

I interviewed Shri Ambekar extensively when he was a bit over eighty years old. It was a semi-structured interview which went on for about three hours, and an audio recording was made. My first question was concerned with my observation that a large proportion of visitors who came to him were primarily concerned about mundane problems and that spiritual seekers seemed to be rare. He immediately corroborated this observation. He basically confirmed that most people came to him for help with the kind of mundane problems that were listed before.

The next set of questions was concerned with the common "remedies" he seemed to offer: (a) giving a few incense sticks to light, (b) a pinch of holy ashes (*bhasma*) to apply to one's forehead or to ingest with water, and (c) in some cases worship a certain deity or read some religious text (*pothī*). How could such simple activities (mostly rituals, one may say) be effective in any way? The thrust of his answer was that it is the resolve (*saṁkalpa*) for doing something to ameliorate the bothering situation, which is the key for bringing about a change. Every time a seeker lights up an incense stick, he or she is repeating that resolve, and thereby moves a step closer to relief. More specifically, one gets detached from the problem on hand for at least a moment, and gradually a sense of detachment gets stronger—and a positive cycle gets initiated. But then, I asked, how is it that he arrives at a particular kind of response to a specific visitor, or comes up with suggestion for a specific course of action? Shri Ambekar was very forthright in explaining what happens in his interaction with a visitor. He said that he intensely concentrates on what the person says, looking first straight into his eyes, then his appearance and his complaint. As he does this, his mind goes blank for a moment, and then something flashes in his mind. One day in the case of a person complaining about the disappearance of a boy in the family, for instance, the image of a boy walking on a street flashed in his mind. So he immediately affirmed that the boy was not lost, that he was walking in a place that looked something like such and such, and assured that he would be found. Such reassurance put the visitor at ease, which made a good beginning. Often he is able to describe the details of what is thus "seen"—the direction in which the boy may be going, the setting such as the time of the day, which sometimes helps in locating the missing person or thing. Quite often he is proven right. When his "visions" usually get verified, it affirms his credibility, and the visitor comes back with some degree of trust or faith.

My next set of questions was aimed at exploring his views about causal effects, if any, of burning incense or applying holy ash on one's forehead. He was very clear that there was no direct effect of such actions; what was effective, he said, was the thought behind the actions. Such acts could even help cure a physical disease, he suggested, although this would happen only when a disease was in a starting phase; it would not work in an advanced stage or in a serious condition. He affirmed that, in his view, mind would work on the body, no doubt.

The conversation then turned to the idea of God. God, he said, is an idea in our minds. What matters most, in his view, is the idea that there is some power behind everything that exists or happens in the world, and that a bit (*aṁśa*) of that power resides in each one of us. It is like the reflection of the sun in each wave of the ocean. And it is that part of the Divine to which we have to reach out. It is in this context that he mentioned *Soundaryalaharī*, a famous mystic work attributed to Ādi Śaṅkarācārya. Following that line of thinking he mentioned three means for reaching out to the Divine within us: *mantra*, *tantra* (technique), and *yantra* (instrument). *Mantra* is not just some sounds; there is a very specific *mantra* or set of sounds that is unique to a given individual, which, when chanted, would produce a desirable effect. Just any *mantra* would not do. This line of thinking could not be pursued further, but it explains part of the remedial strategy, namely the use of chanting of *mantras*.

The conversation then turned to the question: how does an individual turn to a spiritual pursuit? Shri Ambekar's reply was unequivocal; one begins with a selfish motive, whether it is the desire for money or redress of pain. It is quite common among people to have no faith in God; most people turn to praying when desperate, and that too, rather reluctantly. Often when he gives a bunch of incense sticks to a reluctant visitor, he does not prescribe lighting it daily or whatever; it is totally up to the visitor to light them if and when she or he feels like, or ignore them completely. But after a seeker starts to pray or worship, something good may happen, which prompts him to continue with the ritual. A gradual process of change for the better sets in. Most often Shri Ambekar "sees" things in or about the visitor, which are relevant to the problem he or she may be facing. Sometimes he asks for the visitor's birth date and checks the position of the stars on which she or he was born, and that, he says, gives him some clues about the person and his problems. As to his beliefs in the horoscope he says that they are based on the fact that people from the past, such as Bhṛgu and Parāśara, have recorded their mutually corroborating astrological observations at different times and places. Their mutual agreements indicate that the same kinds of things may be true in a given type of case as well. It is his observation that his horoscope-based calculations often come true, and that helps fostering a positive impression in the eyes of the visitor. Then he or she is more likely to follow the rituals as per his suggestions. The more important purpose in doing all this is to bring about a positive change in the person's attitudes and conduct (*vṛtti*). Incidentally he also mentioned that black magic (he called it *devaskī* in Marathi) can also work, but he strongly suggested that one should never turn to such things.

As the interview continued, Shri Ambekar gave several examples of individuals coming in with a great sense of distrust and disbelief in matters of worship or spirituality at the outset, but would gradually overcome their negative feelings. In the course of the conversation he incidentally mentioned the names of various individuals who came to see him often, and described conversations that took place with them. One of them was a widely respected old theosophist, a learned man reputed for free dispensing of homeopathic medicines to visitors at the local theosophical lodge. There were some college professors among frequent visitors, one of them was widely known for his studies of the saint poets of Maharashtra. The discussions with such persons were on difficult passages in texts such as the *Jñāneśwarī*. But such discussions were not common part of events in evenings when one person after another was lined up seeking redress of her or his suffering of one type or other.

Upon further exploration of his views on the nature of positive changes that were said to happen in his visitors, Shri Ambekar said that it was a slow process of overcoming suffering (*duḥkha* or *tāpa*). Some come to him initially saying they did not want to ask any questions, that there was no real purpose for their visit. Often he was able to understand the reason for their coming in spite of their silence about it. When asked how he was often able to say something relevant to the incoming person's problem without the person disclosing it, he said that he feels the vibrations in that person's presence. It was not uncommon for visitors to think that he had some kind of power for "mind reading". There were, however, some visitors who kept coming without really having any problem to solve; they would just sit there without saying anything or asking any questions because they just felt good in his presence.

As to the process of self-improvement, Shri Ambekar did not deny the need for effort (*prayatna*) on the part of the seeker. However, he was not in favour of determined and strenuous efforts such as those demanded by the pursuit of *yogic* meditation. He did not care much for the various *yogic* postures; in his view we naturally adopt a bodily posture suitable for a given activity—such as sitting down to read, or bending down to pick up an object on the floor. One should follow one's natural inclinations, rather than setting up a specific program of action with a specific image of the desired outcome. An enterprise in pursuit of a fixed goal tends to make too much of an image of the expected outcome, and one tends to run after it. It is better, rather, to just let things happen, he said, because spiritual development naturally unfolds in due course. It is important to keep working without expecting much. Listening to, or studying, good ideas, meditating upon them, and becoming singularly engrossed in them (implying the three commonly prescribed steps, namely *śravaṇa, manana*, and *nididhyāsana*) naturally follow one another. You cannot suppress them, he said.

If so, why do they not happen to everybody? That is because many people are too involved in mundane activities and gains, said Shri Ambekar. It was his observation that almost all of those who keep coming to him kept making (spiritual) progress on their own. It is common for people to try to make sure that they continue to make progress. There is no need to worry about markers and milestones along the way; after some time whether or not one is going on the right path automatically becomes clear. It is common among people to keep comparing with fellow travellers—especially fellow disciples—to see if one has become as good as, or better than, someone else. Such comparisons are impediments to progress, and should be avoided. Individuals progress at different rates; some may take a few months or four years or decades, while someone could make the same journey in a few days. Among the many people who came to see him, he thought there were some who had made good progress, up to fifty or even eighty percent of the best that could be expected.

How could we recognize whether someone is spiritually advanced, to the level of "the person of stable intellect" (*sthitaprajña*) described in the *Gītā*, for instance? The most important sign of spiritually advanced persons is that they are not attached to mundane gains and pursuits: my home, my family, my son; they do not think that they must get something or other. The word in the *Gītā* that described such a person best is non-attached (*niḥsaṅga*). It implies being innocent like a child. Often such a person is not appreciated even by members of the family. Indeed, the behaviour of a spiritually highly advanced person looks odd to many people around him. Shri Sahasrabuddhe, for instance, was widely thought of as whimsical or even mad. He was sixty-five years old by the time he was clearly understood as being a truly spiritually advanced person, which was only during the last five years of his life!

Finally, I asked him to describe in simple words what he thought he was doing for hours sitting in his room and entertaining questions from any and all who dropped in. What he was doing, he said in Marathi, was "*mānasopacār*", which in plain English means psychotherapy.

Thoughts and principles expressed in the biographies

The biography of Shri Sahasrabuddhe (Deshpande, 1978) includes a series of reminiscences of a number of individuals that indicate the nature of problems for which they sought the *guru's* help, the nature of advice they were given, and extent of relief they attained. They also contain occasional and incidental reference to concepts or principles that were heard in the course of interaction with the *guru*. Although the biography of Shri Ambekar (Sane, 1988) does not include reminiscences of his disciples, the author does occasionally refer to her *guru's* thoughts which shed light on the philosophical principles on which their lives and teachings were based. Neither of these *gurus* wrote out their own views, but it is possible to reconstruct the principles underlying their healing practices from various references in the biographies.

Shri Ambekar's biography provides some interesting information of the kind of instruction he received in his early days, which may have adequately prepared him to receive guidance from Shri Sahasrabuddhe. Thus, according to Sane (1988, p. 26), Shri Ambekar had met Shri Uplekar Maharaj earlier in his life, and the thrust of the instruction he repeatedly received was: "sit in silence and look inside, and all is obtained". This, it would appear, is quite consistent with the main teachings he received later from Shri Sahasrabuddhe. Sane's conversations with Shri Ambekar also provide pointers to the ideas that guided his behaviour. Thus, when she asked him to explain the secret of the courage with which he had faced many difficult situations in his life, and had usually come up with a prompt and correct course of action as demanded by the occasion, he explained in words that may be paraphrased as follows: "If one has firm faith in God and believes that He does everything needed to get us through, then there is no place for fear and anxiety. Then one automatically develops the attitudes of vigilance and courage needed for right action. One should focus only on the situation on the hand, and the right course of action automatically suggests itself" (Sane, 1988, p. 17). By comparison to such relatively rare gleanings, the longer biography of Shri Sahasrabuddhe provides reasonably extensive information on his thoughts and teachings.

One specific point is repeated several times and seems to indicate the central principle of Shri Sahasrabuddhe's teaching. To paraphrase it in English, it can be described as follows: "One should meditate on the effulgent nature of the Self, and enjoy or suffer as dictated by Providence" (Deshpande, 1978, pp. 37, 330)[3] When asked about what one should do, a common instruction was that one should sit in silence. Sometimes the suggestion was to sit with closed eyes, and gaze at the void in the skies. The common Marathi words he used were "*svastha rahā*" which literally means just stay in silence. As the biographer Deshpande (1978, p. 386) explains it, the word *svastha* is to be understood as *sva-stha* meaning that one should be firmly grounded in the Self, i.e., in *Ātman*, the unchanging principle underlying the continually changing images of the self. At one point, the *Ātman* was explained as the eternal propitious principle (*ātmā eva sadāśivaḥ*, p. 168); and at another point it was indicated that it was the same as the ubiquitous Divine principle (*viśvaṁ viṣṇuḥ*, p. 200). Lest the instruction is understood to mean simply sit down and do nothing, it is repeatedly emphasized that one must learn to "stand on one's own feet" and face the challenges of practical life. The need for repeated and untiring effort (*abhyāsa*) at meditating on the nature of the Self while following the guidelines given by the *guru* is suggested, and it is emphasized that no one can do this but oneself (Deshpande, 1978, p. 335). To describe this form of meditation, the traditional Sanskrit word *ātmānusandhāna*, which means focussed contemplation of the inner Self, is repeatedly used. Such usage would naturally guide a serious seeker to traditional philosophies which explain the correct ways of inquiring into the nature of the Self, particularly the philosophy of the Advaita Vedānta.

It was not Shri Sahasrabuddhe's style to teach through lectures; difficult but crucial ideas were often conveyed through incidental remarks and practical demonstrations. The biographer describes an episode in which the *guru* asked him to fetch a handful of sand from the other bank of the river where they were standing. Lacking confidence in his skill in swimming, the biographer fearfully waded through neck-deep waters, and somehow managed to bring back a fistful of sand. As he handed it over as per instruction, Shri Sahasrabuddhe described the grains of sand as imbued with the principles of *viveka* and *vairāgya* (Deshpande, 1978, p. 381). The two words he used incidentally convey important principles for a spiritual aspirant; first, the principle of *viveka*, which means wise discrimination between the real Self on the one hand, and the ego or the false sense of self on the other; and the principle of *vairāgya*, which means a deep sense of detachment in regard to worldly gains. The incidental reference to such words was enough for the adept listener to get the point; he understood what he was expected to do for his progress on the spiritual path. His fear for life while wading in deep waters would now be understood as a sign of the lack of a sense of detachment to life, for instance. He had enough background to understand the meaning of these concepts in the classical account of the path of knowledge (*jñāna mārga*) described in the Advaita Vedānta tradition of Ādi Śaṅkarācārya.

Interestingly, Deshpande narrates all this as an example of how Shri Sahasrabuddhe never communicated difficult ideas through lectures and discourses, but taught them "through experience" (*anubhava dvārā*). It is hard to say what exactly is meant by "through experience". In the example of fear experienced in wading in deep waters as an instance of learning through experience, it could also mean the need for a direct experience of the nature of the Self. The latter meaning seems to be particularly implied in the fact that he often discouraged — even derided — an overly intellectualized approach (*pāṇḍitya*). It appears from the narrative that the disciple was in the right mood to absorb the message under the circumstances and in the manner in which the words were conveyed. A clearer example of Shri Sahasrabuddhe's practical way of teaching is found in an episode described by Shri Ambekar's son Yashvant. The young Yashvant was one day revising his geometry lesson about the definition of a point. Shri Sahasrabuddhe asked him to explain the idea in his own words. The boy naturally thought of this as a question about geometry, but that was not what he meant. Then the *guru* explained that the *Brahman* is like a point. This was beyond the boy's comprehension; he was totally confused, and asked for an explanation. Then the *guru* put his finger on Yashvant's forehead right between his eyebrows and said, look here and you will see the "point". Yashvant admits in his narrative that he was too young to understand what was involved. However, a reference to a point in the middle of the forehead comes up again in the context of the biographer's conversation with his *guru*, so it deserves a mention here.

Deshpande (1978, pp. 38-39) once asked Shri Sahasrabuddhe to explain what is meant by the expression "the Divine fills up the entire world of moving and non-moving objects, and also transcends the world by a measure of ten fingers".[4] The reference is obviously to the idea that the *Brahman*, the ultimate principle reality, is supposed to be immanent throughout the world and also transcends it "by a measure of ten fingers". To help explain what this means, the *guru* measured the distance across his own ten fingers, then put the tip of his finger point at an equal distance in front of the forehead of the inquirer. As the latter focussed his attention on that point, he experienced bliss beyond description, and realized that this is the bliss implied in the definition of *Brahman* as truth (*sat*), consciousness (*cit*) and bliss (*ānanda*). This episode indicates that Sri Sahasrabuddhe had the capacity to explain difficult concepts of the Advaita philosophy by inducing a direct experience of bliss in a mature inquirer.

This brings us back to Sri Sahasrabuddhe's point that he did not care for scholarly discussion and intellectual exercises, nor did he indulge in lecturing or pontification. His emphasis was on tactfully teaching serious and eligible inquirers the techniques of a deeply personal inquiry that would lead to the direct experiences that are often expressed in terms of abstruse philosophical concepts. No amount of lecturing could be substitutes for truths that need experiential verification. The point is clearly expressed by L. R. Phadke in his reminiscences (Deshpande, 1978, pp. 262-263). He mentions that Shri Sahasrabuddhe used to occasionally ask if any of the visitors had read texts such as the *Dāsabodha* by Saint Ramdās, or the *Jñāneśvarī* by Saint Jñāneśvar. This induced Phadke and some others to start studying them carefully. As their study progressed, they started to ask many questions about subtle points which they had failed to clearly understand. When they asked the *guru* to explain, he got angry, castigating them for failing to meticulously follow his teaching and try to gain understanding of basic principles through direct experience. What is the use of mere reading, and study, he said, unless you follow up your studies through sustained critical thinking (*manana*), and become totally absorbed in contemplation (*nididhyāsana*).

The three steps of study (*śravaṇa*), critical thinking (*manana*) and deep absorption in contemplation (*nididhyāsana*) are clearly the steps toward Self-realization recommended in the *Bṛhadāraṇyaka Upaniṣad*. These steps are elaborately described and developed in the Advaita tradition. There is a quaint reference in Shri Sahasrabuddhe's biography that, while he mentioned this traditional methodology to select visitors who were ready for it, he also hinted at the possible use of other techniques. Thus, Shri Joglekar, one of the senior disciples, mentions in his reminiscences (Deshpande, 1978, p. 214) that at one point his *guru* wrote on a piece of paper the following words: *yantra, mantra,* and *tantra*. These three words were followed by the trilogy of words: *guru*, the great (*parama*) *guru*, and the ultimate (*parātpara*) *guru*. The narrator of this incidence says that these words did not immediately make any sense to him, nor does he explain the meaning in his account of the episode. But readers may recognize that Shri Ambekar had referred to the same three words *yantra, mantra,* and *tantra*, which respectively refer to the instruments, words, and techniques for Self-realization that developed within the *tāntric* tradition. Shri Ambekar mentions that these words occur in Śaṅkarācārya's *Soundaryalaharī*, a reference that suggests the inclusion in his tradition of the teachings of both the *tāntric* as well as the Advaita traditions.

Aside from such incidental mention of *tāntric* techniques, there is no specific indication that they were prominent part of the teaching imparted by either Sri Ambekar or his *guru*. In his overview toward the end of the biography Deshpande (1978, p. 374) suggests that there were two main pathways (*mārga*) to spiritual development that Shri Sahasrabuddhe asked his disciples to follow: (1) the use of chanting of particular words or a "name" (*nāmajapa*), and (2) the practice of meditation (*dhyāna yoga*). On the other hand, there was obvious emphasis on the practice of prayer, worship and other common aspects of the path of religious devotion (*bhakti yoga*). Clearly the teaching of these two *gurus* was syncretic; a combination of various elements of the major paths to spiritual development was recommended as appropriate to the temperament of the specific seeker.

Insofar as a major part of Shri Saharabuddhe's biography involves reminiscences from a number of people, it is natural that what we learn about him is based on the impressions of the followers, which they found worth reporting. A most common impression is that he seemed to always be immersed in a state of bliss. Sometimes the visitors found him lost into his inner experience, oblivious to what was happening in the surrounding. Often he had to be awakened from the trance. According to Deshpande (1978, p. 349), Shri Sahasrabuddhe constantly used to be in the Fourth State of consciousness (the *turiyā avasthā* described in the *Māṇḍūkya Upaniṣad*). While being in such a state, one becomes oblivious to one's physical condition and of the surroundings. As an example he narrates an incidence where the *guru* had been oblivious to burns caused by a cigarette butt as he slipped into a trance in the middle of a smoke. I remember how at one time Shri Ambekar told me that Shri Sahasrabuddhe often walked the fine line between a totally transcendent state on the one side, and normal wakeful state, mindful of the surroundings, on the other.[5] This account is clearly reminiscent of a reference in the *Muṇḍaka Upaniṣad* (3.1), where two birds on a self-same tree are described such that while one thinks of the sweet or sour fruit on the branches of the tree, the other merely witnesses and remains totally uninvolved. It implies that Shri Sahasrabuddhe had attained a state where a *yogi* is able to stay continuously in the Fourth State (*turiyā*) so as to sustain that experience while being in the wakeful state at the same time.

Another common impression recorded in the reminiscences was his whimsical behaviours, which many viewed as signs of madness. When asked about this, the *guru* replied that he had to feign madness to protect himself from unwanted visitors. As soon as he smelled that an undesirable type of person was entering his room, the *guru* would make some sudden remarks or put up a scene designed to drive away that person. One of the things that is repeatedly mentioned in the reminiscences is the child-like innocence manifest in the *guru's* behaviour. Aside from all this, a most significant common observation concerned the *guru's* total selflessness. He had completely overcome the more common inducements for indulgence, namely the desires for the opposite sex (*dāreṣaṇā*), for money (*vitteṣaṇā*), and for fame (*lokeṣaṇā*) (Deshpande, 1978, p. 351). That he had unlimited compassion for all kind of suffering souls is obvious from the large number of people from varied background, young and old, male and female, rich and poor, that kept coming to seek solace in his company. It was only the undesirable visitors who came to him to either poke fun at him or with some ulterior and ignoble motives that were turned away; everyone else was warmly welcomed.

The historical and cultural background

It will be useful now to turn our attention to the historical background of the Dattātreya Sampradāya, which is a spiritual and religious tradition to which belonged the two healers described above. A lot of information is available on this tradition in varied sources, including books (Dhere, 1958/1999; Rigopoulous, 1998), encyclopedia articles such as the relevant article in the *Bhāratīya Saṁskṛti Kośa* in Marathi, as well as the Wikipedia article available online. The historical roots of the tradition go back to stories of the *Purāṇas*, the "mythological" texts of medieval times, which describe the origin of Dattātreya. As noted before, Dattātreya is the name of a Hindu deity characterized by three heads representing the trinity of the Hindu gods, indicating the syncretic character of the teachings in this tradition. More specifically, this syncretic character is symbolically indicated by the story that Dattātreya learned various virtues from twenty-four different teachers collecting gems of wisdom like a honey bee collecting nectar from innumerable flowers. Small wonder that the teachings of this tradition combine elements of the major paths (*mārga*) to spiritual progress. To put it simply, their healing practices are based on principles and philosophies of several rich traditions with a long history. As such, a proper understanding of the teachings and healing techniques of these *gurus* would have to be based on the philosophies and spiritual practices of the many traditions from which they have drawn various elements.

The followers of this tradition are spread across different regions of India. In Maharashtra the tradition is traced to Śrīpāda Śrīvallabha (c. 1323-1353), and Narasimha Saraswatī (1378–1458), the two saints whose life histories are described in the popular Marathi text called the *Guru-caritra*. Narasimha Saraswatī was initiated into *saṅnyāsa* by Kṛṣṇa Sarasvatī, who was connected with the Vidyāraṇya lineage of the Shṛngeri Math. This background puts him clearly in the tradition of the Advaita Vedānta. The lineage of Śaṅkarācārya (788-820) is, in turn, historically traced back to his *guru* Govinda and his *guru* Gauḍapāda — and further back to the *Upaniṣadic* sages. Narasimha Saraswatī was known for healing a large number of people of varied backgrounds. A Muslim king (probably Allauddin II of Bedar) is said to have approached him for relief from the pain caused by a blister. Helping such persons regardless of their background is common to several saints of the Dattātreya tradition, and they are known to have attracted the following of many Muslims. Reciprocally, several Sufi saints had many Hindu followers. Narasimha Saraswatī is followed, in turn, by a long chain of teachers and disciples (*guru-śiṣya paramparā*), and the history of this chain has been published by Dhere (1958/1999). It is to this tradition that the two healers described above belong. According to Dhere (1959/1999, p. 146), Shri Sahasrabuddhe's *guru* was Shri Ramanand Beedkar (1839-1913), who in turn was a disciple of Shri Swami Samarth of Akkalkot (? -1878)[6]. Swami Samarth is a legendary figure whose long life is said be stretched back to Narasimha Saraswatī. On the whole the historical background of the tradition is quite well known. Given that a vast amount of spiritual and philosophical writings of saints and philosophers of this tradition is available, the healing practices described above can be safely placed in the "classical" as distinguished from the "folk" traditions of India.

The modern context

During the life time of the two healers described above, Shri Sahasrabuddhe and Shri Ambekar, practice of modern psychotherapy based on Western models had slowly started to take root in Pune city. By the time of writing this essay in early years of the twenty-first century, signs of clinics announcing the therapeutic practices based not only on Western models, but also of Chinese acupuncture and Japanese Reiki have sprouted in neighbourhoods not far from Shri Ambekar's residence. Given that Shri Ambekar explicitly said that he was practicing psychotherapy (*mānasopacār*), comparison of his approach with imported models naturally arises. Those who follow Western models are bound to view the traditional practices from their own vantage point. Against this background, I wish to offer an interpretation of this traditional approach in the light of principles and idiom of modern psychology.

As a student of modern psychology, and particularly its theory and history, I wish to cast my net wide, taking into consideration the long and rich intellectual histories that have shaped current practices in India and the West. As is well known, the founders of modern psychology were inspired by the success of the natural sciences, and most psychologists today silently share the world view of science. As I understand, there are certain aspects of the traditional approach to healing that do not fit the world view of science, and these misfits may immediately turn away some of our psychology colleagues in disbelief. This is true not only of many psychologists trained in the currently popular approaches to psychotherapy as described in standard texts (e.g., Fell et al., 2004; Feltham & Horton, 2000), but also others who are trained in other disciplines and have imbibed the world view of science. In the next section of this essay, therefore, I wish to consider some of the common objections that are likely to be raised against the traditional healing practice described above, so the ground is cleared for the subsequent discussion. Those who think that considering such objections is unnecessary may skip the next section and continue thereafter.

Some initial objections

Objections due to religious background. Given the strictly secular approach of modern science, the distinctly religious context of Shri Ambekar's healing practices is likely to raise the eyebrows of many. The fact that science had to establish itself in the seventeenth century Europe in the teeth of opposition by the Church, an antireligious feeling has seeped into the world view of science. Psychologists seem to be affected more specifically by this background, because the conflict between supporters of evolutionism versus advocates of "intelligent design" is raging at the same time that neurology and evolutionary psychology are getting increasingly popular among psychologists. I have personally witnessed a gut level reaction against anything connected with religion among my psychology colleagues in not only North America but also India.

To those who have such reactions, I wish to point out that disdain for religion is the result of the historical baggage of Europe, and not of India. Unlike Christianity, whose foundational beliefs were challenged by Copernicus, Galileo and Darwin, discoveries of science have not offended the doctrines or sensibilities of Hindus, Buddhists or Jains. Their religious traditions have felt no need to strictly monitor the beliefs of their followers, nor have they set up watchdogs to identify and punish heretics and apostates. By and large, the pathways to spiritual development promoted by religions of Indian origin tend to be neutral to belief systems. The world wide appeal of *Yoga* illustrates this point. Anybody wanting to practice *dhyāna yoga* or *jñāna yoga* need not renounce their creed before starting to practice. More specifically, the Dattātreya tradition to which Shri Ambekar belongs has not only been eclectic, but tolerant of diverse religious ideologies as evidenced by the large following its saints have acquired among Muslims. In this regard, the tradition is close to Sufism within the Islamic fold. Interestingly, atheists are equally welcome to practice *dhyāna*, *jñāna* or *karma yoga*; indeed, the Sāṁkhya system is itself atheistic; it has had no need to postulate any kind of God.

Do we need philosophy? Shri Ambekar's approach is clearly grounded in Indian philosophy, particularly the Advaita Vedānta, and for many psychologists today, philosophy is anathema. The fact that modern psychology had to "cut the apron strings" of the mother discipline of philosophy has led to an antiphilosophical stance among psychologists. This is not simply a matter of burden of the history of nineteenth century Europe and America; the department of experimental psychology at Pune University, for instance, had to face opposition from philosophers when it was founded in the nineteen forties. Those who take pride in empirical studies in psychology tend to think of themselves as scientists wanting to benefit humanity through their discoveries, and take a dim view of "armchair speculation" that philosophers are supposed to indulge in.

However, if philosophy is understood as providing conceptual foundations for psychology—for instance in providing a favoured solution to the "mind-body problem"—then at least some of the objections to philosophy may be removed. Another important use of philosophy is in providing thoughtful guidelines for assessing the true value of propositions based on sound principles of epistemology, or the philosophy of science.

Are old historical ideas relevant today? Aren't old insights obsolete? Psychologists who follow the natural science model often tend to think that they should try to articulate timeless laws that control behaviour; which means that there is no need to study what happened in the past. The fact that today's psychology itself is a product of the intellectual history and the contributions of the discipline's pioneers and forebears is often ignored. Psychology's ahistoric stance is, unknown to many, informed by an understanding of the nature of development of knowledge in any field proposed by Auguste Comte in early nineteenth century. Comte proposed that knowledge in any field goes through three stages: theological, philosophical, and positive or scientific, such that each subsequent stage is superior to the previous stage. He also suggested that science develops through a continuous process of refinement such that each new discovery makes earlier developments obsolete. Unwittingly following this line of thinking, students of psychology were routinely told that they should not have more than five references older than five years in their research reports. Leahey (1987) has called such attitude to history a "Whig view", and has noted its prevalence among contemporary psychologists.

This idea, that old cannot be gold, militates against the recognition of old insights that might still be relevant and of practical value. Certain *Upaniṣadic* insights are an integral part of the teachings of Shri Sahasrabuddhe. The three-step process of study, critical examination, and contemplation in search of Self-knowledge, for instance, goes back to the *Bṛhadāraṇyaka Upaniṣad*. And it is still found useful by many who have tried it out. Thus, there is no need to be gingerly anti-historical in our approach to psychology—and to methods of healing.

Are you proposing a belief in ESP? The fact that Shri Ambekar used to "see" things beyond his eyesight, that he could often recognize the unasked questions in the mind of visitors, and that he could correctly predict what lay in somebody's future, may be viewed as signs of his extra-ordinary powers—powers such as Extra-Sensory-Perception (ESP), mind-reading, and precognition. Such powers are believed to contravene laws of science, or as anomalies. As Kuhn (1970) has pointed out, the history of science has repeatedly demonstrated the tendency of scientists to routinely ignore observations that do not fit the contemporary understanding of the laws of nature. Indeed, during the past century, numerous studies in the field of parapsychology have amassed lots of empirical data suggesting the existence of paranormal phenomena, especially cognitive anomalies. Many of the studies in this field meet—even exceed—the most stringent criteria of experimental methodology. However, as K. R. Rao (2011) has pointed out, for those who are committed to the world view of science, no amount of corroborating data can convince the actuality of ESP and other such paranormal phenomena.

Looking at it from a traditional Indian standpoint, instances of ESP and particularly mind reading are commonplace. That many holy men (*sādhu puruṣ*) routinely recognize the thoughts of visitors and answer unasked questions is common knowledge. Richard Alpert, the psychologist who was fired from Harvard for his controversial experiments on LSD, has put on record his experience of this sort in his book published under his new name Ram Dass (1974). When Alpert went to see Neem Karoli Baba in the Himalayas to find out if the LSD he was carrying in his pocket could give him *Nirvāṇa*, the first thing Baba asks him was concerned with what he was carrying in his pocket—a paper bag containing LSD. For those who are familiar with the *Yoga Sūtra* of Patañjali, it should be clear that the third chapter lists a number of extra-ordinary powers that an advanced *yogi* is supposed to attain. While affirming their existence, Patañjali also warns that adepts should meticulously avoid using such powers if and when they manifest in the course of their spiritual development. This is because the use of such powers tends to inflate the possessor's ego—which is exactly opposed to the main goal of *yoga*—to overcome, and ultimately dissolve, egotism. Interestingly, as far as I remember, there was no talk about such powers (called the *siddhis*) in Shri Ambekar's presence, which indicates following the caution of such avoidance in the *Yoga Sūtra*.

Effective communication across world views would not be possible unless we are willing to set aside initial misgivings arising from misfits such as those mentioned above. A good way to proceed would be to set aside such misgivings for the time being at least, and focus instead on the fundamental principles as understood from an "insider's" perspective.

Turning to basic principles

As noted, the tradition to which Shri Sahasrabuddhe and Shri Ambekar belonged goes back to ancient times, and to understand the key concepts in their repertoire it is necessary to trace them to their original sources. Let us first look at the most crucial concept in their enterprise of healing, namely the concept of suffering, called *duḥkha* in Sanskrit, and its modern derivatives.

A most well-known work, which aims at understanding the nature of suffering and its radical removal, is the *Sāṁkhya Kārikā* of Īśvarakṛṣṇa.[7] It proposes three basic types of suffering:

1. the *ādhibhautika* type, meaning that which arises from physical causes such as pain caused by falling objects, which is left for the doctors (*bhiṣaj*) to deal with;
2. the *ādhidaivika* type, meaning that arising from haunting by ghosts and other menacing creatures, which is left to the *mantriks* (shamans) to deal with through black magic; and
3. the *adhyātmika* type, meaning that belonging to the self, which in turn is divided between two subtypes, bodily and psychological.

Shri Ambekar's mandate was, clearly, to deal with psychological suffering. According to the Sāṁkhya-Yoga and the Advaita, the systems that have arguably the greatest influence on his tradition, the main cause of psychological distress is the misconstrual of the true nature of the Self (*avidyā*). When misconstrual of the nature of the Self is accepted as basic diagnosis, appropriate therapeutic strategies seeking enlightenment follow. Small wonder, then, that in Shri Ambekar's injunction *"sva-stha rahā"* the key term is *sva*, meaning the self, and its correct meaning is to be understood in light of the philosophies of the Advaita and Sāṁkhya-Yoga.

The Advaita tradition is based on the *Upaniṣads*, where the term for the Self is *Ātman*. The *Bṛhadāraṇyaka Upaniṣad* (2.4.5) suggests an inquiry into the true nature of the Self as the most important thing to undertake in life, and proposes three steps for attaining correct Self-knowledge: "listening to", or studying, the classical teachings concerning this issue (*śravaṇa*), critically examining the implications of the teachings (*manana*), and becoming deeply absorbed in contemplation (*nididhyāsana*). It should be clear that it is precisely this method for Self-realization that Shri Sahasrabuddhe suggested to his more serious and capable disciples. In the Advaita literature (e.g., Dharmaraja, 1972) that follows the lead of the *Upaniṣads*, a more specific guideline for critical inquiry is suggested: make a wise discrimination between the permanent versus impermanent (*nitya anitya viveka*) in regard to the self. What is implied here is that the true Self (*Ātman*) is the principle of unity and sameness underlying the continually changing images of the self. Critical examination shows that the views involving identification with the body, possessions, social roles, beliefs and even highly cherished core values are open to change, and what remains unchanged is only pure consciousness.

In Patañjali's *yoga*, essentially the same theme is repeated, although the specific technique suggested there is different and a different terminology is used. According to the Sāṁkhya system, the unseemly collusion between the primordial principle of pure consciousness (*puruṣa*) and the principle of materiality (*prakṛti*) leads to a fundamental source of ignorance (*avidyā*), and the result is the genesis of innumerable individualized centres of awareness, or sentient organisms of varied sorts. Patañjali follows this line of reasoning and suggests that this basic ignorance (*avidyā*) breeds egoism (*asmitā*), likes and dislikes (*rāga, dveṣa*), and an urge to cling to life (*abhiniveśa*). These are the primary afflictions (*kleśa*) that lead to suffering (*duḥkha*). According to Patañjali, the ego identifies itself with changing thoughts that appear in and disappear from awareness in wakeful and dream states, feeling happy with the gain of likeable things and sad with their loss. Being continually thrown into alternating experiences of pleasure and pain is not taken as a sign of happiness. To escape from the frustrating repetition of the pleasure-pain cycle, bringing the flow of thoughts to a stand-still through concentrative meditation is suggested as a way out. According to Patañjali (1.3), when the flow of thoughts is brought to a stand-still, the true Self (*draṣṭā*, seer) stays into its pristine state [of bliss] (*tadā draṣṭuḥ sva-rūpe avasthānam*).

Shri Ambekar did not recommend this *yogic* strategy of concentrative meditation following a rigorous discipline of postures (*āsana*) and breathing exercises (*prāṇāyāma*). In his view, the same result can be more effortlessly achieved if one simply sits down in silence and tries to remain grounded in the Self. Let us remember now the explanation of remaining *sva-stha* given by Deshpande in his biography of Shri Sahasrabuddhe saying that here *sva* means Self, the unchanging basis of selfhood, and *stha* implying abiding in a stable state or stasis. This should make it clear that the message is essentially no different from that of Patañjali.

Interpreting the teachings in the contemporary context

We may now try to understand Shri Ambekar's teachings and healing techniques in the language and idiom of contemporary psychology.

Note first that according to the traditional teachings passed on by Shri Sahasrabuddhe and Shri Ambekar, the root cause of psychological distress is misconstrual of the true nature of the Self. Let us see how this diagnosis compares with the prominent diagnostic ideas of the West: Disobedience of God's commandments, or sin, as the main cause of suffering according to Christianity; repression of id-impulses by socially imposed restrictions as the cause of anxiety and distress according to Freud; maladaptation to the environment as the main problem of difficulties according to behaviourism; discrepancy between the real self and ideal self according to Rogers, misconception of role expectations in George Kelly's view; being other-directed or being inauthentic from the existential viewpoint. The distinctiveness of this traditional Indian approach should now be quite clear. It is but natural that different approaches to healing and psychotherapy follow from differing views of what goes wrong, and why. Since the Self is the core concept in the injunction "*sva-stha rahā*", we can start the discussion of what that means from Western psychology's viewpoint.

Self (Ātman, Puruṣa). As noted, Patañjali uses the term *draṣṭā* to designate the Self, which means the self-as-seer rather than self-as-seen. A well-known text in the Advaita tradition called the *Dṛg-dṛśya-viveka* (1931) states the same. To put it in terms of modern psychology, the Self is the self-as-subject as distinguished from the self-as-object in William James's (1890/1983) terms. James included the following in the domain of self-as-object: Material Self meaning body and possessions, Social Self meaning one's social roles and reputation, and Spiritual Self, by which he meant one's thoughts, ideas and ideals. To put it in another way, the self-as-object includes all sorts of objects, including objects of thought with which the "I" feels identified. (In this context ideas and beliefs, although intangible rather than tangible like physical objects, are "objects of thought" open to description like other objects.) If we ask someone "who are you?", the common answers she or he would give include one's name, occupation, place of residence, country and citizenship as well as thoughts, feelings, and actions with which one feels identified. What then is the self-as-subject? It implies that in us which has the experiences, the "I" which is aware as distinguished from things he is aware of. This is not very easy to explain, because the seer cannot be seen in turn. To help reach out to the centre of awareness, the Advaita system provides a guideline: find out that in us which remains changeless, in other words the principle of unity and self-sameness underlying the changing body, roles, thoughts, feelings and actions. Another word for this principle of unity and sameness is identity.

Identity. In daily life we wear many masks. In the morning I am a father who takes my son to his school, an employee during the day at work, a member of the tennis club in the evening, a buddy of my best friend with whom I have coffee in the evening, a husband when I go back home in the evening. When I go to the library and borrow a book, the clerk at the desk knows that I am the same as the one pictured on the ID card. Normally, sameness is established across time and place by the way I look, speak, and so on. Establishing one's "identity" is very important not only in ensuring that one is eligible to borrow a book or cross an international boundary, but also in proving someone's guilt or innocence in a court of law. For only the same person who did something right or wrong can be rewarded or punished for respectively his right or wrong actions. Also, we change a lot from year to year over decades of life in various ways. Although we take our different roles and many changes in our stride, it is not easy to say exactly what, if anything, accounts for our being one and the same person.

In modern psychology, Erik Erikson is most well-known for his work on identity. He defines identity, or more precisely psychosocial identity, as an "evolving configuration of roles". In his opinion, we can only develop a "sense" of identity, a sense that is forever revisable. At one point in his writing Erikson (1968) says that "there is in fact in each individual an 'I', an observing centre of awareness and of volition, which can transcend and must survive the psychosocial identity" (p. 135). The idea of "centre of awareness" comes the closest to what is meant by *Ātman* or *Puruṣa* in Indian philosophy, and that is what is meant by Shri Ambekar when he talks of *sva* in the expression *sva-stha rahā*. Interestingly, that in us which sees cannot be seen in turn. However, the sages of the Advaita and Yoga traditions insist that it is possible to reach into the source of experience—and stay there. Several techniques of meditation have been devised over the centuries, although I never saw Shri Ambekar directly teaching any such technique. An interesting technique is suggested in the writings of Sri Ramaṇa Maharshi (1879-1950), a famous sage and a contemporary of Shri Sahasrabuddhe. Here is a quotation of his words:

> To say "I am not this" or "I am that" there must be the "I". This thought is only the ego or the "I-thought". After the rising up of this "I-thought" all other thoughts arise. The "I-thought" is therefore the root-thought. If the root is pulled out all other at the same time are uprooted. Therefore seek the root "I", question yourself "Who am I"; find out its source. Then all this will vanish and the pure Self will remain ever . . . All that you need to do is to find out its origin and abide there. (*Talks with Sri Ramaṇa Maharshi*, p. 168)

Emphasis on sameness versus emphasis on change; Being vs. Becoming. The emphasis on stasis, or seeking to remain in a changeless state, is common to Shri Ambekar and Sri Ramaṇa Maharshi. They represent the continuation of the persistent theme of culture reflected in sources of the literature on the Advaita and Yoga. This stands in contrast with a dominant and persistent theme in the cultural tradition of the West. Aristotle's concept of self-actualization, for instance, suggests that there are hidden potentials in human beings even as the ability to grow into a huge tree is dormant in a tiny seed such as an acorn. Aristotle suggested that continuing to manifest one's potentials is the essence of becoming happy; a well grown and growing oak is a happy tree than a stunted one! It is presumed that the continued manifestation of hidden potentials, which implies continual accomplishment of successes of various sorts one after another, is a good thing. In modern psychology, Abraham Maslow (1970) revived the Aristotelian view of self-actualization. The examples of self-actualized persons that he presents include Eleanor Roosevelt, Albert Schweitzer and other such highly accomplished persons—or heroes. And for Maslow these individuals represent human ideals worth emulating. In a similar vein, Carl Rogers (1961) talks of "On becoming a person", implying the notion that Becoming, or continually changing for something better than before, is intrinsically desirable. Against this background, the emphasis in the Indian tradition on seeking some changeless state would seem odd, especially in current times where seeking more of everything or "endless progress" is a value promoted all over. One must keep improving one's personal worth—or bank balance—even as a country must attain greater and greater Gross National Product.

Indeed, I remember Shri Ambekar saying to me that it is important to recognize that there is no need, really, to *go* anywhere, to keep seeking something or other. "Just be", he would say. What sense does this message make? Is this not a message asking for stagnation, for remaining idle, doing nothing?

The answer to this question is easy to find if we just look at his own life. If it was true that Shri Ambekar's message were to result in idleness, he would not have been so busy. He was carrying a full time job, and looking after a family of two adult children and grandchildren, and was tirelessly facing personal problems heaped at his feet some five to six hours a day after work for three days a week. It is as if he was on an overdrive, and it looks as if his sitting in silence was the key to his working non-stop—and that in selfless service to others.

But does this therapy work, and if so, how? It may be recalled that Shri Ambekar was quite candid and modest in estimating the effectiveness of what he delivered. It is important to recognize that the primary focus of the enterprise is spirituality, and in his own estimate the proportion of people interested in spiritual pursuits is less than five per hundred. And of those, few make limited progress. What then happens to the vast majority of people who seek his help? One way of looking at this issue is to judge by the fact that few of the initial visitors keep coming; not all. Those who keep coming tend to sit in his presence primarily because they simply feel good; which is what is claimed to happen according to the tradition. To my knowledge, some of the frequent visitors say that over the years they feel that they are being guided in the right direction all along. As noted by Shri Ambekar, spiritual progress is quite slow and the rate of progress is highly variable from one individual to another.

But when seen from a modernist standpoint, the evidence of effectiveness of interventions should be measurable, and there is an increasing number of publications reporting assessment of effectiveness of therapy based on varied methods of measurement. And such effort is extended not only to many Western therapeutic techniques but also to techniques of Asian origin, like Transcendental Meditation and *vipāśana*. The possibility, relevance, and worth of application to the Dattātreya-type healing is an open question. It may be noted, however, that the demonstration of effectiveness is partly a matter of marketing, and somewhat of an American obsession, and of little relevance from the point of view of genuine spiritual progress. As Shri Ambekar indicated, to become oblivious to markers of progress is, ironically, a sign of spiritual progress. In any case, seen from the vantage point of contemporary psychology, it makes sense to suggest two aspects of Shri Ambekar's healing technique that seem to be at work: First, there could simply be a degree of relief coming from letting the steam off, a form of catharsis from having spoken out the fact that one is suffering. This may be common to all forms of help, whether speaking to a friend, or a counsellor, or a psychoanalyst for that matter. Second, it is the "unconditional positive regard" for the sufferer, which Rogerian therapy considers as a most essential aspect of effective therapy. Here it will be useful to note the assessment of spiritual healing by Sudhir Kakar (2003), a well-known psychoanalyst. "Theory of cure that makes best *psychoanalytic* sense of spiritual healing is that of Heinz Kohut," says Kakar. In his view, Kohut's approach "cures by restoring to the self the empathic responsiveness of the selfobject" (p. 662). Comparing psychoanalytical healers with spiritual healers, Kakar suggests that "[i]n their empathic identifications, analysts can perhaps never go as far as a few spiritual teachers" (p. 671). He further adds that "the chief obstacle to an analyst's empathy is his phenomenal, sensual self" (p. 673). I tend to agree with Kakar's observation about the difference in levels of empathy in healers belonging to the two different traditions. For a spiritual healer such as Shri Ambekar, overcoming the demands of the sensual self—such as those for wealth, progeny, and reputation—is a basic step on the way to attain the goal of genuine selflessness. His *guru* asked him to help people in distress only after ascertaining that he will not do it to make money. On the other hand, modern psychotherapists, whether of psychoanalytic or other persuasions, are trained to pursue a career that would help them in earning enough to afford a comfortable life style and a good reputation as a successful professional.

For a highly selfless person, who has no expectation from anybody, whether of money or any other reward, the empathy and regard for the other is most genuine, and therefore likely to be most effective. Nevertheless, the role of persons like Shri Ambekar is different from the role of a modern therapist; their roles are embedded in two different social institutions shaped by long historical development of different cultures. It would therefore be useful to examine the differing roles of healers in differing cultural contexts.

The differing roles of therapists in different institutional and cultural contexts

Three evenings a week the door of Shri Ambekar's residence used to be wide open; anybody could walk in and seek relief from her or his pressing personal distress. There was no sign announcing the place as a clinic, although sometimes he used to say that he had opened a clinic (*davākhānā*). This would appear strange coming from a person who was never enrolled in a medical college or a psychology class. Several questions might pop up regarding this, particularly when seen from a contemporary perspective where people are, and ought to be, concerned about the training and qualifications of anyone practicing as a medical or paramedical professional.

The medical context: That Shri Ambekar could think of his role similar to that of a medical professional is not strange if we look carefully at his cultural and historical background. In his commentary on Patañjali's *Yoga Sūtra* (2.15), Vyāsa views the enterprise of *Yoga* as analogous to that of medicine (*cikitsā śāstra*). Thus, Vyāsa explains, suffering (*duḥkha*) is the disease, the mistaken views of the Self is the cause of the disease, and acquiring the correct knowledge of the Self is the therapy. A similar analogy is found in the Advaita literature about its enterprise. Small wonder, then, that Shri Ambekar was well aware of the role of a therapist that was bestowed upon him in the Dattātreya tradition which combined the elements of the systems of Yoga and Advaita. Yet, clearly, this role does not fit the prevailing model, where a medical or paramedical practitioner must be a duly trained and licensed professional.

Surely Shri Ambekar was not a "professional" therapist. He derived his mandate from the Indian tradition, which is very different from that of the West in some respects. Indeed, there is no simple, single name to his role as a healer. It is a common practice in India, however, that some enlightened persons keep helping and guiding people. Sometimes such people earn the informal titles like "*Bābā*" or "*Mahārāj*"—just as Shri Sahasrabuddhe did. I never heard Shri Ambekar being referred that way. Sometimes people who gather around such persons are supposed to be having "*satsaṅga*", which literally means being in the company of a good man—a sage or a saint. But unlike in the West, especially in the Catholic Church, where a person has to be "canonized" as a saint, i.e., officially recognized as having performed miracles, in the Indian tradition there is no such formality of an endorsement of sainthood. Sometimes saintly persons are recognized as "*gurus*"; and of course Dattātreya is the quintessential *guru*. The role of a *guru*, too, is not a matter of being certified or "ordained"; some wise and kindred soul becomes recognized by others for his wisdom, and they seek his advice. The role of a *guru* is sometimes compared with that of a therapist (Neki, 1973). Where does Shri Ambekar fit in this cultural context?

It should be clear that in case of Shri Ambekar, his role as a healer was not what he had sought, nor was he self-appointed in a helping role. As noted, he was "drafted", so to speak, by his *guru* to start helping people. It is Shri Sahasrabuddhe who started sending distressed people to him. There was apparently no training provided to be a healer. This route toward becoming a healer is radically different from the way modern therapists get trained and certified. Insofar as therapists trained in the Western style practice side-by-side with traditional healers like Shri Ambekar, a comparison between them would help in understanding the challenges ahead for both the modern and traditional types of healers.

Tradition and professionalization. A careful look at the professionalization of medicine in the West would indicate that the concept of the regulation of practices of professions like medicine, law, engineering and so on is not that old. The story goes that the work of doctors used to be regulated by the European monarchs till the time of the French revolution in the late eighteenth century. When the revolutionaries replaced the monarch, they were at a loss to know how to deal with issues concerning professional practice, such as dealing with complaints of malpractice. So they assigned the task to the associations of professionals to collectively regulate their affairs. Now in countries around the world there are "Colleges" of doctors, lawyers and engineers which collectively regulate their affairs.

Feltham and Horton's (2000) Handbook of counselling and psychotherapy provides an excellent discussion of the problems in the professionalization of counsellors and psychotherapists in the Western world today. The main issue is accountability. The public, or particularly the clientele who pays for the services of the professional doctors, therapists, lawyers or engineers, deserve to be protected from ill-trained, incompetent, or irresponsible professionals. It is for this purpose that the College or association of professionals perform the important task of ensuring that training provided at universities or training institutes is of high quality; that training programs and their products are respectively accredited and certified to practice; that ethical guidelines for proper conduct as professionals are laid down; and that committees are set up to hear complaints against errant members and disciplined in case of proven guilty. Most governments legitimize the functioning of the professional associations and bestow on the Colleges the authority to fine recalcitrant members or cancel their privilege to practice.

It is clear that in India today there is a crying need to form a credible and legally approved association of professional counsellors and psychotherapists. There is a common complaint that individuals without adequate training call themselves counsellors or psychotherapists without the need for certification, and the danger of abuse exists. It is well known that the government has been approached for support in this regard, but such efforts have not yet been successful.

Now we may ask: what about similar regulation of traditional healers? The field of traditional healers is wide open in India. There are spiritual and religious *gurus*, there are shamans, and many folk practitioners: masseurs, curers of snake bites, many who pedal folk remedies (called *vaidus* in Marathi) for diabetes, jaundice and so on, who are not formally trained as are Āyurvedic *vaidyas*. Many astrologers in fact do psychological counselling, and this has been well recognized by some anthropologists (see Pugh, 1984), but rarely by psychologists. For want of professionalization, the situation is "buyer beware; go at your own risk". There has been no shortage of abuse at the hands of charlatans plying in the name of religion and even spirituality. Scandals about so-called *sadhus* break out in the news now and then. Against this background, it is useful to recognize the distinctive authenticity of healers of the Dattātreya tradition described here.

In my opinion, the key issue is charging money for service rendered. Modern counsellors and psychotherapists are—or rather should be—certified professionals who pursue a career and legitimately charge fees for their services just as lawyers, engineers and architects do. There are of course self-proclaimed *gurus* who charge fees for giving *mantras* to seekers and there are so-called *gurus* who own fleets of expensive cars and live in five star mansions. This is because many people do not recognize that spirituality is not a consumable open for sale. There is an unwritten rule, a convention in traditional spiritual circles, which asks us to beware of *yogis* who claim to have special powers and offer to use them for your (or rather their own) benefit. It must be emphasized that Shri Ambekar did not charge any fees, or expect any returns in kind. Indeed, it is not only the classical healers like him who refused to charge fees in cash or kind; even many folk practitioners worked on the principle of no fees. Puneites may remember a family of masseurs who rendered their fees as a matter of their family obligation (*kulācār*); I know of one of them who used to get very angry if any client would dare to offer him money. It was a common practice for expert healers to teach their techniques only to those who would take a vow not to charge any fees. Some of them were told that the efficacy of their cure would vanish in case the no-fee rule is violated. Whether that was true or not, it is clear that in the Indian culture, this was a way in which attempt was made to instil an ethical code for healers.

But who could, in these days of stark commercialism and high cost of living, afford to provide services for no charge? Why did persons like Shri Ambekar provide selfless service at high cost to themselves and their family members? The answer is that Self-realized persons totally overcome their egos; for them there is no lure of wealth (*vitteṣaṇā*), progeny (*putreṣaṇā*), or fame (*lokeṣaṇā*). Having discovered an unending source of bliss in their inner Self, and having shed their narrow egos, such persons behave in a totally selfless manner. Genuine selflessness becomes manifest in Self-realized persons, and people start coming to them for advice and healing. For such kindred souls, regulations are unnecessary and professionalization is irrelevant.

Where do we go from here?

There are implications here for psychologists. For too long training in psychology is restricted to imported textbooks and models. It is high time that we realise that psychological theories and practices, including therapeutic, developed in the Indian tradition exist, and are providing benefits to countless individuals. Various techniques of meditation devised in Asian traditions have already begun to be incorporated by Western psychologists in their clinical practice. If we do not decolonize our minds, and erase the continuing shadow of Macaulay in our thinking, we may import Indian insights with a "Made in the USA" stamp.

Endnotes

1 A brief account of the Dattātreya tradition of *gurus* and their disciples is available on the Wikipedia online.

2 A biographical note of Shri Beedkar is available on the Internet; just google the name.

3 The words he used in Marathi were *"ātmatejāce dhyān karaṇe, va dehaprārabdha bhogaṇe"*.

4 The words between inverted commas are a paraphrase of the original Marathi words *"sthirācara vayāpuni to paramātmā daśāṅguḷe uralā"* or its Sanskrit equivalent *"atyatiṣṭhat daśāṅgulam"*.

5 The Marathi expression he used was: *"ek pāy nirguṇāt, ek pāy saguṇāt"*. This can be paraphrased to mean that he was simultaneously experiencing a transcendental state on the one hand, as well as a normal wakeful state of consciousness on the other.

6 The reason for the question mark in regard to the birth date here is that Shri Swami Samarth of Akkalkot was a legendary figure who is said to have been a contemporary of Narasimha Saraswatī (1378–1458), meaning that his life extended over some four centuries or more. Simply put, his background is shrouded in mystery, and his date of birth remains unknown.

7 For the original Sanskrit text of the *Sāṁkhya Kārikā* see the Nirṇaya Sāgar edition of 1940, and for an English translation see Larson, 1969.

References

Deshpande, S. R. (1978). *Śrīsadguru Raosāheb tathā Bābāmahārāj Sahasrabuddhe yāṅce caritra*. Pune: Vāsudevānandasarasvatī Caritraprakāshan Samiti.

Dharmaraja Adhvarindra. (1972). *Vedānta paribhāṣā* (S. Madhavananda, Ed.). Howrah: Ramakrishna Mission Saradapitha.

Dhere, R. C. (1999). *Datta sampradāyācā itihās* (Rev. ed.). Pune: Padmagandha Prakashan. (First edition published 1958).

Dṛg-dṛśya viveka. (1931). (S. Nikhilananda. Ed. & Trans.). Mysore: Sri Ramakrishna Asrama.

Erikson, E. H. (1968). *Identity, youth and crisis*. New York: W.W. Norton.

Fell, K. A., Holden, J. M., & Marquis, A. (2004). *Theoretical models of counselling and psychotherapy*. New York: Brunner-Routledge.

Feltham, C., & Horton, I. (Eds.) (2000). *Handbook of counselling and psychotherapy*. Thousand Oaks, CA: Sage.

James, W. (1983). *Principles of psychology*. Cambridge, MA: Harvard University Press. (First published 1890).

Kakar, S. (1982). *Shamans, mystics, and doctors: A psychological inquiry into India and its healing traditions*. New York: Knopf.

Kakar, S. (2003). Psychoanalysis and Eastern spiritual healing traditions. *Journal of Analytical Psychology, 48*, 659-678.

Kakar, S. (2008). *Mad and divine: Spirit and psyche in modern world*. New Delhi: Penguin Books, India.

Kuhn, T. (1970). *The structure of scientific revolutions* (2nd ed.). Chicago: University of Chicago Press.

Lasron, G. J. (1969). *Classical Sāṁkhya: An interpretation of its history and meaning*. Delhi: Motilal Banarsidass.

Leahey, T. H. (1987). *A history of psychology: Main currents of psychological thought*. Englehood Cliff, NJ: Prentice-Hall.

Maslow, A. (1970). *Motivation and personality* (2nd ed.). New York: Harper & Row.

Neki, J. S. (1973). Guru-chela relationship: The possibility of a therapeutic paradigm. *American Journal of Orthopsychiatry, 43*, 755-766.

Pugh, J. F. (1984). Concepts of person and situation in North Indian counselling: The case of astrology. *Contributions to Asian Studies, 18*, 85-105.

Ram, D. (1974). *The only dance there is*. Talks given at the Menninger Foundation, Topeka, Kansas, 1970, and at Spring Grove Hospital, Spring Grove, Maryland, 1972. Garden City, N.Y: Anchor Press.

Rao, K. R. (2011). *Cognitive anomalies, consciousness, and yoga*. New Delhi: Centre for Studies in Civilizations.

Rigopoulos, A. (1998). *Dattātreya: The immortal guru, yogin, and avatāra: A study of the transformative and inclusive character of a multi-faceted Hindu deity*. Albany: State University of New York Press.

Rogers, C. R. (1961). *On becoming a person*. Boston: Houghton Mifflin.

Sane, M. (1988). *Shri Bhausaheb Ambekar*. Pune: Santakrupa Prakashan.

Sāṅkhya Kārikā of Mahāmuni Śri Īśvarakṛṣṇa. (Pandit Sivanarayana Sastri, Ed.). (1940). Bombay: Nirṇaya Sāgar Press.

Talks with Sri Ramana Maharshi. (1955). Tiruvannamalai: Ramanasramam.

16

Concept and scope of *pratyāhāra* in management of mental health

K. M. Tripathi

The last five decades have seen a growing body of research in the areas of mental health and stress disorders on the one hand, and in the potential and promise of *yogic* practices in bringing about positive neuro-physiological and psychological changes on the other. A large number of medical reports showing the efficacy of *yogic* practices in the management of psycho-physiological problems have been published in a variety of journals. As far as the utility of *yogic* practices in managing mental problems are concerned, they are usually applied as an adjunct to other psychotherapeutic systems, or as part of psychosomatic rehabilitation and relaxation training.

The system of *yoga* can be conceptualized as one of self-healing. Following the technical definition of *yoga*, derived from Patañjali's *Yoga-Sūtras*, one could consider *vipāssanā*, transcendental meditation, and *śavāsana* as techniques of *pratyāhāra*, the control of the senses. Through *pratyāhāra*, one can attain complete isolation from both internal and external stimuli. Thus, the practice of *pratyāhāra* can help in managing the stresses of personal life and in regaining composure. *Pratyāhāra* has been described differently by different schools of thought. The *aṣṭāṅga yoga* view, the early and later *Upaniṣadic* view, and the Jain and Buddhist views are described below:

Pratyāhāra in *aṣṭāṅga yoga*

In the *aṣṭāṅga* or Eight Limb *yoga* of Patañjali, there are eight elements:

1. *Yama* (moral instructions)
2. *Niyama* (self-purification)
3. *Āsana* (posture)
4. *Prāṇāyāma* (rhythmic breath control)
5. *Pratyāhāra* (sense withdrawal)
6. *Dhāraṇā* (concentration)
7. *Dhyāna* (meditation)
8. *Samādhi* (higher unitive consciousness)

These eight limbs have been divided into two categories, viz., *bahiraṅga yoga* (exterior *yoga*) and *antaraṅga yoga* (interior *yoga*). Since *antaraṅga yoga* leads to meditation and transcendence as well as to the higher spiritual levels, it occupies a focal place in *aṣṭāṅga yoga*. The process of *antaraṅga yoga* begins with a perception, reflection or query, which finally leads to a momentary or prolonged state of transcendence. The whole course of *antaraṅga yoga* is a cognitive *yogic* practice, and not merely physical exercise as popularly perceived. The cognitive or psychological part of the eight-limb approach of *yoga* begins with *pratyāhāra*, which occupies a special conjunctive place between *bahiraṅga* and *antaraṅga yoga*. Thus, *pratyāhāra* can be seen as the entry point from *bahiraṅga* into *antaraṅga yoga*. In fact, without a proper comprehension of the concept, components, practice and application of *pratyāhāra*, further psychic upliftment in *yoga* is not possible.

The term *pratyāhāra* consists of three Sanskrit parts, viz., *prati* (in response to, obverse, opposed to, against), *ā* (near, towards) and *hṛ* (to bring back properly), and thus it literally means 'the act of collection' or 'to step back purposely in order to attain the right mode of consciousness in a more powerful way'. According to Patañjali,

> The state of physical cutting-off of contact between the sense organs and their respective objects, i.e., the reflections of the sensory world in the mind, is called *pratyāhāra*. Regular practice of *pratyāhāra* leads to attainment of greater control over the senses and the functioning of the organismic system, and gradually the ability of complete attention and concentration is achieved (*Yoga Sūtra*, 2.54–56).

Here, the term *indriya* (translated as senses), used by Patañjali in reference to *pratyāhāra*, should be comprehended within a wider perspective, as all the mental processes and components that intervene in the interaction between consciousness and the material world. All these mental processes or components are subject to the practice of *pratyāhāra*. Thus, the entire process of *antaraṅga yoga* seems to be a continuum of *pratyāhāra* that initially starts with cutting off the interaction of the external sense organs with their respective objects, followed by disconnecting the *manas*, that is, sense-mind, from the senses. Further, at a more advanced level the *buddhi* (intellect), the discriminatory element of the mind, is detached from the mind, and finally the *ātman*, the real Self, is isolated from all mental impacts. Patañjali provides only a very brief account of *pratyāhāra* in the *Yoga-Sūtras*. In the later *Upaniṣadic* literature, the concept and methodology of *pratyāhāra* is duly developed into a more technical and applicable procedure. In modern times it has emerged as a powerful technique for mental health management, working through the modification of the mind-matter interaction.

Pratyāhāra in the *Upaniṣadic* scriptures

Pratyāhāra *in the early* Upaniṣadic *literature*

Pratyāhāra as a process and a continuum leading to self-realization is lucidly depicted in the *Taittirīyopaniṣad*, one of the earlier *Upaniṣads* (chapter 3, *Bhrigu Valli*), as the progressive experience of the five sheaths of the true Self, viz., corporeal (physical), biological (vital), psychological (mental), gnostic (supramental) and the beatific (spiritual). In its second chapter, the *Bhagavad Gītā* emphasizes the need for and importance of controlling the fickleness of mental activities (*Bhagavad Gītā*, 2.58–62, 67–68). While advocating the state of withdrawal from the senses inwards, the *Gītā* asserts that the one who is able to withdraw the senses from their corresponding objects, like a tortoise withdraws his limbs within the shell, finally attains perfection of the intellect (*Bhagavad Gītā*, 2.58).

Pratyāhāra *in the later* Upaniṣadic *literature*

Described below are the conceptualizations, rationale, techniques and outcomes of *pratyāhāra* as proposed in the later *Upaniṣadic* literature, composed between the 9th to the 13th centuries AD:

- *Pratyāhāra* is the introverted state of mind (*Triśikhā-Brāhmaṇa Upaniṣad*, 30).
- Detachment of senses from their respective objects, finally leading to a restrained state of mind, is called *pratyāhāra* (*Maṇḍala-Brāhmaṇa Upaniṣad*, 1.7; *Yoga Cūḍāmaṇi Upaniṣad*, 120; *Darśana Upaniṣad*, 7.1; *Yoga-Tattva Upaniṣad*, 68).
- *Pratyāhāra* is the pleasant state of consciousness that observes the mind preoccupied with the impacts of objects of senses, and requires repeated and sustained practice (*Tejobindūpaniṣad*, 34).
- The same notion is depicted in the *Amṛtanādopaniṣad* (*Pratyāhāra-lakṣaṇam*, 5) with greater clarity. It says that *pratyāhāra* is the practice of realizing that the five senses and their respective sensory objects are the sources of agitation in the mind and consciousness, and it finally deems them as the extension and emanation of the serene Self, just as the divergent beams of the static sun give rise to different colours, shades and forms.

In the *Śāṇḍilya Upaniṣad* (1.17.1: a *pañcavidha pratyāhāra*) and the *Darśanopaniṣad*, five different kinds of *pratyāhāra* are described as follows:

- Forcible withdrawal of the sense organs from the objects of sensual pleasure with which they interact.
- Looking upon everything one sees as the *ātman*, the true Self.
- Giving up the desire to attain the fruits of one's actions and observances, performed as part of daily living.
- Turning one's attention away from all material things and thoughts.
- Projection of *prāṇic* (vital) energy and mind on the 18 vital regions of one's body (*marmasthānas*) by shifting attention from one point to another in a prescribed, sequential ascending and descending order.

Thus, as per the description of *pratyāhāra* available in the later *Upaniṣads*, the popular practices of *yoga-nidrā*, *yoni-mudrā* and *śavāsana*, as well as certain other kinds of meditation practices, are actually different kinds of *pratyāhāra*. These are described in a subsequent section of this chapter.

Role of Jainism and Buddhism in evolving technical and practical strategies

Gautama Buddha evolved a technique of meditation based on certain aspects of respiration and supported by the practice of certain observances, and called it *vipāssanā*. It was widely advocated for modifying one's state of mind as well as for uplifting one's level of consciousness. Presently, it is a widely used technique of meditation, and has shown positive clinical results. Another technique of meditation, prescribed by the *Yoga-Vāsiṣṭha* (10th–12th century AD) and known as *anapana-śati*, also leads to positive and psychotherapeutic effects. The later Jain literature lucidly elaborated a similar and allied process which focused on related problems, and which evolved into the practice called *prekṣā*. The *prekṣā* method (Mahaprajna, 1980; Mishra, 2003–2004) has been found to be a very powerful and effective technique for controlling one's internal functioning, for restraining the five senses, and for getting rid of mental afflictions (Muni Nathamala, 1970). On the basis of the description found in Jain literature and the later *Upaniṣads*, many fruitful techniques modified to suit specific needs can be derived. *Vipāssanā* and *prekṣā* are described in some detail in a later section of this chapter.

Pratyāhāra: Contemporary issues

In recent years, through integrating the *shamanic* and *Upaniṣadic* views, Sri Yogendra and his disciples have made a remarkable contribution towards understanding and conceptualizing the applicable aspects of *pratyāhāra*. Yogendra (1997) defines *pratyāhāra* as 'deconditioning the mind' from its customary activity toward internalization. *Pratyāhāra* serves as a bridge between the control of the external senses through the first four stages of *aṣṭāṅga yoga* and control of the internal senses through the last three stages, viz., *dhāraṇā*, *dhyāna* and *samādhi*. It is an exclusive practice of *yoga* 'to discover one's inner self and experience subtler thoughts and feelings'. Sequeira (1997) emphasizes that *pratyāhāra* is the practice of turning one's sensory orientations inwards, for introspection and for the analysis and re-analysis of one's reflections. After reflection, one is able to prioritize one's needs in order to set one's priorities right and curb the wilful nature of the senses. *Pratyāhāra* is sense-control leading to self-control. It is one's sensations, perceptions, notions, imagination, and other mental activities that become the subject matter of study when the mind turns inwards for introspection. Introspection helps to regulate and modulate these mental activities by understanding their nature and field of operation, and is a means of redirecting their energy. Perfection in *pratyāhāra* confers a deep mental relaxation. The basic procedure begins with attaining a state of physical relaxation (by assuming a relaxed posture) followed by mental relaxation (through *pratyāhāra*), leading to the relaxation of the vital (*prāṇic* relaxation). The greater the relaxation of the body and mind, the greater the ability to communicate with one's internal aspects. In recent years, the term *pratyāhāra* has come to be used to refer to the process of roping in/reining/withdrawing/manoeuvring/marshalling the jumble of thoughts and feelings which tumble about on the screen of the mind in a disorganized and disoriented fashion (Modi, 1997). The process leading to *pratyāhāra* requires one to pay attention to one's thoughts and day-to-day actions, watch the sensory inputs, reactions and behaviour, and observe their interplay. It allows for intelligent and insightful decisions based on observation, and this helps in honing the *buddhi* (intellect). It makes one vigilant against disturbing thoughts, feelings and actions.

Application models for *pratyāhāra*

To facilitate a better understanding of the process and role of *pratyāhāra*, three models are described below:

1. **Children's classroom model** (Modi, 1997): The disorderly crowding of thoughts, emotions and images in the mind when one begins meditation can be compared to a class of mischievous children who have been asked to move out of the room in an orderly queue. Just as a class monitor tries to bring about order and organization in a classroom, *pratyāhāra* is an important preparatory step in the practice of meditation, to bring about order and organization in mental activities.
2. **Recess-time announcement model:** This model proposes a comparison between the scattered romping of boys in the playground during recess time and the swarm of ideas, feelings, images, reactions and thoughts in the mind during meditation. In the case of schoolboys, if an important announcement has to be made, order needs to be restored; similarly, one needs to bring about order in the mind during meditation. To establish order in the playground, a special bell might be rung, the boys might be asked to stand in lines according to the classes they belong to or in increasing order of height; similarly, a step-by-step method needs to be followed to calm the mind.
3. **WRIDASM model for *pratyāhāra***: *Pratyāhāra* involves many psychological techniques, which can be represented by the acronym WRIDASM. The letters in the acronym stand for the following psychological processes:

W Withdrawing the senses followed by witnessing of reflections.
R Rallying and regulation of reflections.
I Introverting attention and introspection of mental activity.
D Detachment of senses from their objects and deconditioning of the mind.
A Attempting abstraction.
S Sensory control leading to internal seeing.
M Manoeuvring and marshalling.

Popular techniques of *pratyāhāra*

In this section, seven popular techniques of *pratyāhāra* are outlined.

Upaniṣadic *technique of* pratyāhāra

The *Kṣurikopaniṣad* (6–10), one of the later *Upaniṣads*, prescribes that an aspirant of *yoga* should bring the senses under control and make his mind and *prāṇa* steady and strong (in the region of the heart) by using the thumb, aided by the little finger and the ring finger, and fixing their tips on the root of the thumb. He should then fix his eye and mind on the different sense organs and the limbs. Finally, the mind and the *prāṇic* (vital) force should be channelized to the *suṣumnā nāḍi*. (The *suṣumnā nāḍi*, *iḍā nāḍi* and *piṅglā nāḍi* are the three channels of *prāṇic* energy flow in the 'subtle body' as described in the *yoga* system, and are referred to as the central, left and right channels respectively.) One shifts one's attention and fixes it in the great support of the heart, shining like a blood-red lotus of *anāhata*. Breaking through that lotus, the attention should reach the throat or *viśuddhi*. Then it should be fixed in the middle of the eyebrows on *ājñā* and finally in the *sahasrāra* at the top of the head (*anāhata, viśuddhi, ājñā* and *sahasrāra* are four of the seven *cakras*, the critical *yogic* points in the *suṣumnā*).

Yonimudrā

Yonimudrā is an important traditional *haṭha-yogic* technique, which forms a continuum with *pratyāhāra*. It starts with the ordinary consciousness but finally reaches a higher, transcendental state (*Dhyānabindūpaniṣad*, 86; *Yoga-Cūḍāmaṇi Upaniṣad*, 59). In the simpler form of *yonimudrā*, after assuming a meditative posture the eyes are closed by the index fingers pressing the eyeballs; similarly, the ears are closed by the thumbs and the nostrils are pressed by the middle fingers. The ring and little fingers are placed above and below the lips respectively. *Yoga* experts prescribe a varied degree of pressure on the respective parts of the face: pressure on the ears 100 per cent; pressure on the eyes 50 per cent; pressure on the nose 25 per cent; pressure above and below the lips 10 per cent.

For the purpose of *pratyāhāra*, *yonimudrā* as proposed by Yogendra (1997) involves strong imagery-building techniques. A beginner in the practice of *yonimudrā* is advised to concentrate on the area of the forehead and build images. The images consist of happenings in the sky, such as the scene of dawn followed by sunrise, the diffusion of sunbeams, the scene of sunset followed by the panorama of dusk, followed by twinkling stars scattered in the whole area of the forehead. The meditator then has to imagine the gradual rising of the moon followed by the gradually increasing and gentle darkness. *Yonimudrā* techniques range from those for beginners to those suited for advanced practitioners.

Yoga-nidrā

Certain references to *yoga-nidrā* can be found in the later *Upaniṣadic* literature (*Śāṇḍilya-Upaniṣad*, 1.17.1), but in modern times the technique of *yoga-nidrā* has been developed and propagated by Swami Satyanandaji (1976), the founder of the Bihar School of Yoga, Munger. The term *yoga-nidrā* means *yogic* sleep. Although the technique of *yoga-nidrā* was developed by the Bihar School of Yoga, it contains a good amount of *tāntric* components and has hypnotic effects. Research pertaining to the medical efficacy and the physiological and psychological effects of *yoga-nidrā* has brought to light many positive findings, which have been reported in prestigious journals. The component of resolve (not to be confused with will-power) plays a significant role in *yoga-nidrā*. A wide range of techniques of *yoga-nidrā* have been developed to suit different needs, and it is very popular.

Vipāssanā

The Buddhist tradition uses the term *vipāssanā*. It is derived from the Sanskrit term '*vipaśyana*', consisting of two terms '*vi*' + '*paśyana*', which mean 'special visioning'. The special feature of *vipāssanā* is profound concentration on different aspects of respiration, which leads to the regulation of subtle internal physiological and mental processes directly or indirectly associated with the process of respiration. The variations in respiration are linked with various affective states and related autonomic functioning. It is difficult to exercise control over one's affective states and their related autonomic functioning, but it can be achieved, albeit indirectly, by conscious control over one's breathing. This control over affective states and autonomic functioning, and consequently the ability to calm one's mind, leads to a blissful state, followed by the attainment of higher stages of consciousness.

Prekṣā

The technique of *prekṣā* was propounded by Acharya Tulsi, a renowned Jain spiritual leader and social reformer, on the basis of ancient Jain literature, and has been further propagated by his disciple Acharya Mahaprajña. The term *prekṣā* means to observe and experience the internal psychic and vital functions in order to regulate them. *Prekṣā* is quite similar to the Western bio-feedback technique, the difference being that bio-feedback is carried out with the help of certain gadgets, while *prekṣā* is done with the help of individual consciousness and will-power. An effort is made to feel and observe internal physiological and biochemical changes and the faculty of resolve is used to regulate them. Jainism does not place much importance on rigorous breathing exercises. Like *yonimudra*, *prekṣā* also has a range of techniques for both beginners and advanced practitioners.

Śavāsana

Śavāsana is a classic Indian *yogic* technique prescribed for psycho-physiological relaxation. The word *śavāsana* is a combination of two words, *śava* and *āsana*, which means the dead-body posture. The description of *śavāsana* may be found in classical *haṭhayoga*

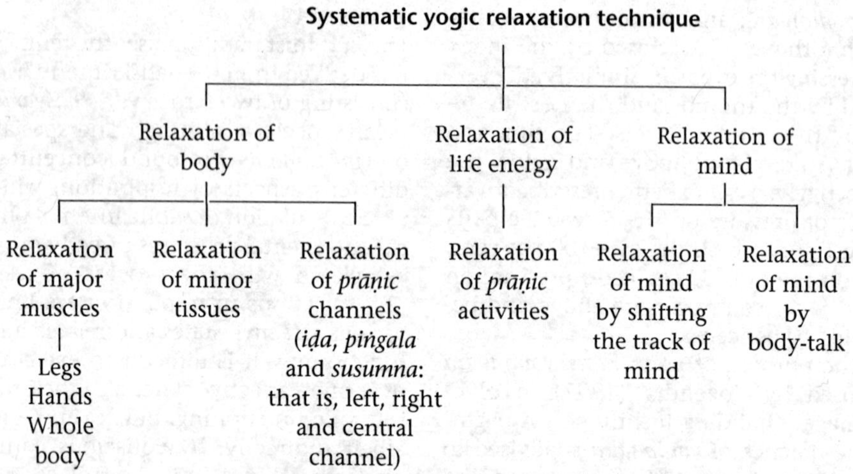

- Start relaxation of major muscles by creating tension in the muscles.
- Sustain the tension in the muscles while holding the breath.
- Release the tension in the muscles while exhaling by jolting the limbs.
- Followed by relaxation of minor tissues by shaking feet, waist, shoulders, hands and head respectively.
- Relaxation of *prāṇic* channels by shaking the limbs 10–12 times in the following order: left leg; right leg; both legs; left hand; right hand; both hands; head.

Figure 16.1. *Kramika śavāsana* (corpse pose)
Source: Tripathi, 1987

literature with varied nomenclature (*Haṭha Pradīpika*, 1.32; *Gheranda Saṃhitā*, 2.4, 2.19), but is mainly depicted as *śavāsana* (corpse pose) or *mṛtāsana* (dead pose). The classical *haṭhayoga* literature does not provide detailed instructions on how to use this technique, which may be due to the fact that the instructions vary, depending upon the teacher and the requirement of the learner. The techniques of *śavāsana* have been developed by health scientists in contemporary times to address the problems of psychosomatic illness. A noteworthy three-stage clinical technique for *śavāsana* has been developed by Datey and Bhagat (1975) and Datey et al. (1969). The first stage of Datey's technique is to lie down flat in a relaxed and comfortable posture. In the second stage, breathing should be unusually deep and long, and one should concentrate on the abdominal movements. In the third and last stage, Datey suggests concentrating on the coolness of inhalation and the warmth of exhalation. In this *śavāsana* technique, a relaxed posture is not sufficient. As the meaning of *śavāsana* is a dead body-like posture, one's body should be, as far as possible, tensionless at the muscular level, passive at the vital (*prāṇic*) level, and relaxed at the mental level.

Another technique of *śavāsana* has been developed by Tripathi and Singh (1984) in the Manasa-Roga and Rasayana Clinic, I.M.S. Banaras Hindu University. In this technique, effort has been made to enhance the psychological efficacy of *śavāsana*. The technique has been developed in such a manner that it not only follows the traditional *yogic* criteria, but also incorporates the fruitful components of other techniques, so as to emerge as an effective, scientific relaxation technique. The description of this technique is given in Figure 16.1.

Three of the most important exercises are as follows:

Relaxation of prāṇic *activity by simple contemplation on breathing*

This technique helps to lower the rate of metabolism, calm the mind and promote 'body-talk' (awareness) to enhance the influence on internal activities.

Procedure: One should lie down in a relaxed manner, like a dead body that has no control over its limbs. After lying down comfortably in *śavāsana*, attention should be turned to the immediate environment. An effort should be made to decipher the tactile sensations, smells and sounds present in the immediate environment. The next step is to expand the circle of attention to the outward environment in all directions simultaneously. At first, the clear sounds originating from the most distant places should be attended to, followed by an attempt to attend to the minute sounds of the immediate environment. The next step is to move the attention inwards and observe the sensation of the breathing pattern. The breathing pattern should be observed in the following manner:

- It should be kept in mind that the duration and amount of air inhaled and exhaled must be equal.
- A soundless and effortless pattern of breathing is adopted, but the breathing is deep and prolonged.
- The effects of inhalation and exhalation are observed, that is, the depth of inhalation is observed at the neck/throat region, at the umbilicus and below the navel. If possible, the pressure (intensity) of the exhalation is measured in centimeters outside the nostrils.
- The physiological and psychological functions occurring during inhalation and exhalation are observed.
- One inhalation followed by one exhalation completes one respiration cycle. It has been found that as the observation of respiration progresses, it becomes lighter, minute and subtle, till it becomes negligible.

Relaxation of mind by shifting the track of mental activities

This stage involves imagining the soul leaving the body. In this exercise, one visualizes the body lying on the ground. Then one visualizes the place around the body and shifts attention to the areas beyond the body. Then one has to imagine the soul gradually levitating and simultaneously expanding in size, which will finally lead to an expansion in the area of vision. One imagines and visualizes the sight of the city, then the outskirts of the city, thereafter the whole region, the whole state, the whole country, the subcontinent, the entire continent and finally, the entire earth. This experience leads to the emergence of a wider range of vision as the smaller one is replaced. Gradually, after the vision of the earth disappears, the soul is imagined to be ascending upwards and passing through the solar system, as well as through the galaxies. After spending some time in infinite space, the soul then begins to descend and everything appears again in their respective order in reverse. Passing through the galaxies and the planet systems, the soul reaches the earth and floats in the air as light as a dry leaf or a piece of cotton. Finally, the soul approaches the body and enters it.

Body-talk

After the above exercise, one experiences an added freshness and energy, and observes a consequent increase in the flow of blood to various parts of the body, starting at the toes and gradually ascending upwards through the heels, calf muscles, knees and thighs. Thereafter, one feels the same in the perineum, below the navel, as well as around the abdomen. Then the concentration moves to the centre of the chest, on to the neck and chin, followed by the lips, the tip of the nose and between the eyebrows. The blood flow then passes through the forehead, the apex of the head, and lastly to the hind part of the head, touching the ground. The same parts of the body are then attended to in descending order, starting from the head. While attending to the head, if thoughts, feelings, ideas and images swarm the mind, they are to be observed for a while. Then the focus of attention shifts to the point between the eyebrows, also referred to as the point of the third eye. A sparkling light is imagined to be shining at this point of focus. Then attention shifts to the eyes, where the reflections of light and colour are to be observed. At the nose, breath as well as smells are observed, at the mouth wetness and taste, at the throat the cool of the inner side of the neck, at the chest the palpitation of the heart and the movement of the lungs, at the stomach the movement of the gastro-intestinal system and the heat at the perineum. Lastly, attention passes through the thighs, knees, calf-muscles, ankles and toes. This leads to a feeling of freshness and energy in the body. This technique requires building strong visual imageries involving all five senses equally. One has to imagine oneself lying on a sloping grass field in a garden under a tree, or by the banks of a lake or pond in full yet gentle sunlight, with the wind gently blowing the fragrance of flowers and birds chirping all around. One then has to attend to all the clear sounds originating from a distance in the environment, followed by the minute sounds in the immediate environment, and only then the immediate sounds, touch and smells. Then attention is turned inwards, and breathing is observed. Finally, one has to open one's eyes, look around for a while and then gently sit up, and before standing and resuming normal activity, the normal active phase is revived by sitting calmly for a minute.

It may be hard to believe that the imagination of death can bring about relaxation, yet the state of death and the experience that follows death are perceived in different cultures as relaxing. Greater relaxation can be achieved through the incorporation of these relaxing components into the instructions of *śavāsana*. The dead body essentially does not breathe. Thus, in the practice of *śavāsana* one has to concentrate upon the pattern of breathing until it becomes too minute to detect. This in turn induces silence in the mind. Although a dead person is in a state of thoughtlessness, it is difficult for most people to keep the living mind quiet because it is a human tendency to think. Instead of interrupting the natural process of thought, it can be allowed to continue on a tensionless path. It is for this purpose that the author uses instructions about imagining the soul leaving the body, travelling and then returning to the body; and the last set of instructions about imagining a pleasant place helps bring about feelings of freshness.

Introspection

The author proposes that this practice be followed before going to bed at night and after waking up in the morning. For this exercise, one either needs to lie down or sit in a cross-legged position in a calm state of mind. The mind is then left free for thoughts to swarm in, and after a considerable amount of time has been spent reflecting on these thoughts, attention should be focused on the routine of the day, beginning with waking up in the morning, the people with whom one interacted, what the interactions were about, the reactions the interactions elicited, etc., till the time one went to bed. Each detail of the day has to be recalled vividly, in a systematic and sequential manner. One then has to observe all the happenings of the day as a neutral observer, the positive and negative events have to be examined, accomplishments stored away, and the things remaining to be accomplished to be planned. After everything has been reviewed, the author suggests that the mind is to be left free for thoughts to come and go, and they have to be observed neutrally without trying to either suppress them or care about them, or feeling good or bad about them. These thoughts can be compared to the rising and falling of a wave. However, if a thought, desire, feeling or memory disturbs the mind, the body has to be loosened and 10 to 11 deep breaths taken. If, at night time, this leads to sleep, one should let sleep overcome oneself. If one wants to remember something or commit something to memory, it can be done before sleeping, and this committed or memorized idea will become rooted in behaviour.

Before practicing this in the morning, the author suggests that one should wash one's face, hands and feet and be seated in a cross-legged position, keeping the back straight. Then the same method described above has to be followed, and plans for the day ahead can be made. Thereafter, one should let the mind relax for five to seven minutes. Finally, 20 to 30 deep breaths need to be taken, the respiration observed, and then one can begin with the daily routine. If at some point during this exercise one feels like noting salient points, that can also be done.

Pratyāhāra as a method of psychic modification and mental health

Elucidating the concept and methodology of *pratyāhāra*, the later *Upaniṣads* assert that just as the practice of *āsanas* alleviates minor aches and pains of the body, the practice of *pratyāhāra* helps in ridding oneself of mundane ills, afflictions and mental disorders (*Yoga-Cūḍāmaṇi Upaniṣad*, 109; *Darśana Upaniṣad*, 7.9). In the *Yoga-Sūtra*, Patañjali emphasized that practising *pratyāhāra* on a regular basis helps in attaining greater control over the senses. Control over the senses not only implies components of the external senses, but also a mastery over the internal senses, including the propioceptive, introspective and kinesthetic senses, and the sensory areas of the mind. All these lead to better control over the functioning of the organism, finally leading to control over the self. Certain traditional practices of *pratyāhāra* (*Śāṇḍilyopaniṣad*, *Darśanopaniṣad* and *Kṣurikopaniṣad*), including *vipāssanā*, provide an opportunity to change the style of thinking and feeling, from a stress-prone to a less stress-prone one. The process and instructions used for *śavāsana*, *yoga-nidrā* and *prekṣā* help the person to forget worldly worries and tensions. Instructions regarding concentration on the body are also included when attention is centred on different parts, from the toes to the head, and then back to the toes. This concentration yields a new energy to both the entire vital system and the body.

During the practice of *pratyāhāra*, when one sits calmly and detaches one's senses from external objects, one conserves psychic energy, which would have been wasted through sensory interaction with the material world, and through a reactive attitude. It is believed that in order to conserve or revive psychic energy, one needs to isolate oneself and go into seclusion. Usually only the lower brain functions are active during external sensory involvement and continuous stimulation, and there is insufficient policing over the regulatory mechanism of the internal psycho-physiological and autonomic sympathetic nervous system. As the external sensory involvement and the resulting reactive tendencies calm down, it gradually brings forth the realization that the actual locus of control lies inside oneself, leading to a greater relaxation of the autonomic sympathetic nervous system. Gradually, with practice, one is able to establish better communication with the regulatory centres of the autonomic sympathetic activities in the brain. Consequently, one's affective states settle down. It is evident that the stressful and hypersensitive contemporary life-style creates a number of emotional problems. One is always reacting to one's environment and situations present around oneself. These emotions, if not observed in the right perspective, can lead to mental disorders or neurosis. Due to lack of time or lack of will, people tend to avoid this introspective technique to locate the causes of the problems, and the consequence is reactivity and the corresponding affective state. The eyes are closed during *pratyāhāra* to de-condition the mind from its usual sensory activities; they bring about a change in the style of thinking and emoting, and categorize mental reflections to regulate mental activity. This effort, by and large, calms the mind. When one isolates oneself for constant and deep reflection, one begins to organize one's notions, emotions, reflections and reactions on one's psychic screen; this not only decreases the complexity of the problems, but also reduces over-sensitivity and reactivity, which in turn encourages a healthier style of living.

The internal physiological functions can be regulated through the practice of *āsanas* and *yogic* breathing, and the regular practice of *prekṣā* and the 'body-talk' of *śavāsana* can regulate bio-chemical changes and endocrine secretions. Further, different *yogic* practices may offer individualized devices to overcome the fears, anxieties and stresses of day-to-day living. Through a sincere and regular practice of introspection, one is able to rearrange one's priorities and needs and modify one's behaviour accordingly. Thus, a composed state, which is considered a favourable environment, is created to resolve conflicts, and a way to manage these conflicts is actively sought. The five sheaths in the *Tattirīyopaniṣad* (described earlier) represent the psychotherapeutic process of *pratyāhāra* in all its depth. In the *Tattirīyopaniṣad* model, at the initial exterior corporeal stage, the practitioner undertakes an analysis of the dietary habits, waking and sleep patterns, and daily routine of the client in terms of proper and improper styles of functioning with the help of appropriate literature and instructed guidance. At the next stage, that is, at the inner vital level, the management of psychosomatic factors and the regulation of autonomic functioning take place through the practice of *āsanas, prāṇāyāma* and *yogic* relaxation. It should be kept in mind that certain aspects of *pratyāhāra* are always indirectly present in all practices of *yoga*, including *āsana* and *prāṇāyāma*; otherwise, their *yogic* effectiveness would be doubtful. If at this stage the problem still persists, one needs to probe into a deeper psychological level. Here, the connative complexity of behaviour is probed to bring about emotional catharsis, followed by the analysis and re-analysis of day-to-day reactions and reflections. Further, cognitive conflicts and complexes are detected and resolved, and problem management techniques formulated. This results in psychic emancipation, accompanied by feelings of relief and delight, which falls within the purview of the beatific level.

Concluding remarks

In general, all psychotherapy aims at the resolution of emotional suffering and promotion of well-being in clients. Thus *pratyāhāra* qualifies as a form of psychotherapy, as it attains these goals and takes the practitioner closer to the larger goal of self-realization. Our conclusion is in agreement with that of Fritjof Capra, who in his book, *The Turning Point*, (1981) notes that *yoga* resembles psychotherapy more closely than it does religion or philosophy.

Classical texts consulted

Yoga-Sūtra
Bhagavad-Gitā
Tattirīyopaniṣad: Bhrigu Valli
Triśikhā-Brāhmaṇa Upaniṣad
Maṇḍala-Brāhmaṇa Upaniṣad
Yoga-Cūḍāmaṇi Upaniṣad
Darśanopaniṣad
Yoga-Tattva Upaniṣad
Tejobindūpaniṣad
Śāṇḍilya Upaniṣad
Kṣurikopaniṣad
Dhyānabindūpaniṣad
Haṭha Pradīpika
Gheranda Samhitā

References

Capra, F. (1981). *The turning point*. London: Flamingo.

Datey, K. K., & Bhagat, S. J. (1975). Management of hypertension by shavasana. *Proceedings of seminar on Yoga, Science and Man* (pp. 103–116). New Delhi: CCRIMH.

Datey, K. K., Deshmukh, S., Dalvi, C., & Vinekar, S. (1969). Shavasana: A yogic exercise in the management of hypertension. *Angiology, 20*, 325.

Mahaprajna, Y. (1980). *Appanam sharanam gachchhami*. Ladanun: Jain Vishwabharati Prakashan.

Mishra, J. P. N. (2003–2004). *Dwi-varshika prativedana* (p. 43). Ladanun, Rajasthan: Jain Vishwabharati Samsthana.

Modi, T. (1997). On pratyāhāra. *Yoga and Total Health, 42*(2), 18.

Muni Nathmala Ji (Acharya Mahaprajna) (1970). *Manonushasanam Churu*. Rajasthan: Adarsh Sahitya Sangha Prakashan.

Satyananda, Saraswati (1976). *Yoga nidrā*. Munger, Bihar: Yoga Publication Trust.

Sequeira, P. (1997). Withdrawal of senses—pratyāhāra. *Yoga and Total Health, 42*(2), 10.

Tripathi, K. M. (1987). *A study of personality and behaviour pattern profile in psychosomatic disorders and the role of certain therapeutic interventions*. Unpublished Ph. D. dissertation. Varanasi: Banaras Hindu University.

Tripathi K. M., & Singh, R. H. (1984). Astangic Yoga—its symmetrical wholeness and mutual interrelations with special reference to *yama, niyama* and *samadhi*. *The Yoga Review, 4*, 27–40.

Yogendra, J. (1997). Editorial. *Yoga and Total Health, 40*(2), 2.

17

Psychotherapy and Indian thought

Alok Pandey

Introduction

Human thought has been preoccupied with the problem of suffering and pain since man became conscious of himself as more than just another struggling animal upon this charming and dangerous earth. Of course, this is not the whole of his evolutionary story. The greater part of his struggle has been to evolve a thinking creature out of the mud, to evolve a rational being out of the animal nature imprisoned by the sense-mind, even a spiritual person who lurks as a vague hint of light behind his familiar surface comprising of turbulent emotions, desires and passions. Still, a part of his evolutionary journey can be written as an attempt to overcome various forms of possible suffering and pain.

This move to conquer or contain suffering has taken two basic forms or approaches. One regards suffering as an inevitable and even natural state of living beings, with life being presented as a constant struggle for survival. Happiness is not intrinsically ingrained in human nature and is something that has to be acquired from the outside, although the urge to seek happiness is part of the human constitution. Here, relief from suffering and its alteration into some form of joy has to be a double approach: first, the eradication of pain through physical and psychological means, and second, the acquiring of happiness through largely external means. The other approach regards some form of joy or bliss as the natural endowment of humanity, even as the very basis of creation, and pain as a temporary imposition. This approach uses both inner and outer means to get rid of pain, but insists that true happiness can only be found in one's own depths. The first approach has led to a multiplication of outer technology and methods to overcome physical and psychological suffering. The other has led man towards inner mastery, through *yoga* and such other inner means. While the first approach is generally associated with the Western outlook on life, the second is usually regarded as Eastern or, more specifically, Indian. However, this is only a generalization. A dispassionate look will show both approaches existing simultaneously across the globe at every point in time, the relative stress on each notwithstanding. For the modern mind, though, the Western world is associated with the advancement of material technology, while in the present era most inner approaches are associated with the Indian subcontinent, which still continues to shed an authoritative light on inner means.

The two approaches

Let us take a closer look at these two approaches with special regard to their relevance to psychotherapeutic methods. If psychotherapy is the science of changing the psychological patterns that give rise to mental distress and disorder, it must base itself on the most complete knowledge and understanding of what a human being is and can become. Much of psychotherapy is, however, based on what a human being was, either in his remote and hoary past (a pack of animals that could speak and think, as some would say) or in his more recent yesteryears of infancy and childhood. Through tracing the roots of present problems to the past, it tries to put a corrective by setting things right there. Although the principle sounds good in its own right, it has two fundamental problems. The first has to do with defining the past itself. In other words, how far back does our past go? The second problem concerns the future. Is the goal of psychotherapy to return the client to his past (when he was healthy) or to what has been till now his maximum possibility; or is it to utilize his crisis to enable an inner evolutionary journey towards a more meaningful future—that is, using the crisis as a learning experience for growth and progress? It is here that we come across the divergent world-views of people and their goals, destinies and scope, views that even provide a different understanding of the past and the future. These can be broadly divided into two main categories (at the risk of over-simplification for the sake of easier comprehension):

- Man is a creature of mud formed by a process of chance evolution. He is essentially a physical, or perhaps a chemical, being. Psychologically, he is nothing more than an erstwhile animal or worm that has somehow managed to form itself through a series of random and accidental mutations. There is no essential goal or purpose to his life except to struggle and survive as other creatures do, and this tussle between his individual instinct to save himself and the social or collective instinct to save others is the source of his inner conflict. The crude animal is his past, the refined animal his maximum scope.
- Juxtaposed to this, and somewhat of a contrast, is the other view, which holds man as a creature of heaven fallen here upon earth, and high and sublime in both origin and parentage. Psychologically, he is a soul, a miniature divinity shut in the prison house of matter, seeking release and escape. His goal and purpose is to find his true and spiritual self. Animal in nature but divine in essence, he is a cross between the two, and that is the secret of his difficulty and conflict. The animal nature is the trap; in freedom from this trap lies his hope of salvation.

As we can see, so different are these two views, so disparate their understanding, that it becomes nearly impossible to think of a reconciling synthesis. They have existed side by side in each civilization and culture in one form or the other, but without any reconciling station. There have been some compromises, such as the one attempted by Descartes himself, giving each idea its scope in its own domain. Sometimes their fortunes fluctuated. The sophists of old, the later-day positivists and the modern materialists try and explain everything on the basis of our material sense-perception and the struggle of animal life, denying every other experience as hallucination or poetic imagination. Equally strong has been the rejection of material life as a vanity, a delusion and nightmare of the soul, by the anchorites and the ascetics.

The evolutionary aim of life

The aim of psychotherapeutic processes is the relief of psychological distress in the individual. Of course, with the emergence of the field of psychosomatics and the recognition of the role played by the mind in physical illnesses, a variety of psychological methods (bio-feedback, for instance) are being used as adjuncts in the management of physical illnesses as well, especially in the case of chronic pain syndrome. The processes involved in the Western model are to do with strengthening the ego, exchanging immature with mature defences, enhancing assertiveness and other survival strategies, increasing adaptability to change, and coping with stress. All these means have evolved essentially from the view of man as an animal who is here for an adaptive survival. The emphasis is on making the body fit, the life impulse healthy and the mind more 'mature' in dealing with the problems of life. Of course, some of the later models, like the humanistic and the transpersonal, which draw heavily from the Eastern philosophies, include strengthening the social and spiritual aspects of health. Still, the stress remains on equipping man for survival and coping with stress. In fact, the overwhelming attention on stress is because it has been found that in physical diseases, stress can be counterproductive to survival when it escalates beyond a point. Needless to say, this is a purely material view, and even though some of the strategies to cope with stress may be superficially beneficial, they may not necessarily be the right strategies from a deeper evolutionary perspective.

What is this deeper perspective? Interestingly, both the traditional Eastern and the modern Western approach converge on one point—that an evolution is taking place behind and through all these processes of Nature. Yet, there is an essential difference, in that the material view of life regards nature as a mechanical, inconscient process with no essential purpose or aim. Whatever evolution we observe (and that is an undisputed fact where material science is concerned) is at the outer level, an evolution of forms governed by pure chance and accident. However, the Indian perspective essentially considers an evolution of the soul, which continues through many cycles of life, changing form one after another, till it reaches perfection. In this view, nature is conscious in its depths, an intelligent force that has a teleological basis. The purpose is not so much material survival (as that has only a secondary value), as a growing perfection of the soul embodying the material case. Interestingly, a deeper observation of the living world clearly points towards the existence of an intelligent force behind even the smallest of cells and the simplest of living organisms. Even the most modern findings in physics point in this direction, which we still fail to acknowledge despite it being self-evident. Is it because this would necessitate a radical shift in our self-view and world-view, which in turn would generate the stress of readjustment? Nevertheless, the Indian perspective has always recognized this evolutionary imperative, and holds that man can consciously participate in it by facilitating and accelerating it.

Thus, the aim of counselling, the processes used, and even the nature of what is considered a malady is different in the two approaches. In the materialistic system, psychological movements like anger, sexuality, attachment and greed are not regarded as abnormal, so long as they are kept within reasonable limits. Even anxiety and fear are regarded as adaptive so long as they do not become counter-productive. In the Indian perspective, however, these are to be conquered for the soul to reach perfection. The aim of psychotherapeutic counselling is therefore not merely to strengthen and assist survival and provide stress-busting strategies, but even more importantly to assist in the soul's evolutionary journey. It is against this background that we can consider some of the strategies and solutions offered to counteract psychological and other forms of human suffering.

The negative *māyāvādin* solution to psychological suffering

There has generally been a tendency to attach the term 'Indian thought' to a process that tries to solve a problem by a radical cutting of the knot of pain, rather than by untying it. This view of the *māyāvādin* and the illusionist rejects the problem by labelling it as non-existent, a fever and malady of the soul, which can be cured by abolishing the world along with the problem. The solution therefore poses a greater problem for those left behind, the cure being radical enough to fell the body along with the disease. All life is summarily dismissed as a painful illusion, and escape from it, the sole remedy. From its radical and extreme perspective, birth itself is seen as an illness, the grandsire of all illnesses, and human life a supreme opportunity to escape from this cycle of birth and death and all that lies in between. According to this view, some form of psychological suffering will remain so long as one chooses to be born on the earth. The reasons attributed to this suffering may be different in different doctrines. Some blame it on the past, not on the individual past of this life alone, but those of other lives as well. Others, taking mercy on the poor soul (which they consider a learner and therefore prone to stumble and fall on its heroic journey), blame the root cause of suffering on a larger, cosmic principle of Ignorance, *avidyā*. It is this child of *māyā* that clouds the soul and keeps it enslaved to Ignorance, leading naturally to suffering. Still others speak of the cosmic principle of desire as the source of all misery, and cessation of desire as leading to a state of blissful calm and freedom, or *nirvāṇa*. In these conceptions suffering refers not only to the conscious suffering experienced by the mind, but to a deeper, unconscious and greater suffering experienced by the soul because it is trapped in this meaningless world of Ignorance. Yet so long as the soul chooses to be part of this *avidyā*, it will continue to suffer in some way.

The task of a counsellor subscribing to these views is to awaken the soul from its earthly nightmare by reminding it of its essential nature. The only solution is to cease from birth. Conscious suffering is used only as a strong point of support, a lever to develop *vairāgya*, a state of detached indifference towards life and world, leading thereby to non-affliction. It is a kind of desensitization or de-addiction programme for our world-addiction and craving for material happiness, which brings much suffering in its wake.

In actual practice, however, one does not take this extreme approach. The client's mind is led through a cognitive framework, starting from his present crisis, to reveal the transient rather than the illusory nature of this world and all its events. The mind is made to note the utter impermanence of things; the wealth, position and fame, family and children, fortune and misfortune, are all too little to grieve for. The believer adds that the only thing worthy in life is that which is eternal and imperishable—the soul in man and the Divine above; some combine these individual and universal aspects of the Divine into a single formula—the *Brahman*. Here, a common misconception needs to be clarified. Some modern writers tend to use the word *Brahman* as interchangeable with the later *Paurāṇika* deity Brahmā, the progenitor of our world. *Brahman* is no particular god, although all gods, and everything else originates from It. *Brahman* is the stable, unchanging and eternal basis of all existence. Even if all creation, including the trinity of the gods, is dissolved, *Brahman* would still remain, as untouched as ever. One of the principal *Upaniṣads*, the *Kena*, describes through the sublime poetry characteristic of that period, how everything originates from *Brahman*, and therefore That alone is the object of our pursuit—*tadeva brahma tvaṃ viddhi, nedaṃ yadidam upāsate*, Know That to be the *Brahman*—and not this that men follow after here. Another *Upaniṣad*, the *Kaṭha*, describes through a beautiful verse the transient nature of worldly goods, attachment to which brings only grief and suffering and, at the end, death. Death, in these beautiful passages, lauds Naciketas, the young aspirant, for his choice of *śreyas*, the true good of the soul, over *preyas*, the momentarily pleasant and transient worldly good. Thus, through examples and narratives drawn from the everyday life of the client, the crisis he has faced and passed through, as well as from the cultural context, the person is gradually led away from psychological suffering and helped to focus his attention within, towards the true and ultimate goal. Even the first step is considered good enough, since by impressing upon the mind the concept of transience and impermanence, the client is able to detach himself from his malady and feel lighter and freer.

However, one may proceed a step further, depending upon the readiness of the client. One may, for example, help the person view the problem more objectively, since he would now be detached from its emotional effects. A certain distancing always helps us see better and understand the situation more clearly. This impermanence, far from being a cause of grief, becomes a positive thing, since it also means that grief and unhappiness, tragedy and suffering are not an eternal damnation or a permanent doom. They are only a temporary setback, an inevitable learning experience for the soul in its sojourn over one or several lives. Through pleasure and pain, happiness and grief, success and failure, the march goes on. The journey of the soul does not end at temporary halting points, but goes on and will go on till one has reached the goal.

Common to all *Vedāntic* systems is the belief that this world is not what it seems to be, and that our values have been misplaced due to the mind's conditioning through centuries of evolution (and a series of births and rebirths). The psychotherapist corrects this cognitive error through a dialectic process involving thought, utilizing the person's experiences to demonstrate this. But there is also a later divergence, which lies in the goal placed before the soul after it has thus disengaged itself and is able to look at the problem and enigma of human life and its events dispassionately. Useful as this is for certain problems, it has its own drawbacks. First, it presumes a certain degree of intellectual development, although perhaps less than is required to understand the complex dynamics of the classical Western models of psychotherapy. Compared to that, it is much more direct and close to the person's experience. However, it does require a forceful mind on the part of the therapist, who should be able to logically lead the person from the events at the surface to the deeper phenomenon, and from the apparent to the real. There is a second and even more serious difficulty. According to the system itself, most souls are trapped in the snare of worldly *māyā*. So how can the blind lead the blind or the trapped rescue the trapped? The average graduate in medicine, opting for psychiatry as a field, is not interested in the high philosophy of life or its ultimate goal. He, like everyone else, the client included, is caught in his own nightmares and delusions. Even if he were to undergo some course, it would serve no purpose unless he was himself convinced, either through an innate sensitivity or through a deeper and calmer outlook, awakened through life experiences. This imposes a serious limitation on who is really qualified to administer this form of counselling. It is evident that outer degrees and qualifications, even a crash course in some *Vedāntic* school, is of little value here. Only that which has been lived through is convincing; the rest is only superficial and cannot bring about an inner and radical change. Third, the solution, if taken to its logical extreme, may induce total indifference towards the world. While this may be appreciated by certain extremist schools, the seers who propounded this thought were careful enough to not create confusion in the minds of the average person. An over-emphasis on this other-worldliness may well lead to inertia, justified under the holy name of *vairāgya*. One often finds such escapists who have joined the *nirvāṇa* bandwagon to avoid responsibilities. A visit to any *āśrama* will reveal quite a few who, unable to bear the stresses and strains of life, have taken recourse to the jungle. Those who have suffered disappointments sometimes espouse the philosophy, but nevertheless continue to nurture secret ambitions, which they find themselves inadequate to fulfil. This hypocrisy creates a serious dichotomy between thought and practice, and may lead to complications. It may, for example, lead to a person no longer being fit for life with its many problems and complexities while s/he waits for *nirvāṇa* to come to the rescue. Such an outcome is obviously undesirable. Individually, it may induce one to lead a double life, a sort of spiritual neuroticism, in other words. However, it is even more undesirable collectively for it weakens the very fabric of the race, depressing its vitality and vigour with its inevitable decline. Even genuine individual victory can lead to the doctrine being misunderstood and used to justify disparate things, leading to a collective social defeat with its attendant psychological and cultural problems.

Therefore, the wise ones insist upon not deluding the minds of the average who are not ready by enrolling everyone in the list of candidates for counselling—*na buddhibhedaṃ janayedajñānāṃ karmasaṅgiṅām*—he who is established in the Knowledge (true Knowledge or *jñāna*) should not create confusion in the minds of the ignorant (who are still attached to their egos and not yet ready). In other words, the doctrine requires a high degree of inner development on the part of the counsellor.

It is important to understand that ancient Indian thought saw in this impermanence only a passage towards a higher Permanence. The illusion was to be understood and torn in order to find the Real and not to rest in a midway house built upon the sands of nowhere. But doing so needs effort, a strong predisposition, a positive seeking that few can command. Yet if such a psychotherapist can take this final and crucial step of turning a negative experience into a positive seeking for the Eternal, it would mean a great and true release for the client. An example of this type of counsel appears in the classical treatise of *Yogavāsiṣṭha*, wherein the sage Vasiṣṭha counsels Rāma while the latter is going through a stage of non-involvement vis-à-vis life in the world.

This form of counselling, while useful for a select group of clients who suffer from depression arising out of life situations, is of little use in other forms of psychological disorders, although it may be useful in the case of those whose suffering stems from the pain of their near and dear ones. To take just one example, the depressed and suicidal mother of a mentally handicapped child was asked how she would have reacted had this child been her sister's, and she had to bring him up for some reason or the other. The reply was evident. She would do all she was doing now, perhaps even more, but without the depression, perhaps even with the joy born from a selfless act. As she replied, she could see the obvious—how to live in this world without attachment or possessiveness. A single short session was enough to change her self-view and world-view. She actually recovered and remained well for years.

The positive *Vedāntic* solution

Indian thought, however, is not only about *māyāvāda* and illusion. Despite the current emphasis on other-worldliness, there have been other, equally powerful and positive streams of Indian thought. In fact, *mukti* of the *Vedāntin* view and *nirvāṇa* of the Buddhist view, which propose discarding this world as a nightmare, are not the only ideals conceived by Indian thought. The *Vedic ṛṣis* were extremely life-affirming. In fact, there have been other equally powerful tendencies in Indian thought. These views propose a more positive outlook and try to reconcile the material and spiritual aspects of existence. Of course, the life affirmation suggested here is not the one attempted in the material model, which is essentially an affirmation of the ego. Here the emphasis is on affirmation of the soul upon nature through a growing inner perfection. From a psychotherapeutic point of view, it is this that can be even more effective in dealing with problems of the mind. Some of these major trends can be roughly classified into the following.

The ideal of inner purification

Indian thought views Nature as not only a single continuous movement, but also as a continuum of ascending degrees or potencies. This continuum presents itself as an evolutionary ladder for the soul to ascend to its own innate perfection. According to this vision, all phenomena can be reduced to a three-fold movement placed one on top of the other, like the steps of a ladder. In this view, the true value and significance of an action or any phenomenon in general lies not so much in its appearance as it does in the level or type of consciousness motivating it. The inward and outward reactions and consequences that follow result from the type of consciousness involved, rather than the actual observed movement or action. Three major movements or modes are recognized: *tamas*, *rajas* and *sattva*.

The source of human misery, according to this view, comes at a certain middle stage of our psychological evolution, called the *rājasic*. In a nutshell, the human soul evolves through at least three levels over several rounds of birth before it is ready for the highest spiritual good. The first level is the *tāmasic* or the darkened state of inertia and resistance to change. Here, the law of the masses or the rules of the herd drive him like a subconscious beast or a half-conscious man. Next comes the *rājasic* or the state of kinesis and dynamic movement. This second stage can be further sub-divided into two: one, the preliminary or the predominantly *rajo-tāmasic*, wherein the being is engaged in self-flattering indulgences of every kind; two, the *rajo-sāttvic*, wherein the individual begins to seek some rule of inner law to govern his unruly nature, which he begins to perceive as the source of internal disturbances. Finally, there is the third or *sāttvic* stage, wherein the individual learns to subordinate his ego and take from life only what is rightfully his. He seeks harmony intuitively and is balanced in his conduct and in the distribution of life energies. In the primitive or *tāmasic* stage the individual does not consciously suffer, although he may be the cause of suffering for many others. The need for violent sensations to feel alive drives some of these people towards alcoholism and violence. Others simply enter a depressed state, refusing to budge from or outgrow this stage. The second stage is one of fiery pleasures and equally swift swings to the blues. An inordinate self-seeking and excessive ambition with its natural fallouts of anger, fear, hope, expectations and frustrations bring in their wake opposite reactions from their environment, and this egoistic narrowness makes these individuals extremely susceptible to misery. This suffering is actually Nature's corrective, aimed at helping them to push forth and find a way out of their miserable existence. So lastly comes *sattva*, the great balancer, after the soul has experienced these lesser rungs of existence and grown through them.

It is the middle stage of the *rajo-tāmasic guṇa* that predisposes human beings towards extreme forms of cruelty, directed both at others and themselves. Many perversions, including sado-masochistic tendencies and drug dependence, arise due to a preponderance of the *tamo guṇa*. Illnesses like depression and some forms of schizophrenia can clearly be seen as gravitating towards the *tāmasic* state of nature with its attendant inertia, inability to exercise one's will, a tendency to not alter one's psychological condition, and to become progressively animal-like and stone-like, dubiously termed regression in modern psychology.

According to this strand of thought, psychological pain and suffering and pleasure and thrill are two sides of the same coin. Further, thrill (*sphuraṇa* or *indriya-sukha*), which is predominantly *tāmasic* and pleasure (*viṣaya-sukha*), which is largely *rājasic*, are clearly distinguished from happiness (*sukha*), which is *sāttvic* in nature, being subtler and therefore closer to the fundamental joy (*harṣa*) of existence. The highest and purest form is of course Bliss (*ānanda*), which belongs to the purely spiritual domain. To strive for thrill and the egoistic forms of pleasure is to invite suffering. We must grow out of such momentary sense-bound joy as well as the equally momentary joy arising through the possession of outer objects and move on to the happiness that can be observed in people whose mind is in a state of balance and satisfaction through moderation. What is necessary, therefore, is moderation and balance through enlightened reason and discrimination, *sattvaśuddhi*. This is the ideal of a sane moderation, similar to Aristotle's golden mean. It is a conscious and deliberate cultivation of positive qualities of the mind and the heart, which help one grow into *sukha* or gladness and *prakāśa* or light of wisdom.

Inevitable to this system is the fact that the nature of the advice given to a client depends upon the stage of her/his inner evolution. A story attributed to Swami Vivekananda well illustrates this point. When approached by a man eager for *sannyāsa* (renouncing the world), a man moved by a desire to escape his responsibilities rather than by a positive call for Truth and God, the great one's reply was: 'What is it that you possess and can renounce? First go and earn a lakh of rupees and then come for renunciation!' Unfortunately, most people today associate renunciation with escape from the struggle and labour of life. In actuality, true renunciation requires far greater inner strength (and is therefore an evolutionary move towards self-mastery) than the struggle necessary to satisfy one's desires. It may be noted that even in modern psychoanalytic thought, certain *sāttvic* qualities like renunciation, non-possession and suppression (as opposed to repression) are regarded as mature defence mechanisms, the signs of a mature and healthy mind.

A counsellor working along these lines will therefore first assess the level of the individual's inner evolution. Elaborate descriptions of the type of inner personality and constitution according to the three *guṇas*, as these three evolutionary stages are better known, abound in ancient Indian thought, especially in the *Gītā* and Āyurveda. While we are all a mixture of the three, there is often a predominance of one or the other *guṇas*, which leads to physical and psychological afflictions. The therapy and advice given, therefore, varies. Thus, a *sāttvic* person who suffers due to his idealism and sympathy for others is advised, helped and encouraged to develop a still deeper and spiritual outlook; the *rājasic* man of a higher order is advised to do his work while placing his trust in God and in accordance with the inner laws of his nature, *svabhāva* and *svadharma*. The *rājasic* man of a lower order is counselled and helped to achieve moderation in habits and outlook, and tone down the excess desires that torment and trouble him. His unruly and excess energy is channelled into healthy activities like sports. The army has learnt to use the *rājasic* type of man and channelize his energies into war. But for the *tāmasic* man, very little counselling works unless something shakes him up, some terrible misfortune, for instance, which affects him and arouses the energies dormant within him. Anything that can stimulate this type of person to work with concentration and perseverance is considered good counsel. Fine crafts and manual work requiring physical concentration help, as can be seen in cases concerning psychotics and extreme forms of depression. Also helpful is anything that can stimulate a sense of joy—like eating a dish they relish, or simple things that heighten pleasure. These people are rarely advised to pursue spirituality of the meditative ascetic type because they might use it as an excuse to remain a recluse or justify inertia and addictions that transport them to altered realms without much inner effort.

These *guṇas* have other sub-divisions, but all people can be classified along the lines of these three types. The utility of this typology in treating certain personality and behavioural/conduct disorders is evident. It is also useful in understanding some of the conflicts that arise when an individual transits from one level to another with divergent pulls in his nature. In such cases, the task of the therapist is to assist the transition to the higher level while working through the conflict. A detailed discussion of all possible variations is beyond the scope of this chapter, but as is evident, this system offers great practical utility. It also settles the question of suitability for deeper spiritual counselling. Besides, it does not require great philosophical capacity or outlook on the part of the client, although it does require inner tact and understanding on the part of the therapist. Finally, this understanding can be combined with other forms of counselling as well, adding to its immense usefulness.

The harmony of body and mind

Illusionism is most commonly (mis)understood as representative of Indian thought, and some kind of mind-body harmony through *yoga* exercises is the most commonly sought after therapeutic technique. The *haṭhayoga* exercises (better known as *āsanas* or *yogāsanas*) *prāṇāyāma* and meditation are among the best-researched imports from India that have already found a place in modern psychotherapeutic systems. Many researches undertaken in both the East and the West from the 1960s (or perhaps even earlier) have demonstrated the efficacy of these simple techniques. While theories pertaining to the exact mechanism of their actions might differ, there is hardly anyone who would deny their efficacy in creating some sort of harmony between the body and the mind. While the West continues to search for material explanations, it would be interesting to know what the originators of these systems thought about the 'mechanism' of their actions. This may only help us to modify them to suit our needs.

First, these 'techniques' were originally not meant to be mere techniques. These exercises were part of a larger movement—that of coming in contact with our own Divine essence, hidden in everything and at each plane of our existence. They were also meant to prolong life, stabilize the life-force and increase mental vigour; however, these gains were not so much for adaptive survival as they were for creating the best possible conditions favourable to our inner journey towards perfection of the soul. Here, it must be clearly understood that the ancient Indian mind viewed the body and its preservation not as an end in itself, but as a means for right conduct and the fulfilment of *dharma*, *śarīram khalu dharmasādhanam*. Although these ancient practices are now being seen as the Indian counterpart of behavioural therapy, they are not so in their true essence, for the simple reason that very few things in Indian thought are divorced from spirituality, least of all the systems of *yoga*. Even atheistic and agnostic conceptions have their spiritual element.

In *haṭhayoga* and *prāṇāyāma*, the practitioner first tries to regulate, and then still, the otherwise restless physical and vital energies. This, however, is a preliminary first step. The next and more important one is where he tries to gather and concentrate these energies in an attempt to reach their divine source and bring out their deeper divine possibilities. Before this divine possibility emerges, and certainly after that, the energies of the body and life-force become forceful, effective, balanced, harmonious and, thereby, curative. This is excellent for those not so psychologically minded, and for those less inclined towards an esoteric spirituality. It is quite effective, and has been used with considerable success in treating psychosomatic disorders. The principle here is that diseases of the body arise due to an imbalance in the flow of *prāṇic* currents (life-force), which moves mainly along five different channels, two lower (*apāna*), two upper (*udāna*) and one in the middle (*samāna*). These practices were meant to regulate the life-force along its five-fold path in a balanced and harmonious way—an occult knowledge that we are only fragmentarily discovering again. The disadvantage lies in the fact that these methods, to be fully effective, have to be practised regularly. They are time-consuming and often need the supervision of a qualified expert. They are best used as adjuncts in treating a wide range of disorders, including psychoses.

Meditation is slightly different, even though it falls under the broad category of 'techniques' evolved by the Eastern paradigm, although nowhere is the range and variation as wide as it is in India. It is a vast subject and one need not go into every detail of the different techniques and their relative efficacy. Suffice it to say that one of its well-known effects, recognized now the world over, is toning down the response of our sympathetic nervous system, creating a sense of calm at the most physical level. There may be deeper reasons though, since the nervous system, more specifically the autonomic nervous system, is a sort of interface between the gross physical energies, and those of life and the mind, which act upon matter and influence it. Two techniques are especially helpful. One is the Buddhist method of witnessing self-reflection and introspective meditation. This technique is useful for undoing certain habitual nervous responses, anxiety states, obsessive patterns of thoughts and behaviour, in anger management, and even in studying and thereby controlling oneself. The essential steps here are thought-observation, witnessing, control and mastery. But this is difficult and usually demands some isolation on the part of the practitioner; further, it is only a somewhat developed mind that can separate one part of it from another. The other, more popular and easier, yet very effective, technique is dynamic meditation and its scientific offspring—guided imagery. This method relies on the faculty of imagination and can be considered a first cousin of auto-suggestion. In fact, the two are often combined together. It is used largely in the treatment of psychosomatic disorders, anxiety disorders, etc.

The integral thought of the *Gītā*

There remain two powerful, widely used, but often misunderstood systems of ancient Indian thought. These systems appear to move along very different lines, although there is an unspoken occult and higher synthesis between them. The first is the ideal of the *Gītā*, often misrepresented as the gospel of *karma*, and further reduced to mean a motivation to duty, regardless of its effect. One can only smile at such summary dealings of a great scripture that has endured centuries of invasion and corruption, and yet continues to inspire and transform mankind. All one can say is that if the *Gītā* were to teach nothing more than mere moral rectitude, it would not be worth the trouble. In fact, quite a few words and *sūtras* in the *Gītā* can be utilized for counselling and therapeutic purposes. This is because unlike many similar scriptures, the *Gītā* is an attempt to synthesize various truths known till then. In addition, it adds something unique, profound and new, enriching the old with a fresh insight.

First among these *sūtras* is the truth that *man is essentially an imperishable soul* who uses the body as a charioteer uses the chariot. This reverses the dependence of our psychological state on the physical events of life by constantly reminding us that we are eternal and imperishable souls that assume a transient body, just as a person wears clothes. This doctrine has had such a great impact through the ages that till date it is the most effective counselling for the grief and pain of death. Millions of people have used the *Gītā* in times of crisis—especially loss—and found solace and strength. This is the first thing to remember—that we are essentially souls that cannot be destroyed by the catastrophes of life and nature.

The second doctrine is that man need not take this soul merely on faith (although faith is a great power, the blind man's indispensable staff till he begins to see the higher truths). He can discover his soul through many ways, one of which, according to the *Gītā*, is the *enlightened use of his intelligent will*. Instead of turning it constantly outward and downward to satisfy our desires or remaining caught up in the web of surface phenomenon, this intelligent will can be turned upward and inward to discover our own sublime realities, which free us from bondage to grief, error, suffering and pain. The *Gītā* also briefly mentions one or two psychophysical practices and forms of concentration to help us go within.

A third principle states that we have not been abandoned upon earth; God Himself is concerned with *the march of civilization* towards some ultimate Good. What that ultimate Good is, has been left unsaid or only hinted at, but the *Gītā* assures us that He is concerned intimately with the earth and men. Each element of the universe has a Divine superconscient (not the super-ego or the conscience, which are human things, aspects of our mind and the ego's constructs) hidden within it, and not just a subconscient animal principle (instincts as the base of everything) as Freudian psychology at one time asserted. The *Gītā* states that Divinity dwells within the human being, and that it is the task of each to bring it out rather than stifle it. This is the great conflict occurring at the macro and micro levels.

The principal conflict, therefore, is between the cosmic principles and powers of Light and their opposites—darkness and Ignorance. This is the fourth principle, that war and conflict will remain unavoidable evolutionary necessities so long as earth and mankind are imperfect. Our inner conflicts are essentially *evolutionary conflicts*, our inner and outer crises are essentially cries for evolutionary change. Man can choose to remain in a darkened state, pursued by suffering, till he once again chooses the path towards eternal good, which is also the collective good. The *Gītā* elaborately describes in the closing chapters the nature of the powers of light and darkness. Thus man, to be free of error and grief, has to consciously cultivate the qualities of light and truth.

A fifth element of the *Gītā*, and the most widely known, is the concept of *niṣkāma karma*. The principle of *karma* and its consequences depend upon the level on which an action has been done. This has already been hinted at. Suffice it to say that according to the *Gītā*, *karma* is an inner evolutionary mechanism and not a summary disposal by a judge through a system of rewards and punishments. If anything, the rewards and punishments come from within, through an ensuing inner psychological state. Thus, acts done under a *tāmasic* state delude our consciousness, making it more dense and impervious to Light and Joy. Similarly, even philanthropic acts done under a *rājasic* state of 'I' and 'My' (committed under the stress of the vital ego) bring in their wake happiness that is transient, and invariably mixed with or followed by suffering. *Sāttvic* acts lead to increased inner happiness and wisdom, *sukha* and *prakāśa*. We can, however, be free of *karma* and its consequences by arriving spontaneously at that high point of our soul's evolutionary career towards which the machinery of *karma* and Nature is driving us, that is, to discover the Divine secret within us. The *Gītā* suggests that we dedicate our everyday actions to the secret indwelling Godhead and Lord who resides within the hearts of every living and thinking creature, Vāsudeva (the indwelling Deity) and *mānuṣīm tanum āśritam*. Thus practised, even our most trivial everyday actions can lead us to a happy state of being, if done in a selfless spirit of dedication to the Divine Master and as long as one remains equal to the fruits that they may bring. This emphasis upon a mind that is tranquil under every circumstance—the seemingly pleasant and unpleasant, in success and victory and in failure and defeat—is a great liberating principle of the *Gītā*, and helps to ameliorate much of our everyday psychological and even physical suffering. This equality is not indifference but a state of joy by dwelling constantly in The Lord's remembrance and abiding solely by His Will.

The establishment of *equanimity* is therefore another practical method prescribed by the *Gītā* to free us from the stress of everyday life. But would it not lead to a casual lackadaisical approach towards life? This question stems from an assumption that desire for a particular result is the sole motivator of human action. While that may be true of certain needs such as hunger and thirst, desire is very clearly a distortion that arises when need turns to greed. Even need, though, is not an imperative. For according to *yoga*, needs are nothing but habits of Nature, conditioned responses of the mind to an object. We can recondition ourselves to such an extent that even the needs of food and water can be done away with (in an extreme form of *yoga*). Still, the question of motivation remains. The *Gītā* commands us to approach all work as the work of God, to do them for the benefit of the world, since He alone knows what is best for all. Our role, or rather the role of nature in us, is to be a faithful and perfect instrument. In other words, the *Gītā* enjoins us to pursue perfection and excellence as part of our instrumentality, but with the sole motive of service and love inspired by a higher knowledge and guidance, arising in a tranquil mind free of the turbulence of desires and passions. The rewards, which are not to be sought after for their own sake, are an intrinsic delight and unconditional peace, wisdom, freedom and, above all, the growth of our entire being towards God. Equanimity is not only a strong foundation for a higher life, but also a bedrock of safety against the harshness of the world. We can arrive at it through several ways, one of which is to practice stepping back. Before rushing to speak or act in haste, we need to hold back for a while and look at the relative importance of a thing from the widest possible frame of reference. If practised sincerely, it will help us to discover the triviality of many things we considered important.

Another method is to look at the essence of events and circumstances, and at the place they hold in the totality of life. For things are often ascribed a place that is out of proportion to their real value when seen from a truer perspective. Setting things in their right place and viewing them from the right perspective helps us avoid troubles and misunderstandings in life. Yet another way is to develop a dispassionate and philosophical outlook, or resilience and fortitude that can endure shocks. However, equanimity can be best developed by a conscious and willing surrender to God's Will in the cosmos.

This brings us to the greatest word of the *Gītā*, which assures us that God will deliver us from all fear and evil if we can learn to *surrender* ourselves into His hands. Modern psychology, born out of a sceptic temperament suited to material pursuits, has little sympathy with the idea of God. It may even regard talking of God in matters of science as blasphemous. But we must remember that psychology is not a physical science. It deals not with physical but with psychological phenomena and, whether we like it or not, the fact remains that the quest for Divinity and all that is good, faith and surrender are all psychological phenomena, as ancient as the mountains, yet at the same time as modern as the quantum theories of space and the universe. Psychology will suffer a great loss if this body of psychological self-experience is left unutilized, for it is not scientific scruples but our blind attachment to Ignorance that prevents us from seeing the Light and offering greater possibilities to man. Whether accepted in scientific circles or not, the empirical fact is that faith in God has continued to relieve and cure people around the world, cutting across man-made and natural barriers. The two views of science and faith are perhaps merely two different ways of seeing the One Reality, which exceeds and fulfils both.

In actuality, there is no real opposition between faith in God and reason. If we are sincere, reason leads us to the doors of agnosticism and even hints at some cosmic Intelligence at work. When we regard this vast and wonderful world of myriad phenomena, we clearly see the workings of a perfect Intelligence that is conscious and precedes its works, even when the object worked upon is not aware of It. It even adapts Itself to Its instruments; it is then logical to say that one's supreme fulfilment would be in the ability to express and manifest that Intelligent Will as perfectly as one can. If we can concede this simple observational and inferential truth, then we have to make only one other logical extension—that this perfectly conscious Intelligent Force is also at once a Being, which we can relate to. In fact, it is our own highest Self, the greatest possibility hidden within us. Several eminent men and women have experienced this essential divinity, which cuts across the boundaries of space, time and education. The difficulty lies in reconciling the various notions of God created by different religions, whose external details do not coincide. However, since science seeks to go beyond appearances, it can learn to look behind the various religious practices and arrive at an essential truth about Divine Perfection and a Conscious Force existing behind this world and Nature.

A bold reconciliation: The path of Tantra or an inner technology

Reconciliation, however, is possible. The first attempt to reconcile the two apparent opposites (the materialist and the spiritual) took place in the great and now lost tradition of Tantra. The *Gītā* seeks to reconcile life in the world (the problem of the practical man) with spiritual realization. Tantra seeks to reconcile the energies moving this cosmos (the field of the scientist) with the Supreme Energy from which these lesser forms, forces and energies originate. Given this, it might be possible to master the lesser energies through the stronger and greater ones. This is the fundamental principle of Tantra—to understand, possess, control and master the forces and powers of nature, as well as those of a greater supernature. From this perspective, it is closer to our conception of science, albeit with a much wider application.

Thus, while science studies and tries to master physical forces and the energies of matter, Tantra goes deeper to study and master other occult energies beyond the play of our material universe. It sees physical phenomena as by-products or the final end result of still deeper occult events occurring at other levels of our consciousness. In the field of illness, for example, it believes that there are entities, beings, and forces of disruption and disintegration on which one can act directly if one has the occult knowledge, thereby curing an illness without physical intervention. Unfortunately, modern insistence on physical causes alone has damaged this highly developed science, which has its own rationale of working. Tantra itself fell into disrepute since few occultists and *tāntrikas* had the required inner purity to handle such intense forces. Many, attracted by the power but unable to pay the inner price, turned to lower and derivative activities like black magic, witchcraft, etc. The worship of power not backed by a solid grounding in the highest knowledge led to a further decline of the discipline, and indulgence in practices that were more in the nature of occult quackery than wizardry. The presence of incompetent doctors or quacks in the field of medicine does not abrogate medical science as a genuine branch of science. So too the modern disrepute of Tantra does in no way mean that Tantra in itself belonged to a lower order, or that its practitioners were indulging in some mumbo-jumbo.

Indian thought and psychiatry

There is a lot that Tantra can offer psychiatry, not by way of our modern misreading of its hieroglyphs through the lens of psychoanalysis, but in terms of increasing our understanding of the subtler causes of illness. Thus, according to Tāntrika knowledge, insanity results from possession by certain entities emanating from the dark and hostile worlds. These turbulent energies first enter the atmosphere of a person susceptible to them (through affinity of some parts of his nature). This is the prodrome stage, when the first stage of occult prevention can be undertaken. They next cast an influence which usually takes one or the other following forms:

- Early influence leads to some personality changes (loss of faith and will, doubts, depression, confusion, perverted religiosity, excessive self-vanity, excess of sexual and other appetites, uncontrolled impulsiveness).
- Epilepsy, which is characteristically due to resistance offered by the affected person against the force.
- Hysteria, especially states of possession, dissociation, multiple personality, etc.

- Active communication with these dark entities through voices and other means, as seen in certain forms of psychosis.
- Finally, frank possession/incarnation of one of these stronger dark entities, leading to a total perversion of thought, feeling, will, action and speech, resulting in personalities known as the tyrant, the psychopath and the pervert.

These dark forces and beings have been elaborately classified in Tāntrika literature. Some of these are the *asuras* (distorters of mind, specifically thought and speech), the *rākṣasa* (those perverting and distorting feelings and will) and *piśācas* (distorting sensations and physical instincts). There are other minor entities, such as elemental beings called *bhūta* and disembodied beings called *preta*, who float in the vicinity of the dead, especially those who have died traumatic deaths. These beings and entities are known everywhere, and are mentioned under different names in Western, Arabic and other spiritual literature.

Now the *tāntrika*, the occultist, the *shaman*, the thaumaturgist—call him whatever you will—knew about these forces and the ways to neutralize them, just as a modern scientist would know about the forces of wind, rain and fire, and how to handle them. The *tāntrika* can be further sub-divided into two main types. The lower type has within its control some powerful entity of the same plane, which executes its will, either for good or for evil. Others have mastered the higher energies through sufficient purity and self-control. These can then neutralize the lower beings with the power of Light. Naturally, it is the latter *tāntrika* who is preferable and also the one whose powers are more permanent, but this type is rare to find as too much inner austerity is called for on the part of the practitioner.

The lost knowledge of Tantra is now being recovered, albeit in forms more suited to the scientific temper of our times—Reiki, *prāṇic* healing, working with body and mind energy, a study of the effects of thoughts and other vibrations upon the body and mind and so on. Despite the onslaught of modern science, this ancient science is not dead; rather, it is being reborn through new sciences such as parapsychology. In fact, physical science itself has entered the threshold of the occult and it would not be surprising if in times to come the old ghosts return in the garb of new names and the buried are raised in a different attire.

The two roads to the one solution

Before embarking upon a synthesis of all these diverse systems of Indian thought, a recapitulation. The practical side of Indian thought can be broadly divided into two main categories. The commonly known method is the way of knowledge—Vedānta—and its child, Yoga. The aim here is to rise above suffering through discovering a level higher than and outside the sphere of our pain and suffering. While this will not help us to end suffering or change reality, we can definitely transcend it. This itself is a significant gain and, for many, it is enough. They say, 'Let the stain remain, the imperfection of our earth-nature and its resultant suffering continue; it is enough if I can escape its psychological consequences. If others too do it, we all can collectively ascend to a level where suffering is not felt or experienced even though all below is disarray and strife.'

The other method is that of power or Śakti and its child, Tantra. An effort is made here to understand the forces that create confusion and disorder, sickness and imperfection, suffering and pain. Effort is also made to conquer them, and therefore this method is known as the *vīra mārga* or the hero's path. But inadequacy can set in here too, since power without knowledge is unsatisfactory. One cannot find the final cure if one is unaware of the ultimate origin. A knowledge of the origins of suffering and evil and imperfection can alone lead to a perfect and radical cure. In other words, in their highest station, Vedānta and Tantra, the Highest Knowledge and the Supreme Power, are essentially one. But somehow they have not been reconciled. The *vedāntin* who knows only one half of the truth dismisses the issue of suffering as an illusion without caring to find out why this illusion was superimposed upon the Supreme Truth. The *Śākta tāntrika*, who has the power, also misses the truth since he does not know how this fall into error and confusion came about and the means to rescue the energies that have seemingly deviated from their true purpose.

The grand synthesis and more

In our own times, a grand synthesis of Vedānta and Tantra, Eastern and Western, the spiritual and the materialist approach has been achieved and effected in the work and vision of Sri Aurobindo. Of course, Sri Aurobindo's *yoga* is not an eclectic combination of different methods and paths, although it embraces the highest knowledge possible to the *vedāntin* and the greatest power possible to the *tāntrika*. And yet it includes something more, something not found elsewhere. What that is and how it can help us in our knowledge and practice of medicine and psychiatry has been discussed in the following section. Sri Aurobindo has shed light on practically every sphere of life, reconciling not only the great streams of Indian thought, but also joining materialism and other prominent ideas with the currents of Indian spirituality. It is therefore rewarding to study it as a prototype in some detail as it can form the backbone of an integral synthesis of ancient Indian wisdom and currently prevalent modern thinking on the subject. For our present purposes, however, we shall confine the exposition to the problem of psychological well-being and view it against the background of this grand vision of Indian thought.

First, Sri Aurobindo confirms the ancient knowledge that man is not just an aggregate of physical cells or chemical reactions. He is that only in his outer material basis. His true self-identity lies in his possession of a soul. Sri Aurobindo does not use the word 'soul' in a vague or general sense. There is a universal Self, but there is also an individual soul that has been projected from the One Self into the drama of earthly life. This individual soul, called the psychic being, is important to our psychological well-being. The psychic being is our true being, the secret divinity present in us. Its very essence is peace, harmony and joy; it has a natural affinity towards the true, the good and the beautiful. However, it remains veiled in human beings by their surface nature and its movements. But it exists even in the crudest of human natures as a ray of light and hope, a spark of undying truth covered by darkness.

One source of psychological maladies springs from our inability to dwell in the *psychic consciousness*. We live our lives mostly upon the surface, where there usually is nothing but confusion and disorder. Our nature, in the absence of guidance, depends heavily upon our outer mind and sense data. Our desires, emotions and passions further corrupt this imperfect, partial and broken knowledge (called Ignorance). The result is a falsification of knowledge, a crass Ignorance about others and ourselves. This wrong identification with the ignorant movements of nature as if that were 'me' is the origin of our subjective sense of the ego which appears so very real. With this notion of the superficial 'me' comes the idea of what is 'not me'. And thus begins a conflict and clash of forces, since no real unity or harmony is possible with the ego, only at best some accommodation, tolerance and adjustment. The sense of ego leads inevitably to conflict with all that is not perceived as myself, whether it be as seen in others or hid in our own subconscient depths, which in essence is the same thing. For we almost instinctively see in others a reflection of our own selves. We also wish to see in others the perfection that we secretly desire, but have not yet achieved. Much of our social and emotional conflict with others stems from the separative ego-sense and its attendant Ignorance, or vice versa. This does not mean that there is no such thing as the individual. On the contrary, there is indeed a true divine individual within us that has been projected to manifest one or the other aspect of the Integral Divine. It is our individual drive and need that leads us to arrive at that manifestation of the divinity within us. The more we do so, the more fulfilled and thereby truly satisfied and happy we feel, and our conflict with others lessens as we begin to perceive them as equally representative of yet other aspects of the One and Infinite Deity. The mutually contradictory parts within and outside us begin to appear as mutually complementary, thus resolving many conflicts and contradictions that arise in our everyday lives, from unresolved internal conflicts to discord in relationships. To put it more precisely, *the outer conflicts of man are the reflections of his inner conflicts.*

Another source of conflict is a tussle between what we are and what we secretly aspire to be, between our animal past and our god-like future. There is no part of human nature that can truly resolve this conflict. Reason, even at its best, often leaves us in a quandary, as happened in the case of Arjuna. What should or should not be done often leaves even sages perplexed, says the Master of the *Gītā*. The standards of reason are those of Ignorance, since reason has not the sure light of perfect truth on which to act. Besides, we are often left to the mercy of our emotions, impulses, passions and desires, which can all too easily override reason. Not all of us are fortunate to have an embodied *avatāra* or *guru* by our side to guide and lead us. But there is in each of us the inner *avatāra*, the Divine spark within, the psychic being which can guide us infallibly. This is the first line of psychological help available to us, the inner healer who can put things straight within us, *yaṃ paśyanti hṛtayechīndoṣa*.

Not content with theorizing, Sri Aurobindo and The Mother have provided us with abundant practical methods to aid us in the *discovery of our psychic being*. To discover and uncover the psychic consciousness is to break through the first rank and file of the army of Ignorance into our own true nature, *svabhāva*, and unleash the knowledge and power of the soul. But this is only the first step. There are other aspects of Ignorance that are important, without which we can never be free of suffering and imperfection. This next step is towards our spiritual evolution. Sri Aurobindo once again affirms the ancient truth of rebirth, but imbues it with a new and unique significance. Rebirth, or rather birth itself, in Sri Aurobindo's vision is neither a chemical nor a spiritual accident. It is not an issueless creation where a stern judge sits over us watching and passing decrees of reward and punishment over souls stumbling helplessly through the dark forests of Ignorance. From one birth to another and through different experiences the soul in us grows till it is ready to manifest its inherent divinity upon the earth. *Mukti*, which amounts to an essential freedom from our lower nature and its reactions, is only a preliminary step towards something higher. It is the manifestation of a higher Super-nature upon the earth. Although our soul is inherently divine and its discovery helps us to recover our inner poise and outlook, the nature the soul gathers around itself is not necessarily perfect. As long as the nature that we wrap around us remains fallen and obscure, life on earth shall be replete with error and suffering. The realization of our individual souls will no doubt save us from personal misery, but the common universal problem will continue, leading to disease and disorder of the body and mind.

So the next step is to *ascend to still higher levels of spiritual consciousness*, and with each ascent to take up the lower levels and elevate these to a higher quality by the touch of the higher descending into the lower. This is the evolutionary aspect of life, which can be best described as ascent and integration towards a greater degree of wholeness. This gives man a new aim and psychotherapy a new goal. This evolution is paralleled by the evolution of the consciousness. While it is an unconscious process in animals, it is a more conscious one in humans. In other words, we are not helpless, mute witnesses or unconscious automatons in nature's hands, being shaped by struggles towards higher development. We are and can be active participants, and our choices can help or hinder the evolutionary pace, although it cannot alter the inevitable outcome. Our evolutionary journey stretches through many lives, and it is here that we discover the real significance of rebirth. Our illnesses are not punishments for bad deeds, they (as everything else) are a learning process, an inner growth through which we learn about our different responses to the different energies put forth by our nature.

Here we discover another source of conflict. The first is a general one between our true being and our lower nature, that is, between our true spiritual self and the false ego. The other conflict is between the different parts of our nature that dwell on different levels of consciousness. Thus, the mind may be ready to evolve while the heart may refuse to move and remain confined in its narrow boundaries. Or the heart may be ready to widen, but the life impulse may be mired in lower motives and the body may refuse to move. This creates an *inner disharmony*, leading to psychological and physical imbalances. If the imbalance is too strong and the psychic development weak, the cosmic forces of disruption and disorder may create more serious imbalances, as seen in psychotics, sociopaths and criminals.

The concept of *cosmic forces* has been present in all ancient mystic thought. The modern mind, unable to see beyond the ego's immediate field of vision, knows nothing about it. But the insight of the *yogi* and the mystic goes deeper and reaches farther into the infinite landscapes of our Consciousness. He sees the hidden forces that move life, the occult sources of our action, both the dark and bright sides to our reality, the play of the gods that lead us to harmony, truth and light, and the evil luring the human heart. From another point of view, we may simply see them as evolutionary challenges, assisting our growth by throwing at us obstacles that need to be overcome. The evolutionary journey therefore presents a double challenge, the outer challenge for overcoming the stresses of our environment, and the inner challenge to the soul to overcome the pressure of cosmic forces. When correctly mastered, the first of these challenges leads to a harmonious adaptation between our nature and the environment. The inner challenge can be successfully overcome through inner growth, leading to harmony between the different parts of our nature and their equation with the cosmic forces.

Finally, Sri Aurobindo has provided the widest possible map of consciousness that can be considered a common matrix for a reconciliation between Science and Spirituality. Both admit to Consciousness, but while one sees it as a by-product of our mental evolution, the other sees evolution itself as the natural outcome and an act of Consciousness that is the immaterial and subtlest of subtle Reality behind everything. It is a new way of seeing and mastering life and its anomalies, a top-down view rather than the bottom-up we follow now, leading to much confusion. To take just one example, in the traditional psychoanalytic model lust and anger would be considered primary forces while love and strength are seen as their sublimated and altered versions, and therefore only a civilizational eyewash. But in the spiritual view, it is Love and Strength that are the original forces (among others), and lust and anger their degraded forms. The difference is radical, since the former implies that in effect, man's natural state is akin to that of a fallen animal, and therefore any humanness in him is merely a temporary and fragile cover for the beast; the other view holds that man is essentially a spiritual being and his animal nature as well as his humanness are only a temporary phase leading towards godliness.

A terrestrial divine perfection: The complete solution

To grow in knowledge (the aim of the Vedāntic *yoga*) and to grow in power (the aim of Tāntrika *yoga*), and through this growth to discover the *ānanda* of becoming is the great human journey. The meeting point of these two seemingly different aspects of existence is Consciousness, which in the ancient Indian conception is at once knowledge and power, *cit-śakti*. A growth in Consciousness is the aim of human life and the solution to our human misery and suffering. The more we grow in Consciousness (that is, towards higher levels of knowledge and power), the more we become progressively free of Ignorance and limitation, and the more we discover the peace and *ānanda* hidden at the base of everything. To discover these hidden springs of *ānanda* is to be free from suffering, to discover the hidden source of Light is to be free from error, to discover the hidden source of Love and Oneness is to be free from disharmony and disorder, and to discover in this ascending scale the divinity of Life is to be free from death.

Illness, in this sense, is a barometer, geared towards discovering our hidden weaknesses that need to be developed and perfected, or, in Darwinian language, challenges thrown to the soul by nature to uncover its own inherent divine potential. Each illness represents the obverse of some potential yet to be discovered. Each shadow of the body or mind in the form of illness conceals some possibility of light. Our illnesses are therefore evolutionary challenges, our crises and conflict means for greater self-discovery. Nature utilizes our pain and struggle so that a greater delight and strength may be born within us. It is the task of the therapist to assist this evolutionary process.

How does he do it? What are his means and tools? The first and most important instrument in this catalytic process is the therapist himself. It is the consciousness of the therapist that interacts with the consciousness of the client to effect this change. According to the ancient Indian conception, such an inner change in another individual can only be effected by someone who has worked out the change within himself. The next best alternative is that the person must at least have a strong conviction and faith in the intended change. When neither alternative is available, this change can be brought about by faith in some past Master or representative of God, in whom the client can trust. In either case, the main task of the therapist is to induce faith in a higher Grace or Power and awaken in the client the will towards the possibility of change. Till that happens, the therapist takes on the role of a spiritual midwife to assist the delivery of the client through his dark and painful passage in the womb of nature. The task is indeed a delicate one: moving from dependence on something outside to the discovery of the only true and authentic freedom, brought about by placing oneself in the hands of the divinity within. This was the original conception of '*guru*' provided in Indian thought, on which so much stress is laid. The *guru* is not merely a counsellor (although he is that as well); according to ancient Indian conception, he is a representative of the Divine who is now veiled to the eye of humanity. He reveals to humanity its own higher aspect, the spiritual self concealed by our surface consciousness. The shock of contact with the *guru* acts as a force to bring forth our hidden self, and inspires us to make the necessary effort to discover the inner *guru*, the Divine within. And since the *guru* embodies not only knowledge but also power, the greatest of *gurus* aid the person in distress to discover his own inner divinity. It is only a modern and vulgar misconception that leads to the *guru's* power being seen as a means of satisfying one's frustrated desires. The *guru* may do that if necessary, but more importantly, he equips the disciple with his own inner power and light, which can weather a million frustrations without breaking down. The *guru's* light also unmasks the hidden weaknesses in the disciple without his needing to undergo the painful and difficult processes of disease and crisis. It is this growth in sincerity through the *guru's* intervention, this stripping off of our subconscious defences so that we may see ourselves as we are and then, with the *guru's* help, grow into our own divine nature that is forever free of afflictions and imperfections, full of harmony, peace and *ānanda*, which is the crucial movement of inner growth. In ancient Indian conception it is not the ego defences (mature or immature) that are strengthened, but the strength of the soul that is cultivated. The ego, however necessary at a particular stage of our evolution, becomes a prison at another stage, and must be replaced by the soul. This does not mean a defeatist attitude of inaction as those who know of no other identity than the surface ego perceive it to be. Defeatism is only another warped expression of the ego. The evolution we aim at is an exchange of our surface orientation, superficial understanding and limited responses with a deeper, truer and more powerful understanding and response to life, people and the world. Life assumes the appearance of a frightening struggle so long as we live in Ignorance and for the ego. It becomes a self-possessed delight when we live in and by the soul and for Truth and God.

The means, the instruments and the tools

The counsellor therefore leads the client through a progressive deepening, heightening and widening of his consciousness, using every experience of life, past and present, as materials to aid in the evolutionary process. Towards this end, he may use any and every means, again depending upon the client's readiness to accept, his natural bent and temperament, and most of all, his constitution and faith. All the methods mentioned above can be used. In certain situations the counsellor may even refer the patient to a particular technique as a temporary aid, say for example *yogāsanas* or *prāṇāyāma*. But he must know that these techniques are merely temporary devices, which will eventually need to be outgrown. The goal of the psychotherapeutic journey is not just to ward off the present symptoms, but to discover the inner healer who can heal all anomalies of life in all times to come. It is this discovery of the true soul, this ascent to our own higher levels of consciousness that will progressively reduce our dependence on the *guru*, since we will have discovered the same *guru* within.

This is no easy task. It requires colossal inner development on the part of the counsellor himself. Outer knowledge matters little in this process; in fact, a lot is not even suited to this process. It needs a certain predilection and temperament; perhaps, to use the ancient Indian language, some are destined for it. It is not a question of inner spiritual achievement or merit alone; along with spiritual self-development, it calls for wisdom with strength, a high degree of faith and conviction, an inner goodwill and generosity, but most of all a deep compassion and love for humanity. It is not a Ph.D. course in spiritual counselling, neither does it provide intellectual mastery of the subject but a real living of the truths that one wants to communicate, that matters.

There are lesser alternatives. A client may have faith in a lesser mortal, and still be helped. His faith becomes the guide and the Divine uses it to lead the student through the medium of the teacher. One could also suggest a guided or direct reading of *Śāstra*, a book rich in spiritual knowledge and power. Millions of people all around the world have been helped by reading the Bible, the *Gītā*, the *Dhammapada* in times of crisis rather than by visiting a professional psychiatrist. The modern medical man with his rational tools is often a poor substitute for faith in our own soul's strength and in the Divine Grace. Depending upon the client's need, he could be a teacher, a father figure, a loving and kind mother, a generous and understanding friend, or even simply one human being leading another on the great journey. A counselling session willing to accommodate all possible variations in human nature cannot be based on rigidly fixed principles. The approach has to allow flexibility and not a uniform prescription, for example meditation for all and sundry. In fact, the counsellor should work as an influence whose personal example inspires the client and instils him with faith. And even his counsel should proceed after due consideration to the client's present level of evolution, his natural seeking, his hopes and expectations, his strengths and his weaknesses. This can be best learned through a long and close association with the teacher rather than through any formal course. Ancient Indian thought understood this all too well, and therefore such learning took place largely informally through living with the *guru*, rather than relying on bookish knowledge and the classroom method. The methods of our reductionist science cannot apply if we are to treat the prospective counsellor and client as a living whole. Our problems are not isolated from our total being. Even when they arise in one aspect, they affect the whole.

The counsellor-client relationship in Indian thought

It must, however, be noted that the *guru-śiṣya* form of counselling in the ancient Indian setting was not just a ritualistic formula or method, but simply a statement of fact. Not everyone can be a *guru*; only the man who has moved far on the path of self or God-realization can do so. The *guru* is not an erudite scholar trained in spiritual dialectics or a master in spiritual philosophy. He may or may not be any of these. He may not be a trained psychologist or perhaps even a man of letters, although these would only work to his advantage. He must, at the least, be a man who has found his true soul and is living consciously in it. If he can transmit this soul experience to another, it would help. This is important because the modern mind often misreads in the *guru-celā* relationship either a dependence of a Freudian type, or else a convenient device to facilitate the psychotherapeutic process through faith alone. Faith is no doubt important in the Indian setting, but the emphasis on faith does not sanction blind and irrational obscurantism. On the contrary, it is a necessary pre-condition to arrive at knowledge. It is an enlightened faith that is necessary, a faith consistent with reason; if there is a Divine sense and purpose in this world, then surely there must be a means to discover it; if there is a soul that can help heal, then surely there must be a means to find it; if one man has found it then, given the right means and method, others too can find it. Above all, a faith that if there is at all divine guidance in this world behind the so-called anomalies of life, then there must be a purpose in each trial and tribulation, behind each crisis and failure, behind every stumble and fall. The *guru* assists in this process of discovering the real meaning and significance of crisis, and through it the meaning of our own life in this seemingly meaningless universe. Faith and surrender to the *guru's* guidance is the starting point of this discovery; will, effort and aspiration, the middle stage; knowledge and union with the truth found, the third and last stage of this process. According to Indian tradition, counselling ideally does not end with immediate recovery from the perceived distress, but is carried further till the person has moved beyond all possibility of distress. Distress is only an excuse that the soul uses to start the great journey. Its end is not temporary relief from the transient stresses and satisfactions of life, but the establishment of permanent peace and an unfading joy in the being, a radical cure from all present, past and future ills.

It needs to be mentioned that the spirit of counselling is not commercial at all. If we revert to ancient Indian thought, we find that there was only one criterion that the *guru* used in taking on disciples—the readiness to evolve along the same lines as the master, the *adhikāra bheda*. But once accepted, all commercial and other considerations were put away. If the disciple offered something of his own will, it was another matter. Indeed, the disciple was expected to offer something by way of *guru dakṣiṇa* at the end of the course, and this may have been something as small as a penny or as big as an empire or an object held dear. The disciple gave it in faith and gratitude, trusting that the master knows best. This gift of love at the end of instructions boded well for the student, since ingratitude towards the master, whose debt can never be repaid, was considered the worst of all lapses. Some masters even shouldered their disciples' burdens, not only for one life but for all lives to come.

How relevant is all this in our modern scenario? And is it practicable at all? We must understand that ancient Indian thought aimed at making the ideal pragmatic and practically possible, and the spirit of ancient India is not dead, despite the onslaught of material thought. Even now there exist teachers, instructors, counsellors and masters who go about their task silently without any considerations of money or fame. The gift of knowledge and the help they provide is the greatest gift of all. By the very fact of it being a gift, it becomes one with love and the two are the most potent powers to effectuate the deeper change that is the goal of all authentic psychotherapy.

The goal of psychotherapy

The goal of psychotherapy can be no different from the general goal of mankind in its great evolutionary journey. A crisis only pushes us further towards the goal. The psychotherapist, in the Indian conception, is only a catalyst in this journey from darkness to light. He provides support through authentic love, compassion, wisdom and strength, but most of all through his inner being rather than through the techniques and processes that he may advise, suggest or prescribe. The end result is not just a temporary restoration of the original status quo, but a growth in consciousness towards greater wisdom, greater love, greater freedom, greater harmony that come through our ascent out of animality into divinity, through the discovery of our secret soul. This is beautifully summarized by Sri Aurobindo (2005, p. 4):

> To know, possess and be the divine being in an animal and egoistic consciousness, to convert our twilit or obscure physical mentality into the plenary supramental illumination, to build peace and a self-existent bliss where there is only a stress of transitory satisfactions besieged by physical pain and emotional suffering, to establish an infinite freedom in a world which presents itself as a group of mechanical necessities, to discover

> and realise the immortal life in a body subjected to death and constant mutation,—this is offered to us as the manifestation of God in Matter and the goal of Nature in her terrestrial evolution.
>
> ... For all problems of existence are essentially problems of harmony. They arise from the perception of an unsolved discord and the instinct of an undiscovered agreement or unity. To rest content with an unsolved discord is possible for the practical and more animal part of man, but impossible for his fully awakened mind, and usually even his practical parts only escape from the general necessity either by shutting out the problem or by accepting a rough, utilitarian and unillumined compromise.

In conclusion: A question of faith

This chapter has touched upon the theoretical framework of Indian thought and its relevance to the psychotherapeutic process. The framework is vast and heterogeneous and, despite several points of agreement, there are important divergences as well. Besides, a number of techniques, processes and methods described in various ancient and modern treatises are too exhaustive for even a summary discussion. Each of these needs sustained and persistent practice for practical utility, and cannot be picked up from a book, however helpful they may be. The repeated message that comes through is that Truth is what is lived and experienced within one's soul, and mere preaching without practice will lead nowhere.

In conclusion, one may say that Indian thought moves along many lines simultaneously, resulting in an extraordinary complexity. While on the one hand it creates difficulties in comprehension, on the other hand this richness can be practically useful in catering to the diverse strands and demands of human nature. Yet, certain general principles can be culled out of this complex structure, which can help mankind in its pursuit of relief from suffering. These general principles are elements common to most systems. Since psychotherapy is more concerned with relieving psychological suffering than with philosophical dialectics for its own sake, the thing of the greatest utility is also that which is closely held in the collective faith of the human race. The role of the psychotherapist is not to convert the sick and suffering to any particular belief or to proselytize for narrow sectarian and evangelical purposes, although that might just happen, given that it is natural for a person to develop a faith in something that has been of help in moments of crisis. Faith is a common denominator in Eastern and Western thought, and in both ancient and modern systems. A philosophical doctrine will remain ineffective unless it seizes and holds not only the mind's interest, but also the heart, faith and will. Therefore, what is first necessary in the practical application of ancient Indian thought is that the psychotherapist lives in a wide catholicity, utilising the intrinsic faith of the patient as an essential means of support in his work. And if the faith is found insufficient to support the change, he will work towards instilling and widening it keeping in mind the client's natural bent and past evolution, rather than trying for conversion. Faith works best when it arises from within, and works poorly when it is superimposed from without. This blossoming of faith is a crucial element in all psychotherapy, without which everything else remains incomplete. So common is loss of faith in psychological problems, especially depression, that one may say that most crises of life are actually crises of faith.

This is the first important element in Indian spiritual thought—an insistence on faith as a key element in life, more so than reason. For in spirituality, it is necessary to suspend all judgement and begin with faith as it transcends the mind. It is said that in the end, this faith is fulfilled and justified by the knowledge that emanates from direct and authentic spiritual experience. In a sense this is true of everything else, including science. One begins with faith in a proposition or a method and works patiently till one finds the answer. Thus, we choose one out of many possibilities to strive for. Widening this intrinsic faith rather than confining it within a fixed system of belief is perhaps the most important task of the therapist. Here we must distinguish between faith and belief since the two are commonly confused; although somewhat allied, they are very different in their power and potency.

Belief is directed outward. It is a system of thought held by a mind or a heart and will be conditioned to respond to certain social movements. Faith is more intrinsic, the very grain and mark of man, as the *Gītā* says. It is the spontaneous cry of the soul, which is often buried beneath dead rituals, mechanical beliefs and professed creeds. It is the psychotherapist's task to patiently extract this intrinsic faith, the inner scripture hidden in every heart. This is the Indian version of cognitive therapy, where a client's mind is approached through her/his soul. To change from within by using the client's own faith is therefore the method favoured by the therapist. Towards this end, he moves from the surface to the depths, from outward and professed beliefs and non-beliefs towards that which is concealed in the secret spaces of the soul. Using the helpful material offered by the client's mind, heart and will, the therapist works patiently, offering timely suggestions and intuitive guidance to recover this faith. And it is in this process that we find the role of cognitive and other aspects of the patient's inner constitution.

Despite the enormous complexity of Indian thought, the common cognitive and emotional structures supporting belief are fairly simple. They can be chiefly summarized as belief in an individual soul, in a personal Divine (whether outwardly professed or not in the corresponding philosophical school), in rebirth as one of the means used by nature to arrive at evolutionary fulfilment, in the existence of cosmic forces that help or harm us, and finally, a belief in *mukti* or liberation or a state of soul-perfection as the final goal which all shall one day reach. At the same time, the Indian mind has one great advantage vis-à-vis this complexity—it has become catholic in its approach since it readily accepts the presence of diverse approaches to Truth and Freedom and God. The Indian mind is more ready to accept the word of an enlightened man. It is not because Indians are more credulous, as is commonly believed, but because of the nature of their inner being, which is awake to subtler and deeper realities and is aware that the mind must subordinate itself before the spirit. They know instinctively that Truth can be arrived at not through reason and analysis, but through faith and practice. Most of all, they believe that God's Grace or the intervention of a highly developed person can help us overcome difficulties. The therapist can use these cognitive structures and emotional bonds, already deeply rooted in the Indian psyche.

Whether faith is scientific or not is not the issue here. But if what we have discovered is nothing compared to what remains to be discovered, then man must indeed proceed on faith, a faith in matter or in the spirit, in reason or in faith itself. Especially when it comes to something as subtle as psychology, we must know that truth is not only an external objective reality but an intimate subjective reality, deeply real to the one identified with it. And of all realities known to mankind, there is none more insistent, attractive and universal than the experience of the Divine within and around us, the one simultaneously objective and subjective experience. To deny it in the name of science is to deny the very roots of life itself, and to deny man and his total existence. This is the great truth that Indian psychology carries within it, if we care to listen to its voice of wisdom and compassion. To deny it and give our material research precedence may harm the progression of the human race and its hope to conquer pain and evil. But let us hope that this denial is temporary, for beyond the vision of our material science waits the spirit of a greater truth in man's heart, ready to free us from grief and suffering. The limits of our sight are not the limits of light!

Reference

Aurobindo, Sri (2005). *The life divine*. Puducherry: Sri Aurobindo Ashram Publication Department.

18

Psychotherapy and Integral Yoga Psychology

Michael Miovic

Introduction

In the last decade, a consensus has been reached that it is important to address existential, religious and spiritual concerns in the daily practice of clinical psychology and psychiatry (Richards & Bergin, 1997; Karasu, 1999; Josephson & Peteet, 2004), as well as in palliative care settings (Sulmasy, 2006). For not only are religion and spirituality pervasive cultural phenomena that can have both positive and negative effects on mental health (Shafranske, 1996; Koenig, 1998; Richards & Bergin, 2000), but it is also quite possible that soul and Spirit actually exist. That is, nothing in science or philosophy definitively *disproves* the existence of a divine reality, and therefore mental health professionals need at least to be acquainted with spiritual models of psychology (Miovic, 2004a). Even if they do not personally ascribe to such models, they will encounter many clients who do and find them useful.

The current author has detailed elsewhere the history and central issues of spiritual psychology, from both Western and Asian perspectives (Miovic, 2004a). With regard to Indian spiritual philosophy, there is a tradition in the West stretching from James and Jung through contemporary transpersonal psychology that has always been sympathetic to the experiential insights of Hindu and Buddhist psycho-spiritual practice (Jung & Jaffe, 1961; James & Marty, 1982; Scotton, Chinen & Battista, 1996; Cortright, 1997; Taylor, 1999). In addition, an increasingly compelling body of scientific research supports the veracity of various parapsychological phenomena, and has demonstrated that consciousness is non-local, that is, not limited to the confines of the brain (Byrd, 1988; Radin, 1997; Harris, Gowda & Kolb, 1999; Braud, 2000; Koopman & Blasband, 2002; Standish, Johnson, Kozak & Richards, 2003; Radin & Schlitz, 2005). Today, the convergence of these two streams of thought is leading to a growing interest in Indian psychology, which has always been interested in methods of expanding consciousness so as to find spiritual liberation and overcome suffering (Cornelissen, 2001; Rao, 2002; Joshi & Cornelissen, 2004; Rao, Paranjpe & Dalal, 2008). Indeed, the present book is proof of this renewed interest in the ancient tradition of Indian psychology, both in India and abroad.

Within this larger context, the aim of this chapter is to explore some of the concerns of clinical psychology, with special reference to the areas of overlap between psychotherapy and Sri Aurobindo's model of Integral Yoga Psychology (IYP). Here, IYP is used as an organizing framework because Sri Aurobindo interpreted *yoga* as being primarily a *psychological* process of self-cultivation and ego-transformation, and expressed his insights in modern English. Like psychotherapists, Sri Aurobindo was deeply interested in the problem of how to change character structure and behaviour; only, he felt the key to this change was ultimately spiritual (Dalal, 2001a). Indeed, many of his letters discuss a variety of neurotic and even psychotic symptoms that today fall under the purview of clinical psychology and psychiatry (Sri Aurobindo, 1970; Dalal, 1987). Since IYP accepts the existence of a divine Being/Reality who supports the relative existence(s) of all subsidiary beings/realities, this chapter will present a more theistic model of spiritually informed psychotherapy. For readers who prefer other metaphysical orientations, Indian psychology is graciously broad and diverse, and other chapters in this book present various approaches to spiritual psychology based on non-theistic yet non-dualistic world-views.

Faith as a developmental milestone

As just highlighted, there are many legitimate conceptual frameworks for spiritually informed psychotherapy, and these can generally be grouped into one of three metaphysical orientations, namely theistic, non-theistic (or agnostic) and atheistic (as in non-local studies based on a quantum model of consciousness). Regardless of one's personal orientation, however, it is useful to consider that if indeed there is a supreme Being/Reality, then to have faith in the existence of It is an important step in psychological development. That is, in a divinely constituted universe, to have spiritual faith is not regressive but progressive, and is a normal stage of psychological development to be followed by a subsequent stage in which one actually perceives, experiences and relates intimately with the supreme Being/Reality.

Perhaps an analogy may help illustrate this point: as Mahler showed, the development of object permanence around months 18–24 of a child's life is a major developmental milestone that allows the infant to separate from his or her mother, because s/he now has the capacity to maintain an internal image of 'mother' despite her physical absence. Object permanence is therefore not a defence against separation anxiety; it is an improved perception of the nature of reality that helps the child to master separation anxiety (Gabbard, 2000). Likewise with faith in the Divine: the correct conviction that the Divine exists even when not physically visible allows adult human beings to master the larger anxieties of living based on an improved internal representation of the actual nature of reality. Thus, genuine spiritual faith is not a psychological defence against existential anxiety; it is a developmental achievement that allows one to master existential anxiety. Admittedly the analogy is not perfect, because the process Mahler described establishes the child's ego as separate from the mother's, while spiritual faith leads beyond the ego towards a relationship in which the ego experiences itself as merging into the Divine. Nonetheless, the analogy is good enough to establish why, from the perspective of a theistic model of psychology, the development of faith should be clinically supported (Miovic, 2001).

While no one has yet managed objectively to prove or disprove the existence of the Divine, it is important to understand the philosophical issue described above in order to develop a critical perspective on the literature about psychotherapy and spirituality. Thus far, most Western psychologists writing on the subject come from either a Judeo-Christian or Buddhist background. Not surprisingly, the Western literature on Buddhist psychology adopts a pragmatic and non-theistic approach to spirituality, much as did the historical Buddha (Molino, 1998; Michalon, 2001; Twemlow, 2001). Meditation and mindfulness practices are empirically noted to improve spiritual, mental, emotional and even physical well-being (Kabat-Zinn, Lipworth & Burney, 1985; Kabat-Zinn, Massion, Kristeller, Peterson, Fletcher & Pbert, 1992; Kaplan, Goldenberg & Galvin-Nadeau, 1993; Miller, Fletcher & Kabat-Zinn, 1995; Carlson & Garland, 2005); and fascinating new work is beginning to elucidate the neurophysiological basis of meditation as well (Newberg, & d'Aquili, 1998; Newberg & d'Aquili, 2001; Lazar, Kerr, Wasserman, Gray, et al., 2005; Cahn & Polich, 2006). Also, psychotherapists report that engaging in non-judgemental awareness of the moment during therapy sessions improves their effectiveness as therapists and facilitates the resolution of emotional suffering in clients, which is the main work of psychotherapy (Epstein, 1995; Finn & Rubin, 2000; Germer, Siegel & Fulton, 2005). However, the question of whether or not soul and Spirit exist, and whether clients might be having experiences or perceptions of such at times, is almost entirely avoided in this literature.

On the other hand, psychotherapists writing from the Judeo-Christian perspective have naturally grappled more with the issue of spiritual faith and the individual's relationship with the Divine. This line of inquiry began with Jung's work on archetypes and the phenomenon of a psychological 'God-image' (McLynn, 1996), although his views had little direct effect on mainstream psychoanalytic thinking because of the historic split between Freud and Jung. However, within the Freudian tradition, Winnicott's notions of transitional objects and transitional phenomenon allowed various analysts to re-interpret what Freud called the 'illusion' of religion as a developmentally necessary need for human beings to find meaning and creative connections in the world around them. Subsequently, Rizzuto advanced this line of thinking by showing how the development of intra-psychic structures of God-representation parallels the development of other object relations and may complete an integrated sense of self (Rizzuto, 1979). Rizzuto stopped short of asserting that God is actually real, but Meissner advanced this trajectory by exploring how faith can be understood simultaneously in psychodynamic terms and as referring to a real Christ, a real God, and a real sacrament (Meissner, 2000). Still, he remained cautious about the following step in the sequence, Spero's introduction of an ontologically real God as a factor both in the God-representation and in the therapy process (Spero, 1992). Meissner was concerned about the dangers of therapists wrongly presuming to *know* the Divine's will in the therapy process, but others have gone on to address these legitimate concerns and articulate appropriate ways to conduct faith-based psychotherapy (Richards & Bergin, 1997, 2000).

This brings us to IYP, which synthesizes the experiential insights of *yoga* and Buddhist phenomenology with the spiritual faith of Western monotheistic traditions and the empirical insights of material science, so as to arrive at what we might characterize as non-dual evolutionary theism. That is, Sri Aurobindo proposes that Matter is a densely dormant involution of the infinitely conscious *saccidānanda* into a poise of apparent unconsciousness, and that evolution is the ordered process through which the Divine then progressively reveals itself across space and time under the conditions of matter. In this world-view, transpersonal and spiritual experiences represent the leading edge of the evolution of consciousness on earth, and presage the future emergence of a supra-human life form that will exceed the human consciousness even as human consciousness currently exceeds that of animals and lower life forms (Sri Aurobindo, 1970). Evidently, this interpretation of the aim of life and the ultimate nature of reality offers an interesting new perspective from which to conceptualize some of the central concerns of psychotherapy (Dalal, 2001b; Miovic, 2008).

Soul and ego

Sri Aurobindo uses the term 'psychic being' to refer to the individual soul, which he equates with the *caitya puruṣa* of classical Indian *yoga* psychology. In *yogic* terms, he defines the psychic being as an eternal but evolving aspect of the *ātman* (non-dual transcendent Self) that the *jivātman* (an individualized but non-evolving aspect of the *ātman*) puts forth into the phenomenal play of *prakṛti* (mutative substance of all the physical and supra-physical worlds of manifested existence). However, in contradistinction with traditional notions of reincarnation, Sri Aurobindo places a new emphasis on the evolutionary aim of the process. He posits that the purpose of reincarnation is not to prepare the soul to transcend the cycle of *karma* (as in the classical definition of *nirvāṇa*), but to increase the soul's capacity to perfect life in the physical world, which, as previously mentioned, is itself a manifestation of the Divine reality. Indeed, he argues that this evolution of consciousness is the real force driving the physical evolution of biological forms that are increasingly able to express higher levels of consciousness, for example, the evolution of the animal into the mammalian brain, culminating currently in the human brain (Miovic, 2004b).

In terms of psychotherapy, this world-view

implies that psycho-spiritual development consists of two broad lines of evolution, one the growth of an eternal psychic being or soul, the other the growth of a transient outer being or ego, which is a nexus of cognition, affect and physiology. Now the concept of the ego is the central, organizing principle among the diverse schools of Western psychotherapy. Although it is temporarily being under-used due to the ascendance of neurobiology and psychopharmacology, informed psychoanalysts have pointed out that the concept of the ego encompasses neurophysiology and can therefore still help to integrate the treatment of even 'biological' diseases such as schizophrenia (Diamond, 1997). In fact, the whole premise of the reigning biopsychosocial model of clinical practice is that biological and psychosocial therapies are both relevant to caring for the total human being. What Sri Aurobindo and others add to this proposition is that spirituality is a fourth dimension of consciousness that needs to be annexed to the biopsychosocial model. Even if one rejects the notion of reincarnation, as long as one accepts the reality of a soul that takes birth on earth at least once, the issues of psycho-spiritual growth outlined in this chapter remain fundamentally the same, the only difference being in how many lives the incarnating soul has to work them out.

So then, what exactly is the relationship between the soul and the ego according to IYP? And what are the psychological qualities and characteristics of each? We shall examine these two questions in order. First, there is the problem of what is meant by 'transcending the ego'. In psychodynamic therapy, the whole aim is to strengthen the ego by repairing deficits (giving 'corrective emotional experience') and making unconscious conflicts conscious. In the vernacular of spiritual practice, on the other hand, people are enjoined not to have 'big egos' and to 'be humble' before God. How does one resolve this apparent antithesis? The key is that the vernacular 'big ego' in psychotherapeutic terms refers to narcissistic vulnerability, an ego deficit well-described by Kohut, which is compensated for with narcissistic defences of grandiosity (Mitchell & Black, 1995; Gabbard, 2000). Sri Aurobindo (1970, p. 1392) touches on the neurotic issues of narcissistic grandiosity vs. a punishing superego in the following letter to a disciple:

> Humility is needful, but constant self-depreciation does not help; excessive self-esteem and self-depreciation are both wrong attitudes. To recognise any defects without exaggerating them is useful but, once recognised, it is no good dwelling on them always; you must have the confidence that the Divine Force can change everything and you must let the Force work.

The stable confidence that Sri Aurobindo prescribes here requires a well-integrated ego that allows for what Rizzuto and Meissner would call a mature object-relationship with God. Therefore, in spiritual philosophy, what is really meant by 'transcending the ego' is not to regress to earlier stages of ego development, but to complete the growth of the ego by adding to it another source of sustenance—the awareness of the soul. Thus, genuine spirituality does not erode individuality in a regressive fashion, as happens in different ways in schizophrenia and cults, but rather heightens and deepens true individuality by bringing out the soul, which is a unique manifestation of the Divine. In Sri Aurobindo's words (1970, p. 1368):

> There is individuality in the psychic being, but not egoism. Egoism goes when the individual unites himself with the Divine or is entirely surrendered to the Divine.... On the higher spiritual planes there is no ego, because the oneness of the Divine is felt, but there may be the sense of one's true person or individuality — not ego, but a portion of the Divine.

This distinction between soul and ego is the theoretical foundation of IYP's approach to spiritually informed psychotherapy. Sri Aurobindo acknowledged that childhood and adolescence are critical periods for ego development, and on that basis—for the most part—did not recommend taking up a serious spiritual practice until adulthood. He encouraged families and schools to accept that children do often have spontaneous contact with their souls (a phenomenon mostly overlooked by Western psychology), but he did not advise undertaking conscious efforts at ego-transformation until later. When people are developmentally ready, however, he described the process of transforming the ego as follows (1970, p. 1376):

> Everybody has the ego and it is impossible to get rid of it altogether except by two things — the opening of the psychic within and the descent of a wider ego-free consciousness from above. The psychic being opening does not get rid of the ego at once but purifies it and offers it and all the movements to the Divine, so that one becomes unegoistic through self-giving and surrender ... but it cannot happen in so short a time.

The complexities of how Sri Aurobindo classifies spiritual experiences according to their subjectively perceived somatotopic organization (that is, opening from within or descending from above) go beyond the purview of this chapter. What bears repetition here is that the final 'unegoistic' state he recommends is progressive and adaptive. While both psychosis and neurosis (to a lesser degree) increase fear and decrease the capacity for intimacy and generative love, spirituality as Sri Aurobindo defines it decreases fear and increases the ability to see reality as it is and love others as they are, because one is psychologically fulfilled in the Divine. As Erikson showed, the ego naturally broadens its scope of concerns to include more and more people as it matures, culminating in the healthy generativity of adulthood (Erikson, 1997). IYP would interpret this natural trend towards un-selfishness and individuation, which connects rather than separates one from the others, as due to the covert influence of the soul (psychic being) on ego development. This interaction effect accounts for the stages of faith development identified by Fowler in his research (Fowler, 1981). However, note again that IYP views the soul as ontologically distinct from the ego; hence, it is possible for people to have mature souls but immature or impaired ego-functioning (as happens, for different reasons, in spiritually gifted children, certain patients with psychotic disorders, and dementia in people with strong psychic development).

The second issue of concern, and one more apposite of the practical needs of psychotherapy, is how to distinguish the psychological qualities and characteristics of the soul from those of the ego. According to Sri Aurobindo, the soul's influence is felt in all that leaves the impression of 'sweetness and light'. By this, he does not mean any artificial pleasantry or niceness, but a deep and genuine inner 'movement' that flows purely from a spiritual fount. To name a few such qualities: sincerity, honesty, compassion, joy, love (in the sense of *agape*), forgiveness, patience, humility, courage, devotion, gratitude and the appreciation of beauty. Most people have felt the soul-touch at least once, if not frequently, in the charming innocence of children, in whom the psychic consciousness is often active, albeit in an unformed fashion. Many people also have openings to the soul when appreciating great music, literature, or art (Sri Aurobindo, 1992), or when communing with nature—flowers, for example, are especially full of psychic beauty (The Mother, 2000). For psychotherapy, the most important quality of the psychic being is that it is inherently joyful and free of ambivalence or conflict:

> Let the sweetness and the happy feeling increase, for they are the strongest sign of the soul, the psychic being awake and in touch with us. Let not mistakes of thought or speech or action disturb you—put them away from you as something superficial which the Power and Light will deal with and remove. Keep to the one central thing—your soul and these higher realities it brings with it. (Sri Aurobindo, 1970, p. 1117)

Significantly, a new school of Western psychology, called 'positive psychology', has recently started to study the sources, benefits and sustenance of positive emotions and character traits such as gratitude, forgiveness, joy, love, courage, the appreciation of beauty, hope, curiosity, team-spirit, and so on (Seligman & Csikszentmihalyi, 2000; Snyder & Lopez, 2002; Fredrickson, 2004). Research in this field is beginning to empirically validate interventions that foster positive emotions (Seligman, Steen, Park, et al., 2005), and has found that such feelings often arise during 'flow' states in which the consciousness of the agent becomes one with the activity, as can happen sometimes during satisfying work, play, sports, prayer, meditation, or artistic expression (Csikszentmihalyi, 1990). From the perspective of IYP, all of the feelings and traits aimed at in positive psychology are due ultimately to contact with the psychic being (soul), and all methods for fostering them simply varieties of *sādhanā*. The main concern from the *yogic* perspective is therefore not theoretical but practical, e.g., actually finding and practicing the method that best helps any given individual or group increase the depth, duration and frequency of contact with the soul.

We have thus addressed the first half of the clinical problem—how to recognize and cultivate the soul-influence in human life. But the second half remains, namely the differential diagnosis of various levels of ego functioning, which is the bulk of what confronts practising clinicians. Therapists have all seen countless instances of false or inauthentic positive emotion, such as altruism that hides unconscious anger, faithfulness that avoids loneliness and fear, hypomanic happiness that distracts one from grief, forgiveness motivated by guilt, etc. What does Sri Aurobindo say about such instances in which apparently positive emotions are being used to defend against awareness of hidden negative ones?

Defence mechanisms vs. transformational processes

Before answering the last question directly, let us review the context first. The notion of defence mechanisms is one of the enduring pearls of wisdom gleaned from psychoanalysis. In his research following a cohort of Harvard graduates over several decades, Vaillant elegantly studied the interaction between defensive styles and Eriksonian stages of adult development across the life span. He found that in general, people tend to grow towards using more mature defence mechanisms as they age, and that those who are stuck behind are unhappy and fare poorly (Vaillant, 1993, 2000). The basic defence mechanisms cluster into four groups: psychotic, immature (borderline), intermediate (neurotic) and mature (see Table 18.1).

1 Psychotic	a. Delusional projection b. Denial c. Distortion
2 Immature	a. Projection b. Fantasy c. Hypochondriasis d. Passive aggression e. Acting out f. Dissociation
3 Intermediate (Neurotic)	a. Displacement b. Isolation/ Intellectualization c. Repression d. Reaction formation
4 Mature	a. Altruism b. Sublimation c. Suppression d. Anticipation e. Humour

Table 18.1. Mechanisms of ego-defence
Source: Vaillant (1993; pp. 36–37)

1 Transitional	a. Witnessing b. Listening c. Going into d. Understanding (Mindfulness)
2 Spiritual	a. Aspiration (Invocation or Remembering) b. Surrender (Offering or Sacrifice) c. Rejection (Purification or Discrimination)

Table 18.2. Processes of ego-transformation
Source: Miovic, 2001

Now, in terms of Indian psychology, what Vaillant has demonstrated is an evolution of consciousness, a growth out of the darkness and turbulence of the inchoate ego to the relative stability and self-mastery of the well-formed ego. Over two millennia ago, the *Bhagavad Gītā* described the same sequence of ego development as in Table 18.1, only in less detail and without listing specific defence mechanisms. In his discourse on *yoga* to Arjuna, Kṛṣṇa described personality growth as proceeding from a *tāmasic* character structure (primitive/immature), through *rājasic* (immature/intermediate), to *sāttvic* (mature), and finally beyond into spiritual. Thus, both Indian and Western psychology agree that mature defences are necessary for the pursuit of happiness: people who know only how to deny and project live in raw misery, while those who can sublimate and deploy humour are much freer to find meaning and spots of joy in life, or, as Freud put it succinctly, 'to work and to love' despite the burden of normal human suffering.

IYP also recognizes the existence of defence mechanisms, but understands them within the larger context of the evolution of consciousness. Take, for instance, the following observation by Sri Aurobindo (1970, p. 1329):

> The vital started in its evolution with obedience to impulse and no reason — as for strategy, the only strategy it understands is some tactics by which it can compass its desires. It does not like the voice of knowledge and wisdom — but curiously enough by the necessity which has grown up in man of justifying action by reason, the *vital mind* has developed a strategy of its own which is to get the reason to find out reasons for justifying its own feelings and impulses.

This passage clearly conveys Freud's idea of the 'id' (although the Aurobindonian concept of the 'vital' is broader than that of the 'id'), implies the existence of the unconscious, and cites the defence of rationalization. Sri Aurobindo did not explicitly catalogue the other defence mechanisms listed in Table 18.1 (although he alluded to some in other letters) because he was more interested in the fact that all of the defence mechanisms depend a priori upon the ego. His primary aim, therefore, was to transform the ego into a centre of individuality capable of manifesting the Divine. The only way to achieve this goal, in Sri Aurobindo's opinion, is to evoke the psychic being (soul) through spiritual practice, and then infuse the psychic consciousness into the outer mental, vital and physical parts of the ego, so as to slowly effectuate a radical transformation of egocentric into soul-centric awareness. From the Aurobindonian perspective, cognitive behaviour therapy (CBT) attempts to change ego-functioning via the influence of the mental being, psychoanalysis via the vital, and psychopharmacology via the physical. However, while each of these approaches has its own relative utility, the problem is that the mental, vital and physical components of the ego are all inherently ignorant and in conflict with each other, and in any case no final solution to the ego is achievable at the level of the ego. Only the psychic being (true soul) is by its very nature capable of lasting harmony and unalloyed happiness, because it is a portion of the Divine, and therefore one must find and harness the psychic consciousness in order to definitively transform the ego. Hence the relevance of the psychic being to psychotherapy.

However, if the psychic being (soul) is real and can actually transform the ego function, then it must have modes or processes of operation that are distinct from the defence mechanisms listed in Table 18.1. Sri Aurobindo explained that such psycho-spiritual functions of the psychic being (soul) do indeed exist, and he named them 'aspiration, surrender, and rejection'. He defines *aspiration* as a conscious remembrance of the Divine and invocation for It to transform all of one's inner and outer awareness and action, while *surrender* is the inner movement of opening oneself entirely to the Divine will, and receiving and following its guidance without any reservations. Finally, *rejection* is the process of actively evaluating the source and quality of one's thoughts, feelings and actions, and discriminating and discarding all that does not express the soul (that is, all that is motivated by the ego or by adverse forces of ignorance and falsehood that seek to oppose spiritual evolution). The essential impulse for these three movements comes from the psychic being; however, if the ego is willing, it can take them up and consciously elaborate them. To do so constitutes spiritual *sādhanā* or faith-practice, and thus, a deficiency in any of these psycho-spiritual movements, or an imbalance among them, leads to an incomplete practice of *yoga*.

Against this background, we can now expand the hierarchy of ego development in Table 18.1 by extending it vertically to add the ego-transformational processes listed in Table 18.2. The definition of transformational processes is that they are psychological movements that approach negative or otherwise painful content (drives, wishes, feelings, thoughts) directly and transmute it, instead of trying to ignore, disguise or divert it as defence mechanisms do. Sri Aurobindo named the 'spiritual' processes in Table 18.2; however, in order to integrate IYP with the existing knowledge of psychotherapy, I have created a bridging category dubbed 'transitional processes'. Transitional processes are already used extensively in both CBT and dynamic therapy, and are synonymous with the analytic concept of the 'observing ego'. These functions are classified here as transformational processes because they are not defence mechanisms per se, but rather adaptive capacities of the ego that derive ultimately from the soul's covert influence on the ego (Miovic, 2004b). Although one does not have to be conscious of one's soul in order to have a good observing ego, if the soul is entirely dormant (as in sociopathy), there will be a weak or absent observing ego.

In terms of definitions, to *witness* means to detach from and observe the flow of thoughts and feelings without interfering, controlling or altering them. Witnessing is taught formally in *vipāssanā* and other meditation techniques, and is used extensively in CBT to identify negative automatic thoughts and cascades of catastrophic thinking. Freud also sought witnessing in his method of free association, in which he enjoined the patient to 'say whatever comes to mind, without holding anything back'. On the other hand, *listening* means to turn one's awareness towards arising content so as to study and learn from it, while *going into* means to consciously experience a thought/feeling as much as possible, particularly if the experience is painful or difficult. Finally, *understanding* is the balanced process of practising witnessing, listening and going into over time, the result of which is that liberating awareness that analysts call 'curative insight' and Buddhists call 'mindfulness'. Prototypically, in psychotherapy periods of witnessing allow painful content to arise, which can then be listened to and later gone into, so as to arrive eventually at directly experienced understanding. This cycle is repeated in miniature within each therapy session, and on a larger scale over time across many visits. Also, clients often initially delegate the transitional capacities of ego-transformation to the therapist, and it becomes the therapist's role to gradually help clients learn and internalize these capacities over time (Miovic, 2001).

Practical implications

One good clinical illustration of the transformational processes listed in Table 18.2 is the 12-step method of Alcoholics Anonymous (AA). Much has already been written about AA from sociological, psychological and scientific perspectives, and we should briefly review these findings before proceeding to amplify this knowledge in the light of IYP. To begin with, AA is the single most used method for treating problem drinking in the world, and the scope of AA's organization is now global. After more than half a century of debate regarding its efficacy, scientific research has recently established that participation in AA is not merely *correlated* with decreased drinking, but actually *causes* it (McKellar, Stewart & Humphreys, 2003). Research has also shown that while both professional treatment with CBT and non-professional treatment with AA are probably equally effective for light to moderate drinkers, for heavy and severe drinkers AA is more effective (Morgenstern, Bux & Labouvie, 2003); and that regardless of drinking intensity, more frequent and prolonged attendance at AA meetings yields greater rates of abstinence (Bond, Kaskutas & Weisner, 2003; Cloud, Ziegler & Blondell, 2004; McCrady, Epstein & Kahler, 2004; Moos & Moos, 2004b; Bottlender & Soyka, 2005). Finally, one of the important mediating factors of AA's effectiveness involves opportunities for recovering alcoholics to help each other and help their communities (Pagano, Friend & Tonigan, 2004; Zemore & Kaskutas, 2004), and neither psychotherapy nor psychopharmacology has ever been shown to be *more* effective than AA (Vaillant, 2005). Thus, the best treatment for alcoholism probably entails a collaborative relationship between mental health professionals and AA, especially for patients who have severe mental illnesses (Brooks & Penn, 2003), and indeed data show that such collaboration can improve clients' long-term participation in AA and thus improve outcomes (Kelly & Moos, 2003; Moos & Moos, 2004a).

As for the spirituality of AA, Vaillant has noted that the individual and group spirituality of AA probably taps into some of the same pleasure and reward circuits in the brain that addictions do, and much more powerfully than professional treatment can, so AA offers something invaluable to the alcoholic. Also, he has argued convincingly that AA is neither a cult nor a religion (Vaillant, 2005). Nonetheless, sceptics may still maintain that the 'Higher Power' invoked in AA may just be a useful fiction for eliciting a placebo response, and that the real benefits of AA derive from the solidarity of group membership, frequent and ubiquitous meetings to provide an alternative to drinking, confrontation by peers who challenge the drinker's defences of denial and deception, and a series of tasks (the 12 steps) to restructure the alcoholic's sense of self and overcome feelings of guilt. However, philosophically speaking, it is important to remember that the existence of such mechanisms of action does not negate the existence of a Higher Power, and if indeed the Divine exists, then these mechanisms of action are simply the channels through which the spirituality of AA works.

From the perspective of IYP, the effectiveness of AA re-demonstrates the perennial wisdom that spiritual groups (including *āśramas*, *saṅghams* and churches) help to propagate *dharma*. The more people convene to seek help from the Divine, the more the Divine answers through all available channels—provided, of course, that the inner call is sincere. Second, IYP would note that the proverbial 'devil in the bottle' is not just metaphorical, but real. *Yoga* has always acknowledged the existence of hostile forces and beings (*rākṣasas*, *asuras*) that seek to slay the spiritual seeker and retard or destroy spiritual evolution (Sri Aurobindo, 1970, pp. 393–398), and IYP posits that these hostile forces frequently use alcohol and other intoxicants as an entry into the vulnerable individual, because intoxicants cloud consciousness and undermine reasoning and judgement (Basu, 2004, and personal communication). Lastly, it is impressive that AA charges its clients no fees and most AA service positions are unpaid; that its organizational structure has no significant social hierarchy; and that its governing principles prevent members from gaining fame or consolidating power (Vaillant, 2005). Few other organizations in the world can claim an equal purity of process and dedication to egalitarian ideals. Also, the Big Book's language is often quite beautiful, and the sincerity, honesty and lucidity of its thought and feeling substance reveals a psychic inspiration. Appreciate, for instance, the penetrating transparency of the following: 'Anonymity is the spiritual foundation of all our Traditions, ever reminding us to place principles before personalities' (Alcoholics Anonymous, 1976). That is pure eloquence of the soul speaking.

Likewise, consider the remarkable 12 steps themselves, which on paper read like *yoga sūtras* that teach the soul movements of aspiration, surrender and rejection. Step 1 begins with understanding, or the observing ego's ability to hold a painful truth without enlisting defences to alter or distort perception, while Step 2 proceeds upwards with an *aspiration* to the Divine for transformation:

1. We admitted we were powerless over alcohol—that our lives had become unmanageable.
2. Came to believe that a Power greater than ourselves could restore us to sanity.

Steps 3 through 7 focus on *surrender*, with aspiration and rejection in the background:

3. Made a decision to turn our will and our lives over to the care of *God as we understood Him*.

4. Made a searching and fearless moral inventory of ourselves.
5. Admitted to God, ourselves, and to another human being the exact nature of our wrongs.
6. Were entirely ready to have God remove all these defects of character.
7. Humbly asked Him to remove our shortcomings.

Steps 8 through 10 focus on *rejection*, or the psychic being's conscious will to transform the faults of the outer personality. In this working-through process, the functions of the observing ego are enlisted and applied inter-personally:

8. Made a list of all persons we had harmed, and became willing to make amends to them all.
9. Made direct amends to such people wherever possible, except when to do so would injure them or others.
10. Continued to take personal inventory and when we were wrong promptly admitted it.

Finally, Steps 11 and 12 consolidate the work and provide a prescription for spiritual living based on the continued application of aspiration, surrender and rejection in all activities:

11. Sought through prayer and meditation to improve our conscious contact with God as we understood Him, praying only for knowledge of His will for us and the power to carry it out.
12. Having had a spiritual awakening as the result of these steps, we tried to carry this message to alcoholics, and to practice these principles in all our affairs.

These last two steps, minus the passing reference to alcoholics, are as concise a definition of *yoga* as any written and integrate the three main approaches to the Divine described in the *Bhagavad Gītā* and reaffirmed by Sri Aurobindo in his *Synthesis of yoga*: *bhakti* (devotion, prayer), *jñāna* (knowledge, meditation) and *karma* (action, work). Thus, whatever the limitations of the human beings who seek the help of AA, from the perspective of IYP it is clear that the 12-step method is a spiritual discipline that seeks to re-awaken the psychic being (soul) slumbering in the alcoholic and save him or her from the devil in the bottle. It is a genuine spiritual inspiration.

A second area of IYP's clinical relevance is in deepening clinicians' understanding of the unconscious and resistance, which are primary issues in dynamic psychotherapy. Sri Aurobindo preferred to call the unconscious the 'subconscious' or 'subconscient', because in his view even inert matter is endowed with consciousness (1970, p. 1597):

> For the subconscient receives impressions of all we do or experience in our lives and keeps these impressions in it, sending up often fragments of them in sleep. It is a very important part of the being, but we can do nothing much with it by the conscious will. It is the higher Force working in us that in its natural course will open the subconscient to itself and bring down into it its control and light.

The Aurobindonian concept of resistance encompasses the entire psychodynamic sense of resistance, plus more. This is why transformative spiritual practice is a life-long endeavour and takes even more time and discipline than psychoanalysis, because its scope is total and its final aim is to manifest the Divine in the world:

> The mind resists with an obstinate persistency in argument and a constant confusion of ideas, the vital with a fury of bad will aided by the mind's obliging reasonings on its side, the physical resists with an obstinate inertia and crass fidelity to old habit, and when they have done, the general Nature comes in and says, "What, you are going to get free from me so easily? Not, if I know it," and it besieges and throws back the old nature on you again and again as long as it can (Sri Aurobindo, 1970, p. 1111).

Thus, we see that without reading a word of Freud or Jung, Sri Aurobindo developed a complex understanding of human psychology, including concepts of the ego, the importance of childhood development, defence mechanisms, the unconscious, the significance of dreams (alluded to above and elaborated elsewhere), resistance and the importance of biology. However, where Sri Aurobindo diverges from Western psychology and psychiatry is in his spiritual realism. The practical consequence of this is that he recommends that people find their souls *before* trying to work through the unconscious, because the psychic being is a more powerful agent of knowledge and action than the observing ego. This was the basis of his objection to psychoanalysis as a disciple explained it to him:

> If one wishes to purify and transform the nature, it is the power of these higher ranges to which one must open and raise to them and change by them both the subliminal and the surface being .... But to begin by opening up the lower subconscious, risking to raise up all that is foul or obscure in it, is to go out of one's way to invite trouble. First, one should make the higher mind and vital strong and firm and full of light and peace from above; afterwards one can open up or even dive into the subconscious with more safety and some chance of a rapid and successful change. (Sri Aurobindo, 1970, pp. 1606–1607)

Note that when Sri Aurobindo wrote this letter in the 1930s, he was criticizing the early analytic preoccupation with quickly unearthing childhood libidinal conflicts. However, since then psychoanalysis has evolved along the lines Sri Aurobindo recommended, such that today analysts are careful to strengthen the observing ego (that is, to 'make the higher mind and vital strong and firm') before exploring Oedipal issues. Also, there are many approaches to dynamic psychotherapy that avoid working directly with the unconscious and focus rather on the conscious, pre-conscious and real-time aspects of transference.

Case material

The following case material from a general outpatient psychiatry practice in the United States further illustrates the principles outlined in this chapter as they apply to psychotherapy:

> A 24 year-old married Hispanic woman, with three young children, presented for treatment of severe panic disorder with agoraphobia, and moderate PTSD from childhood sexual abuse. She was grateful for education about her diagnoses, and obtained moderate relief after 3 weeks on clonazepam and citalopram. Based on this positive experience, she was eager to continue on in weekly therapy and medication management with a female resident, as I was leaving the clinic. At our third and final session, it struck me that the patient had consistently exuded an atmosphere of genuine sincerity, gratitude, trust, and an underlying joy of being despite her obvious anxiety. My counter-transference reaction to her was a peaceful feeling in my heart and the thought 'what a lovely person, such a blessing to meet her.' Further exploration revealed that she had an active Catholic faith but she had recently stopped going to church because she always 'yawned and got sleepy' during the services, and was worried that might be rude to her priest and to God. I asked if she felt bored by the sermons, and her face lit up as she replied to the contrary, 'oh no, the words are sometimes so inspiring, they go right into my heart.' I suggested that perhaps she got sleepy because she felt safe, and that maybe God could accept her sleeping in His arms 'like a little baby.' The patient visibly relaxed and replied, 'Yes, I think He wants me back. Two of my kids have dreamed of the Cross recently. I think it's a sign.'

Contrast that with the following vignette:

> A 48 year-old divorced, Hispanic woman with an inactive Catholic faith, presented with moderately severe panic disorder and PTSD from sexual trauma as an adolescent. She spent 8 months of treatment not tolerating medications, resisting education about her diagnoses, and making me feel very frustrated and irritable. Dynamic exploration revealed many ways in which she had felt oppressed by

her mother and was in turn oppressing her teenage daughter, but progress in therapy was painfully slow. During our last session before I left the clinic, she finally realized that she truly had panic attacks and agoraphobia, and expressed limited appreciation for my help.

The major difference between these two cases is the prominence of the psychic atmosphere in the first woman vs. a stubborn vital ego in the second. I would expect the first woman to be able to use spiritual processes of transformation (Table 18.2) to amplify the action of her observing ego in therapy. As she has active psychic movements, she might need help at times in differentiating these from ego defences. For example, she might confuse true aspiration with the defences of fantasy, reaction formation or altruism; or true rejection (a conscious will to change and grow) with the defences of repression or suppression. Her dreams might be rich and vivid, and one would need to distinguish between common dreams that reveal the subconscious and subliminal dreams that reveal the inner being (as happened when her *children* had dreams with a spiritual message for her). Naturally, resistances would arise at times during therapy and restrict the patient's contact with her psychic being, but the working-through process could be accelerated by offering each session to the Divine in whatever way would be mutually agreeable to both the patient and the therapist. This could be done quickly and simply, with or without a particular theological overlay, but the key would be to do it with sincere aspiration and surrender.

Conclusion

This chapter has introduced Sri Aurobindo's Integral Yoga Psychology (IYP) as one possible model for integrating the wisdom of Indian spiritual philosophy with the insights of Western psychotherapy. The primary focus has been on exploring the relationship between the soul (psychic being) and the ego, and understanding how the soul can transform ego functioning. It is proposed that the psychic (soul) movements of aspiration, surrender and rejection extend the range of ego-functioning from ego-defensive operations to ego-transformative processes. Also, the 12-step model of AA is interpreted as potentially evoking these movements of aspiration, surrender and rejection. While Buddhist psychology offers a valuable non-theistic alternative to IYP's more theistic model of psychology, the strength of IYP is that it has a more richly developed concept of evolution and offers an orientation towards the future. Other frameworks for spiritually informed psychotherapy can and should be elaborated as well in order to suit the diverse needs and interests of patients and clinicians. Also, there is much work to be done in order to integrate culturally diverse understandings of spirituality into the mainstream of modern clinical practice.

References

Alcoholics Anonymous (1976). New York: Alcoholics Anonymous World Services (3rd ed.), 58–60.

Aurobindo, Sri (1970). *Letters on yoga* (3rd ed.). Pondicherry: Sri Aurobindo Ashram Trust. (Original work published 1958).

Aurobindo, Sri (1992). *Letters on art, literature and yoga*. Pondicherry: Sri Aurobindo Ashram Trust.

Basu, S. (2004). Occultism and psychiatry: Implications in clinical practice. *Journal of the World Psychiatric Association, 3*(1), 194.

Bond, J., Kaskutas, L. A., & Weisner, C. (2003). The persistent influence of social networks and Alcoholics Anonymous on abstinence. *Journal of Studies on Alcohol, 64*(4), 579–588.

Bottlender, M., & Soyka, M. (2005). Catamnestic study on the efficacy of an intensive outpatient treatment programme for alcohol-dependent patients: Impact of participation in AA on the abstinence rates. *Fortschritte der Neurologie-Psychiatrie, 73*(3), 150–155.

Braud, W. (2000). Wellness implications of retroactive intentional influence: Exploring an outrageous hypothesis. *Alternative Therapies in Health and Medicine, 6*(1), 37–48.

Brooks, A. J., & Penn, P. E. (2003). Comparing treatments for dual diagnosis: Twelve-step and self-management and recovery training. *American Journal of Drug & Alcohol Abuse, 29*(2), 359–383.

Byrd, R. C. (1988). Positive therapeutic effects of intercessory prayer in a coronary care unit population. *Southern Medical Journal, 81*(7), 826–829.

Cahn, B. R., & Polich, J. (2006). Meditation states and traits: EEG, ERP, and neuroimaging studies. *Psychological Bulletin, 132*(2), 180–211.

Carlson, L. E., & Garland, S. N. (2005). Impact of mindfulness-based stress reduction (MBSR) on sleep, mood, stress, and fatigue symptoms in cancer outpatients. *International Journal of Behavioral Medicine, 12*(4), 278–285.

Cloud, R. N., Ziegler, C. H., & Blondell, R. D. (2004). What is Alcoholics Anonymous affiliation? *Substance Use & Misuse, 39*(7), 1117–1136.

Cornelissen, M. (Ed.) (2001). *Consciousness and its transformation*. Pondicherry: Sri Aurobindo International Centre of Education.

Cortright, B. (1997). *Psychotherapy and spirit: Theory and practice in transpersonal psychotherapy*. Albany: State University of New York Press.

Csikszentmihalyi, M. (1990). *Flow: The psychology of optimal experience*. New York: Harper & Row.

Dalal, A. S. (1987). *Living within* (pp. ix–xxxvii, 30–85). Pondicherry, India: Sri Aurobindo Ashram Trust.

Dalal, A. S. (2001a). *Psychology, mental health and yoga*. Pondicherry, India: Sri Aurobindo Ashram Trust.

Dalal, A. S. (2001b). *A greater psychology: An introduction to Sri Aurobindo's psychological thought*. San Francisco: J. P. Tarcher.

Diamond, D. B. (1997). The fate of the ego in contemporary psychiatry with particular reference to etiologic theories of schizophrenia. *Psychiatry, 60*, 67–88.

Epstein, M. (1995). *Thoughts without a thinker*. New York: Basic Books.

Erikson, E. H. (1997). *The life cycle completed, extended version*. New York: W.W. Norton & Company.

Finn, M., & Rubin, J. B. (2000). Psychotherapy with Buddhists. In P. S. Richards & A. E. Bergin (Eds.), *Handbook of psychotherapy and religious diversity* (pp. 317–340). Washington, DC: American Psychological Association.

Fowler, J. W. (1981). *Stages of faith: The psychology of human development and the quest for meaning*. New York: Harper Collins.

Fredrickson, B. L. (2004). The broaden-and-build theory of positive emotions. *Philosophical Transactions of the Royal Society B, 359*, 1367-77.

Gabbard, G. O. (2000). Psychoanalysis. In B. J. Sadock & V. A. Sadock (Eds.), *Kaplan and Sadock's comprehensive textbook of psychiatry* (7th ed.), (pp. 563–607). Philadelphia: Lippincott Williams & Wilkins.

Germer, C. K., Siegel, R. D., & Fulton, P. R. (2005). *Mindfulness and psychotherapy*. New York: Guilford Press.

Harris, W. S., Gowda, M., Kolb, J. W., et al. (1999). A randomized, controlled trial of the effects of remote, intercessory prayer on outcomes in patients admitted to the coronary care unit. *Archives of Internal Medicine, 24*(1), 79–88.

James, W., & Marty, M. E. (Eds.) (1982). *The varieties of religious experience*. New York: Penguin.

Josephson, A. M., & Peteet, J. R. (2004). *Handbook of spirituality and worldview in clinical practice*. Washington, DC: American Psychiatric Publishing.

Joshi, K., & Cornelissen, M. (Eds.) (2004). *Consciousness, Indian psychology and yoga*. New Delhi: Centre for Studies in Civilizations.

Jung, C. G., & Jaffe, A. (Eds.) (1961). *Memories, dreams, reflections*. New York: Random House.

Kabat-Zinn, J., Lipworth, L., & Burney, R. (1985). The clinical use of mindfulness meditation for the self-regulation of chronic pain. *Journal of Behavioral Medicine, 8*(2), 163–190.

Kabat-Zinn, J., Massion, A. O., Kristeller, J., Peterson, L. G., Fletcher, K. E., Pbert, L., et al. (1992). Effectiveness of a meditation-based stress reduction program in the treatment of anxiety disorders. *American Journal of Psychiatry, 149*(7), 936–942.

Kaplan, K., Goldenberg, D., & Galvin-Nadeau, M. (1993). The impact of a meditation-based stress-reduction program on fibromyalgia. *General Hospital Psychiatry, 15*, 284–289.

Karasu, T. (1999). Spiritual psychotherapy. *American Journal of Psychotherapy, 53*(2), 143–162.

Kelly, J. F., & Moos, R. (2003). Dropout from 12-step self-help groups: prevalence, predictors, and counteracting treatment influences. *Journal of Substance Abuse Treatment, 24*(3), 241–50.

Koenig, H. G. (Ed.) (1998). *Handbook of religion and mental health.* San Diego: Academic Press.

Koopman, B. G., & Blasband, R. A. (2002). Two case reports of distant healing: New paradigms at work? *Alternative Therapies in Health and Medicine, 8*(1), 116–120.

Lazar, S. W., Kerr, C. E., Wasserman, R. H., Gray, J. R., et al. (2005). Meditation experience is associated with increased cortical thickness. *Neuroreport, 16*(17), 1893–1897.

McCrady, B. S., Epstein, E. E., & Kahler, C. W. (2004). Alcoholics Anonymous and relapse prevention as maintenance strategies after conjoint behavioral alcohol treatment for men: 18-month outcomes. *Journal of Consulting & Clinical Psychology, 72*(5), 870–878.

McKellar, J., Stewart, E., & Humphreys, K. (2003). Alcoholics Anonymous involvement and positive alcohol-related outcomes: Cause, consequence, or just a correlate? A prospective 2-year study of 2,319 alcohol-dependent men. *Journal of Consulting & Clinical Psychology, 71*(2), 302–308.

McLynn, F. (1996). *Carl Gustav Jung: A biography* (pp. 398–415, 459–509). New York: St. Martin's Press.

Meissner, W. W. (2000). Psychoanalysis and religion: Current perspectives. In J. K. Boehnlein (Ed.), *Psychiatry and religion: The convergence of mind and spirit* (pp. 53–70). Washington, DC: American Psychiatric Press.

Michalon, M. (2001). 'Selflessness' in the service of the ego: Contributions, limitations, and dangers of Buddhist psychology for Western psychotherapy. *American Journal of Psychotherapy, 55*(1), 202–218.

Miller, J. J., Fletcher, K., & Kabat-Zinn, J. (1995). Three-year follow-up and clinical implications of a mindfulness meditation-based stress reduction intervention in the treatment of anxiety disorders. *General Hospital Psychiatry, 17*, 192–200.

Miovic, M. (2001). Towards a spiritual psychology: Bridging psychodynamic psychotherapy with integral yoga. In M. Cornelissen (Ed.), *Consciousness and its transformation* (pp. 98–119). Pondicherry: Sri Aurobindo International Centre of Education.

Miovic, M. (2004a). An introduction to spiritual psychology: Overview of the literature, east and west. *Harvard Review of Psychiatry, 12*, 105–115.

Miovic, M. (2004b). Sri Aurobindo and transpersonal psychology. *Journal of Transpersonal Psychology, 36*(2), 111–133.

Miovic, M. (2008). Therapeutic psychology and Indian *yoga*. In K. R. Rao, A. C. Paranjpe, & A. K. Dalal (Eds.), *Handbook of Indian Psychology* (pp. 449-470). New Delhi: Cambridge University Press India Pvt. Ltd.

Mitchell, S. A., & Black, M. J. (1995). *Freud and beyond: A history of modern psychoanalytic thought.* New York: Basic Books.

Molino, A. (Ed.) (1998). *The couch and the tree: Dialogues in psychoanalysis and Buddhism.* New York: North Point.

Moos, R. H., & Moos, B. S. (2004a). Help-seeking careers: Connections between participation in professional treatment and Alcoholics Anonymous. *Journal of Substance Abuse Treatment, 26*(3), 167–173.

Moos, R. H., & Moos, B. S. (2004b). Long-term influence of duration and frequency of participation in alcoholics anonymous on individuals with alcohol use disorders. *Journal of Consulting & Clinical Psychology, 72*(1), 81–90.

Mother, The (2000). *The spiritual significance of flowers.* Pondicherry: Sri Aurobindo Ashram Trust.

Morgenstern, J., Bux, D. A., Labouvie, E., et al. (2003). Examining mechanisms of action in 12-step community outpatient treatment. *Drug & Alcohol Dependence, 72*(3), 237–247.

Newberg, A., & d'Aquili, E. (1998). The neuropsychology of spiritual experience. In H. G. Koenig (Ed.), *Handbook of religion and mental health* (pp. 76–94). San Diego: Academic Press.

Newberg, A., & d'Aquili, E. (2001). *Why God won't go away: Brain science and the biology of belief.* New York: Ballantine.

Pagano, M. E., Friend, K. B., Tonigan, J. S., et al. (2004). Helping other alcoholics in Alcoholics Anonymous and drinking outcomes: Findings from project MATCH. *Journal of Studies on Alcohol, 65*(6), 766–773.

Radin, D. (1997). *The conscious universe: The scientific truth of psychic phenomena.* New York: Harper Collins.

Radin, D. I., & Schlitz, M. J. (2005). Gut feelings, intuition, and emotions: An exploratory study. *Journal of Alternative & Complementary Medicine, 11*(1), 85–91.

Rao, K. R. (2002). *Consciousness studies: Cross-cultural perspectives.* London: McFarland & Company.

Rao, K. R., Paranjpe, A. C., & Dalal, A. K. (Eds.) (2008). *Handbook of Indian psychology.* New Delhi: Cambridge University Press India Pvt. Ltd.

Richards, P. S., & Bergin, A. E. (Eds.) (1997). *A spiritual strategy for counseling and psychotherapy.* Washington, DC: American Psychological Association.

Richards, P. S., & Bergin, A. E. (Eds.) (2000). *Handbook of psychotherapy and religious diversity.* Washington, DC: American Psychological Association.

Rizzuto, A. M. (1979). *The birth of the living God.* Chicago, IL: University of Chicago Press.

Scotton, B. W., Chinen, A. B., & Battista, J. R. (Eds.) (1996). *Textbook of transpersonal psychiatry and psychology.* New York: Basic Books.

Seligman, M., & Csikszentmihalyi, M. (2000). Positive psychology: An introduction. *American Psychologist, 55*(1), 5–14.

Seligman, M. E., Steen, T. A., Park, N., & Peterson, C. (2005). Positive psychology progress: Empirical validation of interventions. *American Psychologist, 60*(5), 410-21.

Shafranske, E. P. (Ed.) (1996). *Religion and the clinical practice of psychology.* Washington DC: American Psychological Association.

Snyder, C. R., & Lopez, S. J. (Eds.) (2002). *Handbook of positive psychology.* Oxford: Oxford University Press.

Spero, M. H. (1992). *Religious objects as psychological structures: A critical integration of object relations theory, psychotherapy, and Judaism.* Chicago, IL: University of Chicago Press.

Sulmasy, D. P. (2006). Spiritual issues in the care of dying patients: 'It's okay between me and God'. *Journal of the American Medical Association, 296*(11), 1385–1393.

Standish, L. J., Johnson, C., Kozak, L., & Richards, T. (2003). Evidence of correlated functional magnetic resonance imaging signals between distant human brains. *Alternative Therapies in Health and Medicine, 9*(1), 122–128.

Taylor, E. I. (1999). *Shadow culture: Psychology and spirituality in America.* Washington, DC: Counterpoint.

Twemlow, S. W. (2001). Training psychotherapists in attributes of 'mind' from Zen and psychoanalytic perspectives. *American Journal of Psychotherapy, 55*(1), 1–21.

Vaillant, G. E. (1993). *The wisdom of the ego.* Cambridge, MA: Harvard University Press.

Vaillant, G. E. (2000). Adaptive mental mechanisms: Their role in positive psychology. *American Psychologist, 55*(1), 89–98.

Vaillant, G. E. (2005). Alcoholics Anonymous: cult or cure? *Australian & New Zealand Journal of Psychiatry, 39*(6), 431–436.

Zemore, S. E., & Kaskutas, L. A. (2004). Helping, spirituality and Alcoholics Anonymous in recovery. *Journal of Studies on Alcohol, 65*(3), 383–391.

19

Integral education: An application of Indian psychology

Neeltje Huppes

> At present mankind is undergoing an evolutionary crisis in which is concealed a choice of its destiny; for a stage has been reached in which the human mind has achieved in certain directions an enormous development while in others it stands arrested and bewildered and can no longer find its way .... Man has created a system of civilisation which has become too big for his limited mental capacity and understanding ....
>
> —Sri Aurobindo, *The life divine*, p. 1053

Introduction

Sri Aurobindo wrote this more than 60 years ago, but how true it still is. We see humanity struggling with the issues of individual and collective use (and abuse) of power and their concomitant responsibilities. We are experimenting with values and redefining our belief systems. There is a massive upsurge of both progressive and conservative forces. Each of these movements seems to be seeking to reshape and redefine itself, to search for a new identity, to find and express a new aim in life. They often clash, each proclaiming that its truth is higher or greater than that of the other.

Could it be that all these endeavours and upheavals are pointing to the need for a decisive change? For thousands of years humankind has focused on sharpening, increasing and refining our human capacities. There has been a manifold development of our physical and mental abilities, resulting in great achievements in many spheres of life. The most obvious effect of this mass development has been a remarkable technological progress that, while allowing many comforts, has also brought a tremendous over-stimulation to our lives. With the click of a mouse we can access almost any information we need, or communicate with people anywhere on the globe. Yet, when we read or watch the news, we get the impression that collectively we lack the right approach to handle wisely the enormous powers we have unleashed with our mind. Each of us is challenged. Do we really have the knowledge and wisdom to resolve the myriad conflicts we have created for ourselves? How can we help restore the balance, and create a more fulfilling life and a more harmonious world for all of us?

The truths that have guided us so far are apparently not enough to handle the tremendous powers technology has set in motion. Technology forces us to live globally, and so we must recast our identity in a world in which our self is no longer embedded within the limited context of traditional family values. Education plays an important role in both individual and national development, and so one wonders why education has been unable to guide humanity towards greater harmony, providing fulfilment to all. What is this wisdom needed to bring about that decisive change? We are confronted with the ills of continuing imperialism and rampant commercialism, destroying not only human life but threatening the very life of the planet. Our most urgent need is to replace imperialism with more beneficent forms of globalization, and to realize a deeper understanding of personal freedom—a freedom not gained at the expense of others, but based on unity with others and harmony with Nature.

We can look at our world from many perspectives—economic, ecological, cultural, personal, and so on. Seeing the limited successes we have achieved so far in creating that harmonious world that we long for, we find that none of these perspectives goes deep enough. All are part of the larger whole, but even together they are incomplete; they are not integral enough.

During the last couple of centuries Western civilization has dominated the way our world has been shaped. Its influence remains dominant, and today's problems originate to a large extent from the fact that Western cosmology lost integrality hundreds of years ago. Simplifying history, one could say that it began when science parted ways with the Roman Catholic Church at the time of Bruno, Copernicus and Galileo. When science parted from religion, it also tossed out spirituality, and since science has been so successful, the dominant world-view is now based on a physicalist, scientific paradigm. India did not escape this development, and even now Western psychology dominates the study of psychology at Indian universities. Is it not time to research what the more integral Indian psychology has to offer?

PART I — INTEGRALITY IN THE INDIAN CONTEXT

What is integrality?

Each of us is endowed with various levels and forms of consciousness. We know that we have thoughts and feelings, and are able to take action through the use of our body. At any given moment we can shift our centre of identification between these mental, affective, volitional and physical domains. What is more, each of these domains has not only a surface layer, but also deeper, inner layers. This means that during a day we shift many times, not only from domain to domain but also between our surface nature and the various inner parts of our being. Over the millennia humans have developed an incredible complexity of which most of us are hardly aware. As a result we do not live up to our true potential. Our present fact-based and marks-oriented education makes it worse, as it is very limited and taps only a narrow part of our potential. Integral education strives for a much wider and deeper development. But let us first take a closer look at the philosophical context of integrality.

Integrality in the context of Indian education

Indian civilization has its foundation in a deep understanding of integrality. It sees the universe not as a purely material fact, but knows that a Supreme, although often concealed, consciousness pervades each and everything. In our daily consciousness this Supreme consciousness is mostly covered up, yet each of us carries a spark of the Supreme deep within, called the *caitya puruṣa* or soul. If the soul is allowed to come to the foreground, it can influence the mental, affective, volitional and physical surface consciousness to act more in harmony with this universal consciousness. Our surface then becomes an instrument for the soul to act in this world. All this is part of a life-affirming spirituality which reaches beyond the divisions of religion. In the perennial cosmology of India, the psychological process of human development is seen as *a progressive development; a development that is balanced between the innermost part of the being—the soul—and the outer life.*

In harmony with this, the ideal of integral education combines two lines of development: the revealing and unfolding of the soul, and the development of the mental, affective and physical domains as instruments for expressing that soul in daily life. It calls for an individualized process of education. Of course, we want universal education for all the children of India, but for universal education to work, it must respect individual differences and provide an education that is relevant for every child. Consider the differences in daily inputs and the experiences of children growing up in one of the metros and children in interior rural areas—how can prescribing the same textbook be meaningful for both categories? If 'universal education' could have come about through a standard textbook, it would have been achieved long ago. Consider the large variety in intelligence, capacities and qualities of children. Only an education based on genuine respect for individual differences can provide a meaningful development for each student.

Some theoretical and practical aspects of integral education

Based on his deep understanding of the Indian psyche and his emphasis on integrality, Sri Aurobindo wrote a series of short introductory essays on the general principles of education between 1910 and 1920. He says (1990, pp. 13-14):

> ...true and living education ... helps to bring out to full advantage, makes ready for the full purpose and scope of human life all that is in the individual man, and ... at the same time helps him to enter into his right relation with the life, mind and soul of the people to which he belongs and with that great total life, mind and soul of humanity of which he himself is a unit.

Sri Aurobindo understood that education is a magnificent tool for building up a nation. He and his spiritual associate, The Mother, called their model of education integral education. First, it is centred around the innermost consciousness, the soul. Second, it emphasizes optimum development of the mental, affective and physical domains, not as an aim in itself, but as instruments through which the soul can express itself in the world. The principles of integral education do not impose a belief system or a set of rules to adhere to. They respect the vast individual differences of the students and can be applied anywhere in the world.

Two basic assumptions

The impulse towards self-exceeding is an innate part of being human.

Education needs to implement more methods that facilitate the action of this innate tendency to excel. In sports, the principle of self-exceeding has become so commonplace that records which seemed impossible to be surpassed the year before are being regularly broken. I have experienced similar feats in mental development in a Free Progress school, and saw students excel in solving math problems far beyond the levels of their age group.[1]

Self-exceeding also has a spiritual component, which brings us to the concepts of *svadharma* and *svabhāva*. Here, *dharma* is not used in the sense of morality or ethics. *Svadharma* is action governed by the *svabhāva*, the essential law of one's nature. When we act here on earth according to our highest or inmost *svadharma*, our action emerges from and is an expression of our essential Self, our soul. Integral education trusts that each one of us is able to find his or her own balance between developing, training and refining one's mind, heart and body, and discovering how to live from one's soul.

We perceive the nature of reality according to our state of being. Consequently, everything depends on where we place our consciousness.

From the experiences of daily life, we can easily learn that each mental, affective and volitional domain has its own 'laws'. The 'laws' pertaining to the physical domain are different from the laws that provide structure to the affective domain, and these in their turn are different from those of the mind. During the day, without realizing it, we often shift our consciousness between the various domains. As we observe ourselves, we become aware that our perceptions change according to the domain we identify with. For instance, most of us have experienced the difference it makes when we react to a situation with our reasoning mind, and when we react with our emotional heart. Our soul brings in other qualities yet; qualities that illumine and harmonize whatever we do. Once we realize this, we can begin to live consciously and choose the domain from which we interact, thereby changing what we allow to influence our life. Integrality starts with becoming conscious of all the parts and layers of our being. Integral education aims to help children become conscious of these inner and outer processes without forcing students into a fixed mode. Spirituality is not a subject to be taught. Neither can 'being spiritual' be imposed.

All integral education can do is provide an environment in which students are free to make choices, while encouraging them to do so as consciously as they can. It trusts that self-observation will naturally lead to self-awareness. This can help the student to feel responsible for self-made choices, which in turn can lead to an accelerated self-development, leading to becoming a truly responsible citizen.

Key concepts of integral education

There are four key concepts of integral education:

- Acknowledgement of the fact that *the whole spectrum*, from unconsciousness to divine consciousness, from the surface layer to the greater depths and heights, is present in everyone. It is also present everywhere around us in people and nature, and thus in the classroom we should not narrow it down to the layer of the mind only, but provide scope for developing the other layers as well. The aim is to give students the opportunity to extend their own range of consciousness by heightening, widening and deepening their instrumental domains.
- Respect for the relationship between *being* (to live in the presence of the highest consciousness an individual can perceive) and *becoming* (the outward, surface consciousness in which we usually live).
- The view that each student is a *unique* being who is developing the inner nature and the innermost qualities of the soul as well as the outer capacities in the surface domains—mental, affective, volitional and physical. The progressive manifestation of the soul in the surface nature has to take place in and through daily life. Each student has to be able to find his/her individual level of integration.
- The acknowledgement of the concepts of *svabhāva* and *svadharma* as the essential principles through which a human being can express him/herself in this world.

Reflections

Living according to one's *svadharma* generates true and perfect action in the world. It is the best that an individual can give to society. By neglecting the search for one's *svabhāva* one loses one's true authenticity; neglecting the ideal of *svadharma* leads to both the nation and the individual losing out. The modern consumer society encourages us to live completely in the surface consciousness and wants us to believe that we are happiest when spending money on all kinds of goods. By now, we all know that this attitude has ruined our earth, bringing it almost to a point of no return. It is the task of education to offer students the broadest range of world-views with as little bias as possible, so that they can reflect on the choices they want to make. It is for the students to decide consciously how much importance they give to the soul and to the surface nature, and to work out a personal balance between these in their daily lives (Mirambika, 2013).

A broad-based integral education asks for a shift in educational methodology. Teachers often complain about the lack of motivation in students. But is it really the fault of the students? In our present educational system, students can construct or create a positive self-image only with reference to their success in the material and external world. Education has largely turned into a race for the highest marks, which, it is wrongly believed, will enable children later to make the most money and so be happy. Unfortunately, this system inherently gives importance and provides satisfaction to the natural inclinations of only a few students; it hardly allows other precious aspects of the human nature to be developed in the classroom. Yet, many children know from within that they have other important qualities, and that the value of their life is reduced by not cultivating these. My experience is that students deeply appreciate it when they are getting time to reflect without compulsion. Learning primarily for outer gains, like the highest marks, has reduced students to the level of input-output devices. Not being part of the highest 20 per cent leaves a feeling of being-not-capable-enough in 80 per cent of young adolescents. As long as the educational model complies with this single-track race, the nation loses the great potential and precious qualities of millions of young people.

A clear sign pointing to the need for a shift in methodology is the complaint of employers that young recruits are not creative, and that they lack initiative and responsibility when they enter the job market. The responsibility rests squarely with schools, where rote-learning is still the accepted mode of knowledge transfer, destroying enthusiasm, creative potential and an inquiring attitude. Allotting plenty of time for self-directed learning, as in the project-mode, is an alternative that seems to work well.

Looking ahead

For a long time, educationists have been talking about child-centred education. But even now, in practice, instead of appreciating the faculties and qualities of the child in its entirety, it is the mark sheet of the child that stands at the centre! There can be no doubt that the Western model of education has allowed humankind to make enormous technological progress, but it has by and large ignored the spiritual aspects of life. This one-sided progress has led us close to the destruction of the ecological balance of the earth. The craving for power and wealth is so strong that even now, calls for constraint by eminent scientists are hardly heeded. Can the balance be restored so as to prevent the world-wide disasters set off by indiscriminate human craving? Paying greater attention in education to the qualities of our innermost essence will help us to utilize our scientific discoveries in a more ethical manner. At the beginning of this century a light on the educational horizon has been the fact that the UNESCO has realized this need and appointed a commission to bring out a report on the educational model of the twenty-first century. Significantly, this report is titled *Learning: The Treasure Within*. Basically, Indian education was founded on this concept, even though it was lost during colonial times, the echo can still be heard. India, located as it is at the beginning of a significant economic development, can still avoid making the same mistakes as the West. The inherent strength of the integral world-view that she nurtured throughout the ages needs now to be translated into a new model of education.

India plays an important role in the information society. To remain not only a successful but also a responsible player in this field, both the content and method of schooling have to change. The fact that the changes needed in schools and colleges are so much in harmony with a more integral, more Indian approach to life seems to provide a wonderful opportunity. My experience in working with young adults in colleges showed that they want a curriculum that incorporates time for self-enquiry and self-development, with open-ended discussions that help them to reflect on their role in society. In short, they want a study environment that encourages them to discover for themselves who they are and how they want to shape their lives and become responsible citizens.

PART II — SUGGESTIONS FOR IMPLEMENTATION

Shifts in the content of education

To bring about this integration, two major shifts related to educational content are needed.

The first concerns the way we look at the content of the syllabus. The course content must not be seen as mere information that has to be transferred to the students. Instead, the content must serve as a means to evoke in the students thought processes and personal experiences. In this way, learning can become truly experiential. It is only when a teacher shifts focus and starts concentrating on the *self-development* of the student instead of on the effective transfer of content that learning becomes integral.

The second shift is related to learning levels and modalities. Students are naturally at different levels of both inner and outer development. Moreover, they come from a variety of backgrounds and have various talents. The use of a single textbook approach will not provide opportunities for optimum learning.

Most teachers will agree that in the present system, both the intelligent and the weaker students suffer. Moreover, students with some special gift are not given the opportunity to practise and develop it other than in a few periods of so-called co-curricular activities. There is thus a need for an entirely new approach related to learning material.

A practical solution allowing for the required diversity in learning levels and learning content is a combination of a relatively small compulsory *Minimum Common Syllabus* for all students, combined with extensive periods of self-directed learning in which the student chooses what and how s/he wants to learn. It could be acquiring a skill, working on a quality, speeding ahead in a certain subject, mastering a certain content in depth, using time for self-reflection, etc.

In practice, this can be worked out by daily setting apart certain common self-directed learning periods for all students at a certain level (let's say class 9 and 10) in the school. This makes most of the teachers (including arts and crafts teachers) who teach at that level available to the students during these periods. This also offers students a wide variety of choices and teachers. Students sign up in advance for a certain project, either offered by a teacher or requested by one or more students. One of the requirements for a positive outcome of project work is the availability of a rich diversity of learning materials on various learning levels. This provides individual students with a good choice and allows for a wide range in learning opportunities and optimum development. The project approach has been successfully implemented in several integral schools.[2]

The details of the other half of this method, the Minimum Common Syllabus, has to be worked out with great care, but the total quantity of learning material in the MCS need not be more than what an average student can complete in half the time of the regular syllabus.

Shifts in methodology linked to present day technology

It has been explained that our present situation calls for major shifts in our teaching-learning practices. The major shift here is to acknowledge that *learning is a process*. Several facts point in the same direction. First is the revolution in educational technology, with data readily available on CDs, DVDs, and on the Internet. This calls for an important change in our attitude towards information transfer: it has become more necessary for students to learn *how to process* information than to collect a vast stock of facts learned by rote. Two other important trends need to be considered here. Due to the fast progress of science, data become rapidly outdated and have to be readjusted continuously. Also, knowledge has become so specialized that it is impossible for any educational system to offer inputs that are complete enough. So we find that when a graduate begins a new job, most companies first provide him or her with a specialized training period of several weeks. Thus, the current reality is that any effective system of education must equip students with the skills needed for the fast pace and complexity of the information age, in which memorizing one fixed set of facts useful for all has become less relevant than it used to be.

Shifts in the process of education related to values

When the aim of the educational process is the development of the student, the subject matter is meant to help a student widen and deepen his world, and gain insight into his own qualities, capacities and skills. Applied in this way, it will lead the student to ask questions such as—*Who am I? What do I want to do, to become? What is the required factual knowledge? What type of inner knowledge do I need to reach my goals?* The aim here is not to tell the students the 'right' answer, like in moral education classes, but to be a good facilitator and create an environment in which the student feels safe to truly grapple with these questions, and come personally to the most authentic answers. Only when self-knowledge is thus gained and integrated can we utilize it effectively in our daily actions, and only then do we become self-reliant citizens.

In an integral learning environment, self-reflection can become a natural part of the daily routine. Quiet time can be set aside on a regular basis to create the habit of self-observation. On an individual level, it centres on the question 'Who Am I?' and includes reflection on personal problems and achievements, positive as well as negative incidents. Reflection in a group is beneficial when it relates to a specific event, positive or negative, that occurred in the classroom during the day. This will foster in the students a high level of self-awareness and encourage sensitivity to group dynamics. In this way, students become aware that they are endowed with different capacities and qualities and start utilizing them to enhance the social fabric. Many students start realizing their natural weaknesses and natural strengths. Consequently, they make an effort to overcome their weaknesses and perfect their strengths all the more.

Each one of us is like a doorkeeper (*dvārapāla*). Self-perfection is closely related to self-control. It gives enormous strength when one has learnt, through self-awareness and feedback (not moral judgement), to view the effect of one's actions and one's decisions. The point here is to help a student grow into a conscious young adult, who can make conscious choices about his/her aim in life and live from that strength.

Another important shift that needs to be made is in the attitude towards mistakes. When we stop chiding students for their mistakes and allow them space to see that mistakes do actually facilitate learning and are pointers towards greater perfection, fear and stress will fall away. If we look at ourselves, we have to admit that we never learned anything without making mistakes. So mistakes are a natural part of any learning process. We must end practices that make students feel ashamed or shrink from their mistakes. Instead, we must help students realize that each mistake is an opportunity for further development, a pointer or a road sign to greater accomplishment.

In general, to gain self-control from within, the attitude towards the teaching of values has to undergo a drastic change. Control through punishment and moralizing takes away trust and responsibility from the learner, and deadens motivation. A caring teacher allows students the space to take responsibility for good as well as bad behaviour. S/he allows self-exploration, so that the values can arise from within.

Proven practice

To illustrate these points, I quote here part of an article written in 2006 by a young woman who was for 10 years a student of an integral school.[3]

> Once Damini (a friend) and I did a project on [our school]—we made a whole booklet out of it, with a lot of metaphorical drawings, interviews of students, teachers and the principal. All this was compiled together with our own, very coherent opinions. So, each project included many different facets—a wide variety of ways to learn, apart from just the academic bit. There was a lot of art, fieldwork (like a trip to a marble factory, collecting heavy rocks, etc.)
>
> ... the system [of education] lays a lot of emphasis on freedom; freedom from structures, from prescribed modes of thought, from inhibitions, from fear. But this freedom never came without responsibility. Freedom and responsibility go hand in hand, and together culminate into self-discipline. Self-discipline is to me true discipline, which comes from within a human being and is not imposed or forced on her/him. This constitutes an individual in the true sense of the word—someone who does not do things by being compelled to by others, but simply because her/his convictions urge her/him to do it. Motivation and freedom that are self-realized see much better results than those that are obligatory (Saranda, 2006).

Shifts in procedures of evaluation

Assessment of the students' work has to be in harmony with the process of awakening, and in harmony with the focus on the development of qualities and capacities of the students. Therefore, a major shift to be introduced in assessment procedures of students is that assessment has to be focused on development and not on ranking. The main role of the teacher should not be that of a taskmaster and judge, but that of a guide and facilitator. The new attitude is to help a student make progress, not for the sake of high marks, but for individual growth. In this context, it is important that teachers observe the students with empathy.

The assessment required should be diagnostic and not judgemental. This is an assessment in which the student participates and gains insight into his own learning process. The teacher/facilitator provides positive feedback and helps the student to understand for her/himself if something needs more attention, or if s/he can directly proceed to the next stage, etc. Self-evaluation by the student is an important component of this process (see also Huppes, 2001, pp. 252, 226, 176).

Shifts in teacher education

A shift in the content and methodology in Elementary and Secondary education necessitates a shift in the content and methodology in Teacher Education. This in turn requires a shift in the attitude of teacher-educators—from taskmaster to facilitator. The core issue is that the methodology of the teacher education colleges has to reflect the philosophy of learning for personal growth. Imposition and rote learning, which entails a closed learning process in which we create dependency, has to be replaced by an open learning process of positive suggestion in which student-teachers explore their own capacities and qualities, and simultaneously acquire the knowledge and skills related to the teaching-learning processes that facilitate self-development. It is important to realize that high marks in test papers do not provide certainty for being a good teacher. The length of this chapter prevents detailed descriptions, but some of the major shifts are listed below:

- The methodology of the teaching-learning process of teacher education institutes has to be in harmony with the aim that the student-teacher will learn to become a guide and facilitator instead of a task master and disciplinarian.
- Student-teachers must be empowered with planning skills for optimum individual learning, simultaneously handling a variety of learning materials for multiple levels of learning in the classroom.
- The focus of learning must be learning-for-development, while recognizing that the physical, affective, cognitive and spiritual domains all have a place in the teaching-learning process. The shift in methodology must help the teacher to experience the value of all these domains for her/himself, and through that develop the skills for implementing such learning in the classroom.
- Another important component to be introduced in the teaching-learning process of teacher education institutes is allotting time and structures in their syllabus for self-observation and self-reflection. Keeping a daily journal will lead to self-awareness and self-perfection. It is important to encourage student-teachers to find ways unique to their disposition and develop their style of facilitating learning so that they will continue this while working in schools.
- Implementation of these components will necessitate a change in the evaluation procedures of the teacher education institutes, and make self-evaluation by the student-teachers a component that matters.

Conclusion: *Kurukṣetra* in our own life

We are living in a period of great intensity. Spiritually as well as materially, it is a time of transition and change. How can a positive change come about? Till now, humanity has mainly been busy with what we could call 'outer' changes, in the hope that these would bring a more comfortable life. It is time to realize that happiness will be an elusive aim unless we learn first to live a nobler life. We can go on changing strategies and institutions, but this will have a lasting effect only if we first change ourselves. Sages and social scientists have told us over and over again that inner change has to precede outer change, and that the future of the world will not improve by changing only outer conditions and remodelling institutions. For as long as human beings remain the same, outer innovations will break down rapidly. It is the quality that comes from a profounder state of consciousness that has to be the guiding principle in the new initiatives that humankind is looking for. The changes that we have to bring about in our organizations and institutions have to be founded on an inner truth that is waiting to be expressed. This 'living from within' does not mean an impoverishment in the mental and affective domains. What it does mean is self-knowledge and mastery, which will keep us away from action at the expense of others or the earth. When we live a more integrated life, we naturally create harmony and beauty. Since our lives are still embedded in the old ways of living, it requires effort to make this inner shift. Some parts in us may resist and shy away, or return to the beaten track. Yet, if we look at the present world, it seems to cry out for a qualitative change. The appreciation and cultivation of soul qualities has from ancient times been inherently linked with the Indian civilization. It is one of the most precious gifts that India can give to this world. In the field of education, it is up to administrators, psychologists and educationists to be instruments in this process.[4] The time seems to be ripe for a change in this direction; it is an ideal whose time has come!

Endnotes

1 See, for further details, Anjum Sibia (2006).

2 There are many schools in India, drawing inspiration from the vision of Sri Aurobindo, that have amalgamated the CBSE syllabus with Integral education. However, there are two schools, SAICE (Puducherry) and Mirambika (New Delhi), which have implemented the principles and methodology of Integral education quite radically. Mirambika has an Integral teacher education programme (duration 3 years) on the same campus. The student-teachers do their teaching practice at Mirambika.

3 Sarandha, A Tribute to Mirambika on its 25th anniversary. Published in *The Awakening Ray*, Vol. 10, 4, (2006).

4 The ordinary way of man's individual and social living seems indeed to be a contradiction of these principles; for certainly we bear a terrible weight of external necessity, rule and law and our need for self-expression, for the development of our true person, our real soul, our inmost characteristic law of nature in life is at every turn interfered with, thwarted, forced from its course, given a very poor chance and scope by environmental influences. Life, State, society, family, all surrounding powers seem to be in a league to lay their yoke on our spirit, compel us into their moulds, impose on us their mechanical interest and rough immediate convenience. We become parts of a machine; we are not, are hardly allowed to be men in the true sense, *manuṣya, puruṣa*, souls, minds, free children of the spirit empowered to develop the highest characteristic perfection of our being and make it our means of service to the race. It would seem that we are not what we make ourselves, but what we are made. Yet the more we advance in knowledge, the more the truth of the Gita's rule is bound to appear. The child's education ought to be an outbringing of all that is best, most powerful, most intimate and living in his nature; the mould into which the man's action and development ought to run is that of his innate quality and power. He must acquire new things, but he will acquire them best, most vitally on the basis of his own developed type and inborn force. And so too the functions of a man ought to be determined by his natural turn, gift and capacities. The individual who develops freely in this manner will be a living soul and mind and will have a much greater power for the service of the race. And we are able now to see more clearly that this rule is true not only of the individual but of the community and the nation, the group soul, the collective man (Sri Aurobindo, 1976, pp. 499–500).

References

Aurobindo, Sri (1976). *Essays on the Gita*. Pondicherry: Sri Aurobindo Ashram. (Original work published 1922).

Aurobindo, Sri (1988). *The life divine*. Pondicherry: Sri Aurobindo Ashram. (Original work published 1940).

Aurobindo, Sri & Mother, The (1990). *Sri Aurobindo and The Mother on education*. Pondicherry: Sri Aurobindo Ashram Trust. (Original work published 1956).

Huppes, N. (2001). *Psychic education, a workbook*. New Delhi: SAES.

Mirambika (2013). *Paths to self-discovery: Reflective practices with children*. New Delhi: Mirambika, Research Centre for Integral Education and Human Values.

Sarandha (2006). A Tribute to Mirambika on its 25th anniversary. *The Awakening Ray, 10*(4).

Sibia, A. (2006). *Life at Mirambika. A free progress school*. New Delhi: NCERT.

UNESCO (1996). *Learning: The treasure within*. Report to UNESCO of the International Commission on Education for the Twenty-First Century. Paris: UNESCO.

20

The blending of healing and pedagogy in Āyurveda

P. Ram Manohar

Introduction

The medical tradition of Āyurveda has preserved a rather unique concept of education that blends principles of healing with those of pedagogy. With its intense focus on the promotion of positive health and higher states of well-being, Āyurveda has discovered that elevated states of health can be achieved only through a subtle transformation of the inner personality. Diseases can be cured, managed or prevented by medical intervention and other such physical means. However, higher states of health can be achieved only through self-awakening. The process of self-awakening is essentially an educative development, a psycho-spiritual transformation that enables the individual to not only live with awareness, but also with health. The meeting point of the most refined methods of pedagogy and healing gave birth to the notion of the physician par excellence as the *vaidya*, the one who knows the essentials and educates the individual, enabling him to reach a state of heightened awareness most conducive to knowledge acquisition and a healthy existence.

Healing the sick to cure and the healthy to liberate

The *Caraka Saṃhitā*, the celebrated medical textbook on Āyurveda that dates back to a few centuries before the Common Era, opens the section on the medical treatment of diseases with chapters on *rasāyana* (rejuvenation) and *vājīkaraṇa* (reproductive medicine and eugenics).[1] At the first instance, the reader would find it appealing that the ancient masters emphasize the importance of prevention over the cure of diseases. But on a closer look, it becomes evident that there is a more profound message in this clever arrangement of topics in the medical treatise. The message is that even the so-called healthy individual needs further treatment—'*svastho'pi cikitsyaḥ*'. Health according to Āyurveda is definitely not the mere absence of disease. Āyurveda does not encourage the individual to remain complacent by eliminating the physical or mental discomfort caused by illness. It is not enough to adopt a conservative and defensive approach to life in order to prevent disease. The focus is on empowering the individual to evolve to elevated levels of health and fulfil the higher goals of human evolution. Health becomes synonymous with an awakening of the mind in an invigorated body and with a life lived with an awareness of the spiritual self. The target of Āyurvedic knowledge is the '*karma puruṣa*', also known as the '*rāśi puruṣa*', the acting individual, who has to participate actively and consciously in this programme to soar into the realm of positive health and well-being.[2] Terms that mean diseased—such as *rogī*, *ātura*, *vyādhita* and so on—are only used in the context of grave diseases where external help from the physician is more important.[3] Since the overall goal of Āyurveda is to be a holistic system of healthy living, these passive terms have been replaced by the term '*karma puruṣa*'.

Central to Āyurvedic healing is the notion of the human persona as a three-dimensional composite of body, mind and self.[4] Āyurveda aims to empower the body to invigorate the mind and, consequently, to use the invigorated mind to generate self-awareness. The conscious self shines through every individual, but in different degrees, depending on the stage of evolution of her/his psycho-spiritual apparatus. The ultimate healing, according to Āyurveda, involves a subtle manoeuvre that enables the physical hardware and the psychic software of the human personality to upgrade itself to become capable of manifesting the true nature of the self in all its glory and completeness. This is the true disease-free state that Āyurveda aims to guide each human being to gradually evolve to.[5]

The chapters on rejuvenation and eugenics have been placed before the discussion on the treatment of physical and psychic ailments for the simple reason that Āyurveda considers every individual to be an incomplete and vulnerable entity till the full potential of the inner being has been awakened to perfection through a process of psycho-spiritual transformation.

Āyurveda stresses the importance of begetting progeny by choice rather than by chance, and emphasizes that only individuals enjoying higher states of health should reproduce to ensure that humanity can collectively raise itself to the sublime levels of spiritual awareness. The purpose of *rasāyana* (rejuvenation) is to tone up and empower the physical body as well as invigorate the mind. Eugenics and reproductive medicine are mentioned after rejuvenation in order to indicate that one should plan for progeny only after rejuvenating one's physical and psychic being.

It is very interesting to note that only these two chapters have been divided into quartets (*pādas*), thus partitioning each chapter into four subsections. No other chapter in the treatise shares this feature. Each section represents one of the four *Vedic* goals of human life —the *puruṣārthas*. Rejuvenation and eugenics have been placed on the four pillars of the *puruṣārthas* to indicate that their purpose is to realize the four major goals of life, viz., *dharma*, *artha*, *kāma* and *mokṣa*.[6]

One verse in the section on *rasāyana* explicitly states that the purpose of this modality of treatment is not cure of disease or a long life. One who adopts this regimen is able to follow the path of self-evolution attained by the great sages and becomes one with the supreme *Brahman*.[7]

Psycho-spiritual transformation of the healthy leads to liberation

According to Āyurveda, the conscious self is the immutable awareness[8] upon which no medicine can act. It is entrapped in matter and masked by the delimiting nature of the material plane of existence. The liberation of awareness comes by the transformation and transmutation of matter and not merely by cultivating intellectual thoughts and ideas. Therefore, Āyurveda gives emphasis to physical medicines and physical procedures that aim to transform the material body so that the mind becomes powerful and capable of reflecting the true nature of the conscious self. Mind is not different from matter but is the other side of the material continuum, a finer state of matter itself. By definition, *rasāyana* is the means to clear the path for the smooth transformation of the life sap (*rasa*).[9] The manifestation of consciousness in the relative world of experiences is very much a matter-bound phenomenon; the qualitative state of matter determines the degree of expression of consciousness in living beings. On the other hand, when consciousness manifests itself fully by liberating itself from the clutches of matter, it exerts a direct and transforming influence on the states of matter that delimit it in the first place.

This process of transformation cannot be started by external means. It has to happen from within. Physical illness can be healed, to some extent, with external medical help but to attain higher states of health, there has to be a conscious effort by the individual. The ideal Āyurvedic physician, therefore, has a dual role to play in the realm of healing. He has to first become a healer of diseases—in Āyurvedic terms, a *bhiṣak*, or one who drives away the fear of disease.[10] Second, and most importantly, he has to become a healer of the personality, the knowledgeable *vaidya* who can facilitate self-transformation and impart knowledge of the self.[11]

The dictum 'Physician, heal thyself' underpins the approach to the formal training that the Āyurvedic physician had to undergo in ancient days. Texts such as the *Caraka Saṃhitā* point out that apart from learning about diseases, medicines and treatment, the physician himself has to effect an inner transformation and become the ideal of the healthy existence that he will attempt to invoke in all those who approach him for solace and relief from suffering.

We do come across a method of training of the physician that culminates in the transmutation of the personality and the awakening of a higher awareness, comparable to a second birth of the fully trained doctor who now becomes fit to go out into the world as a healer.[12] It is very pertinent to note that this discussion falls within the quartet on *rasāyana*, an indication that sophisticated modalities of treatment like *rasāyana* should be done by a physician who has transformed himself into higher states of health and well-being.

Healing the healthy is education of the self

We see in the exposition of Āyurveda the emergence of a context where the principles of healing and pedagogy blend naturally to create an approach to self-transformation that transcends the scope of both healing and education as they are popularly understood.

This higher modality of healing in Āyurveda is truly 'self-education', which can mean educating oneself on the true nature of the higher self as well as education that has to be self-initiated and self-completed.

In Āyurveda, we can see a continuum being formed by healing and education, beginning with education about healing and culminating with education becoming a process of healing. The physician par excellence, or *apūrva vaidya*, in Āyurveda is one who eliminates the six faults of the mind and thereby roots out the seeds of disease once and for all.[13] Thus, the true physician is one who can balance the two roles of healing and teaching, who can offer a helping hand to a sick person sinking in the swamp of illness and uplift him to the highest level of healthy existence by facilitating an inner transformation. That is why in ancient days, the physician was considered a manifestation of the Lord himself—'*vaidyo nārāyaṇo hariḥ*'. In due course of time, this higher role of the physician was neglected, even forgotten. The noble vocation of healing became a means of livelihood, a business, a lucrative profession. The *vaidya* who was Nārāyaṇa himself became the brother of the Lord of Death—Yama—who takes away both the wealth and life of the sick people who approach him.[14] The *Caraka Saṃhitā* says that in the long term interests of humanity, such individuals deserve to be punished by molten metals being poured down their throats![15]

The section of the *Caraka Saṃhitā* that deals with nature of the physical body, including anatomical considerations, devotes a full chapter to discussing the psycho-spiritual nature of the individual. It is in this context that serious questions are raised regarding the outcome of healing. Can healing eliminate sickness forever? What is the means to attain a disease-free state in which one is not afflicted by sorrow of any kind?[16]

The answer is *yoga*, the text declares. One can transcend the limitations of relative existence and go beyond disease and sorrow only through the practice of *yoga*. In *yoga* and *mokṣa*, there is freedom from pain. In *mokṣa*, which is the end result of the practice of *yoga*, there is complete cessation of sorrow and freedom from all limitations.[17]

Pain and pleasure are two sides of the same coin and cannot be avoided by living beings. In Āyurveda, both are together referred to by the technical term '*vedanā*'.[18] The practice of *yoga* enables the individual to rise above them and attain equanimity of mind, which eventually leads to self-awakening and liberation. In that state, the individual identity dissolves completely; the individual becomes one with existence and evolves into a cosmic individuality characterized by the experience that he is one with the universe and the universe one with him.[19]

It can, thus, be seen that the higher aspects of Āyurvedic healing aim to take the individual on the path of *yoga*, the path of self-transformation. Interestingly enough, there is no single textbook on Āyurveda that deals with the eightfold path of *yoga*. There is not a single reference in any Āyurvedic textbook recommending physical postures or breath regulation as a means to heal disease or improve health. Not that they are not useful for these purposes, but Āyurveda seems to have understood *yoga* as a process of the psycho-spiritual transformation that leads to union with the higher self.[20] This goal cannot be achieved by practicing *āsanas* or *prāṇāyāma* alone.

Suffice it to say that *yoga* in Āyurveda is, then, the means to psychic transmutation that leads to mental stillness (*sattvasamādhāna*) and, eventually, to complete self-awareness.[21]

Āyurveda advises the physician to become a parent to the sick and to treat the ailing person as one would one's own child.[22] In other words, Āyurveda beseeches the physician to take up the responsibility to facilitate the physical, psychic and spiritual growth of those who approach him for succour.

The twin goals of healing and education

Āyurveda is made an example here to demonstrate the compact manner in which all knowledge systems in the *Vedic* tradition have been organized to serve the dual purpose of material prosperity (*abhyudayaḥ*) and spiritual uplift (*niśreyas*). Āyurveda fulfils the dual purpose of *aparā vidyā* (mundane knowledge) and *parā vidyā* (spiritual knowledge) by defining two modalities of treatment. The lower level of healing diseases is called *cikitsā*, which corresponds to the realm of *aparā vidyā* in the *Upaniṣads*. The higher level of healing is called *naiṣṭhikī cikitsā*, and it corresponds to the realm of *parā vidyā*.[23] Āyurveda thus fulfils the *Vedic* ideal of embracing both the physical and the spiritual in an act of balance, and to guide physical evolution to reach out to the higher realms of spiritual evolution.

The Āyurvedic example also demonstrates the need to complement vocational training with self-transforming education, and conveys the powerful message that any branch of human learning must blend the lower vocational component with a higher self-transforming programme of education. Training in any knowledge system was designed to develop vocational skills as well as facilitate the self-evolution of the student. In the context of Āyurveda, however, the physician is himself expected to become a powerful catalyst of self-awakening.

The principles of higher education in Āyurveda

The Āyurveda accounts that reveal the system of education through which students of Āyurveda were trained to become physicians give very valuable insights into techniques and methodologies that aimed to facilitate psycho-spiritual evolution and the balanced development of the personality.

The main principles of the Āyurvedic approach to education can be summarized in the following points:

1. *Right parenting:* The education of parents, the pre-conception behaviour of expectant couples and the proper upbringing of the child.
2. *Right nutrition:* The nutritional requirements of the child have to be properly met because growth and development of mental functions are dependent on the physical body, which works as a hardware for the mind.
3. *Right medical care:* Higher mental functions can be awakened by appropriate medical care, and defective development rectified to a great extent by suitable medical intervention.
4. *Right teacher:* The teacher makes all the difference between knowledge and ignorance. The true teacher is a facilitator of learning and not a mere transmitter of information.
5. *Right teaching:* For a harmonious unfolding of the inner potential, it is essential to strike a balance between acquisition of professional skills and personality development, and teaching must give equal emphasis to both these aspects.
6. *Right student:* The student should be endowed with the necessary qualities to be able to imbibe the teaching completely and effectively. Preparing the student

to receive knowledge is a key factor in education.

7. *Right environment:* Learning has to take place in an environment conducive to the acquisition of knowledge as well as self-development. Most importantly, the environment must nurture the process of learning in a natural and effortless way.
8. *Right learning process to suit needs of a student:* Each individual is unique. The ideal teaching programme should recognize individual differences and customize the teaching to suit the specific requirements of an individual.

A more detailed discussion on these points will provide better insight into the method of education for self-development advocated by Āyurveda.

Right parenting

The foundation for the complete education of the child begins before its conception. Educating the child begins through the education of the parents. Being born with a healthy physique gives a natural advantage to the individual in the effective pursuit of learning. Āyurveda advises a couple to rejuvenate itself physically and mentally, and to improve the quality of reproductive tissue with special treatments (*rasāyana* and *vājīkaraṇa*). The quality of parental tissues will reflect upon the quality of the reproductive tissues and, consequently, on the child that will be born to them. Āyurveda emphasizes that major developmental handicaps can be averted by proper planning and intervention. Āyurveda has also discovered that neurological development can be influenced by behavioural regimens adopted by the expectant mother during gestation. The pregnant woman is advised to mentally visualize the qualities she desires the child to be born with.24

Two legends in the tradition give an indication that the influence of gestational behaviour on the developing personality of the child was a widely accepted principle in ancient times. One is the story of Prahlāda, the devout child of the *asura* king, Hiraṇyakaśipu, who rebelled against his father and was able to invoke the blessings of Lord Viṣṇu in the ferocious form of the man-lion. Prahlāda, it is said, did not develop *asuric* traits like his father because he was influenced by spiritual discourses delivered by the sage Nārada when his mother was pregnant. Another is the story of Abhimanyu, the son of Arjuna, who learnt the technique of piercing through the *padmavyūha* formation in warfare when he was in his mother's womb. A story from the epics depicts a couple praying to Lord Śiva for a child and facing the predicament of having to choose between a long-lived dullard and a short-lived but intelligent child—they ask for the latter. The role of right parenting in laying the foundation for proper education of the child has been well expounded in the Āyurvedic classics and also finds parallels in the popular culture.

Right nutrition

Āyurveda has discovered the relationship between proper nutrition and balanced growth of the mind. Without being provided with the right nutrition, mental alertness can be hampered and during gestation and early childhood, this could lead to permanent mental disability. A story from the *Upaniṣads* demonstrates the importance of nourishment for the proper functioning of the intellect and the mind. One day, after a teaching session, a teacher advises the students to go on a fast and return with empty stomachs. In the fasting state, the students are unable to remember their lessons. They regain their memories after eating. This was an ingenious way in which the teacher of the *Upaniṣads* impressed upon children that the mind was a product of food—'*annamayaṃ hi soumya manaḥ*'.

Right medical care

Āyurveda recommends medications to enhance the higher mental functions of the growing child so as to facilitate the process of learning. Āyurvedic textbooks abound with lists of formulations for improving mental functions.[25] There is specific reference to the awakening of a faculty called '*medhā*', which is, according to one definition, the enhanced ability to read and understand books, and, according to another, the capacity for constant remembrance and the application of acquired knowledge.[26] There is also reference to the ability of herbal formulations to improve '*smṛti*', or ability to store and recall acquired knowledge.[27] Āyurveda has understood that mental functions have a physical basis and that the mind is but a finer form of matter. Only the conscious self transcends the realm of matter and mind and remains unaffected by the changes that take place in the material plane. Medicines can change the quality of physical matter, including the mind, and make it fit to reflect consciousness in a profound and intense manner.

Right teacher

It is very interesting to note that the ideal teacher described in the Āyurvedic texts is a facilitator of learning rather than one who drills information into the minds of his disciples. The teacher is compared to the timely rain that falls on fertile land sown with viable seeds.[28] In other words, the true teacher helps the student to unfold his inner potential. The relationship between the teacher and student was characterized by the sentiment of *vātsalya*, or deep affection. According to the commentator, *vātsalya* is the intense feeling of affection that a cow feels spontaneously for her newborn calf.[29] The main role of the teacher was to mould the character of the student, much like preparing a vessel to hold water. Knowledge is compared to water and the mind of the student to the vessel.[30] It is easier to transfer knowledge than to organize a student's mind to use it in a benevolent way. The teacher was, therefore, one who was vested with the responsibility of ensuring that knowledge was passed on to only deserving candidates. The quality of a teacher was measured not merely by his ability to bestow knowledge and skills but also by his ability to build character. A student was given the right to examine a teacher before accepting him, just as a teacher would examine a student before enrolling him for study.[31]

Contrary to popular belief, the student enjoyed great freedom in the learning process. We find in the *Caraka Saṃhitā*, for instance, that teaching begins only when disciples raise questions.[32] In many sections, the teaching is in the form of dialogues between the teacher and the pupil. According to tradition, even a teacher's mind is awakened by a student's stimulating question that is asked with the right attitude.[33]

The *vidyārambha* ceremony, which is a very popular event (albeit nowadays only an occasion for celebration), symbolizes the role of the teacher in the Indian approach to education. The *navarātri* festival, which culminates in the *vidyārambha*, or the initiation into the learning process, lasts for nine nights and ten days. During the first three days, devotees worship the Goddess Kālī, the next three days, the Goddess Lakṣmī, and the last three days, the Goddess Sarasvatī. This festival represents the gradual victory over the lower tendencies of the human mind that manifest when *tāmasic* and *rājasic* qualities predominate. Kālī is the fierce aspect of the divine that overpowers the *tāmasic* tendencies of the human mind, Lakṣmī is the dynamic aspect of the divine that conquers the *rājasic* tendencies and equips the individual with the resources of nature. And, finally, Sarasvatī indicates the awakening of the *sātvic* tendencies of the human mind, indicating the maturity of the individual to receive knowledge. The grand finale is on the tenth day, which celebrates the victory of the higher nature over the lower, and represents the rebirth of the individual as a new person. It is no coincidence that these ten days correspond to the ten months of gestation in human beings. Āyurveda refers to *rajas* and *tamas* as the two faults of the mind, and spiritual education as the means to rectify them.[34]

Since true education leads to the mental rebirth of the individual, the teacher became more sacred than one's biological parents and the teaching became sacrosanct. While the biological parents bring forth the physical body of the individual, the teacher brings forth the inner personality to complete the manifestation.

The function of the teacher as a source of information is slowly becoming redundant in this age of information technology and virtual reality. But the role of the teacher as a humanizing and catalyzing influence to facilitate the inner growth of the individual is assuming significance as never before.

Right teaching

The teaching should be appropriate and effective. It should strike a balance between theory and practice. As an Āyurvedic text says, one who is grounded only in theory will become like a soldier who will run away from the battlefield at the mere sight of the enemy; and one who has only practical training will falter in complex situations. Theory and practice are like the two wings of knowledge. A very important concept regarding appropriateness of teaching is *adhikāra*. It is not easy to translate this word, but it would roughly mean eligibility or preparedness. The right teaching is like a potent seed that sprouts spontaneously when it is sown in the fertile mind of the disciple. Teaching becomes effective only when the mind of the student has been ploughed and made fertile. When the sage Bharadvāja approached Indra to get knowledge of Āyurveda, Indra explained Āyurveda in a very brief and suggestive exposition, knowing the powerful and receptive state of his disciple.[35]

Right student

The *Caraka Saṃhitā* mentions in one place that the sage Ātreya had six disciples and that he taught all of them in the same manner, without favouritism. However, Agniveśa, his most brilliant disciple, got an edge over the others and became the first to systematically expound on Āyurveda.[36] There are three types of teachers and, likewise, three types of students—superior, mediocre and inferior. When a superior teacher meets a superior student, the best possible outcome can be expected. The worst scenario is when an inferior teacher meets an inferior student. Yet, a superior teacher can salvage something from an inferior student. The importance of the student putting in the effort to inculcate the necessary qualities to imbibe knowledge cannot be underestimated. Examination of a student was compulsorily carried out before initiation and was known as *śiṣyaparīkṣā*.[37]

Right environment

True learning occurs spontaneously in the right circumstances. Creating the right environment for education alone can bring success. In the ancient Indian tradition, it was customary to send students out on specific tasks without giving them any formal lessons; the students would learn automatically from the situations that they found themselves in. Two stories in the Āyurvedic tradition exemplify how the ancient masters would cultivate professional skills and nurture personality development. Bhikṣu Ātreya told his students to roam around and find a plant that had no medicinal value. Only one of his disciples, Jīvaka, came back empty-handed, declaring that he could not find any plant that did not have medicinal value. Bhikṣu Ātreya announced Jīvaka as the only student of his who had qualified to be a physician. In another story, Nāgārjuna, the famous alchemist, asked two of his students on probation to prepare medicinal linctus. Both returned the following day: one had prepared the medicine while the other one came empty-handed. Nāgārjuna asked his second disciple why he had not followed the instructions. The disciple explained that on his way to collect herbs, he had met an old, ailing man calling for help. He could not ignore the old man's pathetic calls and attended to his needs and, therefore, could not make the medicine. The other disciple confessed that he had ignored the old man, fearing his teacher's wrath, and went on to make the medicine. Nāgārjuna explained to them that compassion and not just the skill of making medicines was the more important quality that a physician must cultivate. He chose his compassionate disciple as his successor and forsook the more skilled one. Nāgārjuna clarified that it was easy to teach the skill of pharmacy but very difficult to nurture the value of compassion.

Right learning process to suit the needs of a student

The teaching most appropriate to an individual's temperament and potential has to be imparted. In other words, teaching has to be individualized. Mass education and uniform standards were not the salient features of the ancient method of learning and teaching. The *Upaniṣadic* tradition itself reminds us of the importance of personalized teaching based on a very close and intimate relationship between the teacher and the student. Āyurvedic texts explain that the teaching should be modified according to three levels of intelligence of the students—the brilliant, the mediocre and the dullard.[38] Teaching should be suggestive to the brilliant, elucidative to the mediocre and instructive to the dullard.[39] The dullard student's training is application-oriented, the mediocre student's training theory-oriented, and the brilliant student's training discovery and innovation-oriented. These three levels correspond to the three-tier structure of a knowledge system dealing with the practice, theory and principles of a particular subject. Further, the Āyurvedic texts proclaim that one who has the qualities of a *brāhmaṇa* can study Āyurveda to teach and propagate science; one who has a *kṣatriya* disposition can learn it to become a health administrator; one who has a *vaiśya* character can learn it to practice and make a livelihood; and everybody can learn it for self-protection and to help the suffering.[40] Once again, the purpose of learning is differentiated on the basis of the inner qualities of the student.

In its approach to the training of a prospective student, the classical tradition of Āyurveda has captured the essence of the Indian approach to education in a vivid and clear manner. The goal of psycho-spiritual metamorphosis and the balance between professional skills and personality development constitutes the core of this method.

Conclusion

Both education and healing have two aspects—higher and lower. The lower aspect of education deals with vocational training and the imparting of professional skills with which one is able to serve society and make a living; this is the breadwinning education that we are quite familiar with. The higher aspect of education, however, deals with personality development that eventually leads to self-realization; it is an education that transforms the human personality and transmutes the beast into the human and the human into the divine. The lower aspect of Āyurveda is to prevent and cure disease; this is the profession of medicine, the so-called noble profession that helps humanity to free itself from the clutches of disease and discover the health of the body and the mind. The higher aspect of Āyurveda is no different from the higher aspect of education in general. Knowledge systems in India used this two-fold approach with a view to impart professional skills and transform personality so as to achieve deeper self-awareness to ensure that the acquired knowledge would be applied for the welfare of humanity and the world at large. In Āyurvedic learning, we have a powerful and suggestive representation of this ancient wisdom.

True education heals. It is not a mere acquisition of information but an unfolding of the personality to actualize inner potential. It is, therefore, hardly a wonder that Āyurveda discovered that the higher forms of healing were synonymous with the process of education itself. In the Indian tradition, the undeveloped state of the inner self has long been considered a disease in itself, even outside the medical tradition. This disease is known as *bhavaroga*, or the disease of relative existence. The one who removes this disease and helps self-evolution is a physician, even if he is not trained in the medical sciences. In this sense, all spiritually awakened individuals become physicians in India. For this reason, even the Buddha came to be known as the '*bhaiṣajya guru*', or the preceptor of physicians, and came to be revered in some traditions of Āyurveda. Both Āyurveda, in particular, and the Indian cultural process, in general, bear testimony to the fact that at the higher levels of expression, education and healing become synonymous in facilitating a profound psycho-spiritual transformation of the embodied being.

Endnotes

1 CS. ci. 1.1–5, *svasthasyorjaskaraṃ yattu tadvṛṣyaṃ tadrasāyanaṃ*—the two modalities of healing that enhance the health of the individual are rejuvenation and reproductive medicine.

2 CS. śā. 1.53, *puruṣo rāśisaṃjñastu mohecchādveṣakarmajaḥ*—the embodied individual is born out of delusion, likes, dislikes and the fruit of action.

SS. śā. 1.16, *yato/bhihitaṃ—pañcamahābhūtaśarīrasamavāyaḥ puruṣaḥ iti, sa eṣaḥ karmapuruṣaścikitsādhikṛtaḥ*—the person who is embodied in the physical body made up of the five great elements is the subject of treatment, the enjoyer of the fruits of action.

3 AH. ut. 40. 64, *ātaṅkapaṅkamagnānām hastālambo bhiṣagjitaṃ*—medical treatment is the helping hand that uplifts those who are sinking in the swamp of disease.

4 CS. sū. 1.46, *sattvamātmā śarīraṃ ca trayametat tridaṇḍavat*—the mind, the self and the body constitute the tripod upon which life subsists.

5 CS. śā. 5.23, 24, *vipāpaṃ virajaḥ śāntaṃ paramakṣaramavyayaṃ, amṛtaṃ brahma nirvāṇaṃ paryāyaiḥ śāntirucyate*—the sinless state of perfect composure, the abode of immortality, was attained by the sages who became free from delusion and attained everlasting peace.

6 CS. sū. 1.15, 16, *dharmārthakāmamokṣāṇāmārogyaṃ mūlamuttamaṃ, rogastasyā pahartāraḥ śreyaso jīvitasya ca*—health is the foundation for the pursuit of the four goals of human life, and disease is verily an obstacle in this path, taking away merit and life itself.

7 CS.ci.1.1.80, *na kevalam dīrghamihāyuraśnute rasāyanaṃ yo vidhivanniṣevate, gatiṃ sa devarṣiniṣevitāṃ śubhām prapadyate brahma tathaiti cākṣayaṃ*—by the use of rejuvenative medicine, one does not merely attain long life but becomes one with the supreme *Brahman*.

8 CS. sū. 1.56, *nirvikāraḥ parastvātmā sattvabhūtaguṇendriyaiḥ, caitanye kāraṇam nityo draṣṭā paśyati hi kriyāḥ*—the supreme self is the cause of awareness and is a witness to all actions operating through the mind, the senses and the five-fold material world.

9 CS. ci. 1.1.8, *lābhopāyo hi śastānām rasādīnām rasāyanaṃ*—rejuvenative medicine is the means to obtain tissues endowed with good qualities.

10 *vācaspatya*, Vol. 6, p. 4701, *bheṣaṃ rogabhayaṃ jayati iti*—the physician is one who removes the fear of disease.

11 The word *vaidya* is derived from the root '*vid jñāne*', meaning to know. The *vaidya* is one who is knowledgeable and can impart this knowledge to others. Vācaspatya defines the *vaidya* as a *paṇḍīta*.

12 CS. ci.1.4.52, 53, *vidyāsamāptau bhiṣajo dvitīyā jātirucyate, aśnute vaidyaśabdaṃ hi na vaidyo pūrvajanmanā, vidyāsamāptau brāhmaṃ vā sattvamārṣamathāpi vā, dhruvamāviśati jñānāttasmād vaidyo dvijaḥ smṛtaḥ*—on the completion of education, the physician is known as the twice-born, and one does not become a physician by birth; on completing education, the mind of the physician is transformed to that of *brahmā* or a *ṛṣi*; therefore, the physician is known as the twice-born.

13 AH. sū. 1.1, *rāgādirogān satatānuṣaktān aśeṣakāyaprasṛtānaśeṣān, autsukyamohārati dañjaghāna yopūrvavaidyāya namostu tasmai*—I bow before the physician par excellence, who eliminated the six diseases of lust and the like, which plague all living beings constantly.

14 A popular verse portrays the physician as a messenger of death—*vaidyarāja namastu bhyaṃ yamarājasahodaraḥ, yamastu harate prāṇān, vaidyāḥ prāṇān dhanāni ca*.

15 CS. sū. 1.131, 132, *varamāśīviṣaviṣaṃ kvathitaṃ tāmrameva vā pītamatyagnisantaptā bhakṣitā vā/pyayoguḍāḥ, natu śrutavatāṃ veśaṃ bibhratā śaraṇāgatāt, gṛhītamannaṃ pānaṃ vā vittaṃ vā rogapīḍitāt*—this verse describes the fate of a physician who commercializes the noble profession of medicine.

16 CS. śā. 1.13, *kva caitā vedanāḥ sarvāḥ nivṛttiṃ yāntyaśeṣataḥ*—a question addressed to the teacher on the complete cessation of pain and suffering.

17 CS. śā. 1.137, *yoge mokṣe ca sarvāsām vedanānāmavartanaṃ*—the teacher answers that in the state of *yoga* and *mokṣa*, there is a complete cessation of all suffering.

18 CS. śā. 1.133, *sparśanendriyasaṃsparśaḥ sparśo mānasa eva ca, dvividhaḥ sukha dukhānām vedanānām pravartakaḥ*—this verse says that *vedanā*, or sensation, has the dual nature of pain and pleasure.

19 CS. śā. 5.7, *sarvalokamātmanyātmānaṃ ca sarvaloke samamanupaśyataḥ satyā buddhiḥ samutpadyate, sarvalokaṃ hyātmani paśyato bhavatyātmaiva sukhaduḥkhayoḥ kartā nānya*

iti, karmātmakatvācca hetvādibhiryuktaḥ sarvaloko/ahamiti viditvā jñānaṃ pūrva mutthāpyate/apavargāyeti—a vivid description of the self-realized state in which one develops a cosmic individuality of oneness with the universe.

20 CS. śā. 1.138, 139, *ātmendriyamanorthānāṃ sannikarṣāt pravartate, sukhaduḥkha manārambhādātmasthe manasi sthire, nivartate tadubhayaṃ vaśitvaṃ copajāyate, saśarīrasya yogajñāstaṃ yogamṛṣayo viduḥ*—a very clear and lucid definition of the state of *yoga*, characterized by liberation in the embodied state.

21 CS. śā. 1.141, *ityaṣṭavidhamākhyātaṃ yogināṃ balamaiśvaram, śuddhasattva samādhānāttat sarvamupajāyate*—one enters into the state of *yoga* and obtains higher mental powers when the mind is calmed and quietened.

22 CS. ci. 1.4.46, *bhiṣagapyāturān sarvān svasutāniva yatnavān, ābādhebhyo hi saṃrakṣedicchan dharmamanuttamam*—this describes the responsibility of the physician to look after the patient like his own son, which is much like how a teacher looked after his disciple in ancient times.

23 CS. śā. 1.94, *hantītyuktaṃ cikitsā tu naiṣṭhikī yā vinopadhāṃ*—the definition of the higher form of spiritual healing.

24 AH. śā. 1.30, *icchetām yādṛśaṃ putraṃ tadrūpacaritāṃśca tau, cintayetāṃ, janapadāṃ stadācāraparicchadau*—instructions to expectant parents to visualize the desired qualities of the progeny they wish to be born to them.

25 AH. ut. 1.42–49, lists several formulations that enhance the higher mental functions.

26 Dalhana on SS. sū. 2.3, *medhā granthāva dhāraṇakarṣaṇasāmarthyaṃ; Hemadri on AH, sū. 5.37, upadiṣṭagrahaṇe śaktiḥ dhīḥ, gṛhītasya vicchedena dhārayituṃ śaktiḥ smṛtiḥ, avicchedena medhā*—these are two definitions of *medhā* in two different contexts.

27 AH. ut. 39. 78, 175 may be referred as examples of two formulations that enhance *smṛti* in a profound manner.

28 CS. vi. 8.4, *evam guṇo hyācāryaḥ sukṣetramārtavo megha iva sasyaguṇaiḥ suśiṣyamāśu vaidyaguṇaiḥ saṃpādayati*—the ideal teacher is portrayed as a facilitator of learning.

29 Dalhana's comments on SS. sū. 1.4, *vatsāḥ iti pakṣapātātiśayatvasūcakaṃ saṃbodhanaṃ, athavā vatsāḥ prathamavayaso gavām putrāḥ, vatsāḥ iva vatsāḥ, anena viśeṣaṇena prathamavayastvaṃ putrasādṛśyaṃ damanīyatvaṃ ca sūcayati*—an elaboration of the concept of *vātsalya*, the sentimental relationship between the teacher and the disciple.

30 AS. sū. 2.12, *śastraṃ śāstrāṇi salilaṃ guṇadoṣapravṛttaye, pātrāpekṣīṇyataḥ prajñām bāhuśrutyena bṛmhayet*—the importance of bestowing knowledge on the right person.

31 CS. vi. 8.4, *...tato/nantaramācāryaṃ parīkṣeta*—instruction to examine the teacher.

32 CS. śā. 1.1, questions about the true nature of the self.

33 Chakrapani's comments on CS. si. 1.5, *apraduṣṭena bhāvena prasannenāntarātmanā, śiṣyena samyaṅpṛṣṭhasya gurorbuddhiḥ prakāśate*—guidelines on how to ask a question of the teacher to get an effective response.

34 AH. sū.1 *rajastamaśca manaso dvau ca doṣāvudāhṛtau*, and 1.26, *dhīdhairyātmādi vijñānaṃ manodoṣauṣadhaṃ paraṃ*, CS. śā. 4.36, *trividhaṃ khalu sattvaṃ, śuddhaṃ, rājasaṃ, tāmasaṃ ceti, tatra śuddhamadoṣamākhyātaṃ kalyāṇāṃśatvāt, rājasaṃ sadoṣamākhyātaṃ roṣāṃśatvāt, tāmasamapi sadoṣamākhyātaṃ mohāṃśatvāt*—various references to the influence of *rajas* and *tamas* on mental states.

35 CS. sū. 1.23, *tasmai provāca bhagavānāyurvedaṃ śatakratuḥ, padairalpaiḥ matiṃ buddhvā vipulām paramarṣaye*—Indra expounds on Āyurveda to the sage Bharadvāja very concisely.

36 CS. sū. 1.32, *buddherviśeṣastatrāsīnnopadeśāntaraṃ muneḥ, tantrasya kartā prathamamagniveśo yato/bhavat*—a difference in the quality of the intellect makes Agniveśa more successful than his counterparts who received the same teaching from the sage Ātreya.

37 CS. vi. 8.8, ... *adhyāpane kṛtabuddhirācāryaḥ*

śiṣyamevāditaḥ parīkṣeta—instruction to the teacher to examine the student before initiation.

38 CS. vi. 8.3, *trividhaśiṣyabuddhihitaṃ*—the ideal text should aim to give an exposition that can be understood by all three types of disciples.

39 CS. sū. 4.20, *etāvanto hyalamalpabuddhīnām vyavahārāya, buddhimatām ca svālakṣaṇy ānumānayuktikuśalānāmanuktārthajñānāy eti*—the scope for the intelligent student to go beyond the boundaries of the formal teachings.

40 CS. sū. 30. *sa cādhyetavyo brāhmaṇa-rājanyavaiśyaiḥ, tatrānugrahārthaṃ prāṇinām brahmaṇaiḥ, ārakṣārthaṃ rājanyaiḥ, vṛttyarthaṃ vaiśyaiḥ, sāmānyato vā dharmārthakāmaparigrahārthaṃ sarvaiḥ*—the knowledge of Āyurveda can be put to different uses depending on the nature of the person who studies it.

Abbreviations of classical Indian texts used

AH *Aṣṭāṅga Hṛdayaṃ*
AS *Aṣṭāṅga Saṅgrahaḥ*
CS *Caraka Saṃhitā*
SS *Suśruta Saṃhitā*
sū *sūtra sthānaṃ*
śā *śarīra sthānaṃ*
vi *vimāna sthānaṃ*
ut *uttara sthānaṃ*
ci *cikitsā sthānaṃ*

References

Damodar, Athvale Ananth (Ed.) (1980). *Aṣṭāṅga saṅgraha*. Poona: Mahesh Anand Athvale.

Sastri, Paradakara Hari Sadasiva (Ed.) (1994). *Aṣṭāṅga hṛdayam*. Varanasi: Chaukhambha Surabharati.

Trikamji, Acharya Yadavji (Ed.) (1994). *Suśruta samhitā*. Varanasi: Chaukhambha Surabharati.

Trikamji, Acharya Yadavji (Ed.) (2002). *Caraka samhitā*. Varanasi: Chaukhambha Surabharati.

21

Situating teacher education in the Indian context: A paradigm shift

Bharati Baveja

The genesis and development of teacher education in India

Discourse in education, particularly teacher education, has its genesis in pragmatic concerns overridden by social pressures in the late nineteenth century. Much like in the field of intelligence, where the testing of intelligence was seen as a social necessity and tests were constructed without the existence of a sound conceptual base, teacher training also arose to meet the demands of providing education to a larger population of the society. Teacher training programmes also lacked an underlying theoretical framework. However, unlike the field of intelligence, there did exist a sound, well-articulated and time-tested discourse on education in the Indian tradition, but this was ignored. The teacher training programmes launched in British India were not rooted in the cultural context and ethos of the soil. Ad-hocism and reductionism characterized the nature of these programmes, with an over-emphasis on the technical skills involved in teaching. Consequently, learning and teaching came to be treated as synonyms. The limitations of such an approach gradually became too obvious to be ignored. It was realized that teacher preparation, which has serious social implications, cannot be based on a random collection of hypothesized ideas about teaching. It is an enterprise which not only involves the academic learning of children, but also provides direction to the development of individuals and society. The need to consider the education of children a serious academic endeavour was realized, and it was argued that a deeper and systematic understanding of the field was a precondition to teacher preparation.

Teacher education essentially required a more intense and systematic effort to understand and explicate the nuances of the educative process. The Calcutta University Commission in 1917 (popularly known as the Sadler Commission) recommended inter alia a significant organizational structure at the university level. The goal was to promote the development of education as a legitimate field of study. The academic pursuits that followed considered teacher training in the psychological, sociological, political and epistemological contexts. The phenomenon of teacher training was expected to be understood according to the varied findings drawn from the cognate disciplines (psychology, sociology and philosophy). Consequently, there occurred a shift in nomenclature from teacher training to teacher education. Epistemologically, as in all other areas, education too followed the 'scientific approach'. Within this framework Western psychology, more specifically behaviourism, came to dominate academic thinking until the 1960s. In its recommendations, the Education Commission (1964–1966) emphasized the creation of new and strengthened organizational structures to facilitate academic pursuits with deeper understanding. Unfortunately, pedagogy and education developed as two distinct branches of education as a social science, just as test construction and theorization in the field of intelligence developed as two disjointed fields. Although the multi-disciplinary nature of education was recognized, education as a distinct area of study was reduced to an applied field. Ideas from 'pure disciplines' such as philosophy, sociology and psychology were generously and unhesitatingly applied. The continued dissatisfaction and attempts at reform were addressed not by creating a holistic discourse emerging from the cultural context, but by adding newer theories from the cognate disciplines. This led to a false sense of efficacy and relevance. The relevance and universalism of content were taken for granted. The role of culture in the process of 'meaning making' remained unattended. For instance, the inclusion of humanistic psychology, which places self-actualization at the centre-stage, was considered sufficient to compensate for the earlier 'excesses' of behaviourism.

A call for change

The compatibility of the western notion of self with that of the Indian tradition was not considered. Even though over the years changes have occurred (in theory), from behaviourism to cognitivism and humanism, and now to social constructivism, the vital issue remains missing—the need for a discourse in education and psychology based on Indian traditions. In the existing teacher education curricula, not only are the concepts of childhood and adolescence derived from Western theories, but their development is also understood from the Western perspective. Needless to say, teacher education is still ineffective and leaves a lot to be desired.

The periodic surveys of research in education in India since 1974 highlights of which are given below stand testimony to the fact that the teacher education programmes have remained largely unchanged.

- The roles and functions of a trained teacher as an agent of change in India have remained unexplored through research. Identification of the goals of teacher education is a relevant theme for further research (First Survey of Educational Research, 1974, p. 444).
- The curriculum of teacher education does not seem to have changed much. It is not adequate for just any one to suggest what changes should be brought about. Researchers with deep understanding and analysis should offer guidance in this regard. It should be within the ingenuity and genius of our researchers to make a dent and develop indigenous approaches (Second Survey of Educational Research, 1979, pp. 421–422).
- In-depth studies of teacher education institutions, training situations and teachers at the micro level are essential to discover new variables for improving the effectiveness of teacher trainees and for exploring the results emerging from a macro analysis of these studies (Third Survey of Educational Research, 1986, p. 789).
- There is a need to know more about the teacher's role expectations, the relationship between the individual teacher's role expectations and her/his social responsibilities, the relationship between the teacher's conception of her/his role and their performance as observed by others in society. To make research meaningful, studies should be comprehensive and reflect rigour (Fourth Survey of Educational Research, 1993, pp. 915–916).
- Research projects aimed at understanding the multi-faceted process of teacher education in its totality need to be undertaken by agencies and organizations like the NCERT, the NIEPA, the UGC, etc., as well as individual researches supported by the government (Fifth Survey of Educational Research, 1998, p. 457).

Empirical support

The early researches in the field were survey-based and quantitative in nature, and provided data regarding the inadequacies and ineffectiveness of teacher education programmes. Besides, these studies also indicated crucial areas requiring immediate attention in education and the school system. This was followed by a large body of research in the field of education technology, leading to a lopsided emphasis on technology in education. The 'organic' dimension of the educative process not only remained untouched, but was also suppressed by the more tangible and attractive idea of technology in education. Consequently, means became confused with ends. For instance, today computer-aided learning has become a goal in itself. Such innovations have only added to the existing behaviourist nature of education.

Some recent qualitative researches (although they are very few in number) have pointed towards the need to focus on individual processes of knowledge construction, the contextual situatedness of meaning-making, ways of strengthening inter-personal communications, the importance of teacher development, and so on. Even when self-development is emphasized in some cases, there is often very little understanding about the concept and the processes of its development.

Research in the field of psychology, particularly cognitive psychology, conducted in the previous century was also in the reductionist-logical-positivistic framework. In its quest to reinstate 'mind' in psychology, the cognitive revolution of the 1960s transplanted a mechanistic mind based on a computational model. The model of mind as an Information Processing System explains the processing of information in fixed ways and assumes isomorphism between external and internal or constructed reality. The complexity and vastness of the mind, the existence of the inner self and its journey across different levels could not be conceptualized within this framework. Furthermore, the context of cognitive development, physical or cultural, was viewed as an external variable, distinctly separate from the mind and therefore subject to external control. Independent researches were conducted in the fields of perception, memory, problem-solving and the nature of the task to be learned, to mention a few. Although these were collectively referred to as mental processes, they were not conceived of as inseparable parts of an indivisible whole. Thus the subject matter, the learner, the context of learning, the process and product of learning were treated as independent units of analysis. In this framework, the learner got separated from learning, the subject matter to be learned and the cultural context of learning (the chronic Cartesian impasse). Although today we do talk of constructivism, distributed cognition, and embedded or situated cognition, which asserts the continuity of context, mind and task, the context is defined in finite, material terms. It fails to capture the Indian view that all entities are inter-dependent and inseparable parts of the same cosmic whole—the Supreme Consciousness—as different manifestations of the same reality—*Brahman*. In the Indian traditions there is an unwavering belief in the unity and mutual relatedness of objects which form a whole that is indivisible, and manifests in all things—the Self.

Concepts such as *Brahman*, *īśvara*, *puruṣa* and *ātman* are rarely understood by contemporary Western thinkers. *Brahman*, the Universal or the Supreme Self, supersedes existence and encompasses everything that exists; it envelops space and time and is thus expanded in the cosmos and beyond. This changeless and imperishable Self is the essence of all existence. When *Brahman* is considered in relation to the Universe, it is regarded as *Īśvara*. *Īśvara* is *Brahman* with attributes—united with its powers. *Puruṣa* is the higher nature of *Īśvara* and is the manifestation of the Supreme Self in all living forms. *Māyā* is *Īśvara's* lower nature or *prakṛti*. When Self as *Īśvara* interacts with *māyā*, *prakṛti* bursts into form and activity and constitutes the phenomenal reality—*kṣetra*. The *Jīva* or Individual Self is only a part of the Supreme Self and is a limited manifestation of the infinite reality. The world is dependent upon *Brahman*, but *Brahman* is not dependent on the world. It is the cause of all activity in the world, yet it itself does nothing. It pervades every entity, living as well as non-living, and sustains everything, yet has a distinct identity. It is in itself the existence, the knowledge, the joy, that is, the *sat*, *cit* and *ānanda*, respectively. If we were to conceptualize situated and embedded cognition according to this perspective, then its meaning, orientation, expanse and scope would change tremendously.

We have consistently failed to acknowledge the richer and more convincing concepts that have existed in Indian traditions since time immemorial; concepts that are not just an outcome of sensory experience, but the result of prolonged and continuous reflection at the higher levels of consciousness; concepts which are robust enough to withstand the test of time. At the same time, they are flexible enough to provide a framework for understanding varied experiences, irrespective of time. Among the galaxy of preceptors, the impact of Sri Aurobindo's thought has been distinctive in the field of education. His views on Integral psychology and the corresponding Integral education provide a well-articulated framework for education based on Indian thought. The emphasis in this system of education is on enabling learners to locate the experience of 'I' within them. Silence is basic to such an introspective and meditative process when one undertakes the journey to discover the true nature of Self, 'the inner I'. The essence of spiritual practice is attaining that state of experiencing the inner feeling where existence is independent of the physical body and the outside world. It is then that one is able to see oneself as part of the Infinite; an unbroken continuity of Universal Consciousness. The unique feature of such a spiritual experience is its motiveless urge. Such experiences have become even more relevant in contemporary times, when personal and social conflicts are taking a heavy toll on both individuals and societies. The addition of a course on Education for Peace in the National Curriculum Framework 2005 testifies to this effect. 'Peace as an integrative perspective for school curriculum is an idea whose time has come' (NCF Review, 2005, p. 183).

The paradigm shift

The previous two centuries witnessed a dominance of quantitative research situated in the experimental research paradigm. Replicability and public verification were at the heart of such an approach, and generalizability its logical outcome. Phenomena, experiences and internal processes that could not be verified by others were not considered worthy of research as these did not lend themselves to observation and measurement. The physical world may lend itself to an explicit demonstration of causality, but the 'inner world', which governs the thoughts, feelings and actions of humans, does not lend itself to the 'hard science' research methodology. In such a situation, there existed only one option—rejection of one of the two, that is, the content of research or the method of research. The intangible, unobservable and immeasurable content of human experience was denied substantive existence and therefore rejected in favour of the scientific method, which enjoyed the reputation of a legitimate approach to inquiry. Consequently, personal experiences, despite being genuinely real, were not acknowledged, and therefore not considered valid enough to be researched. Over-mechanization and dehumanization of mankind was met with resistance by the humanists and took the shape of Third Force psychology, which placed the individual human experience at the core of its analysis. It was increasingly acknowledged that the deeper and subtle issues that govern human life cannot be understood according to the parameters prescribed by the scientific approach. However, since these issues are real to the experiencing self, there must be other methods of enquiry that can deal with them. This view was supported by researches conducted in cultural anthropology, which attempted to analyse and describe the lives of people 'as they lived'. The Fourth Force, namely transpersonal psychology, with its thrust on transpersonal inquiry, further legitimized this emerging argument. It became increasingly clear that the method of science was not only inadequate, but also an inappropriate tool of inquiry for understanding deeper and subtler issues of a metaphysical nature. The need for qualitative rather than quantitative research was strongly felt, and there occurred a remarkable shift from objective to subjective, reductionist to holistic, scientific to phenomenological, experimental to descriptive, and contrived to naturalistic research in the late twentieth century.

Qualitative research derives data from participative observations and verbal interactions with a focus on meanings and interpretations made by the participants. Its major goal is to explore the deeper and intense aspects of the phenomena under study, and essentially involves a search for meaning. Ethnography, biographies and phenomenological approaches are examples of qualitative research. Phenomenology is primarily oriented towards experience and its meaning for the subject—the experiential reality. Emphasis is laid on how the 'life-world' is perceived and described by the subjects themselves. Such a research is not governed by a theoretical priori, but through a construction of meanings and categories or themes emerging in the process of interpretation. The essence of reality is to be understood as it exists. The aim is to capture lived experience with all its emotions and feelings.

Thus, with experiential reality acquiring a respectable position in what are considered legitimate ways of knowing, it seems perfectly reasonable to frame questions and seek answers to what is observed and experienced in everyday life. The everyday observations of most individuals, irrespective of age, gender or class, highlight an effort to contemplate something that is convincingly real, and yet denied as reality by the mainstream intellectual tradition. The need to create space for dialogue on such issues has been expressed silently as well as overtly, and therefore can no longer be brushed aside under the garb of scientifically invalid content or secular education. Observation of this expression itself warrants intellectual deliberation on the subject. It is fitting to note that in a seminar on the theme 'Personal Re-engineering in Management', organized in Bangalore in 1998, an agonized management professional remarked, 'Do I understand right that living (being) is the goal of life? If that be so, why should all that not be told to me at an early age? I am, actually learning to live life after one third or two third of it is gone. Do I have to stumble upon the goal?' The other management personnel also shared their anxieties, feelings of insecurity, loneliness, fears and despair at the same seminar (Swami Dayanand, 1998, p. 35).

While pursuing his teacher preparation course, a physics post-graduate from Delhi University chanced upon a book, *Jnanayoga* (1993), written by Swami Vivekananda. He shared his experience of reading this book with other members of the tutorial group, including the tutor (the author), in October 2005. He reported that reading this book was an elevating experience and remarked in a thoughtful voice,

> I wish I had read this book earlier, I would have been a different person. I have passed through tremendous inner turmoil and state of uncertainty. This book has changed me by putting my mind to rest. It has answers to so many questions which nagged me as a young boy. Today I feel happy—happy without any apparent reason. But I know the reason, I have discovered something, perhaps the truth or the essence of life. There is peace inside and I can look at my experiences objectively. I think this book should be taught as part of our school curriculum. Every child must read this book. There will be more peace and harmony inside and outside.

He then asked the most difficult question: 'Why is it not part of our school curriculum? It is neither religious nor communal.'

Another member of the tutorial group also opened up and said,

> I was feeling terrible yesterday after my practice teaching. Nothing seemed to work, I felt very incapable and dejected since all my plans and theory went down the drain. When I came back home, I cried and was feeling very depressed. Suddenly I turned the pages of the book called *Psychic Education*.[1] I opened it with no intention of reading it seriously but the page I opened described just how I was feeling. I got interested and started reading and very soon I was following the suggestions given in the book. I realized I was meditating. It cheered me up and made me feel light inside. I think every B.Ed. (Teacher Education) student must read this book.

The tutor wondered how a simple act of placing certain books on the table around which the tutees sit, and asking them to glance through them if they so desired, could make such a difference. The students found a space in this tutorial class to share something that the system does not want to acknowledge. Talking about religion, spirituality or inner experiences is not only considered unacademic, but also communal. After all, our education is secular, with secularity defined in curious ways! However, spirituality is part of the human experience, and it is naïve to confuse it with any religion or community. Furthermore, if the aim of education is to address the whole child, it is absolutely imperative that room be provided for understanding inner experiences and integrating them with overall thought and behaviour.

Cultural context

All along, from ancient times to the present, Indian psychology has cogitated on the depths and heights of consciousness, and the inner world has been a major subject of inquiry and analysis. The UNESCO report of the Education Commission, 1996, titled 'Learning the Treasures within', proposed that '... the process must begin with self understanding through our inner voyage whose milestones are knowledge, meditation and practice of self-criticism'.

What clearly emerges from the analysis is the need for reorientation, deconstruction, and a paradigmatic shift in our approach to education and teacher preparation. The importance of a sound theoretical base, and the lack of the same, has been stressed upon by various commissions, committees, and those involved in education. A persisting concern in teacher education has been the enhancement of its 'impact potential'. The urgency to reorganize teacher education courses has been highlighted by all concerned with education. The National Policy on Education, 1986 (revised in 1992), reiterated the same, and emphatically suggested that there is something basic to teacher education programmes that needs to be remedied urgently. These programmes fail to convey a coherent and meaningful view of the school education system. The revised National Curriculum Framework (2005, p. vii) opens with a quotation from Rabindranath Tagore's essay *Civilisation and Progress* (1924) in which the poet asserts that 'creative spirit' and 'generous joy' are key in childhood, and that both can be distorted by an unthinking adult world. As regards teacher education, it suggests a complete overhauling; there is a need for a fundamental change in the approach to teacher education in order to make it field-sensitive and participative in nature. It visualizes the teacher as an 'encouraging, supportive and humane facilitator in teaching-learning situations who enables learners (students) to discover their talents, to realize their physical and intellectual potentialities to the fullest, to develop character and desirable social and human values to function as responsible citizens' (Yadav, 2005).

The agenda of education stands crystal clear. There is a need to redefine the goals of life, self, knowledge, processes of knowing, and processes of enabling others to know and connect with others' selves. This obviously involves a deeper consciousness. Well-articulated views already exist in this regard in the Indian tradition. There is need to capitalize on these before they are sold to us (*yoga* and alternative medicines are good examples). Our society has lost its earlier structure and orientation towards 'progress inside', and lacks the culture to deal with the 'progress outside'. There is a need to build on our culture of 'growth inside' to deal with the growth of the world 'outside'. This requires a cognitive reorientation; a culture of learning to be at peace with oneself; a structure which provides space within oneself, composure within ourselves so that we can view the world objectively and decide about actions in consonance with our basic nature as human beings (see Swami Dayanand, 2002).

The task ahead

As stated in the previous section, the Teacher Education programmes in India were not only reactive, but also mechanistic, and were based on the 'teacher as a technician' metaphor. The goal of Teacher Education was to equip teachers with the tools and techniques effective in 'handling' and 'moulding' children according to fixed, preconceived and, quite often, contrived notions of humans and human life. A system that does not allow space for individual variability systematically stifles creativity, curbs originality of thought and action, and impedes the actualization of potential; it injects intellectual anaesthesia and produces academic robots. Denial of individuality or uniqueness in children is denying the existence of the self; it is tantamount to the denial of the existence of consciousness and thus cannot serve as a valid conceptual base for human development. Therefore, there is a need to reorient teacher education programmes towards a more proactive stance, which will ensure the conceptual, contextual and ethical validity of the teacher education curriculum.

> The immediate response that comes to mind while trying to answer the question of 'how we want our children to grow up' is that we want them to grow into individuals who are healthy, with life-styles conducive to the sustenance and promotion of life in all its forms; who appreciate the beauty and potential of nature, the inter-dependence of all forms of life and the need for harmony; who are happy and at peace with themselves, and consequently 'make peace' with others; who reason dispassionately about natural and social phenomena; who are tolerant to ambiguity and multiplicity and can resolve, or at least understand, the antinomies of today's world; who have understanding and respect for cultural diversity and are able to communicate and cooperate with persons of different origins; who value good human relations and are committed to mutual trust and coexistence; and work towards the common goals of society and mankind. (Baveja, 2005)

To sum up, these are individuals who are competent and self-propelled to undertake the journey of the evolution of self and society in its widest, deepest and highest sense.

In view of the above, there cannot be a better characterization of education than that education is a process of 'drawing out the best in body, mind and soul'. The aims of education flow directly from this immensely meaningful statement of Mahatma Gandhi's. There seems to be no substitute for this eternal definition of education. Although education has to essentially address these major dimensions of the child, they cannot be viewed as independent components that develop and function in isolation from each other. Body, mind and soul form an integral whole not amenable to fragmentation, thus pre-empting a reductionist approach.

Our prevailing education system not only fails to address the 'whole child', but also fragments knowledge into discrete areas of study, rendering life experiences incomprehensible. No wonder research indicates that in comparison to 'unschooled' children, 'schooled' children are better equipped to memorize discrete bits of often meaningless information. Although schooled children are at an advantage given their ability to comprehend symbolic information such as graphs and formulae, they are not better in day-to-day problem solving when compared to 'unschooled children'. 'That students failed to connect their formal symbol manipulation procedures with "real-world" objects represented by the symbols constitute a dramatic failure of instruction' (Schoenfeld, 1988, p. 150). 'People who perform poorly in the test situations show great skill on similar problems in their everyday lives' (Rogoff, 1984). The fact that 'school knowledge' does not connect the child to real life and remains for the most part 'inert knowledge' is too well-known to be emphasized further (Brown, et al., 1989). Teacher education is no exception. The traditional approach in teacher education programmes is to teach the philosophical, sociological, psychological and pedagogical aspects of education as distinctly separate areas of study. Further, there is no explicit attempt to illustrate the inter-connectedness of these areas. As a result, most practising and student teachers not only fail to see the relevance of some of these content areas, but are also unable to comprehend the same. Researches conducted in the last two decades (Behari, 1997; Ramanathan, 2004) indicate that most teachers feel that although the B.Ed. course prepares them for specific subject teaching (which is no doubt the goal of secondary and senior secondary teacher education), it does not address those dimensions of their personality that are important to becoming fully functioning teachers, or, for that matter, fully functioning humans. The existing teacher preparation courses are not focused on preparing 'teachers', but are designed to prepare 'subject teachers'. Subject teachers can only produce academic robots. This is part and outcome of the mechanistic scheme of our teacher education programmes. Most participants in both the researches either directly or indirectly pointed to the irrelevance of foundational courses such as philosophy and sociology of education as they perceived their jobs as subject teachers. The real classroom poses different kinds of challenges for which they are ill-prepared. The need to structure teacher education programmes according to holistic themes emerges clearly, both at the research and experiential levels. It might be more useful to structure teacher education programmes according to broader thematic areas that transcend the boundaries of traditional disciplines and focus on learners, learning, pedagogy, etc. The other major problem sighted by teachers in the above research was how unprepared they were to meet the challenge of variability that exists in actual classrooms. The teachers' own ability to connect positively with children from diverse backgrounds and, in turn, enable children to relate effectively with each other is not nurtured in the existing teacher education programmes. And neither is concern for good inter-personal relationships among teachers a significant focal area.

Given the pluralistic social order, marked by aggressive global forces, communal conflicts and vested political interest, it is essential that education produces critical thinkers who can take informed decisions and act with courage and conviction. '[...] it is vital to prevent social conflict through an education that fosters understanding and respect for cultural diversity as well as communication and cooperation between persons of different origins' (Dasen, 1992). Urbanization, industrialization and cross-border conflicts have generated unprecedented human mobility. Teachers are invariably faced with multi-cultural classrooms and have to communicate with children and parents from different cultural origins, and thereby have to deal with complex intergroup dynamics. 'It is therefore important to train teachers to understand the phenomenon linked to migration, cross cultural communication and social psychology .... Explicit attempt should be made to enable teachers to overcome their own ethnocentrisms by reflecting on their enculturation recognizing their prejudices' (Dasen, 1992). Such goals cannot be achieved through verbal communication alone. They require an experiential and more participative approach to teacher preparation. Internship or school life experiences should essentially include inter-cultural education and provision for self-development and working with the community.

Perennial foundations

> The greatest challenge for human beings is to understand the Self, the inner essence of one's existence. This awareness is totally experiential and not conceptual. (*The Hindu*, National daily, dated 28 December, 2005, p. 9)

The Western traditions look at the concept of self as the potentiality and possibility of development inherent in humans. These inherent potentialities are actualized through interactions with the phenomenal world. Carl Rogers (1951) defines self as an 'organized, fluid, but consistent conceptual pattern of perception of characteristics and relationships of the I or the "me" together with values attached to these concepts'. The structure of the self is formed as a result of interaction, particularly evaluative interaction, with the environment, which comprises significant others and events. 'Self actualization involves becoming whatever one can become through activities determined by one self' (Maslow, 1970). 'The organism has one basic tendency and goal—to actualize, maintain and enhance the experiencing organism' (Rogers, 1951). Although a fully actualized self is allocentric, altruistic and autonomous, its locus of existence lies essentially in the individual. The individual self is the be all and end all; a single point, a unidimensional entity.

The concept of self according to Indian traditions, particularly the *Bhagavad Gītā*, is a multi-layered construct. It simultaneously connotes the metaphysical, spiritual and phenomenal realms of existence. A well-defined hierarchy of the many selves within the composite universal self is conceptualized. *Brahman*—the Universal Self—is the highest layer in this system. *Brahman* pervades everything that exists, organic and material (physical). Human beings are miniscule in the larger cosmic order. *Brahman* can neither be fully known, nor can it be achieved by the 'human form'. *Brahman* is inconceivable or *acintyarūpa*. It is also unmanifested—*avyakta*. It is therefore beyond cognition, experience and comprehension.

Next in the descending order of pervasiveness is the individual self or *puruṣa*. *Puruṣa* is the knower, the cognizing being. It is addressed by different scholars as *ātman*, *jīva*, consciousness or life force. *Puruṣa* pervades only living entities unlike the *Brahman*, which pervades the entire universe. *Dharma* or the nature of *puruṣa* is to illumine all that comes in contact with *buddhi* (reasoning principle), *manas* (mind), *ahaṁkāra* (ego sense), *indriya* (sensory perception apparatus), and the external world with detachment. However, in human life *puruṣa* comes in contact with the *triguṇa*—*rajas* (activity), *tamas* (inertia) and *sattva* (purity)—leading to enjoyment, incurring pleasure and pain. To attain true knowledge of the Self, the limitations imposed by the gross-subtle body and by the three *guṇas* must be transcended. The individual has to become *triguṇātīta*—an individual who is led not by personal choices, but by duties with complete detachment. Surrender or attachment is not to the persons or objects served, but to *svadharma* and *svabhāva*. Lower down this order is the personal self. This conception of self addresses the misconception of self entertained by human beings. Although the true Self of man is the *puruṣa*, yet with the *prakṛti*-borne body-*manas*-intellect-*ahaṁkāra* apparatus, the consciousness principle is conceived as a means to worldly ends rather than as an end in itself. In this process, the ego-sense (mis)identifies with the body, and the cognitive apparatus with the self.

This level (personal self) is akin to the Western notion of self, which includes the physical, social, intellectual and emotional dimensions of an individual's personality. These, according to the *Bhagavad Gītā*, are components of *prakṛti*, and must be transcended for self-realization. The goal of life is to strive for the evolution of the personal self to higher levels, rather than limiting its evolution to the actualization of inherent bodily potentials.

The pursuit of knowledge leads to the discovery of Self, which is the source of liberation. Knowledge is possible only when the mind is free from desire, likes and dislikes, fears and threats. One's commitment to knowledge leads to self-learning, *svādhyāya*, which is pursued for its own sake; the commitment comes from within; the knower or the epistemic subject is intrinsically motivated to discover the truth. Discovery of truth or knowledge is an outcome of inquiry; however, when the learner is not mature enough or is unable to conduct a successful inquiry, he may be taught. *Pravacana* is teaching. *Svādhyāya* and *pravacana* form a continuum, wherein the one who knows shares knowledge with others who are keen to know. Learning requires an inquisitive, perceptive mind which engages in reflection and articulation. It is not ingestion of what is told but is a constructive and a generative process which requires a contemplative mind. A contemplative mind has to be discovered and developed by releasing the mind from the bonds of likes and dislikes. Suitable measures and appropriate means have to be adopted to free the mind from the shackles of personal likes and dislikes. One who is continuously learning and sharing knowledge, that is, engaging in *svādhyāya* and *pravacana*, leads a contemplative life: s/he is a life-long learner who is sincerely committed to enabling others to learn. However, learning and teaching—*svādhyāya* and *pravacana*—are two separate, though intimately related, processes. Learning and teaching both require a contemplative mind. The teacher teaches, but does not indoctrinate or impose. The student must construct his own understanding, decide for himself and assume responsibility for his actions. As described in the *Bhagavad Gītā*, Arjuna asks for advice from Lord Kṛṣṇa and He teaches Arjuna about the nature of action and renunciation while leaving the understanding of the scheme and the consequent action to him. The teacher is a facilitator; he shows the path, provides exposure, but leaves the analysis and contemplation to the learner. The '*adhikāra*' or choice of action lies with the learner. A contemplative mind is fundamental to metacognition and is an outcome of the evolution of the inner self. A developed and evolved contemplative mind, fundamental to metacognition, is free from biases and can embark upon objective decision-making.

The Self is *akartā*, actionless; it neither performs any action nor leads anyone to do so; the knower of the self is indeed the Self. Here, it is not action that is denied; it is the *kartṛtva* or doership that is denied. 'Actions are performed by the body and the wise man is not identified with the body; he knows himself to be actionless Self. So the knowledge of actionless Self is freedom from action' (Swami Dayananda, 1987, p. 4). The discovery of the self involves the renunciation of the sense of doership. Pursuit of '*karma*' (action) involves the sense of doership. *Karma* is action and *vihitakarma*, the enjoined actions known as duties. Nature is in perfect harmony to sustain the Universe. This harmony can be disturbed only by humans as other living beings are not endowed with volition—the faculty of choice. *Vihitakarma* are conducive to the maintenance of harmony in life, which is the duty of every human being. Duty is borne out of maturity and appreciation of one's role in the scheme of things. It can be seen as a mandate until it is internalized. A sense of duty culminates in a proper attitude towards life and evolves into *niṣṭhā*—commitment. Actions that disturb the harmony in the universe and life are '*niṣiddhakarma*'. A true *karma yogi* is one who avoids '*niṣiddhakarma*' and engages in '*vihitakarma*'. A *yogī's* actions are governed by duties performed through detachment from personal likes and dislikes, as well as from the outcome of actions. *Yoga* here implies equanimity of mind.

Concluding remarks

These ideas, taken from the *Bhagavad Gītā*, help us reconstruct the conceptual framework for teacher education. First, it clearly indicates that teaching is not a collection of skills but an ongoing process of contemplation, a continuous process in the search for truth. It is an ongoing quest to understand the learner, the processes of learning, ways of providing learning experiences and inspiration to embark on the inner journey. A teacher has to be a true *karma yogī* who engages in enjoined action in the pursuit of knowledge and is committed to the development of her own self and those of her students; one who makes discretionary use of the faculty of choice.

The development of self is basic to all aspects of development. An evolved self is naturally committed to altruism, justice, diligence and genuine concern for the development of society. Teachers should be facilitated in their journey towards self-development and in helping their students move towards the same goal. Legitimate space should be provided for self-development activities in the Teacher Education Curriculum. A non-evaluative, accepting, threat-free environment is basic to self-development. It inspires sharing, increases receptivity and, most importantly, promotes self-reflection, leading to the development of a positive self-concept. Opportunities for self-expression in different art forms with a view to unfolding aesthetic sensibilities would also lead to a sense of fulfilment. Teachers need to be taught how to create learning environments that are non-competitive and threat-free; permissive environments that inspire and nurture creativity, critical thinking and reflexivity, thereby preparing the child for problem-solving and conflict resolution.

The Teacher Education Programmes should provide space for developing teachers who are conscientious and committed to unity and harmony. A true teacher is one who engages in an ongoing process of self-evolution through contemplation, self-reflection and self-correction; s/he initiates and enables the pupils to engage in these processes with equanimity, taking into account the student's cognitive, cultural, economic and physical characteristics. Knowledge essentially entails the discovery of the Self, as already stated; thus, all the attributes mentioned above can only be realized through experience and reflection. Therefore, it is essential that the teacher education curriculum be experience-based and interactive, with ample opportunities for self-observation and self-reflection, leading to self-development. Only an evolved self can facilitate the evolution of the selves of others.

Vertical development inside is expected to lead to horizontal development outside; the deeper the connection with the inner self, the greater the comfort and ease in connecting with others outside. Biases and prejudices dissolve when realization of the oneness of the omnipresent consciousness dawns.

Endnotes

1 See Huppes, 2001.

References

Baveja, B. (2005). Paper presented during the deliberations of national focus group on teacher education.

Behari, A. (1997). *Teaching behaviour of beginning teachers as related to self actualizing personality and skills of teaching during teacher education programme.* Unpublished thesis. Delhi: Delhi University, Department of Education.

Brown, J. S., Collins, A., & Duguid, P. (1989). Situated cognition and the culture of learning. *Educational Researcher, 18*, 32–42.

Dasen, P. R. (1992). Cross-cultural psychology and teacher training. In J. Lynch, C. Modgil, & S. Modgil (Eds.), *Cultural diversity and the schools. Prejudice, polemic or progress?* (pp. 191–204). London: Falmer Press.

Dayanand, Swami (1987). *Knowledge and action: The two-fold commitment.* Rishikesh: Sri Gangadhareswar Trust.

Dayanand, Swami (1998). *Personal re-engineering in management.* Bangalore: Arsha Vidya Kendra Trust.

Dayanand, Swami (2002). *Need for cognitive change.* Bangalore: Arsha Vidya Kendra Trust.

Huppes, N. (2001). *Psychic education.* New Delhi: SAES.

Maslow, A. (1970). *Motivation and personality* (2nd ed.). New York: Harper and Row.

Ramanathan, S. (2004). *Science teaching in classrooms and its implication for the teacher education programme.* Unpublished thesis. Delhi: Delhi University, Department of Education.

Rogers, C. (1951). *Client-centred therapy: Its current practice, implications and theory.* Boston: Houghton Mifflin.

Rogoff, B. (1984). Introduction: Thinking and learning in social content. In B. Rogoff & J. Lave (Eds.), *Everyday cognition: Its development in social context* (pp. 1–9). Cambridge, MA: Harvard University Press.

Schoenfeld, A. (1988). When good teaching leads to bad results: The disasters of 'well-taught' mathematics courses. *Educational Psychologist, 23*(2), 145–166.

Tagore, R. (1996). Civilization and progress. In S. K. Das (Ed.), *The English writings of Rabindranath Tagore* (Vol. 2). New Delhi: Sahitya Akademi. (Original publication 1924).

Vivekananda, Swami (1993). *Jnanayoga.* Calcutta: Advaita Ashrama.

Yadav, M. S. (2005). Paper presented to national focus group on teacher education. NCERT, New Delhi.

22

The Mirambika experience

Anjum Sibia

Adopting an ethnographic approach, this chapter examines the rich and dynamic life of teaching-learning in Mirambika—a school based on the Free Progress Education as envisioned by Sri Aurobindo and The Mother. The school ideology influences the social environment, the behaviour of its inhabitants, and provides sources and resources of support, guidance and reinforcement. The influence of the ideology of Mirambika is evident in its physical environment and organization of pedagogic processes. The interactions between teachers and children encompass a range of meanings and messages, which are largely governed by this ideology. A selective account of classroom realities in Mirambika is presented as an attempt to build up the school culture through ideas, thoughts, feelings and artefacts.

The school Mirambika attempts to practice the educational views of Sri Aurobindo and The Mother, and seeks alternatives in curriculum, content, as well as in transaction. This chapter attempts to explicate the pedagogic processes taking place in the classroom with a view to examining the relationship between the school philosophy, activities and student outcomes.

Education in India: A brief overview

Concern for education in India can be traced back to the *Vedic* age, from the age of the *Upaniṣads*, the *Gītā*, the Buddhist and Jain scriptures, *Smṛtis*, etc., through the medieval and British periods to the post-colonial systems of traditional education. Education was accorded the highest priority right from the pre-historic days. However, the aims of teaching-learning have shifted in focus during different periods. As described by Altekar (1965), during the *Vedic* period the focus was on imparting sacred literature and family occupation to the children. Memorization was the dominant pedagogical method, along with interpretation and creativity. These, however, became less important during the *Upaniṣadic* period, where the emphasis was on accuracy, correct accent and intonation. In the *Dharmaśāstrik* period, a systematic teaching of reading, writing and arithmetic took place. The focus was also on memorizing the *Vedas*. The *Paurāṇika* period had four types of teachers: the *ācārya*, the *guru*, the *śikṣaka* and the *upādhyāya*. The *ācārya* was the highest level that a teacher could attain. During the Buddhist period, the *upādhyāya* was considered the most revered teacher, and instructed students in proper conduct, morality and notions of *vinaya* (humility) and *dharma* (duty). The nature of pedagogy during the early period was 'oral, repetitive and exemplary' (Altekar, 1965). Prior to colonization, the teacher or *guru* provided practical instruction to students in local village schools, or *pāṭhaśālās*. Reading, writing, arithmetic and Sanskrit were the main subjects. Teachers played an authoritative role and students related to the teachers with reverence (Dharmpal, 1983).

During the colonial period, the British

introduced a complete English system of education in India. Rote learning was encouraged and British knowledge or curriculum (as embodied in the textbook) played a prominent role (Kumar, 1991, p. 14). In *Political Agenda of Education*, Kumar (1991) points out that the British curriculum was not related to the experiences of the Indian child, and represented a discontinuity. As a result of this discontinuity, Indian students were forced to memorize the information. As Clarke (2001) in her work on *Teaching and Learning: The Culture of Pedagogy* states, 'it is difficult to conceive that the British could have transformed this pervasive practice of rote entrenched among us for generations even with curriculum that may not have represented discontinuity with our own culture and traditions' (p. 41). Even though the British attempted to transform pedagogy through a 'more progressive' method of learning (through Froebel's method of instruction), they were not successful.

The assumption that the system of education in its entirety is still completely Western-oriented has been the basis for several reform initiatives for education in India. Innovations in pedagogy after independence were attempts at indigenizing education. It was held that the education system could be transformed and enriched through the inclusion of the core elements of being Indian. One of the early initiatives in the process of indigenization of education was Gandhiji's *Basic Education* (*Bunyadi Talim*) in the 1930s. He believed this was possible through craft learning, not as a subject of instruction, but by imparting the whole process of education through some handicraft specific to the local context. Gandhiji believed that education in India should represent the Indian ethos, and required the teachers to be virtuous. The post-independence period was characterized by a series of reforms 'to give an indigenous identity so as to reflect the Indian ethos and concern for society' (National Curriculum for Elementary and Secondary Education—A Framework, 1988, p. 2).

The educational system of modern India had its beginnings in the nineteenth century. Lord Macaulay could be said to have laid the foundation of the modern Indian education system through his well-known *Minute on Education* in February 1835. It would not be wrong to say that in Indian education, one effectively sees a continuation of an imperial culture; unfortunately, Macaulay's ideas still dominate education in India. Elements of colonialism are evident in the position of authority teachers hold in the class, control over students' responses, and the use of teacher-centred methods, which lead to a passive acquisition of knowledge. 'Teachers, regulated by the primacy of the syllabus, help their students understand and know this syllabus in its entirety through repetition and memorization. Higher order thinking typified by analysis and the reasoning is largely upheld in the Indian educational system' (Clarke, 2001, pp. 166–167). It is suggested that the culturally defined patterns of hierarchical interaction influence the teacher's pivotal authoritative role within the classroom in India. Kumar's study (1991) considers the dominance of the teacher in the classroom a natural outcome of the respect and authority given to age and experience within the religious, social and cultural ethos of the country. From a developmental standpoint, Kakar (1984) described the authority conferred on the adult by children in Indian society. Adults accede to all the demands of the child generally till the child is about five years old. After that the roles reverse: the child is required to respect and obey the adult. It is suggested that teachers are aware of and constrained by these tacit understandings of authoritative adult roles within society, and tend to fashion their pedagogy and classroom organization accordingly. Besides the teacher, textbooks have played a major role in the way teaching-learning is organized in classrooms. The Yash Pal Committee report of the mid-1990s identified the information overload in textbooks used in schools across the country as the major problem in the Indian educational system.

The educational traditions of colonial times still permeate practices in post-colonial India. This is so despite the fact that a number of education commissions and policies, such as the University Education Commission led by Dr S. Radhakrishnan (1946–1948), the Secondary Education Commission headed by Dr A. L. Mudaliar (1952–1953), the Education

Commission headed by Dr D. S. Kothari (1964–1966), and the National Policy on Education 1968 and 1986 were concerned about the state of education. It has been observed that the Westernization of the education system has been far greater since independence than it was under British rule. Even after more than 60 years of independence, we have not been able to liberate ourselves from the colonial mind-set.

In present times, teaching-learning in schools is subject-specific, time-bound, focused on structured forms of learning, characterized by repetitive rote memorization, and examination-dominated. Creating a fear of failure, schools have become merely centres for selection, monopolized by tests and examinations. As Shotton (1998, p. 32) observed, 'what one effectively has in Indian education is a continuation of an imperial culture, something that is essentially elitist and autocratic'. Variations through innovations within traditional mainstream schooling do exist, but are nominal, marginal and peripheral. These alternatives challenge the existing culture of rote learning and cramming, arising from prescriptive teaching, teacher dominance in classroom transactions, learning focused on securing marks, and evaluations that create feelings of inferiority and insecurity. In view of the existing realities, there is a need to address the question: what is the aim and function of education? The educational ideas of Indian thinkers provide a base upon which to build a perspective for a new system of education.

Educational thought: Some Indian views

The philosophical thinking of eminent personalities like Sri Aurobindo, Rabindranath Tagore, J. Krishnamurti, Swami Vivekananda, Mahatma Gandhi, Zakir Hussain, and others has influenced the system of education in India. Gandhi's *Basic Education Scheme* (*Bunyadi Talim*) formed the basis of various education committees that were created during the independence period. Education for Gandhiji 'is one in which the individual develops his character, trains his faculties, and learns to control his passions in the service of the community' (Kabir, 1961, p. 202). Tagore pleaded for an education which would lead to an 'all-sided and well-integrated development of the human personality'. He also felt that in order to be truly creative, education should be in touch with the lives of people in their entirety—economic, intellectual, aesthetic, social and spiritual. Sri Aurobindo too placed emphasis on the all-round development of the personality, which included education of the senses, body and mind, as well as moral and spiritual education. Swami Vivekananda's educational thought laid emphasis on the realization of the perfection already present in man. He placed the greatest stress on education as the gradual unfolding of the intrinsic quality of the individual, and was of the view that no knowledge comes from outside. For Iqbal, the essential purpose of education was to develop man's individuality. He saw education as a process that ensures the possibility of eternal progress. Indian philosophers, according to Kabir (1961), 'regard education essentially as process of drawing out what is implicit in the individual and to develop his latent potentialities till they become actualities'. Indian thought, as expressed in the educational philosophies of Indian thinkers, lays stress on a comprehensive education aimed at the development of the total personality of the individual, in harmony with society and nature.

Amongst the various thinkers and writers on education who contributed to the philosophy of education in India, Sri Aurobindo's perspective is significant in the light of a comprehensive education and an all-round development of the learner. It calls for a shift in the educational paradigm, one where curriculum is individualized, linkages with life experiences established, a love for learning inculcated, and the personal growth of the learner aimed at. It seeks a new approach to schooling: it considers alternatives to curriculum planning, teaching approaches, evaluation procedures, the role of the teacher and the learner in the learning process, and aims to bridge the gap between home and school.

Sri Aurobindo's ideas on education

The educational views of Sri Aurobindo are closely linked to his futuristic vision of human destiny. He maintains that the kind of education we need in our country is 'proper to the Indian soul and need and temperament and culture that we are in quest of, not indeed something faithful merely to the past, but to the developing soul of India, to her future need, to the greatness of her coming self-creation, to her eternal spirit' (1956, p. 7). Sri Aurobindo's concept of 'education' is not only about acquiring information. 'But the acquiring of various kinds of information', he points out (1956, pp. 9–10),

> is only one and not the chief of the means and necessities of education: its central aim is the building of the powers of the human mind and spirit, it is the formation or, as I would prefer to view it, the evoking of knowledge and will and of the power to use knowledge, character, culture—that at least if no more. And this distinction makes an enormous difference.

Sri Aurobindo's chief concern is not merely with the acquisition of information placed at our disposal by the science of the West 'in an undigested whole or in carefully packed morsels', but

> the major question is not merely what science we learn, but what we shall do with our science and how too, acquiring the scientific mind and recovering the habit of scientific discovery ... we shall relate it to other powers of the human mind and scientific knowledge to other knowledge more intimate to other and not less light-giving and power-giving parts of our intelligence and nature (1956, p. 10).

The aim and principle of a true national education, according to Sri Aurobindo (1956, pp. 10–11), is 'not, certainly, to ignore modern truth and knowledge, but to take our foundation on our own being, our own mind, our own spirit'. A truly national system of education according to him will be 'as comprehensive as the European and more thorough, without the evils of strain and cramming'. This can only be done 'by studying the instruments of knowledge and finding a system of teaching which shall be natural, easy and effective' (1956, p. 19).

Sri Aurobindo (1956, pp. 20–21) elaborates certain sound principles of good teaching, which have to be kept in mind when actually engaged in the process of learning. According to Sri Aurobindo, the first principle of true teaching is 'that nothing can be taught'. He explains that knowledge is already dormant within the child and for this reason, 'The teacher is not an instructor or task-master, he is a helper and a guide.' The role of the teacher

> is to suggest and not to impose. He does not actually train the pupil's mind, he only shows him how to perfect the instruments of knowledge and helps him and encourages him in the process. He does not impart knowledge to him; he shows him how to acquire knowledge for himself. He does not call forth the knowledge that is within; he only shows him where it lies and how it can be habituated to rise to the surface.

The second principle of true teaching is that 'the mind has to be consulted in its own growth. The idea of hammering the child into the shape desired by the parent or the teacher is a barbarous and ignorant superstition.' Sri Aurobindo has more faith in the *svabhāva* of the educand, that is, 'it is he himself who must be induced to expand in accordance with his own nature'. He states:

> To force the nature to abandon its own *dharma* is to do it permanent harm, mutilate its growth and deface its perfection. It is a selfish tyranny over a human soul and a wound to the nation which loses the benefit of the best that a man could have given it and is forced to accept instead something imperfect and artificial, second rate, perfunctory and common.

For Sri Aurobindo, the chief aim of education should be to help each and every soul to draw out its best. He firmly believes that everyone has her/his own individuality and potential, with a chance of perfection and strength, however imperfect. As he succinctly observed:

> Every one has in him something divine, something his own, a chance of perfection and strength in however small a sphere which God offers him to take or refuse. The task is to find it, develop it and use it. The chief aim of education should be to help the growing soul to draw out that in itself which is best and make it perfect for a noble use.

The third principle of education is 'to work from the near to the far, from that which is to that which shall be'. As Sri Aurobindo states,

> The basis of a man's nature is almost always, in addition to his soul's past, his heredity, his surroundings, his nationality, his country, the soil from which he draws sustenance, the air which he breathes, the sights, sounds, habits to which he is accustomed. They mould him not the less powerfully because insensibly, and from that then we must begin.

Sri Aurobindo observed that if genuine development is to take place,

> We must not take up the nature by the roots from the earth in which it must grow or surround the mind with images and ideas of a life which is alien to that in which it must physically move. If anything has to be brought in from outside, it must be offered, not forced on the mind. A free and natural growth is the condition of genuine development.

Sri Aurobindo's philosophy of education is based on the principle of evoking the potential of the individual in all its entirety, which should be developed according to human nature. Free Progress Education is based on the assumption that a human being is good in himself, and that positive freedom is a pre-requisite to helping children by allowing them space to experiment and providing opportunities for growth. As The Mother says, 'A free and natural growth is the condition of genuine development'. Free progress is 'a progress guided by the soul and not subjected to habits, conventions or pre-conceived ideas' (The Mother, 1956). According to The Mother (1956), education, in order to be complete, must contain five principal aspects relating to the five principal activities of the human being: physical, vital or affect-related, mental, psychic and spiritual.

In contrast to the educational ideas of Sri Aurobindo and The Mother, the present-day education system in India is purely an instruction-of-information enterprise, supported by a subject and time-bound curriculum that neither relates to the needs or abilities of the learner nor takes into consideration the way children learn successfully. Instead of being child-oriented, it is subject-oriented. The schools focus on competition with others, on mastery of the subject matter for getting better marks or grades than on learning in cooperation with and from one another for personal growth and the welfare of others. This is not an exclusively Indian phenomenon; rather, education all over the world is largely reductionist, materialist, ego-enforcing, and devoid of the joys of the spirit (Cornelissen, 2003). It is in this context that there emerges a need to examine initiatives rooted in the Indian tradition; seek alternatives in curriculum, teaching, learning and measuring success; involve children in the process of learning; and focus on learning from one another and not from an authoritative pedagogue.

Against this backdrop, this chapter seeks to examine the school Mirambika, which is based on the ideals of Free Progress Education as envisioned by Sri Aurobindo and The Mother, specifically with regard to the effect of school philosophy on school organization, teaching-learning processes and student outcomes (Sibia, 2006).

The present research

Located in New Delhi, Mirambika came into being in 1981. The school, with 132 of its students aged between 3 and 12 years and 48 teachers,[1] was studied using a range of ethnographic methods, the aim being to study various school aspects such as organization, culture and teaching-learning processes. It involved examining the roles and responsibilities of school functionaries and their role perception, the study of routine and formal activities (meditation, sports, evaluations, etc.), the way teaching-learning is organized, the involvement of children in the process of learning, and the role of the teacher. Our understanding of the school was built through participant observation, interviews, informal talks and questionnaires, which were used for collection, documentation and analysis over a period of eight months. A thematic analysis of the data revealed the salient teaching-learning features, and interpretations of the classroom were drawn through inductive analysis. Validity of the interpretations was sought in 'triangulation'. The interpretive analysis provided a view of curriculum organization, teaching styles, disciplining techniques, grouping and seating patterns—a kaleidoscopic vision of classroom realities in Mirambika.

It is important to state that the process of entry to the school is to be viewed as an integral part of the ethnographic research undertaken. A brief narrative of our entry into Mirambika offers an important backdrop for understanding the research findings and the possible gaps that remain.

Gaining entry

On my first visit to Mirambika, I talked to the Principal about the nature of the research work—observing the teachers and children in and outside the classroom, as well as the other activities taking place from the start to the end of the school day. The major concern expressed was that the study, especially the presence of the observer in the class, might interfere with the functioning of the school. I was briefly introduced to one of the school coordinators (core group of teachers) to work out my schedule. The teachers gave no straight answers to my questions; instead, they suggested that we get a feel of Mirambika for a couple of days by sitting in the classes, observing, watching the happenings during meditation, games, etc. As they said, 'one does not enter anyone's house till one gets to know the occupants', and Mirambika to them was their home. Informal talks with the coordinators helped us to develop a working schedule. We had our first formal contact with the Diyas (teachers) during one of their weekly Saturday meetings, in which I talked about the proposed research work, its objectives, and briefly about what the research team intended to do. No questions were asked by the teachers, who seemed to know about the research. My early interactions with the teachers were limited to greetings while sitting in the class. I felt my presence probably held an 'evaluative stance', which was erased with time through a deliberate, conscious effort. Our initial contact with the children occurred while observing their daily activities in and outside the class. Although we were silent observers and did not initiate talk, informal talk did develop when the children enquired whether we were the new teachers. We tried to answer their queries honestly. However, the children viewed us as new teachers, and addressed us as Diyas. Total acceptance on the part of the children was the key factor in making intensive observations. Informal contact was established with parents during the initial days in the school. Some of them knew about our research work and were interested in our perceptions of the school activities. Formal contact with the parents was established when interviews were held with them. They allowed us enough time in which to answer our queries and were quite open with their opinions. As the research progressed, the research team began to be viewed as a part of the school, especially by the children, which helped us in maintaining a credible research role.

Mirambika: The physical ecology

Nestled among trees in the premises of the Sri Aurobindo Ashram in South Delhi is Mirambika. The school came into being in 1981. Mirambika is approached through the 'Sunlit Path', which has a statue of Sri Aurobindo, and signifies the road taking Sri Aurobindo's vision to the outside world. Wide open green spaces lined with eucalyptus trees surround the school, which has swings, slides, a *neem* grove—which at various junctures provide the space for learning activities for different groups. Mirambika has a number of resources, physical and material, which are characterized by the principles of 'openness' (Malehorn, 1978), that is, self-directed learning, enhancing uniqueness, encouraging exploration, flexibility in planning, sensitivity and affective awareness. Some of these are provided by the architectural layout of Mirambika, for instance, the wide roof terrace, which is used for various activities during the cooler months of the year. Similarly, the '*neem* grove' and the open spaces surrounding the school are used for multiple purposes like group walks, games, exhibitions, etc. Some common spaces of use located in the school include the teacher training wing, the library, the science laboratory, meditation hall, the art room, stationery room, gymnasium, computer room, talk room, the living museum and the dining hall. The physical facilities may therefore be considered resources in the school, keeping in mind their functions, activities organized, equipment, and the material they provide for school processes.

The architectural and physical organization in Mirambika has a distinct structure, and is an attempt to foster an environment that can keep the interests of all the children alive. The architectural space of the school, that is, its building, surroundings, equipment, materials, services and other resources set certain restrictions, but at the same time offer a certain degree of freedom to its inhabitants. The way each group uses the school's environment as a pedagogic resource is of paramount importance.

> The 30 or more models, charts, experiments, that were made as part of the 'Environment' project were displayed in the 'Living Museum' for a week and the children talked about their display, conducted small experiments, operated their models for other children, teachers and parents who visited (Field Note).

The importance of physical organization in Mirambika is highlighted in the context of the cultural meaning it acquires. The furniture, books, trees, all assume culturally defined meanings, which determine their limits and uses. All these set a range of opportunity, mobility, independence, flexibility and responsibility. The child's experiences in school are thus moulded by her/his surroundings, which may have a personal or special meaning for her/him. The personal meaning the school environment has for the children is expressed in words like *wonderful, peaceful, calm and quiet, different, superb, beautiful, best in the world*. Some children have provided reasons for liking their school environment and related it to trees, the surroundings, building, open fields, cool breeze, etc. In the children's own words:

> I like the building of Mirambika because it is very open and there are so many places to hide when you play hide and seek (Humility Group, 9 years).
>
> I like the building of Mirambika in winters because the chilly air and fog come in the group (Humility Group, 9 years).
>
> I like the playground and the trees, flowers, grass, plants, leaves, fresh air ... ducks and the pond (Progress Group, 8 years).

A day at Mirambika

It is Monday morning, 8.30 a.m. The children, dressed in their daily wear and not in school uniforms, are seen approaching the school building through the Sunlit Path. Some enter; others begin informal games in the grounds. No bell rings. Children move towards the dining hall for a collective breakfast. They have informal exchanges over sandwiches and fruit. Soon they are ready for studies and disappear into their 'groups' (classrooms) ever so quietly. Children and Diyas (as the teachers are called in Mirambika) clean their workplaces, dusting, sweeping, mopping—getting ready for the day. The term 'Diya' has been coined from the words '*didi*' (elder sister) and '*bhaiya*' (elder brother). As explained by a teacher, 'it symbolizes beckoning the light, the one who kindles the light in children'. Music for 'meditation' (concentration) marks the start of the school day, and a tranquil silence prevails. Students and teachers are seen sitting, some standing with eyes closed, a few looking out of the large windows, deep in thought. Children are told to think of what they left at home and what they will do in school. As a Diya said, 'these thoughts help them make a smooth transition from home to school and help them to set the pace for the day's work'. This activity is seen as an attempt 'to help children look inwards, which in turn helps them to evaluate and control one's feelings like anger, jealousy, etc.', as expressed by the teachers. As a child said, 'I feel peaceful after meditation.' Meditation is clearly governed by an ideology that aims at self-reflection, and is in accordance with Sri Aurobindo and the Mother's views on education, that is, that it should be a path towards self-knowledge, self-mastery and inner realization. The purpose of 'meditation' as stated by the school coordinators is to provide 'vital education', that is, control over emotions, impulses and desires, which also helps to link 'psychic' and 'spiritual' education. The school, however, feels that the latter (spiritual education) is a life-long process; yet, by 'creating awareness of it in the child, a small beginning is made'. The mornings are devoted to group work where pedagogic transaction takes place through 'projects', wherein different subject areas are integrated to achieve the project goals. Children work individually, in small groups, or take field trips. The work done in the mornings is evaluated either through self-evaluation sheets prepared by their Diya, or by discussions in a group. Lunch at 12.00 noon is an informal affair where children and teachers sit together on *durries* spread on the floor. Children from each group serve the food voluntarily. After eating, each person cleans his/her own '*thāli*' (big metal plates) and places it in specified stacks. This activity acquires particular significance because it is an attempt by Mirambika 'to develop a sense of responsibility, duty, self-help, dignity of work, self-restraint and co-operation', as expressed by the Diyas. After lunch, from 1.00 to 3.00 PM, there is 'formal training' and 'clubs' for the older groups. During this time mathematics and languages (English and Hindi) are taken by subject specialists, the majority of whom are volunteers (part-time teachers). Twice a week children take part in 'club' activities in areas like cooking, jewellery making, calligraphy, arts and crafts, pottery, etc. The child is free to choose and participate in an activity of his/her interest. The day's work closes at 3.00 PM with a 'home session', marked by the playing of music for concentration. The Diyas said, 'it is meant to prepare the children to get connected to their homes, and reflect on what they did during the day'. This is followed by light snacks and milk or juice, after which the children leave for their homes.

Diyas—teachers in school

The Diyas at Mirambika comprise full-time teachers (those residing in the Ashram), volunteers (part-time teachers) and trainee teachers doing their B. Ed. (at the time of the research project, they were affiliated to Indore University). They are not salaried staff and are paid a token stipend, which varies for full-time and trainee teachers. The volunteers are given a conveyance allowance. The teachers are chosen on the basis of their interest in working with children, affection and motivation to do their job. When asked what their aim in life is, the teachers replied, 'I want to be an ideal teacher', 'be a perfect instrument of the divine', 'work for The Mother and Sri Aurobindo', 'to make my life worthy to live', 'teaching is my *sādhanā* (devotion)', and 'to do *sevā* (service)'. Commitment to the school ideology is a common factor among the teachers at Mirambika. It provides a strong basis for carrying out their responsibilities within the stated boundaries of an ideal teacher. They view themselves as 'reflective' learners, and their role is to help the children discover their potential through guiding them, and helping them to know their interests.

Organising the school processes

Watching the teachers and children at Mirambika, we became convinced that the ideology of the school provides a framework for structuring and organizing its work. The manner in which the classes, the entire day, the teaching-learning is organized, the way decisions are taken, are all influenced by the ideology on which Mirambika is based. As Brunsson (1985, p. 16) states, 'Ideology is important in that it provides the set of ideas that decision makers take with them to guide decision making and to interpret their context.'

Mirambika does not compartmentalize itself into strictly graded or numbered classes; students are grouped together keeping in view their developmental needs. When asked how groups are formed and named, a teacher said,

> Children are grouped according to their age, but each group has an overlap of ages. The five groups for younger children are given names related to colours, namely Red group (3+ years), Blue group (4+ years), Green (5+ years), Yellow (6+ years) and Orange group (7+ years). Colours are chosen because at this age, children can easily relate to them. From seven years onwards the children themselves, keeping in view the qualities and virtues they want to develop in themselves, name the groups. The name decides the focus of the group for that specific year (for example, progress, receptivity, humility, etc.) and the children are encouraged and guided to achieve their group goal. This gives children a focus to their being in that specific group, and at the same time is a constant reminder of what they need to develop, which helps them assume responsibility for their actions.

The day-to-day functioning of Mirambika reveals that the working relationship between members is located in an informal work organization. We observed that there are no records or written memos maintained or sent. All communication is informal, and verbally conveyed to the teachers. The functionaries view their roles in line with their commitment to the school ideology, which enhances identification with the school goals. Hence, they carry out their responsibilities in a collective and collaborative manner. We observed that

> there are no peons to do office work which is normally shared amongst the members; no extra hands are employed to help the children with their personal needs, which the group teachers tend to; no office bearers are appointed to look after the principal's paper work—he himself works on the computer along with some others (Field Note).

Hierarchy in work is not evident, and the school comprises of workers of equal status. Symbols marking special status and embodying authority are conspicuous by their absence in Mirambika. The principal is not regarded as the supreme authority on school related matters. When asked who takes the decisions, the teachers replied, 'We all sit and talk and decide what has to be done'. Teachers and children often seek the principal's guidance and support, and he makes himself available to the children whenever required. His office is a small space with little furniture, often used by younger children as a 'hiding' place during play. This may be taken as evidence of his relationship with the children, irrespective of the role performed by him in the school. The perceptions of the children regarding their principal are: 'is a pal', 'he is great', 'knows everything', 'is a friend', 'like talking to him'. Clearly, the principal is not viewed as a 'supreme authority', deserving deference. As expressed by a teacher: 'he is one of us, we don't see him differently. He discusses everything with us and if we do not want to do a particular activity he does not force us. In Mirambika we are free to decide with our children. But he has a vision which I like hearing from him.' The principal's influence on members of the school, that is, teachers and children, may be attributed to his knowledge, personal skill, charisma and power of persuasion.

The unpredictable nature of teaching-learning at Mirambika makes centralized monitoring difficult. Since there is intra- as well as inter-group variations in the tasks, activities and organization of work, Mirambika finds alternative ways to monitor performance and inspire the members with a sense of purpose and commitment. In line with Sri Aurobindo's philosophy, evaluations in Mirambika are for self-improvement and personal development and not for comparison. Neither are they related to grading, ranking, certification or upward mobility of classes. On being asked how children are evaluated, the teachers said, 'We do not assess the child to show his weaknesses, but to show him how much he has learnt. Sometimes the evaluations are done by children in groups or individually and at times jointly by teachers and children. The idea is to let the child know how much he has progressed.' Joint collaborative efforts during evaluations are influenced by the school philosophy, which stresses the undesirability of comparisons and competition among students in any of the school processes, including evaluation.

As alternatives to authority in school, attempts are made to make teachers and children responsible for their actions by letting the responsibility of action lie with the individual member. Activities like letting the children take the responsibility of serving food, issuing oneself sports equipment and returning it after play, providing medical aid to younger children with minor injuries, issuing books on their own from the library and solving minor fights in their respective groups are some efforts Mirambika makes to inculcate responsibility, cooperation and self-discipline. Therefore, the participants at Mirambika may be seen as autonomously functioning individuals. Accordingly, Mirambika functions within flexible work groups, which have open patterns of communication and coordination amongst themselves through mutual adjustment.

Classrooms: The context of learning

The classroom is where pedagogic interactions take place and apart from the transaction of content, it is the physical organization that affects interactions. The classrooms in Mirambika have a distinct physical structure and a unique organization, which fosters 'openness' in learning and forms the classroom climate.

The physical organization of the classroom bestows a structure on the activities carried out. It is therefore significant to know that the classrooms or workspaces of children in Mirambika are designed keeping in mind the needs of different groups. The three younger groups (classes) have large areas of work, low tables and *durries* for sitting. The younger children's classrooms have an annexe which, their teacher explained,

> is used by children for sleeping or for those children requiring special attention or for attending to a crying child away from the curious eyes of the peers. The round sunken area in the corner of the room is used for activities like singing, story telling, and playing with children. Making children sit in this area helps us to be close to them, to keep them in one place without actually saying anything to them.

Diyas were seen sitting in the sunken area narrating stories and reciting poems, the children often sitting on their Diyas' laps or climbing on their backs. The areas of work for older groups have tables and chairs arranged in a circular manner to facilitate interaction during group discussion. Since the children do not carry books home, each one has an individual cupboard (for keeping books, copies, pens, pencils, etc.). Common cupboards are used by the Diyas (teachers) for keeping dictionaries, other reference materials (maps, globe), books, stationery, colours, chalk, duster, etc. All the groups have spaces for photographs of Sri Aurobindo and The Mother. Low walls separate the work areas of different groups. This gives an impression of one large group space with different groups working in different areas. Large classroom windows are a notable feature of the school, as they create an impression of unobstructed space and at the same time gives the building the benefit of natural light and breeze. The following description provides a view of how teachers and children function within such arrangements:

> Location '*Neem Grove*': Receptivity group (10 years) children and Diyas carry low tables and small mats to the open grounds, which they arrange in two semi-circles. Each group has 4-5 children and one Diya. Movable display boards mark the boundaries of work areas, on which charts and write-ups are displayed. The two groups are working on the project 'Egypt', with one group interested in drawing the map and the other working on making a pyramid, a few sticking pictures on chart paper while others are seen participating in a quiz related to the theme. (Field Note)

In Mirambika classrooms, the traditional pattern of tables and chairs is missing and the physical space is casually organized into interest areas, with children sitting around tables, working in small groups, lying on the rug, reading or drawing alone, wandering around the room aimlessly, or approaching the teacher for attention and help. The activity (curriculum) is not centred round the teacher, but dispersed throughout the room around each child. It can be concluded that the distinctive character of the physical space in Mirambika gains importance in light of the opportunities and experiences it provides.

Teaching and learning through projects

The ideological setting influences pedagogic processes and differentiates Mirambika from other schools in Delhi, thus lending it a special character. The project-oriented teaching in Mirambika has its origin and base in the school ideology, which stresses on education according to the child's needs and capacities and aims to provide an environment conducive to such type of learning. It is based on the school's philosophy that learning at primary levels should not be subject-specific but instead an integrated, multi-disciplinary approach that should be followed within an evolutionary curriculum, which develops according to the needs of the children. Kerry and Eggleston (1996) state: 'The terms topic, project, theme, integrated work are interchangeable labels which describe the approach to teaching-learning and includes all those areas of the curriculum which are explored in a thematic way. Project work exhibits a particular attitude towards the nature of knowledge or epistemology.' Gunning et al. (1981, pp. 83-84) summed up the ethos of the philosophy underlying project work:

> One of the most prolific sources of such information lies within the child's own day-to-day experience. Everyday the child is involved in a vast range of experiences at first hand. These contacts and experiences can be used very effectively by the teacher to provide the child with developing insight into a great range of ideas since they provide very 'concrete' pegs on which to hang important concepts.

In accordance with Sri Aurobindo's philosophy, the projects in Mirambika form the base of Free Progress Education, which is defined by The Mother as 'Education guided by the soul and not by preconceived ideas'. The founder-principal of Mirambika has described projects as 'little ships on which our children explore themselves and the beautiful world around them'. Teachers expressed that 'academics in the conventional way are not the focus, Mirambika mainly aims at an all-round development of personality, that is, the vital, mental, physical, psychic, and spiritual, and projects are the best way to achieve our goals'. The following description provides a view on how the curriculum is transacted through projects at Mirambika.

> Project 'Environment' was taken up by the whole school as the school functionaries felt that the topic was the need of the hour, and that children needed to get acquainted with issues related to the environment. During the planning stage, the Aims, Resources, Activities and Evaluation to be undertaken were written on the 'Planning Sheet'. The goals varied according to the learning needs of the respective groups. Keeping in view the groups' goals, activities were listed by the Diyas after discussions with the children and among themselves. The children were divided into four levels, keeping in view their age, knowledge, and the focus on the content to be covered at a particular level. At each level different subject corners, including arts, were set up to focus on activities related to the specific subject content. For example, in an Alternative Models corner basic concepts to understand the global implications of pollution were discussed. Children traced man's dependence on his environment in the past, the ozone layer, the Narmada Valley Project, etc. Children planned an ideal city in terms of solar energy. Issues like what is real development were discussed, and teachers guided children to envisage the future they desired for themselves. During the first week children experimented

in different corners to choose an area of their interest. The culminating activity of project work took the form of fairs (organized by younger groups), and exhibitions, quizzes and experiments carried out by the older groups for the younger groups. The teachers made each child's profile covering all areas of work undertaken, and no marks or grades were given—progress was measured against the child's own record and not with others in the group. The older children carried out self-evaluations to provide themselves feedback on their work. (Field Note)

In Mirambika, project work implies an approach to teaching-learning that deals with theme-related topics and cuts across all subjects, that is, science, social science, mathematics, languages, arts, etc. The Diyas guide children, individually or in groups, towards the process of inquiry in order to develop certain skills and mental faculties. The focus is on the construction of learning experiences based on children's interests. The choice to work in an area or activity is made by the children, and not just by the teachers. The teacher does not control the time spent on an activity; that depends on the activity undertaken, such as building a pyramid, making a model of solar energy or measuring the length of shadows, or helping to water the plants and clear the leaves. While working on projects, subject boundaries do not exist, and children are encouraged to view the relationship of one activity across different subjects. This is a combination of a 'child-centred' and 'teacher-facilitated' curriculum.

Flexibility in work

At Mirambika, the children and teachers may be seen as united by their shared experiences in a project or activity in their groups. As Thapan (1991, p. 48) states, 'the ideology creates an ethos in which living together necessitates cooperation between participants'. An observation was made during our stay at Mirambika regarding the way teachers and children collectively make collaborative efforts and mutual adjustments while undertaking activities during project work.

Older children are required to go in small groups to the younger groups and get the survey proforma filled. The older children have developed this survey proforma. It has drawings showing the different seasons and the younger children are required to write what they would like to do in a particular season. Children visit the younger classes and one child of the older group tells the teacher the purpose of their visit, and on being granted permission to proceed, s/he explains the purpose and activity to the younger children. The younger children have queries like, 'Do we have to write only?' Or 'Can we draw also?' 'Can I write one word?' 'I want to use coloured pencil ...'. Answers are provided to each query. The children in the older group were later seen helping the younger (Orange) children with their spellings, at times giving examples, clarifying doubts .... The older group teachers stand aside and watch quietly. The younger group teachers take this interruption calmly, helping the children when required. They seem least disturbed by the intrusion and resume work after the children's excitement has subsided. (Field Note)

Project work is a way of planning and organizing teaching material with spontaneity as an essential feature influencing the content of the lesson, which then begins to evolve on its own, as one cannot decide whether the topic will 'take off' from the very point it ended the previous day (Plowden Report, 1967). The curriculum therefore evolves according to the needs of the group. While organizing project work, the Diyas have to deal with open-ended activities, spontaneity, flexibility in organizing work, and adopt an informal style of teaching. It is difficult to pinpoint a teaching style, but the ethos of project teaching is 'cooperative enquiry-based learning', and therefore a range of teacher behaviours was witnessed.

The following observation conveys the relationship of Diyas with the children.

> Location: Sunken Area. Blue Group (4+ years) children are all piled in the round sunken area along with one of the Diyas. They are listening to a story with the Diya dramatizing and enacting some instances. While some children are sitting 'all over her' (one on her lap, one on her shoulders), she seems equally comfortable with them. A solitary young artist is seen sitting in a corner, colouring intently, least distracted by the class activity. The second Diya is cleaning the cupboard and joins in the group's laughter at times. (Field Note)

Project work gains significance in view of the affective meaning it has for the children. Some of the perceptions of 52 children regarding projects in their own words are: 'I like projects because they are very interesting'; 'Project time is nice'; 'In project time I like doing drawing, reading and doing drama'; 'When it's project time, I like it very much, and have a lot of fun also'; 'I feel the best doing project work'; 'Projects help me know lots of things'; and 'In projects the fun is in doing activities'.

Interviews with parents also revealed that teaching-learning through projects help children develop confidence, accept responsibility and take decisions regarding their learning. As a parent remarked, 'Mirambika's system of learning encourages the child to come forward and do whatever they like without the fear of being compared with his/her peer group. This makes the child confident. Confidence in children makes them clear about their goals, likes, dislikes, which helps them to take their own decisions.' Another parent said, 'Children accept responsibility for good or bad decisions, and this is because Mirambika has provided enough space to the child to experiment and learn from their mistakes.'

The child: An active learner

Special aspects of teaching need special mention as they impinge upon project teaching. Rules of work are planned out in consultation with the children; organization of work takes place in small groups, which are formed in accordance with learners' needs and keeping in view the group goals. Diyas work together to create a peaceful conducive environment that emphasizes learning by sharing and the complete involvement of children in constructing reality, that is, in eliciting answers. Children are given the full responsibility and freedom to make observations, personally experience and use the resources in the library; creative use of space is a common feature with children as they are free to work in the open grounds, lobby, library, laboratory, etc. The Diyas stated that 'It is important to know what the child knows and start from that point, build up on the strength of the child. It is no point saying, "You don't even know this".' An interview with another teacher revealed that she believed her work should suit the needs of children. As she said, 'I don't like to think in terms of shaping children in a pre-existing mould. I am trying to help the child develop into a complete human being.' The teachers' concern with the all-round development of children is in accordance with the school ideology.

The Diyas view their role as that of a facilitator, a co-constructor of children's learning experiences, and to build on students' strengths.

Diya: When you go to the library and want to consult a book, how do you look up a book?
Child: Have a look at the chapters.
Diya: That's right. What if it is a big fat book and you have to get information on 'Universe'?
Child (1): See the 'Contents' of the book.
Diya: Yes, that's right. What is it?
Child (2): List of chapters given at the beginning of the book—that is contents.
Diya: Good, what more it contains? (After some time the teacher again asks, is there anything else given or not?)
Child (3): Nothing else is given.
Diya: (Picks up a book and shows it and says) One has a list of tables.
(Children say in some books more information is given.)
Child: Do we have a list of pictures in books?
Diya: Yes! That's right, we have

illustrations and figures also. Now tell me, what will I do if I have to find information on 'orbit'?

Diya: If I see the chapter on 'Life' or 'Earth' I will get the information.

Child: Yes! You mean look at the most appropriate chapter.

Diya: Okay! That's one way. Don't you think it will take a lot of time to search for information in this manner?

(Children collectively agree.)

Diya: Okay! Now let's make small groups of 4-5 students each (Gives each group a book.)

(Children are seen examining the books.)

Diya: What is an 'index'? Where is it?

Child: At the back of the book.

Diya: That's right! What does it contain?

Child: Words are given and nos... is it page nos?... Yes, page nos are given.

Diya: Choose a word and see the page no.

Children: 'Orbit' is given on pages 8, 41, 126 ...

In this excerpt, we consistently see certain qualities that can be said to be the teachers' characteristic ways of behaving with children: patience, giving them freedom to express their ideas and opinions, providing opportunities to search for information, and being basically loving and considerate.

A 'child-centred' orientation on the part of Diyas is also reflected in behaviours such as asking questions, interest in and responsiveness to children's individual needs, a great willingness to give children latitude in responding, and greater tolerance and approval of their behaviour. The discernment and development of uniqueness in children is highly valued by the Diyas. Their view is that 'each child has his/her personality which needs to be developed, and our role is to channel the personality'. This is nicely illustrated in the following excerpt, which shows the interaction between a teacher and children. All through, the children are encouraged to express their personal ideas and opinions.

Diya: We have been doing a project on environment. Let us talk about types of environmental pollution. Can you tell me what causes pollution?

Child (1): Smoke in the air is pollution.

Diya: (Writes this on the board) Do you know other things which cause pollution?

Child (2): Smoke from buses, cars and scooters ...

Diya: Yes, you are right, there are many sources of smoke which cause air pollution.

Child (2): Didi, also smoke from factories and cigarette smoking.

Diya: Good, are there other kinds of pollution?

Child (3): Water pollution, when we throw garbage in water, it causes many diseases.

Diya: That is very good! Who else is affected by water pollution?

Child: Animals in water ... fish, whale ...

(The other children add on).

Child: Didi, even plants in water are affected.

Child: Sometimes animals die and become less.

(A discussion on dinosaurs followed, and how they became extinct.)

Child (2): For this we have to protect animals from hunters.

Diya: What else can we do to help the animals?

Child: The animals can be protected in a Zoo ... or such places.

Diya: You are used to a particular environment, how would you feel if your home is shifted elsewhere?

(A discussion followed on this.)

Child (2): No! I think they should live where they are used to.

Child (3): We should not pollute their environments and let them live in their own places.

(The discussion continued to show the inter-dependence of man, animals and plants.)

Diyas allow each child optimum space, time and context to develop and display his/her interest and personality. Interviews with Diyas revealed that 'opportunities given to each child to come forward encourages independent behaviour in seeking solutions to problems and issues'. Parents felt that for children, 'learning is enjoyable and they develop a strong craving for knowing', which may be attributed to projects, which 'helps them to look at things from different angles and develop a wider perspective by relating one subject to another'.

Mirambika, in view of its educational and philosophical goals, invites the child's participation in various activities, and provides experiences to explore, create, experiment and observe.

Negotiations at work

Exchange or negotiation is the mode of interaction often used by teachers and children to maintain a working relationship. Negotiations, according to Woods (1979, p. 127), 'enable interaction to proceed in a manner agreeable to both sets of participants, so as to achieve their goals and maximize their interests'. Children in the older groups are involved in negotiations to a much greater extent as compared to younger groups, and are aware of the (almost) equal power existing between the teachers and children. This is perhaps the result of the complete freedom they are given to express their opinions, and the absence of teacher authority. As Thapan (1991) states, 'If pupils are encouraged to express their opinions freely they become aware of this bargaining power.' The following observations show how children negotiate during work.

> (The teacher gives them worksheets to work independently.)
> Children: Didi, can we work in pairs?
> (The teacher wants them to work on their own and is not willing to go along with them; discussion follows.)
> Diya: Do you want to work in small groups?
> Child: Please, we want to work together (points to her friend).
> Diya: Convince me.
> Children: We are a free world. We have a right to choose our partners.
> (Children in this particular group had done a project on the 'rights of children'.)
> Diya: Even I have some rights—don't I?
> Children: No, you don't—(laughingly). We want to work in pairs (they insist).
> Diya: Ok, work in pairs. Who are going to be the partners?
> (The children decide among themselves, and the teacher agrees.)

Children in Mirambika are typically frank and expressive. During an interview, a parent revealed, 'The freedom given to the child in class allows them to put forward their views without being "ridiculed" or "laughed at", which makes them express their opinion.' Informal communication lines exist between the teachers and children. 'Power' or 'control' do not lie with the teacher, and negotiations help to maximize the student's effort. Attempts are made to provide children with opportunities to increase their sense of obligation to others, and to encourage the self-reflection that helps to maintain good working relationships.

The teacher (Diya) is not viewed as the positional authority who 'knows best' or is the only one who is relevant and correct, and hence wiser and stronger. The next example illustrates the view of a teacher as learner in Mirambika.

During self-evaluation of the work done, a Diya writes questions on the board.

> Diya (1) writes: Which experiment did not you understand at all and why?
> One girl: Bhaiya, it should be 'you did not'.
> Diya (1): Asks her to sit down (ignores what she has said).
> Child again: Bhaiya, 'wrong language is written', and again points at the mistake.
> Diya (2): Talks to the teacher who is writing the question, who then corrects it.
> (The other children continue writing without reacting.)

Diyas are often heard using the phrase, 'I am also learning, no one knows everything', in order to get the children to move, explore, seek information or facts on their own. This is clearly in accordance with the official version of Mirambika as a learning centre for all, for children as well as teachers. No sharp boundaries are maintained between the one who 'knows' and the one who 'knows not'. This makes children 'independent learners in the sense that they search for information/knowledge on their own', as expressed by a Diya. This suggests a fundamental shift in the teachers' thinking and in the strategies they apply to children's learning.

Disciplining strategies

Interviews and informal conversations with Diyas reveal that Mirambika does not relate teacher success to securing silence and orderliness in their classrooms; instead, it is related to personal (self) and situational control, that is, being 'centred'. We too observed that 'neither corporal punishment nor verbal aggression by teachers play any role in school interactions'. The teachers said that the 'focus in Mirambika is on developing "inner discipline" in students, that is, control of emotions and actions'. As alternatives to punishments, attempts are made to develop inner discipline. Some controlling strategies evolved by the Diyas for the younger groups include calling peace—a symbolic gesture of the hands to quieten children down; asking children to become a 'statue'; symbolic gestures like 'take the rat of fight and throw it out'; putting on music to make children dance and expend their extra energy; playing tug-of-war with the trees in the grounds; and talking softly to get the attention of children and making them in turn lower their own volume. With older groups, the teachers use different strategies. The teachers stated, 'Each child is given five sticks, each time the child speaks unnecessarily, one stick is taken away. Once the child has exhausted all the sticks, s/he is not allowed to participate or ask questions.' Children are also encouraged to form their own rules, and are then asked to adhere to them. Assigning responsibilities to the children seemed to be a popular disciplining strategy in Mirambika; this also helps the children become aware of their actions. Informal talk with children reiterates the school's notion of developing inner discipline. They said, 'If you are given freedom, you don't misuse it but in a strict environment you feel like breaking the rules.'

> The principal had a talk with some 6-7 children from the senior groups after hearing about the use of offensive language by a student in class. He tells them that through their misbehaviour, they are harming themselves and Mirambika. The children say that 'he is always using' such words, and wanted the Principal to take a tough stance. He is not willing to do so, and the children put forth their arguments in their defence. The boy in question is bewildered and explains his point, saying, 'Boys I play with also use the same language but no one checks them'. He, however, shows willingness to make an effort to not use undesirable language. The class is adamant, 'he has earlier made false promises'—no excuse is to be given now. The Principal asks the children to decide amongst themselves how they could find a solution to the problem. He reminds them, 'we all make mistakes, you may also be at fault some day.' Together they fix a date and time to discuss the solutions and opinions put forward by the children. (Field Note)

These attempts are derived from the school's philosophy, which restrains teachers from encouraging conformity to a set of rules.

The findings are suggestive of the strengths of the project work approach followed in Mirambika. In addition to the cognitive aspect, project work also intends to develop the affective and conative aspects of development. Projects help students to become more resourceful, prone to taking initiatives and responsible for their work, and promote searching skills, reasoning power and experimentation. The role played by such experiences in shaping the personal-social development of children cannot be overlooked. The perceptions of parents, teachers and children revealed that teaching-learning in Mirambika attempts to turn children into confident 'thinking individuals', and inculcate values like the dignity of labour, sharing, cooperation and openness to others' view-points. Mirambika children are perceived as being very confident, resourceful, adventurous, dynamic, responsible, sincere, hardworking, and information seekers. The results, however, also suggest the need for preparing and orienting Mirambika students to the prevalent teaching-learning-evaluation system, so as to aid them to adjust better after the students shift to other schools.

Conclusion

The basic premise of teaching in Mirambika is based on acknowledging that students have experiences, insights and talents, and that the role of the teacher is to help find ways to use them in the classroom. The project approach is inter-disciplinary, integrates arts in the curriculum and leads to collateral learning. This is accomplished through an evolutionary syllabi that emerges out of the needs of students. The use of projects is an alternative way of organizing work in such a manner that the activities taken up are designed to fit each student's needs. Since projects are open-ended and flow in a direction determined by the children's interest rather than by a pre-determined schema, they tend to develop the skills of inquiring, investigating and presenting the information in students. This makes children independent, responsible and confident of their learning. Frequent opportunities are offered to children to 'reconstruct knowledge for themselves, rather than receiving it from the teacher'. Such interactions allow for an atmosphere of freedom and informality, in which lies the classroom ethos. In line with Sri Aurobindo's philosophy, teachers at Mirambika attempt to build their teaching on what children know. The approach usually used by the teachers has a number of features: it is based on the student's interests and experiences; it creates a climate of mutual trust and faith in the child's capabilities; it provides the freedom to explore and experiment; and it lays emphasis on collaborative learning. The teacher's role is that of a facilitator, a generalist. Fewer constraints operate on teachers and their success is not measured in relation to the contents covered, but calls for situational and personal control. The teaching style can be labelled as informal, participative, democratic and illuminative. In spite of a wide disparity among teachers—in terms of qualifications, background, experience and expertise—what emerges is a strong consensus to work for the 'divine'. The teacher is a learner; as a teacher aptly put it: 'we all make mistakes and it's never too late to learn'. We also noted in our observations that teachers are constantly in the process of 'self-reflection', which, as Wade and Yarbrough (1996) stated, is a step towards professional growth. It may be said that the success of innovations in teaching-learning is dependent on the overall school climate. The new techniques used at Mirambika originate from its ideology and values, as well as from the motivation and commitment of the teachers. Such experiences at Mirambika help students to take initiatives, be self-disciplined, cooperative and responsible for their work, and play an active role in their learning.

Suggestions for future research

The success of the innovative patterns of teaching-learning followed in Mirambika, based on the educational ideas of Sri Aurobindo and The Mother, is relevant for bringing about a change in the current highly structured, time-bound system, which imparts information and knowledge in subjects separated into tight compartments, and is acquired by the learner in the same manner.

To meet the present-day challenges of the changing, inter-dependent world, there is need for a paradigm shift in the way schools impart education, the methods used by the teachers, and the total function and nature of schooling. Therefore education, besides providing cognitive skills (the traditional 3 Rs), needs to emphasize other aspects of learning that help children develop self-confidence, a sense of personal integrity, and individual personalities capable of helping and relating to others, evaluating one's own learning, understanding relationships with people, being appropriately motivated, etc. The focus should shift to learning how to learn, where to get information, and how to apply what has been learnt in everyday life. This will lead to autonomy in one's learning and promote the development of both cognitive and affective skills—those of taking initiatives, being creative, decision-making and cooperative living. The development of cognitive and affective qualities demands a curriculum that is process-oriented and not content-based. This would require organizing teaching-learning in a manner that is sensitive to the needs of the learner, unlike the current teaching-learning in schools, which is uniformly given and tested within a rigid frame to all learners, irrespective of their liking or capacities. Teaching time and methods will have to be reorganized for self-learning, problem-solving, questioning and fieldwork, so as to encourage learner participation over a flexible time period in an activity most suited to her/his capacities. Grouping students according to their interests and capacities would be a step towards individualizing teaching and learning. The implied role of a teacher in this scheme is that of a learner and not one who 'knows-all' or is the sole purveyor of knowledge. Alternative methods of evaluation would facilitate learner self-evaluation for personal development, cooperative effort and further learning. Self-evaluation helps in knowing one's strengths and weaknesses, is not judgemental, and aims at understanding oneself. The focus of such evaluation is to help the child overcome her/his weakness, which fosters personal development. It also provides the teacher with feedback on teaching techniques, learning methodologies and curriculum planning. Since self-evaluation helps in learning how much the child has covered and what more is needed, it would provide the teacher with inputs for modifying the syllabi and organizing her/his teaching to suit the child's needs and capacities.

Endnote

1. There are three types of teachers who work at the school: full-time, B. Ed. trainees and volunteers. The total number of teachers keeps changing, depending upon the number of volunteers in the school.

References

Altekar, A. (1965). Educational and intellectual methods in Vedic and ancient Indian cultures. In S. Guy & F. C. Metraux (Eds.), *Studies in the cultural history of India*. Agra: Shiva Lal Agarwala and Company.

Aurobindo, Sri, & Mother, The (1956). *Sri Aurobindo and the Mother on education*. Pondicherry: Sri Aurobindo Ashram.

Brunsson, N. (1985). *The irrational organisation: Irrationality as a basis of organisational action and change*. Chichester, England: John Wiley and Sons.

Clarke, P. (2001). *Teaching and learning: The culture of pedagogy*. New Delhi: Sage Publications.

Cornelissen, M. (2003). *The philosophical basis of education. How a small and fundamental change can have tremendous consequence*. Paper presented at the National Seminar on Psychology in Indian Traditions: Conceptual and Methodological Issues for Indian Schools, 22-24 December. New Delhi: NCERT.

Dharampal (1983). *The beautiful tree: Indigenous Indian education in the eighteenth century*. Coimbatore: Keerthi and AVP Publishing Houses.

Gunning, S., Gunning, D., & Wilson, J. (1981). *Topic teaching in the primary school*. London: Arnold.

Kabir, H. (1961). *Indian philosophy of education*. New Delhi: Asia Publishing House.

Kakar, S. (1984). *Shamans, mystics and doctors: A psychological inquiry into India and its healing traditions*. Bombay: Oxford University.

Kerry, T., & Eggleston, J. (1996). *Topic work in the primary school*. London: Routledge.

Kumar, K. (1991). *Political agenda of education*. New Delhi: Sage Publications.

Malehorn, H. (1978). *Open to change: Options for teaching self-directed learners*. California: Goodyear Publishing Company.

National Council for Educational Research and Training (1988). *National curriculum for elementary and secondary education—A framework*. New Delhi: NCERT.

Plowden Report (1967). *Children and their primary schools.* Report of the Central Advisory Council for Education. London: HMSO.

Shotton, J. (1998). *Learning and freedom.* New Delhi: Sage Publications.

Sibia, A. (2006). *Life at Mirambika: A free progress school.* New Delhi: NCERT.

Thapan, M. (1991). *Life at school: An ethnographic study.* New Delhi: Oxford University Press.

Wade, R. C., & Yarbrough, D. B. (1996). Portfolios: A tool for reflective thinking in education. *Teaching and Teacher Education, 12*(1), 63–79.

Woods, P. (1979). *Divided school.* London: Routledge & Kegan Paul.

23

Krishnamurti and value education

Vinita Kaushik Kapur

> The world is in such chaos that even if you deliberately set about to make the world more chaotic than it is you could not succeed.... And it needs a very sharp, clear, decisive, sane mind to resolve such a chaotic condition. I do not think such a mind can come about, except through religious perception.
>
> —Krishnamurti, *The religious mind*, p. 4

Education and the human condition

For Krishnamurti, the means to religious perception is through scepticism, doubt and questioning, and this can come about through right education. All through his teaching years he emphasized the crucial and vital role that education can play in the creative regeneration of the way human beings think, and therefore live. Enquiring deeply into the nature of the mind, he posited that the aim of education must be to awaken an intelligence through which thought and knowledge find their rightful place. Such perception is religious perception. And it is only when the truly religious mind informs the values on which we build our daily existence that there is a possibility of a sane and orderly world, free from conflict and sorrow.

Education, as generally understood, is the movement generated by social systems to ensure their perpetuity through time. It is a process of imparting and acquiring skills for life, at home, in schools and colleges; it is also the total process of psychological imprinting that is absorbed and perpetuated in tandem with the acquisition of such life skills. Wherever human beings have lived in groups, they have created structures, both physical and psychological, in order to ensure the safe continuity and security of their offspring. Workable solutions, ways of being, of understanding the world, have been codified and passed on as a means of coping with inner (psychological) and outer exigencies. These patterns are mostly subject to the needs and requirements of the maintenance of power structures within societies. All new entrants to human groups must necessarily submit to these established structures. They must be programmed to fit into pre-determined and socially approved slots.

Education generally conditions the mind to accept these structures of society. Therefore, such a mind is unable to see beyond this socially constructed reality.

The process begins at home and continues throughout the life of a person. Societies are so particular about the maintenance of social order that deviations are kept in check through formal and informal means of social control. Those considered mad or wayward are re-oriented, even re-parented in order to fit them back into society.

Krishnamurti questions the very basis of this kind of education. He suggests that conditioned human beings can neither bring about nor participate in a society that is free and creative. Hence, for him, the most important concern of education is to help the child enquire into and understand the movement of conditioning as it expresses itself in the individual and in society, and thus be free of it.

In order to appreciate his vision of an education that can bring about deeply religious values, it is necessary to understand the nature of human existence as he saw it. For Krishnamurti, it was axiomatic that the human mind operates from a base that is made up of patterned responses, which themselves are the result of thousands of years of human struggle with nature and with the ever-evolving worldviews that make up our social environment. These responses are so deeply embedded in the fabric of our psycho-physical natures that it has become impossible to meet the movement of life without the filter of these pre-established means of cognition. These means manifest themselves in the way human beings think. Our thoughts are directly linked to the basic assumptions held by the society we are born into. There is a continuous back and forth movement of patterning between the conditioned individual and the conditioned society. And this is what sustains the system.

At a more fundamental level, human conditioning inevitably brings about a sense of fragmentation within the psyche, and separation from other humans, other social groups and from nature. The culture one is born into plays an integral role in the way the instinctive drives take shape, and the child is programmed to respond to fear and approval from a very early age. The personality created through conditioning is the constructed self, the prison in which one is held. Any 'action' that emanates from such conditioning is therefore based on a partial and fragmentary view of a given situation and of the totality of life. And being a constructed piece or 'fragment' that has been plucked out of a whole picture, it must necessarily lead to partial action. Partial, biased equations can never be balanced; by their very nature they will be in conflict with other fragments operating from similar backgrounds.

It is this kind of conditioning that has brought about sorrow, confusion and pain. The wars and battles fought over the territorial identities and interests of religions, nations, corporations and individuals; the escalating stress and misery in every field of life; the momentary relief and pleasure that act as buoys on the ocean of the constructed 'me', all these form the human condition—a prison from which human beings must find a way out if humanity is not to destroy itself and the planet we live on.

Enquiry and human values

The process of educating the mind is generally aimed at conditioning the intellect into predetermined ways; however, for Krishnamurti, education implies a process of un-conditioning. It is freedom from given ways of thinking that allows the mind to observe without a parallel biased movement of interpretation. In this kind of education, understanding the ways of the self is more vital than the accumulation of knowledge.

> The whole movement of enquiry into knowledge, into oneself, into the possibility of something beyond knowledge, brings about naturally a psychological revolution, and from this comes inevitably a totally different order in human relationship, which is society. The intelligent understanding of all this can bring about a profound change in the consciousness of mankind. (Krishnamurti, 1984)

Most of what we know as values are culturally defined ways of responding to life situations. Each social system has its own parameters for socially appropriate behaviour. So, depending on a multiplicity of factors, which include religious beliefs, customs, and the economic and political status of a society, the codes of conduct that are the guiding principles in one society may not be so in another. This is an anthropological truth. Several themes for enquiry emerge from this: are human beings doomed to live by a conceptual relativity where any value system is bound to clash with another unless it shares a common set of assumptions? Or are there values that are true regardless of time, place, culture or situation? Are there universal human values that will bring about an order that cannot be found through identifications such as nationalism, religion, sect and caste and political ideologies? Are there values that cut across the cruel lines of class division and racial discrimination? Is it at all possible for a mind born into the complex web of culture to ever be free of it?

In all the talks and dialogues he conducted over the span of more than half a century, Krishnamurti paid little heed to the details of cultural differences between societies. He examined directly the fundamental reality of the common human condition, the nature of man-made ways of thinking, and the universality of basic instincts as they manifest in forms like greed, fear, envy and the desire for security. Subservience to these movements is the cause of human bondage. He maintained that it was possible for man to be totally free of these bonds so long as he could hold them in awareness, without taking recourse to any means of relief. The moment the mind in distress seeks a way out, it moves away from the reality of its situation (the 'what is' in Krishnamurti's terminology) and gets caught in another pattern. Thus, the original problem gets superimposed with another idea and in effect remains un-addressed because 'Truth alone liberates, not your desire to be free. The very desire and effort to be free is a hindrance to liberation' (Krishnamurti, 2002, p. 108).

How does one discover the nature of this machinery that keeps generating patterns within which we live as subjects? The first step is to observe one's own mind and see how 'cluttered and burdened it is with belief' (Krishnamurti, 1999, p. 6). Krishnamurti points out the sheer absurdity of using systems of 'belief as a hypothesis' (Krishnamurti, 1999, p. 6). A mind that is enquiring must put aside faith, belief, tradition and the learned ways of man. 'When a man is enquiring, he does not start out with a hypothesis, he has a free mind .... He is not bound by any fear. He starts out denying all that and then begins to seek' (Krishnamurti, 1999, p. 6). The very enquiry contains the answers, but they need to be looked for.

It is thus evident that the mind looking at facts as they are cannot possibly look clearly through the prism of fear. Fear in any form bends the lines of perception towards that which will bring security. These barriers to seeing are created by the mind, which seeks security within the confines of thought. It is not physical security that prevents the mind from enquiring beyond known frontiers; it is deep psychological fear that does not allow the movement of seeing to go beyond the known.

'Fear dictates conformity, fear dictates that I must imitate, that I must follow somebody in the hope that I shall find comfort' (Krishnamurti, 1999, p. 8). So, one sets authority up as a guiding light that will show the way out of uncertainty. Thus we barter away freedom for certainty, which promises security but never delivers.

Krishnamurti held that mankind could and must become free of these layers of conditioned responses and come upon the nature of the mind in its natural state. It is '... only a mind that is free from conflict, free from problems, free from sorrow that can find out. And you must find out because that is the only way out of this misery, this confusion that we have created in this world' (Krishnamurti, 1999, p. 7). Hence, meaningful education would be concerned with allowing for the flowering of this kind of intelligence, and not merely with building the intellect.

Academically, it is not very difficult to analyse relations within and between power structures in society. Sociological enquiry into the operating axis of power can reveal the underlying motives, the polarizations and struggles between unequal elements in individual or social schemes. All these and more are possible and essential as pedagogical techniques for the development of a clear mind, but for Krishnamurti, this kind of enquiry is still limited. Modern education stops short with developing the intellect alone. Enquiry must be carried further into the examination of the nature of thought itself. Thought carries memory and belief. It is the vector for the assumptions that further thinking is based on. Thought, in fact, is the attire of the self.

The thousands of years of human thought overflowing with a plethora of ideas explored to their logical limits and their ramifications—intellectual, emotional and, very concretely, physical—are apparent in our day-to-day living. Working from within these given paradigms can only lead to answers situated within these same paradigms. Is there a way of looking that operates from outside the circular confines of thought? If understanding the nature of thought is imperative to a clear seeing of the human situation, if such understanding is essential to coming upon a sense of the sacred, then learning about oneself is a necessary part of education.

Learning about oneself

Krishnamurti makes a distinction between learning about oneself and accumulating knowledge about oneself. Consistent with what has been said, learning about oneself is an awareness of our patterns, beliefs, hopes and fears, as revealed in our daily lives and interactions. Awareness brings its own order without taking recourse to imposing control over it.

> The beginning of the religious mind is self-knowledge—not the knowledge of the supreme self, that is sheer nonsense. How can a petty mind, a narrow mind, a nationalistic mind, a mind that is begotten through fear, through compulsion, through imitation, through authority—how can that petty, shallow mind try to find out what is the supreme self? To seek the supreme self is an escape; it is pure unadulterated romanticism. The fact is—you have to understand yourself first. (Krishnamurti, 1999, p. 9)

The task involves the art of looking, listening and observing choicelessly, neither denying nor accepting what is revealed through such observation. The mind must watch its own functioning to understand the ways of the constructed self. Can the educator learn and help the child learn to observe the myriad ways in which thought creates its own prison? Instead of pushing beliefs, whether religious or secular, as a priori premises for living life, can the educator place the multiple stimuli that storm the brain and senses, within an objective context? Can one learn to see clearly and without bias? In the classroom and at home, an atmosphere that invites the colourful variety in which life and man express themselves and still enables a holding of such questions, may inculcate an enquiring mind.

> It is becoming more and more important in a world that is destructive and degenerative that there should be a place, an oasis, where one can learn a way of living that is whole, sane and intelligent. Education in the modern world has been concerned with the cultivation not of intelligence, but intellect, of memory and its skills. In this process little occurs beyond passing information from the teacher to the taught, the leader to the follower, bringing about a superficial and mechanical way of life. (Krishnamurti, 1984)

Relationship with nature

Relationship with nature is fundamental to the kind of education that Krishnamurti envisaged. Man's relation to nature is perhaps one of the few areas where there is a possibility of direct perception without the interfering noise of thought. Children growing up amongst scrub jungle and animals, climbing trees and eating raw fruit have the possibility of touching and perhaps retaining a sense of being one amongst a 'community of beings' (Gadgil & Guha, 1997, p. 18), an inherent identity within the natural world that is man's genetic inheritance.

With the Industrial Revolution, there has been an accelerating separation between man and nature. From being in a state of participation with nature, mankind now sees itself as manipulator of the natural world. The resulting alienation has brought about the near destruction of the planet. Simultaneously, it has consigned mankind to a state of psychological alienation, where humans are divorced from their real and simple roots. They have become creatures of thought, occupied with creating and solving abstract problems that work well only within the parameters of mental logic.

Therefore, Krishnamurti repeatedly stressed the absolute necessity of a relationship with nature as part of education, in order to provide the ground for coming upon "value", which is an act rather than a concept. After all, to value something is to respect it, care for it and treat it with sensitivity. This cannot come about through the mere inculcation of frameworks and paradigms. Therefore, education is not just imbibing information from books or teachers, not just learning how to manage the examination system and achieve technical proficiency, it is also being vulnerable enough, '... to be able to listen to the birds, to see the sky, to see the beauty of a tree, and the shape of the hills and to feel with them, to be really, directly in touch with them' (Krishnamurti, 1974, p. 14).

Nurturing the individual

Working with children demands awareness and attention on the part of the educator. It means seeing the child as s/he is, without measuring her/him against ideals dictated by one's own ambitions or by society at large. To see the process of life as it is and people as they are without any distortion implies a denial of comparitive modes based on measure and mean, on better and worse, on success and failure. In today's fiercely competitive, achievement-oriented culture, this presents a formidable challenge. In terms of everyday life, this means being aware of one's own conditioned responses in the process of dealing with children. Confronted with a child who is either conforming or reacting to conventional academic structures, a great deal of energy and understanding is needed to meet the situation adequately without judging the child through the social context that exists within the mind of the teacher. It means coming up with the response that addresses that particular child and helps her/him discover the movements necessary to actualize her/his own individual potential.

Individuality, Krishnamurti maintained, is not the same as personality, with its shifting identities. Any kind of identification born out of insecurity and comparison leads to separation. Through our present structures of competition and comparison, we strengthen identity and the alienation that inevitably accompanies it. Individuality, on the other hand, has to do with the inner grain of the person, her/his unique and specific dispositions. Individuality has its own movement of excellence and passion, which does not need competition and comparison to sustain it.

The role of the educator is to pay heed to the inner movements and feelings of the young—who, 'if they are at all alive, are full of hope and discontent' (Krishnamurti, 2003, p. 42)—and in awakening an intelligence that can see the myriad influences one is subject to. Each individual student needs to be helped to watch these movements within her/himself, to observe how personal impulses and ways of apprehending the world are deeply rooted in collective values as well as in one's own habits and patterns. The educator may then guide that flame of discontent, not into reaction but into 'self-knowledge and self-abnegation' (Krishnamurti, 2003, p. 42). In this way, young people can be helped to break free from the ways of the self '... from the craving for self-fulfilment that brings endless conflict and sorrow' (Krishnamurti, 2003, p. 29). Out of this may emerge the truly creative action of the individual.

There are dangers that inevitably arise in a process of deconstructing deeply rooted ways of being. Personalized and idealized interpretations of freedom emerge. The mind, freed from the grosser forms of social regimentation, reacts with a stubborn self-indulgence. Explorations into the pernicious nature of authority, combined with a refusal to use authority, and the withholding of reward and punishment which are generally used as a means of cultivating susceptibility to external control may leave participants in a psychological atmosphere where there seem to be no guidelines.

Like Ariadne's thread, which showed a way through the labyrinth of Minos, the only possible guiding factor is the mirror of relationship. Quite apart from the overt modes of interaction, it is in the subliminal layers of the psyche that engagement with students really takes place. Even an intellectual acceptance of the fact that the use of authority is damaging to the process of education leads to a questioning of one's own self-importance, and the possibility of being free of the burden of authoritarianism. Teachers no longer need to invest energy into projecting images about themselves. The result is an opportunity to develop an open and caring relationship with children who, through this means, learn the value of relationship without the need for dominance. This ground of relationship is where the teacher and the student are learning and moving together and understanding the process of conditioning. There need be no dichotomy between living and learning. There is not even a distinction between the teacher and the taught. In the field of life, teacher and students are both participants in an exploration into an arena that is common ground for them both.

In such an environment of love, there is little need for constructed ways of exercising the control commonly referred to as discipline.

> Discipline is an easy way to control a child but it does not help him to understand the problems involved in living ... with the right kind of educator and a small number of students would any repression, politely called discipline, be required? If the classes are small and the teacher can give his full attention to each child, observing and helping him, then compulsion or domination in any form is obviously unnecessary. If, in such a group, a student persists in disorderliness or is unreasonably mischievous, the educator must enquire into the cause of his misbehaviour, which may be wrong diet, lack of rest, family wrangles, or some hidden fear. (Krishnamurti, 2003, p. 33)

If an educator is able to establish such an atmosphere in the classroom, mischief and natural exuberance can flow together with the flowering of an innate sense of responsibility. Freedom and responsibility are generally perceived as antithetical. In Krishnamurti's understanding, freedom means responsibility. 'Freedom does not mean the opportunity for self-gratification or the setting aside of consideration for others' (2003, p. 31).

> The right kind of educator, aware of the mind's tendency to reaction, helps the student to alter present values, not out of reaction against them, but through understanding the total process of life. Co-operation between man and man is not possible without the integrity which right education can help to awaken in the individual. (2003, p. 31)

Questioning value systems in contemporary India

Today, India stands at the threshold of a major economic leap. Links with global arteries of material nourishment are within reach. Affluence is no longer a far-off dream for a large section at the top of the ladder of wealth and achievement. The millions strung on the rungs below are scrambling to revise their technical skills in order to be part of this chain of wealth.

Yet, even as technical knowledge and skills outpace the best the world has to offer, stride for stride walks a spectre. Paradoxically, it is the spectre of our ancient heritage. Replete with the self-transcending wisdom of the ages, it also carries the most rigid and unblinking adherence to belief and tradition.

Deep cultural imprints, especially when overlaid with semi-tones of religious emotion and 'truths', can begin to masquerade as the real thing. Tradition and custom have a deep hold on the Indian psyche. Known practices rooted in belief systems may appear as prerequisites for a sense of psychological security, but are neither necessary nor mandatory stepping stones for 'coming upon the sacred'. In fact, Krishnamurti has pointed out that the quest for security through these systems of thought is a barrier to clarity, and actually creates insecurity.

As symbols of the sacred, systems of religious belief lend themselves to a host of interpretations. They have been the receptacles of the human being's need for something bigger than her/himself. And in the face of any disturbance, they seem to stand as guarantors for the elusive truth of the universe. In India today, religious values are being interpreted in ways that can provide a counter to the insecurity that social and economic change has engendered. New and varied inputs from the world pose questions that threaten old customs and beliefs. This has led to a revival of deeply separative trends as people cling to known ways that have, for centuries, been concretized in religious forms.

Any system of values, whether rooted in a set of religious beliefs, a vision of Utopia or in the ideology of the marketplace, creates divisions. The result is an increasing hardening of identities that can never reflect upon the very process of identification. In such a scenario, what economic and technological superstructures are we setting up? Factionalism cannot end with material comfort. And the invention of faster and easier ways of doing things cannot bring about an order that embraces a true appreciation of life on this marvellous and wonderful earth, where life can be lived in true freedom and dignity.

In Indian society, the most threatening divisions are between one religious identity and another, as well as that between a society rooted in religious tradition and one rooted in secular, modern values. Both approaches are partial and fragmentary. Each position is content to oppose the other and reiterate its own beliefs without asking more fundamental questions about the nature of the psyche, of relationship and whether there is something sacred that is not put together by thought.

Krishnamurti's approach to the nurturing of values offers a possibility of moving outside the dichotomies of belief—secular or religious. He initiated the process towards establishing values that are deeply rooted in the sacred, in the truly religious. In contrast to other religious thinkers and educators, Krishnamurti provides no prescriptions and no methodology. He did, however, direct exceptional energy and passion into creating educational institutions in India, England and America. The Krishnamurti schools attempt to create conditions that may foster a spirit of freedom, enabling enquiry into the nature of the self because '... it is essential that education should above all, help the individual to understand his own psychological processes'. It is only on this ground that a truly religious mind can be nurtured.

> A religious mind is a mind that has no belief, that has no dogma, that has no fear, that has absolutely no authority of any kind. It is a light unto itself. Such a mind, being free, can go very far. Then you will find out for yourself that extraordinary stillness of the mind—it is not an idea but an actual fact. A mind that is completely still without any distraction, a still mind, but not the romantic mind, a mind that is not begotten through conflict or through contradiction or through misery—it is only such a mind that is completely quiet and therefore completely alive, totally sensitive; it is only such a mind that can receive that which is immeasurable. (Krishnamurti, 1999, p. 18)

Acknowledgements

This chapter has benefited from the contributions of Kabir Jaithirtha and Alok Mathur, Krishnamurti Foundation India, who gently and patiently read the initial drafts and in the process assisted in elucidating Krishnamurti's ideas. Revisions to the text have been based on their suggestions. Thanks to Usha Rao for bringing about order to the first draft.

References

Gadgil, M., & Guha, R. (1997). *This fissured land, an ecological history of India*. New Delhi: Oxford India Paperbacks.

Krishnamurti, J. (1974). *Krishnamurti on education*. Chennai: Krishnamurti Foundation India.

Krishnamurti, J. (1984). *Talk at Ojai, CA*.

Krishnamurti, J. (1999). *The religious mind*. Chennai: Krishnamurti Foundation India.

Krishnamurti, J. (2002). *Commentaries on living, second series*. Chennai: Krishnamurti Foundation India.

Krishnamurti, J. (2003). *Education and the significance of life*. Chennai: Krishnamurti Foundation India.

24

Broadening of consciousness: A healing process among the survivors of the Kachchh earthquake

Kumar Ravi Priya

A massive earthquake, magnitude 6.9 on the Richter scale, hit Kachchh (a district in Gujarat state) on 26 January 2001 at 8.46 am. According to the Gujarat State Disaster Management Authority, 12,200 people died and several thousand were injured. The salient psychological, ecological and social conditions that threaten the well-being of the survivors of a massive earthquake may include the trauma of losing those near and dear to them, fear of aftershocks, the absence of basic necessities of life (food, shelter and clothes), fear of epidemics, the absence of means of livelihood, the emergence of varied cultural norms among the survivors (Acharya, 2000), the dehumanization implicit in taking compensation money (Scott, 2000; James, 2004), and the deformation of family and social support networks caused by the availability of compensation money (Parasuraman & Acharya, 2000).

I used the bio-psychosocial model, or the cultural psychological perspective of health and illness, and the ethnographic method to understand the phenomenon of suffering and healing under such a crisis situation in the post-earthquake period in Kachchh. In this chapter, I attempt to illustrate how the villagers' belief in *karma*[1] (internalized duty towards family, community and nature) aided the healing process by enabling them to transcend the boundary of the 'I' or the ego and making them realize that their selves were part of a pure and eternal consciousness. In other words, their belief in *karma* facilitated healing by 'broadening their consciousness'.[2]

In this chapter, I first provide the perspective of health and illness on which this study was based. Then, after describing the ethnographic method employed in this study, I present and discuss the findings related to how the survivors' cultural beliefs shaped the healing process as a 'broadening of consciousness'. Finally, I also share some of my reflections on how carrying out this study has contributed to my growth as a person.

Cultural–psychological perspective on health and illness

The bio-psychosocial model of health and illness shows how cultural beliefs shape the suffering and healing experiences of people (Kleinman, 1988). First, the meaning of a behavioural symptom and a sufferer's response to it are driven by implicit cultural beliefs. For example, in Western cultures, symptoms of illness are taken to be the outcome of lack of control over the environment (Sinha, 1990; Misra & Varma, 1999). Second, every culture has moral exemplars of how pain and loss should be borne. Not adhering to such culturally-prescribed behaviour may shape suffering as a moral form of agony. In a subsequent work, Kleinman, Das and Lock (2000) have shown that political, economic and institutional power ruins collective and intersubjective connections and thus propagates alienation among sufferers. Indeed, alienation induced by structures forms another kind of suffering.

In accordance with the culture-sensitive conceptualization of terms in the domain of health and illness, 'suffering' may be understood as the experience of pain or agony, within its socio-cultural, economic and political context, which is assumed to be *shaped* by one's cultural belief system with regard to illness and health. Also, healing is conceptualized as gradual recovery from such an experience of pain or agony (Kleinman, 1980, 1988; Kakar, 1982; Stacy, 1988; Ramaswami & Sheikh, 1996). Palsane (1988, p. 7) indicates the roles of beliefs and customs of a culture in the process of suffering and healing, saying, 'The belief system based on tradition helps in immunization against suffering, and in adaptation to and acceptance of suffering with equanimity. The belief together with custom provides the necessary psychological strength in times of crises and also makes available social network resources.'

Kleinman (1988) points out that cultural beliefs orient a sufferer to the questions, 'Why me?' and 'What can be done?' This orientation initiates the healing process as a reconstruction of suffering. Depending on the cultural belief, the healing process leads the person either towards better control (primary or secondary) over the situation or towards harmony with nature. As far as moral suffering and alienation due to socio-economic forces are concerned, providing emotional space to the sufferer initiates the healing process (Kleinman, 1988; Pennebaker, 1991). The verbal expression of suffering within an authentic relationship often helps reinstate a sense of self in the person (Brison, 1997; Ellingson, 2001).

'Broadening of consciousness' as healing: What literature says

Literature on the healing process also points to the 'expansion' or 'reframing' of consciousness as another indication of healing. According to Dethlefsen and Dahlke (1995), transcending suffering means giving up the 'I' or the ego, for wholeness is attainable only when one finally stops dividing off one's 'I' from the rest of existence. Healing, thus, means getting closer to being 'whole'.

Several ancient Indian systems of thought have focussed on how healing begins once a person is aware of his wrong identification with 'I' or the ego. Health, or healing, is a way of life, according to this tradition, where one recognizes and endeavours to realize the true nature of the human being, that is, pure or cosmic consciousness.

The Sāṁkhya system postulates two distinct ontological categories: *puruṣa*, which is pure consciousness, and *prakṛti*, which Larson and Bhattacharya (1987, p. 23, cited in Paranjpe, 1998b) have termed 'primordial materiality'. Although conceived as a single category, the term *puruṣa* refers collectively to innumerable distinct centres of awareness, or individual 'souls'. The basic nature of *puruṣa* is sentience, or the capacity for experiencing objects and events. In and of themselves, *puruṣas* do not act; they are passive witnesses to what goes on in the domain of *prakṛti*. The characteristic of *prakṛti* is to be the object of experience or 'enjoyment' (*bhoga*) for the *puruṣas* and thereby bind them within its domain, and to release (*apavarga*) them from its bonds so that they can remain in the ideal state of 'isolation' (*kaivalya*). *Prakṛti* comprises of three continually interacting components or 'strands' (*guṇas*), namely *sattva* (intelligibility, 'enlightenment' or lightness), *rajas* (activity, energy) and *tamas* (inertia, resistance, darkness). These strands continually supersede one another; one dominates while the others recede, thereby accounting for the constant changes in the domain of mind and matter.

According to the Sāṁkhya tradition, *puruṣa* may mistakenly identify itself with the conditions of *prakṛti* and consider itself happy, sad or depressed, in accordance with the conditions of the three strands of which the mind and body are composed. As long as that mistaken identification continues, one experiences different kinds of affect—feeling happy for some time and sad or disturbed later, and back again, in endless cycles. However, it is definitely possible for the individual to use the inherent capacity for knowledge or correct discrimination and to realize that true selfhood involves being the uninvolved witness, as *puruṣa* is in its nascent state. After this insight, *puruṣa* returns to its nascent condition beyond the ever-changing domain of *prakṛti*, never again to return to the sorrowful experiences of mundane life.

Thus, as Paranjpe (1998b) points out, it is implied that the end of suffering means going beyond pleasure and pain, happiness and sadness. It is the ideal state of 'isolation' (*kaivalya*). After his death, the individual doesn't return to the cycle of birth and death as he has attained release from *saṁsāra*, the wheel of life and death.

The monistic (*advaita*) school of Advaita Vedānta shares the similar goal of attaining 'self-realization', as observed in the Sāṁkhya and Yoga traditions. However, while both, the Sāṁkhya and the Vedānta systems, maintain that the Self is beyond pleasure, Advaita Vedāntists view it as blissful in nature.

The Vedānta tradition emphasizes that pleasure and pain, happiness and misery are a result of cognitive reconstruction, and so is the ego, which is usually mistaken for the true Self. If one performs meditation as prescribed by this tradition, the ego is cognitively deconstructed. When it is realized that the true Self does not believe itself to be a knower and agent, there is no one left to do something, to know whether the results are good or bad and thereby feel pleasure or pain.

In the Buddhist tradition, too, desire is viewed as a source of stress for several reasons (Evans, 1998). First, as in the Vedāntic tradition, it contributes to dualism between the self and the object of desire. Instead of seeing the transcendence of the self with other persons and the natural order, desire sets up a false dichotomy of self and possessions of the self. Not only does this dualism make it hard to appreciate the source of one's suffering, it also creates suffering since desires become self-perpetuating—one can always find more money, more food, more beauty, etc. In this tradition, desire in itself is not necessarily a problem. Desire, but without attachment to its objectives, helps unlock overdependence on sensory stimuli by enabling a person to respond to pleasure and pain with equanimity.

Apart from acquiring an attitude of *equanimity*, Mahāyāna Buddhism provides the concept of *mindfulness* (Sattler, 1998). Mindfulness is becoming aware of how the law of cause and effect functions. Everything we encounter is caused by our former actions. These, in turn, affect the present situation, so we do not look for causes for our *karma* and situation other than in our own past actions. This minimizes our projecting of guilt on others, reduces stress between each other, and encourages mindful behaviour. With this realization, we may expand on these thoughts by becoming aware of all the countless beings we may have related to in our countless lives. As human beings, we depend materially and spiritually on other beings' kindness. By gratefully remembering their kindness, we are moved to repaying it through developing *bodhicitta* (the mind of the enlightened) to help all beings.

It is important to note that Sinha (1990) points out that the belief in *karma* and fate and an attitude of acceptance have their basis not only in the religious-philosophical tradition but also in the nature of the physical environment and the climate that characterizes the Indian subcontinent. Many studies carried out to understand the attribution of illness in India and the Indian subcontinent have revealed *karma* and/or other metaphysical beliefs such as God's will and fate as causal factors for illness or disability (Naidu, 1986; Ojha, 1986; Joshi, 1988; Desjarlais, 1994; Dalal, 2001).

Before we try to understand how the survivors of the Kachchh earthquake were able to overcome the impact of trauma by the broadening of consciousness, here is the method used for this study.

Method

I adopted an ethnographic approach for this study. It was planned that 20 adult members[3] of earthquake-stricken families (in which at least one death had occurred) in each of Selari Village and Bhachau town would be followed up in three phases (fieldwork of 45–60 days once a year over a period of at least three years). The rationale behind selecting these two research sites was that one being rural and the other urban, they differed in their community life and cultural beliefs and customs. Another rationale was the difference in the number of people they lost to the earthquake (thirty three in Selari and several thousand in Bhachau).

I began the fieldwork in November 2001 in Selari. Although I had initially participated in a rehabilitation programme (run by the University of Delhi in the areas of health, earthquake resistant housing, education, etc.) as a volunteer, I had to take up the role of a teacher in the high school at the village. Through the relationship I developed with the students there, it became possible to build trust with the villagers. Throughout the research process, the villagers considered me a resource person in education. Similarly, in Bhachau town, I began fieldwork as a volunteer at 'Child Line', an NGO. It helped me in getting connected with the affected families.

Participants

Of the 20 families that participated in all the three phases of the study at Selari village, 19 were Hindu families and 1 a Muslim family. Of the 13 survivors who were farmers, 5 had pump sets to use underground water for irrigation. The other 8 farmers were solely dependent on rainwater for irrigation. It may be noted that a 'good monsoon' that is 'sufficient' for cultivation comes to Kachchh once in every three or four years. Therefore, these families have to work in the fields of other farmers. Their poor economic condition sometimes leads them to borrow money. The 7 non-farmer families belonged to the lower socio-economic strata. Their traditional occupations were tailoring, sheep-rearing, manual labour and shop-keeping.

Among the survivors in Bhachau, 2 were Muslim and rest 31 were Hindu. They held a variety of occupations, including business, manual labour, government employment (teacher, engineer and water-motor operator), etc.

Data collection and analysis

The interviews were conducted in Selari and Bhachau, in family settings in which other family members also voluntarily shared their experiences. In Selari, one of the key informants, Sudhakar Bhai, helped the researcher by acting as a translator (Gujarati to Hindi and vice versa). The interviews in Selari were conducted during the evening hours, when the men in the family returned from work. In Bhachau, interviews with students were conducted in a school. In the first phase, interviews were tape-recorded; in the subsequent phases, notes were taken during interviews. The interview guidelines were:

1. What were the experiences and constructions of suffering and healing among the survivors?
2. What was the influence of cultural belief systems (about earthquakes, health, life and death) on the experiences and constructions of suffering and healing?
3. What was the role of social support networks (family, relatives, social groups and NGOs) in the healing process?
4. How did the socio-economic conditions influence the support networks and shape the healing process?

Besides the semi-structured interviews with survivors, focus group discussions and participant observations among the survivors and semi-structured interviews of key informants (journalists, social workers, creative writers, etc.) were also conducted in order to provide a holistic understanding of the suffering and healing process, utilizing different data sources through theoretical sampling.

I analysed the experiences of suffering and healing in the light of the cultural beliefs and constructions of health and illness, which is in accordance with the meta-theoretical framework of the bio-psychosocial model (or cultural psychological perspective of health and illness) adopted for this study. A combination of thematic analysis and constructionist grounded theory was utilized to analyse the narratives. The approach of constructionist grounded theory (Charmaz, 1995, 2001; Pidgeon & Henwood, 1997) also enabled me to recognize the influence of my perspective (of existential philosophy) and experiences on the development of themes and categories through an empathic understanding of the experiences of the survivors.

The following section presents constructions of health and illness among survivors in the village, which has been shaped by their belief in *karma*.

Constructions of health and illness in Selari village

The interview with Mansingh Baba (a priest of Selari village and one of the key informants) was of much value as it helped in gaining a better understanding of the phenomenon of suffering and healing.

When I asked him what he understood of the reasons for the suffering caused by the earthquake, he said,

> According to me, the earthquake occurs because gases get accumulated inside the earth and it has to come out due to pressure. But the gases get accumulated inside the earth due to the result of our *karma* (one's duty towards oneself, family, community and nature). Tell me, who saved us (pointing towards himself and Amrit Bhai, the interpreter) from the earthquake? It was nothing but our *karma*. If people lead their lives according to *dharma* (principals of virtue)—and by *dharma*, I mean *mānava dharma* (humane religion), which is above all caste, religion and community—they will achieve *ānand* (joy). If they don't do it, they will suffer.

It was evident from the interviews of Mansingh Baba and the survivors that the notions of 'suffering' and 'healing' were constructed and experienced around *their* 'theory of *karma*', which centred on the following themes. [Themes (*a*), (*b*) and (*c*) emerged from the narratives of all the survivors, and theme (*d*) emerged from the narrative of a priest who was one of the key informants]:

(a) Exercising one's potentialities to the fullest

One of the survivors, Amba Bhai, while sharing his construction of *sukh* (health and/or happiness) and *dukh* (illness and/or sorrow), said, '*mānav dharma* says that we must do our *karma* by doing utmost labour we can to earn our livelihood to take care of our family and serve the society'.

Almost all the men in families where one or more deaths had occurred were back to work after a month or two. Among them were Naresh Bhai, Amba Bhai, Kailash Bhai and Pravin Bhai, whose families had lost two or three of their members.

(b) Diffusion of boundaries between self and other 'beings'

Thus, action should be oriented towards the welfare of not only the self, but also the other 'beings' of nature.

In our interaction about how he construed *sukh* and *dukh*, Jayendra Bhai said, 'Our *karma* should be directed not only towards the welfare of our family and the poor but also towards the birds and animals which are a part of our living. I regularly give *bājrā* (millet) to the birds.'

In this connection, it would be pertinent to take note of the common practice in the village of feeding birds, cows and other animals, apart from helping fellow human beings. This is not merely a ritual to be completed—several survivors (for example, Jayendra Bhai, Maya Ben, Nirmala Ben and Vira Bhai) expressed their serious concern with keeping animals fed. They said that such a practice gave them *santoṣa* (satisfaction) and *śānti* (peace of mind).

(c) Possessing just enough for a 'healthy', non-luxurious living

Amba Bhai told me,

> The disasters like this earthquake take place due to the fact that we commit *pāp* (wrong deeds in violation of *karma*). Having plenty for myself and not bothering about the poor is 'not following my *karma*'. We should have only that much *dhan* (material possession) with which we can take care of our family members. The rest should be given to the needy people and be utilized towards the welfare of the society.

During the days of scarcity two or three days after the earthquake, despite being poor and suffering a death in the family, Vira Bhai distributed all of his stored *bājra* to the homeless. Paras Bhai, a farmer who had lost his 13-year-old daughter, built a bus stop in the village with the money he had received as compensation for her death.

(d) Forces of nature (that cause happiness and sorrow) are beyond human control
How much these forces oppress a human being depends on the nature and intensity of the wrong deeds of his/her past and present lives. Through exercising one's potentialities to the fullest in this life and living in harmony with the forces of nature, one can rise above these forces and merge with the *paramātmā* (the Almighty) to end the cycle of life and death.

The survivors had a firm belief that carrying out one's *karma* (which intricately relates one to family, society and nature through one's duties towards them) is the necessary condition for the attainment of *śānti* (peace of mind) despite one's experiencing *darad* or *dukh* (agony, pain, illness). *Karma* was taken as the key means of maintaining *śānti*. For example, a farmer, who was prevented from farming due to severe asthma, expressed his *śānti* as he was able to perform his duty of 'guarding the house'. That *Karma* or *pravṛtti* is the only medium for *śānti* in their lives is captured well by the following saying:

> *Bhūtkāl no bhulī jāo,*
> *bhaviṣya ni chintā nahiṁ karo,*
> *vartmān mā pravrutti karo.*
> (Forget the past, do not worry about the future and perform your duties in the present.)

Let us now find out how their belief in *karma* aided healing through the 'broadening of consciousness'.

Healing through 'Broadening of Consciousness': Some evidence

An analysis of the narratives provided certain themes about the healing process. They pointed out that (*a*) with their belief in *karma*, they could *re-organize their selves as a continuous process across time* and this process gave them new and positive meaning in life; (*b*) carrying out their *karma* (internalized duty towards self, family, community and nature) made them experience *śānti* (peace of mind or equanimity); and (*c*) the death of a loved one became an *inspiration for them to follow the path of karma*. These themes that show the healing process as a broadening of consciousness are presented and discussed below with verbatim accounts or my observations in their support.

Healing as reorganizing self as a continuous process across time
Survivors construed self as a continuous process across time by attributing their present condition of illness and health to performing *karma* in the past. Krishna Bhai, 38, who lost his 12-year-old daughter, said,

> We are experiencing *dukh* due to our indulgence in *pāp* in the past or in *pūrv janm* (previous birth). In this life also, in the past, we committed *pāp* (sin or non-adherence to *karma*). For example, when the Kargil war4 took place, people of Kachchh didn't give any financial support but, now in troubled time of Kachchh, people from outside have come to provide all kinds of support. I have decided that I am going to build a structure where animals like cows and birds can have some cereals to eat. Let us do something for others. What shall we take with us after we die?

Most participants in the focus group discussion also shared a feeling that the *pāp* they had committed in the past had led to the earthquake and the resulting *dukh*. One of the participants said, 'Our *dukh* is a result of our own *pāp* that we committed by becoming selfish and not caring about poor and weak. If we carry out our *karma*, God will provide us with the strength to endure the difficulties produced by the earthquake.'

It was evident that their belief in *karma* had facilitated a *cognitive restructuring* of their state of loss. Almost all the men of those families where one or more deaths had occurred were back to their work after two to three months. Among them were men like Naresh Bhai, Amba Bhai, Kailash Bhai and Rama Bhai, whose families had lost two or three members. All said that through their work, they attained some *santoṣa*, or satisfaction, that they were taking care of their families. Also, they considered their involvement in *karma* to be the only way to face and transcend *dukh*. Naresh Bhai said,

> *Dukh* is there and it will subside only with time but our *karma* is in our hands which is the only *truth* or the *way out*. It is perhaps because of our *pāp* only that the family members have expired. Through doing our *karma* only, we may attain some *santoṣa* in present and in future.

It is quite clear that health for them is to 'move on' or to carry out their duties towards their families and the society, despite suffering the sorrow of losing their near and dear ones. Atwood and Maltin (1991, p. 375) have noted a similar pattern of healing among Easterners: 'The best way for [Easterner] patients to handle unpleasant feelings is to recognize them, to accept them, and to go about their business. In time, unpleasant feelings will pass .... Just as one cannot hold on to positive feelings forever, one cannot hold onto negative feelings forever. Feelings are temporary experiences.'

Omprakash (1989) points out that belief in *karma* has important psychological implications. These include an uncritical acceptance of misery and hope for a better life in the future through 'right' actions. The patterns of feelings and behaviours observed during the second and third phases of the study indicated that most of the survivors engaged actively in their daily activities. Even those farmers who had to depend solely on the monsoon worked hard in the agricultural fields of others (who could afford to have alternate means of irrigation) to earn their livelihood. They expressed a sense of satisfaction that they were able to earn.

Amba Bhai, a tailor, who suffered an injury in his pelvic joints, said that he had to work for double the hours he used to work before the earthquake because he had to get his sister married and repay the debt he had incurred. It is apparent that the belief in *karma* enabled the survivors to accept their suffering and move towards a *positive meaning in life*, which was to get involved in their work so that they could take care of their families.

Belief in *karma* is widely accepted as a causal explanation for suffering not only in the Buddhist and Hindu philosophical traditions (Radhakrishnan, 1926), but also among contemporary Indians (Sinha, 1990; Kohli & Dalal 1998). Also, as evident from the examples quoted above, it did provide a space for the survivors to reconstruct their loss and move towards a positive meaning in life.

Śānti *through* karma

The survivors expressed a strong sense of self located in relationships with family, society and nature by carrying out their internalized duties towards them. They also shared experiencing *śānti* or peace of mind or equanimity through carrying out their *karma*. Maya Ben, 48 years old, lost her husband in the earthquake and lives with one of her granddaughters in her house. She wanted neither to live with her son, who does some business in Mumbai, nor tried to persuade him to stay with her in the village. She told us that while her son did all the rituals associated with his father's funeral and stayed with her for two weeks, she didn't ask him to stay back as she didn't want him to stay against his wishes. She told us,

> My only son, who lives in Mumbai, calls me there feeling that I would be lonely here. But I do not like to leave this place. I have brought back one of my granddaughters from Mumbai and I look after her. Living in this place, I would be able to do some *puṇya* like, *sevā* or service to animals, birds, cows and poor people. Living here, doing this gives me *śānti*.

Vira Bhai, 52 years old, and respected in the village, lost his mother in the earthquake. He said,

> Due to health reasons, I am unable to go to the field and work hard. Therefore, I stay back at home, guard and manage it. All the rest in the family, my children and my wife are there in the field to contribute to farming. *Dukh* has reduced among them too. *Śānti chhe* (I have peace of mind).

Through their belief in *karma*, survivors experienced *śānti* as they could reorganize (or meaningfully define) their selves in harmony with their family members, community and nature. In some cultures, as in Selari village, a harmonious relationship with other human beings and nature is considered important in order to experience positive health. For example, Torsch and Ma (2000) found that among elderly Chinese-Americans, 'interpersonal harmony' was regarded essential to healthy living. Inter-personal harmony was characterized as caring for others, sharing among people and maintaining a strong family system. Pachuta (1996) emphasized that healing in the Eastern system is *circular*, that is, the universe as well as the individual can be conceived of as a circle that contains every explicit duality as an implicit unity; where oneness with the universe is a given, and one continually seeks balance and harmony within this oneness. Jensen and Allen (1994) noted that 'wholeness' with the world is associated with the experience of health. Similarly, Tolle (2003) emphasized that every form of existence in the cosmos is intricately related. One cannot understand what role a seemingly senseless event may have within the totality of the cosmos, but recognizing its inevitability within the vastness of the whole can be the beginning of an inner acceptance of what *is* and thus a realignment with the wholeness of life. Thus, a socio and eco-centric health belief may help reorganize one's self within a harmonious relationship with some form of existence (family, society or the entire cosmos).

Lewis-Fernandez and Kleinman (1994) and O'Nell (2004) have pointed out that in some cultures, cultural beliefs of health and illness are based largely on a socio-centric ideology, that is, the experience of suffering and healing are situated in the networks of social relationships. Similarly, survivors' belief in *karma* is one such socio-centric cultural belief that also locates one's experiences of suffering and healing in relationship with one's society and ecology. Also, it is generally believed that in the Indian cultural tradition, no sharp boundaries are drawn between the individual and his environment. A healthy individual is one who has a harmonious relationship with the community, surroundings and the supernatural world (Sinha, 1990; Paranjpe, 1998b).

Departed family member as an inspiration to performing one's karma

Some survivors also shared their feeling a sense of self through carrying out their internalized duties towards family, society and nature out of an inspiration gained from the death of a family member. It was evident in the case of Paras Bhai, a 42-year-old farmer who owned a *sūkhī khetī* (farmland completely dependent on rainwater) and who lost his 13-year-old daughter.

Paras Bhai, being a manual labourer, had received Rs 80,000 as compensation for her death. I was filled with a sense of reverence for him when I came to know that he had added Rs 20,000 to this amount and had spent the entire sum in rebuilding the village bus stop, which had been severely damaged in the earthquake. He told us that he had not earned the compensation money, and therefore didn't want to use it for himself. And since the money was associated with the death of his daughter, he wanted to spend it on a good cause. He said, 'My daughter Fuli Ben was very dear to me. She is no more (physically) with me but she still inspires me to do my *karma* which is meant to do good to all the people around us. So, she has inspired me to build this bus stop.'

In the third phase of our interaction, Paras Bhai reiterated the change in his approach to life that was brought about by the death of his daughter. He said,

> The death of my beloved daughter showed to me that our lives and those of our loved ones won't last for ever. Therefore, whatever time we have in this world, we must try to do whatever we can for the society and humanity. That is real *prem* (compassion). Building the bus stop for the village is a small step in that direction.

As maintained in various traditions of Indian thought (Sāṁkhya-Yoga, Advaita Vedānta, Buddhism, etc.), we are not merely bodies or minds: we are a part of, or a manifestation of, a cosmic or pure consciousness (Evans, 1998; Paranjpe, 1998a; Sattler, 1998). A crisis situation like the death of a loved one may, besides inducing a sense of loss, lead to the realization that the sense of loss is because of the belief that we exist only as bodies or minds. Once we realize that we exist as a manifestation of a higher or pure consciousness, we may experience that, irrespective of existing or not existing as bodies or minds, we are *one* as we are the manifestations of *one*. And this experience or realization may be an inspiration that enables us to devote our lives to contributing (or doing our *karma*) to harmony among all beings of nature. This inspiration is reflected in the above-mentioned case of Paras Bhai.

Ramesh Bhai, a 45-year-old businessman in Bhachau town, lost his 38-year-old wife and 14-year-old son in the earthquake. Although he didn't belong to a village and shared a health belief based on *karma,* he considered himself and his loved ones as part of a larger 'process' or consciousness that is continuous over time. That is probably why for him his departed family members became a source of inspiration to do something positive in life by looking after his daughters. He and his surviving daughters, in their constant struggle against standing losses and fighting the discrimination by authorities, had apparently accepted their trauma. They wrote the following couplet below the photographs of their departed family members:

> *Tame āwyā nahotā kain*
> *thodā ghanā varas laīne*
> *tame to jāwso hṛdaymā*
> *bhavo bhavni taras laīne*
>
> Couldn't you come (to this earth)
> for some more years?
> You shall remain in my heart making me long deeply
> (for your physical presence) for eras to come.

Ramesh Bhai said, 'This couplet is a mark of what they (the departed souls) mean to us. They are still a part of our existence and give us strength to face this difficult time and that is why they will be missed.'

When I met him again in the third phase, he looked much calmer and more active. He told me that he had got one of his daughters married and was planning to get another daughter married within a year.

The themes outlined above indicate that healing may be considered a process of broadening of consciousness which enables a person to think of all forms of existence as manifestations of a higher consciousness (continuous over time and space). And the death of a loved one may, in fact, provide an opportunity (despite a feeling of loss) to experience "being a manifestation" of that higher consciousness. It is also evident from these themes that such a realization leads one to act towards the harmony or well-being of all beings of nature, which provides a person the experience of equanimity (*śānti* or *santoṣa*).

Reflections: How I felt 'expanded'/harmonized during the research

In the 'Method' section, I had mentioned that my own subjectivity as a human being was also affected during the process of data collection and analysis. Qualitative methods do accept and provide space to the idea that we, as researchers, cannot remain 'neutral' to or detached from the process of research. I must share with the reader that my inclination towards existentialism did shape the coding process, which made the patterns in the narrative intelligible. It is evident from a theme such as, how a crisis situation re-affirmed the survivors' belief in *karma* with which they could *re-organize their selves as a continuous process across time* and how this process gave them new and positive meaning in life. Besides this, the fact that I could empathize (to whatever extent possible) with the experiences of loss of some of the survivors also lent meaning, or authenticity, to the coding process. Besides aiding to the authenticity of analysis, an empathic understanding of the survivors' experiences also became for me a harmonizing experience of painful personal experiences of the past and the present that were revived in the process of research.

During the first phase of the study in Selari village, I recall sitting in the house of the middle-aged, childless Nirmala Ben, whose husband had died in the earthquake. An ex-*sarpanch* (a relative of hers) and Sudhakar Bhai (my interpreter) were sitting with me. After speaking with the ex-*sarpanch* about whether she had received compensation, I tried to initiate an interaction with her by asking her about the work that she was doing. After a silence of about two minutes, she slowly said something that I took to mean, 'Something ... I do something.' Then tears came in her eyes and none of us spoke for more than 10 minutes. With tears in our eyes, I indicated to Sudhakar Bhai to tell her to rest, and that we would come again. She responded that we would have to take tea, which she then went to make. The intensity and nature of the pain that that single sentence of Nirmala Ben contained was far greater than any pain I have faced till now in my life. It was extremely difficult for me to empathize with the pain she was feeling. Her sorrow and her silence made me feel once again the grief and loneliness that I had felt when my mother was seriously ill (and had to be hospitalized in a different town) following the death of my eldest brother in 1982. I was five or six years old then. I do not remember crying, but I can still feel the loneliness and the peculiar sense of 'meaninglessness' associated with that time.[5] My interaction with Nirmala Ben made me realize the 'littleness' of my suffering in life.

I was, however, happy to see Nirmala Ben in Phase II of the study, when she was managing her life in a much more positive way by regularizing her daily routine, which consisted of worshipping, rendering services to a priest, Mansingh Baba, and organizing religious activities such as *satsaṅg.* In line with what Ellingson (2001) said, this participatory research also provided me the space to positively and compassionately re-experience my own trauma while empathically relating with Nirmala Ben's suffering.

Having met and interacted with Vira Bhai and Paras Bhai (who contributed towards the well-being of others while themselves being in crisis), I was filled with reverence for them. I realized that I too was in search of a positive meaning in life. It was probably that search that led me to the earthquake-affected area in expectance that the survivors would also move towards some positive meaning in life after the crisis. I could empathize with them when they said that they experienced *śānti* by carrying out their duties towards family and society. I, too, had a harmonizing experience—that of being able to contribute towards the healing of traumatized people by providing them, to the best of my ability, with emotional space through our interactions.

Endnotes

1 In this study, although I found the belief in *karma* to be quite prevalent in Selari village, some urban survivors too shared their realization of the temporariness of worldly objects and activities. Furthermore, their action (for example, nurturing younger ones to give a new meaning to life) showed a commitment towards contributing whatever they could to nature's "beings". So, in some of the urban survivors, too, I observed a tendency to transcend the boundary of their 'I'.

2 Although in this paper I have written about how the metaphysical beliefs of the survivors made healing possible, I also found that healing was rare among those survivors who held on to materialistic beliefs. Particularly in the urban setting, I found threatening post-earthquake socio-economic events (e.g., development of the boundaries of caste and class) that were impeding the healing process, as there the individualistic lifestyles and materialistic notions of health and illness disabled them from positively re-constructing their sorrow. I have reported these findings elsewhere (see Priya, 2004).

3 These participants are referred to as 'survivors' throughout this paper. Because of ethical concerns, the names of these survivors and other key informants that have been reported are not their original names.

4 'Kargil war' is a popular term given to an Indian Armed Forces' military operation in 1999 in the state of Jammu and Kashmir to drive out infiltrators from Pakistan who had crossed the Line of Control into India. These infiltrators had constructed bunkers in the Indian state of Jammu and Kashmir from where they waged a mini-war on the Indian armed forces.

5 It took my mother almost a year to recover from meningitis and another year

to completely recover from the loss of memory resulting from the disease and its treatment.

References

Acharya, N. (2000). Double victims of Latur earthquake. *The Indian Journal of Social Work, 61*, 558–564.

Atwood, J. D., & Maltin, L. (1991). Putting eastern philosophies into western psychotherapies. *American Journal of Psychotherapy, 45*, 368–382.

Brison, S. J. (1997). Outlining oneself: Trauma, memory, and personal identity. In D. T. Meyers (Ed.), *Feminists rethink the self* (pp. 12–39). Boulder, CO: Westview Press.

Charmaz, K. (1995). Grounded theory. In J. A. Smith, R. Harre, & L. Van Langenhove (Eds.), *Rethinking methods in Psychology* (pp. 27–49). London: Sage Publications.

Charmaz, K. (2001). 'Discovering' chronic illness: Using grounded theory. In A. Bryman (Ed.), *Ethnography* (Vol. 4, pp. 220–242). London: Sage Publications.

Dalal, A. K. (2001). Health psychology. In J. Pandey (Ed.), *Psychology in India revisited: Developments in the discipline* (Vol. 2: Personality and health psychology, pp. 356–411). New Delhi: Sage Publications.

Desjarlais, R. R. (1994). *Body and emotions: The aesthetics of illness and healing in the Nepal Himalaya.* New Delhi: Motilal Banarasidas.

Dethlefsen, T., & Dahlke, R. (1995). *The healing power of illness.* Melbourne: Element.

Ellingson, L. L. (2001). 'Then you know how I feel': Empathy, identification, and reflexivity in fieldwork. In A. Bryman (Ed.), *Ethnography* (Vol. 4, pp. 52–74). London: Sage Publications.

Evans, G. W. (1998). Costs of coping with stress: East & West. In U. Ram (Ed.), *Suffering and stress management: West versus East* (pp. 17–27). Pune: Deepa Publications.

James, E. C. (2004). The political economy of 'trauma' in Haiti in the democratic era of insecurity. *Culture, Medicine and Psychiatry, 28*, 127–149.

Jensen, L. A., & Allen, M. N. (1994). A synthesis of qualitative research on wellness-illness. *Qualitative Health Research, 4*, 349–369.

Joshi, P. C. (1988). Traditional medical system in the Central Himalayas. *The Eastern Anthropologist, 41*, 77–83.

Kakar, S. (1982). *Shamans, mystics and doctors.* New Delhi: Oxford University Press.

Kleinman, A. (1980). *Patients and healers in the contexts of culture.* California: University of California Press.

Kleinman, A. (1988). *The illness narratives: Suffering, healing and the human condition.* New York: Basic Books.

Kleinman, A., Das, V., & Locke, M. (2000). *Social suffering* (2nd Indian ed.). New Delhi: Oxford University Press.

Kohli, N., & Dalal, A. K. (1998). Culture as a factor in causal understanding of illness: A study of cancer patients. *Psychology and Developing Societies, 10*, 115–129.

Larson, G. J., & Bhattacharya, R. S. (Eds.) (1987). Samkhya: A dualist tradition in Indian philosophy. *Encyclopedia of Indian Philosophies* (Vol. 4), (K.H. Potter, Series ed.). New Delhi: Motilal Banarasidass.

Lewis-Fernandez, R., & Kleinman, A. (1994). Culture, personality and psychotherapy. *Journal of Abnormal Psychology, 103*, 67–71.

Misra, G., & Varma, S. (1999). Introduction: Concerns in the study of stress and health. In G. Misra (Ed.), *Psychological perspectives on stress and health* (pp. 25–38). New Delhi: Concept.

Naidu, R. K. (1986). Beliefs, trust, impulse control and health: Studies in the psychology of health. *Journal of Social and Economic Studies, 3*, 369–378.

O'Nell, T. D. (2004). Culture and pathology: Flathead loneliness revisited. *Culture, Medicine and Psychiatry, 28*, 221–230.

Ojha, J. M. (1986). Expectance and communication in planning for health education: A study of attitudes and beliefs. *The Indian Journal of Social Work, 37*, 153–168.

Omprakash, S. (1989). The doctrine of Karma: Its psychological consequences. *Journal of Community Psychology, 17*, 133–145.

Pachuta, D. M. (1996). Chinese medicine: The law of five elements. In A. A. Sheikh & K. S. Sheikh (Ed.), *Healing east and west* (pp. 64–90). New York: Wiley and Sons.

Palsane, M. N. (1988). Concept of stress from traditional Indian standpoint. In U. Ram (Ed.), *Suffering and stress management: West versus East* (pp. 4–8). Pune: Deepa Publications.

Paranjpe, A. C. (1998a). Merits and limits of East/West integration of concepts and remedies of suffering. In U. Ram (Ed.), *Suffering and stress management: West versus East* (pp. 4–8). Pune: Deepa Publications.

Paranjpe, A. C. (1998b). *Self and identity in modern psychology and Indian thought.* New York: Plenum Press.

Parasuraman, S., & Acharya, N. (2000). Analysing forms of vulnerability in a disaster. *The Indian Journal of Social Work, 61*, 581–597.

Pennebaker, J. (1991). *Opening up: The healing power of confiding in others.* New York: Avon.

Pidgeon, N., & Henwood, K. (1997). Using grounded theory in psychological research. In N. Hayes (Ed.), *Doing qualitative analysis in psychology* (pp. 245–273). Hove: East Sussex: Psychology Press.

Priya, K. R. (2004). Post-quake recovery in urban Kachchh. *Economic and Political Weekly, 39*(38), 4229–4231.

Radhakrishnan, S. (1926). *Hindu view of life*. London: Allen & Unwin.

Ramaswami, S., & Sheikh, A. A. (1996). Buddhist psychology: Implication for healing. In A. A. Sheikh & K. S. Sheikh (Eds.), *Healing east and west.* New York: John Wiley.

Sattler, K. (1998). Tibetan teachings on Buddhist thought transformation as a means of stress management. In U. Ram (Ed.), *Suffering and stress management: West versus East* (pp. 52–55). Pune: Deepa Publications.

Scott, M. J. (2000). Journeying with the traumatized—The Hillsborough disaster. In M. J. Scott & S. Palmer (Eds.), *Trauma and post-traumatic stress disorder*. London: Sage Publications.

Sinha, D. (1990). The concept of psycho-social well being: Western and Indian perspectives. *National Institute of Mental Health and Neurosciences Journal, 8*, 1–11.

Stacy, M. (1988). *The sociology of health and healing*. London: Routledge.

Tolle, E. (2003). *Stillness speaks*. Mumbai: Yogi Impressions Books.

Torsch, V. L., & Ma, G. X. (2000). Cross-cultural comparisons of health perspectives, concerns, and coping strategies among Asian and Pacific Islander American elders. *Qualitative Health Research, 10*(4), 471–489.

25

Resolution of social conflicts: An Indian model

Raghubir Singh Pirta

Introduction

Human social conflicts have both an evolutionary and a cultural past. However, changes in inner (intra-psychic) and outer (inter-personal/environmental) contextual features drastically affect the nature of conflicts as well as their resolution. A conflict arises when two activities are incompatible. It may occur within the individual, when it is termed an intra-psychic conflict. However, more important for our purpose are those conflicts originating from the incompatible belief systems of two or more groups. The resolution of these social conflicts depends on the consonance among the cognitive beliefs. Consider the following examples.

When India was facing the challenge of independence and was fraught with turmoil and social conflict, Sri Aurobindo (1998, p. 90) envisaged taking up the essence of all religions and gathering these streams into

> one mighty river, one purifying and redeeming Ganges, pour it over the death-in-life of a materialistic humanity as Bhagirath led down the Ganges and flooded with it the ashes of his fathers, so that they may be a resurrection of the soul in mankind and the Satyayuga for a while return to the world.

There is yet another important dimension, which includes conflicts between individual and collective interests. These are called 'social dilemmas' or 'social traps', and generally include conflicts between individual and collective preferences embedded in the environment. The ecologist Madhav Gadgil has explored such social conflicts in the institution of local deities in the villages. He writes, 'One often finds associated with such deities a rich body of folklore which can illuminate the history of human groups that worship these deities. Such folklore can be particularly fascinating when it appears to have its origin in conflicts of interests amongst the different human groups' (Gadgil, 2001; p. 164). These two perspectives, the first that of a philosopher and the second of an ecologist, are important in understanding the conflicts involving people in Indian villages.

It seems strange that in India, psychologists have never been especially interested in either Indian mysticism or the material issues troubling Indian people. However, several contemporary thinkers (Sarala Devi, 1982; Chidananda, 1991; Thakar, 1999; Chaitanya, 2000) have observed that this development was perhaps not in consonance with the Indian psyche. According to the Nobel-winning economist Amartya Sen, the process of development has various aspects that should be evaluated in the context of the well-being of people. If we see the elements constitutive of well-being rather than the utilitarian elements, 'much of the task that Nehru had identified remains largely unaccomplished' (Sen, 1997, p. 5). The constitutive elements signified a view of a 'mental state', whereas utilitarian elements signified the 'desire-fulfilment' aspect (Sen, 1999). In the latter, utility is achieved through the objective realization of the 'desired state', while in the former it is achieved through some 'mental state'.

A very significant aspect of human social conflicts is that they are embedded in culture. Western material culture evolved in towns and cities, while Indian culture has its origins in the small village communities of the forests. Material science is therefore of little use to the villages of India, where most of its people live, unless it is assimilated into the indigenous culture. This was a point of discord between Gandhi and Nehru (see Mitrany[1]) at the time of Indian independence. However, even more important is the premise of the famous poet Rabindranath Tagore (1986) that the origin of culture in the forest is the basis for the uniqueness of the land known as *Bhāratavarṣa*. Isolation in dense forests made people turn their minds inward in search of the infinite mysteries of the world. This inward quest is the typical method through which people who make their discoveries in the *tapovans* acquire knowledge.

In the first half of the twentieth century, Mahatma Gandhi successfully tested an ancient discovery, 'the law of non-violence', through his inward quest (Pyarelal, 1959). The use of non-violence as a method of resolving conflict has been validated in the naturalistic observations of Kropotkin (1914) and Lorenz (1976), who are well-known for their explorations of how the laws of the jungle maintain peace in animal societies.[2] For psychologists, there is more to explore in Gandhi's unusual experiments; consider, for example, Bandura's (2001) study of how non-violence can be an effective method for enhancing self-efficacy.

Whether the theory of the 'idiocy of village life' carries any weight in India is a contentious issue, and the noted historian Kosambi (1975, p. 16) asserts that the self-contained village provided 'the material foundation for Indian culture and civilization'. He feels that Indian society has developed more through successive religious transformations (and associated philosophical developments) than through violence.

The people of India have a profound spiritual affinity with the river Ganges, the legendary Bhāgīrathī. And their deep cultural association with the Himalayas as a numinous sacred landscape is also well-known. But over the past several decades, the Ganges and the Himalayas have faced the onslaught of rapacious and destructive policies under the guise of essential development. These activities have had an extremely detrimental effect on the living landscape and its inhabitants. Not only have native residents of the Himalayas been deeply affected, but so also have others in distant places. According to thinker Vidyanivas Misra, this is noteworthy, and the important question is not 'who does the Ganga belong to, but who belongs to the Ganga' (Misra, 1995a). In order to be of the Ganga, it is not material ownership that has a bearing, but the assimilation of the Ganga's rich cultural identity and the determination of our own identity from the Ganga (Misra, 1995b). Through this framework, he has probably resolved the dilemma of some social psychologists about emic and etic approaches (see G. Misra & Gergen, 2002), while introducing the concept of cultural relativism.

One way to achieve cultural sensitivity is through grassroots resistance movements. The idea emerges from two opposite streams—the American social psychologist Kenneth Gergen[3] and the Indian thinker V. Misra (1995b). This way of resolving social conflicts is no different from the affirmative action that *Chipko* social workers took in the 1970s in the Himalayas, which we will soon explore more fully.

The indigenous model

This section describes an indigenous approach towards resolving social conflicts. Our context will be the processes of development currently underway in the Himalayas. In this approach, there is an inherent awareness of the sustainability of life. Besides the physical and environmental aspects, our approach encompasses the social, psychological and spiritual aspects of life, all of which are deeply rooted in the Hindu world-view. The main concepts of the indigenous model will also be related to those found in mainstream psychology.

A note on methodology

This is a qualitative account of people's cognition which follows a holistic approach;

therefore, a short note on methodology should suffice. The study involves the people of the tiny kingdom of Garhwal in the western Himalayas. After independence, it was merged with Uttar Pradesh, and is now a separate state, Uttarakhand A holistic point of view guided the author's explorations into people's thoughts, feelings and actions. Next, an attempt was made to articulate the native understanding of the world through a model of holistic development. A significant fact is the author's involvement in this struggle for over 25 years (Singh, 2001). Thus, this account includes the author's reflections and experiences as a participant-observer. The author strongly identified with the people while joining them in foot marches, attending their meetings, giving interviews on their behalf, speaking for their cause at seminars and writing about their problems. Furthermore, his own experience as a native of the western Himalayas helped him to experience all of this from close range.

An overview of the Chipko movement

Since independence, a large-scale intensification of two development activities, dam-building and clear-cutting, has been taking place in the western Himalayas, with planners showing scant regard for an integrated vision of life. All this has happened with total disregard of the aspirations of the native people, making a mockery of their holistic approach to development.

To really understand the spirit of this social movement, we must visualize the situation in the Garhwal Himalayas in the late 1960s and early 1970s, when the folk poet Ghanshyam Sailani was struggling along with his compatriots to resolve a deep conflict. For many years, forest policies had been a matter of dispute in the Himalayan region and the healthy, symbiotic relationship between the local people and their forests was beginning to rupture. By the 1970s, the trouble was so bad that forests became almost inaccessible to the poor local folks, while a few wealthy contractors from the plains managed to lay their hands on the forest produce of their choice. The scale of denudation of the Himalayas by contractors, facilitated by government policies, was so enormous that the sacred landscape began to die.

Perceiving the helplessness of the local people and the disregard of the government, the deeply wounded folk poet seemed to almost foresee the next turn of events. His insightful solution to the impending threat on the lives of trees and the local folk was written in a poem at midnight. The message of the poem was very clear; there was a call for collective action, '*Hug the trees, don't let them be cut*'. These words, uttered by Ghanshyam Sailani[4] in 1972 during a period of social turmoil truly touched the hearts of the people.

The following years bore witness to the Chipko (hug-the-tree) movement in action, which the poet later declared as 'the War of Dharma'. In this way, an apparently selfish struggle for survival after getting embedded in the indigenous spiritual context took a new turn. This chapter explores the features, dynamics and outcome of this movement—an unusual socio-cognitive invention—a non-violent struggle for justice and sustainability in the Himalayas.

The people of the Garhwal Himalayas became aware quite early of the impending ecological crisis in the Himalayan region. As mentioned above, in the 1970s some local social workers picked up strands from the cultural heritage of India and neatly wove a grassroots environmental campaign known as the Chipko (hug-the-tree) movement (Bahuguna, 1974; Sarala Devi, 1980; Kunwar, 1982). Chipko had its origins in the environmental desecration of the Garhwal Himalayas, which was characterized by large-scale logging operations managed by private contractors, as previously stated. The villagers revolted against the logging policies of the forest department since it made their lives much more difficult and complicated. A hawk and dove conflict ensued. The doves, or native Garhwalis, engaged in a contest with the hawks, the government, by following a non-violent method of protest to save their forests from the axe of the contractor. In this unique, unprecedented game, the doves won the contest. The message of this non-violent struggle of the brave Garhwali people spread to distant parts of the world. The Man of the Trees, Richard St. Barbe Baker, was among the first to pay tribute to the thousands of Garhwali men and women by visiting their far-flung villages (Baker, 1982).

The people of Garhwal applied this non-violent method of resistance to those policies of the government that flouted the basic principles of sustainable development. The first phase of the environmental movement, devoted to the protection of Himalayan forests, continued from the 1970s up to the 1990s. During this period, the social workers of Chipko not only helped to foster an environmental consciousness, but also convinced the government to make a drastic change in its forest policy. The Government of India announced a 10-year moratorium on the felling of green trees in the Himalayas in 1983. The moratorium was reviewed in 1993, but the ban has continued.

During the transition period, approximately from 1985 to 1990, it appeared that the Chipko social workers may have lost interest. However, some of them soon started a new struggle to save the entire ecosystem and culture of the mountains. This new campaign was called Himalaya Bachao Andolan, or Save Himalaya Movement. The main objectives of this movement have been to stop the construction of big dams in the Himalayas and to generate electricity from small hydroelectric projects. The Ganga-Himalaya Kuti (near the upcoming 260.5m high wall of the Tehri Dam in the Garhwal Himalayas) became the centre of the non-violent protest against the aggressive development policies being implemented in the Himalayan region. As planned, the impounded water engulfed the Ganga-Himalaya Kuti in December 2001; however, the spirit of the non-violent struggle remains alive.

Other social workers involved with Chipko have continued their efforts to save the ecosystem of the Himalayas. Some in the Henwal Ghati who had also participated in Chipko have chosen to save the traditional varieties of crops grown in the Himalayan region (Prasun, 1996). Social workers in Gopeshwar and Kumaon have continued their efforts to save the green cover of the hills in various novel ways, including eco-development camps and the publication of a journal, *PAHAR*. Besides these workers, people from every walk of life and from all over the world have at times been involved in Chipko. The major achievement of the Chipko leaders has been to reach the masses directly, through popular media, by publishing small booklets in Hindi narrating the success stories and providing instances of environmental catastrophes.

The Chipko movement has attracted the attention of social scientists from all over the world. One after the other, researchers have climbed the hills of the Garhwal Himalayas and returned with a different story of the Chipko (Shiva & Bandyopadhyay, 1986; Weber, 1988; Berreman, 1989; Guha, 1989; Rangan, 2001). There can be no doubt about the academic excellence of these stories; however, it is unlikely that they have helped in the real cause—the 'upliftment' of the local population and the sustainable development of their precious environment. Although some of the authors of these accounts became 'renowned environmentalists' (for a self-appraisal, see Rangan, 2001), the people are still 'natives' for them, unable to comprehend their Western analytic finesse. This raises a second but more relevant question. Are we really trying to understand and honour the viewpoint of the local people? These academic storytellers have analysed the role of the local people with the untested propositions of other academics in the West. Those whom they study, on the other hand, have at least tested their propositions in the field of real life during their non-violent struggle.

The holistic model of development

The local people of the Garhwal Himalayas look at the developmental process holistically (see Figure 25.1). In their holistic thinking, the development of both the individual and the community is important. In their minds, the goal of the individual is to attain self-enlightenment through a way of life, one where there is harmony in one's knowledge, devotion and action. Following this path, if one learns that oak trees are good for the hills, one has to plant the oak species whenever there is an occasion to do so, and finally, one has to honour and even empathize with oak trees. One example of such integrated devotion, action and knowledge was Mira Behn.

She inspired the Gandhians who later spearheaded the Chipko movement in the Garhwal Himalayas. She also saw in the oak (*banj*) tree the all-important link between the Himalayan ecology and the well-being of hill people (Mira Behn, 1978).

At the community level, sympathetic scientists, poets and writers, social workers and others of a compassionate nature should work towards the welfare and sustainability of all systems, living and non-living. Sarala Devi,[5] another disciple of Gandhi, sacrificed her life for the people of the Himalayas. She ran a school for girls and also inspired and encouraged Sarvodaya workers to take up pro-environmental action. Those Sarvodaya workers were the forerunners of the Chipko Movement. They followed a holistic, sustainable approach to development and paid special attention to the cause of the poor. For instance, 'Bimla Behin and her husband Sunderlal Bahuguna, it will be remembered, chose to set up their ashram in the Simiyana valley because of the high concentration of harijans in that area' (Alter, 2002, p. 122).

The Garhwali people's understanding of development reminds modern man that his 'material development' is a path towards *vikṛti* (destruction). That this life is not intended to be a form of escapism should be clear from the call of Swami Chidananda, a *sanyāsin* and patron of the Chipko movement (Chidananda, 1987): 'We have to wake ourselves up and save the Himalayas and the Ganges'. There are deep spiritual (*Vedāntic*) roots to the Chipko understanding of nature, development and social action, and Chidananda (1991) explains that *prakṛti* has a dualistic nature. As a principle, it affects, or afflicts, *puruṣa*, and *yoga* has been especially developed to separate *puruṣa* from *prakṛti*. However, the phenomenal world in which we experience happiness and sorrow is also *prakṛti*, the Mother who sustains us all. Indeed, in this world, each person is instructed to follow a path that sustains life (*dharma*), pursue some economic means for day-to-day living (*artha*), participate in procreational activities (*kāma*) and work for the attainment of salvation (*mokṣa*).

Everyone has to engage in the *yajña*, the noble cause, of reviving our dying planet (Sarala Devi, 1982). We have to say 'Yes' to life and 'No' to death while following the path towards *saṁskṛti*, culture, characterized by qualities such as peace, happiness and fulfilment (Bahuguna, 1997). The hill people of the Himalayas are against those values that regard nature as a commodity to be exploited in the service of human greed and profit. In their world-view, the all-pervasive modern way of life in which we have acquired enormous information (a big head) devoid of compassion (no heart), and where there is little scope for manual work (feeble hands), is the path towards *vikṛti* or destruction.

The wisdom of the Himalayan people states that the very air, water and soil are the life-blood and main products of the forest, whereas for a silviculturist, the forest and timber exist only as a commodity to be sold for profit. And for the hill people, believing translates into doing. This phrase aptly describes the method of the Chipko social worker in fostering environmental awareness. For example, the Chipko activist would show the rural masses slides of the denuded countryside in the hills, of depleted water sources, fodder scarcity, soil erosion, flooded rivers and more to explain the negative consequences accompanying the destruction of the forest. The images are accompanied by a commentary that blends information from scientific studies with the wisdom of ancient Indian traditions (Tikekar, 1988; Bandyopadhayay, 1992; Pirta, 1994, 2000; Bahuguna, 1996).

In this model of sustainable development, some concepts are used that need further explanation for them to be related to mainstream psychology. The following section deals with this issue. The author's intent is to suggest some broad relationships between native understanding and the apparently similar issues of behavioural scientists.

Implications for psychology

Earlier studies conducted by the author indicate some similarities between certain concepts in the holistic cognitive model and corresponding concepts in mainstream psychology (Pirta, 2003, 2004, 2005a). There appears to be a considerable parallel in the meaning of the concepts and the underlying processes. Some of those concepts and processes are harmony, holism, development, and the relationships between thinking, feeling and behaving.

In recent years, several points of convergence have been visible between the Eastern and Western views of the environment. One is the realization that there is a need for a radical change in the human relationship with nature. To build a new relationship with nature, a holistic approach is imperative—one that is partly spiritual in temperament (Chaitanya, 2000) and is open to the native wisdom of primal societies (Goldsmith, 1998). Deep ecology (Naess, 1989) is also a meeting point for Eastern and Western streams of thought. Another area of convergence is emerging from the acceptance of holistic relationships by biologists and physical scientists, evidenced in the widespread citings of Lovelock's Gaia Hypothesis (Bunyard, 1996). Gaia is the living and all-encompassing whole of the planet earth and its atmosphere. In India, people relate to *dharatī mātā*, the Mother Earth, in multitudinous ways (Tripathi, 2002). We may have to develop a new vocabulary to describe these holistic relationships, because science customarily uses fragmentary language to narrate these phenomena of nature. It holds importance for us because 'The Hindu mind is essentially synthetic. It always analyses a problem into its various aspects, and considers them in their synthetic relation to one another' (Sinha, 1986, p. xvii).

There is some evidence to support a similarity between the concept of harmony as proposed in the indigenous model and as it is used in some theories of psychology. Gestalt psychologists assert that interest in environmental psychology was stimulated by the suffocating experience of the urban environment, leading to the study of living more in harmony with nature (Ittelson, Proshansky, Rivlin & Winkel, 1974). At the micro level, we may find a similarity with the models of Gestalt social psychologists such as Heider and Festinger (Rock & Palmer, 1990). Heider, in his principle of balance, proposes that individuals prefer harmonious cognitive relations. Along similar lines, Festinger's cognitive dissonance model hypothesizes that people seek to reduce inconsistencies in their beliefs, feelings and behaviours. We may also consider two examples where the need for exploring harmonious social relationships has led to the development of indigenous models of organizational behaviour in the Indian context (Gupta, Surie, Javidan & Chhokar, 2002; Batola, 2003). The primary reason suggested for these alternative models is the ineffectiveness of the materialist model of development in certain Eastern cultures. These investigators have independently found that a harmony of thoughts, feelings and actions is important in a variety of interdependent relationships within organizations. The importance of this has already been pointed out in relation to the indigenous model of development.

Our research on four issues related to environmental psychology and mental health provides evidence in support of the assertions derived from the local people's cognitive model. First, it may help us to understand pro-environment action in terms of thinking, feeling and behaving. It appears that the holistic approach of Chipko is likely to be more influential in creating environmental consciousness among people than other behavioural approaches (Goswami & Pirta, 2002). Second, it may be fruitful to examine the displacement of people due to the construction of big dams and their psychological rupture with the indigenous cognitive experience in conjunction with attachment theory (Pirta & Agrawal, 2003). Third, people tend to favour the humanistic approach characteristic of the holistic model rather than authoritarian policies in solving environmental problems (Pirta, 2005a). Fourth, holistic mental health programmes need to honour traditional healing systems, a trend indicated in our preliminary survey of mental health and its association with the institution of local deities (Pirta, 2005b).

Conclusion

In brief, the local people of the Garhwal Himalaya region, while resolving social conflicts, are engaged in a non-violent struggle, a *War of Dharma*, to save their forests and rivers, for ultimately these define their culture. The movement became known as Chipko (hug-the-tree), which later transformed into a broad-based

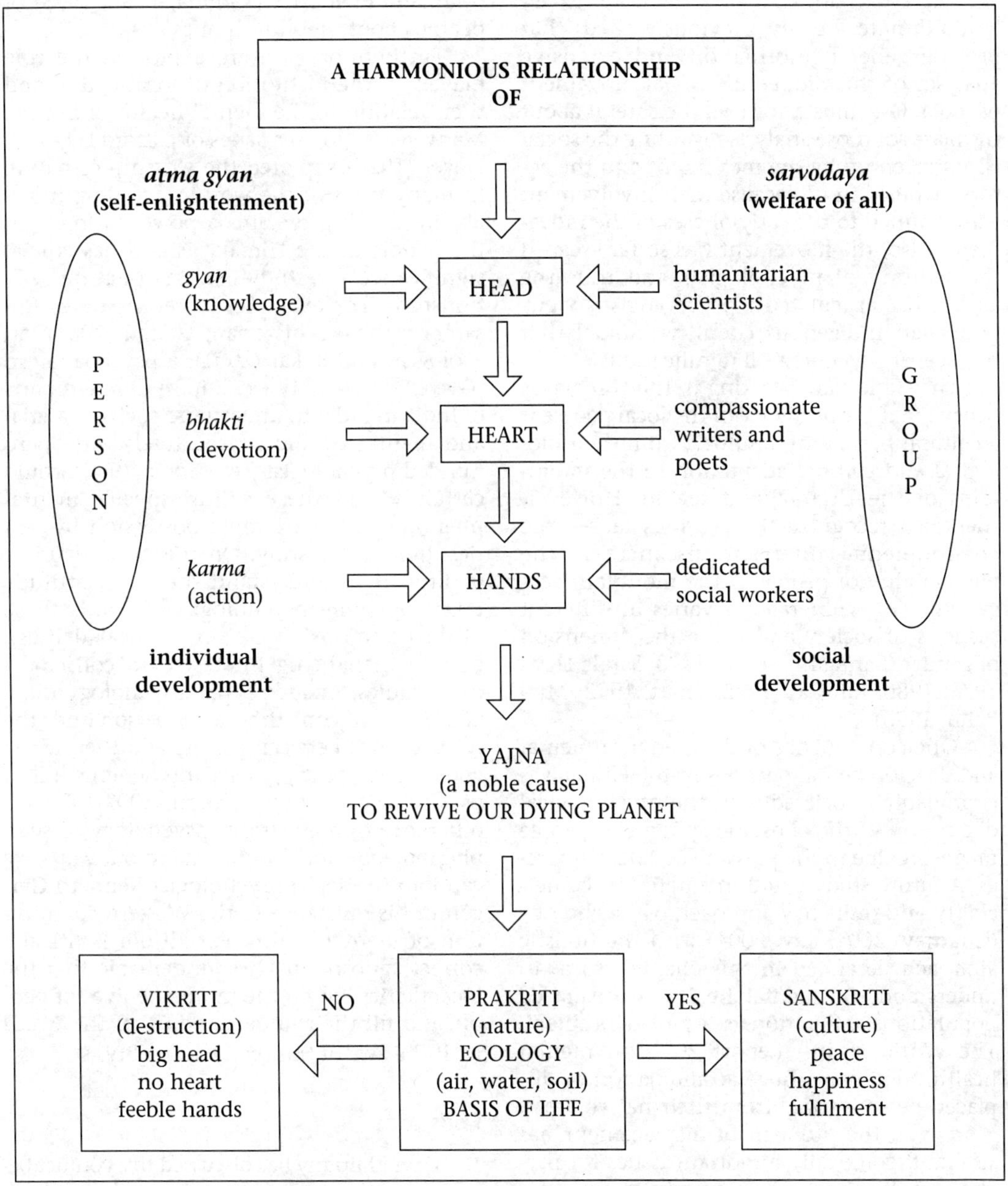

Figure 25.1. The indigenous model of sustainable development
(Adapted from Pirta, 2003, 2005a)

Himalaya Bachao Andolan. There are excellent alternate sources (previously cited) that provide general information and extensive analyses of this pioneering social movement of India. One must, however, be careful about the biases of those analysts regarding the social issues taken up by the movement and the actors involved in it, because their involvement was confined to the early phases of the movement. Also, the movement has so far escaped the scrutiny of psychologists and thus the author has articulated a psychologist's viewpoint—an indigenous cognitive model that has deeper psychological ramifications.

The Gandhians working in the Himalayas believe that the resilience of the local people is a cultural peculiarity resulting from their biological and cultural adaptation to the mountains of the Uttarakhand region. However, they also recognize that various large-scale environmental interventions increase the vulnerability of people in the mountain ecosystem. This vulnerability varies in different sections of society and along the dimension of gender (Bahuguna, 1968, 1973; Sarala Devi, 1978, 1980; Kunwar, 1982; Bhatt, 1992; Mira Behn, 1993).

One consequence of these environmental and developmental changes in the Himalayas is probably associated with the psychological dimension of the allostatic systems of people migrating due to the pressure of external forces. A future study could integrate the vulnerability and resiliency approach of psychology (Charney, 2004; Ray, 2004) with the holistic approach described in this chapter, so as to understand the mental health of displaced populations. Migration is a global problem. The World Health Report 2001 on mental health mentions a huge accumulation of displaced persons away from their native areas. Moreover, the problem of displacement has several theoretically important issues for psychology. Two such issues pertain to the areas of affect and memory. For example, we use Bowlby's theory of attachment (Stroebe, Gergen, Gergen, & Stroebe, 1992; Ciechanowski, Walker, Katon & Russo, 2002) to understand the psychological vulnerability of displaced people. Second, we are also interested in episodic memory (Tulving, 2002), especially the traumatic memories (Yehuda, et al., 1998) of people about their lost homes.

Furthermore, we are exploring the role played by the institution of local deities and their relation to the mental health of people. Many years ago, in a series of Gifford Lectures, Frazer (1926) explored the worship of nature in many parts of the world, including India. Nature worship remains a powerful force for the people in the Himalayas and has crucial significance for studies in man-nature relationships. For example, in recent times Kosambi (1975), a historian, Gadgil (2001), an ecologist, and Kakar (2001), a psychoanalyst, have explored deity worship in different parts of India in order to understand social, material and mental conflicts respectively. An open-minded psychologist (see Crook, 1997) would certainly find these culture-specific mental phenomena, for example possession by deities, quite interesting. On the other hand, it is difficult to understand the elitist attitude taken by some psychologists towards these 'little traditions' (worship of local deities), despite their being interested in consciousness studies, including parapsychology (Rao, 2001). At the same time, a lay person finds the relationships between people and their forest gods, water spirits, ghosts and demons full of psychological content (Singh, 2003). The indifference of mainstream psychology to such phenomena should not come in our way—we can join the social psychologist Kenneth Gergen in his resistance to the Western colonization of mental health. For all our politically correct agnosticism, it is undeniable that the local deities enrich the mundane lives of people and fill their understanding of the world with the awe of transcendent reality.

Endnotes

1 David Mitrany has discussed this conflict between the cognitive beliefs of two great leaders of India in the introduction to Pyarelal (1959).

2 These naturalistic studies inspired Pirta to undertake studies on two common Indian monkeys that have relevance to this issue (Pirta, 1990).

3 From Kenneth J. Gergen (n.d.) and personal communication through email in August 2005.

4 From the famous poem 'Chipko' written by the folk poet Ghanshyam Sailani on the night of December 12, 1972 (see Sunder Lal Bahuguna and Kunwar Prasun in a booklet published in the memory of this famous Garhwali folk poet who was born in 1934 and who died in 1997: 'Yad rhenge Sailani' published by Himalaya Bachao Andolan, Tehri).

5 Sarala Devi (Sarala Behn; Catherine Mary Heilman) and Mira Behn (Madeleine Slade) were European disciples of Gandhi, who chose Himalayas for their social work. They inspired local Gandhians like Sunder Lal Bahuguna, the prominent leader of Chipko Movement, and his wife Vimala Bahuguna (see Bahuguna, 1983).

References

Alter, R. C. (2002). *Water for Pabolee. Stories about people and development in the Himalayas*. New Delhi: Orient Longman.

Aurobindo, Sri (1998). *Essays in philosophy and yoga*. Pondicherry: Sri Aurobindo Ashram.

Bahuguna, S. L. (1968). *Madhya Himalaya: Vikas ki samasyain*. Tehri-Garhwal, U. P.: Parvatiya Navjivan Mandal. (in Hindi)

Bahuguna, S. L. (1973). *Uttarakhand: Pradesh aur prashn*. New Delhi: Himalaya Seva Sangh. (in Hindi)

Bahuguna, S. L. (1974). *Chipko andolan*. Ramnagar, Saharanpur: Garhwal Sabha. (in Hindi)

Bahuguna, S. L. (1983). What man does to mountain, and to man: A healing message for violent times. *Future*, first quarter, pp. 6–11.

Bahuguna, S. L. (1997). *Chipko message. Save Himalaya movement*. Ganga Himalaya Kuti, Tehri (Garhwal), U. P.: Chipko Information Centre.

Baker, R. St. B. (1982). Chipko—hug the tree people. In *The Chipko march*. Silyara, Tehri-Garhwal, U. P.: Chipko Information Centre.

Bandura, A. (2001). Social cognitive theory: An agentic perspective. *Annual Review of Psychology, 52*, 1–26.

Bandyopadhyay, J. (1992). Sustainability and survival in the mountain context. *Ambio, 21*, 297–302.

Batola, B. S. (2003). Ontology of labour and participation of youth in the labour force in north east India or hauntology of strategic action in the periphery. In A. Saikia (Ed.), *Population, environment, and the challenge of development* (pp. 326–344). New Delhi: Akansha Publishing House.

Berreman, G. D. (1989). Chipko: A movement to save the Himalayan environment and people. In C. Borden (Ed.), *Contemporary Indian tradition* (pp. 239–266). Washington: Smithsonian Institution Press.

Bhatt, C. P. (1992). *The future of large projects in the Himalaya*. Nainital: PAHAR, People's Association for Himalaya Area Research.

Bunyard, P. (Ed.) (1996). *Gaia in action: The science of living earth*. Edinburgh: Floris Books.

Chaitanya, K. (2000). Man, nature and cosmos in Vedic India. *The Ecologist, 30*, 21–24.

Charney, D. S. (2004). Psychobiological mechanisms of resilience and vulnerability: Implications for successful adaptation to extreme stress. *American Journal of Psychiatry, 161*, 195–216.

Chidananda, Swami (1987). An appeal to save the ecology of the Himalayas. In *The Chipko Message* (pp. 1–3). Silyara, Tehri-Garhwal, Uttar Pradesh: Chipko Information Centre.

Chidananda, S. (1991). *The philosophy, psychology and practice of yoga*. Shivanandanagar: The Divine Life Society.

Ciechanowski, P. S., Walker, E. A., Katon, W. J., & Russo, J. E. (2002). Attachment theory: A model for health care utilization and somatization. *Psychosomatic Medicine, 64*, 660–667.

Crook, J. H. (1997). The indigenous psychiatry of Ladakh, Part I: Practice theory approaches to trance possession in the Himalayas. *Anthropology & Medicine, 4*, 289–307.

Frazer, J. G. (1926). *The worship of nature*. London: Macmillan.

Gadgil, M. (2001). *Ecological journeys: The science and politics of conservation in India.* New Delhi: Permanent Black.

Gergen, K. J. The self: Colonization in psychology and society. Downloaded on 3 August 2005 from http://www.swarthmore.edu/SocSci/kgergen1.

Goldsmith, E. (1998). *The way: An ecological world-view.* Athens: The University of Georgia Press.

Goswami, K., & Pirta, R. S. (2002). An experimental study on inducing environmental concern in girl students. *Indian Journal of Applied Psychology, 39,* 5–8.

Guha, R. (1989). *The unquiet woods: Ecological change and peasant resistance in the Himalaya.* New Delhi: Oxford University Press.

Gupta, V., Surie, G., Javidan, M., & Chhokar, J. (2002). Southern Asia cluster: Where the old meets the new? *Journal of World Business, 37,* 16–27.

Ittelson, W. H., Proshansky, H. M., Rivlin, L. G., & Winkel, G. H. (1974). *An introduction to environmental psychology.* New York: Holt, Rinehart and Winston.

Kosambi, D. D. (1975). *The culture and civilization of ancient India in historical outline.* Delhi: Vikas Publishing House.

Kakar, S. (2001). *The essential writings of Sudhir Kakar.* New Delhi: Oxford University Press.

Kropotkin, P. (1914). *Mutual aid: A factor in evolution.* Boston: Extending Horizon Books. (First edition 1902).

Kunwar, S. S. (Ed.) (1982). *Hugging the Himalayas: The Chipko experience.* Gopeshwar (Chamoli), U. P.: Dasholi Gram Swarajya Mandal.

Lorenz, K. Z. (1976). *King Solomon's ring.* London: Methuen. (First edition 1952).

Mira Behn (1978). The one remedy. *Himalaya: Man and Nature, 2*(6), 4–5.

Mira Behn (1993). Himalaya ki seekh. In B. P. Nautiyal (Ed.), *Mira Behn: Gandhi ji ki putri evam shishya. Janm shatabdi granth* (pp. 115–129). New Delhi: Himalaya Seva Sangh. (Original article published in Harijan Sevak in 1951). (in Hindi)

Misra, V. N. (1995a). Ganga kiski ...! In S. L. Bahuguna (Ed.), *Jan-Jan ki Ganga-maiya* (pp. 14–16). Silyara, Tehri-Garhwal, U. P.: Chipko Information Centre. (in Hindi)

Misra, V. N. (1995b). Ganga ka shap kab utarega. In S. L. Bahuguna (Ed.), *Jan-Jan ki Ganga-maiya* (pp. 17–22). Silyara, Tehri-Garhwal, U. P.: Chipko Information Centre. (in Hindi)

Misra, G., & Gergen, K. G. (2002). On the place of culture in psychological science. In A. K. Dalal & G. Misra (Eds.), *New directions in Indian psychology* (pp. 405–424). New Delhi: Sage Publications.

Naess, A. (1989). *Ecology, community and lifestyle: Outline of an ecosophy.* New Yok: Cambridge University Press.

Pirta, R. S. (1990). *Cooperation in urban macaques and langurs.* Department of Science and Technology, Government of India, New Delhi (unpublished report).

Pirta, R. S. (1994). *Himalaya bachao.* Rajghat, Varanasi: Sarva Sewa Sangh Prakashan. (in Hindi)

Pirta, R. S. (2000). *Jaivik vividhata ki aor.* Amritsar: All India Pingalwara Charitable Society. (in Hindi)

Pirta, R. S. (2003). Native cognition of sustainable development in the western Himalaya. *Psychological Studies, 48*(2), 30–42.

Pirta, R. S. (2004). A holistic model of sustainable development: An Indian approach to environmental psychology. In K. Joshi & M. Cornelissen (Eds.), *Consciousness, Indian psychology and yoga* (pp. 379–390). New Delhi: Centre for Studies in Civilizations.

Pirta, R. S. (2005a). Folk wisdom and environmental crisis: A contemporary case study from the western Himalaya. In K. Kapoor & A. K. Singh (Eds.), *Indian knowledge systems* (Vol. 2, pp. 516–546). Shimla: Indian Institute of Advanced Studies, and New Delhi: D. K. Printworld.

Pirta, R. S. (2005b). Community mental health approach in rural areas: Developing the traditional institution. *Journal of Personality and Clinical Studies, 21,* 91–108.

Pirta, R. S., & Agrawal, A. (2003). The problem of forcibly displaced people and the psychological solution of rehabilitation. *Journal of Community Guidance and Research, 20*, 13–24.

Prasun, K. (Ed.) (1996). *Beejon ki virasat*. Khadi, Tehri Garhwal: Chipko Prakashan. (in Hindi)

Pyarelal. (1959). *Towards new horizons*. Ahmedabad: Navjivan Publishing House.

Rangan, H. (2001). *Of myths and movements: Rethinking Chipko into Himalayan history*. New Delhi: Oxford University Press.

Rao, K. R. (2001). Consciousness studies: A survey of perspectives and research. In J. Pandey (Ed.), *Psychology in India revisited—Developments in the discipline* (Vol. 2, Personality and health psychology, pp. 19–162). New Delhi: Sage Publications.

Ray, O. (2004). How the mind hurts and heals the body. *American Psychologist, 59*(1), 29–40.

Rock, I., & Palmer, S. (1990). The legacy of Gestalt Psychology. *Scientific American, 263*(6), 84–90.

Sarala Devi (1978). *Swasth arthavyavastha*. Pattikalyana, Haryana: Gram Bhavana Prakashan. (in Hindi)

Sarala Devi (1980). A blue-print for survival of the hills. *Supplement to Himalaya: Man and Nature, 4*(6), 1–16.

Sarala Devi (1982). *Revive our dying planet*. Nainital: Gyanodaya.

Sen, A. (1997). Radical needs and moderate reforms. In J. Dreze & A. Sen (Eds.), *Indian development: Selected regional perspectives* (pp. 1–32). New Delhi: Oxford University Press.

Sen, A. (1999). *Inequality reexamined*. New Delhi: Oxford.

Shiva, V., & Bandyopadhyay, J. (1986). The evolution, structure, and impact of the Chipko Movement. *Mountain Research and Development, 6*, 133–142.

Singh, C. (2001). The search for sustainable development in the Himalayas. An interview with environmentalist Raghubir Singh Pirta. *Mountain Research and Development, 21*, 30–33.

Singh, U. (2003). *Between worlds: Travels among mediums, shamans and healers*. New Delhi: Penguin.

Sinha, J. (1986). *Indian psychology* (Vol. I, Cognition). Delhi: Motilal Banarsidass. (Original work published 1958).

Stroebe, M., Gergen, M. M., Gergen, K. J., & Stroebe, W. (1992). Broken hearts or broken bonds: Love and death in historical perspective. *American Psychologist, 47*, 1205–1212.

Thakar, V. (1999). *Himalayan pearls*. Ahmedabad: Vimal Prakashan Trust.

Thakur, R. (1986). Tapovan. In S. L. Bahuguna (Ed.), *Hamare van hain jeevan pran* (pp. 14–34). Tehri-Garhwal, U. P.: Parvatiya Navjivan Mandal. (in Hindi)

Tikekar, I. (1988). *Shrimad Bhagvat. Aik yuganukool darshan*. New Delhi: Acharya Kakasaheb Kalelkar Smarak Nidhi. (in Hindi)

Tripathi, R. C. (2002). Aligning development to values in India. In A. K. Dalal & G. Misra (Eds.), *New directions in Indian psychology* (pp. 307–325). New Delhi: Sage Publications.

Tulving, E. (2002). Episodic memory: From mind to brain. *Annual Review of Psychology, 53*, 1–25.

Weber, T. (1988). *Hugging the trees: The story of the Chipko Movement*. New Delhi: Viking Press.

Yehuda, R., Schmeidler, J., Wainberg, M., Binder-Brynes, K., & Duvdevani, T. (1998). Vulnerability to posttraumatic stress disorder in adult offspring of holocaust survivors. *American Journal of Psychiatry, 155*, 1163–1171.

26

Spiritual Climate in business organisations and its impact on customers' experience

Ashish Pandey & Rajen K. Gupta

Introduction

In the midst of dynamic economic forces and technological breakthroughs, business corporations are set to play the lead role in shaping and creating modern society. If the revenues of governments and corporations are listed together, 77 of the top 100 are corporations (Assadourian, 2006). The top 100 Trans National Corporations alone account for one-tenth of the gross world product. With their tremendous resources and being embedded in the social system, corporations can exert extraordinary influence over the civic, economic, and cultural life of society.

The source of the market value of firms is shifting towards more and more intangible resources (Henson, 2003). Innovation, tacit knowledge, creativity and perhaps most interestingly, spirituality are recognized as new sources of competitive advantage. The suggestion of Mitroff and Denton (1999) about spirituality as the ultimate competitive advantage is based on their observation that now people, as part of their spiritual journey, are struggling with what this means for their work. Similarly, Nichols (1994) observed that creating meaning and purpose would be the most important managerial task in the 21st century. She emphasized that companies find ways to harness soul searching on the job. From this realization has come a call for nurturing and integrating at work all four aspects of human existence — the physical, mental (intellectual), emotional, and spiritual (Moxley, 2000).

In the Indian culture, ordinary vocations of life are accepted as a medium of spiritual growth. Vocations like farming or trading when undertaken with the intent of larger societal well-being and not only for selfish pursuits become practice of *karma yoga*, one of the three predominant methods of attaining spiritual enlightenment explained in the *Bhagavad Gītā*. This article takes forward these notions, adopting an approach of synthesis of contemporary research in the field of spirituality in management and thoughts in Indian traditional wisdom. A major thesis of this research is that spirituality of employees is reflected in the work climate. This may in turn affect the employees' service to the customers.

This study primarily aims at three things:

- to trace the conceptual underpinnings of the notion of spirituality in different streams of knowledge, particularly relevant in management,
- to present the development and validation process of the inventory to measure spirituality in the organisation climate, and
- to report empirically derived findings about the impact of Spiritual Climate on customers' service experience in business organisations.

With these objectives in view, first we describe

the conceptual and theoretical foundation of spirituality presented in the social science streams of 'well-being', positive and humanistic psychology and the Indian wisdom tradition of Vedānta. We then present some parallel thoughts amongst these streams and their relevance to spirituality in management. Third, we identify the conceptual convergence in 'spirituality in management' and report on the existing state of research in this field. Fourth, we describe how spirituality in management can be conceptualized as the Spiritual Climate at the workplace and also briefly present the process of developing and validating a scale on Spiritual Climate. Fifth, we present the study of the impact of Spiritual Climate on customers' service experience. We conclude by discussing the nature of hypothesized relationships, and the theoretical and managerial implications of this work.

Conceptual and theoretical foundation

Human personality and its functioning are studied in the human wellness stream. 'Human Wellness' literature conceptualizes human functioning as body (soma), soul (psyche) and spirit (pneuma). In the humanistic school of 'wellness', human functioning is viewed as a synthesized whole, and each component is seen as inextricably interrelated with the other components (Addis, 1995). Theorists in the field of well-being (e.g. Bensley, 1991) believe that the spiritual dimension is an innate component of human functioning that acts to integrate the other components. Within this philosophical framework, spiritual functioning has equal relevance to physical, mental, and emotional functioning; one cannot treat an illness or disturbance with one component without understanding the balance and interaction between all the components. Spiritual wellness represents the openness to the spiritual dimension. This openness permits the integration of one's spirituality with the other dimensions of life, thus maximizing the potential for growth and self-actualization. Charlene (1996) deciphers the four components of spiritual wellness:

1. meaning and purpose in life,
2. intrinsic values,
3. transcendent beliefs/experience, and
4. community/relationship.

Many authors, thinkers, and researchers in the field of humanistic and positive psychology have written about one or more of these factors. The following section briefly reviews the notions of some prominent psychologists about the spiritual aspect of human personality.

Spirituality in Positive and Humanistic psychology

Jung viewed religion and spirituality as reflective of the soul and did not discard them as delusion and distortion as Freud did. Religious ideas and experiences are psychically real, fundamental to human experience, and represent psychic evolution for Jung. Psychological problems are essentially religious problems for him. Jung (1978, quoted in: Keating and Fretz, 1990) said:

> A psychoneurosis must be understood, ultimately, as the suffering of a soul which has not discovered its meaning ... the cause of the suffering is spiritual stagnation or psychic sterility.

Jung thought that neither intellectual nor moral insight alone was sufficient and he found that for his patients over the age of 35, the real problem was finding a spiritual perspective.

In the later twentieth century, Freudian views were seriously challenged by humanistic psychologists. Taking the 'potential view' of the human psyche, most humanistic or positive psychologists indicated the tendencies of self-development, reflection, and transcendence in human beings. In his work, *On Becoming a Person,* Rogers (1961) expressed his beliefs about people having basically a positive direction toward their true being, the power to reflect and transcend in the 'fully functioning personality', and the innate capacity to flourish in the right condition.

In the same vein, Frankl (1978), in his book, *The Unheard Cry for Meaning,* recognized that the search for meaning is a vital avenue of human development. The views of Fromm (2003) are particularly important because he examined human development issues in the larger economic, social, and cultural contexts. According to him, humanistic alternatives of development are only a matter of awareness of being human. Describing the path of development for mankind in his book, *The Search for a Humanistic Alternative,* he writes:

> In this frame [humanistic development frame] of reference the goal of life is the fullest development of human powers, specifically those of reason and of love, including the transcending of the narrowness of one's ego.

Maslow (1968, 1971, 1996) expressed his human development views referring to 'being values' like wholeness, goodness, self-sufficiency etc. He considered these values as part of the human self. These being-values are not the same as deficiency-needs. They are meta-needs or growth-needs with which we can never get bored. This is in direct contrast to the basic needs, which we can definitely satisfy. Under good conditions people can integrate these values in daily life. Maslow (1971) described such integration in terms of transcendent self-actualization. For him, transcendent self-actualization carries a spiritual significance and manifests itself in the recognition of the sacred in life.

Positive organisational scholarship and spirituality

A complementary effort that draws on positive psychology is positive organisational scholarship, better known as positive organisational behaviour (POB). Luthans and Church (2002) define POB as "the study and application of positively oriented human resource strengths and psychological capacities that can be measured, developed and effectively managed for performance improvement in today's workplace". POB carves an agenda for how a focus on the positive opens up new and important ways of seeing and understanding organisations (Roberts, 2006). In recent years many studies have been conducted on the human tendency of self-growth and ego transcendence and its positive relation to mental health (Seligman and Csikszentmihalyi, 2000), creativity (Larson, 2000), and learning (Howard, 2002; Senge et al., 2005). Notions of spirituality as an intrinsic drive and motivation to seek meaning in life as having a place in the larger schema of existence are well established in the field of positive psychology and in many other disciplines in the social and natural sciences (Fry, 2003). Spirituality as an aspect of human potential is defined as the highest reach of human development (Wilber, 2004) and is apt to be part of positive organisational scholarship.

Spirituality and work: Drawing from the Indian wisdom tradition

Most of the wisdom traditions in the world have shown concern for spiritual growth. Vedānta, Confucianism, Buddhism, Christianity, Islam, have all emphasized the importance of nurturing the spiritual aspect of the human being. The importance of these traditions lies in the fact that they are based on both philosophical and experiential pillars. In the form of meditation, prayer, zen, or yoga, these traditions have produced many time-tested experiential methods to attain spiritual experience.

In Vedic literature 'truth' is analogue to *dharma*. The word *dharma* has originated from the root word *dhri*, meaning to uphold, sustain or support. The *Bhagavad Gitā* (3-35) teaches that to find out and follow one's own truth of right action (*swadharma*) is the ideal of human life. *Manas, buddhi* and *ahamkara* are the dimensions of the human self that act as modifiers in this search. One never gets fed-up of one's *swadharma*. One is not worried about results when performing one's *swadharma*. A true artist is not worried whether his art is appreciated or not. To him, the act of painting or singing is a reward by itself. One's *swadharma* gives maximum satisfaction and joy to oneself. A deeper connectedness with the work is the reflection of *swadharma* at the workplace. In contemporary literature this state is indicated in the book by Maslow (1971), *Psychology of Being*. He refers to the "intrinsic conscience" and writes that:

> This (intrinsic conscience) is based upon the unconscious and preconscious perceptions of our own 'call' in life. It insists that we be true to our inner nature and that we do not deny it out of weakness or for advantage or for any other reason.

Rogerian and personal growth psychologists also talk about 'discovering' the self. In the organisational change and leadership literature, Quinn (2005) explained that leaders are at their best when performing on the basis of their deepest values. The internal state while performing on the basis of one's deepest values refers to the 'fundamental state of leadership' or 'moments of greatness'. It is like being aware of our true nature or *dharma* and finding ways to express this in the job. Hence we take '*swadharma*' as a sub-construct from traditional literature for explaining spirituality in business organisations.

In Indian culture ordinary vocations of life are accepted to be a medium of spiritual growth. Action with heightened awareness becomes a spiritual pursuit and is called *loksangrah*. Radhakrishnan (1951) translated and defined *loksangrah* as 'doing work for world maintenance'. The *Bhagavad Gītā* says:

> *Saktah karmany avidvamso*
> *Yatha kurvanti bharats*
> *Kuryad vidvams tatha saktas*
> *Cikrsur loksangraham (3, 25)*
>
> As the unlearned act from attachment to their work, should the learned also act, O Bharata (Arjuna), but without any attachment, from the desire to maintain the world-order (trans. Radhakrishnan, 1951).

Loksangrah symbolizes the 'path of action' (*karma yoga*, one of the three major paths of spiritual awakening) and is nested in the thought of interconnectedness in the world. In its discourse on *karma yoga*, the *Bhagavad Gītā* elaborates on the interconnectedness of the world.

> *Annad-bhavanti bhootani*
> *parjanyaad-annasambhava*
> *Yagyaatbhavati parjanyo*
> *yagyah karmsamdbhavah (3,14)*
>
> From food creatures come into being; from rain is the birth of food; from sacrifice rain comes into being and sacrifice is born of work.
>
> *Aivam parivartitam chakram*
> *nanuvartyateehya ya*
> *aghaayur-induryaaraamo mogham*
> *paarrathah sa jeevati (3,16)*
>
> Arjuna, he who does not follow the wheel of creation thus set going in this world (i.e., does not perform his duties), sinful and sensual, he lives in vain.

The *Bhagavad Gītā* suggests that life is to be seen as an integrated, whole system and is to be lived with the awareness of wholeness. Worldly action, performed in harmony with the self (according to *swadharma*) and for 'world maintenance' (not for one's pleasure) becomes a spiritual pursuit.

Spirituality in management: Contemporary literature

Management academics has never been totally blind to the spiritual perspective of work. Quatro (2004) posited this point referring to the writings of Follett (1918) in classical management literature. Weber (1958) also called for developing management theories and practices by de-emphasizing materialism and individualism. In 1997 the Academy of Management (USA) set up an interest group on spirituality and religion at the workplace. Many academic journals like the *Journal of Management Education*, *Journal of Organisational Change Management*, *Leadership Quarterly*, *Organisation*, *Journal of Social Economics*, *Pfeiffer annual of training and consulting*, etc. have brought out special issues or published articles on different aspects of spirituality. Many terms like 'divinity', 'soul', 'managing with love' and 'rediscovering the soul' have started appearing in contemporary management academic and popular literature. Academic management researchers, management consultants and gurus, and practicing CEO's have all written about it. Corporate spirituality may well shape the organisation of the future (Zohar and Marshall, 2004). Organisations and groups like 'Spirit at Work' (www.spiritatwork.org) and Global Dharma Centre (www.globaldharma.com) are tirelessly propagating the ideas of spirituality at work for last many years in different parts of America, Europe, and Asia.

Spirituality at the workplace: The conceptual convergence

Thompson (2001) denotes that spirituality at the workplace has to do with how you feel about your work, whether it is a job or a calling. Sanders et al. (2004) define spirituality in the workplace as the extent to which the organisation encourages a sense of meaning and interconnectedness among their employees. Sheep (2004) defines spirituality at the workplace through four components: self-workplace integration, meaning in work, transcendence of self, and personal growth of one's inner life at work. Viewing the fundamental conceptualization of spirituality and definitions given in contemporary literature indicate that spirituality is a multi-dimensional, multi-level phenomenon. Acknowledging that consensus is lacking in the spirituality literature on how spirituality should be defined, we nonetheless propose that a conceptual convergence can be traced in the workplace spirituality literature: harmony with self, harmony in social and natural environment, and transcendence. While having the relational aspect more pronounced, the feministic view of spirituality also involves these three aspects (Fischer, 1988; Harris, 1989). Spirituality in management is a dynamic balance of these three factors.

Harmony with self

Organisations are places where individuals find meaning for themselves and evolve in their sense of meaning. Spirituality in organisations represents a specific form of connection to work that energizes actions. This aspect refers to the individuals' alignment to their work. It is about finding meaning and purpose in work (e.g. Ashmos and Duchon, 2000). This observation is parallel to the notion of *swadharma* explained earlier. Variables like the quest for feeling good, a profound feeling of well-being, and joy at work also indicate the underlying theme of 'harmony with self' at work. Inner life at work, self-actualization, or development of one's full potential represents this aspect of the literature.

Harmony in the work environment

The second dimension of spirituality the literature suggests is relational. This is manifested in the relation with social and natural environment. This spiritual dimension is manifested through a sense of community, being comfortable with the world, work place integration, connectedness, compassion, respect, humility and courage (Heaton et al., 2004), common purpose, inclusiveness and interconnectedness (Kinjerski and Skrypnek, 2004). This aspect of spirituality in management is seen in the form of a greater kindness and fairness and industrial democracy and shared responsibility (Biberman and Whitty, 1997; Marques, 2005).

Transcendence: The underlying aspect

In management literature, the transcendental aspect is related to a 'connection to something greater than oneself'. Ashforth and Pratt (2003) explain that the "something" can be "other people, cause, nature, or a belief in a higher power". McCormick (1994) talks about meditative work and describes it as the experience of being absorbed in work, losing the sense of self, and becoming one with the activity. Mirvis (1997) explains that the 'individual self' can transcend in four concentric circles of consciousness:

1. consciousness of self;
2. consciousness of others;
3. group consciousness;
4. to organise in harmony with the unseen order of things.

This explanation and observation is comparable with the notion of *loksangrah* explained earlier. Mirvis (1997) explained that transcendence at the workplace results in "company as community" and wrote that "Community is built upon transcendence of human differences rather than on commonalities". Transcendence results in the employees rising above traditionally divisive boundaries of hierarchy, demography, spiritual orientation, etc. (Sheep, 2004).

Impact of spirituality in organisations

The impact of spirituality in the business organisation has been studied in terms of job behaviour of employees and overall organisational performance. The literature correlating workplace spirituality related factors to employees' job behaviour converge into three areas: motivation, commitment, and adaptability (Jurkiewicz and Giacalone, 2004). The study by Scott (2002) demonstrated that organisations high on spiritual values outperform those with lesser degree of that, on the parameters of growth, efficiencies, and returns on investments. Nur (2003) reported in his doctoral research work that organisations managed by spiritual virtues (MBV's) earned better returns in the duration of 5 years. Colvin (2006) in his analysis (in Fortune magazine) of 'Best Places to Work' in the USA does not use the word spirituality but writes that these are the places where people find a purpose to work other than their pay cheques. The meta-analysis of Dent et al. (2005) showed the positive association of spirituality and productivity. Marques (2005) suggested that spirituality results in a unified pleasant performance and quality orientation of workforce which in turn result in excellent output and community orientation.

Need for study

Review of the relevant literature shows that spirituality at the workplace is reflected in the culture and climate. The literature also incorporates the linkage between spirituality at the workplace and certain job behaviours of employees which in turn affect the organisational performance. Our review suggests that conceptualization of spirituality and related constructs is a foundational requirement for better theorizing in the field of spirituality in management. The potential contribution of wisdom traditions is acknowledged in the literature at many places but systematic attempts at examining and integrating this with contemporary thinking are few in number. Predictive studies examining association of spirituality with organisational performance outcome are very few. To address these needs of research, first we made an attempt to develop the construct of Spiritual Climate in Business Organisations and studied the impact of the same on organisational processes like learning in teams (Pandey, 2010), organisational outcomes like customer service (Pandey et al., 2008), and antecedents of the construct (Pandey et al., 2013).

Development and validation of the construct 'Spiritual Climate at the workplace'

Workplace spirituality is intended to provide a means for individuals to integrate their work and their spirituality, which will provide them with direction, connectedness, and wholeness at work. Spirituality is reflected in the values framework of the organisation (Jurkiewicz and Giacalone, 2004) and values are reflected in the organisational climate. Hence, the concept of work climate may be a promising mechanism for understanding spirituality at the workplace.

A work climate is defined by the perceptions that are psychologically meaningful descriptions that people agree characterize a system (Schneider, 1975). The majority of the climate types are aggregations of perceptions of the organisation (Victor and Cullen, 1988). The prevailing perception about the work and immediate work group that have spiritual content constitute the Spiritual Climate. Like most other climate research, this is also grounded in the Gestalt psychology of Kurt Lewin. Organisational climate is a gestalt — 'whole' — that is based on perceived patterns in the specific experiences and behaviours of people in an organisation. A broad definition of spirituality is employed in developing a construct of Spiritual Climate that includes general and pervasive characteristics of the work group, and is defined as the collective perception of the employees about the workplace that it facilitates harmony with 'self' through meaningful work, transcendence from the limited 'self', and that it operates in harmony with the social and natural environment, having a sense of interconnectedness within it.

Variables of Spiritual Climate in business organisations

Connection with and responsibility towards the whole, recognition of the interconnectedness between different forms of life and existence, compassion, concern for the larger social and natural environment, these have been the basic tenets of spirituality propagated in the various wisdom traditions in the world. These variables are also common in contemporary literature on spirituality in management (Pandey, 2008). The construct of Spiritual Climate based on the synthesis of traditional and contemporary literature is elaborated in the current section.

Climate is a gestalt — 'a whole' — that is based on perceived patterns in the specific experiences and behaviours of people in an organisation. The perception of the work environment refers to organisation climate (Rousseau, 1988). These perceptions represent how work environments are cognitively appraised and represented in terms of their meaning and significance for individual employees in organisations (James & Jones, 1974). This is the intervening variable between the context of an organisation and the behaviour of its members, and attempts to understand how employees experience their organisations (Patterson et al., 2005).

Schneider (1975, 2000) suggested general multidimensional measures of climate and advocated a facet-specific climate approach where the climate is focused on something of interest. This line of argument facilitated the development of the measures of several dimensions of climate such as service, innovation (Anderson & West, 1998) etc.

Spirituality is reflected in the values framework of the organisation (Jurkiewicz and Giacalone, 2004) and values are reflected in the organisational climate. Hence, the concept of work climate was considered to be a promising mechanism for understanding spirituality at the workplace (Pandey, Gupta and Arora, 2009). The prevailing perceptions about the work and the immediate work group that have spiritual content constitute the Spiritual Climate. Based on the contemporary literature of spirituality in management and Indic wisdom traditions, the following variables of spirituality in organisations are identified which are proposed to converge into three streams: harmony with self, harmony in team environment, and transcendence or *loksangrah* (Pandey and Gupta, 2008).

- Meaningful work: Meaningfulness refers to work for life, not only for livelihood (Ashmos and Duchon, 2000). The work of Jung and Jaques King and Nicol (1999) suggests that the search for self, and inner self and fulfilment is the individual's spiritual quest which is realized through the medium of the work place.
- Meditative work: This is the deep experiential aspect of spirituality which is deeper than cognition and involves the affective, behavioural part of the self. It involves the experience of being absorbed in work, losing the sense of self, and becoming one with the activity (McCormick, 1994).
- Hopefulness: 'Hope' is an element in the emerging theme of 'workplace spirituality' (Fry and Matherly, 2006). 'Hope' refers to individual determination that goals can be achieved, and the belief that successful plans can be formulated and pathways can be identified to attain the goal (Snyder, 2000).
- Sense of community: This aspect of Spiritual Climate is about interconnectedness and interdependence of employees (Jurkiewicz and Giacalone, 2004). This spiritual dimension is manifested through a sense of community, being comfortable with the world, work place integration, connectedness, compassion, respect, humility and courage, inclusiveness and interconnectedness. These factors are reflected in the ease of collaborative problem solving at the work place.
- Authenticity: Authenticity is not just genuineness and openness, though that forms a central part of being authentic, but it is also socially situated. Authenticity is integral to the inner life which is nourished

through self-reflection and meditation (Gardner et al., 2005). This aspect is operationally defined as alignment of people's actions and behaviours with their core, and internalized values and beliefs.

- Respect for diversity: The Indian wisdom tradition maintains that the ultimate truth can be explained and attained in different ways. Adapting a plural way of accommodating the multiplicities and diversities of societies and individuals, it operates on shared opportunity and shared responsibility (Zohar and Marshall, 2004).
- Transcendence or *loksangrah*: This aspect and construct is drawn from traditional Indian literature; it is about the concern for the larger social and natural environment and defined as working for world maintenance. In the contemporary management literature it is echoed in terms of transcendence which is related to 'connection to something greater than oneself' that can be 'other people, cause, nature, or a belief in a higher power'.

Distinguishing Spiritual Climate from related constructs

As part of our conceptual development of the Spiritual Climate construct, we distinguish it from related constructs of Employees' Engagement, Ethical Climate, and Service Climate.

First, Engagement is similar to Spiritual Climate in that it refers to a deeper involvement in work and a feeling of connectedness at the workplace. However, Engagement and Spiritual Climate have important differences in terms of level of construct and contributing factors of the construct. First, Employees' Engagement (of which Q12 is the most widely used assessment tool) covers both individual level variables like role clarity and learning opportunity. It also covers dyadic level constructs like Appreciation, and collective level constructs like Enabling Environment, whereas Spiritual Climate is purely a collective level construct. Second, a sense of contribution to the larger social and natural environment, authenticity, and meaningful work are constituting variables of the Spiritual Climate which are not part of the Employees' Engagement construct.

Spiritual Climate is distinct from Ethical Environment also. Ethical Climate typically involves rules, laws, codes, along with caring and independence (Victor and Cullen, 1988). Similar to Spiritual Climate, Ethical Climate involves caring, but the scope of the Spiritual Climate construct puts it close to the spiritual aspects of the workplace unlike the Ethical Climate which focuses on the ethical temperament of the people creating the organisational climate.

Spiritual Climate is also conceptually distinct from Service Climate (Schneider, 1994). Service Climate captures the managerial behaviour and branch administration, whereas Spiritual Climate goes beyond the behaviour and captures the employees' experience of work and work group, but does not include administrative aspects.

The Spiritual Climate construct is also distinct from the 'Spirituality in Management' construct proposed by Ashmos and Duchon (2000). Like the Spiritual Climate construct, Spirituality in Management involves inner life, sense of community, and meaningful work. However, conceptualizing spirituality at the workplace as a climatic construct and inclusion of *loksangrah* (concern for social and natural environment), authenticity, and concern for family, extend the scope of the construct from the existing conceptualization proposed by Ashmos and Duchon (2000).

Exploratory factor analysis

Spiritual Climate is a collective (macro) level construct. Data from the employees of the manufacturing sector were used for exploratory factor analysis. This choice was justified based on the theory which suggests that core spiritual concerns remain the same in different walks of life (Maslow, 1996). Data of 162 executives from Indian public sector firms were used for scale development using exploratory factor analysis. The second phase of the study was aimed at validating the scale and to examine the impact of Spiritual Climate on customers' experience of employees and learning in teams.

Development and validation of the Spiritual Climate inventory

A theory-driven (construct-oriented) approach was adopted for the scale development of Spiritual Climate. Sub-construct and related items were decided based on the review of empirical, philosophical and spiritual literature. Perceptions about work and work environment amongst organisational members were collected on a Likert type scale format to assess the Spiritual Climate of the organisation. The development of the 'Spiritual Climate' inventory was completed in three major steps:

- Item creation,
- Validity check, and
- Reliability testing.

Scale development and validation process is given in detail in Pandey et al. (2009). Confirmatory factor analysis on the eight Spiritual Climate variables was conducted by Pandey et al. (2013) using AMOS. To assess whether the observed covariance matrix fits the construct model, we used the comparative fit index (CFI), normed fit index (NFI), incremental fit index (IFI), and the standard root-mean square error of approximation (RMSEA), and found acceptable results supporting the conceptually proposed factor structure of the Spiritual Climate construct. In a separate study Pandey et al. (2013) found similar factor structure of the construct of Spiritual Climate taking data from a cross-section of business organisations through Confirmatory Factor Analysis.

Spiritual Climate of the organisation and customers' service experience

Service satisfaction is a function of consumers' experiences and reactions to a provider's behaviour during the service encounter and service setting (Nicholls et al.,1998). Every service organisation routinely experiences opportunities to personally interact with their customers through their employees. Lack of concreteness of many services increase the criticality of employee service in the formation of customers' perception about service quality (Crosby et al., 1990). Thus, behaviour of the employee plays an important role in shaping the customer's perception of the service quality (Crosby , 1990), which in turn affects the future consumption behaviour (Chandon et al., 1997).

Behaviour is a function of the characteristics of the person and the environment. There has been an increasing awareness of the impact of organisational climate on employee behaviours. Studies examining specific dimensions of climate, such as innovation climate (Anderson and West, 1998), safety climate (Hofmann and Stetzer, 1996), and transfer of training climate (Tracey et al., 1995) have explained significant variance in specific employees' behaviours. In the same way the current study examines the impact of Spiritual Climate of the workplace on employees' service performance.

Literature review suggested that spirituality at the workplace makes the employees motivated, adaptable, and committed to their work. These qualities of employees should logically be reflected in service enounters. 'Moments of truth' are created in these encounters (Carlzon, 1997). During these encounters, the customer is mentally evaluating the service they are experiencing and forming a lasting opinion about the organisation. Additionally, spirituality at the workplace results in a unified pleasant performance and quality orientation of the workforce. Other things being equal, employees working in a Spiritual Climate are more likely to provide a better service experience to their customers. Hence, we proposed that:

H1: Workplace showing higher Spiritual Climate is experienced by the customers as providing better employees' service.

The following sub-hypotheses are proposed based on different aspects of Spiritual Climate:

H1a: Customers experience better employees' service in the workplace where employees find their work meaningful.

H1b: Customers experience better

employees' service in the workplace where employees experience sense of community.

H1c: Customers experience better employees' service in the workplace where employees are concerned about each other's families.

H1d: Customers experience better employees' service in the workplace where employees perceive authenticity in behaviour at work place.

H1e: Customers experience better employees' service in the workplace where employees work with a feeling of loksangrah, i.e., as if they are working for world-maintenance.

H1f: Customers experience better employees' service in the workplace where employees experience meditative work at the work place.

Customers' service experience: Nature of the construct

The logic of Grace and O'Cass (2004) was followed in this study where they describe three contributing factors of service experience, i.e., core service, service-scape, and employees' service. The factor, employees' service, is a function of variables like Prompt Service, Helpfulness, Availability, Trust, Safety, Politeness, Understanding behaviour, Personal attention, Being well informed, and Keeping promises. The statements in the scale were sentences like 'Employees in this branch give prompt service', 'Employees in this branch are polite', etc. Customers' responses were collected on a Likert type (1–5) scale based on these variables.

Responses from 15-20 randomly chosen customers were collected from each branch. Data of 462 customers from 28 branches were used for the study. The value of KMO and Bartlett's test was found 0.923 and the Reliability coefficient was 0.91 for the scale used for customers' service experience.

Testing hypotheses

To ensure the logical adequacy of the proposed relationship, the nature of antecedents and consequents were specified in the previous section. Respondents for the antecedent variable (spirituality in organisation) were employees of the branches, whereas respondents for the consequent variable (service experience) were the customers of the particular branch.

In order to meet the empirical adequacy criterion, variability in the nature of branches of the bank was ensured while collecting data.

Schneider (1987) states that it is the employees' behaviours that make organisations what they are. Drexler (1977) and Schneider (1987) argue for the validity of using employee perception to measure organisational (collective) level characteristics. Based on these recommendations the average scores of Spiritual Climate and employees' service of 28 branches were used to test the hypothesis. In order to check the strength of causality, regression analysis was performed on these scores.

The value of R was 0.411; R^2 and adjusted R^2 were 0.169 and 0.137 respectively. The standard error of estimate (0.195), F change (5.276) was significant at 0.03 p value and corresponding significance level, and the Durbin-Watson statistic value was 1.691.

This output shows that Spiritual Climate explains only 16.9% of the variance in customer service experience for this sample. R^2 is close to adjusted R^2 because there is only one independent variable. Significant F statistics indicate the overall significance of the model.

The Durbin-Watson statistic is a test to see if the assumption of independent observations is met, which is the same as testing to see if autocorrelation is present. As a rule of thumb, a Durbin–Watson statistic in the range of 1.5–2.5 means the researcher may reject the notion that data are auto-correlated (serially dependent) and instead may assume independence of observations, as is the case here.

Correlation between average scores of Spiritual Climate of the branches and their respective average customers' service experience was 0.41 at a p value of 0.03. This correlation score also supports the positive direction of the hypothesized relationship but does not reflect a strong relationship between Spiritual Climate and customers' service experience.

Findings of regression and correlation suggested that the linear relationship between Spiritual Climate of the branches and customers' experience of employees' service, though present, is not very strong. In order to clearly examine the impact of Spiritual Climate and employees' service we did further statistical analysis, i.e., t-test and Analysis of Variance, which are more sensitive and can bring out more clearly the difference in employees' service scores corresponding to Spiritual Climate scores.

Branches were classified as low and high based on their Spiritual Climate scores. Fourteen branches in each category were identified. The average employees' services scores of corresponding branches were compared through a t-test. The difference was found to be significant, p values less than 0.05.

Significant score of t-test for difference of means supports the main hypothesis (H1) that branches showing higher Spiritual Climate are experienced by customers as providing better employee service. Findings of t-test further strengthened the assumption that impact of Spiritual Climate is more pronounced in extreme cases.

To check this possibility the five highest (H5) and five lowest (L5) branches in terms of Spiritual Climate were identified. The difference of the combined mean scores of employees' service was checked through Analysis of Variance (ANOVA). Results of ANOVA showed that impact of Spiritual Climate is more pronounced in extreme cases.

Discussion

Our paper intends to contribute to the relatively sparse, but growing literature on spiritual aspects of work and its connection with business-related outcome, as little is known about the spiritual aspects of work and workplace. Following the suggestion of Whetton (1989), our aim was to parsimoniously organise and clearly communicate about the Spiritual Climate construct.

We hypothesized a positive relationship between Spiritual Climate and customers' experience of employees' service. An important criterion for the explanatory potential of the hypothesis is specificity of the substantive nature of the relationship between the antecedent and the consequent. A note on 'necessary or sufficient' conditions is called for at this stage. Findings of regression and correlation analysis suggest that the linear relationship between the dependent and independent constructs is not very strong. Empirical findings suggest that at least one variable, that is, the 'size of the branch' has also resulted in significant variance on customers' experience of employees' service. Other forms of organisational climate that affect the customer service have also been identified in literature (e.g., service climate, psychological climate etc.). These findings indicate that 'Spiritual Climate' is one of the necessary conditions for better customers' experience of employees' service but not a sufficient one. In furtherance to the discussion section we summarize the key theoretical implications of this research.

Theoretical implications

This study is a response to the call of Gupta (1996) for examining whether there is any place for the sacred in organisations and their development. Spirituality is a sacred aspect of the human self and a form of human potential. For some, it represents the highest reach of human development (Wilber, 2004). This study being focused on an aspect of human potential is aimed to contribute toward positive organisational behaviour (POB). POB scholars also seek to identify the role of organisational climate and its impact on sustained performance (Roberts, 2006). As mentioned in the review section, positive psychologists like Maslow, Frankl, and Rogers indicate that the human tendencies of search for meaning and purpose in life contribute to their larger social and natural environment. Like most of the POB research, this work sharpens the focus of spirituality as a dimension of human potential in the organisational context, conceptualizes spirituality as a climatic variable, and incorporates the generative mechanism of it in the form of employees' service.

This study draws on positive psychology and aims to carve a broader agenda for how a focus on the positive opens up different ways of seeing and understanding organisations and people working with them. Most existing foundational theoretical perspectives draw on agency cost theory and transactional cost theory. Transaction cost theory advocates tight monitoring and control of people to prevent "opportunistic behaviour" (Williamson, 1975). The agency theory subscribes to the assumption that managers cannot be trusted to do their job, which is to maximize shareholder value (Jensen and Meckling, 1976). Management education in general subscribes to these theories. Although the actual theories may not be presented to students and executives directly, they learn to subscribe to these theories and associated worldviews because they have been in the air, shaping the intellectual and normative order (Ghoshal, 2005).

These theories and the world views associated with them are useful in certain ways but do not capture the full essence of humanness (Ghoshal, 2005). The fact remains that human agents, on one hand demonstrate opportunistic behaviour but on the other hand also search for meaning and purpose in their work. In business, share holders' value is a sure deliverable (as transaction cost view suggests), but concern for the larger social and natural environment cannot be ignored. The rising problem of industrial pollution is largely a result of a myopic view of business and its deliverables. Now it is a widely recognized fact that sustainable development is possible only through sensible business with a concern for the larger good. Business organisations on one hand are sites of production and delivery of material and services, but on the other hand they are also sites of living where individual meaning and purpose are created, shaped and shared amongst the organisational members.

Spirituality represents the positive aspect of a human being which goes beyond opportunity-seeking tendencies. Vedānta views human beings as *'amritasya putrah'*, children of immortality. It views human beings as multi-potential, spiritual entities, seeking meaning in life and a place in the larger schema of existence. This view of the human being is an alternate for the 'utility optimizer' or 'opportunity seeking' view of the human being which at best considers a human being as a 'resource' for meeting business objectives. This study demonstrates that spirituality at work, i.e., harmony with self at work, harmony in the social and the natural environment and transcendence are meaningful to employees. These aspects go beyond the opportunity seeking and utility optimizing behaviour of employees. The study also demonstrates within the limitations given below that spirituality at work results in better service to customers. Indian culture, from time immemorial proposes four objectives of human life, the *purushārtha: Dharma* (Righteousness), *artha* (material wealth), *kāma* (satisfaction of worldly desires) and *moksha* (liberation). All these objectives are important and need to be pursued in harmony with each other. The findings of this study indicate that spirituality at work (related to *dharma*) and business outcome (customers' service in this case and related to *artha*) cannot only coexist but can be of complementary nature. The findings also suggest that positive organisational scholarship in general and spirituality in management in particular can enrich the foundational theoretical discourse in management. This may result in theories which can incorporate more wholesome perspectives of individual and organisational realities.

Managerial implications

The findings of this research indicate that facilitating employees to find meaning and purpose in their job can positively impact their service performance. The findings substantiate the observation of Nichols (1994) that creating a sense of meaning and purpose in the job may be the most important managerial task in the twenty-first century. Colvin (2006) in his report on 'Best Places to Work at America' also mentioned that these are the places where people find it meaningful to work. This study empirically validates these notions to some extent. Employees may derive meaning out of their job from the organisational philosophy, the nature of work, the organisational policies, leadership etc. Hence, strategic and leadership issues should be dealt with, keeping in view the human quest for meaning and purpose in life.

Pruzan (2001) suggested that socially responsible behaviour of the organisation positively affects the service quality. Empirical findings of the current study substantiate this notion and point out that a concern for the larger social and natural environment amongst the employees is reflected in customers' perception of the service. If employees perceive their work as a means or opportunity to contribute to a higher purpose toward community, society, or mankind, the work climate will be more positive and the customers' experience will get better.

Schneider et al. (1998) reasoned that specific strategic climates are unlikely to achieve the intended outcomes unless they are built on a strong foundation of generic work-facilitation climate. Spiritual Climate is one of the generic climates on which other strategically important climates (service climate, transfer of training climate, innovation climate etc.) can be built.

Research findings may be useful for Organisational Development (OD) work which aims at creating performance-oriented and humanistic culture. OD efforts can facilitate employees and leaders to find meaning and purpose in their work. Developmental work in the organisation should include efforts for building authenticity, and a sense of community at the workplace for better performance and results.

Limitations

At the level of conceptualization, this study is limited in terms of the number of wisdom traditions it surveys. The study largely refers to the *Vedāntic* traditional wisdom. Acknowledged here is that this is but one of the many wisdom traditions evolved in different cultures across the world.

This study was conducted in the positivist paradigm with the usual limitations of survey research design. This design is suitable for bringing out commonality amongst the respondents and leaves out the uniqueness of the individuals being studied.

This study is limited by its objectives and scope and does not accommodate the aspect of person-organisation fit. The study does not, for example, deal with situations where the people working in the organisation have a higher level of spirituality than the organisation and eventually do not find it meaningful to work with that particular organisation.

ADDENDUM

Spiritual Climate inventory (1 to 5 scale on agreement)

Harmony with self at work

1. My job helps me to understand my life's purpose. (Meaningfulness)
2. Working here makes my life meaningful. (Meaningfulness)
3. Working here is a means for realizing my real self. (Meaningfulness)
4. Work itself is enjoyable for me. (Meditative Work)
5. I am deeply involved in my work here. (Meditative Work)
6. I feel frustrated after working here (reverse). (Meditative Work)
7. People here feel that they are in charge of their own destinies. (Feeling Empowered)
8. People here are able to use their talents at work. (Feeling Empowered)
9. People in the group/department are able to apply their creativity at work. (Feeling Empowered)
10. People generally believe that business targets of the group/department can be achieved. (Hopefulness)
11. People doubt the success of any new plan for business growth (reverse). (Hopefulness)

Harmony in work environment

12. When stuck with a problem, people feel

free to ask for (choose a number for each one): (Sense of Community)
a. advice from colleagues
b. advice from a superior
c. help from their colleagues
d. help from a superior

13. People's actions here are aligned with their words. (Authenticity)
14. People own up to mistakes with others in the group. (Authenticity)
15. Manipulation is the way people perform their jobs here (reverse). (Authenticity)
16. Diversity of views is accepted in my group/department. (Sense of Community)
17. People here are concerned about each other's family responsibilities. (Sense of Community)

Transcendence

18. People here perform their duties as if they contribute to (choose a number for one): (*loksangrah*)
    a. the community
    b. the larger society
    c. mankind in general
19. People here try to avoid wastage of any kind (paper, electricity etc.). (Loksangrah)
20. People are concerned about the natural environment while working here. (Loksangrah)

The 2009 Pfeiffer Annual: Consulting. Copyright © 2009 by John Wiley & Sons, Inc. Reprinted by permission of Pfeiffer, an Imprint of Wiley. www.pfeiffer.com

References

Addis, L. (1995). Holism. In R. Audi (Ed.), *The Cambridge dictionary of philosophy* (pp. 335–336). New York: Cambridge University Press.

Anderson, N. R., & West, M. A. (1998). Measuring climate for work group innovation: Development and validation of the team climate inventory. *Journal of Organisational Behaviour,* 19, 235–258.

Ashforth, B. E., & Pratt, M. G. (2003). Institutionalized spirituality: An oxymoron? In R. A. Giacalone & C. L. Jurkiewicz (Eds.), *Handbook of workplace spirituality and organisational performance* (pp. 93–107). New York: M.E. Sharpe.

Ashmos, D. P., & Duchon, D. (2000). Spirituality at work: A conceptualization and measure. *Journal of Management Inquiry,* 9(2), 134–146.

Assadourian, E.: 2006, 'Transforming corporations', in *State of the World 2006.* New York: W. W. Norton & Company.

Bensley, R. J.(1991). Defining spiritual health: A review of the literature, *Journal of Health Education* 22(5), 287–290.

Biberman, J., & Whitty, M. (1997). A post-modern spiritual future for work. *Journal of Organisational Change Management,* 10(2), 130–138.

Carlzon, J. (1997). Putting the customer first: The key to service strategy. *The McKinsey Quarterly,* Summer.

Chandon, J. L., Leo, P. Y., & Philippe, J. (1997). Service encounter dimensions – A dyadic perspective: Measuring the dimensions of service encounter as perceived by customers and personnel. *International Journal of Service Industry Management,* 8(1), 65–86.

Charlene, W. E. (1996). Spiritual wellness and depression. *Journal of Counseling and Development,* 75(1), 26–36.

Colvin, G. (2006). The 100 best companies to work. *Fortune,* 1, 50.

Crosby, L. A., Evans, K. R., & Cowles, D. (1990). Relationship quality in services selling: An interpersonal influence perspective. *Journal of Marketing,* 54(7), 68–81.

Dent, E. B., M. E. Higgins and D. Wharff (2005). Spirituality and leadership: An empirical review of definitions, distinctions, and embedded assumptions, *Leadership Quarterly* 16(5), 625–653

Drexler, J. A. Jr. (1977). Organisational climate: Its homogeneity with within organisation. *Journal of Applied Psychology,* 62, 38–42.

Fischer, K. (1988). *Women at the well: Feminist perspective on spiritual direction,* New York: Paulist

Follett, M. P. (1918). *The new state: Group organisation and the solution of popular government.* London: Longmans, Green, and Co.

Frankl, V. (1978). *The unheard cry for meaning.* New York: Simon & Schuster.

Fromm, E. (2003). *On being human.* New York: Continuum.

Fry, L. W. (2003). Towards the theory of spiritual leadership. *Leadership Quarterly,* 14, 693–727.

Fry, L. W., & Matherly, L. L. (2006). *Spiritual leadership as an integrating paradigm for positive leadership development.* Paper presented at the Gallup International Leadership Summit, Washington, D.C. Available from http://www.iispiritualleadership.com/index.htm.

Gardner, W. L., Avolio, B. J., Luthans, F., May, D. R., & Walumba, F. O. (2005). Can you see the real me? A self-based model of authentic leader and follower development. *The Leadership Quarterly,*16, 434-372.

Ghoshal, S. (2005). Bad management theories are destroying good management practices. *Academy of Management Learning & Education,* 4, 75–91.

Grace, D., & O'Cass, A. (2004). Examining service experience and post-consumption evaluation. *Journal of Service Marketing,* 18(6), 450–461.

Gupta, R. K. (1996). Is there a place for the sacred in organisations and their development. *Journal of Human Values,* 2(2), 149–158.

Harris, M. (1989). *Dance of the spirit: The seven steps of women's spirituality.* New York: Bantam

Heaton, D. P., Scmidt-Wilk, J., & Travis, F. (2004). Construct, method, and measures for researching spirituality in organisations. *Journal of Organisational Change Management,* 17(1), 62–82.

Henson, R. (2003). HR in the 21st century. In R. Henson (Ed.), *Headcounts: An anthology for the competitive enterprise* (pp. 257–269). Pleasanton, CA: People Soft, Inc.

Hofmann, D. A., & Stetzer, A. (1996). A cross level investigation of factors influencing unsafe behaviour and accidents. *Personnel Psychology,* 49, 307–339.

Howard, S. (2002). A spiritual perspective on learning in the workplace. *Journal of Managerial Psychology,* 17(3), 230–242.

James, L. R. &. Jones, A.P (1974). Organizational climate: A review of theory and research. *Psychological Bulletin,* 81, 1096-1112

Jensen, M., & Meckling, W. (1976). Theory of the firm: Managerial behaviour, agency costs and ownership structure. *Journal of Financial Economics,* 3, 305–360.

Jung, C. G. (1978). *Psychological reflections,* Princeton. NJ: Bollingen. Quoted in: A. M. Keating and B. R. Fretz,1990. Christian anticipations about counselors in response to counselor descriptions, *Journal of Counseling Psychology,* 36, 292–296.

Jurkiewicz, C. L., & Giacalone, R. A. (2004). A values framework for measuring the impact of workplace spirituality on organisational performance. *Journal of Business Ethics,* 49(2), 129–142.

King, S., & Nicol, D. (1999) Organizational enhancement through recognition of individual spirituality. *Journal of Organizational Change Management,* 12(3), 234-242.

Kinjerski, V. M., & Skrypnek, B. J. (2004). Defining spirit at work: Finding common ground. *Journal of Organisational Change Management,* 17(1), 26–42.

Larson, R. W. (2000). Toward a psychology of positive youth development. *American Psychologist,* 55, 170–183.

Luthans, F., & Church, A. (2002). Positive organisation behaviour: Developing and managing psychological strengths. *Academy of Management Executive,* 16(1), 57–75.

Marcqus, J., S. Dhiman and R. King: 2005, 'Spirituality in the Workplace: Developing an Integral Model and a Comprehensive Definition', *Journal of American Academy of Business* 7(1), 81–92.

Marques, J. (2005). Redefining the bottom line. *The Journal of American Academy of Business, Cambridge,* 7(1), 283–287.

Maslow, A. H. (1968). *Towards a psychology of being.* New York: Van Nostrand Reinhold.

Maslow, A. H. (1971). *Farther reaches of human nature.* New York: Viking.

Maslow, A. H. (1996). Higher motivation and new psychology. In E. Hoffman (Ed.), *Future visions: The unpublished papers of Abraham Maslow*. Thousand Oaks: Sage.

McCormick, D. W. (1994). Spirituality and management. *Journal of Management Psychology,* 9(6), 5–8.

Mirvis, P. H. (1997). "Soul Work" in organisations. *Organisation Science,* 8(2), 193–206.

Mitroff, I. I., & Denton, E. A. (1999). *A spiritual audit of corporate America: A hard look at spirituality, religion, and values in the workplace.* San Francisco: Jossey-Bass.

Moxley, R. S. (2000). *Leadership and spirit.* San Francisco, CA: Jossey-Bass.

Nichols, M. (1994). Does new age business have a message for managers? *Harvard Business Review,* 72(2), 52–60.

Nicholls, J. A. F., Gilbert, R. G., & Roslow, S. (1998). Parsimonious measurement of customer satisfaction with personal service and the service setting. *Journal of Consumer Marketing,* 15(3), 239–253.

Nur, Y. A. (2003). *Management by virtues: A comparative study of spirituality in the workplace and its impact on selected organisational outcomes.* Unpublished PhD Dissertation in Proquest database, Indiana University, USA.

Pandey, A., & Gupta, R. K. (2008). Spirituality in management: A review of traditional and contemporary thoughts. *Global Business Review,* 8(1), 65–83.

Pandey, A., Gupta, R.K. and Arora, A.P. (2009). Spiritual climate of business organizations and its impact on customers' experience. *Journal of Business Ethics,* 88, 313–332.

Pandey, A., Bhattacharya, D. P., & Bose, S. (2013). Impact of spirituality of leaders at work and leaders' reputation on teams' spiritual climate. Accepted for presentation in Academy of Management Meeting, Orlando, Florid, Aug. 2013.

Pandey, A. (2010). Impact of spiritual climate on learning in teams in business organisation, International Conference on Science and spirituality: The growing interface, Aug. 2010, Sri Sathya Sai International Centre for Human Values, New Delhi.

Patterson, M., West, M. A., Shackelton, V. J., Dawson, J. F., Lawthorn, R., Maitlis, S., Robinson, D. L., & Wallace, A. M. (2005). Validating the organizational climate measure: links to managerial practices, productivity and innovation. *Journal of Organizational Behavior,* 26, 379-409.

Pruzan, P. (2001). Corporate reputation: Image and identity. *Corporate Reputation Review,* 4(1), 50–64.

Quatro, S. A. (2004). New age of age old: Classical management organised religion as underpinnings of the contemporary organisational spirituality movement. *Human Resource Development Review,* 3(3), 228– 249.

Quinn, R. (2005). Moments of greatness: Entering the fundamental state of leadership, *Harvard Business Review,* 83(7/8), 74-83

Radhakrishnan, S. (1951). *Indian philosophy.* London: George Allen & Unwin.

Roberts, L. M. (2006). Shifting the lens on organisational life: The added value of positive scholarship. *Academy of Management Review,* 31(2), 292–305.

Rogers, C. (1961). *On becoming a person.* New York: The Riverside Press.

Rousseau, D . M. (1988). 'The construction of climate in organization research'. In Cooper, C. L. and Robertson, I.T. (Eds) *International Review of Industrial and Organizational Psychology,* 3; 139-159. Chichester: Wiley.

Sanders, J. E., Hopkins, W. E., & Geroy, G. D. (2004). The spirituality–leadership–commitment relationship. *Journal of Management, Spirituality and Religion,* 2(1), 21–30.

Schneider, B. (1975). Organisational climate: An essay. *Personnel Psychology,* 28, 447–479.

Schneider, B. (1987). The people make the place. *Personnel Psychology,* 40, 437–453.

Schneider, B. (1994). HRM – A service perspective: Towards a customer-focused HRM. *International Journal of Service Industry Management,* 5(1), 64–76.

Schneider, B., Bowen, D. E., Ehrhart, M. G., & Holcombe, K. M. (2000). The climate for service: Evolution of a construct. In N. M. Ashkanasy, C. Wilderom, & M. F. Peterson (Eds.), *Handbook of organizational culture and climate,* 21-36. Newbury Park, CA: Sage.

Schneider, B., White, S. S., & Paul, M. C. (1998). Linking service climate and customer perceptions of service quality: Test of a causal model. *Journal of Applied Psychology,* 83, 150–163.

Scott, Q. (2002). *Organisational spirituality normativity as an influence on organisational culture and performance in fortune 500 firms.* Unpublished Ph. D. Dissertation, Iowa University, USA.

Seligman, M. E. P., & Csikszentmihalyi, M. (2000). Positive psychology: An introduction. *American Psychologist,* 55(1), 5–14.

Senge, P., Flowers, B. S., & Scharmer, C. O. (2005). *Presence: Human purpose and the field of the future.* New York: SoL edition.

Sheep, M. L. (2004). Nailing down gossamer: A valid measure of the person organisation fit of workplace spirituality. Academy of Management, Best Conference Paper MSR.

Snyder, C. R. (2000). *Handbook of hope.* San Diego: Academic Press.

Thompson, W. (2001). Spirituality at work. *Executive Excellence,* 18(9), 10.

Tracey, J. B., Tannenbaum, S. I., & Kavangagh, M. J. (1995). Applying trained skills on the job: The importance of the work environment. *Journal of Applied Psychology,* 80, 239–252.

Victor, B., & Cullen, J. B. (1988). Organisational bases of ethical climate. *Administrative Science Quarterly,* 33(1), 101–125.

Weber, M.: 1958, *The Protestant ethic and spirit of capitalism* (transl. T. Parson). New York: Scribner's. Quoted in B. Dyck and D. Schroeder (2005). Management, theology and moral points of view: Towards an alternative to the conventional materialist-individualist ideal-type of management. *Journal of Management Studies,* 42 (4): 705-735.

Whetton, D. A. (1989). What constitutes a theoretical contribution. *Academy of Management Review,* 14, 490–495.

Wilber, K. (2004). Integrating spirituality at work: An interview with Ken Wilber (Interviewer T. C. Pau-chant). *Journal of Management, Spirituality and Religion,* 1(1), 113–130.

Williamson, O. E. (1975). *Markets and hierarchies: Analysis and antitrust implications.* New York: Free Press.

Zohar, D., & Marshall, I. (2004). *Spiritual capital: Wealth we can live by.* London: Bloomsbury.

Glossary of words of Sanskrit or Pali origin

List of Contributors

Index

Glossary of words of Sanskrit or Pali origin

For abbreviations, see list at the end of the Glossary

A

abhidharma, (Sanskrit), *'abhidhamma'* (Pali), the Buddhist philosophy.

abhva, nescience, non-being; usually translated as 'terrible', 'monstrous' etc.

ācārya, a teacher, a spiritual guide who knows what to do and how to proceed, from *ācāra*, 'practice'.

adbhuta, transcendental, beyond being/becoming, 'wonderful'.

adharma, that which is not upholding existence, a-*dharma*, or not in accordance with *dharma* (see *'dharma'*).

ādhibhautika, belonging to the five elements, elemental.

ādhidaivika, belonging to the gods, or faculties of consciousness known as *'annam prāṇam cakṣuḥ śrotraṃ mano vācam'* (TaitUp 3.2); see also KeUp 1.1-9 etc.

ādhyātmika, belonging to the Self; in epistemology of consciousness, psychological.

aditi, infinite Consciousness, the divine Mother, the mother of the godheads named Ādityas; in the later philosophical language she is known as *parā prakṛti* (*Gītā* etc.).

āditya-gaṇa, the group of solar deities, children of Aditi: Varuṇa, Mitra, Aryaman, Bhaga, Dakṣa, Aṃśa, Sūrya or Savitṛ; later there were mentioned a few more: Indra, Viṣṇu, Dhātṛ etc., the number of which grows up to 12 in the later literature of *Brāhmaṇas* symbolising the Sun in the 12 months of the year (ŚBr 4.5.7.2 etc.).

āditya, a solar deity, a child of the Infinity, Aditi; there are seven original Ādityas mentioned in the *Veda* (see *'āditya-gaṇa'*); in the later literature it is used as the name of the Sun.

ādityas, see *'āditya-gaṇa'*.

advaita, non-dualistic, unique, monistic, identity of spirit and matter.

āgama, a tradition handed down; Tantra of the Śaiva and Śākta traditions.

agni, a sacrificial fire; universal godhead growing within the creation, incarnating and manifesting the gods.

ahambhāva, see *'ahaṃkāra'*, ego-sense; lit. 'saying or making "I"'; conception of one's individuality, self-consciousness (ChaUp etc.); the making of self, thinking of self, egotism (MBh etc.); the third of the eight sources of creation; the conception of individuality, individualization (in Sāṁkhya phil.).

aitareya, prop. name of *ṛṣi*; son of Itarā, he is known as Mahīdāsa Aitareya, the author of the *Ṛg Vedic* tradition of *Aitareya Brāhmaṇa*, *Āraṇyaka* and *Upaniṣad*.

ājñā, a command, an order; the fifth *cakra* in *sūkṣma śarīra*, subtle body, located in-between the eye brows, the *cakra* of will power, known as the third eye.

ājñāna, one of the four major faculties of consciousness, the operation by which consciousness dwells on an image of things so as to hold, govern and possess it in power (see *'prajñāna'*).

akṣara, 'imperishable', sound or syllable AUM. In the eighth chapter of the *Gītā*: *akṣara* and *kṣara puruṣa*: imperishable and perishable spirit.

amṛta, immortal, immortality, the nectar of immortality.

aṃśa, N. of one of the seven Ādityas; lit. 'a portion of the divine'; a soul created for the sake of manifestation on the Supramental plane.

anāhata, lit. 'unbeaten', the fourth *cakra* in the heart centre of the *sūkṣma śarīra*, subtle body.

ānanda, bliss, the transcendental Bliss as a part and result of relation of *sat* and *cit*, divine Being and Consciousness.

anātman, not self, another, 'having no self', 'something different from spirit or soul'.

annamaya, material, lit. 'made of matter'.

annamayapuruṣa, 'self of material body', *puruṣa* made out of matter (TaitUp 2).

antaḥkaraṇa, the internal organ, the seat of thought and feeling, the mind, the thinking faculty, the heart, the conscience, the soul.

antarātman, the inner self, the psychic being (SA), the soul, the internal feelings, the heart or mind (MaitrS etc.).

antarikṣa, the space between heaven and earth; the internal space of life, vital plane of consciousness.

apāna, the breathing out; one of the five major *prāṇas*, the lower breath located in the navel and connected with *mṛtyu*, death; it is by *apāna* that *ātman* could come into material body, by death it could stay in the material form (AitUp 1.3); in the later literature it is located in the anus.

aparā, lit. 'not higher', 'lower' nature.

artha, aim, purpose, meaning, reason, object, thing, wealth etc.

aryaman, one of the seven Ādityas, always mentioned together with Mitra and Varuṇa; the light of the divine Consciousness working as Force (SA).

āsana, lit. 'sitting'; sitting in a particular posture (eighty-four postures are mentioned, such as: *padmāsana*, *bhadrāsana*, *vajrāsana*, *vīrāsana*, *svastikāsana* etc.).

asmitā, lit. 'I-ness', egoism.

āśrama, a hermitage, a place in the forest for ascetics and sages to live; four major periods in the life of a *Brahmin*: *brahmacārin*, 'the student of the *Veda*'; *gṛhastha*, 'the household'; *vānaprastha*, 'living in the woods'; *sannyāsin*, 'the ascetic'.

aṣṭāṅga, consisting of eight parts; the *Yoga-sūtra* of Patañjali is sometimes called 'aṣṭāṅgayoga'.

asura, lit. '*asu-ra*', 'having power of being'; *asu* is a power of existence. In the *Veda* the great godheads, such as Varuṇa, Mitra, Aryaman, Agni, Indra etc., are called *Asuras*. They have their own power of existence. In the later literature this power to endure was assigned to the spirits of the lower hemisphere only, to the demons and the whole interpretation of the word has changed into a-*sura*, lit. 'no light'. In the *Purāṇas*, *Asuras* are the elder brothers of the gods and are in constant battle with them. *Asuras* belong to the first stage of creation, the fall of the Spirit, and therefore are older and stronger than gods in the field of manifestation. Gods belong to the second stage of creation, who came down to upraise the fallen spirits.

asūyā, envy, jealousy.

aśvins, *aśvinā du.*, lit. 'two charioteers', two gods, who come in a golden chariot in the sky before dawn; they bring treasures and cure illnesses; they are known as the physicians of heaven (RV).

ātma-bhāva, lit. 'becoming of the Self'; existence of the soul (ŚvetUp); (in Buddhism) the self, proper or peculiar nature; the body.

ātmabodha, lit. 'knowledge of the Self'; the work of Śrī Śaṅkarācārya.

ātman, the self; the soul, the principle of life; used often as the word 'self' is used in English; distinguished from and one with *Brahman*, universal Spirit. When *Brahman* becomes self-aware it is distinguished as *ātman*. *Ātman* has three major poises: 1) *Paramātman*, the supreme universal Self, 2) *Ātman*, the supreme individualised Self, unborn and everpresent and 3) *Antarātman*, the individual soul involved in manifestation, the evolving Psychic Being (SA).

avatāra, lit. 'descending down', incarnation of a deity on earth; 10 *avatāras* of Viṣṇu are well-known.

avidyā, lit. 'not knowing', 'not finding', searching but not finding; partial knowledge as compared to *vidyā*, 'full knowledge'; ignorance; partial knowledge in time and space (ĪśUp 9-11).

avyakta, lit. 'unmanifest'; in Sāṁkhya philosophy 'the unevolved (Evolver of all things)', the primary germ of nature, primordial element or productive principle whence all the phenomena of the material world come into being (KaṭhUp, Sāṁkhyak etc.).

āyu, living being, a group of living beings (mankind); a life force.

āyurveda, the science of health or medicine (it is classed among sacred sciences, and considered as a supplement of the *Atharva-veda*).

B

bhaga-vat, Nom. '*bhagavān*'; lit. 'the Possessor or the Lord of Bliss', usually translated as 'Blissful Lord', Śrī Kṛṣṇa, Viṣṇu etc.

bhaga, a Bliss; from the root *bhaj*, 'to share the enjoyment'; one of the seven Ādityas; a solar deity, a godhead representing bliss in the *Veda*.

bhagavad-gītā, lit. '*The Song of the Blissful Lord* (Kṛṣṇa)'.

bhāgavata, lit. 'about the Blissful Lord (Kṛṣṇa)'; N. of one of the major *Purāṇas*.

bhakta, lit. 'shared', or 'whose joy is shared', implying 'with the Lord'; a devotee.

bhakti, lit. 'sharing', implying 'joy with the Lord'; devotion, devotional love.

bhaktiyoga, 'the *yoga* or union with the Divine through love and devotion'.

bharadvāja, N. of a *ṛṣi*; in the *Ṛg Veda* he is the author of the sixth book.

bhāva, lit. 'a state of being'; can be any state of emotion, feeling etc., in the later literature means mainly the emotion.

bhaya, fear.

bhoga, 'enjoyment', from the root *bhuj*, to enjoy.

bhoktā, 'the enjoyer'; phil. the one who partakes of all the happenings, sacrifices or offerings (see '*adhiyajña*' in the *Gītā*).

bhū, 'earth', lit. 'a level of being/becoming'.

bhūmīḥ, 'earths'; *tisro bhūmīḥ*, 'three earths' are supporting the three spaces, *trī rajāṃsi*, which support the three heavens, *tisro dyāvaḥ*, which are projected from the three luminous worlds of *Svar*, *trī rocanā*, which are the product of the triple power of the Supermind, *tri aryamā* (RV 5.29.1).

bhūta, lit. 'that which has become', ppp from root *bhū*, to become, to be; 'the past', 'creature which is born on earth'; an element, there are five great elements, *pañca mahābhūtāni*, known as ether, air, fire, water, earth: *ākāśa*, *vāyu*, *agni*, *āpaḥ*, *pṛthivī* (TaitUp 2.1); a spirit (good or evil), the ghost of a deceased person, a demon etc. (Up, Mn etc.); see also '*ādhibhautika*'.

bodhisattva, m. 'one whose being is awakened', one who is on the way to the attainment of perfect knowledge (i.e. a Buddhist saint when he has only one birth to undergo before obtaining the state of a supreme *Buddha* and then *Nirvāṇa*). The early doctrine had only one *bodhi-sattva*, viz. Maitreya; the later reckoned many more.

brahmā, Nom. from *brahman* m.; lit. 'the speaker of *brahma*, a *mantra*'; a priest in the sacrificial ceremonies; 'a creator' known in the later literature as Prajāpati; in the *Purāṇas* he is spoken of as part of the divine Trinity of Brahmā-Viṣṇu-Śiva, Creator-Preserver-Destroyer.

brahma, Nom. from *brahman* n.; *Veda*, lit. 'expanding one', a *mantra* rising from the heart, the lord of which is Brahmaṇaspati, the *Guru* of the gods in the *Veda*. In the later literature Brahma is the all-embracing Spirit.

brāhmaṇa, n. *Brahmanic* literature (*Aitareya Brāhmaṇa*, *Taittirīya Brāhmaṇa*, *Kauṣitaki Brāhmaṇa* etc.); m. a person in the *varṇa* of *brāhmaṇa*, *Brahmin*.

brahmāsmi, one of the *mahāvākya* of the *Upaniṣads*: 'I am Brahman'.

bṛhadāraṇyaka, N. of *Upaniṣad*, which is a part of *Śatapatha Brāhmaṇa* of *Śukla Yajurveda*.

buddhi, f. reason, intellect (Mn, MBh etc.); comprehension, apprehension, understanding. The second *tattva* of 25 *tattvas* of Sāṁkhya philosophy; the higher mind as distinguished from the sense-mind, *manas*.

C

caitanya, lit. 'conscious'; soul, spirit; N. of a reformer of the Vaishnava tradition (1485 AD).

caitya, (fr. cit) the individual soul (BhP iii, 26); the Psychic Being (SA), see '*antarātman*'.

cakra, wheel, discus; there are seven *cakras* in the *sūkṣma śarira*, these are *sahasrāra*, *ājñā*, *viśuddha*, *anāhata*, *maṇipūra*, *svādhiṣṭhāna*, *mūlādhāra*.

carakasaṃhitā, Caraka's book on medicine.

cārvāka, N. of a materialistic philosopher (whose doctrines are embodied in the *Bārhaspatya-sūtras*).

cetana, percipient, conscious, sentient, intelligent; soul, mind; (*ā*) f. consciousness, understanding, sense, intelligence.

chāndogya, doctrine of the *chando-gas*, 'the singers in meters'; a *Brāhmaṇa* of the *Sāma Veda* (incl. the ChaUp).

cikitsā, medical attendance, practice or science of medicine.

cit-śakti, the power of Consciousness or 'Consciousness-force'.

cit, thought, intellect, spirit, soul; pure Thought; the divine Consciousness.

citta-vṛtti, state of mind, feeling, emotion; continuous course of thoughts (opposed to concentration), thinking, imagining.

citta, lit. 'noticed', 'perceived', 'realised in consciousness'; the stuff of consciousness realised as memory.

cūḍāmaṇi, lit. 'a jewel worn by men and women on the top of the head' (MBh); N. of the work of Śaṅkarācārya.

D

dakṣa, one of the seven Ādityas; represents the power of Thought, the all-discerning and all-distributing power of the divine Mind (SA).

dakṣiṇa, able, clever; right (not left); south, southern (also N. of a fire on the altar of *Agnihotra* rite) (RV); a donation, gift (for the priest of the sacrificial ceremony), reward.

darśana, lit. 'view'; 6 major philosophical systems: Pūrva-Mīmānsā by Jaimini, Uttara-Mīmānsā by Bādarāyaṇa, Nyāya by Gotama, Vaiśeṣika by Kaṇāda, Sāṁkhya by Kapila, Yoga by Patañjali.

dehin, lit. 'one who has a body', corporeal, man, a soul.

devās, gods, divine beings; lit. 'shining beings' from root *div*, to shine.

dhairya, intelligence (from root *dhī*, to think); firmness, steadfastness (from root *dhṛ*, to hold).

dhammapada, Buddhist treatise on *dharma* (3rd century BC).

dhāraṇā, lit. 'holding', 'concentrating (mind upon)'; the sixth stage of Patañjali Yoga before *dhyāna*, 'meditation'.

dhātu, lit. 'an establishment or placement' from root *dhā*; a basic layer, stratum, constituent part, ingredient; element, such as *mahābhūta* or a constituent element of the body or primary element of the earth; in gram. a verbal root or stem.

dhī, thought, esp. religious thought, reflection, meditation, devotion, prayer; pl. holy thoughts personified (RV); understanding, intelligence, wisdom; personified as the wife of Rudra-Manyu (BhP).

dhṛti, lit. 'holding steady' from the root *dhṛ*, to hold; steadfastness, steadiness, firmness etc.

dhyāna, meditation, thought, reflection; the seventh stage of Patañjali Yoga before *samādhi*; (in Buddhism) divided into 4 stages.

diti, lit. 'dividing'; in the *Veda* the Creatrix of a lower hemisphere of darkness and division in opposition to Aditi, the infinite Consciousness-Power; in the Epics daughter of Dakṣa and wife of Kaśyapa and mother of the Daityas; the Maruts are also described as her progeny.

draṣṭā, seer.

dṛṣṭi, from root *dṛś*, to see; a vision, revelation, direct knowledge.

duḥkha, lit. 'difficult or spoilt space'; suffering, sorrow, pain.

durgā, lit. 'the inaccessible or terrific [goddess]', N. of the daughter of Himavat and wife of Śiva.

dvaita, lit. 'dualism, duality'.

dveṣa, hatred, dislike.

dyaus, lit. 'shining one' from root *div*, to shine; heaven, sky, in the *Vedas* the father of all creatures whereas the earth, *pṛthivī*, is the mother; very often the *dvandva* is used: *dyāvapṛthivī*, heaven and earth, indicating the higher and lower hemispheres of the world, many times called as *rodasī*, 'two shining ones'; when used in feminine gender they indicate the mental and physical being (SA).

dyāvaḥ, heavens; in the *Veda* three heavens are mentioned, *tisro dyāvaḥ*, 'two are in the world of Savitṛ and one in the world of Yama' (RV 1.35.6).

E

ekāgratā, lit. 'onepointedness', concentration, the state of absorption.

G

garbha, the inside; a fetus or embryo, child (RV, AV); *hiraṇya-garbha*, 'the golden child', 'the golden embryo', is a symbol of the divinity growing within its own manifestation.

gītā, lit. 'a song', ppp of root *gai*, 'to sing'; *Bhagavad-Gītā*, the song of the Blissful Lord (Śri Kṛṣṇa).

gotra, lit. 'enclosure for the cows', a family, family name, lineage; all *brāhmaṇas* are supposed to have a *gotra* descending from the ancient sages such as Gautama, Kaśyapa, Bharadvāja etc.

gṛhastha, lit. 'staying home', a household; the second *āśrama* in the life of a *brāhmaṇa*, the period of marriage.

guṇa, a single thread or strand of a cord or rope; a garland, a bow-string; the string of a musical instrument, chord; subdivision, species, kind; a quality; an attribute of the 5 elements; (in Sāṁkhya phil.) three major qualities of *prakṛti*: *sattva*, *rajas* and *tamas*, i.e. tranquillity, activity and inertia; (in Nyāya phil.) a property or characteristic of all created things.

H

harṣa, (from root *hṛṣ*) excitement, erection (esp. of the hair in a thrill of rapture or delight); joy, pleasure, happiness (also personified as a son of *dharma*).

hāsa, laughter, a joke.

hāsya, lit. 'laughable', funny, comical etc.

haṭhayoga, lit. '*yoga* of persistence'.

hetu, a motive, a reason, a course, a manner.

hiraṇya, gold, golden.

hrī, modesty, shyness; also personified as daughter of Dakṣa and wife of Dharma.

I

icchā, wish, desire.

indra, the Lord of the Divine Mind (SA), who in the *Veda* with his striking Lightning destroys all the demons: Vṛtra, Vala, Śuṣṇa etc.

indriya, lit. 'the power of Indra', cognitive faculty of consciousness, sense: hearing, touch, sight, taste and smell, known in Sāṁkhya as *jñānendriyās*, the senses of cognition corresponding with five elements: *pañca mahābhūtāni*: *ākāśa*, *vāyu*, *agni*, *āpaḥ*, *pṛthivī*.

īrṣya, envy or jealousy.

īś, master, lord.

īśvara, master, lord, king; the Lord of Creation manifesting himself through his *Śakti* with no difference between Him and Her (SA).

J

jāgrat, lit. 'waking', a waking state of consciousness; there are also *svapna*, a sleeping state with dreams, *suṣupti*, a sleeping state without dreams and the transcendental state of *turīya* (MāṇḍUp 3-5).

jāti, lit. 'birth'; position by birth, lineage, cast, family, kind, class, species etc.

jijñāsā, lit. 'desire to know or realize oneself'.

jijñāsu, lit. 'one who desires to know or realize oneself'.

jīva, lit. 'living being', from root *jīv*, 'to live'; the principle of life, the living or personal soul (as distinguished from the universal soul, see '*jīvātman*'); the individual soul involved in manifestation.

jīvātman, the living individual soul, not involved in manifestation but present as witness from above, distinct from the *paramātman* or universal soul.

jñāna, lit. 'knowledge', 'self-realization' (SA); there are many types of self-realization of consciousness: *saṃjñāna*, *ājñāna*, *vijñāna*, *prajñāna* (AitUp 3).

jñānayoga, the *yoga* of knowledge; the last six chapters of the *Gītā*.

jñānī, lit. 'the knower'.

jugupsā, dislike, disgust.

K

kaivalya, lit. 'alone-ness', the state of being alone, where there is no other; absolute unity; detachment of the soul from matter.

kālī, black, of a dark colour, dark-blue; the goddess of utmost power of destruction, most powerful, furious and intolerant goddess, destroying the demons, also the universe and all creatures. The divine Mother in the form of divine Love, most intolerant of falsehood (SA).

kāma, (fr. *kam*), wish, desire, longing; desire for, longing after (gen. dat., or loc.), love, affection, object of desire or of love or of pleasure; pleasure, enjoyment, love, especially sexual love or sensuality; N. of the god of love (in *Purāṇas* represented as son of Dharma and husband of Rati). In the *yogic* literature it is considered to be one of the major enemies of the *yogin* (BhG etc.) together with *krodha*, anger, and *moha*, bewilderment.

kāraṇa, lit. 'what causes to do'; a cause, reason; motive, origin, principle; an element.

karman, lit. 'work'; from root *kṛ*, 'to do'; duty, occupation; any religious act or rite; labour, activity; product, result, effect etc. In linguistics it is the second *kāraka* of Accusative case, indicating an object of action. In the *Vedic* literature it mainly means a 'sacrificial action', for the sacrifice in general was seen as the only right action to be performed here in the lower hemisphere, which is to accommodate the higher powers of consciousness (the gods) into the narrow life of Ignorance and thus to transform it into its higher prototype.

karmayoga, *yoga* of works; the first six chapters of the BhG describe it in great detail; according to Śrī Kṛṣṇa, the long forgotten path of the Ancients, where the dynamic way of self-discovery and self-realization was accepted as the most efficient way to reach the Divine. There are three major liberations in *karmayoga*: 1) freedom from the fruit of action; 2) freedom from attachment to any particular action; and 3) freedom from the notion of the doer.

kartā, lit. 'a doer'; in linguistics the first *kāraka* of the Nominative Case.

karuṇa, pity, compassion.

kḷeśa, pain, affliction, distress; (in Yoga) five *kleśas*: *a-vidyā*, 'ignorance', *asmi-tā*, 'egotism', *rāga*, 'desire', *dveṣa*, 'aversion', and *abhiniveśa*, 'tenacity of mundane existence'; (in Buddhism) ten: three of the body (murder, theft, adultery), four of speech (lying, slander, abuse, unprofitable conversation), three of the mind (covetousness, malice, skepticism).

kṣara, lit. 'perishable', 'what is melting away', in opposition to '*akṣara*', imperishable. In the *Gītā* *kṣara puruṣa* and *akṣara puruṣa* are mentioned. *Kṣara* represents the world of becoming where nothing is permanent, whereas *akṣara* the transcendental world of permanent existence.

kṣetra, lit. 'a field', land, county; a field for manifestation of the soul; the body.

kṣetrajña, lit. 'a knower of the field', the embodied soul, the indwelling spirit.

kuṇḍalinī, lit. 'a coiling one'; in Tantra the power hidden in the *mūlādhāra cakra* coiling in three (or sometimes in three and a half) coils, which, when awakened, rises to the *sahasrāra cakra*, opening on her way all the *cakras* in the *sūkṣma-śarīra*, to meet and to unite with her Lord, Śiva, seated above in *sahasrāra cakra*. *Mahākuṇḍalinī* is the *mahāśakti* which is descending from above (*sahasrāra cakra*) and opens all the *cakras* one by one from above (SA).

kuṭumbaka, family.

L

lakṣaṇa, lit. 'indication', characteristic, a mark, sign, symbol, token, attribute, quality; definition, illustration etc.

laukika, lit. 'belonging to the world', worldly, common, habitual, not sacred (in opposition to *vaidika* etc.).

līlā, a play, amusement, 'child's play', pretence, disguise; in the Vaiṣṇava tradition it is the *līlā* of Kṛṣṇa which creates the world.

liṅga, a mark, characteristic; the male organ or phallus; in ling. 'gender'; the image of a god, an idol.

loka, lit. 'shining [space]'; from root *ruc*, 'to shine'; in the *Veda u-loka* or *uru-loka, ava-loka*, 'the vast world' is mentioned; country, world; in the *Purāṇas* seven *lokas* are mentioned: *bhūrloka*, the earth; *bhuvarloka*, the space between heaven and earth, the sky, inhabited by *siddhas*; *svarloka*, the heaven above the Sun and below the Polar Star, Indra's kingdom; *maharloka*, the great world above the Polar Star, inhabited by Bhargavas and other *ṛṣis*; *janarloka*, the world of Bliss, *ānanda*; *taparloka*, the world of Consciousness-Force, *tapas*; *satyaloka*, the world of the divine Existence, *sat*.

lokāyata, (*śāstra* or *mata* or *tantra*) materialism, the system of atheistic philosophy taught by Cārvāka.

M

madhyamaka, or '*mādhyamika*' lit. 'middle', 'middlemost'; N. of a Buddhist school.

mahābhārata, epic of the Bhāratas.

mahārasa, lit. 'great essence'.

mahas, lit. 'the great [world]'; the fourth world of the *Taittirīya Upaniṣad*, the world of *Brahman*, known as *Vijñāna*, translated by Sri Aurobindo as 'Supermind'.

mahāyāna, lit. 'great path', or 'great vehicle' (opp. to *hīnayāna*); N. of the later system of Buddhist teaching by Nāgārjuna in the *Mahā-yāna-sūtras*.

mamakāra, lit. 'saying "my"'; selfishness; interest in oneself.

manana, lit. 'thinking'.

manas, sense-mind or mind (in its widest sense as applied to all the mental powers), intellect, intelligence, understanding, perception, sense, will (RV etc.); in philosophy the internal organ or *antaḥ-karaṇa* of perception and cognition, the faculty or instrument through which thoughts enter or by which objects of sense affect the soul; in this sense *manas* is always regarded as distinct from *ātman* and *puruṣa*, 'self or soul' and belongs only to the body. In RV sometimes joined with *hṛd* or *hṛdaya*, the heart; or with *cakṣus*, the eye; thought, imagination, reflection, opinion, intention, inclination, affection, desire, temper, spirit.

mānava, lit. 'the descendent of Manu', man, mental being.

manomaya puruṣa, lit. '*puruṣa* made out of *manas*', the self of mind, mental being, mental self in man; in the system of five *puruṣas* it is the third puruṣa (TaitUp).

marut, usually in pl., prob. the 'flashing or shining ones'; the storm-gods (Indra's companions; said in the *Veda* to be the sons of Rudra and Pṛśni, or the children of heaven or of ocean; and described as armed with golden weapons, lightnings and thunderbolts, as having iron teeth and roaring like lions, as residing in the north, as riding in golden cars drawn by ruddy horses; in the later literature they are the children of Diti, either seven or seven times seven in number, and are sometimes said to be led by Mātariśvan).

māruta-gaṇa, lit. 'the host of Maruts'.

mātā, Nom. from *mātṛ*, lit. 'a measuring one', creatrix, mother.

mati, lit. 'thought'; worship, hymn, sacred utterance (RV, VS); intention, determination, inclination, wish, desire; opinion, notion, idea, belief, conviction, view, creed; the mind, perception, understanding, intelligence, sense, judgment.

māyā, lit. 'creative power', 'measuring power'; in the *Vedas* it is a 'power manifesting the Supreme'; later in the post-*Vedic* literature an 'illusion'.

māyāvāda, the doctrine of *Māyā*, based on the belief that the material world is an illusion, asserting the permanence of the Spirit, and the temporality of material creation, *brahma satyaṃ jaganmithyā*, (Śrī Śaṅkarācārya).

medhā, mental vigour or power, intelligence, prudence, wisdom, (RV. etc.).

mīmāṁsā, lit. 'desire or wish to think over'; an examination of the *Vedic* texts, having two great divisions *Pūrva Mīmāṁsā* or *Karma Mīmāṁsā* by Jaimini, and *Uttara Mīmāṁsā* or *Brahma Mīmāṁsā* (*Brahma sūtras*) by Bādarāyaṇa with Śaṅkara's commentaries which constitutes Advaita Vedānta, known also as Śaṅkara Mīmāṁsā.

mokṣa, liberation, ultimate emancipation, (see '*mukti*').

mūḍha, lit. 'unconscious', 'bewildered'; ppp. from *muh*, to become unconscious.

mudita, lit. 'delighted', ppp from *mud* 'to be happy'; joyful, glad, rejoicing etc.

mukti, liberation, from *muc* 'to free'; setting or becoming free, release, liberation; final liberation or emancipation, final beatitude (= *mokṣa*). The concept of *mukti* is changing over the period of time from the *Vedic* understanding, where *mukti* is only a condition for a more effective action in manifestation of a freed spirit, to the concept of *mukti* where the manifestation itself is seen as an ultimate prison which is to be gotten rid of altogether as soon as possible (Māyāvāda doctrine).

mūlādhāra, lit. 'the foundation of the root of being', the lowest *cakra* in the *sūkṣma-śarīra* (see '*cakra*').

mumukṣutvam, lit. 'a tendency towards freedom', a desire to be free.

muni, a sage, seer, monk etc.

N

nāḍi, any tube or pipe, (esp.) a tubular organ (as a vein or artery of the body); there are 72,000 *nāḍis* in the *sūkṣma deha*, subtle body, of man, of which 5 major *prāṇas* are mentioned: *prāṇa*, *apāna*, *vyāna*, *samāna*, *udāna*.

naiṣṭhikī, from *ni-ṣṭhā*; forming the end, final, last; highest, perfect, complete.

nāma, a name, a characteristic mark or sign, form, nature, kind, manner (RV, VS, AV); name, appellation (RV); in ling. a noun (as opp. to a verb) (Nir); substance, essence (in the Mīmānsā phil. opp. to *guṇa*, as accidental quality). In the *Upaniṣads* it is that which presents the being in its proper meaning and purpose, whereas *rūpa*, form, addresses its formal manifestation.

nara-loka, lit. 'the world of men'; earth or people of earth.

nara, a man, a hero, an individual soul, (from *nṛ*); in the *Veda nṛ* is the power of the soul, which is assigned to different gods and godheads in their sacrificial actions. Many great gods, such as Mitra, Varuṇa, Aryaman, Maruts etc. are called by this name *nṛ*, expecially when they are participating or expected to participate in the sacrifice.

nārada, N. of a sage, known as *deva-ṛṣi*, the divine *Ṛṣi*.

naraka-loka, hell (distinguished from *pātāla*); people of hell.

nārāyaṇa, N. of Viṣṇu; the universal Soul, whereas *nara* is the individual soul.

nāṭyaśāstra, a treatise of *nāṭya*, drama, by sage Bharata.

nididhyāsana, profound and repeated meditation (*Vedāntas*); from Desir. of *ni-dhyai*, 'to think over in depth'.

nidrā, lit. 'deep sleep'; from *ni-drā*, 'to fall deep into sleep'.

niḥsvabhāva, lit. 'without one's own characteristic or essential nature'; want of property, poverty; void of peculiarities etc.

nimitta, from *ni-mā* 'to measure totally'; mark, target, sign, omen; cause, motive, ground, reason; (in philosophy) instrumental or efficient cause; opp. to *upādāna*, the operative or material cause (*Vedāntas*).

nindā, hate, blame, defamation, outrage.

nirguṇa, void of qualities, or beyond any qualities; when applied to *Brahman*, Spirit, it means 'pure Spirit', which is beyond manifestation, in opposition to *sa-guṇa brahma*, 'spirit with qualities', or *ananta-guṇa brahma*, 'spirit of infinite qualities' (SA).

nirodha, lit. 'total obstruction', from *ni-rudh*; restraint, check, control, suppression, destruction; aversion, dislike etc.

nirvāṇa, lit. 'extinguished state', 'without a breath'; from *nir-vā*, 'to blow out', to live without life, as it were; a state of ultimate peace in which the whole world is seen as unreal, as if in a movie (SA); the ultimate goal of Buddhism and Jainism as an absolute extinction or annihilation (= *śūnya*) of individual existence or of all desires and passions; perfect calm or repose or happiness, highest bliss or beatitude.

nirvikalpa, lit. 'without any modification'; not admitting an alternative, free from change or differences; there are two major kinds of *samādhi*, *sa-vikalpa*, including temporal modulations, and *nir-vikalpa*, excluding all temporal modulations of consciousness, which is considered to be the highest.

niṣkāma, lit. 'without desire'; desireless, disinterested, unselfish.

niṣprapañca, subject to no expansion or manifoldness.

niṣṭhā, lit. 'totally stable'; situated within.

nitya, one's own; continual, perpetual, eternal (RV); constantly dwelling or engaged in, intent upon.

nivṛtti, returning, ceasing; disappearance; leaving off, ceasing from worldly acts, inactivity, rest, repose.

niyama, lit. 'fixed rule' or 'vow'; the second stage in the eightfold discipline of Yoga: *yama-niyama-āsana-prāṇāyāma-pratyāhāra-dhāraṇā-dhyāna-samādhayo aṣṭāva aṅgāni* (YS 2.29); five *yamas* are: *ahiṃsā-asatya-asteya-brahmacarya-aparigrahā yamāḥ* (YS 2.30); and five *niyamas*: *śaucha-santoṣa-tapaḥsvādhyāya-īśvarapraṇidhānāni niyamāḥ* (YS 2.32).

nyāya, lit. 'going to the bottom of things', a logic; an original type, method, rule, esp. a general or universal rule, system; a logical or syllogistic argument or inference, consisting of five members: *pratijñā* (a proposition), *hetu* (an argument, deduction, or reason for an inference), *udāharaṇa* (example), *upanaya* (application), *nigamana* (conclusion); a system of philosophy delivered by Gotama or Gautama (see also '*darśana*').

P

padmapāda, lit. 'lotus-foot'.

pāpa, bad, wicked, evil, low; sin, crime, guilt etc.

parā, lit. 'beyond', 'transcendent'; supreme.

parama, see '*parā*'.

paramātman, lit. 'transcendental self', 'the supreme universal Self' as in opposition to the individual self which is *ātman*, or *jīvātman*, 'unborn or uninvolved individual self' or *antarātman*, 'an involved individual self'.

paramparā, a tradition; an uninterrupted lineage, succession, continuation.

paśu-loka, 'the world of creatures who can see/perceive', the animal world in general.

patañjali, N. of the author of *Yogasūtras*; N. of the author of *Mahābhāṣya* on *Pāṇini Aṣṭādhyāyī* (2 cent. BC).

piśācas, the lowest kind of demons, who like to eat flesh (*piśa*).

prahlāda, lit. 'delight'; N. of a pious *daitya*, son of the Asura Hiraṇyakaśipu.

prajñā, 'discrimination', 'knowledge by apprehending cognition'; wisdom etc.

prajñāna, one of the four major operations of consciousness, *saṃjñāna*, *ājñāna*, *vijñāna*, *prajñāna*, mentioned in *Aitareya Upaniṣad* (3.2); according to Sri Aurobindo, *'the outgoing of apprehensive consciousness to possess its object in conscious energy, to know it'*.

prakāśa, lit. 'light', 'shining forward'; illumination, elucidation; clear etc.

prakṛti, lit. 'making or placing before or at first', the original or natural form or condition of anything, original or primary substance; cause, original source; nature, character etc.; (in Sāṁkhya phil.) 'the original producer' of the material world (consisting of 3 constituent essences or *guṇas* called *sattva*, *rajas* and *tamas*); Nature as distinguished from *puruṣa*, Spirit, just as *Māyā* is distinguished from *Brahman* in the Vedānta.

prāṇa, lit. 'breath'; there are five major *prāṇas*: *prāṇa*, 'breathing in', *apāna*, 'breathing out', *vyāna*, 'pervading breath', *samāna*, 'equalizing breath', *udāna*, 'rising up breath'.

prāṇamaya puruṣa, lit. 'self made out of vital', the self of the vital sheath of the *puruṣa*. According to the *Taittirīya Upaniṣad* there are five selves, *ātman* in the form of *puruṣa*, *puruṣa-vidhaḥ*, which constitute the manifestation of the Divine in the individual frame (TaitUp 2.): *annamaya* (material), *prāṇamaya* (vital), *manomaya* (mental), *vijñānamaya* (supramental), *ānandamaya* (transcendental, blissful) *puruṣa*.

prāṇāyāma, 'breath-exercise'; there are three major breaths on which *prāṇāyāma* is built: *pūraka* (breathing in), *recaka* (breathing out), *kumbhaka* (holding).

prapañca, lit. 'spreading forward'; from root *pañc*, 'to expand'; expansion, development, manifestation; phenomenon; (in philosophy) the expansion of the universe, the visible world.

pratibimba, a reflection, reflected image, mirrored form; a resemblance or counterpart of real forms, a picture, image, shadow.

pratyāhāra, lit. 'withdrawing'; in Yoga 'withdrawing of the senses (*indriya*)' from the object of sense (*artha*). It is the sixth stage of Patañjali Yogasūtras (see '*niyama*').

pravacana, recitation, oral instruction, teaching, expounding, exposition, interpretation.

pravṛtti, lit. 'rolling forward'; moving onwards, advance, progress; coming forth, appearance, manifestation; rise, source, origin.

prayatna, effort, endeavour, activity, action.

prekṣā, seeing, viewing, regarding; consideration, reflection.

prema, love, affection, kindness.

preta-loka, lit. 'the world of the dead'.

preta, lit. 'gone', dead.

preyas, lit. 'more loved', more desired; desirable.

pṛthivī, earth.

puṇya, moral or religious merit.

purāṇa, lit. 'ancient'; N. of a class of sacred works. 18 major *Purāṇas* are grouped in 3 divisions: 1) Brahmā of the *Brahma*, *Brahmāṇḍa*, *Brahmavaivarta*, *Mārkaṇḍeya*, *Bhaviṣya*, and *Vāmana Purāṇā*; 2) Viṣṇu of the *Viṣṇu*, *Bhāgavata*, *Nāradīya*, *Garuḍa*, *Padma*, and *Varāha Purāṇa*; 3) Śiva of the *Śiva*, *Liṅga*, *Skanda*, *Agni* or in place of it the *Vāyu*, *Matsya*, and *Kūrma Purāṇa*.

puruṣa, a man, a principle of man, a person; in the *Vedas* the transcendental or universal Man, embodying all the faculties of Consciousness, who was sacrificed (RV 10.91) or whose faculties were sacrificed (AitUp 1-2) projecting the universal Consciousness in the terms of faculties of consciousness into manifestation and thus evoking the evolution of individual being; in Sāṁkhya the principle of the Soul, a witness whose engagement with *prakṛti* creates the Universe.

puruṣārtha, lit. 'an object of human pursuit'; pl., the four aims of existence: *kāma*, the gratification of desire; *artha*, acquirement of wealth; *dharma*, discharge of duty; *mokṣa*, liberation or final emancipation (Mn etc.).

puruṣottama, lit. 'the highest *Puruṣa*', the supreme Person, Soul, transcendental to the transcendental, as it were, who oversees and rules over both *vyakta* and *avyakta*, *kṣara* and *akṣara*, *vidyā* and *avidyā*, who is simultaneously transcendental, universal and individual and greater than all of them.

R

rāga, lit. 'colour'; red colour, redness; any feeling or passion, (esp.) love, affection; a musical note, harmony, melody. In the later system a particular musical mode; Bharata speaks of 6 *rāgas*: *bhairava*, *kauśika*, *hindola*, *dīpaka*, *śrī-rāga*, and *megha*; other writers give other names, sometimes 7 or 26 *rāgas* are mentioned.

rāhu, lit. 'a seizer'; N. of a *daitya* or demon who seizes the sun and moon and thus causes eclipses.

rajāṃsi, airy spaces or vital spaces, in the *Veda trīṇi rajāṃsi*, three vital regions are mentioned.

rajas, 'coloured or dim space', the sphere of vapour or mist, region of clouds, space; in the *Veda* the lower and higher atmospheres; sometimes also three vital spaces; (in phil.) the second of the three *guṇas* or qualities (see also '*sattva*', and '*tamas*'); sometimes identified with *tejas*.

rājasika, of the quality of *rajas guṇa*, energetic, full of passion etc.

rājayoga, lit. 'the King Yoga'.

rākṣasa, lit. 'of *rākṣas* quality'; an evil or malignant demon; in the post-*Vedic* literature divided into 3 classes: a semi-divine nature and ranking with Yakṣas; corresponding to Titans, relentless enemies of the gods; demons going about at night, haunting cemeteries, disturbing sacrifices and even devouring human beings; this last class is the one most commonly mentioned.

rāmāyaṇa, great epic poem of Vālmīki about Rāma and Sītā; it contains about 24000 verses.

rasa-bhāva, the feeling of *rasa* (see '*rasa*').

rasa, lit. 'essence', a juice, a marrow, a liquid; taste, flavour, there are 6 original tastes — *madhura*, sweet, *amla*, sour, *lavaṇa*, salt, *kaṭuka*, pungent, *tikta*, bitter, *kaṣāya*, astringent. In Rhet. the taste or character of a work, the feeling or sentiment prevailing in it, *śṛṅgāra*, love, *vīra*, heroism, *bībhatsa*, disgust, *raudra*, anger or fury, *hāsya*, mirth, *bhayānaka*, terror, *karuṇa*, pity, *adbhuta*, wonder, *śānta*, tranquillity or contentment, *vātsalya*, paternal fondness.

rāśi, a heap, a pile.

rati, lit. 'rest' from root *ram*, 'to rest, to calm'; repose; pleasure, enjoyment, delight; the pleasure of love, sexual passion or union, amorous enjoyment; one of the two wives of Kāma-deva, together with Prīti.

raudra, lit. 'belonging to Rudra', 'having Rudra's qualities'.

ṛg, from *ṛc*, the sacred word or hymn of the *Ṛg Veda*.

rocanā, lit. 'the shining ones'; there are three shining worlds of Svar world, known in the terminology of Sri Aurobindo as Overmental Gnosis, Overmind and Intuition, which constitute the link between the Supermind and the lower hemisphere. The three heavens of the mental consciousness are the highest layers of the lower hemisphere, *tisro dyāvaḥ*; in Sri Aurobindo's language these heavens are the Illumined Mind, Higher Mind and Mind proper.

rodasī, lit. 'two shining ones', usually applied to *dyāvāpṛthivī*, heaven and earth.

roga, a disease, sickness.

rogī, ill, sick.

ṛṣi, a seer, an inspired poet, a composer of the *Vedic* hymns. There are two kinds mentioned in the *Veda*: *pūrva ṛṣayaḥ*, the first *ṛṣis* and *nūtanāḥ*, the modern ones. In the *Brāhmaṇas* seven *ṛṣis* are often mentioned; according to ŚBr xiv, 5, 2, 6, these are: Gotama, Bharadvāja, Viśvāmitra, Jamadagni, Vasiṣṭha, Kaśyapa, and Atri. In astronomy the seven *ṛṣis* constitute the Great Bear constellation. For each *manvantara* there is a different set of seven *ṛṣis* who bring the *Veda* into action within the human consciousness.

ṛta, the dynamic Truth, divine law, divine truth in its dynamism, manifesting the world. The concept of the dynamic truth, *ṛtam*, was lost in the post-*Vedic* literature and only the static truth, *satyam*, remained. All what was related to the action of *ṛtam* was seen only in the context of illusion, *māyā*, and thus lost its true value, and manifestation of the Divine was thus regarded impossible and unnecessary. The aim of life changed from manifesting the Divine to escaping from his manifestation and dissolving oneself in his static truth, *satyam*.

ruci, light, lustre, splendour, beauty.

rudra, lit. 'roarer', by some 'the shining one'; N. of the father and ruler of the Rudras and Maruts in the *Veda*; he is closely connected with Indra and still more with Agni; he has also the epithet Śiva, 'benevolent', which later replaced the name of Rudra.

rūpa, a form, shape, figure; in the *Brāhmaṇas* it is mentioned together with *nāman*, 'name', as two major means for manifesting *Brahman*, (ŚBr). It represents the visual faculty of consciousness whereas *nāman*, its auditory faculty of knowledge.

S

saccidānanda, Existence-Consciousness-Bliss; the transcendental Divine.

ṣaḍ-darśana, 6 major philosophical systems: Pūrva-Mīmānsā by Jaimini, Uttara Mīmānsā by Bādarāyaṇa, Nyāya by Gotama, Vaiśeṣika by Kaṇāda, Sāṁkhya by Kapila, Yoga by Patañjali.

sadānanda, perpetual bliss, N. of Śiva.

sadguṇa, lit. 'having good qualities'.

sādhaka, effective, efficient, accomplishing, fulfilling, completing, perfecting, finishing; an efficient or skilful person, an adept, magician; the follower on the path of *yoga*.

sādhanā, means of realising the goal, a discipline of *yoga*.

sādhāraṇīkaraṇa, making equal.

sādhusaṅga, 'communion with *sādhus*'.

saguṇa, lit. 'with qualities', as in opposition to *nirguṇa*, 'without qualities'.

sahasradala, lit. 'thousand-petalled' lotus; the *cakra* at the top of the head; the seat of Śiva in Tantra, where Śiva and Śakti meet and become one.

sahasrāra, see '*sahasradala*'.

sahṛdaya, lit. 'with the heart', sincere etc.

sākṣī, lit. 'with an eye', a witness; in phil. 'subject'; *puruṣa*, unborn soul, witnessing silently the actions of *prakṛti*.

sākṣibhāva, the state of witness.

śākta, belonging to the tradition of Śāktas; relating to power or energy, or worshipping the *śakti* or divine energy, especially as identified with Durgā, wife of Śiva.

śakti, lit. 'force, power, ability', from root *śak*, 'to be able to'; the power of the Divine, known as Mahāśakti, in the post-*Vedic* tradition known in her four aspects: Maheśvarī, Mahākālī, Mahālakṣmī, Mahāsarasvatī, representing Knowledge, Power, Beatitude and Perfection, respectively (SA).

śaktipatha, an initiation into the sacred power of *guru*.

samabuddhi, esteeming all things alike, indifferent.

samādhi, lit. 'becoming one with', union with, completion; concentration of the thoughts, intense absorption or a kind of trance; profound meditation, intense contemplation of any particular object (so as to identify the contemplator with the object meditated upon); this is the eighth and last stage of Yoga; (in Buddhism) the fourth and last stage of *dhyāna*.

sāmājika, social, related to the social gathering etc.

samāna, see '*prāṇa*'.

samatā, equality, equanimity etc.

sambandha, lit. 'binding together'; association, relation, relative, friend etc.

saṃjñā, lit. 'knowledge in complete agreement with all possible views'; consciousness, clear knowledge, understanding, conception (ŚBr etc.).

saṃjñāna, see '*saṃjñā*'; 'the essential sense'; according to Sri Aurobindo, '*the inbringing movement of apprehensive consciousness which draws the object placed before it back to itself so as to possess it in conscious substance, to feel it*'.

sāṁkhya-yoga, *yogic* practice based on the Sāṁkhya philosophy, *yoga* of Sāṁkhya.

sāṁkhya, N. of a philosophical system, ascribed to the sage Kapila, meaning lit. 'enumerating' the major essential categories or twenty-five *tattvas* (twenty-three of them evolved out of *prakṛti*, 'the first-producer', these are *buddhi*, *ahaṃkāra*, *manas*, the five *tan-mātras*, the five *karmendriyas*, the five *jñānendriyas*, the five *mahā-bhūtas*; the twenty-fifth is the *puruṣa*, spirit or soul, which is neither a producer nor production); there are many *puruṣas* and one *prakṛti*; each separate *puruṣa* causes by its union with *prakṛti* a separate creation out of *prakṛti*; the object of this philosophy is to effect the final liberation of the *puruṣa* from the bondage caused by that creation. The Yoga branch of the Sāṁkhya recognizes a supreme spirit, the universal *puruṣa*, dominating each individual *puruṣa*. The Tantras identify *prakṛti* with the wives of the gods, esp. with the wife of Śiva.

saṃsāra, a course, passage, passing through a succession of states, the world, secular life.

saṃśaya, doubt; in Nyāya, doubt about the point to be discussed; difficulty etc.

saṁskāra, lit. 'putting together' or 'making perfect', accomplishment etc.; a sacred or sanctifying ceremony; faculty of memory, mental impression or recollection; impression on the mind of acts done in a former state of existence (one of the 24 qualities of the Vaiśeṣikas); (pl., in Buddhism) a mental conformation or creation of the mind (such as that of the external world).

saṁyoga, lit. 'uniting together', union, conjunction, connection etc.

sañcāribhāva, a transitory feeling.

saṅga, 'coming together', community, association etc.

saṅkalpa, intention, determination; conception or idea or notion formed in the mind or heart.

śaṅkara, lit. 'making peace' or 'causing prosperity', beneficent; N. of Śiva; N. of Śrī Śaṅkarācārya (788 and 820 A.D.), the founder of Advaita Vedānta philosophy.

sannyāsa, lit. 'dropping totally off', resignation, renunciation of the world; the fourth *āśrama* in the life of a *brāhmaṇa*.

sansārin, the one who is in *sansāra*, in the worldly life.

śānti, peace.

santoṣa, 'happiness', total satisfaction.

sarasvatī, lit. 'who possesses the stream'; N. of a river; the river-goddess who in the *Vedas* has seven sisters and is herself sevenfold; in the *Brāhmaṇas* she is identified with *vāc*, 'speech'; N. of the goddess of eloquence and learning in the post-*Vedic* period; truth-audition, inspiration, the divine word (SA).

śarīra, body, physical body.

śāstra, instruction, rule, order, a manual, a treatise, a book of knowledge etc.

sattva, lit. 'the quality of that which is'; true existence, the highest of the three *guṇas*, qualities, of *prakṛti*, that of purity and knowledge (see '*rajas*' and '*tamas*').

satya, truth; 'that which is'; in the *Veda* distinguished from *ṛta*, the dynamic truth.

satyayuga, lit. 'the age of Truth'; the first and the longest of the four *yugas* in every *manvantara*.

śava, a corpse, a dead body.

śavāsana, the *āsana* of full relaxation.

savitṛ, lit. 'the impeller', from root *su/sū*, 'to press upon, to push on, to compel', or 'to create' etc.; in the *Veda* the god of the Sun, the Divine in Manifestation, who represents all the godheads in their rising movement towards the Truth.

sāvitrī, a verse in *gāyatrī* meter addressed to the god of the Sun, Savitṛ, (RV III. 62, 10); the daughter of Savitṛ, the divine Word (SA); the wife of Brahmā, the creator of the world; the wife of Satyavān, in the story of *Sāvitrī* in the MBh.

sevā, service, attendance to, worship etc.

siddha, lit. 'realised', 'whose goal is achieved'; semi-divine being of great purity and perfection who possesses the eight supernatural faculties, *siddhis*; they inhabit, together with the *munis*, the *bhuvar-loka*, the space between heaven and earth; in the later literature they are regarded as *sādhyas*.

siddhis, accomplishment, fulfilment, complete attainment; there are eight *siddhis* usually mentioned, given in the following *śloka*: *aṇimā laghimā prāptiḥ prākāmyam mahimā tathā īśitvaṃ ca vaśitvaṃ ca tathā kāmāvasāyitā*; sometimes 26 are added, e.g., *dūra-śravaṇa*, *sarvajña-tva*, *agni-stambha* etc., (Sāṁkhyak, Tattvas, Sarvad).

śikṣaka, a teacher, instructor.

śilpa, any manual art or craft, any handicraft or mechanical or fine art (64 such arts or crafts, sometimes called *bāhya-kalā*, 'external or practical arts', such as carpentery, architecture, jewellery, farriery, acting, dancing, music, medicine, poetry etc.; and 64 *abhyantara-kalā*, 'secret arts', e.g., kissing, embracing, and various other arts of coquetry) (Mn. MBh. etc.).

śloka, a verse in *anuṣṭubh* meter, probably from root *śru*, 'to hear'; Vālmīki seeing the death of a bird in the forest, experiencing deep grief and compassion, composed the first *śloka*.

smaraṇa, memorizing, remembering, recollecting; mental recitation, remembering the name of God.
smita, smiled, smiling or smile.
smṛti, memory, the whole tradition which was handed down by composing and memorizing the text, in opposition to *śruti*, a direct revelation of the inspired Word, which was not composed but 'heard' by a deeper listening of the soul.
śoka, lit. 'burning', from root *śuc*, 'to burn'; flame, glow, heat; sorrow, affliction, anguish, pain, trouble, grief etc.
sphuraṇa, lit. 'trembling', 'bursting out', breaking forth; expansion, manifestation.
śraddhā, lit. 'holding one's heart'; having faith, believing; faith, belief, trust etc.
śrama, austerity, labour, toil, exercise, hard work of any kind whether mental or physical.
śravaṇa, lit. 'hearing', from root *śru*, to hear; learning, study etc.
śreyas, lit. 'better', 'more splendid', from *śrī*; in *Kaṭha Upaniṣad* it is used as a concept of the ultimate good, in opposition to *preyas*, which is 'more desirable', so that one can choose the path between what is 'liked or desired' and what is 'better or best', respectively.
śrī, probably from *śri* 'diffusing light or radiance'; light, lustre, radiance, splendour, glory, beauty, grace, loveliness; wealth etc.; the N. of Lakṣmī the wife of Viṣṇu.
śṛṅgāra, the *rasa* of love and affection.
śruti, the body of the *Vedic* canon, the literature which was not composed by men (*apauruṣeya*) but revealed to his inner hearing (*śruta*), consists of *Saṃhitā, Brāhmaṇa, Āraṇyaka, Upaniṣad* in different branches (*śākhā*).
stambha, pillar, column etc.
sthāyibhāva, a feeling or a state of steadiness.
sthāyin, stable, steady etc.
sthitaprajña, lit. 'whose wisdom is steady'.
śuddhi, lit. 'purity', cleanliness, purification etc.
sukha-duḥkha, happiness and unhappiness; the *yogin* is to be equal to both according to the *Gītā*.
sukha, lit. 'good space', from *su-kha*; happiness, well-being; in opposition to *duḥ-kha*, 'bad space', as suffering, grief, unhappiness, sorrow etc.
śūnyatā, lit. 'emptiness', void, nothingness etc.
śūnyavāda, the doctrine of nothingness.
supta, 'asleep', ppp. from *svap*, 'to sleep'; sleeping etc.
sura-loka, the world of the gods.
sūrya, the sun; the Sun god in the *Veda*, symbolizing according to SA the supramental consciousness force.
suśrutasaṃhitā, the collection of verses dedicated to medical studies by Suśruta, who is its author and a son of Viśvāmitra (see also another medical treatise *Carakasaṃhitā*).
suṣupti, 'a state of deep sleep without dreams'.
sūtra, 'a thread', a cord, a string, which connects or holds many beads; a short sentence or aphoristic rule; major works of *smṛti* literature were composed in this style; we have *śrauta-sūtras*, *gṛhya-sūtras*, *dharma-sūtras* etc.
svabhāva, lit. 'one's own nature'; according to the nature of the individual soul.
svadharma, lit. 'one's own law or way of action'; according to the law supported by one's *svabhāva*.
svādhyāya, lit. 'reading for oneself'; a technique of reading the scripture for oneself in order to realize its deeper significance.
svapna, dream, a 'sleeping state with dreams' as in opposition to *suṣupti*, 'a state of deep sleep without dreams'.
svar, the sun, sunshine, light, lustre; bright space created by the rays of the Sun; sky, heaven as distinguished from *div*; there are three luminous regions of *svar* in the *Veda*: *trī rocanā*. It is distinguished as a higher region from *div*, which is also triple, *tisro dyāvaḥ*. *Svar* is linking the Sun with the lower hemisphere, bringing the dynamic truth, *ṛtam*, into the manifestation. In the later tradition this region becomes regarded as a region of *māyā*, an illusion, and as such loses its creative aspect, becoming unimportant. The Sun itself becomes a part of the lower hemisphere and heaven, *div*, takes a higher position than the Sun, thus the Supramental region disappears altogether from the memory of post-*Vedic* tradition.

T

tamas, lit. 'darkness'; mental darkness or ignorance; one of the three modes of *prakṛti* constituting inertia and dullness in the being.
tāmasika, 'that of the *tamas* quality', dull, ignorant, inert etc.
tantra, lit. 'the principal or essential part', characteristic feature, model, type, system, framework; a class of works which presents the *Vedic* knowledge in the *kali yuga*. There are three kinds of Tantra: Vaiṣṇava, Śaiva and Śākta.
tāntrika, the *tāntric* who practices Tantra.
tattva, lit. 'that-ness'; the essential quality; a true principle; truth etc.; in Sāṁkhya there are 25 *tattvas*: a-*vyakta, buddhi, ahaṃkāra, manas*, the 5 *tan-mātras*, the 5 *mahā-bhūtas*, the 10 organs of action and perception, and *puruṣa*.
theravāda, N. of a Buddhist school.
titikṣā, endurance, patience.
trāsa, fear, terror.
triguṇa, lit. 'of three qualities', of *sattva, rajas* and *tamas*.
triguṇātīta, lit. 'gone beyond three qualities'; liberated etc.
tṛṣṇā, thirst.

turīya, the fourth state of spirit; pure impersonal Spirit.

U

udāna, one of the five *prāṇas* of the human body (that which is in the throat and rises upwards).

udāsīna, lit. 'sitting above'; sitting apart, indifferent, free from affection.

uddīpana, lit. 'lighting up'; inflaming, exciting, illuminating.

unmāda, mad, insane.

upaniṣad, lit. 'sitting down close to'; the sacred texts which are a part of *Brāhmaṇa* literature.

upāya, lit. 'coming near', 'approaching'; 'that by which one reaches one's aim', a means, way, craft.

upekṣā, overlooking, disregard, negligence, indifference, contempt.

uṣas, dawn, morning light; in the *Vedas* the sister of Ādityas and the twin sister of Naktā, Night; also daughter of Heaven, Dyaus. She is the beloved wife of the Sun, Sūrya, who follows her path to the lower hemisphere, where he realizes all his desires with her. She is the symbol of spiritual illumination of consciousness.

utsāha, effort, resolution; perseverance.

uttara, lit. 'higher'.

V

vaidya, lit. 'belonging to *Veda*'; medical: a learned man, a doctor.

vairāgya, lit. 'loss of colour'; disgust, distaste for; freedom from all worldly desires, asceticism.

vaiśeṣika, philosophical doctrine by Kaṇāda about the distinct nature of the nine substances: air, fire, water, earth, mind, ether, time, space, and soul, of which the first five, including mind, are held to be atomic.

vaiśya, lit. 'belonging to people, *viś*', one of the *varṇas* of traders and agriculturists.

vajrayāna, lit. 'the diamond path' in Buddhism.

varuṇa, lit. 'covering', 'enveloping'; all enveloping sky (cp. Uranus in Greek mythology); one of the greatest Ādityas, symbolizing the manifestation of infinite Existence, later known as *Sat* (SA).

vāsana, lit. 'clothing', 'dress'; or from Caus. of *vas*, 'causing to dwell'.

vasu-gaṇa, see '*vasu*'.

vasu, lit. 'bright'; wealth, goods, riches, property (RV etc.); N. of the gods, esp. of the Ādityas, Maruts, Aśvins, Indra, Uṣas, Rudra, Vāyu, Viṣṇu, Śiva, and Kubera (RV, AV, MBh, Rm); N. of a class of gods, whose number is usually eight, and whose chief is Indra, later Agni and Viṣṇu; the names of the Vasus, according to the *Viṣṇu-Purāṇa*, are: Āpa, 'Waters', Dhruva, 'the Pole-star', Soma, 'the Moon', Dhava or Dhara, 'Earth', Anila, 'Wind', Anala or Pāvaka, 'Fire', Pratyuṣa, 'the Dawn', Prabhāsa, 'Light'.

vāsudeva, lit. 'the son of Vasudeva', N. of Kṛṣṇa.

vāyu, wind; the second element in *pañca mahābhūtāni*, five great elements; in the *Veda* 'the god of wind', often associated with Indra; in post-*Vedic* literature is considered to be the essence of *antarikṣa*, the space between heaven and earth, as Āditya is the essence of *dyauḥ*, and Agni is the essence of *pṛthivī*; the union of Agni, Vāyu and Āditya is considered the aim of the *Vedic* Sacrifice.

vedanā, lit. 'letting know' or 'announcing'; perception; pain.

vedānta, lit. 'the end of *Veda*'; *Upaniṣads*; there are different interpretations of Vedānta: Advaita, Dvaita, Viśiṣṭādvaita.

vibhāva, any condition which excites or develops a particular state of mind or body; any cause of emotion occurring in the persons and circumstances represented in a drama, as opp. to the *anu-bhāva* or external signs or effects of emotion.

vidyā, knowledge; as in opposition to *avidyā*, ignorance or partial knowledge; knowledge of phenomena in time and space; *vidyā* and *avidyā*, according to the *Īśopaniṣad*, are both necessary for the realisation of the Supreme Consciousness.

vijñāna, lit. 'knowing or realising oneself in detail'; in the TaitUp it is indicating the Supramental Consciousness (SA); according to Sri Aurobindo, '***Vijnana** … holds an image of things at once in its essence, its totality and its parts and properties*'. See also '*prajñāna*'.

vikalpa, variation, difference in perception, doubt.

vikāra, alteration, distortion, modification, transformation. In Sāṁkhya *vikāras* are derived from *prakṛti*; there are 7 *vikāras*: *buddhi*, *ahaṃkāra*, and the 5 *tan-mātras*, these are also producers; from them come the 16 *vikāras* which are only productions: the 5 *mahā-bhūtāni*, 5 *buddhīndriyāṇi*, the 5 *karmendriyāṇi*, and *manas*.

vinaya, lit. 'leading away' or 'separating'; leading, guidance, training, education, discipline, control; in Buddhism the rules of discipline for monks; decency, modesty.

vipassanā, (Pali) lit. 'seeing clear'; Buddhist technique of meditation.

vīra, a hero; strong, powerful.

viṣāda, depression, despair, disgust, fear, dullness.

viśiṣṭādvaita, philosophical doctrine of Vedānta by Rāmānuja (12th century AD), lit. 'specified nonduality', where the souls of men have and preserve their own unique identity in the *Brahman*, in opposition to Advaita Vedānta of Śaṅkara, where the souls of men lose their separate identity in *Brahman*, like the drop of water in the ocean.

viṣṇu, lit. '*vi-ṣnu*, who broadens the oneness'; in the *Veda* the godhead of vastness, Overmental Consciousness, the younger brother of Indra, who is the godhead of the Divine Mind (SA). In the post-*Vedic* literature is described as having 10 *avatāras*, becomes one of the major gods of Hinduism.

viśve-devās, lit. 'all the gods collectively'; a class of gods; according to the *Viṣṇu Purāṇa* and other texts they are the sons of Viśvā, daughter of Dakṣa (RV etc.).

vitarka, lit. 'guess', 'supposition'; reasoning etc.

vivasvat, lit. 'with the light shining forth'; N. of the Sun, Āditya; in the *Veda* the eighth son of Aditi.

viveka, lit. 'discrimination', distinction; in Vedānta the power of separating the invisible Spirit from the visible world (or spirit from matter, truth from untruth, reality from mere semblance or illusion).

viyoga, lit. 'dis-union', separation.

vṛtti, lit. 'rolling', 'that which is repeating itself'; conduct, behaviour, character, practice etc.

vyādhi, lit. 'sickness', from root *vyadh*, 'to be pierced'.

vyādhita, sick.

vyakti-viṣaya, *vyakti*, lit. 'appearance', distinctness, individuality; *viṣaya* lit. 'extention', sphere, scope etc.

vyāsa, N. of a legendary *ṛṣi*, the composer of *Mahābhārata* and a compiler of the *Vedas* and *Purāṇas*.

Y

yajña, sacrifice, lit. 'the conscious act of advancing towards more conscious manifestation'; 'manifesting the Spirit in a conscious way'; 'bringing the powers of light into the darkness'; 'offering the powers of darkness to the Light for transformation'.

yama, lit. 'restrain', (see '*niyama*'); In the *Veda* he is one of the Aṅgirasa *ṛṣis*; the first of men who was born from Vivasvat, the god of the Sun, and his wife Saraṇyū; in Post-*vedic* mythology he becomes the lord of Death, judging and punishing people for their deeds after death, whereas in the *Veda* he is the saviour of the soul in the time of death rather than the Death incarnate.

yoga-nidrā, lit. 'sleeping *yoga*', 'meditation-sleep', a state of half meditation/half sleep (which admits the full exercise of the mental powers); light sleep, esp. the sleep of Viṣṇu at the end of a *yuga*.

yoga-sūtra, N. of a work by Patañjali (2nd cent. BC).

yoga, (fr. *yuj*) the act of yoking, joining, uniting (RV, MBh); an abstract contemplation, meditation, (esp.) self-concentration; practised as a system taught by Patañjali and called *yoga darśana*, it is the second of the two Sāṁkhya systems, its aim is to teach the means by which the human spirit may attain complete union with Īśvara; in the practice of self-concentration it is closely connected with Buddhism (Up, MBh, Kāv etc.). In Sāṁkhya it means the union of soul with matter (one of the 10 *mūlikārthās* or radical facts, *tattvas*); with Jainas, contact or mixing with the outer world; in astronomy, conjunction, lucky conjuncture (MBh etc.). There are many kinds of *yoga*. *Karmayoga, bhaktiyoga, jñānayoga* are dealt with in detail in the *Bhagavad Gītā*. There are also other kinds of *yoga*: *dhyāna-yoga, rājayoga, haṭhayoga, kriyāyoga, pūrṇayoga* etc. Patañjali defines *yoga* in the *Yogasūtra* as ceasing the activities of *citta*: *yogaś-citta-vṛtti-nirodhaḥ*, which can be translated as: 'yoga is a cessation of the habitual movements of consciousness.' Generally speaking, any practice which leads the practitioner eventually to union with the Divine can be called *yoga*.

yogavāsiṣṭha, N. of a work on *yoga* in the form of a dialogue between Vasiṣṭha and Rāma as his disciple.

yogī, lit. 'one who practices *yoga*'.

yoni-mudrā, N. of a particular position of the fingers.

Abbreviations of source-texts used in the Glossary

AitĀr	Aitareya-Āraṇyakam
AitBr	Aitareya-Brāhmaṇam
AitUp	Aitareya-Upaniṣad
ĀśvŚr	Āśvalāyana Śrauta-sūtra
AV	Atharva-veda Saṁhitā
BṛhUp	Bṛhadāraṇyaka-Upaniṣad
BhP	Bhāgavata Purāṇa
BhG	Bhagavad-Gītā
Buddh	Buddhist
ChaUp	Chandogya-Upaniṣad
Gṛ	Gṛhya-sūtra
ĪśUp	Īśā-Upaniṣad
JaiUpBr	Jaiminīya-Upaniṣad-Brāhmaṇa
Hariv	Harivaṃśa
KaṭhUp	Kaṭha-Upaniṣad
KātyŚr	Kātyāyana Śrauta-sūtra
KauṣBr	Kauṣitakī-Brāhmaṇam
KauṣUp	Kauṣitakī-Upaniṣad
KeUp	Kena-Upaniṣad
MaitrS	Maitrayaṇī Saṁhitā
Mn	Manu Smṛti
MāṇḍUp	Māṇḍūkya Upaniṣad
MuṇḍUp	Muṇḍaka-Upaniṣad
MaitUp	Maitrī-Upaniṣad
MBh	Mahābharata-yuddham
Nir	Niruktam
Pāṇ	Pāṇini
PraUp	Praśna-Upaniṣad
Rm	Rāmāyaṇam
RV	Rig-veda Saṁhitā
ŚBr	Śatapatha-Brāhmaṇam
Sarvad	Sarvadarśanasaṅgraha
Sāy	Sāyaṇa
SA	Sri Aurobindo
Sāṁkhyak	Sāṁkhyakārika
ŚvetUp	Śvetāśvatarā-Upaniṣad
Suśr	Suśrutasaṃhitā
TaitĀr	Taittirīya-Āraṇyakam
TaitBr	Taittirīya-Brāhmaṇam
TaitUp	Taittirīya-Upaniṣad
TS	Taittirīya Saṁhitā
Tattvas	Tattvasamāsa
Up	Upaniṣads
VS	Vājasaneyī Saṁhitā
VP	Vākyapadīya
Vedāntas	Vedāntasāra

Other abbreviations used in the Glossary

Abl.	Ablative case
Acc.	Accusative case
aor.	aorist
Caus.	Causative
cent.	century
cp.	compare
Dat.	Dative case
Desir.	Desirative
du.	Dual
esp.	especially
Freq.	Frequentative
f.	feminine gender
fr.	from root
fut.	Future Tense
Gen.	Genitive case
ger.	Gerundive
gram.	Grammar
incl.	including
inf.	Infinitive
inj.	injunctive
imperf.	Imperfect (Past Tense)
Imp.	Imperative Mood
Inst.	Instrumental case
ling.	linguistics
lit.	literally
Loc.	Locative case
m.	masculine gender
n.	neutral gender
N.	name
Nom.	Nominative case
opp.	opposite
Opt.	Optative Mood
perf.	perfect
phil.	philosophy
pl.	plural
ppp.	Participle Perfect Passive (Participle II in English)
pres.	Present Tense
Rhet.	Rhetoric
sg.	singular
subj.	subjunctiv

The contributors

For up-to-date contact information, please write to mail@ipi.org.in

Priya Ananda

Priya Ananda's interests are in transformational psychology, Buddhist philosophy and comparative religion. An engineer by background, she has been exploring various philosophies and practice systems for many years. Coming across Buddhism changed her perspective dramatically. Traversing the path of Yogic tradition of Buddhism, she trained under eminent Tibetan Buddhist masters like HH Penor Rinpoche, Khenchen Pema Sherab, Khenchen Namdrol and Khenchen Tsewang Gyatso. She teaches emotional management methods. She was instrumental in establishing Thubten Lekshey Ling, a Buddhist Centre of Learning in Bangalore.

Bharati Baveja

Bharati Baveja, Ph.D., former Head and Dean is working as a Professor in the Department of Education, University of Delhi. Currently, she is also the Director Women Studies and Development Center. Her experience in the field of Teacher Education and engagement with research in the domain of Learning and Pedagogy in the past two decades finds expression in the research papers and articles published in journals of repute. Her participation in the National Focus Group on Teacher Education constituted by NCERT has led to the development of rich insights in the field. She led a major curriculum reform in Teacher Education at the University of Delhi while she was the Dean.

William Braud

William Braud earned his Ph.D. in experimental psychology at the University of Iowa in 1967. At the University of Houston, he taught and conducted research in learning, memory, motivation, psychophysiology, and the biochemistry of memory. At the Mind Science Foundation (San Antonio, TX), he directed research in parapsychology; health and well-being influences of relaxation, imagery, positive emotions, and intention; and psychoneuroimmunology. He was Professor and Dissertation Director, Global Programs, Institute of Transpersonal Psychology (Palo Alto, CA), where he directed doctoral dissertation research, and continued research, teaching and writing in areas of exceptional human experiences, consciousness studies, transpersonal studies, spirituality and expanded research methods.

R. M. Matthijs Cornelissen

R. M. Matthijs Cornelissen teaches Integral Psychology at the Sri Aurobindo International Centre of Education in Pondicherry. He is a Dutch physician who settled in India in 1976. From 1977 to 1992 he worked in the Delhi Branch of the Sri Aurobindo Ashram, where he co-founded Mirambika, a research centre for integral education. In 1992 he moved to the main Sri Aurobindo Ashram in Pondicherry. Presently he is involved in a variety of projects concerned with the development of a new approach to psychology based on the Indian tradition. To this end he founded the Sri Aurobindo Centre for Consciousness Studies in 2001, and the Indian Psychology Institute in 2006. He edited two earlier volumes on Indian Psychology, *Consciousness and its transformation* (2001), and *Indian psychology, consciousness and yoga* (2004), the latter together with the then Chairman of the Indian Council of Philosophical Research, Kireet Joshi.

Ajit K. Dalal

Ajit K. Dalal is Professor of Psychology at the University of Allahabad. He has obtained his doctoral degree from the Indian Institute of Technology, Kanpur, and has published in the areas of causal attribution, health beliefs and indigenous psychology. He received the Fulbright Senior Fellowship and worked at the University of California, Los Angeles, and at the University of Michigan, Ann Arbor. He is also a recipient of the UGC Career Award, Rockefeller Foundation Award and ICSSR Senior Fellowship. He was a visiting faculty at many places, including Queen's University, Canada; National Institute of Health and Family Welfare, New Delhi; Indian Institute of Management, Ahmedabad and Calcutta University, Kolkata. His books include *Attribution theory and research, New directions in Indian psychology* (Vol. 1), *Social dimensions of health* and *Handbook of Indian psychology*. Presently, he is the editor of the journal *Psychology and Developing Societies* published by Sage.

Rajen K. Gupta

Rajen K. Gupta is Professor of Human Behavior & Organization Development with Management Development Institute, Gurgaon, India. He has successfully guided more than twenty PhD scholars and have more than a hundred research publications to his credit in areas of organization culture, Organization development, learning in organizations etc. He has designed and implemented developmental interventions for several business organizations and educational institutions.

Neeltje Huppes

Neeltje Huppes was born in the Netherlands. After post graduation in the sixties, she taught in a progressive school and at a young age became a member of a special Commission set up by the Dutch Government to revamp education in Secondary schools. Her search for in-depth innovation led her to Sri Aurobindo and The Mother. The urge to live in India increased and in the seventies she came to Puducherry. She lived for fifteen years in the Sri Aurobindo Ashram, Delhi Branch where she founded, together with Matthijs Cornelissen, a Research Centre for Integral Education, focusing mainly on teacher education. The urge for a more intense inner quest brought her back to Puducherry where she is presently teaching in the Sri Aurobindo International Centre of Education. She wrote *Psychic education, a workbook*, New-Delhi, SAES (2001). She has lectured in India and abroad on various aspects of Integral Psychology. In February 2006, she opened together with Matthijs Cornelissen the Indian Psychology Institute.

Vladimir Iatsenko

Vladimir Iatsenko, a Sanskrit scholar in Auroville since 1993, is working as a researcher at the University of Human Unity, Auroville. He has graduated in Sanskrit and General Linguistics from St. Petersburg University, Russia and studied Panini Ashtadhyayi in Poona University in 1991–1992. He is a life-member of BORI in Pune, and a teacher and facilitator of on-line courses at ICIS in Delhi, IPI and SACAR in Pondicherry.

Kapil Kapoor

Kapil Kapoor, Ph.D., is former Professor of English, Centre for Linguistics and English, and Concurrent Professor, Centre for Sanskrit Studies, Jawaharlal Nehru University, New Delhi. He was Dean of the School of Language, Literature and Culture Studies, JNU, from 1996 to 1999 and Rector (Pro-Vice-Chancellor) of the University from 1999 to 2002. His teaching and research interests include literary and linguistic theories, both Indian and Western, philosophy of language, nineteenth century British life, literature and thought and Indian intellectual traditions. He has been lecturing on these themes and has written extensively on them. He has been teaching for almost fifty years now. His two books, *Dimensions of Pāṇini grammar: The Indian grammatical system* and *Text and interpretation: The Indian tradition*, have been published in 2005. *Indian knowledge systems* (2 Vols.), edited by him, has also been published (2005). *Literary theory, Indian conceptual framework* (1998); *Canonical texts of literary criticism* (1995); *Language, literature and linguistics*; *The Indian perspective* (1994); and *South Asian love poetry* (1994) are among his earlier publications. He has been a member of the Governing Body of Indian Institute of Advanced Study (IIAS), Shimla and of the Governing Body of Indian Council of Philosophical Research (ICPR), a member of the Academic Council of Indian Institute of Higher Tibetan Studies, Sarnath and Central Institute of English and Foreign Languages, Hyderabad and of the Executive Councils of Central University of Hyderabad and of Gurukula Kangri, Haridwar. He has delivered lectures by invitation in several universities in India in the areas of Indian philosophy, grammar, aesthetics and literatures. He is currently Chief Editor, the Sahitya

Akademi *Encyclopaedia of Indian poetics*, a UNESCO project, and Chief Executive Editor of the Indian Heritage Research Foundation (USA) sponsored *Encyclopaedia of Hinduism*. He is a nominated Visiting Professor at the Irish Academy of Cultural Heritages, University of Ulster, U.K. 2005-2009.

Vinita Kaushik Kapur

Vinita Kaushik Kapur was a doctoral student in Social Anthropology at the Institute of Advanced Studies in Sociology, at the Delhi School of Economics. She gave up her studies when she found academia to be in conflict with the way she was thinking about life especially in the context of several new philosophical perspectives that she was engaging with. She instead chose to translate into action the new meanings that had begun to inform her life. She became a subsistence farmer at Geddai in the Nilgiri hills. She then formed a small alternative school on the farm using several innovative pedagogical styles. She also taught at The Valley School of the Krishnamurti Foundation for several years. At present she is working as an ethnographic researcher.

P. Ram Manohar

P. Ram Manohar is an Āyurvedic physician and has an MD degree in Āyurvedic Pharmacology. He is currently the Director and Chief Scientific Officer, AVP Research Foundation, Coimbatore. He was research advisor to Indian National Science Academy and member of Central Council of Indian Medicine, and has served in the editorial board of *Indian Journal for History of Science* and *International Journal of Āyurveda Research*. He is currently Chief Editor of *ASL Musculoskeletal Diseases* Managing Editor of *Ancient Science of Life*. He was the PI on the Indian side of first ever NIH, USA funded research grant to study Āyurveda outside the United States, which received the Excellence in Integrative Medicine Research Award from European Society of Integrative Medicine. He has published research papers and books both in India and abroad and has made research visits to USA, UK, Canada, Germany, France, Netherlands, Austria, Italy, Switzerland, Denmark and Belgium for the promotion of Āyurveda.

Michael Miovic

Michael Miovic, MD, is a Harvard-trained psychiatrist with extensive background in psycho-oncology (the care of cancer patients). He has a special interest in spiritual issues in mental healthcare, and has published a number of case studies, articles and book chapters on that topic. He has collaborated with colleagues in the United States, Europe and India to help develop the field of integral psychology, and is now focused on expanding the scope of that endeavor to encompass a geo-spiritual understanding of the Earth consciousness based on Sri Aurobindo's philosophy.

Girishwar Misra

Girishwar Misra, Ph.D., is currently Professor of Psychology and Dean, Research (Humanities & Social Sciences) University of Delhi. During his academic career spanning over four decades, he has earlier taught at the Universities of Bhopal, Allahabad and Gorakhpur. He has been a Fulbright Fellow at the University of Michigan, Ann Arbor and Fulbright-Nehru Lecturer at New School of Social Research, New York. The Government of Madhya Pradesh has conferred upon him Pandit Jawaharlal Nehru National Award for contributions to social sciences. He was awarded National Fellowship by the Indian Council of Social Science Research (ICSSR). His research interests include self-processes, well-being, emotions, and qualitative methods. He has authored or edited over several books including *Psychological Consequences of Prolonged Deprivation*, *Applied Social Psychology In India*, *Perspectives on Indigenous Psychology*, *Psychological Perspectives on Stress and Health*, *Psychology and Societal Development*, *Psychology In India: Advances in Research* (4 Volumes), *Handbook of Psychology in India* and *Psychology and Psychoanalysis*. He is a Past President of the National Academy of Psychology, India and edits its journal *Psychological Studies* (Springer). He is currently editing the Sixth ICSSR Survey of Research in Psychology.

Alok Pandey

Alok Pandey, MD, is a psychiatrist by profession who has served with the Indian Air Force for twenty years before taking premature retirement. He has held several important assignments including Associate Professor of Psychiatry at Bangalore University and Head of the Neuropsychology division of the prestigious Indian Institute of Space and Aviation Medicine. He has written and lectured extensively in India and abroad on issues relating to Yoga psychology, health, stress management, education. He has conducted workshops on the Gita and Sri Aurobindo's Yoga. His book *Death, dying and beyond* was published in 2006.

Ashish Pandey

Ashish Pandey is Assistant Professor in Shailesh J. Mehta School of Management in Indian Institute of Technology Bombay in Mumbai, India. He has published in areas of spirituality in management, collective consciousness perspective of organization, Appreciative Inquiry, spiritual climate and learning in several national and international journals like *Global Business Review*, *Journal of Business Ethics*, *AI Practitioner*, etc. He also facilitates leadership and organization development interventions based on synthesis of contemporary management thoughts and Indian traditional wisdom for variety of organizations and institutions.

Anand C. Paranjpe

Anand C. Paranjpe is Professor Emeritus of Psychology and Humanities at Simon Fraser University, Burnaby, Canada. He obtained his Ph.D. from the University of Poona in India; did post-doctoral work at Harvard and taught at Simon Fraser University from 1967 to 2001. His main research interests are self and identity, theoretical psychology and psychological concepts from the intellectual and spiritual traditions of India. He was awarded Smith-Mundt and Fulbright scholarships for post-doctoral research under the direction of Prof. Erik H. Erikson in 1966-67, and was elected Fellow of the Canadian Psychological Association in 2004. His publications include: *In search of identity* (Macmillan/Wiley Interscience, 1975), *Theoretical psychology: The meeting of East and West* (Plenum, 1984), and *Self and identity in modern psychology and Indian thought* (Plenum,1998).

R. S. Pirta

Raghubir Singh Pirta, Ph.D., formerly Professor at the Department of Psychology, Himachal Pradesh University, Shimla received training in experimental psychology. The theoretical understanding of Pirta refined in several brief sojourns to the Center for Ecological Sciences, I. I. Sc., Bangalore, however, it is with the Chipko activists in the Himalayas that he imbibed the humane spirit about Nature. His research publications in the area of animal behaviour and ecology also include two volumes: *Ecology and human well-being: Nature and society in Himachal Pradesh* (2007), and *Pastoralism and the tribesman of mountain: Arung zet sa of kanaor* (2009). He is currently exploring the institution of local deities in the western Himalayas.

Ajith Prasad

Ajith Prasad's principal areas of interest are Buddhist philosophy and the study and practice of its methods of psychological transformation. Ajith teaches methods from Buddhism for managing emotions and developing mind. He also gives lectures on philosophy in various forums. After completing his post-graduation from the Indian Institute of Science in 1994, he had a career in technology and management. He also continued his personal quest for understanding consciousness. This led him to Buddhism. From 2007 onwards, Ajith is focusing fulltime on the study and practice of Buddhist philosophy and path. He took to the Yogic tradition of Buddhism and trained under the guidance of many Tibetan masters, particularly with HH Penor Rinpoche, Khenchen Pema Sherab, Khenchen Namdrol and Khenchen Tsewang Gyatso. He was instrumental in establishing Thubten Lekshey Ling, a Buddhist Centre of Learning in Bangalore.

Kumar Ravi Priya

Kumar Ravi Priya, a Ph.D. from the Department of Psychology, University of Delhi, is presently serving as an Associate Professor of Psychology at the Department of Humanities and Social Sciences, Indian Institute of Technology, Kanpur. His research interest lies in studying the psychology of social suffering and healing processes by locating human suffering caused by environmental, social and political forces in its cultural and historical context.

K. Ramakrishna Rao

K. Ramakrishna Rao is currently the Chancellor of GITAM University and Chairman of the GITAM Institute for Gandhian Studies. His previous assignments include Chairman, Indian Council of Philosophical Research, Professor of Psychology and Vice-Chancellor of Andhra University, Executive Director of the Foundation for Research on the Nature of man, USA, Advisor on Higher Education and Vice-Chairman of Andhra Pradesh State Planning Board, Government of Andhra Pradesh. His publications include over 200 research papers, nearly 50 book chapters and 20 books including *Consciousness studies: Cross-cultural perspectives* (McFarland, 2002), *Cognitive anomalies, consciousness and yoga* (Matrix Publishers, 2011), and *Gandhi and applied spirituality* (Indian Council of Philosophical Research, 2011).

Kiran Kumar K. Salagame

Kiran Kumar K. Salagame is currently a Professor of Psychology at the University of Mysore. He was a Fulbright Post-Doctoral Fellow (1990-91) and Fulbright Nehru Visiting Lecturer (2011) at USA. He is a Fellow of the Indian Association of Clinical Psychologists, and Member, National Academy of Psychology, India. He is an Associate Editor of *Psychological Studies* and has been serving on the Editorial boards of many national and international journals. He is an Honorary Professor and Member of Scientific Board, Yoga Federation of Serbia, Belgrade; Member of the Board of International Transpersonal Association, USA. Integrating Indian psychological concepts with mainstream psychology is his current focus. His publications relate to meditation and *yoga*, states of consciousness, Indian psychology, holistic health, positive psychology, transpersonal psychology and social cognition. He has authored *The psychology of meditation: A contextual approach.*

Peter Sedlmeier

Peter Sedlmeier, Ph.D. is a Professor of Psychology at the Chemnitz University of Technology, Germany. He teaches mainly courses on research methods and evaluation, but also on computer modelling, judgment under uncertainty, and cognitive science. He has written and edited five books, among them, *Improving statistical reasoning: Theoretical models and practical implications*, as well as numerous book chapters and articles in leading international psychology journals and edited books. His research focuses on the processing of time and frequency, psychology of music, judgmental errors, associative learning and, more recently, Indian psychology. He has held a two-year Humboldt-Fellowship at the University of Chicago, USA, and was a guest professor at Pondicherry University, India.

Bahman A. K. Shirazi

Bahman A. K. Shirazi, Ph.D., is currently a faculty member and archives coordinator at the California Institute of Integral Studies (CIIS) in San Francisco and an adjunct faculty at Sofia University, USA (formerly the Institute of Transpersonal Psychology). He has taught in the areas of integral psychology, research methodology, psychology of Sufism, and developmental psychology among other areas. His publications include book chapters and articles in the areas of integral psychology and Sufi psychology, including a book chapter titled: 'Integral psychology: The metaphors and processes of personal integration' (in *Consciousness and its transformation*, Sri Aurobindo Ashram, 2001), and two book chapters on integral psychology: 'Integral psychology: Psychology of the whole human being' (in Consciousness and healing: Integral approaches to mind-body medicine, Institute of Noetic Sciences, Elsevier pub., 2005) and 'Dimensions of integral psychology' (in *Unity in diversity: Fifty years of cultural integration*, Cultural Integration Fellowship, 2004). He has been a guest editor for *ReVision* journal and is a contributing editor to the online journal *Integral Review*.

Anjum Sibia

Anjum Sibia is Professor of Psychology at the National Council of Educational Research and Training (NCERT), New Delhi. She has conducted researches, published and presented papers/book chapters in the area of emotions and learning, innovative school practices, teacher questioning, peer tutoring, emotional intelligence and prepared monographs and exemplar materials. Her publications include research monographs, *Life at Mirambika* and *Valuing teacher questioning* and chapters in *Introduction to psychology,* textbooks for senior secondary stage. She has co-edited *Handbook of personality measurement in India, Functional assessment guide: A handbook for primary teachers* and self learning module *Assessment and appraisal in guidance and counselling.* She is also associated with training counsellors in the area of Assessment and Appraisal for Guidance and Counselling. Her other areas of interest/work include qualitative case study, caring in teaching, aesthetics in education, and evaluation of psychology textbooks.

Kundan Singh

Kundan Singh, Ph.D. is an Associate Core Faculty at the Institute of Transpersonal Psychology, Palo Alto and Adjunct Faculty the California Institute of Integral Studies (CIIS), San Francisco from where he obtained his doctorate in Humanities. Kundan is specifically interested in translating spiritual practice for inner and outer transformation, which includes building a new consciousness for global and local social change. Author of a book titled "The Evolution of Integral Yoga: Sri Aurobindo, Sri Ramakrishna, and Swami Vivekananda," and a few book chapters and journal articles like "Beyond Postmodernism: Towards a Future Psychology," "Relativism, Self-Referentiality, and Beyond Mind," "Relativism and Its Relevance for Psychology," and "Beyond Mind: Towards a Future Psychology," his areas of research include Integral Yoga of the Mother and Sri Aurobindo, Contemporary and Traditional Vedanta, Theravada and Mahayana Buddhism, Sufism of the Indian subcontinent, Spirituality and Social Action, Globalization, Social Change and Personal Responsibility, Indian Psychology, Transpersonal Psychology, Postcolonial and Postmodern Psychology, Integral Psychology, Yogic Psychology, Cultural Psychology, Theoretical Psychology, Social Psychology, Depth Psychology, Postmodern Philosophy, Philosophy of Science and Epistemology, Critical Thought and Deconstruction, Cross-cultural Psychology and East-West Studies among a few others.

K. M. Tripathi

K. M. Tripathi is a clinical psychologist by training. Presently, he is Deputy Director in Centre for Yoga, Malaviya Bhawan, Banaras Hindu University with which he has been associated for the last 24 years. Repeatedly elected as Secretary, Indian Academy of Yoga during 1990 to 2000, he has been the joint editor of the quarterly journal of the Academy, *The Yoga Review,* for 3 years. Besides editing the book *Yogabhyasa avam swasthya—Ek kshetra pustika,* he has contributed 7 chapters in books and authored and co-authored 34 papers and articles. His main area of interest is Indian approaches for the promotion of mental health.

Suneet Varma

Suneet Varma is Associate Professor in the Department of Psychology, University of Delhi. His research interests include philosophy of psychology/ theoretical psychology, the Indian perspective on psychology, and integral psychology. His most recent writing is titled, 'Bhakti and well-being: Healing and beyond'.

Index